MAKING THE MOST OF MARRIAGE

Fifth Edition

PAUL H. LANDIS

Prentice-Hall, Inc., Englewood Cliffs, New Jersey

Library of Congress Cataloging in Publication Data

LANDIS, PAUL HENRY
  Making the most of marriage.

  Bibliography: p.
  Includes indexes.
  1. Marriage.   I. Title.
HQ734.L266 1975   301.42   74-28246
  ISBN 0-13-547968-1

© 1975, 1970, 1965, 1960, 1955 by Prentice-Hall, Inc.,
Englewood Cliffs, New Jersey

Printed in the United States of America

10 9 8 7 6 5 4 3 2 1

Prentice-Hall International, Inc., London
Prentice-Hall of Australia, Pty. Ltd., Sydney
Prentice-Hall of Canada, Ltd., Toronto
Prentice-Hall of India Private Limited, New Delhi
Prentice-Hall of Japan, Inc., Tokyo

CONTENTS

VI PARENTHOOD 397

VII MARRIAGE PROBLEMS 467

PREFACE

The writing of a text dealing with social behavior is an unfinished task in a rapidly changing society; before it has reached the classroom, new social policies are being developed and new social programs being launched. Since the fourth edition of this text appeared, the codes of centuries have been remodeled in significant ways to create a new social climate for marriage and the family: trial marriage, group marriage experiments, communal living, "open marriage," more permissive sex codes and practices, an earlier age of majority, a revolutionary feminist movement, an equal rights amendment nearing final ratification by the states, social acceptance of out-of-wedlock births, "no-fault" divorce, legal right to contraception information and assistance in every state, nationwide right of women to control over their bodies as to abortion, the crusade for child-care centers, and even the adoption in practice of the goal of "zero" population growth.

Each of these revisions in the culture and in social behavior is revolutionary enough, but they also profoundly affect other areas of marriage, family, and social life. Only the persistence of the deep underlayer of custom and moral and social tradition make possible the use of any material published five years ago. As is always true in an era of rapid change, the underlayer does persist. Otherwise there would be no guidelines at all.

The focus of this edition, as the previous one, is on role relationships of mates and of parents and children; on the problem of developing love and security in the child which later makes the close bond of marriage possible for him; the adjustment problems of male and female as they move from the parent family toward marriage and a family of their own; the adjustments within marriage as romantic illusions are replaced by the more stern but deeply rewarding realities of adulthood. This means merging with the kin group of inlaws; adjusting to role expectation which the community holds for the marrieds; adjustments in married sex life; and assuming the economic load which comes with family formation. And finally, there is the transition to the most important problem—as children are born the necessity to socialize them and make them at peace within themselves and with the society in which they will function and carry on the generations.

I am still committed to the view that marriage can be wonderful, that parenthood can be fulfilling, and that there is room for optimism in looking forward toward these great ventures.

Child development is still stressed as a major purpose of preparing young people for marriage. The American Institute of Family Relations finds that disputes over how children will be handled and trained is one of the most frequent issues between modern husbands and wives. Research shows that parenthood is a disillusioning experience, in part because there is little anticipation of its realities. In the pair marriage, the socialization of the child—his very destiny—is in the hands of the pair to a degree it has never been in large family systems where child-rearing is by the kin group, rarely by the pair alone. The great failure of our society, with its rightful claim to a high level of education, is the ignorance and incompetence of parents, which are exhibited in maladjusted, poorly socialized children who later fill the courts, the penal institutions, the clinics, and the mental institutions. Increasing numbers fail to identify with their own sex category and many feel alienated from society altogether.

College students need to learn how love is built or blunted to understand their own development (I have found the autobiographical term paper, the outline for which appears in the appendix, a valuable help to students in this area). Understanding this gives greater understanding of their own later task of parenthood. Students need to see marriage and family beyond the veil of romantic illusions and the glamour of dating and fun seeking if our society is to achieve its potential and if they are going to realize their own potential as husbands and wives, parents, and grandparents.

I would like to thank Ruth E. Albrecht, University of Florida, S.L. Harris, Tarrant County Junior College, and Cole V. Smith, San Antonio College, for their helpful criticisms of the manuscript for the fifth edition.

PERSPECTIVE

VALUES AND GOALS OF MARRIAGE

1 Marriage provides for a stable pair relationship to assure the socialization and rearing of children, to provide them with legitimate status, and to assure the transmission of family name and family possessions to them. Only so can the continuity of generations be realized. Such needs are quite universally recognized. Each culture adds or subtracts from these goals in different ways so that to appraise marriage fully, and to understand its significance to a people, one must study it within its cultural context.

THE COMPANIONSHIP NEED

In the United States, a man builds a house in which to spend his old age, and he sells it before the roof is on; he plants a garden and rents it just as the trees are coming into bearing; he brings a field into tillage and leaves other men to gather the crops; he embraces a profession and gives it up; he settles in a place, which he soon afterwards leaves to carry his changeable longings elsewhere.

DE TOCQUEVILLE, *Democracy in America,* 1831

Each year 35–40 million Americans change their residence—for some it will mean a switch to a new house or apartment close by; for others, across the

3

continent, or even an international move. The U.S. Census shows that only 35 percent of the heads of families in the nation are living in the place of their birth. Of those aged 30, 60 percent have already moved from the place of their birth. One family in five is living over 1000 miles from the place of the head's birth. Five million families a year move across state lines. In western states more than half of family heads were born elsewhere. College graduates are twice as likely to move as grade school educated persons.

Vance Packard (1972) in his *A Nation of Strangers,* finds us nomadic, with a fifth moving at least once a year, and reports that the pace is increasing. This leads to "feebly rooted lives" and Packard questions whether this is "civilized." No sooner do Americans sink roots, making themselves a congenial area, than the roots are torn up, and the nomads are again surrounded by urban strangers. The average American, he finds, moves 14 times during his lifetime. Some schools lose 40 percent of their pupils annually. Over six million Americans live in mobile homes—even if such homes are not moved often, the occupant feels little sense of commitment to community. At any given time, half the 18–22 year olds in many communities live away from home. Aerospace communities are so highly mobile that they are often plagued by infidelity and alcoholism. Nomadic values take over, and mobility, Packard finds, is associated with both mental and physical illness. An anonymous people become more aggressive.

Jack Anderson, popular political columnist, in writing of "gross mismanagement" of the military (Jan. 22, 1973) cited the practice of the Navy needlessly moving men and their families. Among the 623,248 people on its roster in 1971, there were 525,132 relocations at a cost to the public of $240,-722,000, not to mention the uprooted lives and communities, and the emotional cost to wives and children.

Mobile Insecurity   "Mobile insecurity" affects couples, small children, teenagers, and grandparents not tough enough to take it. The stability that place gives to children and adolescents is lost with mobility. Young couples must learn to adapt to new attitudes and standards in attempting to meet the expectations of new groups in new social climates. The elderly must accept the loss of authority and respect as their wisdom and experience are eclipsed by new generations moving not only horizontally but also vertically, gaining the experience so necessary for survival in the competitive struggle with their peers.

Mobility, and consequent anonymity, affects the typical American, particularly the urban dweller. Migration takes him, in the course of a lifetime, far from the intimate circle of his birth. This has created in the human spirit a longing for a close emotional tie such as those who lived in a world of kin and neighbors never knew. The joint family system, the close tribal unit, the integrated primary group neighborhood give the individual continuous social support. He never bears his burdens alone. His crises are shared from cradle to grave, giving his emotional life a sure anchor. He need not demand a close love-life or the compatible association of a mate in marriage to guarantee a full social and emotional life.

Loneliness   The loneliness of the great city, its social isolation for the stranger, creates in the mind of man a sense of isolation and futility that has driven many persons to suicide, and others to the companionship of dogs, cats, parrots, and even silent, nondemonstrative pets or objects such as fish, turtles, and flowers. Those most deprived of companionship even talk to these silent, unresponsive companions to hear their own voice and keep in touch with the flow of language which makes man social. A filling station operator in a neighborhood gas station recognized this problem when he said, "People come here to have someone to tell their problems to." Many a bartender feels that his place serves the same purpose.

Little wonder that marriage has had to take on new meaning and that almost everyone seeks marriage today and seeks it early. The family home is a launching platform into the competitive world outside. As young people grow older and sense more keenly the impersonal character of the adult experience of our time, they understand more deeply the need to establish a close tie—one that will guarantee them not only companionship but sociability itself—stable, tangible, and ever-present sociability.

More than 45 years ago, Harvey Zorbaugh (1929) described life in the "furnished rooms" section of Chicago, where young people from farms and small Middle West towns landed on their arrival in the city in quest of fame and fortune. Here, where the turnover of residents was very rapid and anonymity was characteristic of social life, many of the couples living together as married were not married at all. Excuses given were that they wanted to have "someone to come home to," "someone to talk to," "someone to tell my troubles to."

Morals cannot always stand the test of the great loneliness and the feeling of being cut off from social life. Marriage is modern man's best arrangement for avoiding the solitariness of adulthood. Marriage is the institution which provides for permanent companionship. A mobile society provides no other source of enduring companionship.

Those who find marriage so miserable that they cannot endure it and seek a way out in divorce, do not survive the single state long in our society. Very soon they seek another mate, some even return to the former mate to make another try. The widowed, too, seek another mate in our day, when to be outside the fold of marriage is to be lonely in a sense that people are not lonely in societies with deeper ties in family and locality groups. As will be shown by data in Chapter 28, the divorced are more likely to marry than are the single; the widowed also are more likely to marry than are the single of comparable age.

Ever-Present Companionship   The need for the companionship of a marriage partner in the industrial world cannot be written off as a spurious value. In terms of a different kind of society, it may be an unnecessary value, but not in terms of the world in which modern urban industrial man must live his life. The human being, to remain human, needs someone with whom he can interact on a continuing basis, expressing his deepest joys and fears, plans and failures, hopes and needs. The more that is known about human nature through the study of psychology and sociology, through clinical experience, even from an understanding of suicide—lonely man's last desperate resort—the more clearly it is understood that the human being who can talk frankly and freely with a confidant travels life's journey most safely.

Those who lack companionship and who have no direct way of expressing their hopes, fears, anxieties, and longings to another human being are in danger of losing their sense of personal direction, meaning, and rationality. Normality is determined by the opportunity one is given for constant, meaningful communication with other persons.

A rural couple celebrating their seventy-second wedding anniversary was asked how they had managed a successful marriage. The wife's answer to the question was, "We did litle fussin'. We said little. Mostly we just set." This may not be too unrepresentative of many rural marriages of yesterday. But today's couple has much greater need to communicate with each other—to fuss, to do, and above all, to talk. A marriage of silence and sitting would fall far short of success in terms of meeting the modern person's needs.

A Confidant The democratic marriage creates an atmosphere of confidence and trust in which free communication on a person-to-person level is continuously possible. Even law courts preserve this confidence by refusing to require a person to testify against his spouse. Only the companionable couple can attain a really confidential level of expression, and only they realize the most from the marriage relationship.

One of the best indices of the effect of social isolation and a sense of anonymity on personality is the suicide rate. Data for a three year period indicate that the married are by far the least likely to suicide. Of white males, only 21 per 100,000 of those married committed suicide, compared to 80 of those divorced, 76 of those widowed, and 44 of those single. Comparable rates for the white female are 7 of those married, 19 of those divorced, 13 of those widowed, and 8 of those single. This is striking evidence that marriage is an insurance factor, as far as the individual's hold on his own life and the future is concerned—a vital hedge against anonymity (see Figure 1–1).

The very personal nature of the modern couple's hopes for marriage in our society is illustrated by Strauss' study of 173 engaged or newly married men and 200 women with a checklist of 26 needs they had hoped to find fulfilled in their pair relationship. Here are the 15 items most often checked (Strauss 1945): [I]Wish someone to:

love me
confide in me
show me affection
respect my ideals
appreciate what I wish to achieve
understand my moods
help me make important decisions
stimulate my ambition
look up to

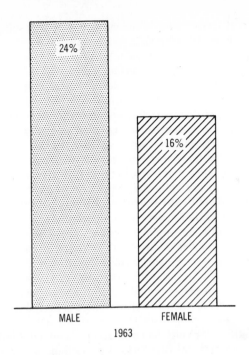

FIGURE 1-1

Higher mortality of unmarried over persons ever married—by sex and age (20 and over) United States, 1963. Marriage is related to health and longevity. Better conditions of living, more to live for, a full expression of basic wishes are all undoubtedly factors in the greater longevity of married persons even though biological selectivity may also operate. United Nations' data show that marriage is related to longevity everywhere, not just in the United States (*Demographic Yearbook, UN*).

give me self-confidence
stand back of me in difficulty
appreciate me just as I am
admire my ability
make me feel I count for something
relieve my loneliness

HAPPINESS AS A GOAL

Happiness as a primary life goal is a luxury of peoples in a culture of abundance. In most cultures man has been much concerned with survival. Life is a serious struggle in which securing food and shelter consume most of human energy. In the United States 150 years ago, happiness was not the primary concern of marriage. A person was more likely to pick a mate for qualities that wore well and to be concerned about the practical aspects of the marriage. But people also worked 14–16 hours a day to make a living. They struggled for the conquest of a frontier. Life was rigorous. A puritanical attitude toward all levity still carried over in the culture. Life was serious and the stake was survival itself. Pleasure seeking as such was condemned, and condemned no less in marriage than in all other aspects of life.

In our culture, abundance of goods and leisure have become the lot of the majority, and life moves in terms of a different set of values. With the increase of luxury and leisure, moderns have come to look upon happiness as a desirable goal not only for marriage but for all of life. Recreation and pleasure are considered man's just due; they are even considered rejuvenating and worthwhile—the proper rewards of work and of earned leisure.

In terms of such contemporary values, who is to say that this goal of marriage happiness is a spurious one? Most students of American marriage prefer to accept the contemporary values, and hold not only that happiness in marriage is a worthy goal, but also that it represents a new and higher level of human aspiration than earlier generations dared hold.

The fact that youth can make happiness the first demand of marriage testifies to the luxury enjoyed today, both in material blessings and spiritual values. On the material side, the human spirit has been freed from the overwhelming burden of incessant work and duty. On the spiritual side, modern concepts of well-being provide a culture in which man dares dream that he can be happy. It is logical that marriage is placed at the center of this dream.

It is doubtful that humanity has ever sought a goal in marriage so difficult to realize and yet so worthy of realization as "happiness." One must grant the psychological necessity of many people compromising the ideal with the demands of reality in everyday living as man and wife, but even so, about three couples in four live out their life span without completely shattering this dream. One cannot claim that all who remain loyal to their marriage pledge fully realize happiness. But many studies that have measured the happiness of married couples show that about two marriages in three are either happy or very happy.

Some critics challenge such research, saying one cannot depend on people's ratings of their own happiness or success. But some studies have used not only self-ratings, but have had friends rate the marriage too. Self-ratings and rating by others agree. This suggests that a couple knows whether or not the marriage is happy, and that the great majority of marriages that survive actually realize happiness. A few generations ago no one would have thought of asking couples whether their marriages were happy.

Even legal grounds for divorce today indicate how seriously the value "happiness" is accepted in the culture as the standard for marriage success. Many divorces are granted for "mental cruelty," an intangible quality but one which well expresses the opposite of happiness. The Mosaic Law recognized no such treatment for dissolving marriage, nor did our nation's customs and laws of 1890. The philosophy of marriage has changed to the point where even the law recognizes that marriage is a dynamic interrelationship of two individuals with personal destinies and must produce happiness or fail.

At the beginning of the century, few farm couples who were considered successful in their family life manifested any affection. Some of them battled and nagged at each other chronically. The community did not worry about these marriages breaking up. The couple had land, children, and the respect of neighbors and relatives. No one expected that they would run to a lawyer simply because they did not like each other. In the good religious neighborhood, few couples acted as though they did like each other, but they had enough mutual activities to keep them occupied and interdependent. They had a farm to operate and children to raise; this was all they demanded of marriage.

Perhaps part of the impression they gave was the customary reserve of farm folks of the day in expressing affection. There was a reticence among all but the teen-age group about admitting in public any interest in the opposite sex. Even the teen-agers were shy about it. Nowadays, the male admits quite openly that there is no creature on earth quite so interesting to him as woman. The once-reserved female now lets her own sex know quite frankly that the opposite sex interests her, and likely as not she acknowledges this interest to the male.

Well within the memory of some of our older citizens, boys and girls were kept on separate playgrounds for fear they would discover that there was a natural fascination of the sexes for each other. Now, from early teen-age up, young people are taught to seek happiness with each other. The relationship of male and female has become the most important one in life.

THE NEED FOR LOVE

Our culture is passing through a sensuous cycle in which the terms love and sexual intercourse are often used with synonymous meaning. This, of course, greatly underrates the significance of both. Love is much more than sex, and sex without love demeans personality. But love is the subject of a later chapter. Suffice it to say here that we are not discussing love in this restricted sense.

A few years ago a group of practicing psychologists were guests at a ministers' institute at which ministers and psychologists gave papers in turn. After three of each had spoken, it was very apparent that the psychologists were making a better case for love as a key to personality than were the ministers. There has been much recent writing of psychiatrists and clinical psychologists in which the love theme is as prominent as in the New Testament. That love has a therapeutic effect, few can doubt today. That it is the key factor in making man's life complete and worthwhile, few question.

If this is true of mankind in general, in an industrial society love of a mate must be recognized as a supreme value, because so many aspects of life have become competitive that much social experience is the very antithesis of love. The human being of our time and place on earth must find a love focus that is dependable and sure. In such a world, the "love marriage" is not merely a nice arrangement, it is a necessity.

A human being is in a dismal state indeed when he begins to feel that there is no one in the world who cares deeply about him or about whom he cares very much. A person's life is most meaningful when it means a great deal to some other person or persons. This need for unqualified love is fulfilled in the normal childhood home by the parent–child relationship.

Parent-to-Mate Transition   The love of a member of the opposite sex comes gradually to replace the affection parents expressed in so many forms during childhood. This affection is not the one-sided affair parental love often is. Parents often give, expecting nothing in return. Mature love involves not only the feeling of being cared for by others, but even more important, of caring for others. It means not only wanting others to feel deeply about oneself, but also feeling a personal responsibility for their happiness.

It is through an understanding marriage that one can be most fully assured of an enduring love in adulthood. The husband–wife relationship becomes for the adult the most important outlet for affection. Here, as in all human relationships, affection is gained by giving affection.

There are other kinds of close comradeship, but our society recognizes none as full, close, and complete as the marriage tie. It brings emotional security. If the marriage meets this need, it provides a place to relax and feel free from competition and assault. It is a refuge from trouble and a hiding place in a world that often brings rough treatment. Those with a normal childhood have been trained for this kind of inner security by their child–parent relationship. It is easy for them to find the psychological counterpart of parental affection in marriage.

Those who have not been permitted to form a close emotional attachment to parents in childhood often find it difficult to realize emotional security in marriage. But if a sense of security can be realized at all, through any human relationship, marriage is designed to bring and maintain it. One without emotional security always feels that he has a flank exposed to the enemy, that he lacks defense against his own misgivings and fears. Failure to realize emotional security is failure indeed.

Complete realization of love does much to put ego-striving in its proper place. The love-starved personality often works itself out in inordinate ambition, intolerable vanity, unreasonable demands for the service and respect of others. The personality that has found itself in a secure emotional relationship is mellowed and matured. The ego takes a more subdued place in the scheme of living, and other people are given a larger place. It is in this sense that love, with the inherent sense of emotional security it brings, is not only the savior of the world but of the marriage relationship. It is the antidote for belligerence, conquest, conflict, competition, and self-seeking.

Willard Waller (1929) observed that spouses going through the alienation process leading up to divorce develop overwhelming egos. The security and fullness of love is vanishing and in its place the ego emerges and makes overwhelming demands. The ego-subduing love element of marriage must, in the process of divorce, be replaced by compensatory ego fictions. The mate must be blamed and the self, justified. The wife who has never written a line declares she is going to write a best seller. The husband of modest wealth or ability is going to become a financier or inventor. Grandiose purposes and plans represent the struggle of the personality to fill the void left by the loss of emotional security in the marriage.

With women, particularly, the sense of belonging emotionally is associated with the desire to have and to give to children. The desire for motherhood, which may be in large part socially cultivated, is a normal yearning of woman as she reaches the years of maturity. She desires the full life which motherhood promises. In motherhood she sees the closest kind of human relationship and also a chance to contribute to her own future happiness and security in having children who belong to her, and to whom she belongs. Many young couples also share this feeling to the extent that it becomes a major aspiration in their lives together.

Many, of course, cannot visualize family life this clearly in advance of marriage. Men generally have to be taught to be parents. Couples who seriously undertake parenthood in faith and confidence, however, do develop a deep sense of emotional security from it and thus enrich their marriage. The total family becomes the area of emotional expression and unity. The marriage relationship itself is strengthened by the extension of the bonds of affection to include children and by the joint aspirations which parents hold for them in planning their development.

In a world that too often seems filled with pessimism and gloom, children give the couple a vital stake in the future. One who senses the world of childhood and its simple hopes has difficulty being pessimistic about the future or about man's and his own high destiny. Although these realities are often only vaguely sensed in early youth, they are a part of the reality which makes marriage and family the basic institution of mankind and one which, when a substantial part of its goals are realized, promises the fulfillment of the greatest possible range of emotional needs.

The Need for Ego Support

Harold Summers, of the guild of London hairdressers, declared in a press release, "modern women no longer require love—what they want and constantly seek is reassurance." Man's craving for recognition of his personal worth is a perpetual hunger. As has been suggested in the preceding section, love and a deep sense of belonging do much to feed the ego and put it in its proper place, but do not annihilate it. The Strauss study (1945) indicated that men, more than women, hope for ego support in marriage.

Social changes have radically modified the ways of satisfying ego needs. In generations past a man was known to many people in many ways. The village shoemaker was not just a shoemaker to his acquaintances—he had a name, a past, a reputation, and a family connection by which he was identified. He might be thought of, for example, as gentle and honest, a good father, a steady citizen and a devout churchman, a practical joker and an all-around good fellow. Acquaintances judged him not only as a shoemaker but also as a person and a neighbor. Today the man behind the counter at the local shoe-repair shop excites little interest in his many patrons. They are not concerned about his personal life or interests. They only want to know if he can repair shoes.

But man does not fit well into this impersonal and indifferent atmosphere that he has created for himself. He is no more an insensitive robot than he was in the past. The neighborhood cobbler has interests, values, hobbies, abilities, and opinions about which he needs to feel proud, but who even knows of them?

If he is fortunate, his wife does. From her he receives the praise, the encouragement, the constant reassurance that reminds him that he is after all an individual, that he is someone special—apart from the mass—that he is a "somebody" rather than a "nobody." This description of life does not fit all people even today, yet modern living provides relatively few with recognition in abundance. Those who make a big splash probably get more publicity and acclaim than they did in the past. With urbanization and increased vocational specialization, however, the majority of individuals are likely to feel like strangers even among their acquaintances. Without a feeling of significance, of amounting to something, many forms of personality distortion develop, because the human ego must have satisfaction. Marriage today is one of the most certain ways to fulfill the need to feel significant.

Marriage must above all things help both man and wife meet the need for status and recognition. Even when there are many other channels through which ego satisfaction can be realized—and there are, particularly for the male, and for the female who can continue a career along with marriage—most persons today are very dependent on marriage for a share of their ego satisfaction. The male who strays has the standard excuse, often real, "My wife no longer understands me." The woman who strays feels, "My husband no longer talks to me." In each case there has developed a lack of ego support for which all hunger, and which outside liaisons give, at least temporarily. In the routine of married life, couples come to take each other too much for granted, and unwittingly leave each other stranded for appreciation.

If marriage and homemaking are a major part of her life, the demands of the wife on the spouse for ego satisfaction through her relationship with him will be great. In dating, the successful male succeeds in making a woman feel that she is the most important creature in the world because she is a woman. He makes her feel that she is beautiful, wise, comfortable to be with, understanding—that she in fact embodies all that makes life beautiful and worthwhile. If homemaking is to be her primary role after marriage, he must continue not only to express such sentiments but to actually hold them if she is to be content and feel significant.

Because this goal is so difficult to achieve in modern marriage, the wife often feels compelled to seek outside activities as means of acquiring status and recognition. Very often she must do so or succumb to feelings of inferiority and uselessness, particularly if she has been in the limelight prior to the marriage.

If a work outlet is blocked for the wife whose ego is suffering in marriage, she is likely to unwittingly turn her frustration toward tearing down her husband's achievements. By criticizing, ignoring, or belittling his satisfaction in his own achievements, or in other ways working out her feeling of defeat she tries to draw her husband down to her own level. This is particularly true if the love bond had also weakened.

Finally, both men and women want in their mate someone who will command the approval and respect of others—parents, relatives, friends, colleagues at work, even strangers. And just as important, both want a mate who will bring credit, not shame and embarrassment. A proper mate draws social approval to the spouse and lends dignity and worth to the marriage motive.

Marriage is our society's only sanctioned outlet for the sex drive. Religion and custom sanction the joining of man and wife in the flesh as normal, natural, and moral. Sex is a value not only with biological meaning, but also with emotional content. The most comfortable, enduring, and responsible sex relationships are still within the marriage bond, and probably they always will be. With modern contraception, both husband and wife can enjoy the sexual bond with little fear of unwanted pregnancy. It has never been so before. Women, particularly, have experienced great dread of the consequences of the act of sexual intercourse no matter how vital it was to them and their husbands.

Sex needs are real physical needs. Their mutual expression in marriage is one of the elements in the fulfillment of one's need for feeling successful, safe, and whole. In this sense of bringing personal unity, sex needs are psychological as well as physical and organic. The romantic marriage integrates the psychological and physical aspects of sex and makes them inseparable. It is in this sense that mates must be able to satisfy each other. Neither prudes nor the unconventional, who use sex merely for excitement, adventure, or domination, can meet the sexual requirements of marriage.

The periodicity of sex hunger, the frequency with which this need must be met by release in sexual contact varies from individual to individual. But the need is there and can be completely satisfied in American society in no other way as satisfactorily as in the constancy of the marriage relationship. Once marriage is entered into it becomes the habitual way of bringing relief, pleasure, relaxation, comfort, and closeness.

Only in marriage does sex become a responsible act, involving for the woman the possibility of motherhood with the obligations and joys which this entails. Thus in marriage she too can participate in the sex act without feeling that she is risking the future of the child who may be born. For the man it carries the responsibilities of parenthood, with the age-long requirement that the male care for and support the female and her young, an arrangement that is as old as human history and probably predates mankind.

Sex as a factor leading to marriage is probably a much more important and conscious factor for the male than the female. At least this is so if one is considering sex as physical appetite. Even women who cannot accept sex as a pleasure generally look upon it as a means to marital security and ultimately to parenthood.

Studies of contemporary mores suggest that for several reasons, the married pair is capable of realizing more in this area than in any previous period of history: (1) The spacing of children is approaching the level of a practical science. The sexual union is now an act of pleasure, release, and mutual satisfaction, which it could never be in an atmosphere of fear and anxiety about an unwanted pregnancy. Unwanted births have declined precipitously since the mid-1960s, among all groups, but particularly among those who had been most overwhelmed by unwanted children, i.e., blacks and Catholics. By 1970 the rate of unwanted blacks dropped by 56 percent and Catholics dropped by 45 percent. Their exposure to risk is still higher than for the more favored socioeconomic groups, and those more free of religious taboos, but the pill and the interuterine device have been rapidly equalizing the situation (*Family Planning Digest* 1972). A national fertility study conducted by the Office of Population Research at Princeton University in 1970 found that more than two-thirds of Roman Catholic women were using birth control methods disapproved by their church. (Even so, there are still some 10–13 million fertile women who must improve their contraceptive practice to achieve their goal of family limitation.)

(2) Psychological impediments to mutual sharing have been greatly reduced. The taboo-ridden female, taught to be passive, felt it was a sin and she was ashamed to be sexually assertive. The young wife of today, if she is fortunate in having been given adequate sex education, looks forward to the sexual life of marriage. She views this as a form of close sharing, of appropriate sensual delight. Rather than merely catering to the male, she is an active and responsive partner. This is the ideal. (In Chapters 20 and 21 we shall indicate how difficult its realization is.)

The lowered fertility rate—confining childbearing to a short span, usually less than 10 years—and the increasing length of life make possible a sharing of sex life for a period of 40 years or more in the average marriage. With sex interest no longer denied by the culture, sex activity for many persists throughout their lifetime, rather than women no longer being concerned much after age 45 and men terminating their sex life early in conformity with cultural expectations (Bernard 1972).

NEGATIVE MOTIVATIONS FOR MARRIAGE

The positive aspects of the motivation to marry have been stressed, for it is assumed that these are the most compelling, yet motivations are rarely unmixed. Many marry in part, or perhaps chiefly, with an avoidance motive. To cover pregnancy is one of the motives in our culture, perhaps for 10–25 percent of the population (Christensen et al. 1953). In this classification are to be found many of the teen-age marriages. Marriage may have been in the thoughts of one or the other or of both but the actual precipitating event was the pregnancy.

Many youths reach the decision to marry when they find the situation at home increasingly unbearable. They want greater freedom than they can have under the parental roof. They hope to find it in marriage. This probably explains in part why young people from large families and underprivileged families so often marry young. Crowded conditions of the parental home, the constant conflict with brothers, sisters, and parents, the rather authoritarian patterns that of necessity prevail in such homes, lead young people to choose early marriage as the better of two alternatives.

Some young people marry from a sense of loneliness which has developed because of neglect or lack of affection during childhood in the parental home. They are insecure souls fleeing loneliness and seeking warmth, closeness, and affection that will shield them from the anxieties and fears of a world in which they have always felt exposed to fear, anxiety, and unearned guilt. Marriage for them is often a mistake, for these feelings are exaggerated as frequently as they are cured by a youthful marriage. Often they become too demanding and monopolistic of the mate and thus invite marital failure.

Some marry to cover a feeling of sex guilt. Their sex drives or acquired sex appetites, or habits, have become a constant source of guilt and anxiety. They seek marriage primarily as a sexual outlet—to sanctify desires which have plagued them from the time of earliest adolescence, sometimes even before. Some such individuals have been haunted by a sense of guilt over masturbation or other types of sexual exercises which are harmless in and of themselves, but which have proved to be harmful because of feelings of deep anxiety induced by teachings to the contrary. Others feel keenly guilty because their sexual desires, even their sensuous thoughts, seem to conflict with the teachings of their parents or the church. Others hasten into marriage to cover feelings of guilt and fear involved in a sexual relationship already begun with the future spouse.

Some marry primarily for spite, or self-justification. The loneliness, the rancor, the bitterness of a breakup are buried in a new, drastic plunge into the risky security of a hasty marriage. Today many remarry to cure an intolerable loneliness following divorce or widowhood. They seek also to find the satisfactions which they once had and lost, or never found in a previous marriage. This statement refers to the one in five marriages which are contracted by persons who have been widowed or divorced.

It is said that some people marry for pity. One finds this the theme of an occasional novel, so one must suspect that it happens in real life. The individual marries another in order to save him from some real or imagined fate, perhaps nothing more than the fate of failure to achieve marriage. One finds it hard to account for the marriage of the physically normal to the severely handicapped in terms of a motive other than that of pity, or altruism.

Probably every motive of which human beings are capable enters into one marriage or another: escape, fortune, prestige, economic security, or status seeking. Both man's negative and positive drives affect almost every decision he makes. Although one cannot say that it is wrong to marry for any of these motives, one must recognize the weakness inherent in marriage based on some of these.

NEEDS THWARTED BY MARRIAGE

Very fundamental needs are fulfilled in marriage as in no other human relationship, yet marriage drastically interferes with other needs. The need to be loved, for example, often runs counter to the need for self-realization and ego satisfaction.

Certain hostilities inevitably develop when the demands of love become so great that they thwart one's desire to attain economic or vocational status and success. The shelter of marriage, which makes one feel secure, may at times interfere strongly with one's desire to be free of ties and obligations, to be foot-loose, so to speak, to venture and experiment and seek new experience. The need to be reassured and comforted is all-important at times, but at other times, when one feels more sure of oneself, a sense of self-sufficiency takes precedence. Independence replaces the need for a refuge. At such times one is ashamed of former weakness and does not want to be reminded of it.

So the changing needs manifest themselves from day to day in the up-and-down fluctuations of moods and the adversities of the world in which we live and work. Marriage is, therefore, a constantly shifting pattern, ever new and in a certain sense never fully adequate for balancing the human being's dual need for oneness and for personal freedom. There are numerous mainsprings to motivation and behavior, not all of them are conscious, but all of them are purposeful in terms of meeting the individual's particular need at a particular time.

Often the marriage is called upon to fulfill needs that have been thwarted in outside activities. The husband who comes home feeling uncertain or unsuccessful in his work may be in need of consolation and reassurance. The mate in this case is expected to rally to the occasion when perhaps she has even greater need for reassurance herself. Yet the husband's reactions are not irrational. They are purposeful in terms of his monetary needs, even though contradictory to the self-sufficient man he may have appeared to be in the morning when he left home. The wife may have greater difficulty in accepting him as the humble child, needing comfort and strength, than as the strong man she respects and honors.

Needs are not always rational and often cannot be expressed in words, but the human organism always moves in response to them, even though they are quite contradictory from one time to another. Marriage is, therefore, a moving equilibrium in which two personalities work to find fulfillment of each other's needs, with love the overall bond facilitating adjustment.

Marriage is as potentially capable of creating deep hostilities, animosities, and frictions as it is of giving happiness and mutual satisfaction. Because of the high aspirations that center in it and the close intimate demands that are made upon personality, hostile tendencies are always latent. When they come to the surface, they can be of the most violent nature.

It is for this reason that marriage, designed to meet more needs than is any other institution, is also capable of producing more misery, suffering, and personal torture than any other relationship developed by man. The pair relationship has throughout history been laden with tragedy where failure has replaced success and where defeat has replaced hope. The tragedies of married life have been the favorite themes of drama and fiction, ranking second only to love itself. This kind of plot is always fascinating, for every person can as readily identify with this phase of the marriage relationship, as with the comedy and glory of marriage.

Of all murders committed in the United States, 38 percent are within the family. The family, being the closest of all relationships, is capable of "failure, hostility, and destructiveness. They are as much a part of the family system and relationships among members as success, love, and solidarity are" (Rossi 1968). Much of the police work in lower-class sections of cities, and in the ghettos particularly, is settling family quarrels and interfering in family violence.

Marriage at a distance often looks much less attractive than it is, particularly to the young, who in the throes of happy romance lose sight of the realities of life. Marriage is not a one-way street to happiness, and the pronunciation of a marriage ceremony is no guarantee that personal needs will be met.

OUR PROBLEM-CONSCIOUSNESS

As a people, we make much of our problems, and in so doing sometimes exaggerate them. Having cast aside tradition, we pursue elusive goals and entertain lofty hopes and dreams, often too romantic, and beyond reach. This is especially true of marriage. Long ago we ceased to believe that fate ruled our destiny, and began to seek remedies for our problems.

Almost every woman's magazine and some magazines written for the more general public carry articles that outline and suggest help for some critical marriage problem. Divorce statistics are much quoted and the pro and con of the sex revolution is considered.

An outsider to our culture, particularly one from the more institutionalized, custom-controlled, Asian cultures, where marriage adjustment is not an accepted concept and where it is never discussed, might well think our marriage institution is but the ruins of some earlier state of equilibrium. Safe and relatively unchallenged by change, the joint family system of these cultures is based on the secure foundations of centuries of custom. Little wonder that they see in our nuclear marriage–family system, where so much is left to the individual choice and so little to ancestral heritage, little pattern at all.

Recognizing that problems exist is the first step toward improvement. Traditional family systems will never improve until they become problem-conscious. They are fate-oriented, believing that what has been must always be. The fact that our society exhibits concern for the welfare of husbands and wives, parents and children, represents a vast leap forward. The numerous minor miseries of the pair and their children have become social concerns.

Failure Often Reflects High Hopes

If the view that couples aspire to more in marriage than they did in earlier generations is accepted, then it is easy to believe (1) that the successful realize more satisfaction in marriage than did their ancestors and (2) that many suffer defeat because they expect marriage to bring more in the way of happiness than is possible.

By the same logic, it is understandable too, that failure is more likely to lead to decisive action than in earlier generations. There is little doubt that many divorces today result from overly idealistic expectations for marriage. Many expect the impossible. As English novelist Somerset Maugham has said, the American wife expects to find in her husband "a perfection English women only hope to find in their butlers." And what perfection in romantic attraction, home management, and social competence American men expect of their wives! It is doubtful that marriage has ever been asked to pass such a high test.

If a culture makes happiness the goal of marriage, it must grant the right of divorce to those who fail in its attainment. Only by this means can they be freed to seek fulfillment in another marriage, or to return to the single state. The right of divorce is important in the new system of marriage values. It recognizes two facts: first, human judgment is fallible in mate choice, and second, those who "fall in love" may also fall out of love.

Divorce is doubly serious when it represents the failure of high aspirations, but is not more tragic than living together in bitter conflict and frustration. In an earlier day, when a more stoic marriage philosophy prevailed, personal clashes may well have brought less torture than now when marriage values are different.

Divorce and its meaning in the modern scheme of values are discussed in Chapter 28. It is enough here to say that divorce is a recognized adjustment device in the modern marriage–family system—the ultimate, desperate, but sometimes necessary one. Divorce is, in fact, a part of all marriage–family institutions, historic and contemporary. In ours, its causes are related to our new marriage values. Marriage is a dynamic interrelationship of two individuals with personal destinies.

Margaret Mead (1968a) has suggested that we try to make all relationships, even in marriage, too intense. Too much is demanded, and we despair too easily. She believes America does not even accept the fact of divorce yet, we are so loyal to the monogamous ideal. Children are disturbed and women feel abandoned and hurt if a marriage fails even after 20 years. Yet historically most couples did not live together that long before death. The ideal of a lifelong union, she suggests, was fine when vigorous men buried a succession of three wives and when sturdy wives survived a succession of husbands.

It is a remarkable testimony to our monogamous ideal that marriage is still looked upon as a lifetime partnership.

The picture of marriage failure is compounded by the 10 percent or so who cannot tolerate any marriage for very long. Should these people be eliminated from the marriage market as tests for marriage fitness become more reliable? This is an ethical question involving social welfare versus individual rights, an issue which is not likely to be settled soon. These marriage misfits are subject to the same pressures toward marriage as others—would it be fair to disallow them the chance to fulfill cultural expectations?

Compulsions to Marry   There are still many social compulsions to marry. One of the most important is the realization, as one leaves the parental home, that the only way one may feel complete again is by establishing a family of one's own. Only by establishing a home can a person enjoy again the pattern of living he himself experienced or longed for as a child. Only thus can life seem fully proper and adequate; only thus can he find again the intimacy, warmth, and sharing that are so much a part of the satisfactions of the socialized human being.

One's drive to marriage begins in childhood in one's own home. Children learn about family loves and hates, rivalry and cooperation, and carry these lessons over into their own homes. The most perfect marriage will fail if it does not meet childhood expectations.

Women undoubtedly feel greater social compulsion to marry than do men since their upbringing is much more family-oriented. Even so, there are pressures on the male to marry. There are few jolly bachelors. After a certain age, a man feels out of place without a wife and children. So he gives up sex variety and many little freedoms for a regular relationship. Marriage is never the all-absorbing thing for him that work is, but it is part of mature life for the normal male.

Another powerful incentive to marry today is the general social expectation that, particularly in recreational affairs, people will participate in pairs rather than as individuals. In the earlier agrarian economy, all age groups associated in social life, but this is rarely so in urban industrial society where all social groups are stratified by age and where pairs are the normal unit of association in adulthood. One reason the older adolescent feels a little out of place is that it is expected that he will attend any private function with a member of the opposite sex. This is more true of women than of men, since it is assumed that a woman will have an escort in her attendance at public and private functions.

The extent to which a person of a given age feels social pressure to marry depends a great deal on the kind of community in which he lives. The college girl of 20 with two years of school remaining will sense no social pressure to marry; rather she will sense considerable pressure of parental and peer group opinion not to marry. The girl of 18 who has left high school for a job may sense great pressure to marry.

Then, too, the social prestige of marriage in some communities is very great. In rural communities where large numbers of young people marry in or immediately out of high school, great social pressure is exerted on girls to marry early and on parents to see them married. To be able to acquire the status of marriage and begin homemaking and childbearing is one of the higher values of the community.

A countertrend may well be emerging. Owing to the population explosion, commentators on the social scene are becoming bolder in expressing views to the effect that it would be better if fewer persons married. In large cities singles' clubs and apartment houses for singles have multiplied. There is an increasing attempt to fill the time of the single person and to cater to his needs. These ventures are profit motivated, but the fact that they prove profitable may be an indication of a move toward the single life as a satisfactory state. It is possible, however, that these institutions are still primarily places to find a suitable marriage partner. Many are nonetheless delaying marriage.

PROBLEMS

1   The modern marriage is usually expected "to meet the individual's needs for love and emotional security, status, recognition, companionship, and sex." Marriage is also sought for negative reasons—as a means of escaping certain undesirable circumstances. These needs vary in importance from one person to another, depending upon his personality and background.

      Analyze your own personality needs as best you can. Which of their various items—love, emotional security, status, recognition, companionship, sex, or negative motives—do you think will rank first in determining whom you marry?

As you analyze your development why do you feel this one need is of first importance in your life?

2 Among your various personality needs, are there some which you would expect to satisfy in relationships outside of marriage? Discuss possibilities of need fulfillment through such avenues as job, friends, children, church, parents, brothers and sisters, hobbies, community activities, girls (or boys) you've previously dated, pets, etc.

3 *Research exercise:* Prepare a list of expectations concerning your marriage (kind of relationship expected, kind of needs to be satisfied, kind of family life planned, number of children expected, and level of living expected).

To ensure frankness, lists should preferably be anonymous with sex of respondent indicated on the sheet. Tabulate and discuss results. Compare tabulations of men and women separately.

What do results show with regard to marriage values in this generation? Do men and women seek substantially the same goals? Far different ones? If different, are they complementary rather than contradictory? Appraise the various answers given from the standpoint of their being (a) practical, (b) realistic, (c) consistent with the expectations of the average community.

4 *Sociodrama:* A young woman is talking with her happily married sister, seeking help in deciding whether or not she should accept the marriage proposal of the night before. Her sister tries to help her decide by asking a number of questions based on contemporary values in mate selection. Their grandmother enters and adds her advice, which is largely based on the criteria of her own youth.

5 Define "anonymity." Briefly indicate why it is so characteristic of many sectors of society today and show how it affects marriage and family life.

6 Once a modern couple have married do you consider that each is obligated to "love, honor, and obey" the other for a lifetime? Explain.

7 Read the following statement and select one of the four conclusions below which you feel best describes a realistic philosophy of marriage. Explain your choice briefly. If you believe that there is a fifth alternative, state it and defend it.

It has been said that "when you don't expect anything of your marriage you can't be disappointed." Do you believe that couples would be happier in the long run if they:

a Expected nothing of marriage but a working arrangement for the purpose of raising a family?

b Expected to fulfill most of their needs other than for sexual satisfactions in relationships outside of marriage?

c Continued to expect complete need fulfillment, as most do today, but worked harder at attaining their goal?

d Tempered their expectations with an understanding of the limitations of all human beings and all human relationships?

8 Have you known persons to marry for motives you would consider with suspicion? Did they succeed?

9 Have you known persons whom you considered unmarriageable? What was the basis for your conviction?

10 *Sociodrama:* A friendless young woman marries to escape her lonely world. Her husband is a popular, out-going person whose need for companionship is

satisfied by his friends and work associates. He thinks of a wife primarily in terms of her role as a housekeeper.

Act out a situation or conversation in which the expectations of each are pictured. If possible have the husband and wife reach a new understanding of one another as a result of the conversation.

PERSPECTIVE ON AMERICAN MARRIAGE AND FAMILY

2 The frankness with which we discuss marriage and family problems in our society today, may well lead to an exaggerated conception of their shortcomings. Historically any breakdown in marital and family relationships, as Dicks (1967) has pointed out, "was studiously concealed as a blot on the whole kinship group." A philosophy teacher told a class, "if you wish to worship the past, don't study history too closely."

CHANGING PERSPECTIVES

Culture change has until recently been measured in terms of centuries. Now it is measured in years or decades, because the old is replaced by the new and experimental so rapidly in both material things and social arrangements.

Institution to Companionship

Burgess et al. (1971) used the "institution to companionship" terms to describe the characteristic trend of the American marriage–family system. Their conceptualization has been quite generally accepted by sociologists. It designates the radical transition from conceiving of marriage and family in terms of customary formal arrangements and traditional values to conceiving of them in terms of personal relationships and values.

Both the old and new systems have many names, depending on their expression in various periods of history and depending on the particular aspect of the marriage–family system being stressed. In the broadest sense, the institutional family system includes all systems in which the institution is given priority over individual inclinations and wishes. The *joint family* system of Asia and the *affiliated* family system of Latin America represent the extremes in submerging the wishes of the individual in the traditional family system. The elders dominate mate choice, provide the joint residence, and provide a joint economic security. The large family is governed by the patriarch.

The farm family of our recent past demanded less of the individual, included fewer relatives, and gave more freedom; but even so, the family and its traditions were the beginning and the end of marriage. Personal whims were not of first consideration.

Asians, viewing our current urban industrial marriage–family system, describe our marriage as the "love marriage." It is significant and surprising to them that mate choice would be left to youth, rather than being in the hands of elders, and that love rather than social status and wealth should guide mate choice. Sociologists focusing on this aspect of our marriage system call it the romantic marriage type. This concept of marriage stresses the individual's supreme right to love and be loved in a romantic, sexual sense. This is considered the essence of happiness.

In a broader framework, sociologists use the term *nuclear* family to describe the new independent family unit, consisting of the pair and their offspring. This family system has reached its most ideal form in the United States, with its high standard of living and high level of personal income. There is no need for the pooling of family funds as in the joint family, or even the pooling of family effort as in the rural economy of an earlier day. Personal insurance programs, company fringe benefits, and government security provisions liberate the individual and the pair from the economic bonds of kinship. The separate living arrangement provides the setting for the nuclear unit.

In fact, the separate abode is considered a prerequisite to independence. The pair is free to work out their relationship unhampered by close-living in-laws and rear their children with minimum interference from parents and other relatives. The stress on interpersonal relationships in marriage and family has led to the current emphasis on companionship as a major test of mate relationships. The institution is of secondary importance, romance is the lure by which mates are drawn together, but the quality of the relationship which binds it together, if it is to be durable, is companionability. Those who not only love, but who also have enough common characteristics and interests to share each other's life as companions are the ones who are destined for the happy, durable marriage.

In a 1967 study of 581 couples, at least one of whom had taken a course in marriage at the University of California, under Judson T. Landis, ability to "communicate with each other" was most universally associated with marriage in the minds of the subjects (Landis and Landis 1973). Love, meeting each other's emotional needs and satisfactory sex relations were also mentioned by most couples. But almost every pair mentioned the importance of communication.

This communication need may be a more significant item in marital happiness for the college group than for those of less education. The college group may well talk more than those who are not college-educated and than those involved in occupations where physical rather than communicative interaction is basic. But it is most certain that communication is essential to success. Landis also found that peaceful discussion of problems with the spouse was a way of reacting to crises employed by 69 percent of successful couples, but by only 35 percent of a group receiving counseling because they were in marital difficulty. Peaceful discussion had been used by only 45 percent of divorced persons studied.

The meaning of any goal is relevant to the culture in which the family functions. It is within the framework of urban industrial culture that marriage must be understood.

The Radical Transitions of a Decade

No short period in the history of our culture has seen such a rapid shift of perspectives, the spawning of so many new life styles, so many challenges to conventional arrangements in sex roles and sex relationships, and the innovations in living together of the sexes. Judge Ben Lindsey (1927) advocated a sort of two-step marriage (*Redbook,* March, 1927). He called it the "companionate marriage." The young would be permitted to live together on a trial basis. Termination would be voluntary until finalizing steps were taken. He became a very unpopular man. Margaret Mead (1968b) seriously advocated "marriage in two steps," and her ideas have been put into practice widely. In 1967, Virginia Saitr proposed before the 75th Annual Convention of the American Psychological Association that marriage be a "statutory five-year renewable contract."

The hippie contraculture (counterculture) proposes no new marriage theories, but practices a form of group life, which includes communal living, communal sex relations, and acceptance of the offspring into the group. The hippies deny conventional aesthetic, monetary, sanitary, and health norms, yet they, and their offshoot groups, have probably more profoundly affected marriage and family norms than any theories propounded by social analysts.

The New Feminism   Women's Liberation, the new feminist movement, exceeds that of the early part of the century in both militancy and comprehensiveness of goals. Likening their plight to that of the pre-Civil Rights blacks, the leaders of the new women's movement have used the militant tactics of the Civil Rights crusade, and in the long run promise to bring more profound reforms in the American social structure than has the Civil Rights movement. The women's movement involves half the population, the Civil Rights movement involved only about 15 percent of the nation's population. Women are sensing new power, analyzing their place in the conventional social structure, taking a more critical look at the male and at his place in the marriage relationship. There is a new disenchantment with marriage, particularly among attractive women, whom Klemer (1970) reports dominate the counseling room. Plain women may be less disenchanted, having less attractive alternatives to marriage, and perhaps also they have more realistic expectations.

The "Pill" Culture   The "pill" and all the other contraceptive freedoms, for the first time in human history make the sex act free of the high risk of pregnancy, and if failure does occur, abortion is now a legal right. The sexual joys without the heavy tax, so much a part of the male's willingness to prowl and of society's giving him the right, is no longer his sole domain. The more aggressive female is frightening to the average male, who prefers to be sheltered by the conventional female modesty and passivity from a test of his masculinity. No doubt this new female creature has done more to break up sexual communes than hunger and disease and the usual privations. Most males cannot stand the test.

The Escape Route   The escape route from conventional marriage has been widened too. Divorce by "irreconcilable differences," the so-called "no-fault divorce," does not take care of financial, psychological, emotional, and custodial problems, but does make the legal process of shedding a mate easier than ever in our society. Now the poor have a right to counsel free of charge, so they too can get divorced rather than using the traditional means of ending marriage by desertion. There has been an upward climb in the divorce rate, indicating that many are taking advantage of the new right.

Newsweek (1967), commenting on "divorce, American style" expressed the trend succinctly: "What underlies the failure of so many mature marriages is not a new form of friction—but an unwillingness to tolerate the old frictions. In the age of the pill, sexual revolution and the feminine mystique, the notion that happiness takes precedence over family solidarity has clearly captured the female imagination."

Shaking the Foundations of Role Relationships   There is in the air at this moment in history a cultivated dissatisfaction with marriage among women. Part of this must be attributed to the Women's Liberation movement in its various manifestations. The unflattering image of the male has also contributed much. He is a "chauvinist pig," in the vocabulary of the few feminists who are not merely for women but against men. Gloria Steinem (1972), leader of the women's movement, describes the masculine myth as *machismo*,—"the idea that the male must prove himself as a male by domineering everybody—in the boardroom, in the bedroom, and on the battlefield." She believes we must forget the myth of the "dominant male and submissive female" and feels that when we do, "both sexes will be free to function as human beings to discover their individual talents, to be happier and better parents."

It is a time when Mrs. is becoming Ms.; chairman, chairperson; his and him, herm; they, te; their, ter; them, tem; and in God we trust, in Goddess we trust. Such radical steps in obliterating sex identity are overwhelming in their implications to a culture so long rooted in clear lines of demarcation, and so clearly favoring masculine dominance.

The challenge of women to the male-dominated marriage goes very deep into the structure of American society. For a long time the male has been yielding power sparingly. Now it is demanded that he be converted to a new way of life without further quibbling. The transition in roles is a just demand in many areas of male–female relationships, but without extreme pressures he will not make it now. This is the history of revolution, power is never yielded willingly, and there are always casualties of the revolution. Many marriages are not able to survive the new demands.

Few of the liberators and the liberated prefer the single life or the lesbian relationship to the heterosexual marriage bond, but they do require that their marriage be in the new framework of revised norms and role relationships.

OUR MARRIAGE–FAMILY-ORIENTED SOCIETY

Our society is still very much marriage- and family-oriented. Practically everyone expects to marry, and more than 90 percent reach this goal. This means that practically all who are anywhere near normal in physical, mental, and emotional makeup marry and some who vary far from these norms do also. Although the family has fewer functions which are exclusively under its full control than ever before, it is still considered the normal and necessary relationship for all human beings. In our culture, happiness is still identified with marriage more than any other human relationship.

Although some express skepticism about the future of marriage, it is still the most significant contractual bond in our society not only in terms of its near universality, but also in terms of its psychological and emotional bonds. Most women seek marriage from the teen years on until they achieve the goal. Although men seek it less purposefully, they do marry, and marriage is a positive factor in their major life goal, that of success in their chosen vocation. John E. Tropman (1972) of the School of Social Work at the University of Michigan, studying 6000 men aged 45–54, concluded that being married almost triples a man's chances for success in a job.

It is well-known that married people live longer, enjoy better mental health, and less often resort to suicide than those who are unmarried. This is particularly true of males (Renne 1971). The death rate of bachelors is about twice that of married men. There is no doubt a selective factor in marriage itself, which helps explain such statistics. The more healthy marry, and if divorced, they remarry. But the marriage relationship itself must undoubtedly be given some credit. It is a protective institution, particularly in giving the individual a needed assurance that his life is meaningful to others, that he is an intimate and vital part of the life of another, or of others. The base is broadened as children enter the marriage.

Individualistic as we are as a people, there is no satisfactory alternative to marriage and family in our culture. This no doubt explains its all-time height of popularity. A brief review of the functions which marriage and family perform for all peoples will convince one that although they are not as invariably tied in with marriage in our society as in some cultures, they are most successfully performed there.

Providing a Sexual Outlet   All peoples control sexual behavior. The survival of a society is dependent on its control. Even in an anonymous society, with relaxed sexual codes, regular sexual relationships are most successfully realized in marriage. The ultimate consequences of the sexual relationships are provided for only in marriage and family. There are substitutes today, but none as satisfactory as the pair relationships for caring for and rearing the child.

Providing Legitimacy   Closely allied to the preceding topic is that of providing legitimacy for the child. Legitimacy involves all the protections of law, of economic benefits, including inheritance, and of the right to the father's name and social respectability. Marriage is the only way to provide legitimate status.

Providing for Division of Labor   In all cultures, there is, and must be, a division of labor. This involves a certain amount of specialization, with the efficiency this brings. Marriage provides for the basic specialization of labor in all cultures. Cultures differ very much in the assigned tasks designated for male and female, but each culture shapes male and female for their concepts of tasks each should and will perform. Even with the great interchange in roles in our culture, there is still much shaping of male and female personality toward anticipated roles in family and society.

Providing Social Supports   In our mobile society, with its great anonymity, social and emotional support have become the principal bond of the man-wife tie. The mate is the main support in times of crisis, illness, emotional stress, and personal catastrophe. The bonds with the parental family have weakened with the migration from home, and with the differentiation in personality produced by special education and special experience of children which create a gap of understanding that widens between the generations. In a similar way, the primary group ties are severed as the individuating influence of unique experience shapes and reshapes personality. The mate becomes the one from whom understanding, sympathy, and counsel are sought.

Sense of Community   Marriage creates a sense of community for both man and woman. When a person settles down to marriage, he views all institutions of the community in a new light. Now he becomes interested in schools, churches, neighborhood relationships, a steady job, a place to call home. He thinks in terms of a future and sees that these community facilities will determine the future of his children. And once marriage takes place, members of the larger society give man and woman a new appraisal. They expect the married couple to be more dependable in handling credit, participating in leadership, providing moral support, and building for the future.

Socializing the Child   By far the most significant function of marriage and family is that of socializing the child. This function is more dependent on the married pair than ever before. In the family systems of preindustrial society, there was a large primary group of relatives to help. In our society, it is very much man, wife, and child. The main focus of this all-important drama is the mother and child, with the father in a supportive role. To fail in bringing the helpless child to an effectively functional adulthood is failure indeed.

EXPERIMENTS IN MARRIAGE–FAMILY FORMS

Marriage–family has always been a conventional arrangement in its given culture. Normally few variations are sanctioned by the mores. In complex societies the mores are embodied in codes and creeds of church and/or state with penalties for flagrant violations. A unique development of recent years has been the widespread and open challenge to the conventional norms of marriage and family. The challenge has been so extensive and so varied in form that legal norms are no longer enforced and religious norms, though never enforceable in the strict sense, are no longer as condemnatory in the area of conscience and in the church climate.

The Hippie Life Style   Much of the revolutionary behavior began in the hippie subculture, which operates in a nonconventional world that denies a wide range of long-accepted social forms. It is drug-oriented, communal in living arrangements, defiant of the work ethic, neglectful of the antiseptic cleanliness norm and cosmetic culture, and has reverted to rough and patched garments once associated with dire poverty—in fact, in diet and level of living it is a poverty culture.

The culture has paid the price for its neglect of sex and cleanliness norms by suffering through epidemics of venereal disease and hepatitis, and for its inattention to diet through many health problems. Its disregard of the sex ethic has led to exploitation of the young who have joined the communes, and to crimes of violence in certain instances, and to living outside the law. On the whole, however, it is a peace-loving culture and one which gives a great deal of social support to the strays from home and family. Its total effect on the new generation, most of whom have not and could not join its ranks because they stand for different values, has been profound.

The Low-Class Urban Commune   Many urban communes have been plagued with venereal disease, hepatitis, and crime as transients move in and out and the complexion of the group changes. Of course, many such groups are havens for the misfits of society, the runaways from home, the disillusioned, people for whom conventional marriage and family offer no attraction.

The Rural Commune   The rapidity with which the experimental marriage–family forms shift to new forms or vanish altogether may well indicate that they have little survival value for either the individual or society. Most rural communes, which Thoreau-like have sought their Walden, have failed within a year or two. The dream of subsisting together off the land, of rearing children in a large-family climate, of providing joint security, has faded under the hard reality of grinding toil, human selfishness, and malnutrition (even with the welfare food budgets, which have made survival possible). These have perhaps been the most idealistic of all the experiments in group living.

One reason the contraculture commune has been so diffuse in its influence is that it readily accepts visitors, and many college students visit communes during their summer vacations. Their informal ways, their revolt against middle-class restrictions, and their professed ideals appeal to many of these visitors, who on a casual visit can scarcely visualize what real life in such a climate is like. Daniel Yankelovich, Inc., reports that 40 percent of students polled said they would like to live in a commune and "live off the land." They do not realize that none of the contraculture communes succeed in this ideal.

The Jesus Communes   The Jesus communes tend toward the ascetic extreme and generally hold high standards of conventional morality. The more stable part of this movement, H. H. Ward (1972) thinks, will persist. They are, in fact, on the way to becoming a formal denomination, with missions overseas, conventions, central financing, and other aspects of formal organization. Although they often draw support from organized churches, and some members are supported by their families, Ward says all branches of the Jesus movement tend to have two things in common: They are hostile toward the church and hostile toward the family. Many members have formerly been on drugs, and most are emotionally disturbed, or rebellious, and find in the close-knit group a personal bond that was lacking in their experience.

The Professional-Level Commune   Not all the marriage–family experiments are at this level of the human strata. Some professional people have formed joint households in order to share rental costs; to broaden the base of child care, giving each mother greater freedom; to lessen the loneliness of the mate whose spouse is away at work for long hours. Such joint households generally confine sex relationships to the married pair, and live their lives by most of the conventional standards.

It is not among the alienated alone that certain aspects of communal living have an appeal. Ramey reports the motives of a group of 80 academic and managerial couples of high social class, who investigated the possibility of entering into a communal living arrangement. Most did not do so. They advertised for responses for those of like mind in the *Saturday Review,* and screened the responses by questionnaire, eliminating "swingers." Few of the group wanted the commune to include sexual intimacy. The concern of wives was escape from the isolation which child-rearing entails, relief from overdependence on the husband for adult contacts, and opportunity to make greater use of their training. Men sought greater freedom from the "rat race" and hoped to gain a higher standard of living by the joint expenditure. Some couples wanted a richer environment for their children, and assumed a communal household would provide it.

Children in the Commune   The ideal of a large-family group as a substitute for the nuclear family has merits. It gives the child a broader range of social experience both with adults and age mates, and the child's socialization is not so fully dependent on the mother, father, and siblings. Yet the contraculture commune is grossly neglectful of children as to diet, education, and general care. It also introduces them to the use of drugs. The single woman with a baby is an asset in getting food rations and other welfare benefits, including cash payments for aid to dependent children from which the group can benefit. The older child is a nuisance—his schooling is much neglected, and his diet, like that of other members of the "self-sufficient" commune is insufficient. S. Cavan (1972), in her study of California communes, describes the ranking in the communes: at the top are the males, then adult females, and then children and dogs. She concludes that sometimes a distinction between children and dogs is not made.

The communes that actually do provide a superior climate for child-rearing are the few "straight" ones, like the Koinonia Partners near Americus, Georgia, which has existed for more than 30 years. It is strictly monogamous, is tied to the outside world by sale of its industrial and farm production, and the education and rearing of its children is one of its main objectives (Velie 1973). It is not part of the contraculture, which at a distance seems so appealing to so many young people.

Pervasive Effects of New Patterns   Change, like waves from a pebble dropped in a pond, ripples throughout the social order. The relationships of the sexes both before and after marriage have been profoundly modified. Personal choice has been extended; young people assert the right of a wider range of alternatives in relationships between the sexes and in marriage forms. Most still choose the conventional for their own reasons: moral, aesthetic, rational, religious, respect for parents, respect for themselves, etc.

This book is, of course, addressed to those who intend to mold their lives in the more conventional framework of the American marriage–family system. This is the area where research has been conducted by sociologists by which one is given some guide as to the effect of given forms of sex behavior, of given forms of role relationships and husband–wife interactions, and of conventional patterns of parent–child relationships in effecting happiness and well-being.

It is assumed that some fairly established form of conventional, and, therefore, predictable relationships, is essential to the well-being of man and wife, parents and children, and ultimately the society of which they are a part.

Sociologists have studied many varieties of groups involved in some form of marriage–family venture. There is little indication that any one of them will become the norm of our society, yet all such ventures do affect the pattern of the total society. So far the effect seems to have been, as has been implied, to bring a relaxation in marriage–family norms, to shift the family further toward the position of giving the individual or the couple a greater number of options as to how they will structure their relationships both before and after marriage.

The body of law and custom is still based on the assumption that the couple will found their separate residence, their children have the right to legitimacy, their inheritance rights be protected, and they have the security which a harmonious husband–wife relationship provides. The statistics indicate that this is the hope, plan, and promise of the masses of this generation.

The trend of history seems to be against communal living. Everywhere in the world, as urban industrial development makes it economically possible, movement is away from the joint family system toward the separate residence and the self-contained nuclear family. It is hardly possible to conceive that any experiments in communal living in our highly individuated society can long survive. This kind of life is not compatible with the personalities shaped in our society. Individualism is too precious and the desire for privacy much too great for survival under such conditions.

Communes Are Not Utopia   Elia Katz, in his examination of a number of experiments in group living of communes, finds that such living does not cure all the problems of the pair marriage and nuclear family. He found greed, striving for success, male tyranny, bullying, sexual hypocrisy, and escapism fairly common. These aspects of human disposition cannot be eliminated by idealistic dreams and revolutionary social movements.

Others report that where communal sexual activity is expected many girls sense great guilt in trying to be promiscuous and have to withdraw from this aspect of group participation (Velie 1973). Certainly it must be that many males, faced with the polygamous challenge, find themselves wanting, as girls of the commune compare the males in terms of sexual performance. Not all males can be equal in these matters and the male self-image is much affected by such judgment.

STRESSES OF A REVOLUTIONAL TIME

Inevitable Conflicts   During this period of rapid change, there are inevitably many conflicts between institutional and personal values. Institutions are built for stability, to perpetuate the ways of a people in traditional patterns so that life may have a routine by which the elders live and which they can project into the future by socializing their children in the routines. Perhaps at few times in the history of man have institutions been so severely challenged and their routines so much disrupted by protest, defiance, and behavior contradictory to their norms.

There is an unprecedented demand for individual freedom. At times the demands have been so extreme that they were self-correcting. The overthrow of social control on the campus was short-lived, as more sober-minded students soon learned that a certain discipline must prevail if an atmosphere of learning is to be maintained. Even the black revolution, in its more militant phase, brought the serious realization that it was the blacks who were losing most property in looting, burning, and killing, and that the whole race would lose unless social controls were exercised over extremists.

The marriage–family institution has borne the challenge of Women's Liberation, and the removal of taboos on abortion, adultery, and fornication.

Marriage is tolerated in many forms. The legal form exists, but living together outside wedlock is no longer viewed as a crime, and children are born out of wedlock in increasing proportions. Welfare institutions have taken over the responsibilities for support as surrogate fathers for a large group of the new generation. The emphasis is in the direction of personal freedom at the expense of the institutions of marriage and family.

Are new social controls needed, or will the new generation find themselves returning to the more secure framework of social control where they can be assured greater continuity in personal relationships and where the traditional economic arrangements for the support of wife and small children is assured by the male worker?

Dominance of the Conventional   For most young people still, both the preface to marriage and its consummation are conventional arrangements. They think and behave within the framework of the mores. Conventional morality has been internalized, marriage aspirations are for a lasting conventional arrangement, and they hope to give children a secure and permanent climate in which to grow to maturity.

Certainly what sociologists know from research was learned in this framework of norms. Any guide or precedence comes from this, and it is to help the young people who think and feel within this framework of norms and aspirations that courses in marriage are planned. There is really no guide for the so-called new forms of marriage. Those who seek them must do so with all the risks which experimentation brings.

In all cultures, marriage and family are among the most conventional arrangements. It is assumed in the presentation of this text that for most young people they will continue to be, although the new patterns will slowly cause significant changes. Society could not function if all suddenly were to make a revolutionary break from the conventional in so basic an area as marriage, family, and parenthood arrangements.

Wave of the Past or of the Future   We may well be in the last phase of the "drifter" revolution. Young people seem to be seeking more privacy in living arrangements. It may be that an increasing number are becoming aware that some degree of "establishment" authority is essential to their personal well-being, and that a depth of satisfaction is possible through the pair relationship that is unknown to the "drifters" and "shoppers" in the sex and marriage mart.

PROBLEMS

1   Do you think problems of marriage are overstressed today? Or do we indulge in too much idealization of the marriage relationship?

2   Do you think individual considerations are primary in marriage rather than institutional ones? Should they be? Relate to marriage stability.

3   Do you feel that communication is one of the most significant bonds of marriage? Need it be all verbal?

4   Appraise Women's Liberation in its various manifestations and give your views of its implication to marriage. Do you think it has increased disenchantment of women? Of men? Which sex do you think has the best deal in marriage today?

5   Summarize some of the significant psychological implications of the "pill." How has it affected male–female role relationships?

6   Do you favor "no-fault divorce"? What arguments may be raised against it?

7   What is your reaction to vocabulary changes directed toward eliminating sex differences? In Nebraska a woman need not take her husband's name at marriage, but may retain her own. What is your reaction? Whose name should the child bear in such a situation?

8   Is there any evidence that marriage and family are destined to disappear in our society? Justify your answer in terms of advantages or disadvantages of marriage.

9   Appraise various forms of communal living from the standpoint of the pair. Of the child.

10   How do you think the commune idea has affected the attitudes of young people who would never consider membership? Do you think conventional marriage types will predominate in the future?

MALE AND FEMALE: PREDISPOSITIONS AND ROLES

MALE AND FEMALE: BIOLOGY

3 Freud said anatomy is destiny. The sociologist is more inclined to the view that culture patterns are destiny for mankind, so much do they mold the child into the image of the adult needed to fit into and function with the group of which he is to become a part. Yet even the sociologist dares not ignore anatomy in analyzing the relationships of male and female. In very critical areas of their relationship anatomy is destiny indeed.

Each of the thousands of cells in the human body have 46 chromosomes except the egg and sperm cells. They have only 23. The chromosomes of the female egg cell are all alike and are called X chromosomes. The sperm cells of the male carry either 23 chromosomes or 22 X chromosomes and 1 Y chromosome. It is this Y chromosome that accounts for the male's beginning.* If a sperm with the Y chromosome fertilizes the egg cell, the male results.

Nature provides in the male a ratio of about 60 Y sperm to each 40 X sperm, so that more male conceptions take place. In some marriages, however, all children are females, in others all males. It is now known that some males produce almost no Y chromosomes, others almost no X. One

---

*A recent genetic development is the discovery that some males have, instead of a simple XY chromosome makeup, an XYY or even an $XYYY$ composition. Preliminary study suggests that prison populations have a relatively high ratio of the excess Y group. This may revive theories of the "born criminal type" made popular by Lombroso. The XYY seem to be tall and thin, highly excitable, given to uncontrollable violence. The extra Y chromosome has already become a legal issue in court procedures involving trial of criminals with the extra Y characteristic. No such behavioral characteristics have been associated with extra X chromosomes in the female.

family had produced no males for five generations. A young man in this family was found to have 96 percent X chromosome sperm. The Y sperm are small, round-headed, and move more rapidly than the X sperm, which are larger and long-headed. The reason some families run to males and some to females is that these ratios are probably hereditary.

This is the biological beginning, but biology alone is not a guarantee that the individual produced will be classified psychologically, or sociologically in the sex class which the chromosomes foretold. The making of a male and of a female is a process involving hereditary determinants, glandular activity (including hormonal balance), and social conditioning to assure proper role identification by self and others. If either the biological or sociological sequences fail, a misfit individual results.

GENETIC CLASSIFICATION

External genitalia are critical in sex identification. The doctor and parents are dependent upon them for the immediate classification of the newborn child into one or the other sex category. The first question of all concerned is certain to be, "Is it a boy or girl?" It would hardly be appropriate for the doctor to reply, "I do not know," yet in a small proportion of cases he cannot know, the child being a *hermaphrodite*. This term comes from the Greek word meaning half man, half woman, child of the gods Hermes and Aphrodite.

When external genitalia are not clearly definable, confusion in sex classification takes place. Currently in hospital births, doubts are allayed by a microscopic examination of bucal cells scraped from the mouth. Every cell in the male is male and in females, female. The hermaphrodite is of one sex by gene determination. However, since hormonal balance is not realized because of inherited malformations or prenatal injury, particular sex characteristics fail to develop. Failure to realize anatomical development may be in external sex organs, internal organs, or both. A few hermaphrodites produce both egg and sperm cells, but there is no known case where a human being has been capable of being both mother and father.

Each embryo starts with the rudiments of sex glands in the form of genital ridges. The chromosome makeup determines which will go forward in the development of the embryo, male or female. The actual development seems to be controlled by the hormones produced by the primitive gonad (undifferentiated glands) and later, it is believed, by other hormones of the adrenal cortex. If the primitive gonads develop a liberal amount of male hormones (testosterone and androsterone), the direction of development is toward maleness; if they produce a sparse amount, it is toward femaleness. Research seems to suggest that all embryos could develop in the direction of femaleness if it were not for the secretion of the testes which lead embryos toward masculine development.

Adult males and females carry in their genitalia marks of the opposite sex. The male carries a seam down the underside of his penis and across his scrotum which could have opened, during the embryonic stage, into the labia of the female's vulva. The female carries rudiments of the penis—the bud-like clitoris, which contains the same kind of nerve plexus as the male glans penis.

Both sexes produce the same hormones but in different quantities. Even after adult development, if the hormonal balance is disturbed, modifications in the somatic structure may occur. Some women at menopause, when male sex hormones are excessive, and the imbalance is not medically corrected, tend to develop moustaches and beards. When a male is castrated, the production of sex hormones is reduced and the male may develop a disposition often identified with the female in our society.

After birth, rearing must be in the appropriate sex category or the individual will not be able to function in the social group, even though biologically complete for his genital sex group. In the past, where gender classification was made at birth on the basis of external genitalia, physicians had to make an on-the-spot decision which determined sex-rearing. This sometimes led to an error in sex-rearing.

THE CRITICAL PERIOD IN SEX "IMPRINTING"

Wrong sex classification is not unalterable during the first two years of life (J. P. Scott 1962). In fact, experience shows that the sex category of a child can be changed with little disturbance until he is two and a half years of age. Psychologists refer to certain ages in the psychological development of the individual as "critical periods." Apparently the critical period for internalizing his sex category comes prior to age two and a half, a time when he is learning language and beginning to take an interest in play with his own group. Any attempt to shift the child from one sex category to the other after this age is accompanied by increasingly severe disturbances. By age six, sex identity is for all practical purposes irreversible.

> As gender role and identity become fully differentiated, they become permanently indelible and imprinted, and subsequently, irreversible and powerful in influencing behavior as if innately preordained. . . . The evidence from hermaphroditic cases of sex assignment is that the critical period of gender imprinting is in early childhood, beginning with the onset of the mastery of language. The die is cast, pretty well, by the age of six, after which major realignment of gender role and identity is rare (Money 1963).

SUBCULTURE REARING

Role modeling for male and female subcultures begins so early that it very soon takes on the finality of a genetic trait in its persistence. Subculture rearing can apparently alter the sex psychology of any individual so much that it will be difficult for him to assume the behavior suited to his biological constitution. The sociological process of role indoctrination is a process so smoothly handled that it seems automatic. So effective are the means by which the male and female internalize attitudes, behavior, and expectations of their sex that subculture identification becomes practically irreversible.

A girl who is brought up as a boy and treated as a boy, no matter what her genetic and hormonal structure, comes to think of herself as a boy, to act as a boy, and will, if allowed to develop very long in this direction, find it almost impossible to ever develop the appropriate attitudes. The same is true of the boy reared as a female. Many individuals have inappropriate gender identification in much or in part of their psychological orientation, even when the family and other social groups handling them fully intended that they would identify themselves psychologically and sociologically with their own sex.

GENDER IDENTITY—A DELICATE BALANCE

The sex a person feels himself to be may be opposite to his anatomy. Herein lies the responsibility of the family for helping the child internalize the correct conception of his gender. The preceding brief summary indicated that interacting biological, parental, and subcultural forces enter into the making of a male or female, and that the achievement of sex identity is an intricate process involving all these factors.

The well-balanced, biologically distinct male or female is produced by heredity and proper glandular functioning during the interuterine period of development. Right sex classification is determined by those who place the child in one sex category or the other. Gender self-identification is a product of the sex roles played by the individual, and these roles, when wrongly typed, need not fit glandular makeup of the developed male or female.

The individual must be so handled that he will internalize his gender as a prerequisite of assuming the roles of the subculture of his own sex. Otherwise an individual with all male characteristics may have the psychological constitution and sexual proclivities of the female. Gender identification is likely to follow the sex-rearing of the individual, no matter what his biological sex, but if it does not conform to his sex, conflict is certain to result. It is also possible that his erotic dreams, fantasies, and practices will conform to his biological sex, even when he is reared in the wrong sex group, inducing further conflict.

Hormonal composition alone will not overcome wrong sex-rearing. Role training is made easy only if one is trained from the beginning for roles in the subculture he will occupy. The general deportment of male and female, as they are shaped in their respective subcultures, takes deep roots from the standpoint of social obligation and expectation.

In 1972, for the first time in the history of the Olympic games, competition of women was restricted to those genetically classified as females by the "hair test"—analysis of the chromosomal content of a single hair determines with certitude the genetic character of the person. The reason for this test was that in the past nearly half the world records in some events were set by hermaphrodites who were socially classified as females, but who were male in chromosome and glandular components. In track competition at Budapest in 1967, sex testing was introduced, and five of the 11 women champions were found to be dominantly masculine in glandular functioning.

Since marriage involves the interrelationships of male and female in their biological constitution, psychological orientation, and role conceptions, each of these areas will be explored as a basis for understanding both the preface to marriage and adjustment during marriage.

It is now believed that homosexuality is a psychosocial development and not a biochemical or hormonal one. Failure in gender identification manifests itself in many degrees of divergence, from transvestism (desire to dress like the opposite sex) to different degrees of latent and overt homosexuality. Even overt homosexuality varies in degree from the desire for a sex partner of one's own sex as an element of sexual variety, to an attraction to one's own sex exclusively.

Gender confusion, when it takes the form of homosexuality, becomes a serious problem in societies such as ours, which expect clear-cut identity with one's own sex and the appropriate sex behavior.

A study of 300 homosexuals by the New York Mattachine Society (1968), a group of homosexuals, showed that only six answered "yes" to the question "If you had a son, would you want him to be a homosexual?"

Homosexuality is a development of the parental home. It is the product of certain types of relationships that exist between parent and child, and between husbands and wives. A nine year study of homosexual males by Dr. Bieber, Associate Clinical Professor of Psychiatry at New York Medical College, concludes that the roots of homosexuality are in disturbed situations in the early family relationship. In almost every case he found "a close-binding intimate" mother and/or a hostile, detached, or unrespected father, or other parental aberrations. In a majority of cases he found the father hostile to the child. He concludes that a warmly supportive, constructive father neutralizes the effect of "seductive, close-binding" attempts of the mother (Doty 1963).

The study of the Wydens (1968) stresses the importance of developing the child's sense of masculinity or femininity between the ages of three and ten. With boys and girls this is largely a matter of normal relationships with parents and setting a good example. The homosexual daughter seems to be produced by the presence of a feared and puritanical father who secretly shows a sexual interest in the daughter, much like the close-binding mother in the case of the male child.

Dr. Harvey E. Kaye and associates made an intensive study of 24 homosexual women and found in their background fathers who were "puritanical and explosive." Daughters feared them, although not from physical abuse. The fathers were overly possessive, interested in the daughter physically, and both mothers and fathers tended to discourage their daughters' development as adults.

Other environmental conditions may contribute to homosexuality, but it is generally considered impossible for a homosexual to be produced in a warmly loving home of sensible parents who are themselves sexually adjusted.

The Wydens suggest that the following factors are important in addition to setting a good example for the child:

1   Breast feeding if possible, although the affection accompanying feeding may be the important factor.
2   Unemotional toilet training. Enemas and rectal suppositories should be used only if medically necessary.
3   Separate sleeping room away from the parent after the first year, or even sooner. The child should never be taken into the parents' bed.
4   Parents should not become excited about the child's masturbation.
5   Children should have plenty of contact with other children.

6   Children should be helped to feel free to discuss sex.
7   Boys should get into competitive activities, but not where they are sure to fail.
8   The child should know that he is loved without being smothered.
9   He should be made proud and happy with his own sex and comfortable with members of his own sex.

BIOLOGICAL RHYTHMS AND SEQUENCES

Female Rhythms   The sexual life of the female moves through complex changes which have no counterpart in the male. As pointed out by Margaret Mead (1949), "Coming to terms with the rhythms of woman's life means coming to terms with life itself." The imperatives of the body are her most pressing realities; they cannot be ignored, and must be reckoned with by society and by the marriage partner as well as by the woman herself.

The major developments are, first, the arrival of puberty with the event of menstruation—the primary sex-life rhythm; second, defloration, on first intercourse; third, pregnancy, with its disturbance of body function and social habits; fourth, childbirth—an event of great biological and sociological moment; fifth, lactation, which has both physiological and psychological effects; and sixth, menopause, or the change of life, which marks the cessation of ovulation, menstruation, and fertility, and which is accompanied by glandular changes and, often, strong emotional reactions.

Defloration, pregnancy, lactation, and menopause will be discussed later. The most significant of the biological events, in terms of adjustment during a large portion of adult life, is menstruation. This marks puberty, beginning suddenly and continuing more or less without interruption, except when pregnancy takes place, for a period of 35–40 years.

The physiological process itself has often been made a great impediment to woman. Many cultures have declared this a period of uncleanness and surrounded it with taboos. Numerous restrictions have been imposed, not only on physical activities, but also on social intercourse. Anthropologist Ashley Montagu has listed some of the common menstrual prohibitions and beliefs on which they are based: Menstruating women cause flowers to wilt and wither, preserves of every sort to spoil, dough to fail to rise, seeds to become sterile, meat to decompose. In Europe women are excluded from many occupations on this account. They are not allowed to work in French perfumeries when menstruating, to pick mushrooms in commercial growing places, or to tend silk worms. Rhine women are barred from handling vessels in which wine is to be fermented. They are also excluded from sugar factories.

He believes that there is some scientific basis for these prohibitions, arising from observation of the effects on living plants. Sweat secretions at this time do kill or damage certain kinds of living tissue. In some cultures anything menstruating women touch must be purified by religious ceremonials. They may be entirely barred from religious participation during menstruation, and among some primitives must even live apart during this period.

Fewer concessions to the menstrual period are made now in our culture than formerly although it is still referred to as "the curse," and more rarely as the "sick time." The use of modern sanitary protections, the daily bath, and higher standards of personal hygiene have removed "uncleanness." Modern drugs and the stress on physical activity for women have removed the taboo on activity. For a few women it remains a critically painful period.

Menstruation is an inescapable fact of women's life from about age 13 to 49, month in and month out, with its moods, its discomfort, its requirements for special sanitary precautions, its limits on contacts with the male. No matter what her time cycle, menstruation is part of her life, and any cessation of it is a matter of concern. If she has been involved sexually, either before marriage, in marriage, or after widowhood, cessation may be due to pregnancy. The cessation may also be due to factors of health or emotional strain, but even so the suspicion of pregnancy is likely to be present.

Jessie Bernard has concluded, from studies on physiology in the experience of women, in the United States at any given time 8.5 percent of women of child-bearing age are pregnant. Of the rest, one-fourth of those not breast feeding are menstruating. Another 10 percent are in the throes of premenstrual tensions. This means that at all times half the women in the child-bearing age group are reacting to stimuli that do not exist in the male body (Bernard 1972).

Male Development   The male's sexual development and decline is a gradual thing without marked periods of change.* Prior to puberty his capacity to reproduce gradually develops. Maturation of sexual capacity comes at puberty accompanied by rather marked body changes. From early adolescence on, his sexual drive gradually declines but rarely disappears until well beyond age 60, often not until 80, or in certain cases not until death in extreme old age. Some men when in their 90s have sired children. Men's decline is a gradual aging process which seems to affect the whole organism rather than sex characteristics as such. Nature spares women the strenuous toil of reproduction in old age. The male need not be spared. His role is primarily economic and he is often more able to provide for children after 50 than before.

There is no physical damage to the male from first sexual intercourse to mark the end of his virginity, and he has no physical responsibility for offspring other than the act of copulation itself. Copulation is an end in itself rather than

---

*Although the above statements are true of the general stages in the development of male and female, a more detailed tracing shows that the development of sexual maturity is not as climactic in either male or female as these obvious stages indicate. The concept "adolescent sterility" has come into the scientific literature in recent years primarily because of research among primitive peoples and among animals. It is evident that the boy is capable of semen ejaculations before ripe spermatozoa are produced. Menstruation begins in the girl also before ovaries are fully developed, and ova are often produced before the womb is sufficiently well-developed to carry a fetus.

It has become particularly evident, from the study of primitive peoples, that among those who permit free sex play prior to marriage, pregnancy is not frequent during the early years of adolescence. In many such tribes, sex play continues uninterrupted until the girl does become pregnant and thus attests to her readiness for marriage and parenthood. In these societies it is evident that fertility rarely comes with the beginning of menstruation. Maximum fertility in the female probably is not reached until the early 20s. For a brief, nontechnical statement on this subject, see Benedek (1953).

a beginning, as for the female. Society places on him the responsibility for the care of the female and her helpless offspring, but this is a social obligation, not a part of nature.

The male is spared the stress which may characterize the female menopause. The decline of potency and fertility in the male is a life-long process once full maturation is reached prior to 20 years of age.

APPETITES AND DRIVES OF MALE AND FEMALE

In this field it is most difficult to separate biology from cultural conditioning. No man or woman is permitted to grow up as designed by nature. From earliest infancy, personality is subject to the molding influences of culture. Manifest drives and appetites are certain in most instances to reflect some degree of modification of biological forces by education.

Glandular Factors   Biological forces in and of themselves are, however, decisive factors in the shaping of the male and female personality. The profound effect on the sex glands and their hormone secretions on the male personality, particularly on such traits as aggressiveness and courage is illustrated throughout the animal kingdom by marked change in psychology, as well as in physical build, of the animal which has had the gonads (testes) removed. The potentially courageous, sinewy, heavy-necked bull, when castrated as a calf, becomes a fat, placid, soft-tissued steer. A similar transformation is seen in the castrated rooster. Instead of a crowing cock, the capon becomes a tender-meated passive-dispositioned fowl much like the hen in temperament and tenderness of flesh.

A comparable change takes place in the human male when he is castrated at a prepubertal age. Such males (eunuchs) become pliant in disposition, fail to develop masculine secondary characteristics such as beard and body hair, become soft and girl-like in voice, and flabby in muscle. Such males lose most of their interest in the opposite sex and become entirely different in psychological makeup from normal males.

Many cultures in the past have, and some still do, make much of this transformation in the male. One of the most cruel aspects of African slavery was the castration by the Arab captors of large numbers of boys to become servants in the harems of the Arab world. The crudity of the operation lead to a very high death rate. The Byzantine State based its vitality as an empire in part on the practice of the extensive employment of eunuchs in key government and military positions. Great numbers of boys were castrated for state positions. Eunuchs had no ambitious sons to place in office and could, unmotivated by nepotism, be objective in administration. In the temples of Judaism, eunuchs were used because they could possess a purity of mind unmatched by males controlled by normal glandular pressures. Eunuchs are the entertainers today at christenings and other special occasions in Pakistan.

The removal of both ovaries in the young female produces marked changes also. The modified female, both among animals and human beings, tends to become more masculine in appearance and characteristics, indicating that these glands and their hormone secretions have a decisive effect upon the development of the female. Some women at menopause, with the decrease of female hormones, take on certain masculine characteristics such as facial hair growth and deepening of the voice. In such instances there seems to be an increase in the secretion of male hormones that are always present in the female.

The sex glands with their hormonal secretions, in fact, affect the growth of the body and account for many differences in height, weight, and tissue formation of male and female.

There is undoubtedly a biological basis for man's urge to pursue and woman's passivity. Certainly these traits are widely observed among most creatures in nature. Even so, culture can, with great difficulty, blunt the male's ardor if tradition so dictates. Where sexual intimacy in childhood and adolescence is a part of the culture pattern, frigidity and impotence will be rare. If too great taboos are built about sex, both male and female may lack interest. The Manus tribe, for example, looks upon seminal discharge as a form of excretion and treats it with repugnance and shame. The birth rate in this tribe is extremely low and the tribe is on its way to extinction (Mead 1954). Female sexual enjoyment has been subject to cultural restraint in many societies, and apparently it is readily curbed.

Psychosexual Development   The rate of psychosexual development differs for male and female. Sex interest for the male is at its height in the teens. Masturbation and other sexual expressions are nearly universal for the young male. Often the teen-age girl has little or no localized sexual desire and she is much less likely to masturbate.* Female sex interest reaches its height near age 30, long after sex sensation has been localized by sexual activity. The teen-age girl is interested in being cuddled but in most cases is not interested in erotic expression as such. Of course, the range of difference in psychosexual interest in both male and female varies from individual to individual. Some mature in sexual interest earlier than others. Some have very weak sex drives; others are often overwhelmed by them.

It is in the consequences of the sex act that one of the most important sex differences inheres. Women house the embryo and nurse the child. As Margaret Mead (1954) has stated, "Men have to learn to want to be fathers. Girls are committed in every cell of their bodies," for the mother role. Sexual intercourse for both man and woman is a matter of a few minutes, but for the man those few minutes end. For the woman, they are "laden with commitments before and commitments afterward."

Coitus is the most intimate and private human activity, yet in its consequences it is of great public importance. This is particularly true for women. From early adolescence and throughout adulthood, women are much more concerned with their bodies and their personal appearance than are most men. It is their biological function to attract the male and bind him to the responsibilities of parenthood. Men are much more concerned with affairs and

---

*Kinsey and his co-workers found in their studies of thousands of males and females that at age 22, 40 percent of females had never experienced a sexual orgasm, whereas 80 percent of males had experienced an orgasm by 15 years of age, and 98 percent by 18 years of age.

activities external to themselves than with their own bodies and feelings. These are, in part, matters of conditioning in American culture, but probably not entirely so.

Cultural Adaptations to Biology   One of the most penetrating analyses of organic differences between male and female as factors in their respective sexual training and behavior is that by Shuttleworth (1959). The essence of Shuttleworth's view is that male and female are conditioned differently sexually because they are so different in their biosexual makeup. Differences in conditioning begin in infancy and continue through childhood and adolescence. At least five biosexual differences lead to the differences in conditioning.

First, the female is a childbearer and has the mammary equipment for nursing. This Shuttleworth states as a fact, but he does not elaborate on the significance of it.

Second, the male has the greater height, weight, and physical prowess, which Shuttleworth feels most societies make a great deal of. He believes that sex aggressiveness is part of the total pattern of the male's superiority in physical build and energy.

Third, the male sex organ is the erectile penis, which, being external, is exposed from earliest childhood to stimulation from bedding, clothes, and later from self-manipulation. The male infant has frequent erections. These continue throughout childhood, and friction brings gratifying response. Thus, there is a profound difference between the baby boy and the baby girl, as well as between the male and female child and adolescent. The boy is aware of this organ and of the sensation which it brings. He develops genital responsiveness very early and cultivates it through maturity.

Female children have no such awareness, because of the different formation of the sex organs themselves. The first sexual arousal of the male comes early, Kinsey (1948) suspects between the ages of six and eight. The first sexual arousal in the female comes later, usually between eight and 13 (Kinsey 1953).

In later childhood, masturbation begins. It usually is learned from other boys; but if it is not, the boy learns it by himself. Girls do not masturbate in nearly as high a proportion of cases; and when they learn, it is often from boys, rarely from other girls. Very few learn from self-discovery.

Nature has prepared the male for instant readiness. His desires are easily aroused by a wide range of psychic stimulation. This is nature's way of preparing him for the sex act, for his part in reproduction depends upon his readiness to take the initiative when the opportunity is offered. To fail to be able to respond to opportunity is one of the greatest threats to his masculinity.

The Kinsey researchers find, for example, that although male and female are alike in their ability to experience sensation of an erotic nature in various parts of the body and that there is no difference in the time male and female require to reach orgasm, once the sex act has begun, there are striking differences in the kind of psychological stimuli to which the two sexes respond and, therefore, in psychological preparation for the sex act.

They studied men's and women's reactions to a list of psychological phenomena: seeing the body of the other sex, seeing the other's sex organs, viewing one's own body, erotic art, motion pictures, etc. In all, 33 different types of psychological stimuli were presented, and the male was found to respond to 29 of the 33 items more fully and more quickly than did the female. In one they were equal. The only three items to which the female responded more readily were motion pictures, reading romantic literature, and being bitten. Differences on these three items were not great.

The male's erotic dreams are usually accompanied by sexual fantasies concerning untried situations. The female can also have erotic dreams that end in orgasm, but they usually involve the recall of experience. Some women can have orgasm by imagining situations, men rarely can.

The male progresses in sexual development by learning more effective ways of erotic stimulation, until he eventually reaches the ultimate satisfaction of sexual intercourse. His sex life begins in the nonerotic masturbation at ages three to five. It recedes, and then reaches another peak at six or seven years of age, when it again subsides. Responsiveness to sex talk reaches its peak in boys of 10–11 years of age, and then this interest declines. Homosexual responsiveness reaches its crest at around 12. Masturbation reaches its peak at about 15, after which come responsiveness to female nudity, day-dreaming, dancing, and so on. Nocturnal dreams seem to increase up to the late teens or early 20s. Petting experiences are more common in the 20s. And finally, of course, the male experiences the more perfect means of sexual arousal and orgasm that comes from sexual intercourse.

By contrast, Shuttleworth finds that the sexual development of the female is a slow gradual learning process, encouraged by the male. Most of what women know about practice in the area of sex is taught them by men. In many tribes, initiation of girls to sex experience is by older men, men experienced in the arts of stimulation.

Fourth, there is a major biological difference in orgastic response. In males it is an inherent reaction; with females it is not. Males are more often rewarded than are females. In nature there is nothing in female reproductive physiology that requires an orgasm. The ancestors of the male who cannot reach an orgasm are long since extinct, since to reach an orgasm is a part of the reproductive act with the male. Shuttleworth believes that few females in the animal world respond to orgasm—that there are probably human females who are biologically incapable of orgasm. Universally, males respond to an orgasm in very much the same way. It is a part of their natural response. The variation in females is from none to multiple orgasms.

Fifth, seminal fluid is a biological factor which affects the differences in sexuality of male and female. Shuttleworth presents extensive evidence, recalculating some of the Kinsey data for various groups of males and females, to show that one of the major reasons for the male's constant and persistent sexuality is the buildup of sexual fluids. The method for stimulating the discharge will vary by social class, education, religion, and other environmental factors, but the regularity of the discharge is more or less constant throughout all social groups, by age level. The frequency of discharge will depend on the particular male. It may be in the form of a nocturnal emission; it may be induced by masturbation, homosexual contacts, petting, or heterosexual intercourse. But the regularity of the male seminal discharge is an incontrovertible fact. Whether the man is married or unmarried, these discharges take place.

Shuttleworth presents strong evidence to the effect that the frequency of the outlet for the male is governed by the production of seminal fluids and not by sociocultural factors. Religion seems to be one of the most effective sublimating factors, for there are actually fewer total outlets among the religious than the nonreligious. The nonreligious less often find an outlet in nocturnal dreams than the religious.

Shuttleworth does not feel that the five factors discussed are the only biological ones, which may be of importance in male and female differences in sex behavior. He does present a very strong case for the fact that some of them are of great importance in understanding the difference in the sexual development and expression of males and females.

Confirming evidence of male persistent sexuality is found in studies of male sex activity. The Kinsey research group reports that men who are divorced continue to have about the same number of sexual outlets as during marriage, and most of the outlets involve heterosexual coitus. Goode (1956) finds that although the folk conception of a divorced woman is that she is a "loose woman," divorced women may cease sexual activity altogether and most are much less active sexually than they were in marriage.

POTENCY AND RECEPTIVITY

These are the conventional terms for the role of each sex in the performance of the sex act. The male's potency is the measure of his ability to perform. The concept of receptivity implies a willingness to yield, to receive, on the part of the female.

Potency   Sexual potency is the key to masculinity in most cultures. Destroy it, and the male's confidence and assurance are lost. The male's satisfaction is derived from activity; the female's from receptivity. The male is easily distracted from one erotic object to another; the female is not. He devotes a great deal of energy to sexual pursuit and performance. In nature, and to a more covert extent in human society, this leads to roaming, aggression, assertiveness, and the defense of territorial rights and sexual property. The glandularly impelled differences even show up in the higher death rate of male children due to accidents (see Chapter 4).

Margaret Mead (1949) has pointed out that a civilization that goes too far in denying the male sexual spontaneity will destroy itself, since the male's performance is dependent on his spontaneity. Female ardor is unimportant in race for survival, provided she will yield to the male's advances for the sake of motherhood.

Receptivity   The rhythm of sexuality throughout nature is pretty much determined by the female and her seasons, although in some species the male's sex interest and potency are also seasonal. Her seasons, in turn, are determined by the period of ovulation and the consequent flow of hormones and genital secretions which increase her excitation and attract and excite the male, challenging him to win or overpower her. The female is receptive only in the period of heat. His is normally the problem of pursuit.

In human beings, where the sex act, because of romantic connotations, becomes conditioned by psychological and aesthetic considerations, biological rhythms are for the most part lost, and sex stimulation becomes associated with tenderness, wooing, caressing erotic areas of the body, and other such types of excitation which operate the autonomic nervous system.

Among humans, the female may become an active, rather than merely a passive, participant in the sexual act. The pattern will vary according to the culture. Even so, the female is generally the less active partner in initiating as well as in performing the sex act. Many cultures have depreciated her sexuality by various psychological and physiological means. The Victorian philosophy, to which our culture is heir, illustrates the psychological; clitoridectomy and infibulation are examples of physiological means.*

The female's role in the performance of the sex act can be much easier than that of the male, for she can be a passive partner. All she has to do is avoid blocking the male's advance and make herself so attractive that she will interest the male and assure his readiness to perform the act of fertilization when social circumstances make this appropriate.

The female learns to value many other rewards apart from sex, and modifies any natural period of receptivity she has by these other rewards. All that receptivity requires is relaxation of her body. She needs none of the readiness which must be sustained by the male. She can easily fit into the sex pattern of the culture by compliance, "balancing the mood of the moment against the mood of tomorrow, and fitting her receptivity into the whole pattern of a relationship" (Mead 1954).

For most women, the physical act of sex is an inadequate expression of love. Woman demands a much broader sense of completion, since sex for her involves a range of feminine roles, the climax of which is motherhood. From early childhood she is taught the risks of coitus. She knows the penalty of an ill-advised relationship. She develops a modesty based on fear of what sex can cost her unless she behaves wisely and confines it to the type of relationship with the male that gives her maximum security. Often she even carries this reserve over into marriage, for the ceremony does not have the magic power to remove many of her built-in inhibitions.

The fending off of the male's advances has been in part a reaction of the female to a fear of pregnancy. This has been no less true in marriage than outside marriage. Family standard of living, as well as the advance of civilization itself in terms of improvement in conditions of life, is dependent on the control of her fertility. She is much more aware of this problem than is the male, who becomes lost in the momentary satisfaction of the sex act itself. It is women the world over who must limit offspring, who destroy unborn infants, who practice infanticide if custom or personal wishes so dictate; and it is women

*Clitoridectomy involves cutting off the labia and clitoris at the time of puberty. It is practiced among a group of Australians and by many groups in Egypt and the Upper Nile. Infibulation involves sewing up the entrance to the vagina. It is opened in part by the husband at the time of marriage, and fully just before childbirth, then partially closed again after childbirth. See Ashley Montagu (1968).

who pioneer the family limitation movements by crusading for and adopting practices of birth control and abortion.

The female has much greater tolerance both for sexual excess and for sexual deprivation than does the male. In general, she has coitus more under volitional control. Havelock Ellis (1915) long ago observed the tolerance of women for sexual excesses. Kinsey (1953) has shown their greater variability compared to the male in sexual activity, and has also indicated that many married women do not suffer from the sudden termination of a regular sex life. The male does.

The Practical Problem of Potency and Receptivity   Basic differences in potency and receptivity are one of the troublesome aspects of dating relationships. The female adolescent can rarely fully understand the male. Surveys of high school girls indicate that they consider the male "sex-driven." This may be a shocking discovery, but there is a natural basis for it. The college male is no different.

The male identifies his sex drive with localized glandular tensions. Culture teaches him to sublimate and control, yet he constantly seeks more satisfactory sexual outlets. To elevate sexual attraction to the level of romantic love, the goal of our marriage system, requires the suppression and sublimation of the male's physical desires.

The female without sexual experience, by contrast, is less likely to be aware of localized sexual tensions. She tends to be romantic by nature; her love impulses are more diffused and less identified with sex drives.

Much misunderstanding between the sexes in dating is due to the fact that they do not comprehend or accept the differences in the way they view the natural sequence of steps following sex attraction. For women, there are generally three steps: (1) friendship, (2) respect and love, and (3) sexual intercourse. Most men can skip the first steps. A man is attracted to a "sexy" woman physically even though he does not respect her otherwise. A woman may be sexually attracted to a man by physical qualities but more likely senses sexual attraction after she respects him and is to some extent in love with him.

With a woman, friendships grow into love relationships. Men often claim "love at first sight." When lightly claimed, this is a man's approach for sexual exploitation without love being involved at all. When serious, some authorities believe that love at first sight, without previous friendship having been established, is indicative of a pathological state—"symptomatic of profound disorder in the love life."

The female is more cautious in yielding to sex attraction at each step, since at the end of the consummated love relationship, there is always the risk of pregnancy, with the biological and social obligations it entails. This is why the female generally requires a permanent relationship before yielding completely to the sexual demands of the male.

PROBLEMS

1   Do you think that this chapter gives too much weight to biological factors in male–female development? Explain.

2 Do you feel that women still suffer discrimination in our culture because of their so-called infirmities?

3 Discuss the importance of male–female biological differences in drives as they bear on marriage relationships.

4 *Research exercise:* Poll members of the class or some other student group on (*a*) color preferences, (*b*) favorite recreation, (*c*) favorite hobby (other items may be added). Tabulate results for men and women separately. Analyze, discuss, and point up significance of findings.

Are innate or conditioned factors involved? What differences are probably attributable to peculiarities of American culture? How do certain differences bear on the relationships between men and women?

5 Custom is still somewhat opposed to women in certain positions: high government posts, the ministry, executive positions in business, campaigning for office, practicing law, etc. (*a*) Tell why the customs came into being. (*b*) Describe assets or liabilities women possess for these activities.

6 Do you think anxiety about being homosexual is a common feeling among college students?

MALE AND FEMALE: PHYSIQUE AND EMOTIONS

4 Masculinity and feminity are products of culture and, therefore, normal responses to social expectation. Consequently they differ from society to society and are modified within a society with the passage of time. In our society there has been great change in the last decade. Much that was masculine has become feminine, and much that was feminine has appeared in the behavior patterns of males. New norms violate many of the prior assumptions of what many considered an inevitable product of human genetics. Even so, it is appropriate that we consider to what extent and in what ways genetic factors persist in male and female behavior.

PHYSICAL STRENGTH AND STAMINA

It is easy to take for granted the superiorities of the male and the inferiorities of the female in our culture, where the male has almost always been the favored sex. Science now probes more deeply to try to learn what men and women are capable of—physically, psychologically, temperamentally. It is not always possible to detach innate factors from those grafted on by male and female subcultures, but complete isolation of these factors would serve only a theoretical purpose, not the functional one which is the concern of this book.

Although the female is less muscular than the male and falls short in tests of physical strength, she is more durable and has greater resistance to fatigue.

She can stand more suffering and go longer without sleep. At every age of life from birth to old age, the death rate of the male exceeds that of the female (see Figures 4–1 and 4–2). Even prenatal deaths of males exceed those of females; more males are stillborn. Nature offsets this in part by a sex ratio at birth which, in most countries, is about 105–106 male births to each 100 female births (105.7 in the United States). The higher general mortality rate and war together explain why men are in the minority in all of the older nations and

Death rates of males and females—per 1000 mid-year population—by age, United States, 1967. At all age periods the male death rate far exceeds that of the female. During the teens and early 20s it is more than twice as high. It is almost twice as high in the years 50–70. Source: *Vital Statistics Report,* Vol. 17, No. 12, Supplement, March 25, 1969, U.S. Public Health Service, Table 7, p. 9.

FIGURE 4–1

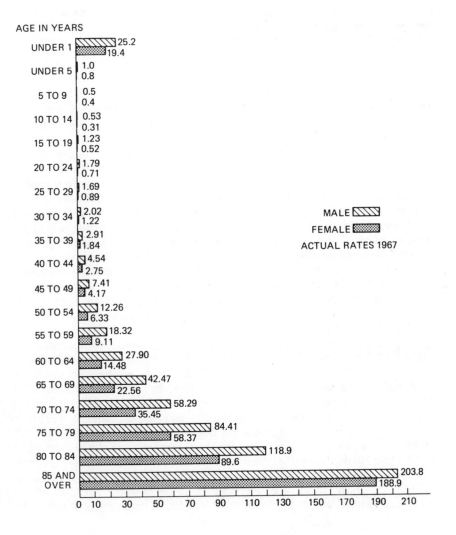

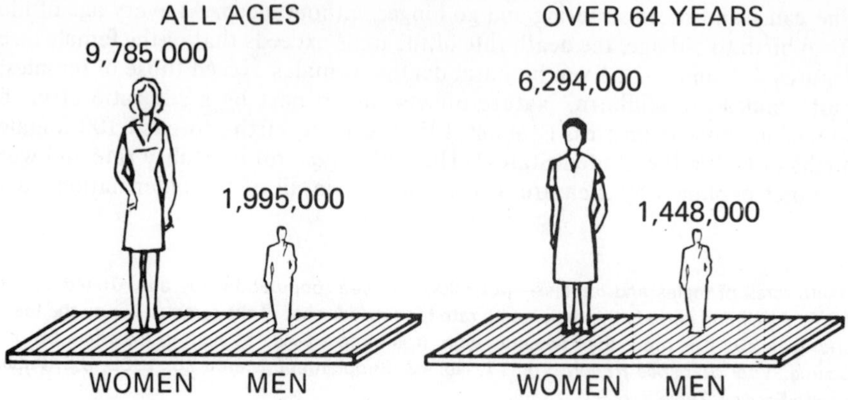

ALL AGES

9,785,000

OVER 64 YEARS

6,294,000

1,995,000

1,448,000

WOMEN   MEN

WOMEN   MEN

FIGURE 4-2   Widowed men and women. Sex ratio of widows and of the widowed 65 years and over. At all ages females are greatly in the majority. Much of the difference is explained by the higher death rate of the male. Source: U.S. Department of Commerce, Bureau of the Census, "Marital Status of the Population: 1960," *Supplemental Reports*, PC(SI)-39, December 28, 1962.

why with the cessation of immigration from other lands (long-distance migrations are always dominated by males) they have, since the early 1940s, become so in the United States.

Women's operative rate runs 46 per 1000 compared to 38 per 1000 for men. Rates run about the same for the common ailments like the removal of tonsils, adenoids, and appendix. Surgery on the genital organs is four times as frequent on women as men, but hernia operations are five times as frequent on men as on women. Coronary thrombosis almost always involves the male. Vital statistics data show that during the years 25–44 the death rate of men from diseases of the heart runs 63 per 100,000 and for women only 18 per 100,000. Between ages 45 and 64, the rate for men is 647, for women only 216. A hospital study of the frequency of 365 diseases found that 245 of them almost always occurred in men.

The sex hormone, estrogen, gives the female protection against many diseases. After menopause, when this hormone decreases, her disease rate goes up. Women have minor illnesses more often than men. Before the days of psychosomatic medicine these were known as "female complaints." But women survive them. They do have a much more complicated glandular makeup to reckon with than do men. Much can go wrong with the female urogenital mechanism because it is so complex. In advanced societies, where diagnosis and treatment prolong life, many women have difficulty in connection with menstruation or childbirth, and some undergo operations involving some part of the reproductive mechanism. Men rarely have difficulty in this part of their anatomy except for the enlargement of the prostate gland in later life. No doubt another reason for women's most frequent complaints is that they get more of a hearing in social intercourse—their operations certainly bring more social acclaim than do those of men. Men, at least in American culture, get no credit for their frailties. Women are now getting less credit for them than in an earlier day when their role in society was a more passive one.

Even so, the differential in length of life is increasing. Today women can expect to live 7 years longer than men—76 compared to 69 years. In 1926, white males in the United States averaged 57 years, females 59.6, a difference of 2.6 years (Figure 4-3 shows the long-term trend of longevity).

Women's greater longevity may be in part due to the fact that they visit doctors more, even aside from calls related to childbirth, and that they are able to take better care of themselves, because they are not so often under the pressure of a scheduled job as are men.

In our culture, men are more definitely committed to the work world than are women. A man's ego satisfaction is found there; he measures his success by the achievements of work and by the advancements in his work position. The warning to the aspiring executive sometimes given is "promotions can kill you." This is indicative of the high pressure which may be inherent in great success in the work world.

The extent to which men are committed to the work world, particularly to heavy manual labor, is partly a matter of culture, rather than biology. In peasant economies and primitive cultures, women often are thought to be as fit for hard labor as men; in some, even more fit. Ethel M. Albert (1963) reports that she was advised in Central Africa that: "Everybody knows that men are not suited to heavy work, that women are stronger and better workers. Men drink too much and do not eat enough to keep up their strength; they are more tense and travel about too much to develop the habits and the muscles needed for sustained work on farms."

Woman is physically awkward, by man's standards. But man is thinking

Increase in average life span. The increase of average length of life in 450 years. The child-rearing span is but a fraction, enabling a mother to begin a new career during the "empty-nest" period of family life. Source: Irving Fisher, U.S. Public Health Service and U.S. Department of Commerce, Bureau of the Census.   **FIGURE 4-3**

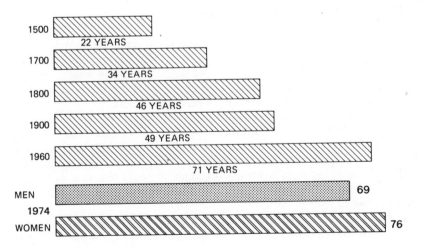

of the way he throws a baseball. If a graceful man were forced to unfasten a back-zippered garment, as women often must, he would soon learn how awkward he is. The male reaches over his shoulders to skin off a sweater; the female, around her ribs. He pulls his gloves on from the front; she, from the back of her hands. He doubles his fingernails into his upturned palm to look at them; she turns her palms down and straightens her fingers to look at the fingernails. He strikes a match toward him; she, away from her. He carries books hooked in a hanging hand. She cradles them on her stomach. He is hinged for certain movements; she, for others. Different, but unequal only if one prefers one style of movement to the other.

In our day when many industrial jobs take nimble fingers, employers have long since learned that many women have physical skills unequaled by many men. Employers sometimes pay women less than men, but this is a survival of custom rather than a denial of equality in ability to produce.

HISTORICAL PERFORMANCE

The male's greatest claim to superior natural endowment over the female is the record of history. The chronicle of humanity's long past is studded almost exclusively with the accomplishments of the male. Even women who achieved enduring fame generally did so by influencing the activities of men rather than by achievements of their own. Yet history shows that now and then a woman has demonstrated superior accomplishment.

What the worshipers of precedent forgot in making historical comparisons of male–female accomplishment is that it is no less a product of opportunity than of genetic inheritance. Few cultures have allowed the female to assume what they considered creative and administrative roles; practically all cultures have placed the male in these roles. The infrequent references to women in history probably prove little except that women in most cultures have been excluded from all but the subservient or domestic activities of the group.

PSYCHOLOGICAL DIFFERENCES

Among the first comparative scientific studies of male and female were those of the anthropologists and psychologists which compared brain weight, reaction time, and sensory acuity of the sexes. The brain-weight test favored the male—more grams of brain, therefore more brain capacity. By such simple logic was the die cast in favor of male superiority.

It remained for the intelligence test, and the competitive situations provided by coeducation to correct this error. The notion that men have superior innate ability as a gift of nature seems so absurd now that few would even attempt to argue the case, yet the proof on which the modern notion of equal ability of the sexes rests is little more than 50 years old. It is not surprising that many still act as though they did not believe women were equal to men in mental ability.

In certain sensory abilities there are slight differences between the sexes. Women, at least as trained in our culture, are generally better coordinated in speech. They rarely stutter. Men inherit a sensory defect, color blindness, which women carry in the genes, but pass on in body characteristics chiefly to the male. Watts (1963) finds that the male tends to "spotlight" knowledge, whereas the female tends to "floodlight" it. The female senses a variety of things simultaneously. He finds that our culture tends to specialize in and reward the spotlight kind of performance.

Male infants are more active than female infants; they cry more, sleep less, and require more attention. The baby girl is more sensitive to touch, sounds, and cold, and is more passive and content. Research shows that female infants smile more and learn more rapidly. As early as 12 weeks they are more interested in pictures of faces than geometric shapes. Later, boys begin to show more interest in geometric forms than in faces. As they develop, girls are more interested in people, boys in things and activities (Krause 1971). In nursery school and in the home, boys quarrel more than girls, are more destructive, and are more aggressive.

Researches of Harvard psychologist Jerome Kagan show that young girls cry more often than boys and drift toward their mothers when placed in a strange laboratory situation. Boys look for something interesting to do. Faced with barriers, boys try to knock them down, girls cry helplessly. Similar differences in aggressiveness between the sexes is seen among primates as well as among human children, leading Kagan (1972) to suggest that they may be due to subtle biological differences. The male takes chances more often. Among males 15–24 years of age 60 percent of the deaths are accidental, among females of the same ages only 35 percent (Metropolitan Life 1966). Deaths from falling are twice as high among males as females during childhood (Metropolitan Life 1968). Throughout life, the male accidental death rate far exceeds the female (see Table 4–1).

Margaret Mead believes that the work cycle of the female in most cultures tends to be adapted to the rhythm of her biological nature. Not all cultures do adapt their work cycle to the natural rhythms of the female, that is, to the rhythm of the monthly cycle and the cycle of pregnancy, nursing, and so on, although it is more convenient if they do so. Man is under no limitations of this kind.

She finds evidence that the man tends to work by spurts of great effort, and that the activity–rest pattern of the male may be related to his endocrine

Accidents in the Male and Female Death Rates, 1962   TABLE 4–1

AGE GROUP (YEARS)	PERCENTAGE OF ACCIDENTAL DEATHS	
	MALE	FEMALE
1–4	31.3	22.7
5–14	23.4	9.9
15–24	90.2	21.0
25–44	65.4	16.5
45–54	78.8	27.0

Source: Adapted from *Statistical Bulletin*, Metropolitan Life (1964, p. 6). (Data are for the white population only.)

MALE AND FEMALE: PHYSIQUE AND EMOTIONS

58　system. Women tend to work at a more constant pace, although Mead cites cultures in which women also work in a spurt–rest cycle. Women have greater capacity for monotonous, repetitive work and bear up under it with less psychological expense.

In the area of interests there are measurable evidences of significant psychological differences between male and female.

Eleanor E. Maccoby (1963), Stanford University psychologist, reports that girls develop greater interest in people than boys do and are more concerned about what people think of them. They are more conforming and more influenced by the opinions of others.

Years earlier, other Stanford psychologists, after covering more than 40 of the best researches made by scientists in different fields, reported (Johnson and Terman 1940):

> Women are consistently more intimate and personal than men. They are strongly interested in persons and spend more time and thought on people and personalities than men do. Excellent studies of young children show that girls very early are more interested in relationships with others, while boys are more interested in material things.

Studies made by eavesdropping show that women talk mostly about personal things—other people, their friends, themselves, or their feelings and loves; men more often talk about activities—politics, business matters, sports, their sexual exploits, and their accomplishments.

Theodor Reik (1960), Director of the New York Society for Psychoanalytical Psychology, has observed that a woman is rarely separated from her husband or lover in her thoughts and emotions, even when at work. Women do not like impersonal work; they want to be working for someone—husband, boss, child, community, or they may want to impress a man through their work. Men are always trying to produce an effect; they want to change the world. For the woman the nicest words are, "I love you," for the man, "I am proud of you."

Research on college dating shows that the bright coed will often deliberately "act dumb" to keep from outdoing her less brilliant date. Of course, a part of this is a woman's sense of the practical in human relations. In this, as in so many of her relationships with the male she must masquerade.

A woman will express herself in terms of how she felt on a certain occasion; a man, in terms of what he said, did, or at least thought. Characteristic female reactions might be "I was embarrassed to death," or "I could have died, I was so humiliated." But in talking about a similar situation, the man boasts, "I told the guy to shut up or I'd knock his teeth down his throat."

If the conversation turns to generalized traits of human nature—like selfishness, greed, obstreperousness, or goodness, for that matter, the woman immediately says to herself, and maybe to others, too, "Am I like that?" She personalizes generalizations about people. A man shifts the generalization to someone else who fits the picture. It never occurs to him that he might be that way himself.

Women are more frequent readers of fiction, for they identify themselves with characters and situations much more readily and completely than do men. If asked to criticize a bit of fiction, a woman appraises situations in terms of how she has acted or thinks she would act under similar circumstances. A man is more likely to rationalize his criticism in terms of principles and universals rather than his own experience.

A man must always be careful in making any criticism of women in the presence of wife or sweetheart, for she immediately feels that his abstract criticism is really meant for her. A man, on the other hand, may fail to get the point when a woman's criticism, aimed at "men," is really meant for him. Likely as not he recognizes that men are that way, but is equally sure that he does not share these imperfections of his sex. His ego is too well-fortified to be punctured by so dull a weapon.

A male, in meeting others, tries to influence them by his conversation and behavior. The female is more often interested in making an impression by her appearance. Women are seldom as direct in stating what they think as are men. For instance, if a man does not like what another does, he is likely to tell him so. A woman is more likely to tell someone other than the offender, thus approaching the issue indirectly. Of course, she hopes her remarks will eventually get around to the right party without her receiving the blame for them. Men are more inclined to be competitive, to outdo others, to achieve success and fortune. Women are more interested in getting along with people, although this pattern is changing because of coeducation and women's work experience.

EMOTIONAL DIFFERENCES

Romantic Inclinations   There is little doubt that the inhibiting of sexual impulses has much to do with romantic feeling. In American culture, at least, perhaps in most cultures of the world, women have more cultural inhibitions imposed upon them in the matter of sexual expression than do men. This explains in part why women are much more romantic in temperament and outlook, why their sex impulses more often take on the character of fantasy, day dreaming, and other forms of covert erotic expression which are in themselves often more satisfying than the physical sexual experience.

This tends to enrich a woman's erotic life and bring to her a more diffused sexual sensation than that of the male, who approaches sex more directly. It has been proposed by some psychologists that such a diffused development of sexuality may actually, in the case of some women, interfere with physical expression of love or make the physical expression seem much less important when experienced than is the enriched sexual fantasy. Eroticism may more readily, in the case of women, also lead to a degree of narcissism, or self-love, which expresses itself in adoration of the body, excessive pride in personal appearance, and general self-absorption as a substitute for sexual love.

It is possible that the female finds it easier to develop masochistic traits than does the male. The male is the active, aggressive partner in the sexual relationship. The female by nature is the passive partner, and these psychological traits may more readily be converted into a masochistic self-torture, which carried to an extreme becomes a perversion. A masochistic personality tends to develop if a father is cruel to his daughters or employs overly stern discipline and physical punishment (see Chapter 6). The tendency of the female to psychologically identify with the male and feel herself a part of him and his activities, which is a natural part of so many cultures, creates a psychological climate which makes it easier for her to develop a martyr complex than it is for the male.

Helene Deutsch has suggested that women who commit suicide because of the breakup of a love affair often do so, not because they are suffering from a loss of the love object, but because of narcissistic injury to their ego.

The connection between woman's sexual and emotional life is quite different from that of the male. Nature has provided him with an insistent and easily aroused sexual desire, and it may be quite emotion-free in the larger connotation. He is vulnerable if his readiness fails him. The woman's problem is that of attracting the male she wants as a mate. Her role is that of surrender, but surrender has a price—she wants coitus identified with love.

When cultures choose to make the female highly aggressive, as among the Zuni Indians, stories of fear of the wedding night are about grooms, not brides. In polygynous cultures of the world the universal quest is for an aphrodisiac to bolster the male's prowess in sexual performance.

The Premenstrual Syndrome   The emotional life of the female must be reckoned with in part because of her biological rhythms, which may be reflected in moods. The temperament cycle of the female tends to affect her energy and sociability during the 28 day menstrual cycle. The first peak energy period is shortly after the menstrual flow, the second is near the mid period at about the time of ovulation, and the third is just before the onset of the menstrual flow, when there is a rise in basal metabolism rate. Each of these energy periods are found to be associated with secretions from the ovaries which are evidenced by increased work performance of women. Generally speaking, during the rebuilding of the uterine wall following menstruation, there is a period of great activity, vitality, and sociability. This is known as the estrogen phase of the menstrual cycle. It is climaxed by a slight rise in temperature near the time the ovum is released. After ovulation, the progesterone phase begins and the woman is more likely to be moody and suffer some tension. Her tensions increase as the time of menstruation approaches, although just before menstruation there is an upturn in physical energy due to a rise in the basal metabolism rate.

Tension may express itself in various moods and in various antisocial reactions. Some women become depressed prior to menstruation, a few so much as to be almost suicidal. Others become overtly hostile. Some of the most violent conflicts between mothers and teen-age daughters come at the premenstrual period of the daughter, when she becomes unmanageable and uncooperative. Roommates, husbands, and friends must come to understand this transitory behavior. The more mature woman who is well-adjusted readily brings herself under control, but even so, she may need an unusually sympathetic husband at times previous to menstruation.

The subject of premenstrual tensions has received much study by gynecologists, internists, and psychiatrists, since they have been concerned with the "premenstrual syndrome." The majority of women have some elements of the syndrome.

Morton found that 80 percent of 249 women prisoners had elements of the premenstrual syndrome (Perr 1958). Eichner found that 70 percent of nurses had symptoms (Perr 1958). Several other studies show 30–75 percent of women polled. Pennington found 95 percent of 1000 high school and college students had symptoms. Proportions showing symptoms depend on the interviewers' descriptions.

Most symptoms appear in the premenstrual week; some women have emotional symptoms at the beginning of menstruation, a few at the midmenstrual period, and a few past the midpoint. Early in the new menstrual phase relief from tension comes to most, although some experience physical and emotional stress in the first quarter of menstruation.

On the other hand, Julia A. Sherman's (1973) studies of college women showed the ovulation phase was the period of mood elation, especially the day of ovulation. In 85 percent of cases the time during the midcycle was when mental and physical activities were at their height, and for 68 percent the day of ovulation was one of elation. She found some increase in suicide attempts during midcycle, too.

American studies summarized by Katharina Dalton (1964), as well as by Sherman, show a significant increase in suicide attempts, crime, assaultive behavior, accidents, decline in quality of school work, decline in visual acuity and in response speed, and absence from work during the premenstrual period. Some 62 percent of violent crimes among women prisoners took place on premenstrual or menstrual days. About half of the admissions to hospitals for medical or surgical treatment, and also of admissions to psychiatric hospitals take place during the menstrual or premenstrual phase.

W. R. Cooke (1945) reported that most crimes of a group studied in Paris were committed during the premenstrual period. J. H. Morton (1953) and colleagues report that at New York State Farm for women prisoners 62 percent of crimes of violence occurred during the premenstrual week, 17 percent during menstruation.

The most common theory is that premenstrual tension is due to low levels of progesterone and to high levels of unantagonized estrogen. The estrogen–progesterone ratio seems to be most disturbed at this time in those with symptoms. The premenstrual syndrome is more severe in women with neurotic constitutions. It is also more severe, Cooke found, among women who have a fear of becoming pregnant.

Frequency of symptoms as reported in several studies dealing with the premenstrual period are seen in Table 4–2. Note that headache is the most common experience reported by various groups. Fatigue, depression, and irritability are often reported, as is swelling and tenderness of breasts.

Although sexual desires of women tend to be weak during the period of menstruation, the sex content of dreams is highest according to studies of undergraduate women by Ethel Swanson (1967) at the University of Wyoming. Women have quite different dreams during different phases of the menstrual cycle.

Katharina Dalton (1972) finds that not only does the premenstrual syndrome affect the wife's behavior, but also that of those around her in the family setting. Husbands' attacks of migraine, asthma, or giddiness, and their efficiency in work correlates with the wifes' menstrual cycle. Visits of children to the family physicians' office for minor health problems coincided closely with the mothers' menstrual cycle.

Temperament   Because of women's biological constitution, as well as by unique cultural conditioning, there may be truth in the folk conception that the

TABLE 4–2   Symptoms Found in the Premenstrual Syndrome

	GREENE AND DALTON† PATIENTS (PERCENT)	REES‡ PATIENTS (PERCENT)	EICHNER AND WALTNER§ NORMAL SUBJECTS (PERCENT)	EICHNER# PATIENTS (PERCENT)	LANDIS¶ COLLEGE GIRLS (PERCENT)
Headache	69.5	63	—	—	33
Nausea	29.7	37	—	—	10
Lethargy (fatigue)	13.1	63	59	—	44
Rheumatism	16.7	—	—	—	—
Vertigo (dizziness)	10.6	—	—	—	—
Depression	6.0	80	62	—	—
Irritability	6.0	100	51	—	48
Edema (congestion)	6.0	73	32	72	43
Rhinorrhea (excessive mucous secretions from nose)	7.2	—	—	—	—
Mastalgia (swelling or tenderness of breasts)	2.4	63	69	—	44
Tension	—	100	—	—	—
Emotional liability (inability to concentrate, etc.)	—	—	—	56	39
Anxiety	—	73	—	—	36
Insomnia	—	40	—	—	—
Pruritus (itching and skin eruptions)	—	40	—	—	58
Marked thirst	—	20	—	—	—
Physical discomfort (chills, cramps, etc.)	—	—	—	58	23

Adapted from Irwin N. Perr, Medical, Psychiatric, and Legal Aspects of Premenstrual Tensions," *American Journal of Psychiatry*, 115:211–219, September, 1958, with additions.

† R. Greene and K. Dalton: *British Medical Journal*, 1:1007, 1953.

‡ L. Rees: *British Medical Journal*, 1:1014, 1953.

§ E. Eichner and C. Waltner: *Medical Times*, 83:771, August, 1955.

E. Eichner, "Premenstrual Tension Syndrome," Presentation at N.Y.S. Academy of General Practice, October, 1957.

¶ Judson T. Landis, "Physical and Mental-Emotional Changes Accompanying the Menstrual Cycle." *Research Studies of the State College of Washington*, 25:155–162, June, 1957.

female is more highly keyed, sensitive, and gifted with emotions which lead to protective behavior of the infant and child. Women may be more intuitive. They no doubt are less ego-centered and live less in bold and courageous action than do the men in most cultures. They may be vain, but they are not as ruthlessly ambitious as the male.

Crying remains a part of the female subculture. It is strictly taboo for the adult male of American culture (this is not so of the Latin cultures, where crying as an expression of joy or sorrow is much more acceptable). The American male is not as stoical as the native Indian but he is very stoical compared to the female when it comes to expressing emotions.

These subtle emotional differences are the theme of many works of fiction and of some scientific literature. These supposed traits, and many like them, may be myth or reality, but it is known that a feeling of need for security, emotional and economic, is very strong in women of our culture. Whether this is innate or learned, or a combination of both, is not yet known.

Stanford psychologists found that women are more temperamental, for the female glandular system is much more complicated than is that of the male. Women are given to up-and-down moods during the monthly cycle of glandular functioning and during pregnancy. Their moods exceed the temperamental deviations of the male. Women are also more given to tears than are men. These traits are, in part, culturally determined, of course. Cry, they do, but when emotional problems must be faced, women have more toughness than do men. During World War II, they stood the strain of air raids better than men.

Built-In Shockproofing   Although women have more emotional problems, or at least are more aware of their problems, it is men who most often get ulcers. Even during the teen years, girls are much more aware of problems and tensions in the parental home and in their social relationships generally than are boys. Tradition holds that women fret and worry more than men throughout life, but only about a third as many of them take their anxiety seriously enough to commit suicide.

Even so, far more women than men attempt suicide in the United States (see Table 4–3). Whether they do not have the courage to do it effectively, use the wrong tools, or for some other reasons of a more subtle nature fail, is a matter of speculation. It is very probable that many do not seriously wish to kill themselves. They may use suicide as an attention-getting device, to spite someone, to get publicity, or for other such reasons, and plan the act, perhaps subconsciously, so they will be discovered before it is fatal.

Autocide accounts for much unreported suicide today. Although such deaths are reported as accidental, they are in fact suicide by automobile. This means is probably used more by males than females.

There is increasing evidence of stress in the experience of contemporary woman if we are to use the suicide index. More women are committing suicide and using more decisive means, according to a Los Angeles study. In 1960, 35 percent of suicides there were women; in 1971, 45 percent. A Wisconsin study of women psychiatric patients suggests that more complain of anxiety, depression, alienation, and inability to cope with stress than did ten years ago.

There seems to be no comparable increase of stress among men patients (*Time* 1972a).

Men and women fall victim to nervous breakdowns and mental illness in about equal numbers, but women are more likely to respond to psychological treatment and to recover. It seems very probable that men, because they are disciplined in ignoring pain and discomfort, and are taught to be tough, neglect nervous problems longer than women do and reach the clinician after the disease is much further advanced. Women express their feelings more than men; therefore, men may get in a much worse emotional state before they or others recognize it. Our culture denies men the safety valve of tears, tantrums, and other such releases permitted to women.

Male and female differences in temperament, emotions, and physical strength and stamina are not all a matter of folk myth. Some differences do exist and they are important to man–wife relationships. In some respects women are the stronger sex, in others, men. Their strengths and weaknesses may complement each other, but cultures do not always take advantages of differences in defining male and female roles. In the area of emotional differences, the female biological constitution may be a major factor.

UNISEX: HAS IT A FUTURE?

Sociologists and anthropologists have been inclined to attribute sex differences almost exclusively to role patterning except for the maternal capacity of the female. The great variety of roles assigned the sexes from culture to culture makes such a conclusion logical. Research into infant behavior casts doubt on this premise, and scientific voices are heard favoring significant built-in sex differences. Young, Goy, and Phoenix (1964) report evidence "that part or

TABLE 4-3 Suicide Deaths and Suicide Death Rate—by Sex, Color, and Means of Suicide, United States, 1960–1962[a]

| | WHITE | | NONWHITE | |
MEANS OF INJURY	MALES	FEMALES	MALES	FEMALES
Suicide—Total				
Average annual number	13,812	4,458	745	218
Rate per 100,000	17.5	5.5	9.1	2.4
Percent	100.0	100.0	100.0	100.0
Poisoning	19.3	40.7	10.6	24.0
Hanging and strangulation	16.8	15.5	17.0	17.0
Firearms and explosives	54.7	25.3	52.7	25.9
Other	9.2	18.5	19.7	33.1

Source: Metropolitan Life Insurance Company, *Statistical Bulletin*, 45:8–9, July, 1964a. Data from reports of U.S. Division of Vital Statistics.

[a]Observe that three times as many males as females commit suicide among whites; almost four times as many males as females commit suicide among nonwhites, where the suicide rate is much lower than it is for whites. Women, however, attempt suicide more often. Do you see a possible explanation for the sex difference in success of means used? Are there other reasons?

parts of the central nervous system are masculine or feminine, depending on the sex of the individual." Anthropologists Tiger and Fox (1971) express belief in ingrained behavior patterns they call "biogrammar." And it differs for male and female. "The human mother is a splendid mammal—the epitome of her order." (See also B. Campbell, 1972).

To the extent that these observers are correct about human biology, unisex has little chance. On the other hand, as sex roles change, there seems to be a movement toward unisex on the psychological level. Clinical psychologist Fred Browan of New York's Sinai Hospital no longer obtains responses on the Rorschach ink-blot test comparable to past male–female patterns. There is a distinct shift of men toward what were once female responses and of women toward male responses (*Time,* Sept. 6, 1971, p. 49).

PROBLEMS

1   Discuss the proposition, "Custom, rather than native endowment, is probably responsible for the fact that men hold more positions of authority in our society."

2   Women are frequently credited with having a greater capacity for "spiritual love" than are men. Explain the probable basis for this belief. Do you think it is justified?

3   Do you believe men and women differ in any or all the following traits: mental superiority, reasoning ability, emotional stability, quick thinking, sense of humor, ability with figures, practical common sense, sensitivity, sympathy, efficiency in work, submissiveness, stubbornness? Those who believe in differences should offer proof for their views. Note whether each sex always considers the opposite sex deficient.

4   Philip Wylie has written a book entitled *The Disappearance* in which he alternately describes our country suddenly left peopled only by women, and then, only by men. He speculates about government changes, social changes, even changes in war and international behavior. Make your own statement on such a world as you visualize it.

5   Is it true that studies have proven that there are practically no native differences between men and women other than those of anatomy? Explain and illustrate.

6   For what reason have women traditionally been referred to as the "weaker sex"? Upon what grounds might it accurately be said that women are the "stronger sex"? Read Ashley Montagu (1968) for a point of view.

7   Do you think women stand the stresses of family life better than men?

SEX IDENTIFICATION

5 Today there are many proponents of a "unisex" society—one in which no sex role differentiation would exist. The approach of the sexes to similarity in hair style, cosmetics, color of attire, and dress itself give androgyny as a life style encouragement. Homosexuals, a despised and harassed minority group in our society, have become more open in protesting mistreatment and have sought redress under law. They crave public sympathy and understanding for a malady which they feel is socially imposed. A major problem of the Women's Liberation movement has been to keep itself from becoming identified with a lesbian crusade. Few of its active members want to be known as lesbians, for most are not, and they know this would seriously discount the influence of the women's movement. Lesbian activists are becoming more open in their protest, and public sympathy, which has always been more tolerant of them than of the male sex invert, is growing.

In this climate of change, it is still important to understand how the child becomes identified with his proper sex, or fails to do so. This is one of the most vital concerns of all societies, and all cultures provide a framework of customary practices and educational forms for seeing that the child becomes, not merely an adult human being, but either an adult male or an adult female. There is no neuter gender in human genetics, and there is none in human societies. Ours is no exception. Some cultures have been very tolerant of that small group of its members who cross the sex line and practice the role and sex behavior of the opposite sex. Few have been as rigorous in their censure of the invert as has our society, particularly in its censure of the male homosexual.

The Greeks during the classical period sanctioned male homosexual attachments, considering this kind of love and companionship superior to the heterosexual bond. The term lesbian, applied to the female sex invert, comes from the Mediterranean Island of Lesbos, where women exalted female love and sexual attachments, after the Greek poet Sappho, who addressed some of her ardent lyrics to other women.

We are no doubt approaching a time of greater tolerance for the sex invert of both sexes, but we are still too far distant to deny the need for the child becoming strongly conscious of his sex identity. College students restrain even normal expression of affection toward their own sex for fear of being labeled inverts. Many who have abnormal attraction toward their own sex fear that they may be inverts. The increasing similarity of male and female roles exaggerates the anxiety. The stigma and personal torture of being a misfit is so great for some inverts that long, painful, and costly transsex operations have become more frequent. These hundreds who feel so strongly "I am a woman inside a man's body," or "I am a man inside a woman's body" that they seek to have their body altered are symptomatic of the complex problem of helping to fix the child's conception of his sex in conformity with his hormonal content (Green and Money 1969).

SEX ASSIGNMENT

Cultures do amazing things to human beings by virtue of sex assignment. What is appropriate for the female in one culture may be strictly masculine in another culture, and vice versa. Granted clear-cut biological differentiation, the male and female are cultural products and a great deal of socialization is required to form the appropriate male and female personality. In every known society, male and female subcultures are different, and an individual growing up in one subculture is never quite at home in the other, no matter what the biological sex category is. The boy becomes a man by participating in the male subculture and imitating males; the girl becomes a woman by living in the female subculture and imitating females.

It is only when the training process goes astray that its striking significance is made apparent, and often it does go astray, for in spite of the best efforts of society to condition the female toward female attitudes and expectations and the male toward masculine patterns, many failures result.

On the genital level, failure to develop sex identification leads, as we have seen, to homosexuality. On the social level, such failure produces women who identify primarily with the male role, have male interests, and feel frustrated in living by the female life patterns; and it produces males whose social training has been such that they identify in their secret wishes and often in their external behavior with the opposite sex.

THE GENITAL STAGE OF SEX IDENTIFICATION

Very early in childhood the striking fact of genital sex differences impresses itself upon the child. How early this comes depends greatly on whether the children are allowed to see each other or their parents nude. If so, within the first two or three years of life, consciousness of male–female genital differences dawns on the child. It is possible that the significance becomes apparent to the girl at an earlier age and presents a greater challenge to her, leading to questions and a need for explanation. The small child lives in an environment of absorbing mysteries which challenge his investigation. By investigating, he learns. It is a fortunate child whose parents, recognizing the critical but at the same time random and incidental character of the child's interest, allow free and unemotional exploration.

Probably few parents—or, for that matter, few adults—are capable of objectivity in this area. Children sheltered in infancy from the knowledge of sex differences may become aware of body structure only after starting school. Many modern nursery schools do not segregate the sexes for toilet use. Teachers of young children have themselves been taught the great importance of handling the innumerable curiosities of their small charges with naturalness and honesty, and without shock. The teachers can help the "delayed learner" to catch up, but the school situation, no matter how enlightened, cannot adequately substitute for enlightened parents.

Freudian psychologists have emphasized *penis envy* as a factor in female inferiority. This presumably develops when the young girl first observes that the young male has an external organ which she lacks. This makes her feel deficient and is the beginning of her feeling of inferiority to the male. In more severe cases penis envy leads to what is described as *genital trauma.* This in turn tends to build up female passivity in the sexual relationship. Whether this is a bit of imaginative fiction or fact has been long debated, and skeptics increase with the years.

Helene Deutsch (1944) points out that young children envy anything the other child possesses and that penis envy, therefore, is normal and more or less inevitable. She points out that many girls claim they once had a penis and lost it. Other young girls, seeing a boy's penis, may try to take it away from him. Penis envy, therefore, is the same kind of envy that arises from the possession by another of any kind of property.

It is possible that the girl feels something is lacking in her body when she first becomes aware of the male difference. Whether her awareness develops psychological significance depends largely on the way in which it is treated. If parents explain frankly, honestly, and without any sense of shock, "Yes, a boy does have more on the outside, but you have much more in the inside. You can be a mother. A boy never can," she is usually able to accept the difference without being psychologically scarred. A fact of life has been established that takes on no more significance than difference of hair color or any other physical trait. If the parents are shocked at this query or shocked when the girl, first observing the male organ, touches it and asks questions, if they hush her and shame her, the difference may become of vital psychological significance.

It is possible, too, that the necessary differences in toilet training of the boy and girl may have a psychological impact on sex identification. The girl may envy the boy's standing position in urination. The expanding use of standing facilities for both sexes, as is evidenced in some modern schools as well as in other public buildings, may well mark the beginning of a decline of cultural difference here. Other cultures have long experience in identical toilet posture for the sexes.

Finally, one may well question whether observing the sex organs is for the child any more surprising, or shocking, or any more a part of awareness of sex identification than observing the length of hair on the head or the mother's breasts. The adult who registers shock in connection with the child's observation of genital differences assumes that the child is equally shocked. Of course, if the child's first knowledge of genital differences comes from observing another child, then the problem is unique in that the child of the opposite sex shows no other differences in physical form.

THE OEDIPUS COMPLEX

Freud saw sex identification as a deeply complex, incestuous struggle. He coined the term *Oedipus complex* to describe it, taking the name from a famous Greek myth. The infant Oedipus was exposed to die in the ancient Greek fashion of disposing of a child who did not appear to be strong at birth. A shepherd found the boy and adopted him. He grew to manhood and became king of a state rival to that of his father. Later, he conquered his father's kingdom and killed him, not knowing it was his father. Becoming king on his father's throne, he married the queen mother, his own mother, and had four children by her. Eventually the truth became known. His mother–wife killed herself, and Oedipus tore out his own eyes in guilt.

Freud used this Greek myth to symbolize the love attachment between mother and son, an attachment which the child, when he reaches the age of social insight, has to fight and destroy within himself.

The *Electra complex,* based on another Greek myth—the story of Electra's love for her father—involves the same mechanism of love and guilt in the relationship between daughter and father.

Freud carried these concepts over into the theory of "parent image" in heterosexual love. The male and female child, he held, are attracted to the person who represents the parent of the opposite sex—the boy to the image of his mother, the girl to the image of her father.

To begin with, both sexes love the mother because she satisfies their needs. They resent the father because he is regarded as a rival for the mother's affections. The development of the male Oedipus complex begins with the boy's incestuous craving for the mother and his growing resentment toward the father which brings him into conflict with his parents, especially the father. He imagines that his dominant rival is going to harm him, and his fears may actually be confirmed by threats from a resentful and punitive father. He is afraid that his jealous father will remove his genital organs because they are the source of his lustful feelings. Fear of castration or, as Freud called it, *castration anxiety,* induces a repression of the sexual desire for the mother and hostility toward the father. Castration anxiety also helps to bring about an identification of the boy with his father. By identifying with the father, the boy also gains some vicarious satisfaction for his sexual impulses toward the mother. At the same time, his dangerous erotic feeling for the mother is converted into harmless tender affection for her.

The sequence of events in the development and dissolution of the female's Electra complex is more involved. According to Freud, when the girl discovers that a boy possesses a protruding sex organ and she has only a cavity, she can have varying reactions of disappointment. It is a traumatic discovery for her and has several important consequences. She holds her mother responsible for her castrated condition and transfers her love to the father because he has the valued organ which she aspires to share with him. However, her love for the father, and for other men as well, is mixed with a feeling of envy because they possess something she lacks. Penis envy is the female counterpart of castration anxiety, and collectively they are called the *castration complex*. She imagines that she has lost something valuable, whereas the boy is afraid he is going to lose it.

Unlike the boy's Oedipus complex, which is repressed or otherwise changed by castration anxiety, the girl's Electra complex tends to persist although it undergoes some modification due to the realistic barriers that prevent her from gratifying her sexual desire for the father. But it does not fall under the strong repression that the boy's does. These differences in the nature of the Oedipus–Electra and castration complexes are the basis for many psychological differences between the sexes.

These Freudian conceptions of the complexities of sex identification may or may not have a basis in reality, but to read intelligently one must understand them, for these are a part of the heritage of psychoanalytic theory. Although they have been widely propagated and have influenced much writing in the field of child development, they are as far from scientific verification as when first propounded.

SOCIAL PRESSURES IN SEX IDENTIFICATION

The social pressures to assure proper sex identification actually begin prenatally. First, males and females are labeled with different names. These names are usually tentatively selected before the birth of the child. Second, a layette is planned with a difference of color for boy and girl. Thus, the social stamp of approval is put on sex identification from the outset.

If the child of two or three does not begin definitely to move toward identification with his own sex, parents make deliberate attempts to push him in that direction. The boy interested in dolls, dressing-up, and other feminine interests is cautiously pushed toward cowboy gunplay and other masculine pastimes. To encourage him, the parents buy a special costume or toys for masculine activities.

Similarly, the girl who is too absorbed in masculine types of play is steered toward feminine interests, encouraged to imitate her mother, provided with dolls and equipment for baby care so that she can practice the accustomed roles of motherhood. With the girl, however, more latitude is permitted than with the boy. Her "tomboy" interests are of less concern to parents than are the pursuits of feminine interests by the boy.

Usually, by the age of four (often earlier), the affection a child feels toward members of both sexes is strongly colored by his own identification with one sex. A boy feels tender love and dependence upon his mother, but if he has lived around a domineering and demanding father, he may also treat his mother with what he considers proper male condescension. He feels a strong attachment to members of his own sex but is careful to display his feelings only in a very masculine manner. From about eight to 12 or 14 years of age he thinks of girls as sissies—and in his attempt to be the complete man, scorns not only the activities and ways of women, but women themselves. He teases and fights his sister and her friends.

This period of rebellion against the opposite sex makes identification with his own sex more complete. It does not, however, kill interest in the opposite sex. The very fact that the sexes wish to fight and tease each other indicates that the interest is still there, even though it is negatively defined.

The instances of going steady among preadolescents has little to do with any real affection. The eight- or ten-year-old girl (or boy) who admits to being in love generally does so in order to further imitate grown-up behavior. Any strong attachment felt by a child of this age toward members of the opposite sex is more likely to be directed toward an adult—a girl may have a strong romantic interest in a rock and roll singer, a movie star the age of her father, a teacher, or her own father. The general rule is, however, that until late childhood or early adolescence, the strongest attraction is to members of one's own sex.

THE ADOLESCENT'S PREOCCUPATION WITH HIS BODY

The growing boy takes increasing interest in the penis and the satisfaction which results from its manipulation. In spite of certain prohibitions, fears, and a sense of guilt that may center around it, the penis becomes a source of great sensuous enjoyment and a symbol of manhood.

This development is so important in the life of the male that Freud saw masturbation guilt being converted in the mind of the adolescent boy to a *castration fear*. This castration fear, Freud felt, reflects the high evaluation the boy is beginning to place upon his genital organs. This presumed fear, which has no scientific basis, Freud defined as the *phallic phase* in the boy's sexual development.

Much of the adolescent male's preoccupation with role identification at this period has to do with physical prowess in all areas: capacity for sexual expression (usually through masturbation), testing muscles in games of skill, flexing muscles and comparing them with pals, testing himself in feats of daring, torture, or endurance. He has come to see maleness as physical toughness and endurance.

In rural culture, male and female subcultures are so completely differentiated by division of work that special channels for male development are not needed. The boy works and hunts with his father and thus avoids the world of women. In urbanized society, where the boy has no contact with his father's work, and is often exposed to his mother's activities, sports are used to build male identity. They may become the consuming passion of the boy from Little League through college.

Attention to the physical prowess of the male was even observed by the Harlows (1958; 1962) in their studies of monkeys. They find that the young male often initiates rough-and-tumble play and more often engages in copulatory play, indicating that these inclinations in the human male may have a strong natural base.

The female becomes preoccupied with her person and its care during the period of adolescence, since with the maturing of sexual functions her body becomes her stock in trade in mate seeking and in realizing the deepest interest of human life, that of childbearing. This interest in the body is not narcissistic in character; it is a normal interest which accompanies social awakening and interest in the opposite sex.

The technique of attraction is, of course, greatly stimulated by cultural values which encourage attractiveness and display and by the informal training in the art of being alluring. Cosmetics culture has been, until recently, largely female; scents, style, powders, and paints are much more her speciality than the male's. Here again the Harlows find a parallel in the behavior of monkeys, where the play of the young females involves a great deal of mutual grooming. Even throughout her adult life, the next most time-consuming activity of the female monkey after motherhood is mutually relaxed grooming (Jay 1963).

That culture plays a profound part in developing feminine techniques, for example, is definitely shown in regional comparisons within the United States. Historically, the Southern girl was trained well in the art of flirtation. In the Far West, where women were scarce and men competed for them, the development of these characteristics was at a minimum. In fact, women could be independent and unconcerned and still succeed in attracting a man. The culture of the West, therefore, neglected the development of the mate-attracting traits in the female.

It is during adolescence that direction in sex-role identification becomes most pronounced. With the coming of puberty, the society insists on greater separateness and greater role identification with one's own sex. Most societies have provided rites of passage designed to impress deeply upon the young adolescent his maleness or femaleness. The male in primitive societies may be put through torturous initiation ceremonies to test his capacity for suffering. When he has demonstrated by suffering that he is worthy to be a man, he is accepted as such. Females in these cultures are often isolated for the initiation rites of puberty. They may be taught about sex, marriage, and the roles of womanhood. This period may involve sex initiation and modifications in hair or dress, even body mutilations. For example, among the Kikuyu of East Africa, there is circumcision for the male and clitoridectomy for the female. In some tribes sex initiation may involve the splitting of a labia for the female. It may also involve, for both male and female, extensive scarification of the body, modification of hair style, and other such ritualistic procedures.

In modern society less attention is given to initiation rites. In certain social circles, debutante balls are in order; in the school program, there is often a break between junior high and senior high school at this period, but sex identification by elaborate ceremony scarcely exists.

There are, however, at this stage, some marked psychological transitions symbolic of sex identification of the period. Some psychologists feel that all adolescents at this time become homosexual in their attachments, and many

MALE AND FEMALE: PREDISPOSITIONS AND ROLES

homosexual activities are actually engaged in. On the emotional level one observes evidences of such behavior; the close pal relation of boys with boys and girls with girls, the small intensely loyal clique groups, and other such phenomena are nearly universal. The constant association between these pals, their lengthy conversations on the telephone when absent from each other, their frequent desire to spend nights together, are indicative of the deeply emotional loyalties which are characteristic of this period.

With girls, custom permits a considerable amount of physical expression without casting suspicion of homosexuality; putting arms around each other and hugging and kissing each other are common behavior. For boys, such overt expressions are less common, but there is the close intimate palship and sometimes mutual masturbation and other sex activities.

The psychology of this transition seems to be that the young person, becoming emancipated from the emotional ties of childhood, tends to cast his parents aside, except at times when he feels abandoned by friends. He seeks a love orientation outside the immediate family. The transition toward attachment to members of the opposite sex seems to be too great for the average adolescent, so he transfers intense, extrafamilial loyalty to his own sex and only gradually does he emerge from this period into true heterosexual relationships. Some never get beyond the homosexual stage. Their love life becomes fixated there. Those who move into heterosexual love eventually move into marriage and complete the full cycle of sex identification by taking on the roles of father and mother.

FORMAL TRAINING FOR THE MALE ROLE

At the turn of the century a majority of men, particularly in urban occupations, spent most of their waking hours away from home. The 12 and 14 hour work days were not uncommon. Men had little if any time to spend with wives and children. As a result, parenthood required of men little preparation. Today a seven or eight hour work day and a five day work week are standard practice. The future holds promise of even more free time. Males find themselves in the wife's domain for long weekends, and sharing evening hours. Many feel awkward and out of place; some feel guilty about not helping but embarrassed at the very thought of domestic tasks. All too many are bored and completely unprepared to enjoy this new opportunity for sharing in family life.

E. E. LeMasters (1957b) has shown that for most young fathers, fatherhood is a crisis of real significance, partly because the male has little conception of what it involves. Other studies have indicated that marriage is more disillusioning for the male than the female, because the male is untrained in the responsibilities he is undertaking. Child expert, Dr. Benjamin Spock, has commented on the lack of training of the young male for the parenthood role and the need for it. It has been found that where boys are allowed to indicate subjects in which they are interested, without fear of shame from peers, they place study of marriage and interpersonal relationships high on the list.

Some college males still have difficulty in accepting females as their full equals. Their feelings are comparable to those of the late Richard Neuberger,

U.S. Senator from Oregon, who admitted that when his wife was elected to the same legislative body, he accepted her for the first time as an equal and came to respect her as a person of real competence, rather than as "just" a wife, companion, and mother of his children. An important bill was before the house and Mrs. Neuberger was to speak on it. He confessed taking her aside and coaching her carefully in what to say. She was new in the legislature; he knew all the ropes, or so he thought. His wife thanked him generously, but having ideas of her own, she prepared her own talk. It proved to be more effective than the attack he had planned.

One of the traditional aspects of male role preparation has been the conditioning in the direction of sex exploration. Some fathers in the older generation encouraged boys to visit a prostitute as a proper initiation to sex life. Even now some boys visit prostitutes in their early teens as a way of proving their manhood. Often they do so on dares, usually in groups, since none of the boys really intends to go, and sometimes older boys take younger boys.

From his study of a small number of cases, Kirkendall (1959) believes that it is a male group experience through which the boys are trying to achieve a group purpose. It results often from trying to prove that they are grown-up, daring, and worldly wise. Curiosity about how a prostitute operates is also a factor. For the most part, the sex experience is unsatisfactory. Because of fear they are often unable to carry out the sex act.

In an earlier day, when the male sexual role was one of conquest and dominance, when the wife was supposed to be passive, this kind of training may have had some place. Today in the setting of the romantic marriage bond, where mutuality is the goal of marriage adjustment, such training is inappropriate.

Even though the criticism directed at the training of the American male for adult family roles is deserved, it is only fair to state that his role preparation for family life is much more adequate than given the male in many other cultures. For example, it is doubtful that the British male ever feels really at home in the family in the sense that the American male does. His training is for administrative duty. His discipline in the boys' school, often away from home, is under the stern master. It is designed to make him immune to many of the personal sentiments, interests, and pleasures of our culture. As an adult, he will probably feel more at home in the office, club, army, and pub than in the domestic scene.

FORMAL TRAINING FOR THE FEMALE ROLE

When the domestic role was the only culturally predestined one, the forming of personality in women was clear-cut. A woman knew her place and her roles and was trained for them. Only the rebellious and unconventional felt thwarted because roles were so completely institutionalized. Here is a comment, made a century and a half ago, on the direction the education of women should take (Moore 1883):

> The profession of ladies, to which the bent of their instruction should be turned, is that of daughters, wives, mothers, and mistresses of families. They should be

therefore trained with a view to these several conditions, and be furnished with a stock of ideas, and principles, and qualifications and habits, ready to be applied and appropriated as occasion arises. . . . An early habitual restraint is peculiarly important to the future character and happiness of women. They should, when very young, be inured to contradictions. . . . They should be led to distrust their own judgment; they should learn not to murmur at expostulation; but should be accustomed to expect and endure opposition. It is a lesson with which the world will not fail to furnish them. . . . It is of the last importance to their happiness in life that they should early acquire a submissive temper and a forebearing spirit.

One cannot deny that the role of the woman who chooses to marry and devote herself, for a period of 20 years or more, to homemaking is vastly different from the role of the woman who will spend all her active years in a career role similar to that of the male. The difference involves attitudes and values as well as roles. After her years of competition with men in school and at work, many an intelligent and ambitious woman has found the role of wife and mother most frustrating. Many of the most competent and competitive women have found themselves ill-prepared psychologically and emotionally for the maternal role, and even awkward in its routine demands.

The conflict of her two roles is one of the most serious dilemmas in the life of modern woman and of modern education. The problem has been of great concern to educators who believe that women must be prepared both psychologically and technologically to assume both roles.

Education must give more attention to qualifying women for the parent-hood role. LeMasters' (1957b) study showed that young mothers had no conception of what they were getting into with their first child. For them, parent-hood constitutes a real crisis and demands many attitude changes that women trained to anticipate the role of motherhood would have found less drastic. Such a situation is uncalled for in a culture which takes up so much of a young person's time in training him, presumably, to meet life's situations. (For a discussion of problems of adjusting to parenthood, see Chapter 25.)

MATURE SEX ROLES

For those in whom the process of identification with their own sex-group roles has been adequate, moving into adult roles is relatively easy. These roles are motherhood for the woman and fatherhood for the man.

Motherhood, Margaret Mead (1949) found, requires very little encouragement from civilization. Fatherhood, on the other hand, is a social invention and requires a lot of cultural conditioning. It consists, essentially, in the tie between male and female based on the economic arrangement of the male providing for the female and her young. Among primates, to some extent, the male shares in the protection of the young, but only among human beings does the male share food with the female and her young as a consistent practice. This is a practice found in all cultures. Although the female may do much of the actual raising of the food, men do the things that are considered to be most essential to the economic survival of the group.

SEX IDENTIFICATION

Margaret Mead believes that the marriage system predates the knowledge that there is a relationship between the sex act and offspring. The marriage system may be closely related to the willingness of the female to grant sex favors in return for food and protection. "In every known human society," she finds, men learn as they grow up that to be a full member of society they must "provide food for some female and her young." However, this does not necessarily mean that a man cares for a wife—he may have to care for his sister instead.

She points out that in all societies there are some tramps, ne'er-do-wells, and recluses who refuse to accept the burden of fatherhood. There are also culturally accepted ways in which a man may avoid the social obligation. He may join the priesthood, a monastic order, the Buddhist priesthood in Burma, the army, or the navy. For women, on the other hand, motherhood is so natural that only complicated social arrangements can break it down entirely—only the Catholic Church has been able to do so on a large scale, with the chastity requirement for its nuns. It is interesting to observe that both priests and nuns are rebelling in great numbers against the chastity requirement and dropping out to marry.

Margaret Mead also points out that under certain conditions society may raise the status of the single woman so high that women will strangle their children with their own hands. Also, illegitimacy may be such a shame in the culture that women resort to abortion or give their children away secretly. Thus there are exceptions to the general rule of a mother nurturing and protecting her child.

PROBLEMS

1   Are you aware of any of the training that entered into your conception of your sex role?
2   What do you think of Freud's views in the area of sex identification?
3   Do you willingly and naturally accept most of the roles assigned your sex in our culture?
4   Contrast male and female adolescent interests.
5   Do you agree that the key male role in our society is that of provider for women and children?
6   Contrast two cultures in their shaping of males or females: British, German, American, Latin.
7   Compare developmental play of male and female monkeys.
8   Appraise the "unisex" trend among youth.

FEMALE ROLES IN TRANSITION

6 In any culture there must be complementary roles between the sexes. Historically girls have moved quite naturally into feminine roles, having been shaped from early childhood for marriage, parenthood, and dependence on the male. The feminist extremist now sees this as shaping women for the use of men, and leading to womens' loss of identity as persons. As women repudiate the traditional norms, they face some of the problems and uncertainties men have always faced in establishing their identities. The male child has not as easily become masculine, as has the female become feminine. To become masculine, he has to act manly. This requires vigorous rebellion against female roles and, in childhood, against girls as persons. Girls are soft and sissy, and too good to be boys' equal. Boys are rough in speech, dirty, and unkempt compared to girls. Boys have to take the bumps as they come. Girls may keep up tomboy roles without too much censure, but no boy can long be identified with dolls, dressups, and other aspects of the female subculture.

Females in most cultures have been conditioned to carry out the reproductive function. They are trained to carry out the roles of birth, nurture, protection, gratification, and giving comfort to children and to men. Theirs is the "stroking function." These functions have to be given priority over self-expression in the ego sense, and work in outside vocations. If we recognize the full implications of the decline in significance of reproduction to the survival of modern man, and the separation of sexual intercourse from reproduction, a revolution in roles is both possible and likely. The one part of the division of labor that is irreversibly fixed is the nurture of the child in the womb. After that short interval, child care becomes a human task, not necessarily confined to women except as tradition dictates.

Implications of Liberation   If women come to see conventional marriage as a trap, they are certain to become more wary and to begin to reformulate the rules. Men have long thought it was a trap—designed by women to fit their special needs—but a trap into which they allowed themselves to be led. If large numbers of women feel that "they have been sold a bill of goods" in the traditional role relationships of marriage, both sexes must begin to reappraise marriage roles.

Will this mean that men play many more domestic roles? That women play many more roles outside the family? Will children be reared communally in nurseries and child-care centers so that both men and women may be freed to a greater extent from the demands of the young child? Will there be some combination of all these alternatives? Certainly we must face the fact that there are many marriage, family, child-nurture, and child-rearing roles that must be performed by someone, and if the old pattern of reciprocal roles is no longer compatible for either sex, or even one of them, alternatives must be found. We are now in a revolutionary period when middle- and upper-class women are seeking these alternatives; lower-class women have never had many options and still do not.

The Resistance Movement   One would be in error to assume that all middle-class and affluent women have joined the more vocal crusaders and their followers in the present feminist crusade. Midge Decter (1972) has spoken for those who like arrangements much as they are. She holds that women are the architects of marriage, not the victims of fate; they have made the arrangements and men acquiesce. She believes women do not want to work of necessity, and have to face the stress and anxiety of making their own way in the world. "They cherish smaller ambitions" than the militants pretend to seek. They seek "the obligations of an impersonal lust they did not feel but only believed in" an unwanted freedom. They do not see the home and family, the attentions to building a home and caring for a wife and children, as sinister "plans from which he (the male) means to construct a towering edifice to his own vanity." Decter sees the current women's movement as "putting women down." She views the wife with three children, not as doing something inferior to her husband, but as doing something different. The wife made the choice to have the children; if she finds it hard, she must be made to understand that "life is hard." As to equating the women's movement with the minority racial movements, Decter feels that women are trying to get "moral credit" for being a minority, which they are not. She sees the women's problem as one of too many "terrifying" choices—they have more options than ever before. She sees danger in the movement in that it provides "a substitute way for young women who don't need a substitute way." Decter sees the ultimate result to young women being a self-imposed "self-hatred."

Black Women's Resistance   "Women's Lib has no soul," according to *Encore,* calling the feminist movement "little more than the hysterical exhibitionism of spoiled children." This black newsmagazine considers Women's Liberation "a playtoy for middle-class white women." *Time* (1973) correspondents checked these views with black women across the country and found that many black women agreed. Reasons given: Black women feel their oppression is by white society, not black men. The joint concern of both sexes of the black group is employment, housing, education, and the psychological impact of discrimination. When asked about the right of abortion, many answered that they consider it genocidal, a way of limiting black population. The Black Muslim group especially believes in having more children. As to the Equal Rights Amendment, many consider it a "liftin' and totin' bill." It may free white women but put more black women in homes as servants to take care of liberated white women's children. Black women have never had to seek a chance to work; they have always worked outside the home. They have not had a chance to get tired of white middle- and upper-class comforts, or to get bored with the big house and the country club, according to *Essence* editor. Underlying all this resentment among black women is also resentment of white women "stealing their men" by marrying them in increasing numbers.

It would be interesting to have a comparable reaction of lower-class white women to the current feminist movement in its various aspects. Do they, too, feel that it fails to represent them? Does it hold promise for the poor woman? Does it even understand the issues most vital to them? Of this much we can be sure, they will likely reap side benefits more quickly than the black woman.

Male Resistance   It may be a long time before extreme positions on appropriate roles for the sexes are reconciled. Certainly, the male is not blameless in the too restricted roles women have played. One reason for her restriction has been the fact that the female can be raped and can conceive. These experiences can drastically change her life and that of her family. Society is affected since it may have to bear the economic and social burden the male ordinarily carries. One can certainly attribute too much to biology, but viewing women's roles in terms of our cultural history, it appears that many limitations on female roles had their origin in this presumed need for sheltering the female. It is probable that there is still a lurking fear of her being violated sexually in the new areas of freedom grudgingly given. The most extreme example in our culture historically was the protection of the Southern white woman from the black male by devices of segregation.

A second important factor is that the male has never liked to be in a position of direct competition with the female. He resents and fears her initiative since he needs to feel that there are many things he can do better than women can. The way to prove his superiority is to keep women from trying. He has been typically less willing to admit women to new roles than women are to enter them. Finally, he has formulated the rules of sexual passivity for women to protect himself from the sexual challenge so threatening to his masculinity.

ROLES IN HISTORICAL PERSPECTIVE

Sociologists view roles as cultural creations rather than biological imperatives. The biological imperatives are few indeed, as even a casual review of cross-cultural comparisons shows very clearly. Within the same culture, too, sex-role typing may be very different, as, for example, the role difference of male and female among the upper and middle classes and the lower classes. The upper and middle classes are given to much sharing of roles between men and women; in the lower social classes, roles are more strictly segregated. Their roles remain anchored in historical tradition, and women of the lower class are less concerned with liberation, for they have never been able to aspire to roles designed for ego satisfaction and personal identity through careers. Many work, but it is to earn and to survive, not to escape from the home, express rebellion, or broaden horizons.

Preference for the Male Child   Throughout much of history, in many cultures female infants have been unwanted. This is so today in much of the world. The male child, it has been assumed, brings advantages to his family; the female, disadvantages. Female infanticide as a way of reducing girls in the family has been common. For a wife to bear sons is to be honorable in the eyes of the husband and his relatives and to rise in status in the community. Having daughters only, in some societies, is sufficient grounds for divorce.

Various studies spanning several years, show that American culture is not free of preference for the male child. This preference is strongest in wanting the first child to be a male. Gerald E. Markle (1974) has studied attitudes of students in three colleges in the Tallahassee, Florida area and of adults whose names were taken from the city directory. He finds the preference for a male as the first child very strong among all religious groups, all ethnic groups, and all levels of education. And it is true of both men and women. He also finds an overall preference for boys for all children, not just the first born. The more education, the less strong this preference.

These studies raise the question of whether there is as much equalitarian philosophy in American life as we usually hold, when even the college population shows little evidence of accepting the girl on the same basis as the boy. The studies also cause speculation as to whether or not we can expect couples to treat the male and female children equally under such a value system, and what might happen when it becomes possible to control the sex of the child.

For the first time, the sex of the child can be predicted with 100 percent accuracy by tapping fetal water and examining the cells. The cells of a female fetus contain a chromatin mass not found in the male fetus. It is now possible to know the sex in time to have an abortion if the wrong sex is found in the fetus. In rabbits, researchers have already succeeded in controlling sex with 100 percent accuracy, and with techniques that could in time be applied to human beings. It is interesting to speculate how couples will handle the choice when it is offered.

The subservience of the female to the male, the denial to her of common rights and privileges, her lack of place in the esteem of both men and women, and even of children, has been and is so commonplace that only violent social revolution can revise her status in any particular social order. In many cultures it is still appropriate for her to be the hod carrier, water carrier, and tiller of the field, in addition to her domestic tasks and function as mother.

Scandinavian women have progressed furthest toward genuine equality in every sphere, even in the area of jobs, and in freedom from subserviance to the needs of the young child. In the Scandinavian countries, supportive institutions to free women from the home are most extensively developed.

CUSTOMARY ROLES VERSUS EXPECTED ROLES OF WOMEN

Customary roles are learned largely from the family. It is through the attitudes, expectations, and habits formed in the family that a young person gets his basic training in role attitudes and role expectations, both for his own sex and for the opposite sex. In our time these customary roles are often in direct contradiction to the expected roles of the peer group.

The peer group is for the most part oriented toward new attitudes and expectations for both sexes. The high school and university experience of today's youth has probably been the main influence in the creation of new role expectations in America. The interaction of men and women in school situations, where they function for the most part as equals, has tended, in the course of three generations, to break down much of the customary role expectations of the past. From this teen-group culture has emerged a new concept of equality such as feminists of an earlier day could never have conceived. More and more young men and women are participating in similar kinds of recreation, intellectual endeavors, and even in similar vices. Here, in playing up to the role expectations of their peers, they tend to part company with the role expectations of the family group.

It is at this point that much of the conflict between the generations has come. Parents of the succeeding generations have seen their daughters moving into types of role behavior foreign to their concept of "young lady." They have registered shock as the daughter has taken on new role behavior considered appropriate for her in the urban industrial community. To many parents, her informality of dress, her companionship with the male, her ignoring of the impediments of female biology have been symbols not merely of an emancipated generation, but of a wayward generation.

Three Perspectives on Women's Roles

There are three major perspectives on the place of women in society and the significance of their roles. Adler believed that women carry an inferiority complex in relation to the male. According to this view, there is a secret wish in women to have been born men. Adler (Ansbacher and Ansbacher 1956), a Viennese psychoanalyst, in developing the concept of inferiority feelings, identified power with masculinity and weakness with femininity. Inferiority was created with unmanliness of femininity, the compensation for which he called the *masculine protest.* Overcompensation, he believed, is indulged in by both men and women when they feel inadequate and inferior. He may well have reflected a traditional masculine bias. However, his views have been a part of the intellectual culture for some years.

Margaret Mead (1949) and Ashley Montagu (1968) both view women's role as superior. Mead believes men do also. No man can ever attain the sense of reality which his childhood conception of the role of motherhood has given him. Men must, therefore, be given work roles, and the culture defines these roles as superior to fortify his ego and make him think that his life is worthwhile. Only in this manner can he gain a sense of "irreversible achievement" which his childhood knowledge has taught him women have by motherhood. Only as men can be allowed to surpass women in some work sphere can they be made to feel important. Cultures, on the other hand, have to work very hard to make women want anything more than motherhood to make life full for them. Most societies, in fact, find in motherhood the model for the mystic, artist, and saint.

Ashley Montagu stresses not only the physical superiority of women but also their moral and spiritual supremacy. He visualizes a better world to the extent that masculine virtues disappear and feminine values and dispositions take over family, state, and international affairs.

Betty Friedan (1963), in *The Feminine Mystique,* revived the masculine superiority position, but saw a way for women today to become "self-fulfilled" by entering a "fourth dimension." In her view the housewife role is servile, helping others to perform the more vital and stimulating ones outside. She believes that women, to live with the fullest significance and the greatest sense of fulfillment, must take on the added dimension of outside achievement. Perhaps she voices the appraisal of women's roles as seen by a certain group of professional women, and of an increasing proportion of middle- and upper-class women.

With the more ambitious and perhaps more talented women, there is some drive toward fulfillment in roles of distinguished achievement. To be happy, they want and need to cultivate their special aptitudes. But the great mass of women, even the college-educated women, want a family, are interested in human relations, and want to take their place in the community, but have no intention of entering into ego-serving conquests in a fourth dimension. Their orientation is toward rearing capable children, helping achieve financial goals for the family, becoming a better person for the sake of their families, being useful in the community, rather than winning personal laurels.

The desire for a fourth dimension finds very little expression among the thousands of student autobiographies which have passed through the writer's hands during the last 20 years of teaching a marriage course. At the outset of teaching in this area, he felt quite sure that many college women had dreams of vocational conquest, and had a need to feel productive in the creative sense. If college women do have such aspirations, they develop after marriage. College women do not claim them.

Freshmen women are still very conventional in their life outlook if a 1970 study of over a thousand at the City University of New York is at all indicative. Asked what they would like to be in 15 years, only 2 percent wanted to be an unmarried career woman, and only another 2 percent a married career woman without children. A total of 28 percent wanted to be housewives. Most (48 percent) expected to combine a career with marriage (Epstein and Bronzaft 1972). Perhaps time and the disillusionment of marriage, as they experience it, are factors in the emergence of the career women. Certainly the social climate created by feminine leaders and agitators encourage it.

Even so, Louis Harris' 1971 poll of 3000 women throughout the nation showed that 71 percent felt that taking care of the home and rearing children was more rewarding than having a job, and most expressed joy in being "homebodies."

Role Conflicts

Young women with children visualize greater happiness when they can pursue roles outside the home. But women who are involved in work outside the home think in terms of the time they "can return home where they belong" and "always wanted to be" (Lopata 1966).

In the life of each sensitive woman today, there is likely to be a great deal of confusion in her concept of her role due to her exposure to conflicting value systems. Part of her concept of what her role ought to be is internalized in the parental home. Yet, in the early adolescent years, the pressure of the peer group has supreme meaning to her. If she cannot measure up with this group, she has lost her closest and most vital tie, binding her to her generation. Therefore, she is likely to play roles consistent with peer group expectations. This, in turn, often brings her into open conflict with her parents, and she is forced to rationalize her concept of how a girl "ought to behave" and how she must behave to get along in her group.

Her role concept is extended as she becomes acquainted with male friends and dates, and later moves into betrothal and marriage. Often she finds that her husband's concept of the female role fails to coincide with any of her previous concepts; neither her parents', her peers', or her own. She often finds herself resisting role concepts that her husband gathered in his own family from observing his mother or sisters, or from association with other young women during the dating period. Since any woman, to have a successful marriage, must try to reproduce in her personality some semblance of her husband's image of what a woman should be, she must yet again try to recast her values, philosophy, and behavior to fit new role concepts.

Children often cannot reconcile the various activities of their mother with the concept of motherhood they see represented in the homes of some of their own playmates. Although most married women work at some time during their marriage, and the work role seems to be a well-established practice, a study of eighth- and twelfth-grade children showed that boys were more often opposed to their future wives working than the girls were opposed to working.

If those close to a wife and mother do not see eye to eye with her regarding her own role expectations, she will probably internalize their standards to some extent. As a consequence, she may feel considerable guilt and anxiety, and build within herself the feeling that she is neglecting her children, husband, or household duties. Yet, at the same time she must, to satisfy herself, continue to play her roles in the larger world, for she knows from previous experience that if she drops these roles she is less than the person she must be to retain her self-respect and to feel herself productive, useful, and significant.

It may well be that the mother-in-law will have a part in the wife's role conflict, particularly if the woman crosses class lines where role expectations are different. This influence may come in the form of direct criticism from the mother-in-law or through her husband who wants her to be like his mother. Many a wife is forced, in facing the realities of marriage adjustment, to modify her behavior for no better reason than that it must fit her husband's concept, or his mother's concept, of what her role as a wife should be.

Finally, in the broader circles of the community, she must face new roles

FIGURE 6-1   Every third worker is a woman. Of the new roles for women, none is more important than the work role which takes them outside the home and family circle. Increasingly, women have entered the field of profitable employment. This modern trend brings with it both new freedom and new responsibility. Source: U.S. Department of Labor, Women's Bureau, *American Women,* Report of the President's Commission on the Status of Women, Washington, D.C., (1963, Chart 10, p. 28), and Special Labor Force Reports, 1970.

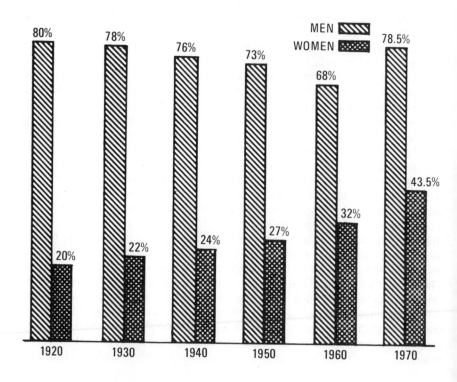

MALE AND FEMALE: PREDISPOSITIONS AND ROLES

defined in the particular segment of the community where she is active. In industry, appropriate role conceptions are demanded. They represent not only work-role situations, but also interest-group activities of which she must become a part (see Figure 6–1).

There is always, of course, the ultimate dilemma. "What do I do if I do not get a chance to marry at all?" A college girl expressed it in this way, "I have a double set of life goals; one set is for if I get married, the other if I remain single." Ambitious college girls seem to go through a crisis during their junior and senior years of college; they become anxious about marriage and develop a fear of competitive success in demanding vocations. (Turn to page 96 for a further discussion of this topic.)

Marya Mannes (1963), in a discussion panel on the roles of modern woman commented, "I believe whatever decisions one makes, one pays for. Therefore, there is such a thing as complete acceptance of choice but no such thing as finite and complete fulfillment. We make a mistake in thinking, 'Will I be happy if I do this or that?' We cannot be entirely happy all the time, and conflict, in a creative woman, often makes for pain and difficulty along with its joys. We must accept a degree of unhappiness, which I think is a natural condition of man."

This analysis of the female dilemma may seem pessimistic. It is not so intended, nor is it intended to suggest that we return to the former customary roles for women. Women could not go back to their former position, even if it were more satisfying, which it most probably would not be. The modern industrial world has left no place for the secure, family-absorbed woman of previous generations. Today women, as well as men, must function as individuals and, through performing significant roles outside the family, achieve their own distinct social status.

The militant American woman is fighting the discriminations long common to her sex. In wages and in occupational rank, she is gaining. In dating and in marital choice, the initiative is still the man's. In sex matters her unequal status is most blatantly obvious. The siring of a child out of wedlock by the male brings little personal or social guilt. The conception of a child by an unmarried female is still looked upon as one of the most serious of moral offenses. The double standard obviously remains at the point where it hurts most.

Women are not now considered an inferior group, looked down upon by men, treated as subjects, humored, and used, as once they were, but at times men still like to think of women in the traditional way. Many men want their wives to be ornaments and clinging vines, even those who expect their wives to support them. They miss the honor and respect that were once considered their inherent right. Today the male must earn these from his wife and children as well as from his male associates. In most cases, however, men are becoming aware of the more-than-compensating advantages that equality has brought. They want the strength, support, intelligent direction, advice, and companionship that only the modern woman can provide.

The threat to the male ego is great and many men still cannot take it. Yet the trend is in the direction of greater equality in sex roles, and both men and women are growing in their understanding of each other under the new philosophy. Once the successful wife was often a shrewd student of the male personality, for most of her wishes had to be realized by manipulating him indirectly. Subtly she acquired whatever prestige and advantage she held in the household and in the pair relationship. Today, women need be much less subtle. They approach men on a different level.

The Female Sex Game

Jessie Bernard (1972) sees in the female sex game a source of woman's "profound sense of inferiority." The woman's role is always a waiting game. The male must be permitted the initiative. So she has the agonizing wait for the telephone call, letter, or invitation. She must employ humiliating attraction strategies, and only the most attractive girl dares to use sexual initiative, even subtly. The unattractive woman and the older woman will only drive the male away, making both herself and him look ridiculous. Her sex act is dependent on his readiness, and her aggressiveness may inhibit his sexual performance. If she puts him to the test and he fails, it is the failure of both, and may subject him to ridicule.

LIFE PLANNING: AN IMPERATIVE FOR MODERN WOMAN

Men have always had to plan. Marriage was women's lot and there were few contrary expectations. "The ever-widening variety of occupations now opening for them makes more comprehensive planning a requirement for satisfactory living" (Harbeson 1972). Women now have love, work, and marriage; if they are not to drift, they must learn to deal with the future.

The lifetime alternation between roles "inside" and "outside" the home, and the identification of self in new orientations is the essence of the role problem of modern woman. Some never move "inside" and some never move "outside." However, most assume both roles more or less successfully, but not without stress. During their lifetime most women have to make the transition rather completely from one role to the other and back again, and must accept themselves in the roles chosen for the particular stage in the life cycle in which they are functioning.

In school the female is the equal of the male, competing with him in the classroom and sharing with him in extracurricular activities. She moves into the work world as a temporary worker to remain there until children come. For most, motherhood brings a radical change. The woman retires temporarily from work to become submerged in the lives of husband and small children. The ego-satisfying roles are lost; competitive achievements are abandoned.

But motherhood is also a temporary period. Childbearing is confined to a span of about six years. Perhaps soon, perhaps in 15–20 years, she moves back into the work world where she will stay until retirement age forces her back to the home. This state is terminated in widowhood in the later years.

The problem of woman's roles is that they are not and cannot be structured by tradition, and yet no culture can shed the persistent past, which so often affects the emotions and even the overt behavior of the individual. Maximum flexibility is required if she is to retain her identity. And facility in learning the skills for the role shifts, and for self-acceptance in adopting them, are a necessary part of her adaptation to marriage and family. Victor L. Christopherson (1965), addressing the annual meeting of the Arizona Home Economics Association, visualized the lifetime training task faced by teachers of women thus: "We must plan for the entire life cycle, from infancy through the gerontological stage. . . ."

The Female Life Cycle in Role Adjustments

The customary roles defined for a particular group may ease the transition through various phases of the life cycle, or make them unnecessarily difficult. It appears that in the United States the culture has tended to create difficult periods of adjustments for the female. The first critical stage comes when she moves from her adolescent beauty in the late teens into mature womanhood. This transition has been analyzed by Sirjamaki (1948), who sees the woman's highest point in status in the United States at the college-age period. Then, as never again, she is the center of attraction—the envied coed, the beauty queen, spending her time in dressing-up, dating, and dancing. In this, our culture contrasts decidedly with most other cultures in which the highest status role for women is motherhood. Supreme ego gratification prior to maturity may well leave a young woman feeling let down as she takes over mature roles.

Where the girl reaches her climax in social status prior to marriage, as in our culture, the marriage is often blamed for the eclipse in popularity which would have come in any case with increasing age and more limited social circulation. For the popular college girl, particularly, the quiet and unspectacular role of housewife is a striking and often unsatisfactory contrast. The ego suffers and she may feel rebellious against the limitations family and motherhood have imposed upon her. Many neuroses originate here. Popular articles lead one to believe that the campus beauty queen does not often prove to be the contented, happy, satisfied housewife. It must be recognized, however, that few reach the beauty queen level of ego satisfaction in the teens.

American culture defines the male peak role much more realistically. He does not achieve his maximum point of recognition and respect until he is somewhere in his 30s and has won it by social placement through occupational achievement and by home and family.

The status peak for both sexes, when contrasted with other societies comes strikingly early. Elsewhere, it is more usual for the aged—regarded, to use A. G. Keller's phrase, as "repositories of wisdom"—to be the most revered of all age groups. Where elders are so revered, they have a secure place in the bosom of their families. Where their wisdom is regarded as the outmoded folk wisdom of yesterday, they frequently must spend their last years outside the family in loneliness.

Finally, the "empty-nest" crisis for the devoted mother marks the beginning of her loneliness. With the loss of her children, the most vital role of her midyears goes. Grandmothers are suspect in our culture if they interfere with the relationships of husbands and wives or if they so much as hint about how young Johnny should be brought up. The loss of work at retirement sends the aging male and female into eclipse. No longer can they manipulate others or expect to be respected for their know-how. Youth in a technological age soon outstrips the wisdom of experience.

For the aging woman, roles shrink so much after widowhood that she considers herself fortunate to maintain her own household and takes pride in self-maintenance.

The Statistical Picture of Woman's Life Cycle

Analysis of census data by Paul G. Glick makes possible the charting of the life cycle of the average marriage, thus indicating the role shifts that will occur in the life of the average woman. The pair stage is fairly short for most couples. They are inclined to begin their family early. This may be changing, with the current emphasis on restricting birth. Even so, once childbearing begins, the span is likely to be short.

In the modern family of from one to three children, childbearing will likely be over in five to eight years after the date of marriage. Statistically speaking, according to census data, in the average United States marriage childbearing is over by age 29. This short period, when small children keep the mother more or less restricted to the home with a rigid domestic routine, is such a distinct break from the freedom of girlhood which preceded it that it requires considerable adjustment. For the woman who planned to work after marriage, it is also a trying period; this is the period when it is most essential that she give her full attention to babies.

The wife may console herself with the fact that it is a five to eight year period for her rather than a 25 year period as it was formerly. If she can adjust to the rigid routine it imposes, it may be one of the happiest periods of her life. It should be, for no period is more deterministic in the personality formation of the child. Her happiness with her child, as well as her full emotional acceptance of the mother role, is basic.

If the average wife finds domestic life less than fully satisfying, she may, after her children are well along in school, reenter the work world herself, at least on a part-time basis. If she has hobbies or club interests, she will probably spend an increasing amount of time in them. The husband too may begin again the cultivation of old or new interests that do not involve his children. This will help prepare both parents for the next stage, the empty-nest, or more technically, the postparental period. The children leave home and the couple is again alone. The final stage is widowhood, for rarely do both members die at the same time.

Marriage, for most couples, passes so rapidly and naturally from one of these stages to another that the problems or pleasures shift before they realize it. In Figure 6–2, the various stages of the typical four- or five-member family of today are shown. It is assumed that the family is unbroken by divorce or death until the years when death normally takes one member of the pair, usually the husband, since women live longer and the husband is usually the older.

Glick's (1955) calculation of the life cycle for the average family for 1950

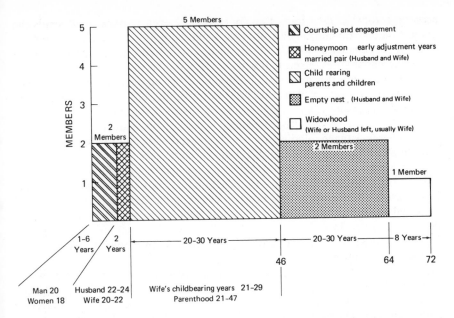

Role changes of women during life cycle (family with three children). Childbearing for most wives ends by age 29. Child-rearing is over by about age 47, requiring only about a third of the life cycle of modern women. As the life span increases, the time after the responsibilities of parenthood have terminated may well become almost half of an average lifetime. Reentry into the working world, often after retraining, is one choice now open.

FIGURE 6–2

shows the median age for husband and wife at marriage is 22.8 years. The last child comes at 28.8 years, making the childbearing period only six years. Marriage of the last child comes at age 50; death of one spouse at 64; death of the other spouse at age 72.

EMANCIPATION BY WORK ROLES

No doubt the most influential factor in the emancipation of women, aside from education, has been their entry into the work world. Work roles are of profound significance to role interaction of husbands and wives today. Women work not only prior to marriage, but early in the marriage, and then typically enter the labor market again after a period of childbearing. Childbearing is over for most at about the age of 29. When the mother is 34, the youngest child is in school, so the mother enters the labor market again. A third of all married women work, and they are still working as grandmothers. Half of the group of married women over 40 work. In fact, as many grandmothers work as do teen-agers.

For the most part, middle-class married women do not work for economic reasons primarily, but rather to fulfill other wishes which homemaking leaves unsatisfied. As much as 40 percent of their earnings is likely to go for taxes. If there are dependent children, the costs of child care and household help take substantial sums. Transportation, special clothes, and other incidentals reduce the margin of profit (see Table 6-1).

Employment outside the home brings social contacts, a chance to use skills and capabilities, a sense of work satisfaction, a chance to dress up, a real need for beauty parlor care, and numerous other satisfactions. Work gives life a satisfying routine which the housewife sometimes lacks in an age of household technology, and it also brings status and independence.

For many it brings a routine which insures them against the neurosis of a purposeless existence. Nadina Kavinoky, gynecologist and former president of the National Council on Family Relations, once said, "Much of the neurosis among American women would vanish if they had to leave for the office every morning at 8:00 AM." Psychiatrists in London prior to World War II had a large case load afflicted with what they called "suburban neurosis." Most of it vanished when war work drew women into group-shared activity in a common cause.

One can scarcely conceive of all the social and psychological implications of the developing work role of American women. It has brought them great freedom, for only those able to earn and support themselves can have any real freedom of choice. Marriage is optional now, as is divorce, for the threat of de-

TABLE 6-1   **Gross Versus Net Income of Working Women**

Couple	Husband's income	$5,000	Wife's income	$3,900
	After taxes	4,245	Tax	845
			Costs[a]	850
			Net	$2,205
Husband and wife with one child	Husband's income	$5,000	Wife's income	$3,900
	After taxes	4,365	Tax	833
			Costs[a]	850
			Maid or nursery school	1,250
			Net	967
Couple	Husband's income	$15,000	Wife's income	$3,900
	After taxes	12,095	Tax	1,265
			Costs[a]	850
			Net	1,785
Husband and wife with one child	Husband's income	$12,000	Wife's income	$3,900
	After taxes	9,965	Tax	1,137
			Costs[a]	850
			Maid or nursery school	1,250
			Net	633
Couple	Husband's income	$35,000	Wife's income	$10,000
	After taxes	25,304	Taxes	5,181
			Costs[a]	3,000
			Net	1,819

Source: "Does It Really Pay for the Wife to Work," analysis by *U.S. News and World Report*, 42:154–158, March 15, 1957.

[a]Transportation, lunches, clothes, laundry, dry cleaning, beauty shop. Costs are considered conservative and allow for no more eating out as a couple than before.

pendency in the absence of male support has been greatly reduced. With economic independence a woman can tell a man to get out and mean it.

A study of professional women found them expressing "great satisfaction" in being able to combine marriage and a career. They find combining two worlds stimulating, and do not rebel against their domestication. The study showed that the 20–30-year-old women did not differ from those 50 or over in their appraisal of the dual roles. Most of the workers did not have to work (Poloma and Garland 1971). For this group of women at least marriage is not "oppressive" as the militant feminist contends.

A common difficulty created by women's entrance into the work world is its psychological effect upon some husbands. When wives become seriously interested in their own jobs they are thrown into competition with their husbands on two counts: (1) the husbands feel they are losing their wives' love and devotion, and (2) they fear their wives may beat them at their own game. Few men of an earlier generation could stand this kind of competition, men are becoming accustomed to it today, although it is particularly difficult for the American male to maintain his self-respect while being outdistanced by his wife. The attitude that a man who cannot support his wife adequately is a

Percentage of working women who are married. During the venturesome early days of women in the working world it was the unmarried career women who sought profitable employment. Today over 60 percent of the female working force is married. Then, the career versus marriage dilemma was one for the unmarried girl. Now, working out a marriage in which roles of homemaking and working are synchronized is a lifelong problem for an increasing number of women. Source: U.S. Department of Labor, Women's Bureau, (1963, Chart 11, p. 29), and Special Labor Force Reports, 1970.

FIGURE 6–3

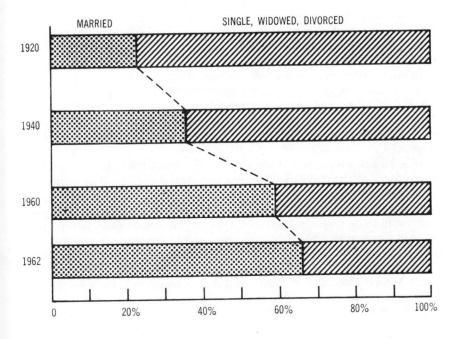

FEMALE ROLES IN TRANSITION

failure has disappeared with the rising level of aspirations and family living standards. But some husbands fear, and others actually sense, the development in their wives of assertive, individualistic, aggressive traits.

On the positive side, the work role of women has increased their insight into a man's life and problems. There is some evidence that successful work experience prior to marriage is favorable to success in marriage. No doubt the insight gained into work roles is a factor. The new work roles have increased woman's incentive to acquire an education, with the privileges and breadth of experience which this brings. Competition in the classroom has increased men's respect for women and their capabilities as even their competition in the work world could not have done.

Male prejudice against women's activities outside the home has decreased, although one must grant that each new venture of women has been marked by initial sneers and vulgar suspicions. Although this country has not permitted women to fight alongside men, as some nations did when involved in World War II, women were taken into the armed forces for special duties in offices and hospitals. When the Equal Rights amendment passes, some new role definitions will have to be made in the military.

For women's venture into World War II, they were not accorded the same patriotic respect as servicemen, or credited with a motive of sincerity. It was assumed by many that the only women who joined were those of questionable character seeking male association. Certainly, in many quarters their morals were questioned and their characters suspected. So it has always been when women have ventured beyond the accustomed roles of the social order. Virginia Gildersleeve, speaking of the Waves, said, "If the Navy could possibly have used dogs, ducks, or monkeys, certainly the older admirals would probably have preferred them to women."

Contrary to what one might expect, the wide-scale entry of women into the work world served as an incentive rather than a barrier to early marriage. As the work world opened to younger women, regardless of their marital status, the economic handicap to early marriage was largely removed. By the careful use of contraception and by both working, young people may marry immediately after high school or college. They will have a struggle economically, and the chance of marriage success is relatively low. Some may even, in fact, marry and continue in school, each working part-time and during summer vacations, or if the wife seeks no further schooling, she works and sees her husband through college or graduate school. (This is discussed in Chapter 14.)

The highest proportion of working women whose husbands are living with them is found in the middle-income brackets, white and nonwhite, rather than among the very poor and the affluent (see Figure 6–4). At all levels, there are more nonwhite and white women working whose husbands are living with them. In all these respects, therefore, the entry of women into the work world has been an incentive to early marriage, and to marriage in general. Once again, as in an agrarian society, a wife can be an economic asset rather than an economic liability.

In March 1967, 39.7 percent of all married women living with their husbands were in the labor force. The percentage of those in the labor force was greatest among those with the most education and smallest among those with

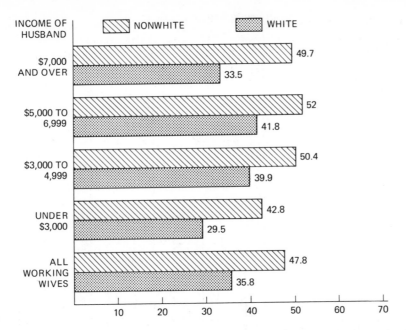

Percentage of working wives based on husband's income. Data deal with marriages in which the husband is present. A much higher percentage of nonwhite wives are in the labor force than of white wives. There are fewest in the labor market when the husband earns the least. Source: "Special Labor Force Report No. 94," U.S. Department of Labor, Table J, p. A–15.

FIGURE 6–4

the least education. For example, in March 1963, of those with less than five years of schooling, 20 percent were in the labor force; of those with grade school training, 27 percent; of the high school trained, 35 percent; of the college graduates, 50 percent (see Figure 6–5).

THE CAREER DILEMMA

The career dilemma is largely history. Yet the college woman must still weigh the alternatives in deciding whether to marry, and what to do about a career. It is known that each year's delay reduces the probability of a woman's marrying (see Figure 14–4). It is also known that college women in general have greater difficulty in marrying than do noncollege women. A special table (Table 6–2) developed by the Bureau of Labor Statistics shows the marital status of women aged 35–44, by education.

To college women, the choice of career or marriage often comes, not as a major theoretical decision, but as a personal choice of whether they should accept a good opportunity to marry before finishing college.

There is no one answer to this question. Some women are more strongly motivated than others toward academic and vocational achievement, and they could not possibly find happiness in terminating college for marriage. For

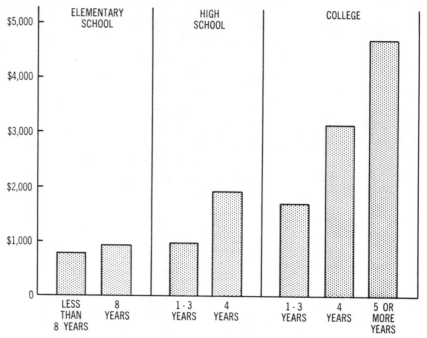

FIGURE 6-5   Relationship of education and earning power. Education is an economic elevator for women as it is for men. (For income of men by schooling see Figure 23-1.) Source: U.S. Department of Labor, Women's Bureau, *American Women,* Report of the President's Commission on the Status of Women, Washington, D.C. (1963, Chart 20, p. 68).

them, marriage would represent more an end than a beginning. Others, in spite of parental pressure, should at this point marry, even though it costs them their college degree.

There is greater tolerance than ever before in our society of the woman who chooses to delay marriage, to be highly selective of a mate, or to remain single. This is a freedom won by the women's rights movement and its exaltation of woman as a person with full right of choice. She has these options and is respected whichever she chooses.

The woman who wishes to marry must consider that after college graduation there are comparatively few opportunities to meet marriageable men on an intimate and long-time basis. However, the choice need not be "either, or" for marriage need not represent the termination of a girl's opportunity for schooling.

Whether a girl continues her college education or terminates a college course prior to graduation seems to be in part a matter of social class background, according to Christensen and Swihart (1956). The girl from the more privileged home is inclined to rate marriage above graduation, if the right opportunity comes along; whereas the girl from a family that is fighting its way

| YEARS OF SCHOOL COMPLETED | MARITAL STATUS | | | |
	TOTAL	SINGLE	MARRIED (HUSBAND PRESENT)	OTHER	PER-CENTAGE EVER MARRIED
Elementary school					
Less than 5	399	37	263	99	90.7
5–7	829	36	631	162	95.7
8	1,326	57	1,086	183	95.7
High school					
1–3	2,463	88	2,042	333	96.4
4	5,160	238	4,495	427	95.4
College					
1–3	1,314	56	1,134	124	95.7
4	903	100	741	62	88.9

Prepared by U.S. Department of Labor, Bureau of Labor Statistics, September 1964.

up the social scale is more likely to finish her college education, even at the risk of losing a marriage opportunity.

It is increasingly possible for women to have both career and marriage. Children must have affection and care, but this does not mean that the able and talented mother must spend all her time with the children. With help in the home she often can carry on her career with only short interruptions. Moreover, she can often start her career before marriage, have it during marriage before children come, and (with the increased length of life) continue it after the children are in school, even if she drops out completely during the period when her children are small. The small family of today—two or three children born close together—takes up only a short span of the mother's life.

A change of attitudes in this area will go a long way toward correcting frustrations in marriage centering around problems of parenthood. Confinement of the mother to the care of the young child is the most trying, particularly for the college woman whose life pattern is changed with the coming of the first child. Many roles are set aside in favor of those centering on the demands of the child. Orientation is definitely inside the home for a time.

WOMEN'S SHORTCOMINGS IN ROLE-STATUS ACHIEVEMENT

Matina Horner has observed a "will to fail" among capable young women in college. In 1969, while Assistant Professor of Clinical Psychology at Harvard University, she studied girls at Radcliffe College who were selected "because of their high ability, achievement, motivation and previous success." Her findings were that many arrived at Radcliffe with high hopes for a career and then "changed their plans toward a less ambitious, more traditional feminine direction." Testing them with a Thematic Appreciation test, she found that more than 75 percent "showed evidence of high fear of success" (*Time* 1972). She found that men do well in competitive situations; women do not, particularly when competing with men. She believes that women associate success with being unpopular, unmarriageable, and lonely, and with guilt about not being a normal woman.

In their junior year in college, many women begin to think in more conventional terms, and by the final semester of the senior year they become anxious if they are not already engaged. Whether the present climate of Women's Liberation has substantially changed this situation is not known. Women are still marrying in a high proportion of cases, but the age has been delayed somewhat. Whether this is from career motivation, lack of men of marriageable age, desire to prolong single freedom, or other reasons, only time can tell.

Women seem to be quite as vocal as men in pointing to areas where modern woman has failed in role-status attainments. Margaret Mead (1960), in lectures to college audiences, has criticized American women because they no longer want to be wives, but only mothers. European women, she has pointed out, want to be wives. She has seen American culture caught in an "extreme reproductive cycle," which might be a threat to national survival. Men have been drawn very much into the inner circle of caring for children. Early dating, early mating, early parenthood have threatened individual development. She has pointed to the verdict of history, suggesting that no civilization has survived which allowed men to get "too close to children." They must be free to venture, explore, invent.

The "extreme reproductive cycle" is over. The birth rate is dropping and women's values have changed. The U.S. Census Bureau reported (April 15, 1972) that the number of women remaining single into the early 20s has risen about a third since 1960. The birth rate is now the lowest level in the nation's history—15 per 1000, compared to 24 in 1961.

Perhaps this will show up soon in a higher level of aspirations and achievements for women of great competence. Although we have more women college graduates per capita than any nation on earth, the proportion of women entering the professions and other creative work endeavors is much less than a generation ago. The National Manpower Commission concludes that only one in 300 women capable of earning a doctoral degree gets one. Only 12.6 percent of all doctoral degrees are granted to women today compared to 15 percent in the 1920s. Packard (1968) finds only 16 percent of doctoral degrees and 24 percent of masters degrees at the University of Chicago Department of Sociology given to women during the period 1960–1965. At the University of Pennsylvania Graduate School of Fine Arts, women make up only 7 percent of the enrollment in Architecture and 40 percent in Fine Arts.

Today young women are more ready than ever to take jobs, yet few want to risk marriage and family for career aims like medicine. The contrast is often made between our output of trained women in medicine and that of countries with far fewer proportions of women privileged by the opportunity of college and university training. The Soviet Union is heavily staffed with women doctors, some 65 percent being women compared to 7.71 percent in the United States and 24 percent in Great Britain (Sadock 1972). A third of the Soviet Union's engineers are women compared to 1 percent of ours. Soviet higher education staffs are 35 percent women; even biological and chemical sciences employ many women. However, we should consider that Soviet women do not usually advance to higher ranks, and that four-fifths of the female labor force is involved in physical labor, primarily agriculture.

There is increasing opinion among critics that American women should "perfect themselves as human beings," that this is the only road to happiness and often is the surest way to a really successful life and marriage.

Marya Mannes (1963), discussing the problems of creative women, comments, "The United States is plunged into an orgy of domesticity and childbearing." Britain, Scandinavia, and Russia, by contrast, are pushing more and more women into intellectual attainments. She feels that in the United States there are "hidden pursuaders . . . cultural forces telling a woman it is unladylike to use her mind."

While Mannes presumes that women throughout history have found their fulfillment in motherhood, she asks whether many women in our society with its alternatives would not have been happier and had a greater sense of fulfillment as doctors, mathematicians, etc. She feels that our culture should recognize that procreation is a luxury today, not a necessity for all. She believes that mass media must recognize that many women are not satisfied with domestic roles, and that we must no longer stifle the creativity of the girl of great capacity by making her feel that creativity is unfeminine. She says that "the identity of women as human beings is as essential to them as their identity as wife and mother."

Betty Friedan (1963) has perhaps received more attention for her views than any contemporary writer and lecturer. She feels women have slid back from the feminist achievements of an earlier day and become involved in the "feminine mystique," which identifies fulfillment with motherhood. As a result, she finds them unhappy and disenchanted. Friedan feels that the talented woman must make a genuine commitment, not just to a job for a job's sake, not just to community busywork, but to a job she can take seriously as part of a life plan, "work in which she can grow as part of society." She recommends in 1973, that men join the women's movement to help assure women their full potential as women for the sake of both sexes.

Rosemary Park, Barnard President, believes that the woman's college is still necessary for women today, for it is so difficult for a woman to develop a "sense of independent individuality." In the background of a girl's mind lurks the traditional thought "that someone will take care of her, that some man will come along and give the answer" (Ferrer 1963).

"Most of you," Park says, "will probably live to be 100. If you want to keep from being a stuffy old bore for forty years, that is, between sixty and 100, then you've got to learn something now. . . . To be young and feminine at sixteen is no achievement. To be a respected person at sixty is."

This long-run failure of women is often expressed in both learned opinion and in research findings. Too early and too complete commitment to motherhood without an awareness of the long-term perspective of life is often tragic to marriage, to parenthood, and to every following phase of the life cycle. Only the purposeful individual can survive happily the later phases of the life cycle in our day of increasing longevity.

Finally, we know that the woman who has enthusiastic interests in work and creativity is not handicapped for marriage or parenthood. Those with a purpose other than marriage make good in marriage and family life. Long ago Burgess and Cottrell (1939) found a high correlation between educational achievement and marriage success. Contemporary studies show that women who prior to marriage and childbearing were "most taken up and bound to their jobs are the ones who are most enthusiastic and committed as mothers when they do have children" (Maccoby 1963).

Serious commitment to intellectual pursuits, to a profession or other career may well be indicative of prospective success in marriage and parenthood. Psychologists describe this process as "feeding from one facility to another."

THE AFTER-PARENTHOOD RECONSTRUCTION OF LIFE GOALS

The longevity of modern woman, combined with the fact that childbearing and child-rearing are limited to so short a span of her life, creates problems of life-long adjustments. Millions of women become grandmothers by age 45 (Foote 1961). Even before that age their major task of rearing children has been completed, and the school and other community institutions have taken over most of the load. Large numbers must move into the work world or feel that their lives are filled with frustrated uselessness and boredom.

Many have lost contact with the work world during the child-rearing period, yet they constitute a skill reserve of immense dimensions. Often they can, by very brief retraining programs, enter the work world, or enter it on a higher level than if such training were impossible. Often women who had specialties in college or in the work world prior to childbearing, have, due to their experience as mothers, developed new interests or values and wish the kind of training which will help them move in the direction of these new interests.

A survey (E. Peterson 1963) of 15-year alumnae, showed that after this span of years following graduation, a third were employed and five out of six were either seeking positions or thinking of doing so. Many wanted to go into teaching though they had not considered becoming teachers when they were in college. Many were interested in preschool teaching, feeling that a great need for competence exists at that level of teaching.

It is apparent that many of these women at midlife are anxious to go in the direction of acute social need, provided that the opportunity for training and for work are open to them. It may be assumed that there would not only be a social gain if short courses for retraining would make the fulfillment of their aspirations possible, but that these women would get greater psychological and financial reward by being upgraded in their work. It is not expecting too much to hope that as happy, creatively useful persons they would also be better wives.

It is apparent that in the training of all women from the beginning we need a program that will feature "flexibility and adjustment to change." The life cycle is becoming quite definitely marked by a series of steps which most women will follow:

1 coeducational schooling
2 a brief work-world experience
3 home and family
4 return to work world (preferably after a short retraining course)
5 retirement and return to domesticity
6 widowhood

The U.S. Department of Labor finds a strong trend back to school of women in the 25–34 year age bracket. In the five years prior to 1970 the number almost doubled, with the total well over a half million. Diminishing home responsibilities are cited as a reason. For those who marry early, the confinement imposed by the need to care for small children is over, and the women returning to school report a "whole new sense of values and priorities" from those they had when they left school. Many found that the home curbed their intellectual and emotional growth. Back in school ideas change, experience widens, and the woman becomes more independent. Unless the husband accepts the idea of the more independent wife, the marriage can become strained.

Kinsey (1953) and his research team suggested that during the years 16–30 in women "the reproductive mechanism overshadows the intellectual interests." They found that women do better in college between 35 and 50. Whether they are dealing with biological verities or merely customs and motivation, certainly the idea of women returning to school for either personal or professional reasons is of great merit to women and to the society.

THE HARD LIBERATION ISSUES

Economic Equality   The Civil Rights Act of 1964 guaranteed equal pay for equal work, regardless of race, creed, or *sex*. It also provided for equal opportunity for job training, promotions, fringe benefits, etc. Law and realization in practice are far different. Injustices are being corrected, but genuine equality must still be fought for.

Status difficulties are most apparent in woman's climb in rank and income within all social and economic structures—business administration, Civil Service, government and political administration, top leadership in church, and prestigious salary and rank in the colleges and universities. There is always the excuse "advancement depends on tenure," and few women acquire tenure equal to men because they drop out for childbearing and perhaps also for child-rearing. There is a point to the argument, as Eli Ginzberg (1966) and associates show (Table 6–3), but it is too often used as an excuse for keeping good women down in the ranks. The higher ranks of authority have

TABLE 6-3   Achievement Level of Educated Women by Career Patterns

| | WORK HISTORY (PERCENT) | |
ACHIEVEMENT LEVEL	CONTINUOUS	BROKEN
High	23	7
Good	41	10
Medium	29	47
Low	7	36
Total	100	100

Source: Ginzberg et al., *Educated American Women* (New York, Columbia University Press, 1966) p. 100.

been held by the male clan, and males feel safer keeping it that way. Women are also strong in their expressions of a preference for a male boss.

Another field of discrimination has been credit. Banks, savings and loan associations, and numerous other credit institutions have discriminated against women in making loans and issuing credit cards. This area is only now being subjected to scrutiny and exposure. Many states have joint property rights for man and wife. Others discriminate greatly against the wife in finance management and in inheritance rights.

Exclusion altogether from many fields has been based more on custom than biology. Still much exclusion is so. Women have been protected from work requiring heavy lifting, for example, so this specification is added to many jobs where heavy lifting is not required to keep women out. Legislators quibble now about women being made subject to the military under the Equal Rights amendment, yet most men in the military never see field action. In fact, much of what the military does in the way of use of personnel can be done as well or better by women.

Equality of Privilege   Perhaps the greatest weakness of the nuclear family is its inability to meet the needs for emotional nurture of the young child and at the same time give the young wife and mother some reasonable degree of freedom to ease the frustration of withdrawing to the family nest. NOW has vigorously sought a solution through the expansion of nurseries and child-care centers. Some progress has been made, but this was not made an important priority by the president, who vetoed an appropriation bill for the needed expansion. We have day-care centers for 650,000 preschool children, yet there are 6 million such children whose mothers work.

Sweden and Denmark have long provided at least some of the social institutions that help emancipate the working mother from the child. In these countries large apartment houses, some exclusively for working couples or for unmarried mothers, with home service for the care of children and for the care of living quarters is provided. Some of these housing projects are cooperative; some are privately supported. For low-income groups the services are subsidized by the state or municipality—even the building itself is subsidized.

These housing units have nurseries which are open 6 AM to 8 PM. Here young children are given the best care by trained nurses and yet may spend the night with their families. For every age group these units have summer play schools, after-school play schools, and provisions for an after-school snack, homework study, workrooms, shops, sewing rooms, kitchens, libraries, art rooms, and recreation rooms. Each group through the teens can be occupied creatively and under supervision until the mother and father return from work. In this way children are given constant care by professionals during the period when mothers and fathers are required to work.

To have genuine sex equality, it must be generally recognized that motherhood is a worthwhile activity and an end in itself entirely apart from other work. This requires that the mother have help available through the community, help which will permit her to obtain some freedom from the home, perhaps an annual vacation whether she can afford it or not, and other benefits.

In Sweden, couples who cannot afford baby-sitters may turn their children over to professionals without expense to themselves and with small expense to others, for an evening each week. Mothers who need it are given a two week holiday at municipal expense, completely apart from husband and children. The children are usually sent to camps.

While these measures are helpful in relieving mothers from the constant strain of caring for young children, their psychological importance probably far exceeds their physical benefit. Homemaking and motherhood are recognized as vocations of social importance, and are granted the same social status as other vocations.

Even freeing mothers from work during a longer period before the child is born may become socially desirable. Several studies, particularly in Great Britain, show that the success of a pregnancy drops significantly when women work during pregnancy. Census data indicate that in 1963 one-third of all births in our nation were to women working during part of their pregnancy.

Norway is now experimenting with the husband and wife holding the same job and spending alternate weeks working and staying home with the children. One father of a two year old said, "I was scared I would lose my masculinity if I did the housework and changed the baby's nappies. But that soon changed." The wife thought the new arrangement "marvelous," and noted that the young son no longer hung around her all the time (*Time* Nov. 22, 1971, pp., 72–73).

Many new experiments can be tried to strengthen the nuclear family as a more effective child-rearing institution, and in their success there may well be found ways to more satisfactory marriages.

PROBLEMS

1   *Sociodrama:* A husband has just come home from work, tired, hungry, and in need of a little sympathy after a difficult and frustrating day. He finds no dinner, an untidy house and a wife who has spent her afternoon electioneering for a friend. The husband's first line is an angry one:

"What kind of a wife are you? Women didn't used to be like this!"
The wife answers indignantly:
"You're right; times have changed and so have women!"

FEMALE ROLES IN TRANSITION

Go on from there to show how confusion and disagreement in role behavior can be at the bottom of marital conflict.

2   *Research exercise:* Poll a student group on the following (other questions dealing with roles may be added if desired): *(a)* favorite work, *(b)* greatest ambition, *(c)* what I want to be at age 50. Tabulate and analyze results by sex. Are marked differences apparent in the roles of men and women? Do they reflect cultural conditioning or biological inclination primarily? If differences appear in life patterns of men and women, do they seem to be supplementary rather than contradictory? What implications do they suggest for the relationships between men and women of this generation?

3   It is sometimes asserted that the more choices we have, the more problems we have. If this is true would you say that the young woman of today has greater or fewer problems than young women of the past?

4   List several choices a young unmarried woman might consider that were never open to women of generations past.

5   Think about the merging that has already taken place and is taking place in male–female roles. Now do a little speculative thinking about the future if this merging continues. Elaborate on such topics as the following:

a   "The man of the future . . ."
b   "The woman of the future . . ."
c   "The marriage of the future . . ."

6   Outline the lifetime shifts characteristic of women's roles in our culture today.

7   Men: Present your views on the proposition below which you are willing to defend:

a   "I would rather marry an 'old fashioned' girl because . . ."
b   "The 'modern' girl, in my opinion, makes a more ideal wife because . . ."

8   Women: Present your views on the proposition below which you can conscientiously defend:

a   "The men of yesterday were a different and better breed than their modern counterparts. I would rather marry the kind of man who lived about _____ than a modern man because . . ."
b   "Men have changed but mostly for the better. I'd prefer to marry a 'modern' man because . . ."

9   Discuss the implications of points of view expressed in Problems 7 and 8. Do you think a young person's view on these alternative questions reflects primarily *(a)* his upbringing, *(b)* his experience with the opposite sex, or *(c)* other factors.

10   Describe several areas in which the line of demarcation between male and female roles seems to be disappearing.

11   Can you name roles that are still primarily one-sex roles?

12   Which sex seems to be changing the most in terms of traditional roles? What do you think accounts for this situation? Do you approve?

13   In what occupations and activities will you find women who have moved further away from the traditional female role?

14   In what occupations and activities will you find men who are most determined to live up to the traditional concept of the "masculine role"? In what occupations and activities is one most likely to find men who have adopted some traditionally feminine interests and activities?

MALE ROLES
IN TRANSITION

7 Women's roles demand less proof than men's. The boy must achieve masculine status by special performance. Cultures seldom if ever grant it to him by the mere fact of his being born a male. He must perform athletic feats, do daring things, earn the right to swagger, prove masculinity by earning, or whatever the culture defines as masculine, and above all he must earn it by sexual conquest. Having attained it, he must still retain it by proof. *Machismo* demands continuous performance—siring offspring, bringing in "the bacon," outdoing competitors in drinking, gambling, physical combat, or whatever the culture demands. Let a man of long record as a provider lose his job, as many do during periods of depression, and soon both wife and children lose respect for him, and reject his authority. This was one of the family tragedies of the depression of the 1930s. In some cultures the male dares not favor birth control, for to reduce the flow of children from the womb is to remove an important symbol of verility respected in the community.

Masculinity and femininity are in essence the typing of role patterns for each sex. All cultures have conceptions of what male and female must be like to fit adult life expectations. To be masculine in American culture has meant physical courage and sexual aggressiveness, but not to the extents they are stressed in many other cultures. We have not stressed physical courage to the extent some militaristic cultures have, or as much as the traditional Masai culture of East Africa, where manhood was marked by killing a lion with an iron spear. In the area of sexual aggression, we disapprove of whistling at or pinching the girl on the street, as Latin cultures do, but the "girl-watcher" theme is a popular one.

As women become more aggressive sexually, no longer accepting the timing of the sex act as an exclusive male prerogative, the male must meet the challenge or face humiliation and retreat into impotency. The definition of his sex role is not likely to change in terms of what is expected of him or of what he expects of himself. Psychiatrists have seen their case load of impotent males rise. The sexual commune is beyond the capacities of many males.

Males are confused about what women expect of them in the way of dominance, as in many other areas. Most women seem to want a strong man to lead them, and to lean on when they feel weak, but they will accept none of the domination that used to be the husband's prerogative. The line between weakness and dominance is a thin one indeed, and a man can risk his standing with women by being either too yielding or too overbearing.

It may well be that in an age of rapid male role changes, the disturbance of masculine roles has been far more serious than has been realized, and that some of the role problems exhibited by wives and mothers reflect failure on the part of their fathers to adjust to the new requirements of marriage and parenthood (J. T. Landis 1962). (We have discussed the father's influence in the development of homosexuality in both male and female in Chapter 3.)

In spite of the conflict and confusion over unisex, the end result of role adjustments of men and women may lead to the development of a more warm, supportive father, and a new kind of sociological fatherhood. Montagu (1958) thinks the culture should move in this direction—the male becoming more like the female in disposition and attitudes. Josephson (1969) has criticized the long-held myth of the matriarchal black family, and suggests that a "warm fatherly pattern" is emerging among blacks in the nation. There seems to be developing throughout the culture more of a tendency for the male to express tenderness toward children and women than our historical traditions considered proper. Certainly feminism at its best expects this of the male, and it is becoming easier for these traits to develop in the male without masculinity being threatened.

Certainly we have reached a point in the development of the culture of leisure where sociological fatherhood is becoming more important than either biological or economic fatherhood. A child can be conceived by artificial insemination or by egg transplant, and many women succeed as the sole support of a child or children. But there is no substitute for a father in the adequate socialization of the child. From the time of primitive society, this has been his main function. In a complex society, where role identity and the complexity of social adjustments are so overwhelming for the young, both girl and boy need a father who is certain of his sex role and supportive of them in learning theirs.

PENALTIES OF DEFICIENT MALE ROLE PERFORMANCE

Deficiencies in female role performance, particularly that of mother, and their effects on children, have been studied and discussed. Inadequacies in male role performance have been neglected, particularly regarding their consequences in the personality formation of children. Tess Forrest (1968) of the William Allan White Foundation claims that the father, in not taking his proper role, is a factor in manic-depressive psychoses and alcoholism. Julian Bergas of St. Justine Hospital in Montreal finds "paternal deprivation and deficiency in father–daughter relationships" a factor in the background of a high proportion of attempted suicides in adolescent girls.

Psychologists Biller and Weiss (Biller 1971) conclude that "the father's role in the family seems to be of great significance in the process of feminine identification and personality formation in the female." A healthy identification with the father is highly important to the personality development of the girl, as they see it. Biller has reviewed some 1500 publications, and concludes that "a warm relationship with a father who is himself secure in his masculinity is a crucial factor in the boy's masculine development."

The Gluecks, in their studies of delinquency, stressed the importance of a strong, concerned father in keeping a boy from delinquency, and also reported that delinquent boys who form a close relationship with a father-surrogate resolve their antisocial tendencies. Child clinics and juvenile court personnel have long recognized that seldom is a child in court if his father is decent, kind, and responsible. Psychiatrists at Walter Reed Army Hospital find that boys whose fathers failed to take their proper role tend to exaggerate masculine behavior to cover their femininity and even have dreams and fantasies of a feminine quality. Those who could not accept their fathers, could not choose a career.

Lack of fathering seems to be one of the most significant factors in the high rate of suicide among college men, according to a study at Harvard University and the University of Pennsylvania. The study dealt with those committing suicide during or soon after college. The risks increased by 50 percent for males who had lost their fathers by death or divorce during precollege years. Another factor in suicide was boarding school attendance before college, an index of paternal deprivation. Loss of the mother was not as critical in the suicide of boys as loss of the father (*Family Life* 29:5, May, 1969).

The Challenge to the Male Parenthood Role

Self-esteem in the male is very closely related to occupational success and work accomplishment. For many, work becomes too consuming, interfering with the parental role. Part of this overemphasis is due to our cultural norms which measure a man by his productivity and monetary success. These values tend to be placed above family for the male; not so for the female. The financial pressures of the family may lead to paternal neglect. There are also time–distance factors in industrial society.

The commuter may leave home before small children are up, and return after they are asleep. The young professional man or executive may have weekends consumed by a full briefcase or by social obligations of business or professional significance. The good citizen father, may accept too many community leadership obligations to have time for his wife and family. Companies often exploit the willing volunteer, encouraging him to be a community man for the sake of the corporate image. Moonlighting is necessary for many, since only by holding two jobs can the father adequately support the family. The underemployed man, or the unemployed may have to vanish to protect himself from shame heaped upon him by wife and children, or to make it possible for her to draw extra welfare payments.

The "organization man" is often guilty of a superloyalty to the corporation. Such loyalty still exists in some companies, perhaps more so in all companies than is generally recognized. *Time* (1972) writing of loyalties in the International Telephone and Telegraph Company, speaks of the mystique which dominates management. The "men consider themselves an elite corps dedicated to a single cause: operating profits shall increase every quarter. . . . To that cause they are expected to sacrifice, if need be, their outside interests and family life." *Time* quotes one executive as saying, "It is a whole way of life to work for ITT, like joining a monastic order . . . a feeling that you are working for an order and not just a mortal company."

No doubt our society could well afford to make time for fathers to be parents if we were sufficiently aware of the need.

Conflicting Expectations in Male Role Behavior

The male has maintained throughout the centuries a pattern of more nearly uniform role behavior than has the female. Yet he has not escaped, in this age, the pressure to conform to new roles. Modifications of behavior, which have been strenuous, embarrassing, and sometimes disastrous to him have been necessary. No doubt the male would have preferred to remain in his traditional role as patriarch of his family, master of his household, and guardian of the family property. This role, so long given community support and so long unchallenged, has had to be sacrificed in part to the newer values of the equalitarian marriage and the democratic household.

The wife has, often in spite of his protests, moved into the work world. He has thus had to share the provider role. He has also had to give up his position as custodian of family wealth as the wife has come to share in the spending. The husband has come to recognize his wife's equality and sometimes her superiority as she has become more educated and more aggressive in community affairs. With her increased knowledge of child training and psychology she has educated him in the belief that children have rights equal to his own and that the fullest development of the child's personality is achieved, not by authoritarian methods, but by the counseling, developmental approach. The big deficiency in men's training is their lack of preparation for the role of parenthood and family life. Women are much more adequately prepared. Men's training ignores this reality of their adulthood.

The Domesticated Male

In the broadest sense, the American male is more domesticated than in any previous period of American history. On the frontier, the masculine virtues were valued far above refinements. The strength of a man's arm and his physical performance in field and forest had survival value, and because they did, such qualities were rated highly in the culture. The virtues of brute strength and accomplishment have always been rated highly where man is pitted against nature. These values still survive, particularly in the logging and mill towns of our West, and to some extent in all of rural America.

In direct contrast to these traditionally masculine values are the so-called effeminate characteristics of the urban male today. Some attribute the increasing effeminacy of the male to childhood training. Because of the long daily absence of the father from the suburban home, the training of the child is left largely to the mother. Added to this has been the sparcity of male teachers in grade schools with the consequence that the training of the child in the formative years in the schoolroom has usually been carried out by women. Those who criticize this trend feel that the effeminate development of the male personality makes for softness and is a disadvantage to national survival.

Masculinity Appraised

Montagu (1958) has no fear of the effeminization of the male. He believes that the culturally induced, so-called masculine qualities of "self-assertiveness, aggressiveness, and bluntness" are not the qualities that build the kind of world we want. He sees love, sympathy, compassion, and the "desire to conserve"—predominantly feminine qualities as our culture rates them—as the key virtues in human survival. He attributes the failure of humanity to achieve greater happiness to the fact that women have been denied the opportunity for "active participation in the government of human affairs."

He would also organize the work world so as to permit men greater time for fatherhood. He would reduce the work day of fathers with young children to four hours a day, with no pay cut and supplementing income and family allowances to help with the economic burden of child care.

Swedish women are beginning to demand some of the goals which Montagu sets forth. They ask that men be freed from demanding work roles so they can participate more fully in domestic life. According to an Associated Press release, Swedish wives want husbands to be free from work more often to cook dinner, do the washing, take the children to the dentist, and in other ways share the chores of homemaking and parenthood. This would require shorter work hours and educating the man to be more domestically oriented in his activities. The wives want their husbands to have leaves of absence with pay so they can spend more time in the home while the children are young. (In Sweden, 70 percent of the women have jobs.)

Masculine values in the United States have changed profoundly. In an earlier day all of the arts and all things domestic were defined as effeminate and were shunned by the male. The boy talented in music could expect the scorn of his father, maybe even of his mother, and certainly of other boys and adults of the community, if he indulged this talent. As vocations, all of the arts—drama, sculpture, painting, even writing and scholarship—were looked upon as effeminate. Few males aspired in these directions. No boy dared dream of these kinds of accomplishments and expect to be accepted in his neighborhood. Thomas Wolfe, one of the greatest of American novelists, who grew up in Asheville, North Carolina, describes in his book, *Look Homeward, Angel,* the disappointment he was to his parents and to his father, particularly, when he chose to write. His father thought his gifted son should go into law.

Many boys hesitate, even now, to indulge their desire to cook. That activity, perhaps especially in rural cultures, has traditionally been effeminate. In urban life, the arts are more often considered as natural to the masculine temperament as to the feminine. In radio, stage, and screen, in sculpture, writing, and music, and also in cooking, the doors are as open to men as to women, and the roles are as readily accepted by men as by women.

With the entrance of women into numerous vocations, it is not impossible for the male and female roles to be reversed in the field of parenthood itself. There are a few families in which the mother is a driving, ambitious person, and the father has actually taken over the maternal role insofar as his becoming the emotional center of the household is concerned. In such cases, the father actually mothers the children, giving them the affection and intimate attention children require. While these instances are rare and perhaps not yet fully approved by the culture, they do represent the extreme to which the male role has been and can be modified in our day.

The twentieth-century democratization of the American home has played a significant part in refashioning the domestic role of men. This new pattern of family life encourages the maximum involvement of the father and husband in family affairs. Thus not only do modern wives demand greater involvement on the part of their husbands, and modern occupations allow time for this greater domestic involvement, but, most important of all, the modern male actually seeks this involvement for his own satisfaction.

When marriage and family relationships are based upon companionship rather than upon economic considerations and rigidly patterned institutional roles, the male is found to seek the company of his wife and children more than in the past. The husband who, for example, bathes the children while his wife washes the evening dishes, does so not only out of a sense of obligation or because of his wife's insistence. He enjoys this opportunity to play with his youngsters and to feel that he is contributing to their daily care and development. By reducing the number of his wife's after-dinner tasks he also ensures their maximum number of hours together as a couple.

An occasional cartoon still features the aproned, bedraggled, domesticated husband, but such cartoons are becoming fewer and less popular. The apron, dustpan, dishcloth, and diaper pins are symbols of his new domesticity, it is true; but today we are coming to realize that they may also be symbols of a deeper and more satisfying family life than men have ever had before. Even the child-training function, traditionally considered a female one, is shared by the male today. This trend admittedly is more characteristic of the middle classes than of the lower classes.

STRAIN IN CONTEMPORARY MALE ROLES

Helen Hacker (1957) sees that the masculine role has been greatly modified by the new role demands of the female, and somewhat to the male's disadvantage. She finds, first, that many of the role demands of an earlier period still exist and may have been increased by the numerous status pressures now centering around the traditional role of bread winner. Second, she feels that the male may suffer from feelings of inadequacy because of the uncertainty and ambiguity of his role expectation. She finds that he is particularly confused about his own masculinity. It is sometimes hard to know what is masculine today, and what kinds of masculinity will be accepted. Finally, she finds that there are problems in adapting male roles to the new freedoms and responsibilities of women.

Hacker feels that man's status as a lover has been challenged. Man's evaluation of himself from time immemorial has been supported by his dominance in the sex act. Historically this has been an almost unilateral male expression. Today his sex prowess is being determined more and more by his ability to evoke a full sexual response from the female. The new sexual emancipation of women has in a definite way been a threat to this key aspect of his masculinity. She believes male ego adequacy is dependent on sexual success. The female's is not. A woman can have status and not live up to any of the standards of femininity. A man cannot be a man without living up to standards of masculinity. A woman can be unfeminine and still be important as a person. To use Hacker's phraseology, "there is a neuter category for women, but not for men." She sees increasing homosexuality as part of the flight of men from the stigma of their inadequate relationships with women. She sees the male's position in society being challenged in many subtle ways. Women are concerned with survival; men with honor, but man's honor in many areas is now subject to question.

The New Impotence

Historically the monogamous marriage has placed few tests on the male's sexuality, particularly in cultures which dulled the sexuality of the female by many taboos and inhibitions. It was only in polygynous cultures that he was forced to seek aphrodesiacs in an attempt to share himself adequately with his various wives, and even there it was not unusual for the wives to avoid the watchful eye and seek other outlets. In the monogamous marriage the male seldom faltered before midlife, when the wife's desires might equal and in some instances exceed his own, and put him to the test. Impotence was a disease of few, and those usually in the upper years of marriage.

Now impotence is much on the rise in our society and the new case load is of young men. The men blame "these newly freed women" and their demand for "sexual performance."* The male who cannot meet the test feels his manhood challenged and his self-esteem lowered. He seeks psychiatric help.

One of the serious problems for the average sexed male, and the below average, who live in communes which share sexual life among group members is that women compare the males in terms of sexual performance, and men know that they are being compared. The male's readiness and ability is

---

*Marijuana is another factor in the new male impotence, according to recent research. Rather than increasing sexual satisfaction, as once was thought in the youth culture, over time it diminishes it and in the long use may produce greatly reduced response.

psychologically induced. Unlike the female, who may perform and even simulate enjoyment when indisposed or uninterested, the male cannot. It takes few failures on the part of the male to rob him of his capacity altogether with a particular woman, and in time with any woman. This, in the masculine value system is indeed failure. The culture provides no comfortable place for the psychological eunuch.

Unique Male Roles

Lower-class males and females become aware of their sex roles early, for in this social class traditional definitions of masculinity and femininity persist. Among the middle classes the strong, domineering, aggressive, pugnacious male of frontier days has been modified, just as the gentle, passive, submissive female has become a character of yesteryear. Yet there is little doubt that men of the middle classes are still trained to be more worldly, more materialistic, and more success-minded than are women. Men still seem to be more politically and community-oriented than women and to find less support in religion and virtue. Although their interests in domestic tasks and activities have greatly increased, and they are more aware of the psychological and social needs of their children, they are still less gentle in disposition, less family-centered, and certainly less domestically oriented than are women.

Strength, courage, the ignoring of minor infirmities, are still values of the male subculture, not the significant values they were and are in agrarian culture, but still genuine values. Men still rate themselves and each other more in terms of efficiency, competence, material success, and prowess in sports and in sex than in terms of beauty, refinement, virtue, and goodness. It is probable that the average man still rates leisure below work, and luxury below the tools of productivity.

It appears also that woman expects many of these traits in man even though she has encroached on all his prerogatives. Many women still want the male to be strong when the test comes; many wish at times to feel dependent. They want to be treated as an equal; they do not wish to be dominated ruthlessly, pushed around, made subservient, and made to feel lower in status, but, if college class discussions are indicative of female attitudes, they still admire and feel more safe with a strong male. If these assumptions are correct, men still have to display some of the traditional elements of courage and roughness to meet the expectation of the female subculture.

These expectations of masculinity have not spared the male a certain amount of conflict and anxiety. In a strictly male-dominated culture he did not have to be careful in drawing the line in his dominance. If he overstepped, the woman was not likely to challenge him. Today, even those elements of masculinity approved by the female must be displayed with discretion. How masculine he must be in order to win and hold her depends on the particular woman and her conception of the male's place in the family relationship. He risks being the offender in the delicate balance of role relationships, but she is more likely to be the one to take issue and to decide when he has overstepped his bounds. Women take the initiative in most of the divorce actions although the ratio has declined with the no-contest divorce.

Prior to any marriage, the average young woman is likely to display considerably more interest in performing joint roles in a sharing basis than she will be willing or able to continue after the marriage is concluded. The great emphasis on companionship, a value which serious couples rate above love as a basis for mate choice, has led the young woman to go all out in being a pal in the man's world. She has adopted the short haircut and donned slacks; she goes hiking, hunting, skiing, hot-rodding, and fishing. Many of her clothes have become more utilitarian, less delicate, and less alluring. She has adopted the male's manner of speech, even his strong language. (A part of the shock of protest movements of the late 1960s, as far as police and public were concerned, was what might be called the "creative cussing" by women. It was as filthy, vile, barnyardy, and sacreligeous as the vocabularly of the old-time lumberjack living in isolation from female subculture.) She may sometimes share his broad humor; she patronizes the tavern; she smokes. Her liberties in the area of sublimated sex behavior are very broad, catering to males' recognized sex needs.

In her youth the gun, fishing rod, skis, golf clubs, and other paraphernalia of the rugged outdoor type are indicative to the male that she shows the same eagerness for speed, blood, and gore as he. She has become a worker beside him and is perhaps more likely than he to lay by a nest egg for establishing a home. Thus she proves to him that she is a real companion and that this companionship is likely to cost him nothing. He retains the traditional statuses; enjoys the traditional recreational forms; and she is a real pal to him, undemanding, enthusiastic, making him feel that life is complete.

It would be unfair to claim that all of this is part of the deceptive technique of the female in winning her man. Many modern young women thoroughly enjoy these activities, but many who participate in them do so as part of the necessary game for capturing the kind of male they want. After marriage, however, the requirements of home and family will most likely make this type of mutual role participation difficult, if not impossible, except on rare occasions. Then the male finds that he must seek other companionship, usually of his own sex. At the same time he will find himself drawn more tightly into the inner circle of the family. The role demands of the female, so unapparent prior to marriage, may become very great. Whether they are greater where the palship has been established prior to marriage is a matter of speculation. Certainly much of the after-marriage palship must be in relation to domestic activities, yard- and home-centered.

The male may find also that most of his pal relationships, rather than being in the field, on the golf course, or in a boat, are at social functions, church, PTA, and other institutionalized relationships which are more carefully structured, and which may or may not be pleasing to him, depending on his own inclinations. Many males who have been very much outdoor-oriented, or sports-oriented, once they are married become oriented toward domestic activities and family-centered institutional activities to a point they never dreamed possible. If they make the adjustment readily, there may be a definite gain to the family. If they make this transition with resentment, feeling they have sacrificed their roles and liberties as men, or if they feel they have been denied the right to function in the male subculture, it may create issues that are quite disastrous to the marriage. The same thing may apply to a woman who feels she has been denied her right to work, or other role activities.

The adjustments required after marriage are undoubtedly related to the degree of honest understanding that couples have of their expectations in these areas. This analysis is presented, not as a criticism of women or in justification of men, but rather as an effort to clarify marital role expectations that may not always be understood by either sex before marriage.

The Strain of Harmonizing Roles

The strain put upon a wife in meeting role expectations of her husband and his family, in adapting to the demands of his work schedule, in moving to the location of his work, and so on, are the most severe adjustments made. Women bear the brunt of marriage adjustment. But there is a case for the male's problem which seems to be of increasing significance. The crux lies in his taking a wife from the college, school, or work situation in which she has established roles and statuses precious to her and his being blamed for doing so. With most women today, entering marriage from either the work or school situation has become a near universal situation.

To make the problem concrete and illustrate how the role shift of the female impinges on the man marrying her, we take the situation of the boss who marries his secretary. In the office, her role as secretary has been well-defined. He gives her orders and makes the decisions. She does his secretarial work, buys small items from petty cash, keeps a list of his appointments, and reminds him when they come due. She controls the coming of persons for interviews and conferences. She is his confidante in many important business decisions. Then they marry. Is he still her boss or does he now become her equal? Who is to give the orders? Who decides the coming of guests? Who handles the money?

What about the role changes of the boss? He has been used to pressing the buzzer or switching on the intercom and having a woman appear to do all his office chores. She has been a pleasant person, always neatly dressed and properly made up in the appropriate cosmetics. She has treated all his business as confidential. She has been willing to stay overtime and sacrifice her own interests for his at times when work was pressing. He has learned to shift all routine to her, to depend on her for his memory work.

Now he is her husband rather than her boss. There is no buzzer or intercom. He makes his own telephone calls and shares the home work by answering some of the calls coming into the home. He shares money matters with his wife, and likely as not is expected to help her with the home chores and baby care. Most often, she rather than he makes the social engagements in which they will spend their leisure time. In the office he says without fear of contradiction: "Tell them I'm not in. It's too nice a day not to be on the golf course." Does he tell her that at home now and go unchallenged?

This example shows how marriage roles differ from many other roles in everyday life, and how impossible it is to handle roles of husbands and wives by custom. They have to be worked out by each couple for themselves. A good secretary may or may not be a good wife, and a good boss may be a wretched husband—will be if he tries to demand of a wife the same kind of loyalty, obedience, and sacrifice he expects of a private secretary. Secretaries like to work for the big boss who manipulates men, materials, and money on a large scale, but wives do not like to be manipulated.

PROTECTED MALE DOMAINS

When cigarette smoking was first becoming common among women, an anthropologist predicted that it would soon become a strictly feminine pastime; that once the female took up the practice, it would no longer be appropriate for men to smoke cigarettes. He was basing his judgment on the tendency of all cultures to assign certain practices to one sex or the other. He failed to take into account either that the cigarette habit is very hard to break or that we are approaching a time when men do not resent encroachment on their cherished prerogatives; for men did not give up the smoking of cigarettes with the growth in cigarette smoking by women.

When women can take over men's vices and men still do not drop them, does any protected reserve of male prerogative remain? LeMasters (1957b) contends that there is still a tavern society that is basically the male world, that there are male organizations that constitute the male club society from which the female is excluded; some athletic clubs, some luncheon clubs, some hunting clubs are a unique part of this male society.

Expense-account society is a male world which women, and particularly wives, rarely share. A survey by the Dartnell Corporation shows that the typical top-layer businessman travels some 30,000 miles on 19 trips, with 54 days away from home per year. Louis Harris and Associates estimate that 86 of every 100 airline trips are business trips. The corporation bill may run as high as $4 million for travel; many companies have a bill running $1 million or more. (*This Week,* 1964, pp. 14–16).

While there are men who really hate travel, and some who refuse jobs with extensive travel, these jobs do carry status. Travel itself is a status symbol. Many who enjoy it, picture its dismal aspects to their wives, telling them of the boredom and loss of sleep. To the home-bound wife the romance of it, the adventure, the breadth of experience, may inspire envy. Often too, it is the basis of suspicion and distrust as she reads of the call-girl society. Few companies are willing or able to pay the cost of travel for the wife, and even if they could, the wife with young children is not free to join her husband in the expense-account world.

Much of the business world is a male society. There is undoubtedly much in the world of the man that most women do not understand and do not want to understand. The operation of the stock and commodity markets, the phenomenon of inflation, or the significance of interest, are matters much less likely to concern her than the male. There is also a world of mechanics, with torsion bars, gear ratios, and a thousand other details of mechanical precision that are primarily male interests. It is not that women do not have the capacity to understand these refinements of technology, merely that their interests are more likely to be devoted to other matters.

Bossard (1955) pointed out that sex distinctions are apparent in the very vocabulary that survives in the male and female subcultures. The male uses a language of stronger terms, while the female uses her own more gentle adjectives. For example, the adjective "lovely" is used extensively by women, rarely by men. The stock phrases of men and women differ, as well as the subjects they discuss. The child grows up learning the appropriate phraseology of his subculture.

PROBLEMS

1   Do you feel that men in America are becoming more effeminate? Is this equally true of all sections, or is it an urban phenomenon? Is it as true of one region as another?

2   If you consider that men are becoming more effeminate, how do you explain this and what are some of the risks, if any?

3   Do you agree that at times most women want their men to be the strong commanding type whom they can look up to?

4   Occasionally one sees a very strong female type married to a very flexible and spineless male. Do you think there is a tendency for the stronger female to seek the weaker male in marriage?

5   "Momism" is sometimes referred to as a curse of American society. Appraise this view.

6   Do you agree that there is considerable confusion in male roles today? Illustrate.

THE PREFACE
TO MATE CHOICE

FOUNDATIONS
OF LOVE

8 Much is being written and spoken today about the importance of human touch; "sensitivity training" and "encounter groups" are very fashionable. Our rather cold social climate has come to recognize the importance of touch, stroking, snuggling, even the rough and tumble movements of play as very meaningful ways of communication. For some, intensive group processes, rather than bringing closeness and the benefit of warmth, bring fear or revulsion, or even severe shock. Why, if touch and intimacy are the keys to man's sociability, do such negative reactions come?

The answer is often complex and differs greatly from individual to individual. But the essence of it is that there are those who were never taught to love, and who are so estranged from the group that any attempt to break down the barrier is frightening.

At the outset, love in the infant seems to be stimulated by physical warmth and comfort. Food is incidental to this warm body of the mother when given food. Studies by Harry F. Harlow (1958) leave little doubt that it is the warm, comfort-giving, body-to-body contact that actually triggers the emotion of love, and with it the feeling of security and safety.

He experimented with newborn monkeys, providing an unheated wire mother for one group and an electric-light-bulb-heated, cloth-covered, sponge-rubber mother for another—a mother soft, warm, and tender. Each substitute mother performed the nursing function. The contact with the heated cloth mother proved to be the one that built the affectional response. This also proved to be the contact to which the young monkeys fled when fear-producing stimuli were introduced. The older the monkeys became, the more they fled to this warm substitute mother for comfort. Evidence of some psychosomatic development was indicated where monkeys had only the wire substitute mother.

Harlow concludes that the main factor in the emotional development is the infant–mother body contact, rather than the nursing contact as such.

BUILT-IN SECURITY THROUGH MOTHER LOVE

The length of these warm contacts and their certainty probably has much to do with the feeling of security the person has as he faces the colder situations life brings. Anthropologists and psychologists have commented on the great security of children reared under certain types of child-rearing practices.

Here is LeBarre's (1949) appraisal of child rearing among American Indians and the resultant effect on personality:

> There was an old army man in the 1890's, James Mooney, who was involved in the Sioux wars—The Battle of Wounded Knee and Custer's Last Stand—who from a lifetime of experience with various Indian tribes, came to the kind of understanding that I think is essential to the issue.
>
> "The Sioux," he says, "are direct and manly, the Cheyenne high-spirited and keenly sensitive, the Arapaho generous and accommodating, the Comanche practical and businesslike."
>
> And the reason clearly is that the Sioux, the Cheyenne, the Arapaho, and the Comanche have different ways of bringing up their children. . . .
>
> In the most primitive groups, because of their pediatric backwardness and lack of Frigidaires, a child is ignorantly suckled a minimum of two or three years—and, worst of all, he is fed whenever he is hungry, in a hopelessly unscheduled fashion! (Some American Indians are permitted an occasional visit to the breast even up to the age of five.) Is the dignity, the inexpungeable security, the settled self-judgment and self-possession of such American Indians a surprise to us, then? I have known American Indians whom the threat of the atomic bomb itself would not disorganize; upon knowing the worst of all imaginable situations, they would continue to adjust to them. I know one American Indian who conducted himself through the terrors of a modern war with a really distinguished aplomb. We would mistakenly call it courage—for him it was something to be taken for granted like his own manhood; he simply lacked these reservoirs of neurotic anxiety which flood us in stress situations. He lacked the culturally defined guilts that would lead him irrationally to anticipate punishment; he had not experienced the frustrations and hence did not have the hostilities to project and to be persecuted by as neurotic fears; he had not had his childhood ego systematically attacked and traumatized so that he had any doubt of his ability to cope with any current situation. . . .
>
> The really serious thing is the kinds of human being we make, and the ways in which we go about making them. The child, we say easily, is the father of the individual man. But more than that, in the larger sense, the child is the father of all future mankind.

With the infant, it is not long before the warmth of body contact becomes associated with other stimuli that broaden the base of love—the voice, the smile, the caress by the mother are all a part of the broadening process. Then comes play with the mother and other members of the family—the father, sister, brother, grandparent, and others. Others enter into this circle as the infant develops the ability to smile and thus respond to attention. The association of safety and well-being with the mother gradually spreads out to include "people." At this early stage in his development the child is already learning that love and happiness are associated with the interdependence of individuals. He is developing a physical concept of love. For him, there is nothing complex in the manifestation of affection—it amounts to nothing more than physical comfort, gentle voices, and warm caresses.

The Heartbeat and Security

The rhythmic sound of the mother's heartbeat seems to be a factor in the emotional security of the infant, apparently helping to allay its fear of abandonment. Dr. Lee Salk, clinical psychologist, found that infants in a nursery with recorded heartbeats transmitted to them cried less and showed greater depth and regularity in breathing and less restlessness than the control group.

With the infant, ease of feeding and depth of sleep are the evidences of security. Dr. Salk found that babies who had trouble getting to sleep were helped by the recorded heartbeat. In the experimental group exposed to the heartbeat, 70 percent gained weight. In the control group not exposed to it, only 33 percent gained weight on the same amount of milk. Salk has developed a mechanical heartbeat which is used in hospital nurseries.

Separation Anxiety

Studies of animal psychology have shown that young creatures develop impressions that have a lasting effect on their subsequent behavior. This fixing of the impression is called imprinting. The time span during which it takes place in a given creature is brief. With the duckling, the tendency to follow an object, be it a hen, box, or human being, begins at 13–16 hours after hatching and ends when at about 24 hours old. With puppies, the imprinting period is somewhere during the time span of three and a half weeks to 13 weeks. It is at the imprinting period that association of creatures with human beings makes them identify life-long with human beings. Once the imprinting attachments are formed, fear of strangers normally develops. Thus fear of the unknown becomes a counterpart of the close tie.

With the human infant, tie to the mother is firmly fixed by five or six months. Previous to that time most children do not differentiate between mother and others. They need the close warm tie, the giving of comfort, the cuddling, but do not suffer severe separation anxiety and fear of others. It is after five or six months that separation anxiety is severe, and it will last until the child is around three years of age. Until then he needs her as an ever-present companion.

John Bowlby (1958) believes the anxiety problem at this stage in development arises from the child's inability to grasp time. To him "a short time may seem like an eternity." After about age three the child begins to learn to maintain a relationship with his mother for short periods during her absence. By age four or five he can usually tolerate absence for a few days under favorable conditions. By seven or eight he can accept absences for longer periods of time with less strain.

Studies (Harlow and Harlow 1962) of monkeys and of apes indicate that after a period of constant association with the mother, the infant begins to stray by gradual steps until he becomes acquainted with others of his age. The mother in time tends to push him away, encouraging his attachment and association with peers.

This is the normal situation with human beings. After the close mother-child attachment stage, the range of love bonds extends to father, brothers, and sisters, and eventually to peers, with the ultimate step that of moving away from adults as a primary attachment and to closer attachments with peers.

LOVE DEPRIVATION

Sociologists have long been interested in the study of "feral men," the product of isolated rearing, some with animals, some shut in cellars and attics away from human contact. These reports range from myth to fairly well-substantiated accounts. Introductory texts cite them as evidence of the importance of social contact to human development. Other studies have focused on retarded socialization due to loss of senses, particularly hearing. Sociologists, psychologists, and child specialists have also observed the tendency of orphanages of the traditional type to produce children lacking important aspects of socialization and prone to delinquency.

More precise studies were begun during the 1930s by John Bowlby (1966) in England. Independent studies in other parts of the western world have added to our knowledge of the effects of social deprivation. These studies have revealed that an undue proportion of delinquents come from orphanages. Also children from emotionally deprived backgrounds tend to be unfeeling, aggressive, violent, and are difficult to help. They show little capacity to relate positively to others. Their feelings are shallow, they lack capacity to respond to or establish close attachments with others, even though some of the children give boisterous shows of affection. Some of the socially deprived children are pathologically withdrawn.

Separations by war can cause emotional starvation resulting in the emotionally withdrawn and isolated child. The phenomenon was widely observed in England during World War II with the evacuation of London and separation of young children from their families. On the continent during the occupation, parents were deported and their children shifted to foster homes—often from one such home to another.

Dr. Marie Meierhoffer (1972) filmed 500 babies in Zurich nurseries recently in a study of depressed infants (infants who exhibit low levels of activity, have compressed lips and wrinkley forehead, frequently cry and cover their eyes when approached). She concludes that depression in the first months of life is due almost exclusively to isolation.

Love deprivation can take place in the home for a lack of mothering, or from mothering by a cold or neurotic type of woman. It may appear due to extreme conflict in the relationship of parents. It may be avoided even in institutions if a mother-type long-term contact with a mother-substitute is present during the years of primary socialization. The important point is that to become a creature capable of love and closeness with others, the child must have been loved.

The child is soon able to evaluate the quality of the relationships about him. As Benedek (1960) has stated:

> It does not take long for the child to begin to know what are the actions for which the mother will like him and those which will increase the expressions of her love—thus enhancing his security—and he also will soon realize what are the actions which bring about punishment, that is, a reduction of love and thus a reduction of his basic security. . . .

Studies of affectionless persons indicate that they have experienced a lack of affection during the period of primary socialization due to parental absence, parental neglect, mobility that disturbed the family situation, or other factors which denied them affectionate relationships. The most serious period is apparently the last half of the first year, but denial is serious until the child is beyond three years of age.

Here is a summary of a filmed study by René A. Spitz (1947), an American psychiatrist, of children in a South American orphanage who were almost completely denied love and close human association:

> Foundling Home was an excellent institution from the standpoint of hygiene. The food was varied, adequate, and carefully prepared; no person whose clothes and hands were not sterilized could approach the babies. A well trained staff of physicians and many consulting specialists checked daily on the infants' health. This institution harbored babies from birth to the sixth year. Up to the fourth month the infants in this institution developed well, even better than the average of a family child. The average baby up to four months in this institution was a month ahead of its age level.
>
> From the fourth month on, however, this picture changed radically. The developmental level of these children dropped more and more until at the end of the first year the average child of Foundling Home was alarmingly retarded. A 12-month-old child in Foundling Home showed the picture of an eight-month-old child.
>
> What happened to bring about this change in the developmental picture of the 69 children in Foundling Home, without any exceptions? All the conditions of hygiene were identical for younger and older children. There was only one factor which had changed. The presence of the mother. The practice in Foundling Home was that mothers brought in their children at birth and stayed with them until the end of their fifth month. They took care of them and breasted them. After this time the mothers had to leave the institution. Trained

nurses took over the care of the children. However, the financial provisions of the institution provided only one nurse for 12–15 children. Therefore infants in Foundling Home from their fifth month on had only a twelfth or a fifteenth part of a mother. Their emotional interchange with human beings was drastically reduced, their response to it was drastic deterioration.

Unfortunately the limited duration of my stay in the country in which the institution was situated did not permit me to follow these children after their first year. An assistant I trained during my stay was entrusted with the follow-up. Although these data seem superficial they are revealing.

The most striking result of this study was that 27 children of those observed originally had died. This is really an alarming figure considering the utmost precautions which were taken in regard to hygiene. It seems that in spite of good food and meticulous medical care these children had too little energy left to resist minor and major ailments.

Besides the 27 children who died, some other children could not be accounted for, as they were adopted, placed in other institutions or simply lost from sight. My assistant had only the opportunity to observe 21 children who ranged from 2 1/2–4 1/4 years. These children were all undersized and underweight. Only 3 of these 21 children had the normal weight of a 2 year old and only 2 attained the length normal at this age. Their mental performance was no better. Of these 21 children, of whom the youngest was 2 1/2 years old, only 5 could walk unassisted, only one had a vocabulary of a dozen words and only one, a 4 1/2 year old, used sentences. On the other hand, 8 of these 21 children could neither stand nor walk, 6 could not talk at all and 11 were limited to the use of 2 words. Even this superficial sketch reveals these children as ranging from mental debility to idiocy.

Psychotherapeutic intervention was tried in a few cases by other investigators to abolish or at least to mitigate the consequences of such early institutional care. The result was nil. The damage inflicted to the children's systems seems irreversible.

This tragic consequence of deprivation of the mother represents not only a theoretical challenge to the scientist who investigates the dynamics of early childhood, but also an important challenge to anyone concerned with the future of a nation, with the future of the world. . . .

Presence or absence of the mother is the to be or not to be for the development of the baby. If a society wants to guarantee the health of its young generation and with that its own survival it has to guarantee an average amount of motherly love to the average child.

This is a striking picture of the meaning of love. Its denial presents in this instance a stark picture of the destruction of personality, and in many instances of life itself.

The mother is the key person with whom all love experience begins. As Spitz (1949) concluded from his research with infants, "During the first year of life it is the mother, or her substitute, who transmits literally every experience to the infant. Consequently, barring starvation, disease or actual physical injury, no other factor is capable of so influencing the child's development in every field as its relations to its mother."

THE PREFACE TO MATE CHOICE

The reporting of extreme physical deterioration has been challenged in Spitz' study. The basis for this challenge was the discovery that this particular area of South America is deficient in certain soil elements necessary for producing foods adequate from a dietary standpoint. However, his work is widely confirmed as to emotional deprivation as a factor in mental and social growth.

Yet Spitz was not entirely wrong in his inferences regarding physical results of emotional deprivation. Pediatricians have coined the term "deprivation dwarfism" (also called *marasmus,* meaning "wasting away") to describe stunted growth for which they find no cause other than unhappy home conditions. They suggest that if the child is placed in a situation of tender care, such emotionally starved children experience a spurt of growth. If returned to the same cold emotional situation of the home, growth slows down. The typical situations producing deprivation dwarfism in complete families are alcoholism, sexual incompatibility of parents, illness, beating of the child, unwanted pregnancy, unemployment with accompanying unhappiness and conflict. Stunting may begin as early as two years of age in such homes.*

Keeping Close Body Contact   The mother's close holding of the infant to her body when feeding, her touching and petting, her joyful face, her sighs and loving words are most certainly a significant part of the socialization process by which social attachments are developed. These, along with the sounds, smells, and tastes that characterize the mother–child relationship, are what Dr. Peter Neubauer, of the Child Development Center of New York calls the "urgent requirements of infancy" (Cadden 1971).

Singing, nonsense talk, the exchange of smiles, hoisting, rocking, cuddling, and laughing are the expressions of love between mother and child which are all essential to his socialization. This builds what Dr. Neubauer calls his "emotional sturdiness."

The mother, as Dr. Eric Erickson points out, builds a "sense of trust vs a basic mistrust." Trust is built by the "consistency, continuity and sameness of experience" which she provides. It is built by the mother's dependable feeding, bathing, and response to needs as expressed by his cries.

Perhaps Back to the Rhythm of the Rocking Chair and Cradle   Anthony Ambrose, Director of the Behavior Development of Research Unit of St. Mary's Hospital Medical School in London, England has experimented with rocking as a factor in the emotional security of the child. He rigged a crib that could be automatically rocked at different speeds and found that crying babies always stopped at around 60 rocks per minute. They became "more peaceful, with less muscle tension, slower and more rhythmic breathing, heartbeats and eye movement." He calls attention to the fact that deprived children rock themselves back and forth and in the absence of rocking rhythmically bump

*It is not known why emotional factors so drastically affect growth. Various hypotheses are advanced: happy conditions may slow down the closing of cranial sutures; the pituitary gland which controls growth may be affected drastically by the emotional climate of the home; the digestive processes may be so affected as to limit the absorption of food.

FOUNDATIONS OF LOVE

their heads against the crib or wall. He questions the stationary crib of modern hospitals (Kee 1971).

Forging the Social Bond   The beginning of communication with the infant is his smile in response to the human face. This is the dawn of social development. It also marks the beginning of attachment to another human being. Seriously neglected infants do not smile. By the end of the first month the average baby begins to smile at people, and will even smile at a mask or white paper with black dots for eyes. By four months most children can distinguish between familiar faces and those of strangers. Dr. Benjamin Spock, famed author of *Baby and Child Care* (1968), states that as early as two months a baby on the examination table may keep his eyes glued to the mother and ignore the doctor. By five months, he finds, the child distinguishes between familiar persons and strangers, and will be disturbed by the mother's absence. The process of attachment to the mother is well under way.

It has long been observed that in orphanages children will run to anyone. They have no sense of attachment to any particular person. Thus, they are lacking in personal security.

Cassel (1972) believes that the absence of strong social support of infants is a factor in the high infant death rate and the high incidence of disease among ghetto dwellers generally. He believes absence of affectionate social relationships can markedly alter hormone levels and change the nervous system in ways that create susceptibility to disease and premature death. In fact, he believes this is an important factor in the high death rate of divorced males.

The Point of No Return

It remains to be determined how long social deprivation and lack of love can continue during the critical period of the child's socialization before recovery becomes impossible. The Harlows' (1962) studies show that monkeys isolated for six months are irreversibly socially and sexually inadequate, but that 60–90 days is not too long to expect recovery under favorable conditions of socialization. They point out that this latter period would be equivalent to six months' isolation of the human infant. They suggest that up to a year of age the situation with the child might be remedied, since the child has little social awareness until he is six months of age. He may retain emotional scars, but will recover. By two years of age, the child may have reached the point of no return. Their tentative conclusion is not entirely based on the assumption that children react like monkeys, but on a knowledge of researches with deprived children.

The answer is not an easy one. Monkeys were kept under rigidly controlled conditions—children rarely are. Interaction with other children, a kindly neighbor or relative, even pets, may in part fill the gap for many emotionally deprived children. Time is no doubt an important factor, for the critical period is a time span, but a child's isolation is seldom complete, nor is the denial of the human touch and affection ever totally lacking.

On the other hand, any degree of neglect may mean that the child will be a step or more short of being the loving human being he could have been with adequate human relationships.

TRAGIC RESULTS FROM EMOTIONAL CRIPPLING

The more psychologists, sociologists, and biologists study the human personality, the more apparent it becomes that any severe denial of love is costly, particularly where this denial is by the mother. Those denied must find substitutes if they are to reach any practical degree of social adjustment.

The sexually delinquent girl, the homosexual individual, the juvenile delinquent, the insecure individual who is a likely candidate for the mental institution or for suicide, the potential alcoholic, and the drug addict, the poor marriage risks—the majority of these types are persons who have been afflicted by a denial of love. The degree of denial is in a general way related to the seriousness of their deficiency in social relationships. Many of their errant ventures are in a quest of love, or are compensations to gain recognition and ego satisfaction to balance their lack of love.

Research shows that the home atmosphere, the relationship of parents to each other and to the child, is the key factor in juvenile delinquency. A long-time study of delinquent children, following them into adult life, indicates that where the home situation is lacking in warmth and harmony, community efforts, social-work programs, and counseling show little results in improvement.* Denial of love as a disciplinary device seems to help produce a personality prone to suicide.

But if this is the true story of human growth, how do so many survive who seem to have been greatly denied love? Fortunately there are parent substitutes in many families and social groups outside the immediate family. Many a child has found love in the close tie with the motherly parent of a peer. Others have found it in an older brother or sister. In primary groups there are neighbors, relatives, and grandparents, whose capacity to love is often very great indeed. In the growing years beyond childhood, buddies or army associates may have great emotional meaning. Pets are very demonstrative of affection, particularly dogs and horses, and even cats to a degree. With the small child, the warm blanket is a comforting substitute when there is a feeling of denied love.

In the teaching of marriage courses, it has been the practice of the writer to require autobiographies of the students based on the outline which appears in the Appendix. Every semester in every class there are papers from those who clearly recognize in themselves an impaired capacity to love. Their experience can be classified into two types: (1) impairment because of a lack of affection between child and parents, usually the mother (their lack results

*William McCord, *Origins of Crime* (New York: Columbia University Press, 1959). This is a report of the Cambridge-Somerville Youth Study begun in the early 1930s with 650 boys—a delinquent group of 325 and a matched control group. The one was subject to all the reform efforts which money and social-work knowledge could provide. Reform for the most part failed utterly, yet it was probably the most intensive and costly ever attempted in this country. For an analysis of the relationship between love frustration, guilt, and suicide see Andrew F. Henry and James F. Short, *Suicide and Homicide* (Glencoe, Ill.: Free Press, 1954).

from emotional rejection, the child's capacity to love not having been developed, which causes much hostility in the personality); and (2) a denial due to folk cultures (in these cases young people come from families, usually immigrant families or stern rural families, in which the tradition of covering up affection is strongly ingrained). In these families there is often deep loyalty between family members, but there is no affectionate expression of this loyalty, and therefore young people feel crippled in not being able to express affection overtly.

Slocum (1963), studying 2500 high school upperclassmen in Washington state, asked about the affection patterns in their immediate family. Of the boys, 23 percent classed their families as unaffectionate; of the girls, 30 percent. Girls apparently are more aware of the emotional climate than are boys. At the other extreme, 27 percent of the boys and 33 percent of the girls classified their families as affectionate. The remaining group said that their families were sometimes affectionate, sometimes not.

THE FATHER IN LOVE DEVELOPMENT

The broadening of the range of love is brought about in part by the father and his contacts with the growing child. In this the mother has a part in encouraging sharing of the child, his comfort giving (like that inherent in bathing and changing the diapers), and his play with the father. Thus the mother helps provide the opportunities for emotional growth which will not come if she monopolizes the child. The child becomes accustomed to the larger physique, the rougher touch, the deeper voice of the male.

If the father remains a stranger or primarily a disciplinarian in the minds of his children it is easy to understand why boys may develop distorted concepts of the role of the male in family and society, and undesirable attitudes about the relationship of man and wife.

Judson T. Landis (1962), studying family patterns, finds closeness to the father predictive of positive family values. The Cambridge-Somerville youth study showed poor relationships of fathers to boys to be highly predictive of criminality: "Warm fathers and passive fathers produced very few criminals. Parental absence, cruelty, or neglect, however, tended to produce criminals in the majority of boys."

We have already discussed the role of the weak father in the development of homosexuality in the male child, and of the too physically interested father in the development of homosexuality in the girl (Chapter 3).

A girl who has lived under a harsh or brutal father may not be able to respect and love a kind man. She may actually be capable of loving only a brutal man and may love him most deeply after he has given her a beating. The love life of a person can actually be so formed. The book and film, *The Quiet Man*, depicted well how such a process of conditioning is elevated to the level of custom in a locality of Ireland.

Psychological studies of "critical periods" in development orientation of young animals show that "imprinting" during critical periods need not be accomplished by pleasant association; the only requirement is that the time be right in the cycle of development of the individual and that the emotional association be strong. During the imprinting period, hunger, fear, pain, and loneliness are effective just as are love, comfort, food, and other pleasant stimuli. Whatever the stimulus, it becomes self-enforcing after the critical period is past, and in time becomes irreversible. Scott, commenting on the implications of this research for human beings, states that this may explain why neglected children often have "strong affection for cruel and abusive parents."

One may speculate a step further and guess that children who develop such a love orientation beyond the irreversible point could love only an abusive mate. Observation of human cultures leads one to believe that the female is more easily turned in the direction of a masochistic orientation of love than is the male.

Girls are also affected in their ability to relate to other males by the role their father plays. Attitudes can vary from love to hatred and defiance, depending on the relationship established. Whether or not a girl can love the opposite sex is very much affected by her concept of how men act as determined by her relationship with her father. A father has it in his power to develop in the daughter the capacity to love or to hate his sex.

CHILDHOOD LOVE ACQUIRES NEW DIMENSIONS

During the first two or three years of life, the child understands and expresses love almost exclusively in terms of physical manifestations. At this stage in the development of the capacity for love, the parents' attitude toward the infant's bodily eliminations is considered by some authorities to be critical.* If his physical eliminations lead to disgust or to punishment by the mother, it is believed that the capacity to love may be damaged. Bowel and bladder voiding should be accepted with praise on the part of the mother, as it is the first experience of the child in giving. Its control should be left until later and should never be treated authoritarianly. The more love and affection denied the small child, the more likely that voluntary control of bowel and bladder will be delayed far into childhood.

As the child grows, his range of association widens and so also do the stimuli which evoke the love response. He watches the play of his brothers and sisters and their friends; gradually, he takes part in their play himself. He begins to include giggles, laughter, loud but happy voices, rough treatment, and occasional bruises in his concept of affection interaction. He learns that the funny-faced frown and the playful spank of his mother are just as loving as her kiss or gentle hug, but in a different way. He is learning of companionship, a nonphysical kind of love.

*To many such Freudian views seem fanciful. Freud believed that the child passes through a series of dynamically differentiated stages during the first five years of life which are decisive for the formation of personality. The *oral stage* is the first stage of development and lasts for about a year, during which time the mouth is the principal region of dynamic activity. The *anal stage* follows, during the second year when toilet training is usually initiated. During this period the child has his first decisive experience with the external regulation of an impulse. He has to learn to postpone the pleasure that comes from relieving his anal tensions. Depending upon the particular method of toilet training used by the mother and her feelings concerning defecation, the consequences of this training, according to the Freudian view, may have far-reaching effects upon the formation of specific traits and values such as stinginess or generosity.

Less is known about the ultimate effect of the rough-and-tumble play of childhood on love development in humans than in monkeys. The Harlows' (1962) studies show clearly that if monkeys are denied such play with their age mates, they never develop normal adult sex and parental patterns. In childhood the male monkey more often initiates play than does the female, and he is the aggressor in rough-and-tumble play. As age increases, his activity often takes the form of copulatory play. The female's role is more persistently in the direction of grooming playmates.

Placed in individual cages, with no chance for play with age mates, monkeys in the experimental situation fail to develop normal sexual patterns upon maturity. Neither sex is able to master the copulatory act even under the tutelage of an experienced mate. A few of the females did become pregnant with experienced males, but proved very inept mothers, as likely to crush and kill their babies as to pick them up gently. Similar defects from isolated rearing were observed with young chimpanzees. These defects in sexual and parental behavior do not appear if the monkeys are allowed spontaneous play for at least 20 minutes per day.

One cannot assume that the same defects in personality result with the human child, but Money (1963) has raised the question as to whether suppression of play, particularly childhood sexual play, among children may adversely affect sexual development in adulthood.*

We do know that in the case of the human child, only-child rearing is a definite liability to normal love development. The only child has more dating problems, less often feels secure in dating relationships, less often marries, and when he marries is less often successful than are sibling-reared children. How much of these love deficiencies are the product of lack of contact with age mates and how much a product of other factors in the only-child situation is unknown.† In many only-child families sufficient contact with other children is no doubt provided to offset serious damage.

From the time a child is able to toddle alone across the lawn toward a neighbor or a group of children at play, the wise parent has stepped aside and let the youngster begin the development of new relationships. Encouraging him in the formation of friendship throughout childhood and adolescence; helping him develop loyalties to his friends as well as to his family; understanding that as he forms closer ties outside the family, the family ties themselves are bound to loosen—all are important ways in which normal parents help their youngster in the normal process of emotional growth.

The love and companionship of infancy and childhood have a bearing on the love given and sought in marriage. A childhood barren of these important experiences in affection does little to prepare individuals for marriage and family happiness in later years. When a child is born unwanted or grows up in a family that has no time or inclination to love and play with him, his attitude toward people is likely to be suspicious, overly demanding, or one of fear and utter dependence. He has difficulty in dating and in building the attitudes, rela-

---

*Some sexual play takes place in the experience of most children even in our inhibited culture. See Reevy (1961).

†More attention to the only-child problem is given in Chapter 27.

tionships, and ties that lead to an affectionate relationship. In the worst cases, he finds it impossible to do so.

When these first experiences in love have been happy ones, the infant develops into a child who can easily accept new people—first pals and grown-up friends, then teachers, scoutmasters, and complete strangers. He looks upon the world with trust because he has no cause to fear it. The exact importance of the early months of life to later happiness has never been accurately appraised, but all of the evidence indicates that a child born into a loving devoted family goes into marriage with a better chance for happiness than a child whose first steps were taken in an impersonal, unloving world. In most families, certainly in the ideal family, love is given as easily as companionship and as naturally as food, clothing, and shelter. It is not something which a child must demand or even earn. It is his birthright. This is why most human beings develop with considerable capacity to love and be loved.

DIRECTION IS NEEDED

Brothers and sisters, parents, teachers, friends, and even casual acquaintances all play an important part in helping or hindering an individual in the growth of his capacity to love. Older brothers and sisters as well as friends and acquaintances of both sexes are frequently responsible for the attitudes and behavior a young person develops toward the opposite sex. A boy whose older brother, or whose pals, brag of their sexual conquests is apt to develop attitudes of exploitation toward female companions. Tenderness, respect, and selflessness—characteristics commonly associated with the concept "true love"—are neither natural nor inevitable in themselves. There is much in the upbringing of the average male to make him less than he ought to be as a lover. Usually, a girl, by imposing restraint and requiring affection, teaches him to love intimately, if as an adult he is to love in a true sense at all.

A child who, by formal or informal learning, has picked up attitudes of disrespect or condescension toward the opposite sex, cannot be expected to make an about-face when the time comes for his own engagement and marriage. Conditioned attitudes, whether good or bad, are deep-grained and pervasive. They affect one's capacity to love and be loved.

DEVELOPMENTS AT PUBERTY

The physiological changes of puberty make interest in the opposite sex take on new dimensions. But most young people do not immediately become interested in the game of pursuit. In fact, the transfer of the primary core of love from parents to a member of the opposite sex seems to be too great to be made in one step. Close attachment to a member or members of their own sex is usual for both adolescent boys and girls. This transition stage is sometimes referred to as the homosexual stage. At a later time the young person begins to show an increased interest in age mates of the opposite sex. This occurs somewhat earlier among girls than among boys, but even within one sex the age of budding interest in the opposite sex varies considerably.

Actually, there is no way of knowing how much of the awakening is due to physical maturation and how much is a consequence of social customs. Both operate. Young people begin dating early or later, as their community dictates. The conformity of the young teenager to the customs and expectations of his group suggests that the part nature plays in determining when love begins is only one aspect of the total situation.

Regardless of the basic motivations for this transfer of affection from one sex to the other, the transition does take place in all but a small minority of young people. When it does, most adolescents are able to move on with relative ease into heterosexual love. When there is a fixation of interest on the parents or on a member of one's own sex, the development of heterosexual interests is blocked.

Human parents are not always as intelligent as monkeys in knowing when to release the child. The Harlows found that this mother rejection was essential to the development of normal sexual behavior. The young had to have the rough-and-tumble play of their own age group. Anyone who has observed domestic and wild animals has observed the rejection pattern. With seasonally breeding animals, like deer, the male often aids in the rejection process by fighting off the young. Human parents sometimes bind their children to them too long.

The growth of affection in the adolescent in the contemporary family is made possible by cooperation, fairness of discipline, and democratic management of the family. The father, particularly, seems to have much to do with the adolescent girl's attitude toward the opposite sex and her capacity to love in a normal way. The father in a very real sense becomes for her a symbol of men.

PROBLEMS OF TRANSFER OF LOVE OBJECTS

Even when a younger person is eager to and completely capable of a growing interest and attraction to the opposite sex, problems frequently arise to complicate the process. Some young people, because of acquired attitudes, have been habituated to depreciating the opposite sex and find it difficult to reverse themselves. After all, it is hard to admit, even to oneself, that the little girl who only yesterday was scorned, now seems both beautiful and interesting.

Some adolescents have grown up in such a tightly knit family circle that they find it new and awkward to form relationships with other young people.

At this stage in emotional growth one of the most common stumbling blocks is raised, not by the young people themselves, but by one or both of their parents. Well-meaning fathers and mothers, in their attempts to protect their children, frequently stand in the way of the normal development of their sons and daughters. In some instances they set up rules and regulations around social life and dating that make normal interaction with the opposite sex virtually impossible. In other cases they use ridicule, shame, or an appeal to family loyalty and affection to hold their teenagers back. In either case, they only complicate and delay a process which must begin before normal heterosexual love can be cultivated.

Some parents meet this period in their teen-agers' lives awkwardly because they have exaggerated notions of the dangers involved; others, because they know too little about the part they can and should play in helping their youngsters safely to the next stage. Some parents get panicky because they are made suddenly aware of broad areas in child training that they never bothered with; they are uncertain of what the results of their neglect will be. In some instances the parents are thus awakened to the fact that their children are almost grown. They think ahead to the years of loneliness that await them when the children are gone, and they hope that by delaying the social development they can hold them back for a little while longer.

Parents who set up harsh or unnecessary restrictions at this point seldom accomplish the results they desire. The youngster whom they hope to hold is more often driven to open rebellion. The parent–child ties, instead of being strengthened, are often irreparably broken by the youngster in anger and disgust. This may drive the child to seek love desperately, often through sex experience.

At this point the wise parents realize that in order to keep their children— their love, respect, obedience—they must give a greater measure of freedom and self-direction. This is a time when counsel may be welcomed by the younger person, but dictates and commands are despised.

The mature parent ceases directing the life of the young person and gives him experience in making his own decisions and suffering the consequences of his own mistakes. He even stands by at times and sees his teen-ager take risks which may not be safe. This is a part of the upbringing of children in our time, when a great deal of independence and self-reliance is required of them as they grow into adulthood. Unwise and experimental love affairs may be a part of this venturing in a quest to replace the lost affection for parents.

During adolescence, young people normally grow progressively more independent of parents and home. Most of their waking hours are spent in the outside world. Most of their favorite activities and keenest interests are shared with age mates. Their life becomes almost completely absorbed in the teen group. Their need to feel loved and to love in return is as strong as ever, yet custom and circumstances are carrying them even further from the parents. One of the most common phrases by which the girl expresses her attitude toward her mother is, "Oh, but you wouldn't understand." Boys are less likely to say it, but they feel this way also. Their confidant is their close friend, and not adults.

As the strong childhood attachment to his parents weakens, the teen-ager revolts against his parents and may consider the family old-fashioned. He finds it necessary to defy the traditions of the parents and start life on his own, with different aspirations and more distant goals than his parents ever dreamed of having. This is a necessary step in attaining freedom from the emotional attachments of the family. While parents sometimes look with alarm and fear at the spirit of rebellion which often characterizes the teen-ager, the wise parent will look upon this with favor as long as it does not get completely out of bounds. This rebellion increases his need for a strong attachment to the teen group and intensifies his need for love of the opposite sex to replace the strong parental love that no longer seems appropriate.

The young person who cannot go through this period of revolt is seldom able to break his ties with the parental home and establish a home of his own. To fail to make this break is to remain so attached to parents that marriage becomes difficult, if not impossible. When the adolescent emerges from this stage of rebellion, his childhood affection and devotion to his parents, his blind worship of them as the only people in his life, is gradually replaced by mature respect and affection. He looks on them, then, as equals rather than as authoritarian superiors.

Once family ties begin to weaken—as they must and should—they can never be completely restored. The older adolescent in college or on a job may feel an ever-growing need for the kind of love he used to feel at home, but if he is healthy and growing in maturity, he realizes that he must seek it elsewhere and not attempt to return to the past. He begins to see marriage as the chief means for satisfying this need.

It may well be that only after marriage will the child be sufficiently mature to view life as an adult. Then the parents are seen in a different light. The young person begins to see that the parents were not as far out of step as he thought.

PROBLEMS

1 Describe briefly the reaction of your own parents to your early ventures in love. Did they seem eager or reluctant to help you transfer your affections outside the family circle? What effect did their reactions or expressed attitudes have on you?

2 Develop a comprehensive definition of love.

3 Suppose that you are a parent keenly aware of the loathing most people feel toward homosexuals. You observe that your 12-year-old daughter is very much attracted to another girl in the neighborhood, carries her picture in her wallet, talks about her, imitates her, and prefers her company to that of any other person. As a parent would you:

a Forbid her to associate with the girl?
b Arrange for a medical examination?
c Seek psychiatric aid?
d Try to interest her in dating boys?
e Encourage the relationship?
f Warn her about the dangers of the relationship?
g Recognize it as a transient phase of development?

4 Explain your choice of alternatives in terms of the material presented in the chapter.

5 Which alternative represents the worst possible course you could follow? Why?

6 *Sociodrama:* A man and woman visit a family-relations counselor and explain that, try as they may to make their home a joyful place and themselves interesting, their adolescent children (aged 15 and 17) seem bored with them and eager to be out with their friends most of the time.

Present the drama so that it emphasizes the attitudes of the parents as well as the explanation and advice given by the counselor.

7   The "movie magazine" craze is often thought of as a normal part of an adolescent girl's development toward mature love. Do you consider this belief justified on the basis of the facts presented in this chapter? What is it about these magazines that is appealing?

8   Upon what grounds is it often argued that the first few years of life greatly affect the success or failure of many marriages?

9   State your views on each of the following propositions:

   a   Custom has provided that marriage should occur sometime during an age period of 18–22 because this is the time when the emotion called love begins to manifest itself.

   b   The most unselfish-appearing lovers (those who willingly suffer in order that their mates can be happy) may be shown to be fundamentally selfish.

   c   Nature has devised a scheme whereby individuals grow normally from one stage of love to the next. It is therefore undesirable for the school or parent to interfere with the affectional development of the youngster.

10   Select and defend one alternative. Children brought up in orphanages:

   a   Are probably incapable of adjusting to marriage since they have not known parental love.

   b   Are likely to be unusually successful in adjusting to marriage because it provides them with an intimate relationship such as they have not previously known.

   c   Will probably have a more difficult time adjusting to marriage than children from a happy home.

ROMANTIC LOVE

9

Romantic love is a cultural creation, and therefore is far from a universal human experience. It differs from the love discussed in Chapter 8—love as the essential core of human well-being and of socialization itself. Romantic love is a peculiar fusion of sex attraction and sexual frustration which comes from the cultural expectation that sex must be associated with love to be proper. In our culture, romantic expectation is more fully cultivated among the middle classes than among the lower classes, among the educated than among the uneducated.

CHARACTERISTICS OF ROMANTIC LOVE

Romantic love is difficult to define, and even to describe because of its ethereal quality. It is of the heart, more than the mind, of the emotions more than reason, and presumably often beyond one's voluntary control. It lifts sexual attraction beyond the animal, to the level of the personal. Perhaps the most serious attempt to define love among college students was that of Goode (1959). He found a wide range of definitions, but 40 percent fell under the following categories:

> "Love represents a magnetic attraction between two persons."

> "Love is a feeling of high emotional affiliation . . . which sends a person's ego into dizzying heights."

"Love is the emotional feeling two people receive when they both have sexual and Platonic love in proportions."

Other definitions stressed companionship and compatibility, the giving of oneself, security of being wanted, and still others stressed realistic and practical considerations like "cooking for him," "providing security," "faithfulness."

No doubt young people define romantic love differently for different stages of a given relationship and for relationships with different persons. It is likely too that male and female definitions vary somewhat, each reflecting male and female subcultures as well as personal experience. Kephart (1967), studying 1079 white college students, reports that although females have more romantic experiences, they are less controlled by romance than is the male. They are matrimonially directed and as they grow older reject romantic experience in favor of more rational values.

In the United States, romantic love is one of the major concerns of the teen years, and interest in it does not cease with the twentieth birthday. Throughout most of Asia, on the other hand, romance is not considered a significant part of relationships between men and women. This has been true since ancient times. Sensuous desire is known and looked upon as a kind of human madness. People in many cultures have considered romantic love a sign of weakness and have ridiculed the people who yielded to it; others have glorified it in poetry, fiction, movies, and in adolescent experience.

Since our culture has staked so much on romantic love, each individual of necessity does so. He acquires his values as naturally as though these values were in the nature of things, and were meant to be. But love is a trait that must be cultivated in human nature, and the patterns of romantic love, too, are formed by custom. Even the key points of allure are culturally defined. Whether this be the trim ankle or the hidden ear lobe depends on what culture has defined as romantic.

Sex Attraction

Romantic love begins in sex attraction. The list of additional elements which may enter into the love of man and woman is endless. The happiest love affairs are those including such qualities as respect, admiration, and the desire to please, protect, share, and assist. Many other qualities may characterize a relationship. Sympathy, even pity, is occasionally an important part of love. The desire to dominate or to be dominated is also common. The desire to have children may be uppermost, or the desire to have money, status, adventure, or security.

In a sense, one has no right to condemn any of these motives or elements in love. When they are sincere, they represent nothing more than the manifestations of an individual's personality needs. The only thing that can justifiably be said against the more selfish motives is that they less often produce mutually satisfying love affairs and seldom lead, in themselves, to successful marriages.

Numerous writers have described components of sexual love in various language—the language of poets, scientists, philosophers, lovers. Like life itself, love is most difficult to put into words.

The great English philosopher, Herbert Spencer, in his *Principles of Psychology,* classified love of man and woman into nine distinct elements as follows:

1 physical sex impulses
2 feeling for beauty
3 affection
4 admiration and respect
5 desire for approbation
6 self-esteem
7 proprietary feeling
8 extended liberty of action from the absence of personal barriers
9 exaltation of the sympathies

Sexual Desire

Dr. Walter R. Stokes, marriage counselor, has said, "The only sound motive for a happy marriage is being overwhelmingly in love on a frankly sexual basis, centering about physical desire." Had Stokes stopped at that point many an infatuated young couple would have had excellent argument for combating paternal opposition to a youthful marriage. But Stokes went on to add that fundamental though sex is, "there is much more to a good marriage."

Sex alone is hunger—raw animal appetite. Love is a combination of sexual desire with all the other impulses that go into the highest type of association between the sexes. Love is a synthesis of friendship, tenderness, self-surrender, altruism, kindness, loyalty, self-sacrifice, and, in fact, of all the finer traits of human nature combined with the feeling of sexual need.

In sexual desire, the ego motive is dominant, the desire to conquer and force to surrender, or to be conquered and to surrender. The physical appetite is animal; love is social in the finest sense. Sex need is the basis for reproduction; it is Nature's way of assuring that passion will lead to fertility and from fertility to the reproduction of the species. Physical desire is concerned with no more distant goal than this.

Love is social, humanized, institutionalized, and becomes the basis in one way or another for almost every activity of the human being. It is, in fact, the basis for society. Love is sexual desire idealized, controlled, and made to conform to social living. Physical appetite is self-centered. Love is other-centered. Physical appetite is craving for an intimate sharing with another.

The most significant aspect of sexual love is that it becomes socially purposeful as it is harnessed and directed by culture. Sexual need is the biological motive for marriage. As love expands in the personality, it brings with it a sense of shared obligation to the mate and to offspring. This provides the social basis for the loyalty of marriage and for the permanence of family life as expressed in the care of dependent children.

An exceptional few rush into marriage with little more than an overwhelming desire for one another and, years later, are still in love. Motion pictures and popular fiction would have us believe that the experience of these few is very common. Part of it is; most of it is not. Many people do marry, particularly during wars, solely on the basis of sexual attraction, but these marriages are seldom successful over a period of time. Either new and more lasting reasons for love are soon discovered or the marriage falls apart. Men and women are so constituted biologically that, demanding though their sexual desires are, they are quickly satisfied. Once an individual has obtained sexual satisfaction, his partner must be much more than beautiful or desirable to hold his continued interest. The existence of strong sexual attraction does not diminish the importance of shared interests, values, and expectations. Neither does it guarantee their existence.

While love may not be blind, it is most certainly often blinding. The man or woman who mistakes physical attraction for complete love frequently does so because of a sincere, though inaccurate, conception of what a complete love is like.

Romance and Physical Restraint

Romantic love at its best is a game of double make-believe, and it flourishes best at a distance. The term "romance" comes from the French word *roman,* which meant a novel or play set in the provincial style of southern France. The idea of romance was spread by the twelfth-century troubadours as a "remote love," separated by great distance and obstacles, which precluded its consummation. This left the imagination free to enlarge upon it, nourishing it to a "happy reciprocal passion" (de Rougemont 1960).

It has always flourished most where there are great obstacles, or intervening circumstances to hinder its consummation: feudal restrictions, caste, Christian law, an existing marriage, for example. It is scarcely to be found in cultures permitting sexual freedom.

If this analysis is correct, romantic love will be expected to diminish in our culture to the extent that sex becomes unrestrained. It may well have diminished already with the increasing physical contact in dating, even though this contact usually stops short of coitus.

THE PSYCHOLOGICAL ADVANTAGES OF ROMANCE

Havelock Ellis defined romantic love as the synthesis of sex and friendship. The female is so constituted that, unless conditioned otherwise, sexual attraction, respect, and deep friendship tend to give her a love feeling that is diffused throughout her body, something far more than a localized sexual need. With the male, sexual attraction tends to create localized sensations which are no more diffuse and meaningful than a desire for the sex act itself. In the male, sex is specific, local, glandular. The synthesis of sex attraction through love and friendship, where it involves restraint of sex expression in the form of coitus over a period of time, seems to have the effect of diffusing love feeling much more widely in the male, sublimating sex desire, sanctifying it, making it a thing of supreme importance in the personality, preparing the male for the ultimate unifying of the pair in the sex act when marriage is consummated.

It is a sound psychological principle that the more interpersonal love becomes, the more a matter of mutual interest and sharing, the more sublimated in character, the more it grows in personality. A tribe of Plains Indians discovered this to their great satisfaction. The young bride was wooed for weeks after marriage before the sex act was consummated. Warriors often talked with nostalgia of the first weeks of marriage when they would lie awake all night "quietly talking to their young wives" (Mead 1949). Some tribes developed the chastity-blanket as an encouragement to restraint, and perhaps as a way of birth control. Couples were expected to seek the pierced blanket from the chief, since sexual intercourse required use of the blanket. Other cultures use the locked chastity belt, with parents retaining the key.

Ernest Van den Haag (1964), analyzing the cultural prerequisites to the growth of romantic love, concludes:

> When sexual objects are easily and guiltlessly accessible, in a society that does not object to promiscuity, romantic love seldom prospers. For example, in imperial Rome it was rare and in Tahiti, unknown. And love is unlikely to arouse the heart of someone brought up in a harem, where the idea of uniqueness has a hard time. Love flowers best in a monogamous environment morally opposed to unrestrained sex, and interested in cultivating individual experience. . . .

If there is any truth in this view, the restrained dating relationship and the restrained engagement which stop sex activity prior to consummation would seem to be the logical preparation for the romantic type of marriage–family system developed in our culture. It is significant that, to date, studies show that chastity prior to marriage is the best preparation for successful marriage. The subtle psychological factors discussed above may well be important here.

THE COURSE OF ROMANTIC LOVE

The idea that one "falls" in love is widespread. This concept of American culture probably carries over from the day when love was looked upon as something instinctive and inevitable, something that swept one off his feet against his wishes and carried him into a blind and blissful state from which there was no return. The more informed young person of today recognizes this as an idea which has little likeness to the more durable relationships of modern life.

While a person may suddenly be swept off his feet once in his lifetime, most individuals are more wary the second time and control their emotions until they are surely channeled toward a person who has the traits, attitudes, and life aspirations which make the relationship appear to be safe.

The idea that love is a fate from which one cannot escape is held by comparatively few informed young people and by none of those who have had variety in dating experience. Such persons know that an enduring love must be something that is cultivated, and that the soil in which it is grown must be appropriate. It usually begins with friendship which continues until respect and admiration develop. Only then may the emotions be given free play.

Ralph Eckert, teacher and counselor, has stressed the view that a young person should expect to grow in love, putting aside the notion of falling in love as a phenomenon of immaturity.

Love is rarely an unmixed emotion. One tends to resist its involvement. It is an up-and-down affair in most pair relationships. In fact, it is often very complicated. It is not always a thing of excitement and discovery. It is certainly not always a thing of novelty. There are long periods when the thrill is absent and life takes on prosaic routines. Love becomes what people make it by constant interchange through communication and contact of personalities with each other.

Love does not stand still, neither does it continue on the same level nor at the same intensity for a lifetime, but this does not mean that all loves are destined to die. The normal course of love may be compared to a wave. The successful loves surge upward; the unsuccessful affairs fall away. Regardless of their ultimate outcome, most loves begin alike with a strong attraction involving physical awareness between the partners. This initial attraction may characterize the couple's first meeting or it may come after months or even years of casual contact. In either case, no real heterosexual love may be said to exist until some feeling of sexual attraction has been aroused.

From this point on, the affair may move to a quick conclusion or develop very slowly. In instances where physical attraction alone unites a couple, the spiral generally begins a rather early downward course. The highest point of love in such an affair is either at the beginning or soon after. With increased knowledge of one another, the attraction lessens and the interest subsides.

Unfortunately, many marriages take place before the course of the spiral has been revealed. In other instances, couples decide to marry in spite of the fact that they are each aware of a slackening interest in one another. One disillusioned young bride described the logic of such a marriage in this way:*

> Ken and I were madly in love for about three months. We were together almost constantly and found it difficult to keep from getting too involved physically. We necked quite a bit, I guess you'd say, but both of us wanted to avoid doing anything wrong.
>
> When we began to quarrel and disagree and get on one another's nerves, we thought it was probably due to the fact that we both were constantly restraining ourselves. We decided that if we would hurry up and get married all of our tensions would be relieved and we could easily save our dying friendship.
>
> That's what we did and for the first two months everything was grand. Now we've discovered that the quarrels we had amounted to more than we thought they did. Marriage is no solution to an affair that is dying.

Other affairs begin with an immediate, upward spiral. Initially, they may grow very rapidly. As the couple discovers more and more reasons for loving one another, the love itself grows in intensity. If the affair continues into a

*From a student autobiography in the author's collection.

happy marriage, their love may continue its upward spiral for a lifetime, although seldom if ever at its initial pace. When the first few years of mutual discovery have passed, the love spiral develops more slowly. Each event or situation that brings the couple together, or gives them a new understanding or appreciation of the other, causes their love to grow, but new events and new insights are likely to decrease in number as the years pass by.

Love can only grow with increased acquaintance, but at any point in this process of "getting acquainted," what one person learns about the other may cause him to cease to love.

TESTS OF LOVE

Bergler (1946) has cataloged eight characteristics of love as follows:

1   subjective feelings of happiness
2   self-torture
3   overvaluation of the love object
4   undervaluation of reality
5   exclusiveness
6   psychic dependence on the love object
7   sentimental behavior
8   predominance of fantasy

Popenoe (1943, Ch. 3), founder of the American Institute of Family Relations, has listed five factors that characterize the well-rounded attitude toward love:

1   biological impulse leading to sex attraction
2   tenderness and affection
3   comradeship
4   a developing desire for children
5   a desire for economic interdependence

Biological impulse, tenderness, and affection may come early in an affair; but real comradeship, the desire for a family, and economic interdependence generally develop only as a result of long and mutually satisfying acquaintance.

Popenoe has also devised a scorecard test that he has found "goes a long way toward determining whether the basic and most essential elements of real love are present." The scorecard is designed as a series of questions one should ask concerning the other person. The questions may easily be reworded to apply to oneself, however, and they are equally effective in revealing the intensity and maturity of one's own state of affections:

1   He seems to take pride in you and wants to show you off, to introduce you to his friends and relatives.
2   He tries, when you are in a group with him, consistently but inconspicuously to put you in a favorable light.
3   His plans seem to keep organizing themselves around you as well as around his own personal ambitions.
4   He seems to defer to your judgment and give full weight to your views.
5   He is eager to share his experiences with you.
6   He shows respect and consideration for your family and friends.
7   He seems eager for your success and fulfillment of your own plans and ambitions.
8   He seems to find intellectual as well as emotional stimulus in association with you.
9   He acts as though he really wants to love you—that he is not doing so against his better judgment.
10 He gives you to understand that he wants children.

Analyzing their love affairs in terms of factors such as Popenoe suggests in these questions will convince many young people that, exciting though their loves may be, not all affairs can or should lead in the direction of marriage. Love relationships that are terminated short of marriage need not be looked upon as unfortunate experiences nor as failures. Since each new relationship can contribute something to the personal development of both parties, we might even safely say it is fortunate that few first loves are so successful as to be last loves.

THE CYCLE OF THE UNSUCCESSFUL LOVE AFFAIR

Most events that enter man's experience have their ups and downs. All are familiar with the business cycle, with its booms and depressions. Even one's mood has ups and downs.

Love affairs also move in a cycle. The pace will differ from person to person, and with the same person in different affairs. Kirkpatrick and Caplow (1945) plotted the cycle of love affairs with a group of University of Minnesota students. The 455 students (141 men and 314 women) were given a sheet of graphs and asked to check the one which pictured best the progress of their emotions during the courtship period. They were given four additional graphs to check which indicated the trend of their feelings after breaking up. In case none of these graphs fitted his case, the student was asked to draw a chart which did (see Figure 10–1).

The group plotted their total 582 love affairs by this means. Most students followed the steady up-and-down pattern, with no radical fluctuations; that is, the love rose to a climax, from which it fell in an uninterrupted line. Only a few went through a whole series of ups and downs. A gradual rise to the point of love, followed after a longer or shorter period of time by a steady decline would seem to be the pattern for most couples who fail to continue in love.

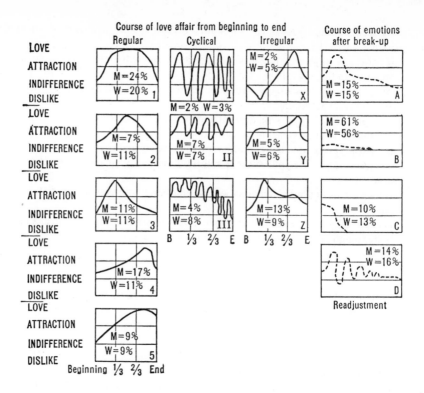

FIGURE 9–1   Emotional patterns in broken love affairs of college students. Graphs presented to students to represent patterns of their broken love affairs. Percentages indicate proportion of men (M) and women (W) selecting each graph. The regular graphs (left column 1–5) were selected by most students. Most often selected was number 1—attraction to a period of love, followed by a gradual cooling off to indifference. About 15 percent followed the up-and-down fluctuations represented in the cyclical charts (second column I–III). Less than 20 percent selected the irregular patterns of charts in column three (X–Z). The graphs in the column at the right represent their ways of getting over a love affair. Well over half picked B to represent their experience—one of indifference. Of both men and women, 15 percent experienced an after flare-up of love, as in graph A; about the same proportion, the hot and cold fluctuations of D. A few experienced a strong dislike of the former lover, as in C. Source: Clifford Kirkpatrick and Theodore Caplow, "Emotional Trends in the Courtship Experience of College Students as Expressed by Graphs, with Some Observations on Methodological Implications," *American Sociological Review*, 5:619–26, October, 1945.

On breaking up, some couples (15 percent) rise to a new height of idealized love (Graph A) after which decline takes place. (Historically, many inexperienced lovers failed to return to earth, if one is to take fiction and biography seriously. The idealized love and phantom lover continued to live on, making interest in further loves impossible. Most college young people seem to be able to avoid this.)

Graph B is a pattern of complete indifference after the breakup. Over half of these college loves ended this way. Graph C is a pattern in which indifference turns to positive dislike (10–13 percent ended so). Graph D is a pattern of repeated, but gradually weakening flare-ups of love (15 percent of students checked this pattern). In all, 90 percent of these student love affairs terminated in what the researcher considered a normal pattern. In a later chapter, breaking of the engagement and its consequences will carry the study of this aspect of the love experience further.

The writer has collected data in graph form of several thousand love affairs of college students over the past 15 years. They follow regular patterns similar to the typical ones described in the chart. Occasionally one finds a relationship in which the initial contact is one of hostility, rather than attraction. "I couldn't stand him when I was introduced to him. I thought he was the most obnoxious, egotistical person I had ever met." But later the miracle of attraction takes place, then love, and in some cases even marriage.

THE CONTROL OF ROMANTIC LOVE

Most cultures have distrusted romantic love. Where the institutional family structure is in existence, romance tends to create many awkward relationships. In the institutional family system, marriages are for social status, for guaranteeing the family inheritance, and improving economic status. People with this conception of marriage cannot let romantic love interfere with parental arrangement. Therefore, they tend to laugh at romantic love or consider it shameful, and they transmit this idea in the culture.

After marriage, romantic love is distrusted in the joint family. Through romantic love, parents lose first place in their children's affection. In patrilocal family systems, where the husband brings the wife into the family home, the mother and sister try to outdo the wife in holding the son's and brother's affections and attention.

Most cultures also put numerous impediments in the way of romantic love prior to marriage. They may require marriage between relatives, usually cousins. They may employ child betrothal, often bringing the engaged into the home as a servant long before the marriage is consummated. They may limit betrothal to persons in a certain social position or class. Segregation of the sexes, precluding secret romances among the young; the veil; the harem; selection of mates by parents or other elders; stressing the value of chastity before marriage; and many other such devices have been and are a part of folk cultures, one important purpose being to control the romantic impulse and keep it from disturbing customary arrangements (Goode 1959).

While we have come to recognize romantic love as a legitimate basis for mate selection, we have had to face the reality that romantic love is not enough. One of the chief advantages of marriage courses has been to help young people discount romantic love as an independent value and force them to check it against some of the realities of human experience. Research in the field of marriage and the family has concentrated largely on the problem of trying to determine the kind of background factors and social–emotional traits which help or hinder success in marriage. By presenting young people with this factually derived information, which, although tentative, far exceeds folklore in authority, teen-agers are helped to temper romantic expectation with realistic ones. It is not unusual for such teaching to break up existing romances, and to cause young people to appraise future relationships in other than romantic terms. The marriage-counseling clinic is another device that has emerged in answer to the needs of our modern urban–industrial culture in which total strangers often meet and date. These clinics are available for helping young people critically appraise each other before marriage. The inquiring couple usually faces a battery of tests that evaluate their emotional, background, and personality factors. The clinician then tries to give them some objective awareness as to their likelihood of success or failure in marriage.

Those who study marriage and the family have learned to consider romance as only one of various prerequisites for mate selection. They realize that some of the most fabulous romances end in the most tragic marriages. The film *This Charming Couple* presents a wonderful romance. The man is a dreamer, an interesting classroom lecturer, a bohemian by disposition. He is sophisticated, profligate, his economic values are unrealistic. The girl in the pair is the systematic, thrifty, conventional secretary whose life must be ordered according to plan, whose future must be made economically secure and framed in a familiar niche of people with familiar patterns. The romance is out of this world. Their very differences fascinate the couple and make their moments together moments of supreme joy. Their marriage, however, is tragic, for they have no basis whatever for a life of similar habits, expectations, and plans.

Many a romance between the American GI and the foreign girl reaches a romantic peak which is impossible for couples of similar backgrounds. The girl's spoken accent is sexually attractive to the man and charms him, but, making a marriage with one of vastly different cultural background is quite a different matter from romance. Romance often flourishes brilliantly across racial lines. Many persons have a deep sexual affinity for members of a race of a different skin color. Their hearts flutter, their imaginations run rampant, they feel a compelling sexual urge—being drawn to the member of the contrasting race with an almost hypnotic fascination. This is ground for wonderful romance, but not necessarily for a successful marriage.

One might go on with examples to show that romance is not enough, nevertheless, marriage without some romance would be dull indeed. Older cultures have recognized this for centuries and have often reserved romance for the mistress, not for the wife, thus ensuring family stability. Wifehood and motherhood are recognized as institutions, not merely as flighty emotional experiences. They are symbolic of the persistent, systematic, demanding, routine aspect of life.

In trying to combine romance and marriage in the marriage–family system, Americans have made some gains, but these can be had only as realities of married life are projected into romance.

ROMANTIC LOVE AS A BASIS FOR MARRIAGE

One of the exciting and yet dangerous aspects of the romantic love situation is the influence of what psychologists characterize as "halo effect"—assessing of personality entirely in terms of some particular trait. Given one or several attractive traits, the personality is wholly accepted on the basis of these traits. Or, conversely, given one or several unattractive traits, the personality is wholly rejected on the basis of these traits.

Halo effect operates in the love relationship more than in any other social relationship. Sex attraction and the appeal of certain superficially valuable "dating skills" provide a brilliant halo that obscures all other personal qualities. They symbolize to the attracted partner the ultimate of everything that is desirable. If the love is not pursued to the point where the halo can be penetrated, permitting a reasonable appraisal of the romanticized one's true capacities, the risk is great indeed. This is a hazard of marriages that occur without an adequate period of acquaintance. Disillusionment following marriage is an inevitable consequence of marriages that have occurred in the glow of the halo effect.

Margaret Mead (1949) sees the American concept of romance as a factor in marriage instability. After marriage, in our culture, even casual flirtation is considered a threat. In cultures where marriage is a permanent institutional relationship, however, as in Europe, flirtations and even heated extramarital affairs are not serious threats to the marriage. In our marriage system romance is put to the test after marriage as well as before.

Even if Mead is right in assuming that our romantic marriage leads to too much temperature-taking after marriage, the essential elements of the romantic mate-choice system are likely to continue in our way of life—with, perhaps, some tempering by other values.

Actually, it appears that romance, as a method of mate selection, is on the wane in the United States, although much on the increase in some other countries. In Japan, where for centuries mate selection has been by proxy and go-betweens, romantic love matches are greatly on the increase, and there, where society is in transition between old and new philosophies of marriage, a Supreme Court Justice has estimated that marriages made by parents and go-betweens end in divorce four to five times as often as "love matches" (Blood 1967).

Sociologists Burgess and Wallin (1953), studying 1000 engaged couples in the United States, expressed the belief that romantic love is on the decline in the United States as a major factor in mate choice, and that an increased emphasis on companionship and compatibility are in evidence. They found that 12 percent of men and 15 percent of women even go so far as to think that it is all right to marry a person when not in love with him.

One suspects that a reason for the emergence of this view is the emphasis upon romance and thrill seeking during the dating period. Many young people learn during this period that highly excited romance is often a temporary thing, so that when they settle down to selecting a mate, they are more interested in the enduring qualities that can survive in a day-to-day relationship. This means ability to get along together in social and recreational life; ability to make plans together for children, family, and an economic future.

There probably is more realism in mate seeking today, at least among the more intelligent groups of the population, than there was a generation ago. Of course, professors in the field of marriage and family like to think that they have played a part in this, in that for more than two decades the emphasis in marriage education through books, magazine articles, and lectures has stressed the desirability of realism. But one must grant that if professors thought love was all that mattered, there would be no reason for their writing books and articles on marriage or teaching about marriage. Nature would handle the job of mating and marriage.

PROBLEMS

1 Draw curves of your various love affairs. What kind of up-and-down pattern do they show? Are they all similar in trend? Do all move at the same speed? Can you mark the relationship or act that brought about the termination of former love affairs?

2 As a group project, devise what you believe to be an adequate test of love. With one person at the blackboard as recorder, have members of the class suggest behavior, attitudes, etc., which an individual should expect of himself or his loved one before concluding "This is love." For example:

a "I am physically attracted to him or her."
b "I am proud to have my family and friends meet him or her."

3 Make three criticisms of the dating customs of your campus or community. Briefly describe how these shortcomings could best be remedied by individual or community action.

4 Have the class divide into sections for an informal discussion concerning the most desirable function of dating. Have one group support dating as "preparation for marriage"; have the other defend dating as "a form of amusement." At the end of the discussion decide as a group whether the two interpretations seem irreconcilable or not.

5 Do library research on the dating or mate-choice customs of other countries and report.

6 Pick the three items which rate highest with you. In asking for or accepting a date I am most interested in someone who:

a Is good looking.
b Is popular among individuals of my sex.
c Is courteous.
d "Rates high" on campus or in the community.
e Is modest and unassuming.
f Shares my religious and cultural background.
g Would live up to my parents' standards.
h Enjoys a good time and isn't too prudish.

What does your choice suggest with regard to your background? The kind of marriage you are likely to have? Does the consensus of male and female students differ? If so, discuss the significance of this fact.

7 The dean of women in a small coeducational college described the following situation to a gathering of the dormitory house-mothers. She did so to get their suggestions for improving the situation. Read her description and consider possible action that could be taken:

Girls on our campus outnumber boys almost two-to-one. Competition among the young women for the available dates is intense and of an alarming character. Girls from the finest homes seem to lose all of their respect for propriety, modesty, and fair play; those who do not, are left dateless.

The mode of dress on the campus is changing from that of traditional college simplicity to one of open suggestiveness. Drinking and petting are becoming the rule instead of the exception on off-campus dates. Girls are willing to risk open criticism and poor grades by cutting class in order to keep coke dates with the fellows.

Girls who came to our college seriously concerned about an education seem to have lost their heads in this mad scramble for male attention.

One's first inclination is to "crack down." We have seen that done on many campuses. I came here to speak to you, hoping that we might avoid this by immediate action of a more positive and constructive nature.

DATING

10 There are two countertrends in teen-age dating culture. One is toward more group activity, less serious personal involvements, and less monopoly of the single dating partner. Casual parties, picnics, beach parties, rock music fests are the major social activities. But another trend is toward greater intimacy, taking sex for granted as a right for those whose conscience or desires permit, and less peer group censure of those who violate the traditional moral code. There is more premarital pregnancy resulting from dating, more inclination to see the pregnancy through to childbirth, and more rearing of the child by the single woman. All in all teen-agers have vastly increased freedom of personal choice and, therefore, more personal responsibility for choice, than ever before.

DATING—A STEP IN PSYCHOLOGICAL WEANING

Ceremonial rites (rites of passage) marking the transition from childhood, or adolescence, to manhood have been extensively practiced among primitive peoples. Such initiations for boys often take the form of ordeals testing a youth's capacity to suffer. In many societies the period of puberty is spent in isolation from parents in special shelters or camps. In these bachelor quarters the boys are initiated into the roles and philosophies of adulthood in their community, and are taught their new relationships to women, work, and children.

Girls in similar camps are in the custody of wise old women who teach them what it means to grow up and become mothers and administrators of tribal households.

There are no such formal rites in American culture unless coming-out parties, mixed social gatherings, dances, and such could qualify. These functions unquestionably help to push young people out of the family nest. More significant, however, is the sanction of informal dating relationships which permit the growth of heterosexual attachments.

The roots of emotional life are in the family. They remain there throughout childhood, the parents and siblings being the natural center of emotional attachment. During adolescence there must be a gradual shift of this attachment from the family focus to members of the opposite sex. The ultimate attainment of emotional maturity depends in large part upon the effectiveness with which the adolescent succeeds in making this transfer of his deeper emotional attachments to a member of the opposite sex. Those who fail to make the transfer and who remain permanently "tied to the mother's apron strings," fail to achieve the kind of emotional maturity that is necessary for establishing a new, independent family.

Dating is not necessary to this weaning process, but it does seem to provide a normal and natural shift to heterosexual emotional alignment outside the family.

Dating, with its close personal ties, is a factor in developing the psychosexual nature of the individual, particularly today when concrete expressions of emotion are expected. Kissing and necking, when they express genuine emotion, become overt steps in a young person's emotional transfer from the family circle. The stimulation such contacts provide often represents a desirable preliminary to the growth of natural heterosexual interests. The way is paved for a normal responsive approach to members of the opposite sex. Without dating, the young person lacks this experience and is to that extent retarded in emotional development.

Dating has evolved as the natural and logical product of the anonymity, urbanization, individualism, secularization, and emancipation of young women from chaperonage that has gradually come to characterize American society. Courtship patterns of the past were built around a relationship involving two people who had known one another more or less intimately for years—usually since childhood. There are today few city residents who have known their neighbors and friends very long.

Traditions of mate seeking were not so ingrained and sacrosanct as to withstand the numerous contacts of teen-agers in the modern city. Gradually, the rules and regulations in most families relaxed, and newly acquainted young men and women began building together new codes of behavior and new concepts of right and wrong to govern their associations with one another. Somehow they had to get acquainted, and, since conditions did not allow for the growth of familiarity through inevitable day-to-day relationships, a more casual type of initial relationship was demanded. Thus, dating—a means of getting better acquainted, looking one another over, and indicating interest but with no strings attached—has gradually become the rule.

Dating received a further impetus as high schools and colleges brought together increasingly large groups of young people of the same age. The daily association of young people in coeducational schools made dating the central activity of social life for this age period, and hence, also, the key to much of happiness or disappointment.

It is possible for a person to date through high school and/or college without ever having any serious intention of selecting a mate. Although potentially any date may develop to the point of serious interest, dating is now a part of the normal social activity of young people. By dating, they size up members of the opposite sex and extend their close acquaintance with them long before they have any intention of choosing a partner for marriage. It is in this setting, nonetheless, that romantic love has become exaggerated out of all normal proportions, as viewed historically and as viewed by most other peoples in the world.

THE VALUES IN CONTEMPORARY CAMPUS DATING

Blood (1956) tried to arrive at the values which college people held uppermost in their evaluation of a date. A group of 95 men and 134 women, a cross-sectional sample of the undergraduate students at the University of Michigan, was presented with a checklist of 37 items pertaining to dating values. They were asked to check values for both casual and serious dates. The six items selected by almost all men and women students for both casual and serious dates were:

1   is pleasant and cheerful
2   has a sense of humor
3   is a good sport
4   is natural
5   is considerate
6   is neat in appearance

A study of unmarried students at the University of Colorado showed the traits these young people rated highest in characterizing a good mate. Both men and women rated companionability as the most important characteristic of a good date and a good mate. Men and women differed somewhat in certain values. Men rated physical appearance fairly high, whereas women rated social graces higher than looks.

SEX ROLES AND SEX CODES IN DATING

Changing sex roles and codes find their most conspicuous expression in dating on the college campus. Certain inhibitions have been shed, and role definitions have been modified in substantial ways. Even the rules of social relationships have been subject to revolutionary revision. Yet it is not possible for the male and female to play the game of dating by the same sex rules. Biological differences have been discussed. Even more important is the difference in the subcultural values of male and female as instilled from childhood. They cannot play by the same rules, as they do not view the outcome with equal objectivity.

Roles Played in Dating

The American dating pattern is one in which favors are exchanged between the sexes. Although it is not a strictly commodity-oriented activity, there is something of this element present in dating in that values are exchanged. The man invests money and time. He expects sex pleasure in return. It is a matter of degree as to how much sex pleasure is expected and how much is given. Some men look upon every date as an opportunity for sexual conquest, and boast of success to male peers. Research suggests than an increasing number, perhaps the best adjusted, are more interested in confining their sexual life to close relationships, as most young women are inclined to want to do. The part each sex plays in dating and the way the other sex reacts to the role played determines the nature of the game, its interest, and outcome.

Male Initiative

The college man looks upon dating as a form of entertainment by which he postpones marriage until he is established in a career. The college woman is interested in dating as a means of securing a partner from the freshman year on. Men who do not date avoid it because they are not interested in it. Women who fail to date ordinarily have no opportunity to date. Women rarely choose not to date; men do choose not to date.

In college situations, dating often centers around particular activities, and may not lead to a romantic relationship. College dating also involves certain codes that are more or less standardized on the campus, in addition to whatever personal codes the individual may have. Such group codes offer considerable moral protection to the female in the dating of relative strangers on the college campus.

The chief problem in dating is the sex problem. Anything from a goodnight kiss to necking, light and heavy petting, or in some cases even sexual intercourse may be involved. Men take the aggressive role; women appraise it in terms of whether it is accompanied by affection. The woman is more likely to "draw the line" than the man. Women are more interested in the moral reputation of the men they date than are men in the moral reputation of the women they date. Fear of acquiring a bad reputation acts as a factor in sexual restraint on the woman's part.

This is, of course, an area where profound changes are taking place. Women are taking more initiative in the relaxed dating atmosphere which has emerged in suggesting dates and in initiating what is done on a date. In the matter of sex relationships, it is still primarily an area of male aggression, with the female most likely setting the standards. The usual, and perhaps natural tendency of the male, is to see how far the female will go. The woman is more restrained because she fears society's unsympathetic condemnation of premarital pregnancy, and because of her awareness of her role as a potential mother.

Some believe that the male's tendency to take sexual initiative, and the female's role of being seductive and alluring, rather than aggressive, have their roots in biological evolution. These characteristic male–female traits are in evidence in many animal species. Those who hold this theory believe that the female is unnatural when she tries to assume initiative, and becomes aggressive. They believe such a woman hinders her cause in dating and marriage. This is certainly less true today with the emergence of the more aggressive female.

Male–female roles are still definitely typed in American culture and affect the reaction of the sexes to particular approaches. In large cities where the sex ratio, from the standpoint of mate choice, is greatly in the male's favor, the female not only has become more aggressive, but is expected to be. In rural areas, where men are in the majority and where the traditional attitudes toward the female still persist, the aggressiveness of the urban female would be spurned.

Physical Contact in Dating Success

In dating, the question of how far to go in physical contact is a matter of considerable importance to women. Because they customarily play the passive role in dating, having dates represents a kind of competitive achievement. Being able to hold the interest of the male is a constant problem. Sex plays a part in this.

Women who indulge in close forms of physical intimacy rationalize that only if they do so can they have dates. Women holding the opposite view, however, seem to be correct. Studies of attitudes on college campuses over many years show that most college students do not believe moral compromise necessary for popularity: of 364 students at Cornell University in 1941, 94 percent did not consider that "a girl must pet on dates to be popular"; in 1947, of 2000 students at Michigan State University, 77 percent of the men and 94 percent of the women said, "no"; in 1952, of 450 students at the University of California, 82 percent of the men and 92 percent of the women said, "no." Very few at any school answered, "yes." A number were undecided.

Current research is more likely to deal with the question of the proportion of male and female students having had sexual intercourse, frequency of intercourse, number of persons with whom they have had intercourse, and related behavior and its consequences. This topic is discussed in Chapter 17, and data for college students is presented there.

LeMasters (1957a) is skeptical of research reporting sexual activity or lack of it. He believes women reply in the negative, for to reply otherwise would reflect on their confidence in their other charms. Also the "no" reply fits the mores better. Men also say "no"—otherwise it would appear they cannot rise above sexual conquest in their dating relationships. Men want women with sex appeal. LeMasters believes it is the unusual woman who can be popular without the use of such devices of sex attraction.

Although most young people state that petting is not a factor in holding a member of the opposite sex, it is common practice, as are other forms of intimate sexual contact. This is due partly to social sanctions, and partly to cultivated interest in sexual excitement. One suspects, too, that it is an indication of an effort on the part of many women to prove to themselves that they are adequate—neither frigid nor lesbian.

So much is made of sex in contemporary culture, and the average male's drives are so specific and intense, that many women feel inadequate. They fear their lack of specific sexual feelings and want to play a compensating part, not knowing that most women in their teens have little or no recognizable sexual desire. The nature of women's sex drive is discussed more fully in Chapters 20 and 21.

Ehrmann's (1959) extensive study of college behavior, with particular attention to sexual behavior, found that physical contact in dating tends to go through certain stages, with increasing degrees of intimacy. The male usually initiates; the female usually determines the limits. The male with extensive dating experience tends to be the one with most experiences in erotic behavior. For the "female, sexual expression is primarily and profoundly related to being in love and to going steady."

Technically virginity has been the norm of the more educated middle classes. It has been less so for the lower social classes and lower educational group. Data of the Kinsey (1948; 1953) research team strongly suggest that necking, petting, and masturbation are sublimating devices, primarily of the middle class, which help this group to delay coitus and marriage for the attainment of goals realizable through a college education. Women enforce the limitations on sex, which stop short of coitus, but the middle-class male believes in this standard, too, since he expects conformity to it of the woman he becomes serious about. Even heavy petting seems to be primarily a substitute for sexual intercourse, rather than a stimulus to it. It permits sexual excitement of a high degree without defloration.

Physiological and Psychological Reaction to Petting   After long petting sessions, many young people report negative physiological and psychological reactions. Shipman's (1968) study of 400 college students shows that 40 percent of the males suffered pain in the testicles, about one-fifth experienced nervous reactions, and about one-fifth developed negative feelings toward the female partner. Of the females, about 38 percent experienced tension and 18 percent developed negative reactions toward the male partner.

Such physiological symptoms are relieved by sexual intercourse. For some, particularly women, sexual intercourse may bring psychological reactions of a more serious character.

Male and Female Conceptions of Sex in Dating

Kirkendall (1965) has stressed the fact that the woman misconstrues the man's concept of sex. She lures him by various devices of sex attraction and in doing so arouses him sexually. If possible he involves her in sexual intercourse.

If she yields, she thinks it is the beginning of affection and a lasting relationship. Often she gets "contempt and abandonment."

If she pushes for a steady dating relationship, the man is likely to fight back. This is particularly likely if pregnancy results, so she is left without emotional support or loyalty. If the woman suggests engagement, the man may take advantage of the situation to press for sexual intercourse, even when he has no intention of continuing a steady relationship. It is his opportunity, for she may have reached the point where she is willing to yield to any of his wishes. If intercourse takes place, the man may drop her. He is then likely to tell his friends, who try to date her with the express purpose of entering into a sexual relationship with no serious romantic interest at all. Kirkendall says the phrase "lost respect for her" is used very loosely by men, and that it often means he never did have any respect for her. All he ever wanted was sexual intercourse. Having achieved that goal, and the excitement of the physical act, disgust comes to the surface. Disgust, he finds, is often intensified when his friends make lewd remarks about the woman, and make the relationship the butt of their jokes and teasing. Often he brings it on himself by making boasts of his conquests.

Kirkendall finds, too, that the male's disgust is triggered if the woman is too willing. The male's interest often ends with the woman who ceases to be coy and resisting. When the challenge of seduction is gone, so is the male's interest; it may cease even more quickly with the aggressive seductive woman.

Other areas of misconception, he finds, involve the woman's use of dirty language, often offensive to the male, even though he uses it. Similarly, the woman who becomes quite free with intercourse may provoke in the boyfriend a fear that she is so interested in sex that she will not be his exclusively. Once sexual intercourse has taken place, a woman may begin to pressure the man for engagement and marriage. But the thought of marriage is frightening to the male, and may be grounds for terminating the relationship.

It is quite evident from various research samples, that only in cases where both are deeply involved emotionally does sex mean the same to male and female. In general, the man is interested in sex for itself. The woman believes that as a person she means something to the man. It is more difficult for her to imagine that he would be interested in sex if he did not care for her. Admittedly, she may realize at times that she is rationalizing for giving in to his wishes, or using sex in an attempt to win the affection she wants from him and is not sure she has. Sociologists believe that middle-class women rationalize more in this area than do lower-class women, who have less ego involvement in whether the male cares for them as a person.

Riesman (1959) feels that sexual intercourse with campus couples occurs less often from desire of men to present trophies of their vanity than to "secure themselves against the anxiety that they may not be truly and deeply loved, or capable of love." If this is true, the situation is more nearly equal than off campus, or, than it has existed historically.

Balance in Dating Interactions   Cultivating emotional responsiveness while maintaining standards of morality is the chief problem of modern dating. Many young men who initiate sexual relations with their dates prefer to marry women who have never compromised their own standards. At the same time, young women who participate in intimate premarital relations seldom do so as a matter of principle or preference. More likely, they succumb to momentary excitement, or they yield to men they respect, or they have a mistaken notion of "what a girl must do to hold her man." Few do so because of an overwhelming desire.

In our society the whole business of male–female relations is complicated for some young people by this contradiction between values and behavior. The woman or man who gets off to a good start in interpersonal relations, has an outgoing personality, and makes friends easily, is seldom faced by the problem. The unsuccessful man or woman, on the other hand, who wants friends but does not know how to make them, wants dates but feels that he or she has little to offer, generally stumbles into this dilemma. The problem is not just "what others will think," but also what the promiscuous individual thinks of himself. An individual cannot long live happily believing one way and behaving in another way.

With emotionally insecure young people, the love–sex element in dating is particularly risky. Having no deep anchor in parental love, the dating game becomes a substitute for the love these young people missed as children.

But even the emotionally secure youth runs a considerable risk of becoming prematurely involved in an emotionally exaggerated relationship. The intense loneliness and uncertainty produced by living in a highly mobile, ever-changing group, drives many young people to desperate lengths to find a sense of permanency, security, and belonging that emotional involvement seems to promise. Some of the most striking examples of this are to be noted among soldiers, who, in times of war, quite seriously propose marriage to women they have known for as little as half a day, or for only an evening.

In novel circumstances and situations of psychosocial isolation, deep affection for a member of the opposite sex is likely to be used as a device for restoring self-assurance, and for protecting oneself against the apparent hostility and coldness of the world. For such an individual, love comes to stand for success in social adjustments.

In the long run, certain attitudes on the part of the male or female do more than anything else to ensure the success or failure of their dating relationship. The double standard in sex matters is a relatively insignificant factor, for example, as compared to the more general attitude of the individual toward members of the opposite sex.

Many men still cannot genuinely accept women as equals. This is bound to affect their behavior in dating situations. It is also true that many women do not as yet accept themselves as the equals of men. Some intelligent women feel that in order to succeed on a date they must play down their intelligence and competence, lest they overshadow the male ego and in that way threaten his loyalty to them. There is no doubt some carryover in the male of the days of chivalry. Some want the female to be a clinging vine. The male likes to be admired and to have his ego flattered. Some college women actually do play down their intelligence, skills, and competence as persons in their dating relationships. It is doubtful that such tactics, however, can in the long run win or hold a man. Almost any man, in the final analysis, respects a woman for being what she is, without pretense.

TABLE 10-1 Significant Discrepancies between the Female Rating Complex at the University of Michigan as Perceived by Women Students and the Actual Dating Preferences of Men Students[a]

| | PERCENTAGE OF RESPONDENTS CHOOSING ITEM | |
FEMALE CHARACTERISTIC	WOMEN'S PERCEPTIONS	MEN'S CASUAL DATING PREFERENCES
1. Is popular with the opposite sex	86.6	54.7
2. Has a car or access to a car	2.2	11.6
3. Doesn't have a reputation for necking	62.3	29.7
4. Doesn't have a reputation for petting	68.9	38.9
5. Is willing to pet on occasion	29.1	58.9
6. Is willing to join in a group	97.0	82.1
7. Is a well-rounded person	91.8	81.1
8. Is a good listener	97.0	87.4

Source: Robert O. Blood, Jr., (1956), "Uniformities and Diversities in Campus Dating Preferences," *Marriage and Family Living*, 18: 37–45, February, 1956.

[a]Differences between percentages are considered statistically significant when the probability of their occurring by chance in a sample of this size is not greater than 0.05.

The dating situation is one of changing sex roles, and in an area of locally defined—often campus-defined—custom. Although certain sex roles in dating are fairly well-defined, all are subject to challenge.

Sex Practices in Dating   One of the great complications of dating is that men and women approach their dates not only with different conceptions of what their roles should be, but also with different conceptions of what the opposite sex expects their role to be. Nowhere is this more evident than in the area of sex behavior. Blood's (1956) students at the University of Michigan were asked to indicate from a checklist their perceptions of what the opposite sex expected of a date. They were also asked to check their own ideas of traits a good date should possess (Tables 10–1 and 10–2).

It is little wonder that the sex problem has become the most critical one in modern dating relationships. It must continue to be so as long as attitudes of men and women are as far apart as those shown in the tables.

"We Do Not Sign Contracts!"

If the woman, prior to consenting to sexual intercourse, were to ask, "Are you willing to enter into a contract to support me and our child, whether we marry or not, should I become pregnant?" the atmosphere would quickly cool and some realistic consideration be brought to bear.

Sophia Derbyshire, formerly of Orange Coast College, says she has asked young men in her class how many would enter into such a contract and has

Significant Discrepancies between the Male Rating Complex at the University of Michigan as Perceived by Men Students and the Actual Dating Preferences of Women Students[a]

TABLE 10-2

MALE CHARACTERISTIC	PERCENTAGE OF RESPONDENTS CHOOSING ITEM	
	MEN'S PERCEPTIONS	WOMEN'S CASUAL DATING PREFERENCES
1 Is popular with the opposite sex	77.9	61.2
2 Has a car or access to a car	57.9	11.2
3 Doesn't have a reputation for necking	44.2	70.9
4 Doesn't have a reputation for petting	50.0	78.4
5 Is willing to pet on occasion	53.3	8.2
6 Is willing to neck on occasion	74.7	34.3
7 Is affectionate	77.7	54.5
8 Belongs to a fraternity	50.5	11.9
9 Is prominent in activities	49.5	17.2
10 Has plenty of money	34.7	6.7
11 Has plenty of clothes	20.0	4.5
12 Has polished manners	81.1	68.7
13 Dates popular students only	12.6	3.7
14 Goes to popular places	77.9	38.8
15 Knows how to dance well	76.6	49.3
16 Is good looking	86.2	61.2
17 Is willing to drink socially	50.0	32.8
18 Is natural	90.5	98.5

Source: Robert O. Blood, Jr., "Uniformities and Diversities in Campus Dating Preferences," *Marriage and Family Living*, 18:37–45, February, 1956.

[a] Differences between percentages are considered statistically significant when the probability of their occurring by chance is a sample of this size is not greater than 0.05.

received a universal negative; the women seemed a little shocked by male reactions to this question.

Society has only one protective contract in the sex relationship, the marriage license. The woman who settles for less in a society as mobile as ours is not using very good sense. This is true no matter how persuasive the argument about safety of birth control methods, the safe period, and other such considerations. The fact is that an increasing proportion of women do get pregnant out of wedlock, about three times as many as 30 years ago when ignorance of birth control was more common and when methods were less effective.

A woman who is pregnant in her teens and decides to see the pregnancy through and care for the child, must immediately write off most of her life plans. She drops out of school, or may be unable to obtain and hold a regular job. She is likely to marry from necessity, rather than choice, someone who can give her little if any security. Had she not taken the risk, she could have had many choices in life which by this one event are closed to her (A. Campbell 1968).

There are those who would make dating synonomous with sexual intercourse, who consider that in a permissive society all young people are promiscuous, and that virginity is indeed outmoded. Perhaps this is a normal reaction of the older generation; suspicious of the great freedom young people have in visiting each other in apartments, their living in coed dormitories, and in their assumed right to make their own decisions regarding sexual conduct, independent of parents and school administrators. There is no research evidence to support such assumptions. Young people exercize an amazing amount of self-restraint, particularly college youth.

There is more sexual intercourse among college young people than among earlier college generations during the dating experience. Part of this is certainly due to the more permissive social climate. Part of it is likely due to the invasion of the colleges by a larger proportion of the lower socioeconomic classes among whom family and religion have never imposed such restrictive standards as those prevailing among the middle classes. Chastity for the girl still carries over some of the traditional family interest in guarding family status. To marry well, a girl must be discreet. The male need not be; for he will most likely marry within his social class in the end, no matter how many lower-class girls he cohabits with prior to settling down to marry.

Research suggests that among college students there is far more tolerance for those who engage in premarital sex relations, than actual practice. That is, those tolerant toward their peers' activities do not necessarily hold the same standards for themselves. Women still must be very discreet in their behavior if they are to maintain a favorable reputation among their peers of both sexes. The woman who is promiscuous becomes known for it, and the status rating is not favorable. Sex, therefore, is not a matter of indifference. It is a social concern of deep meaning still, and a deep personal concern, too, in its many implications.

The Permissive Attitude   It is among college students that measures of permissiveness have been studied. Stone, studying attitudes of members of her classes in family relations from 1967 through 1972, found that in 1967–1968 only 17 percent of her classes approved of premarital sexual intercourse (Table 10–3). The ratio increased rapidly through her 1971–1972 classes, which approved 61 percent. This marks a rapid modification in sex mores over a short period of time. The full meaning, of course, is not clear, as there is no indication as to whether their approval applied to a dating relationship, a love relationship, or was confined to an engagement relationship. Earlier comprehensive studies of Reiss (1967) and Ehrmann (1959), and those of many others, indicate that attitudes toward permissiveness relate to the degree of commitment in the relationship.

Premarital Sex Relations During Dating   Most research does not mark the stage of the relationship when sexual intercourse takes place, whether on a date, only when the couple is in love, or only when engaged. A nationwide study

Attitudes Toward Premarital Sexual Intercourse Expressed by University of Washington Students in Family Relationships Classes, 1967-1972

TABLE 10-3

ATTITUDE TOWARD PREMARITAL SEXUAL INTERCOURSE	PERCENT OF CLASS				
	1967-1968	1968-1969	1969-1970	1970-1971	1971-1972[a]
Do not approve for men or women	57.8	46.3	32.7	29.5	18.3
Approve for men only	10.4	5.2	2.0	3.8	0.8
Approve for engaged couples only	14.6	19.6	15.3	15.4	7.5
Approve for both men and women	16.7	22.7	48.0	41.0	60.9
. . . but only if affection exists			43.3	35.9	52.6
. . . with or without affection			4.7	5.1	8.3
Other, e.g., depends on circumstances	0.5	6.2	2.0	10.3	12.5
Total	100.0	100.0	100.0	100.0	100.0
Number	192	97	150	78	180

[a] Includes summer and fall quarters, 1971, and winter quarter, 1972. Carol L. Stone.

of 4611 women from all social levels, by demographers Melvin Zelnik and John Kantner, classifies sexual intercourse by age. They conclude that almost half of American women are nonvirgins before 20 years of age. Much of this group is engaged prior to 20, so it still does not reflect the sex experience of daters only. They found that at age 15, 14 percent had already had sexual intercourse; at age 16, 21 percent; at age 17, 27 percent; at age 18, 27 percent; at age 19, 46 percent (Kantner and Zelnik 1972).

They found race differences to be pronounced, attributing them partly to social class rather than race as such. At age 15, 32 percent of black women had already had intercourse, compared to 11 percent of whites; at age 19, 81 percent, compared to 40 percent of whites.

Even among this sample of the general population, the researchers found no evidence of promiscuity or rampant sexuality. Over 60 percent had had sexual relations with only one male and half of them were planning to marry him. Those most likely to have sexual intercourse were young people from farms who had moved away from home, and metropolitan young people in the central city. As to family composition, the highest proportion of women having had sexual intercourse were those from households headed by the mother, the least proportion were in households headed by the father, and those in households headed by a stepfather were in between. More white than black women were promiscuous, 16 percent compared to 11 percent, promiscuity being defined as sexual intercourse with four or more males.

TABLE 10-4 Percent of Unmarried Young Women Aged 15-19 Who Have Ever Had Intercourse, for Single Years of Age, by Race and Education[a] of Female Parent or Guardian

	BLACK			WHITE			TOTAL		
AGE	ELEMENTARY	HIGH SCHOOL	COLLEGE	ELEMENTARY	HIGH SCHOOL	COLLEGE	ELEMENTARY	HIGH SCHOOL	COLLEGE
15	36.9	33.0	19.4	9.2	12.1	5.4	14.3	15.0	6.6
16	49.9	45.6	29.5	17.7	17.5	17.6	23.2	21.3	18.3
17	60.7	53.4	61.5	17.2	22.0	23.3	26.6	26.2	25.9
18	66.5	58.9	58.2	41.9	30.9	35.5	47.7	34.4	37.0
19	91.6	80.9	b	43.7	34.2	50.7	54.1	41.3	51.0
15-19	60.8	52.4	42.2	24.4	22.0	26.4	31.8	26.2	27.4

Source: Kantner and Zelnik (1972).

[a]Elementary = Grades 1–8; High School = Grades 9–12; College = 13 or more completed years of education. Percentages are based on totals, excluding 1.3 percent who did not specify intercourse status. Education of the female parent or guardian was not reported in 2.2 percent of the cases.

[b]Unweighted N = <20.

TABLE 10-5 Percent of Unmarried Young Women Aged 15-19 Who Have Ever Had Intercourse, for Single Years of Age, by Race and Education[a] of Male Parent or Guardian

	BLACK			WHITE			TOTAL		
AGE	ELEMENTARY	HIGH SCHOOL	COLLEGE	ELEMENTARY	HIGH SCHOOL	COLLEGE	ELEMENTARY	HIGH SCHOOL	COLLEGE
15	33.6	30.5	13.5	12.9	11.5	8.4	17.2	14.0	8.6
16	57.4	50.6	13.8	19.6	19.0	14.3	26.0	22.4	14.3
17	56.3	55.9	41.1	21.7	23.9	16.2	27.6	27.9	17.7
18	62.4	66.2	41.9	37.4	31.9	34.4	42.1	35.6	34.8
19	85.8	77.7	b	42.7	36.8	42.0	51.7	42.6	43.9
15-19	58.0	53.4	37.4	26.1	23.0	22.4	32.1	26.7	23.2

Source: Kantner and Zelnik (1972).

[a]Elementary = Grades 1–8; High School = Grades 9–12; College = 13 or more completed years of education. Percentages are based on totals, excluding 1.3 percent who did not specify intercourse status. Education of the male parent or guardian was not reported in 6.7 percent of the cases, 4.7 percent for whites, and 19.6 percent for blacks.

[b]Unweighted N = <20.

Of all young women in the United States aged 15–19 in 1971—there were 2.4 million of them—the researchers estimate on the basis of their sample study, 28 percent had had some coital experience. Deferred sexual gratification during dating is closely correlated with education, and to the extent that educational level of the home is associated with social and economic status, with favorable life conditions. This is true for both blacks and whites. Tables 10–4 and 10–5 relate sexual intercourse of women aged 15–19 to level of education of the female and male parent or guardian.

Sexual Knowledge and Pregnancy Prevention   One of the most startling facts about sexual intercourse during dating is the lack of preventive measures to reduce the risks of pregnancy. Part of this is due to ignorance, part to carelessness and inconvenience, and part to the feeling that it interferes with the "fun." Some think they are too young to get pregnant, others that the danger period is just before and just after menstruation. Of the white women, 42 percent knew the greatest period of risk was midcycle; only 18 percent of the blacks knew this. Zelnik and Kantner found "chance taking" to be pervasive.

Some women, of course, make no preparations for having intercourse, it being an event they do not plan in advance. The build up of emotional events overwhelms them. To prepare in advance would be to admit weakness of self-control. Others would, of course, sense overwhelming guilt to plan sexual intercourse in advance. These same women are likely to experience remorse afterward, since conscience is active.

As a result of contraceptive neglect and naiveté 41 percent of the black women and 10 percent of the white women in the Zelnik and Kantner study had been or were pregnant.

These researchers recommend the giving of adequate sex and contraceptive information to teen-agers as preventives. An impediment to preventive measures has been legal restrictions on giving minors contraceptive help, but the present trend has been toward legislation making minors eligible for contraceptive help without a parental consent. By mid-1972, 39 of the 50 states had passed legislation permitting women 18 years of age to seek contraceptive help without parental permission, and 19 states permitted them to do so at earlier ages (*Family Planning Digest* 1972).

The Emotional Toll—Premarital Pregnancy   The openness of sex in modern society, particularly in the teen-age community, the air of permissiveness, and the increasing frequency of sexual intercourse is interpreted by many as a healthy sign, a wholesome release from puritanical traditions that are now outmoded. Intellectual acceptance by the few or even by the many have not succeeded in changing the mores to the point where young people never suffer from their ventures. The parents' generation in the majority of cases still holds the chastity standard, and therefore have taught it to their children. For women, particularly, sex taboos are deeply instilled.

There is a rapidly rising rate of suicide and attempted suicide among teen-agers. Ninety percent of attempts are among women, and of these, "guilt over sexual acting out" was a major participating factor, according to the *Bulletin of Suicidology.* Gabrielson (1970) and associates, reporting a study of 105 pregnant mothers 17 years of age or under, state that 14 made one or more attempts or threats of suicide. Sex guilt, of course, cannot be considered the only factor. Pregnancy in and of itself brings overwhelming problems to young teen-agers.

Seymour L. Halleck, psychiatrist at the University of Wisconsin, states that students who are psychiatric patients, are likely to be promiscuous. They tend to be alienated, and neither male nor female seems to receive satisfaction from his sex activity. The females rarely experience orgasm, and males complain of impotence, premature ejaculation, and inability to ejaculate. Whether the promiscuity preceded or followed the neurosis is left to speculation.

That one cannot take sex from the list of moral values is strongly suggested in a study by psychiatrist Daniel Offer of 1500 middle-class teen-agers residing in various sections of the country. He finds most do not experiment much with sexuality and finds them very much controlled by sexual taboos.

Social Concern with Premarital Sexual Intercourse

Personal concern with problems of sexual freedom involves such factors as getting hurt emotionally, having life plans disrupted by pregnancy, preoccupation with sensuous values at a time when preparation for life is essential to laying a foundation for the future, building habits and attitudes that may be hindrances in consummating and maintaining a stable marriage in which children will feel secure, etc.

Social concerns have a somewhat broader base. There is the important code of legitimacy, and there is the problem of economic security for the child and for the mother during the long period when the child is dependent. Perhaps the most severe social cost is the lack of a complete environment for the socialization of the child.

Providing Legitimacy   The legitimacy norm defines proper sex relations as those which exist with marriage. Without a socially sanctioned marriage, there is risk that the child will be born without protection for his social and economic rights, and that parental obligations will become society's burden. This is the point of sexual morality as a factor in the mores.

The rights to the father's name, to share support, and to inherit whatever property exists at the time of the parents' death are important birthrights. Legitimacy helps to ensure the father's participation in socialization, and is important to the child's proper sex identification.

The principle of legitimacy has been important to the male—he must know that the child born, which he is to support, is his own. Most societies have had more strict codes for the married woman than for the married man. Although such codes may be in part an attempt of the jealous male to protect sexual property and defend territorial rights, his liabilities for support of woman and child are real.

There are psychological problems centering about legitimacy in our romantic culture. Distrust and threat to the self-image of the mate is a likely result of even a suspicion of disloyalty. Adultery has been the most readily acceptable "cause" for divorce in the mores and in the courts.

Providing Economic Support   Our system of division of labor provides that the father be primarily responsible for the support of the child. The whole economic order is built about this assumption. For a time the mother is incapacitated for its support. And its socialization requires her close presence for the first three years in our culture where it is difficult to find adequate surrogate mothers. If he does not carry the economic load, society must, and today it is not the parent family which does so for the young woman with a child born out of wedlock, but the welfare system. The burden assigned normally to the male is placed on the society. This often involves inadequacies for both mother and child.

The Threat of Inadequate Socialization   Family environments are rarely perfect for the socialization of the child, even with male and female both present in a stable marriage. To have the male figure entirely absent, as in the case of the unmarried mother, is certain to be damaging in many respects. A strong supportive father is important to the normal heterosexual development of the male child, and also for the girl's development of a normal image of the male and her relationships to him (Biller 1971). And many young mothers, although the child may give them a sense of significance much as a kitten or puppy would, cannot cope with the emotional problems of child care and rearing. They are not mature enough to provide a secure and stable atmosphere for the child.

The Venereal Disease Consideration

Students of marriage call attention to the risks of premarital sexual intercourse, knowing quite well that fear of unwanted consequences is not the most effective control. The negative incentives are important in total awareness, and the degree of sex ignorance in our culture is such that they must be stressed.

Venereal disease has reached epidemic proportions, and its spread is not primarily by prostitutes, as some might think. Its greatest incidence is now among teen-agers of all classes. During the year ending June 31, 1971, U.S. Public Health officials reported 623,371 new cases of gonorrhea and 23,336 cases of syphilis. The U.S. Public Health officials believe that less than one of every five actual cases is reported; this means that the venereal disease epidemic is exceeding more than 2.5 million cases a year. In early 1973, the U.S. Public Health Service reported a 15 percent increase above these figures, and stated further that the rate of gonorrhea infection was the highest recorded since records were first kept in 1919.

Venereal diseases spread from person to person almost exclusively by sexual intercourse; one infected person often spreads the disease to many others. Teen-age boys sometimes, on a dare or to prove themselves manly, go to a prostitute. Most prostitutes sooner or later acquire venereal disease. The pick-up girl or sexually promiscuous girl runs the same risk of contracting the disease and in turn may pass it on to a great number of males, as the infected prostitute does.

Syphilis is the most destructive of diseases, having been called the great killer of the human race. It is a crippler as well, yet all the medical knowledge and skills are at hand for its complete eradication. President Kennedy set the year 1972 as the date when it would vanish from the nation. President Johnson reaffirmed that goal. It is paramount that doctors cooperate with the U.S. Public Health Service in reporting infected persons, and that all those who suspect they have the disease report to a reliable physician rather than depending upon unreliable "cures."

About 29 days after sexual contact a cancerlike sore appears at the point of infection. There may also be body rash, sore throat, headache, or other symptoms. The disease may quickly go underground but the destructive germs continue to multiply in the bloodstream. Later it will reappear, often imitating other diseases. It may cause blindness, heart trouble, crippling, or general paresis, a mental disease caused by the destruction of tissue of the central nervous system. Early detection by examination even on suspicion of the disease is the only safe course. Detection is by the Wasserman Test, such as is required in the premarital medical examination in almost all states.

Gonorrhea is by far the most common venereal disease, and it has more apparent symptoms in the male. The female may have it and spread it widely without knowing she has it. Or her first knowledge may be acute abdominal pain, with fever and a low white blood count, and be mistaken for appendicitis. The fallopian tubes are clogged with infection already. The male, once the *vas deferens* become affected, suffers severe burning sensation when urinating and painful spasms. Both sexes develop a puslike discharge and burning during urination. Gonorrhea is a frequent cause of sterility in that it may close the egg and sperm ducts. A byproduct has been *blennorrhea,* blindness caused at the birth of an infant. A routine dropping of a silver nitrate into the eyes of the child has eliminated this cause of blindness.

Early treatment by reliable medical practitioners offers a remedy for both venereal diseases that is sure and relatively inexpensive, provided the infected person seeks help promptly. Negligence, using self-administered drugs, or going to quacks for treatment gives the disease a chance to do great damage, and eventually cure may be difficult or impossible. There is no permanent immunity to either disease, and having the disease does not build immunity. Repeated infection is possible.

Crab lice, a flat louse which gathers in the pubic hair, is another plague of the unsanitary conditions of promiscuous intercourse.

Drinking and Sex

Drinking is one of the problems of modern dating. A comprehensive study of the drinking habits of 5000 American college women and 10,000 American college men in 27 colleges scattered throughout the country indicates very clearly that college is not to be blamed for the drinking habits of very many young men and women. An overwhelming majority of college young people who use liquor, used it before they came to college. It was a pattern in their homes; it was embedded in the customs of their families. The study shows that those who drink tend to associate with each other. It shows that drinking increases with the amount of income; almost as much excess drinking results from the use of beer as from stronger liquors. Comparatively few college men or women drink to the point of becoming drunk.

In clarifying the effect of drinking on dates, this study is inconclusive. While the authors recognize the folk belief that alcohol stimulates sex activity, breaks down inhibitions, and facilitates intimate contact in dating, they find that there is a counteracting tendency also; that young men who are tempted to drink to excess often restrain themselves for fear that they will be involved in violence, and that young women who may drink to excess often restrain themselves sexually for fear of the pregnancy and reputation risks involved. They find that few students attribute school problems, encounters with law, accidents, or social difficulties to their drinking. Six percent of the students who drink, however, already show tendencies toward alcoholism.

The study shows that 17 percent of men and 10 percent of women have considerable anxiety about their drinking, apparently fearing its consequences. For the most part, this group was made up of the heavy drinkers. The study also shows that drinking has greatly increased in recent generations.

Rather than alcohol being a stimulant, the authors of the study, after a review of medical research, conclude that it has a depressant effect, bringing loss of sensitivity, reducing speed of reaction, and tending to cause loss of control. They find also that it tends to reduce discrimination.

Drugs and Sex

Drugs have invaded the grade schools, high schools, and college campuses. This brings a new series of problems into dating behavior and mate choice. Drugs are used as a way of releasing inhibitions, of relaxation and escape, in much the same way as alcohol. For those who become victims of drug addiction, the ultimate consequences to personality, marriage, and family life are as bad as or worse than alcoholism.

The effect of drugs on genetic material and on the fetus is as yet unknown. It will no doubt depend on the particular drug or drugs used, and may depend on the quantity. There is evidence that LSD, particularly, is destructive to fetal development. (This problem is discussed in Chapter 14.) Research suggests that it destroys chromosomes, much as the fatal blood disease, leukemia. Both heroin and methadone create addiction in the unborn child in addition to affecting fetal development, as these drugs cross the placental barrier and affect the unborn child. It is likely that drugs expose the woman to greater risk of pregnancy. A reason for the use of drugs with sex, given by young people, is that the drugs make coitus more enjoyable. This may reflect primarily a release from inhibitions. In part it may be the disorienting and illusory effect of chemically induced reaction to the drugs themselves.

SEXUAL AGGRESSIVENESS AND PERSONALITY

Although dating is not always mate-choice-oriented, it may eventually become so. The question as to whether sexual aggressiveness is associated with qualities that are likely to fit well in marriage is one which has not been studied thoroughly. Kanin (1967) found sexually aggressive males most successful in obtaining sexual relations, but also found them sexually frustrated and dissatisfied. He feels that peer-group associations with males of similar aggressiveness is a factor in their feeling of frustration, in that erotic expectations exceed accomplishment.

Dana L. Farnsworth, of Harvard University Health Services, reports that nonconformists in sexuality are more given to depression, emotional conflict, and loss of self-esteem than others.

Riesman (1959) believes a new fear may lead some to sexual quests—the fear that they may be homosexual. This fear "haunts the campuses." Males are particularly fearful in their contacts with teachers and male friends, and may seek out heterosexual relationships to reassure themselves.

No doubt the extent to which sexual quests represent variations from the norm in personal adjustment depends on their motivation. The above suggests that this is an area of very complex motivation. Female motivations are equally complex, and often much different.

PROBLEMS

1   Poll the class on the five traits they most desire in a date. Tabulate the results and compare responses of men and women. Do the standards held by the group appear to be spurious and superficial or genuine and durable? Do preferred traits mentioned seem to be of the kind on which a sound mate choice could be made? Are the values of men or women more sound?

2   Discuss the extent to which women on your campus feel they must play the role of temptress or coquette in dating. What effect does this have on their personal adjustment? The views of both men and women should be sought on this problem.

3   *Research exercise:* Poll the class with the following brief questionnaire (other questions may be added if desired). Indicate your sex but do not give your name.

    a   I have on occasion drunk while on a date.

        _____ yes

        _____ no

    b   I did so—because I enjoy drinking _____.

        I did so—because I wanted to fit in with the others _____.

    c   I believe drinking among students on the campus is_____ common_____ .

    d   I believe a woman who won't "neck" a little on a casual date is too prudish.

        _____ yes

        _____ no

    e   My feeling is "you're only young once," so if you can have some sexual thrills without running much of a risk I say go ahead._____ yes _____ no

    f   I would resist heavy petting because I know it would

        —displease my parents _____.

        —be unfair to my future mate _____.

        —leave me with less self-respect _____.

        —soon "get around" and spoil my reputation _____.

Compare results for men and women. Discuss the significance of findings to marriage and family life.

4   The following statement was made by a popular college senior who, by the way, did not drink. Analyze it and discuss its merits: "The reason so many of us get in trouble about drinking is that drinking is always associated in our minds with 'being adult' but 'moderation' is a virtue we cannot understand. I believe that if drinking were permitted during adolescence as is smoking, it would soon lose its mysterious appeal. Girls who want to should be able to learn to prepare a decent cocktail in college as well as a full-course dinner. Fellows who want to drink on their date should have access to decent cocktail lounges where moderation and propriety are the rule; this would make secretive drinking unnecessary and unexciting."

5   A college sophomore woman is urging her friend to accept a double date with a fellow who has a reputation for drinking and petting. Present both arguments, as each woman sees them, in a convincing manner.

6   Discuss dating regulations on your campus. Are they:

a   Reasonable?

b   Too lax?

c   Outmoded?

d   Overly authoritarian?

7   When young people of high school or college age begin to drink on dates or in mixed groups of their age mates, do you consider that they are trying to make a bid for status in their group's eyes, or to imitate Hollywood, or what are they trying to do?

8   The male animal in most species, and in most human societies, is the aggressor in male–female relationships. Do you consider that it would be against nature's design, and therefore undesirable, to encourage female initiative in dating and courtship behavior, or is this merely a matter of modifying customs? Discuss.

PART **IV**

MATE CHOICE

LIMITS ON
MATE CHOICE

11 It would be rare to find people without restrictions of custom affecting mate choice. In some cultures there is the bride price to be negotiated, and those who cannot pay cannot wed. There are the boundaries of tribe and caste. There are the incest taboos, which may extend beyond blood relatives, and religious and totem restrictions, to mention only a few.

Even though finding a future spouse by our love method may look easy to one unfamiliar with the American cultural pattern, it is not. Each person must relate himself closely with another during a period of trial and error. Few dates produce a person who meets the test for a prospective mate. Karl Wallace (1960) reviewed studies in this field over a period of 25 years. Few men and women meet and become acquainted with more than three or four persons whom they consider suitable mates; rarely do women receive more than two or three proposals of marriage. The conclusion of even those who have dated very widely is that there are few persons in one's dating experience who could be considered really eligible.

From the background of these studies and from his own experience in operating a dating service, Wallace concluded that the problem of finding a suitable mate is most serious for the American middle class. This is because their moral code eliminates many of the methods of meeting mates used by the lower class and because they are more demanding in mate choice. He lists nine factors that limit their mate choice:

1   Conservative attitudes toward methods of meeting mates. They tend to taboo efforts to meet suitable persons, and "wait for the right person to come along." Wallace finds that marriages more often result from the type of secondary contacts tabooed by the middle classes than in approved contacts—bars, night clubs, and so on.

2   The cultural emphasis on beauty and sex. These values are especially prominent in the male. They hinder many in finding a suitable mate.

3   The unbalanced sex ratio in various localities.

4   Social stratification and segmentation. Class, race, and religious differences act as barriers.

5   Urbanization. Its complexities make the finding of a suitable mate extremely difficult because of isolation and anonymity.

6   Sex differences in attitudes and expectations which make it difficult to meet on common ground.

7   Our competitive courtship system which tends to award the aggressive, dominant, and ambitious type and to bypass the quiet, reserved, unsocial person.

8   The widowed and divorced, of whom there are 13 million, encounter special problems.

9   Hereditary differences in glandular activity, IQ, health and energy, height, weight, etc., not to mention disfiguring defects. For example, the woman who is 5 feet 10 inches tall will be excluded from the eligible list of 90 percent of the men she meets.*

There is also the matter of compatibility, which has its base in part in hereditary factors, such as glandular functioning. As Wallace says, "such biological differences help explain many of the common problems and conflicts in mating and marriage: why one spouse is always active—bubbling with excess energy—and the other is inactive, quiet, and phlegmatic; why one spouse can't get going until late afternoon and doesn't want to go to bed before midnight, and the other works best in the morning and likes to be in bed early; why one partner wants sexual intercourse daily, or twice daily, and the other finds weekly or even monthly intercourse adequate."

The practical problem of meeting a suitable mate is not solved merely by meeting or by dating a number of people at random. There must be a matching of many social, cultural, biological, and temperamental factors.

The principle of "preferential mating" has operated (Freeman 1962; Middleton 1964) throughout history. Incest taboos usually bar kinsmen, although in some cultures certain kinfolk are eligible. Brother and sister marriages were the rule for certain royalty in Hawaii, Egypt, and among the Incas. Cousin marriages are not unknown in the United States and have been common in the Arab world. Many cultures have added taboos, sacred restrictions, endogamous-exogamous rules, parental obstacles, sororal laws, rigid barriers of rank or caste, in addition to factors of age, race, religion, or nationality.

*How severe extreme problems of height can be for a girl is illustrated by the case of a 6 foot 1 inch Ontario, Canada, girl who had her legs shortened by three inches. This required three operations and a total stay of six months in the hospital. Before the operation she said, "Boys would flee after a single dance," and "I felt like a freak!" "Now I can at least have happiness, marriage, and children—all the things every girl dreams of—now that men no longer have to look up to me" (*Ladies Home Journal, 1968*).

MATE CHOICE

Even though few persons are ineligible by law or custom in our society, choice is still limited by virtue of the individual's own attitudes and values instilled largely by his own family. He finds few persons of the opposite sex whom he would care to marry. If divorce statistics are indicative, he may in the end choose the wrong person. It would be fortunate indeed if some genius could develop a color chart or statistical device by which couples who find their dating becoming serious would know at once whether or not they were suited to pursue each other into the pleasant but painful depths of romantic involvement.

In this area, women's insight is greater than men's. A study of marriage failures showed 70 percent of the husbands whose marriages failed felt very confident in advance that the marriage would succeed; but only 48 percent of the wives. Even the girl's family and her best friends are better prophets than the boy's family and his best friends.

SCIENTIFIC EFFORT TO ASSIST IN MATE CHOICE

As early as the 1930s, sociologists set out to direct mate choice toward success. Burgess and Cottrell (1939) did the research which laid the foundation for the first *Marriage Prediction Scale*. This scale has been perfected by others, and similar scales have been developed. Norms have gradually been built. The scales are not as reliable yet, as for instance, American College Entrance Examination, which predicts college performance, but the ACE test is built on norms of hundreds of thousands.*

Sociologists believe that marriage can be predicted as accurately as college performance, job performance, and any other area of social behavior by the building of norms by which persons and pairs can be measured. Most marriage clinics, like guidance and vocational placement clinics, now use some kind of measuring devices which give couples a tentative profile of their temperaments and personalities, and interpret findings as they relate to marriageability. These tests, along with personal guidance, and medical examinations, are used to appraise likelihood of success. These are standard procedures for those who seek such guidance. The body of research knowledge still accumulates and will provide a better guide for the future.

Not all persons are marriageable. Many persons—and these cause much difficulty—are marginal in marriageability. Unfortunately, datability and marriageability are not synonymous. A person may seem very interesting on a

---

*Adams and Packard (1946) listed traits on which both men and women should check themselves; also other traits by which a couple could match their personalities by totaling up the score. Many of his traits are from the Burgess–Cottrell *Marriage Prediction Scale,* which itself was a tentative measurement device for predicting marriage adjustment. For many years Paul Popenoe and his colleagues in the American Institute of Family Relations in Los Angeles have used Roswell Johnson's *Temperament Test* as a means of helping a person to understand himself and as a guide to his marriageability. Both Adams and Popenoe report very favorable results from the use of these instruments, supplemented by premarital counseling and medical advice. How much of their success in guidance is due to the measurement devices and how much to the intangible aspects of the counseling experience is unknown. Burgess and Cottrell, as a consequence of their pioneer research, developed a *Marriage Prediction Scale* which has had wide usage in various modified forms. Karl Wallace (1957) has attempted to put dating on a scientific basis with his Introduction Service.

short-time acquaintance, but become intolerable as a long-time companion. On the other hand, many people who have little or no opportunity to date are very marriageable persons. So the winnowing process goes on, not always logically, and certainly with much error in judgment, as the rate of marriage failures shows.

In movie-made romance, impulse is assumed to be a safe and infallible guide. Few intelligent young people, particularly those who have had some variety in steady dating, can believe in impulse as a safe guide. They know from experience that one must be alert to the long-term values in the man–woman relationship. Unless they get completely carried away, young couples know that differences in ideas and values, aspirations and life goals are basic in determining the success or failure of marriage.

On college campuses, young people are very much aware of these long-term values when they begin to face the serious business of mate selection. For example, a group of students were asked to rate 18 factors in order of importance in mate selection. Both men and women put "dependable character" first. They rated emotional stability and maturity second. Pleasing disposition was rated third. Mutual love and attraction was fourth on the list, showing that this group was well aware that love is not all that matters. Here are some other traits in the order in which they were listed: good health, desire for home and children, refinement, neatness, ambition and industriousness, good cook and housekeeper, chastity, education and general intelligence, sociability, similar religious background, good looks, similar educational background, favorable social status or rating, good financial prospects, similar political background.

Engaged men and women rate compatibility and common interests much higher as factors conducive to success in marriage than either love or sex as such (Burgess & Wallin 1953).

During the last 30 years, sociologists and psychologists have directed a great deal of research to the problem of sorting out the marriageable and unmarriageable on the basis of personality traits, social background, developmental history, parental relationships, and other such factors. This research has also called attention to the problem of matching—that is, of learning what kinds of people can safely marry. For example, is there anything to the notion that like backgrounds, like temperaments, like religion are desirable? Or is variety truly the spice of life?

Since experience is the only safe guide, research has attempted to bring together the experiences of hundreds of persons who, successfully or otherwise, have run the gauntlet of mate selection. Although the experiences of a multitude could never give an infallible answer to anyone, they can at least clarify the nature of the mate-selecting problem.

IS THERE AN IDEAL MATE?

In the dreamy days of adolescent romance young people are likely to feel that their love is heaven sent, that they were created for each other. The idea that there is somewhere in the universe a "one and only" for everyone is deeply rooted in fiction and tradition. Probably due to the dating custom, this idea is fast losing ground. Even so, in romantic dating there is much idealization of the prospective mate. This leads to the placing of a halo about him or her, and attributing to the mate qualities desired, even though they may not actually be there. This self-deception is incorporated in the folk saying "love is blind." There is much also in mass media communication about the ethereal nature of romance, particularly in popular songs.

A more practical view is that the loving, well-adjusted person can marry any one of a number of people and be happy, whereas the maladjusted, unhappy person can be successfully married to no one. This view emphasizes the thought that one needs to be the "right" person. It agrees with marriage counselors and students of marriage who know that one finds in marriage much of what he takes into it. Ceremony has no magic power to make people over. Happy and successful persons make successful marriages.

While the view that no one is predestined for any specific member of the opposite sex is generally accepted today, young people nonetheless have some concept of the traits and qualities they want their mate to have. Study of college young people shows that almost a third of the men and almost a fourth of the women are very conscious of the characteristics of their ideal mate. Almost equal numbers have a vague consciousness of such ideals. Very, very few are entirely without any awareness of what their ideal mate should be like.

Research has attempted to define the ideal mate in terms of general background. Here are the ten factors in the background of a person which will tell most about his marriageability (Terman 1938):

1   superior happiness of parents
2   childhood happiness
3   lack of conflict with mother
4   home discipline that was firm, not harsh
5   strong attachment to mother
6   strong attachment to father
7   lack of conflict with father
8   parental frankness about matters of sex
9   infrequency and mildness of childhood punishment
10 premarital attitude toward sex that was free from disgust or aversion

Any person who possesses all ten of these is a much better than average risk in marriage, according to this in-depth study of 792 married couples.

It will be seen at a glance that all of these important background factors indicating favorable marriage prospects have to do with interpersonal relationship in early home life, with the example the parents have provided, and with the attitudes and training they have passed along to their children. Of all the factors listed, happiness of parents' marriage and one's own childhood happiness are most deterministic. This was indicated not only by the research cited above, but is further confirmed by several additional studies. Few children from unhappy homes make happy marriages.

Marriage happiness runs in families; so does unhappiness and divorce. One judge of a divorce court, addressing an audience, felt this so strongly that he said, "I sometimes think divorce is hereditary." Heredity, of course, is not the primary cause of the problem. The vital factor is rather the pattern of adjustment set in the home. But marital unhappiness and divorce do, nonetheless, run in families. Parents who are happy, are well-mated, and settle problems together, set a pattern of relationships children learn and carry into their own homes. Families characterized by constant bickering between parents and brothers and sisters also set a pattern that children are likely to imitate in their associations with each other and carry over into their relationship as husbands or wives. Families which are unhappy, in which husband and wife are dissatisfied with each other, in which there is pessimism and gloom, pass these traits on in the habits and attitudes of their children. This, in turn, complicates the job young people face in establishing and maintaining a happy home and a desirable place for rearing their own offspring.

Close relationships between child and parent are shown to be favorable to marriage. Yet a boy may not fall in love with a girl without a feeling of guilt about forsaking his mother. There are the girls who cannot possibly leave home because father and mother need them. Too strong family attachments take on the character of fixation and make marriage impossible. This is one of the most important reasons why otherwise normal people do not marry. Good relationships with parents must be within the normal range of emotional attachment, which means that the young person, when the time comes for mate choice, must be capable of making the chosen member of the opposite sex the first person in his affections.

THEORIES OF MATE CHOICE

Sociologists and psychologists have propounded various theories of mate choice, some dealing with more obvious environmental factors, others with subtle and largely unconscious forces in the personality.

Value Theory   Coombs (1961; 1962) has expounded a "value theory" of mate choice which he feels incorporates most other theories, or at least explains the factors which make them a reality. Briefly, he holds that each person possesses a value system which consciously or unconsciously guides him in mate selection.

Propinquity Theory   Considerable study has centered around the idea of propinquity as a major factor in mate choice. The theory originally was applied to those living in the same general neighborhood. Some would now include those who go to school or work together. This theory states that people must and usually do meet each other by some form of daily association—same neighborhood, school, church, or office. To stress propinquity and engage in extensive proof, as has been so often done, would seem to be an elaboration of the obvious.

Parental Image Theory   Freudian in origin, this theory holds that the child tends to develop a deep affection for the parent of the opposite sex: boy for his mother, girl for her father. In certain instances, the tie may be between a brother and sister or other sibling. In the mate chosen the youth sees the image of this childhood attachment. This puts mate choice largely on a level below consciousness. The theory has not been well-substantiated. To accept it at face value would be to make the study of mate choice largely meaningless, for it would remove choice largely from the voluntary level, assigning it to the predestination of childhood parental attachments.

Coombs concludes that since the parents are the agents of socialization, the parents and child hold similar values. This becomes a basis for choice of a mate who has characteristics and values similar to those of the parents. Strauss (1946) found little similarity per se, but he concludes that parents do influence choice in that if the child has shared meaningful relationships with his parents, he wishes to find similar traits in the mate; if hostile relationships with parents have persisted, he seeks different traits in the mate.

Complementary Needs Theory   The theory of complementary needs has been propounded by Winch and given some testing, but it lacks objective support. It assumes that the individual seeks out a mate to complement his own personality.

All students of the family accept the view that wish fulfillment is the strongest motive for marriage. Folk knowledge too takes this for granted. But Winch (1958) introduced the theory to explain why a particular person picks the mate he does. He holds that "in mate selection the need-pattern of each spouse will be complementary rather than similar to the need-pattern of the other spouse." It is as though the mate is chosen to fill out weaknesses of one's own personality. In these psychological needs, opposites tend to attract, thus complementing the self.

Although this theory is a challenging one, and Winch found some support for it with a small sample, other researchers have failed to confirm it. In fact, the preponderance of evidence to date leads to the conclusion that the theory has no foundation. Quite to the contrary, couples want to satisfy similar needs in each other.

Homogamy Theory   This theory is concerned with whether choice is of like economic, racial, religious characteristics. In general, we know that like marries like, particularly in general social characteristics, and that the more homogamous pair succeeds most often in marriage. Similarity in church background, education, economic background, social class, age, race, moral and religious background is important. Even the divorced and the widowed tend to marry their kind. It is in this general area that most fruitful sociological research has centered.

"Ideal Mate" Theory   This last theory assumes that the individual has some more or less tangible idea of the perfect mate for him. Coombs would hold that one's conception of an ideal mate for oneself is within the framework of one's value constructs.

A person with dating experience learns that some personalities clash, while others supplement each other, creating a feeling of completeness. The "battle of the sexes" is a frequently heard phrase and has some meaning, yet antagonism cannot be the rule of successful pair relationships. Some couples may profit from a flare-up once in a while. In temperament and disposition couples need not be alike, but they must supplement each other, giving a sense of need fulfillment.

It has even been found that the extrovert may successfully marry the introvert, but this does not mean that all extroverts will be satisfied with introverts as mates. More often the socially active marry others with the same interests. One person may find a sense of security and the satisfaction of emotional needs in a person of like temperament; another may find his own personality filled out by someone quite his opposite in temperament.

One person may need a mate to lean upon while another needs to feel that he or she is the tower of strength in any relationship. One person needs the center of the stage and wants to marry an admirer rather than a competitor; another feels more secure when he or she can stay in the background and bask in the mate's accomplishments.

Most men, in persistent traditional patterns, prefer to be the strong member of the household. Probably most women like them to be. Women of dependent disposition must marry this kind of man in order to be happy. The sensitive, insecure, cautious man may need a maternal type generous with comfort and sympathy. This man will often marry a woman considerably older than himself. A high-strung person may need a placid mate, or he may want one with whom to race through life. Two strong-willed persons may date, but may have so many clashes of will that the relationship ends short of marriage. If they marry, one or both will have to learn to give ground, and they may still agree to disagree in certain compartments of their lives. The chances are they may be happier with more yielding partners, although even here rules are hard to make.

Personality tests help some people in understanding themselves and their prospective mate. Counselors' advice, based on test results, is often even more helpful. There is, however, no substitute for an extended period of going steady, followed by an engagement of at least six months, to test compatibility of personality types in real-life situations. In the early days of going steady, couples are on their good behavior. It is only after long acquaintance that the mask is laid aside and the real self begins to show. When this stage is reached, the serious couple will know if they antagonize or complement each other. The adjustment that results will be symptomatic of future marriage relationships.

BACKGROUND FACTORS

The approach to wise mate choice by studying specific personality traits has not been particularly rewarding. Various personality and temperament traits considered in constellation, as is done with tests in premarital counseling services, can be very indicative of one person's marriageability and the likelihood of a pair's success in marriage. But they take careful administration by experts and even more careful interpretation.

Students of marriage have found that the most critical sociological factors in determining success are what may be called general cultural background factors. Marriage requires the blending of two ways of life, as represented by two families, into a common way of life. A marriage is, in a very real sense, a continuation of family patterns already existent in the personalities of the couple themselves. Sandra Hochman (1968) commented, "When people in love swap childhoods, they will either get married or never see each other again."

Chapters 12 and 13 focus attention on broad sociocultural factors as they affect marriage.

PROBLEMS

1   Recently the Master of Ceremonies of a radio quiz show asked a female participant how she met her husband. She answered, "I was brought up very strictly and although I dated a number of young men, none of them ever lived up to my high standards. I was 32 and on vacation in New York when I finally met the right one. It was just as I knew it would be. A friend introduced me to this fellow and after one date we were sure that we were meant for each other. We got married immediately and we haven't been unhappy for a moment since then." "How long ago was that?" the Master of Ceremonies asked in amazement. "Last month," the woman replied. "We're on our honeymoon."

In your opinion is this woman one of the rare few to find her ideal mate? Was there anything in her statement to suggest that the future may be less rosy?

2   In the light of evidence in this chapter, would you say similarity of background is generally more significant in marriage success than similarity of temperament? Discuss.

3   Try to type men and women whom you feel should never get married.

4   After hearing the statement below from a young bride-to-be, a marriage counselor urged the young couple either to postpone their marriage for a while or else to consider continued counseling after the marriage should take place. Read the statement and decide whether or not the counselor's requests seem justified. What do you think were his reasons for urging a delay?

"I think I'll make Ted a pretty good wife because I'm not sloppy and unstrung like so many girls I know. I like to get up at exactly 6:45. In fact, I always get up then. It upsets me until I'm almost ill if I have to stay in bed later for some reason.

"The first thing I do is make my bed. That takes about 12 minutes, because I like it perfect. If I see a wrinkle or a crooked sheet it bothers me all morning. Then I wash my hands and face and scrub my fingernails with a disinfectant soap.

"There won't be any germs in our house! I rinse the plates and cups off too and I rub each spoon and fork with a clean napkin. I'm just that way with everything. It takes all my time but it pays off. I'm healthy and strong and I'm determined to keep my Ted healthy too."

5   Do you think most young couples fear what a premarital counseling session in a marriage clinic would reveal about themselves? Should they?

RELIGION IN
MATE CHOICE

12 Bride, groom, father, son, brother, sister, mother, and child are central symbols of the great religions of the western world. The values and goals for human attainment are quite the same for both the family and the religious body. The fellowship in both is described in similar terms. In fact, each of the three major faiths is comprehensible in terms of family interrelationships.

There is every reason to expect, therefore, that those who are trained in the values supported by religion would succeed in marriage, that religious people would have the values, beliefs, and expectations internalized as guidelines for themselves that would help make marriage and family a success. There is the added fact that the religious body gives support to morality, stability, kindness, self-sacrifice, cooperation, goodness, in all aspects of human behavior. Church leadership is often able to provide wise counsel from the pulpit or in private, lending further social support in the direction of success in marriage and family life.

Religious bodies, stripped down to their bare ideal for humanity are quite alike. Unfortunately, elaborate creeds are built up, and systems of taboos and procedural routines often become the main concern of the conscientious adherents.

THE SOCIOLOGICAL PROBLEM

As practiced, religion has become one of the great cultural barriers in the western world, and the sabbath, the holy day of "segregation," with each major religious group going its separate way. This separate procession leads all the way to the cemetery. Among the dominant Protestant group, there are over 200 denominations and sects, each with slightly different creed, many of them claiming to be the "only way." A framework of ritual, taboos, and beliefs, by which to justify their separateness, is maintained.

Each Protestant denomination has erected its own barriers by which it resists unity with the whole Christian body. Comparatively few of these barriers are ever torn down to allow merging to take place. Each perpetuates its teaching, bringing up a child in "the way he should go." Each depends largely upon the success of the upbringing of children in the faith for its growth and even its survival. Each strives to see that young people choose mates from the "in-group," if not the exact denomination, then one with similar tenets and sociomoral systems.

All church bodies are concerned with the mate choice of members and even more so with the way children of their members are trained in religion. The Jew and Catholic tend to require religious training. The Protestant groups are more permissive, even if no less concerned. They are more likely to depend on persuasion than on oaths or commandments, or canonical pronouncements, but the goals are the same—to retain a body of believers through the generations.

Part of the reason for Protestant leniency is the more democratic approach to all matters of personal choice, the very essence of Protestantism itself. But Protestant bodies have less to fear, being the dominant group, proportionately few marry outside their faith. They are less exposed to membership loss than either Jew or Catholic.

The sociologist's perspective considers the effect of religion on marriage and family outcome. The church is concerned for the survival of the religious institution as well. The sociological problem is the impact of religion on the total complex of family relationships; the church, life itself, and human destiny.

Although the religious and sociological perspectives are different, they overlap. The very concern of church bodies about marriage, family life, and child training often interferes with the marriage relationship itself, particularly where there is a conflict of loyalties, as in the interfaith marriage. No matter how critical one may be about any given religious body's aggressiveness or arbitrariness about increasing the flock, many church leaders, perhaps most of them, have a deep human concern about the success of marriage and parenthood of their adherents. In their practical way, they are students of the marriage relationship and are more closely involved than sociologists possibly could be in marriage and family interactions and the problems involved in interfaith marriages.

THE ECUMENICAL TREND

This decade has brought a strong ecumenical trend. The Catholic Church has accepted the reformation, not for itself, but for Protestants. Protestantism is becoming more merger-minded. The doctrine of segregation has been attacked in all fields of human relationships. Strong secular influences in American life have created a skepticism of church taboos and even ancient teachings, where these do not seem to tally with sociological knowledge and current concepts of human welfare. It has become much easier for young people, particularly young college people, to choose the rational at the cost of the traditional.

In this kind of world the question may well be raised as to whether religion is any longer a factor of concern to the student of marriage and family. Certainly most of the research in the field is outdated in the rapidly changing social climate of today. Even if it were fully current, it might well have less applicability to tomorrow than yesterday. However not all past research is invalid as a guide for the future.

Similar problems exist which have not been eliminated by changes in institutions or personal value systems. Marriages which cross barriers of faith still have certain unique problems to overcome that are not present in a marriage between persons of similar religious beliefs. Marriages between believers and nonbelievers have even more. Marriages of two people with no religious background will have greater difficulty still, as in the past. Sociological measures of degree of difficulty are faulty, but they point clearly toward special marriage problems in the interfaith marriage and those without a church tie.

MEASURABLE INDICES

There are various measurable indices of church–religious influence. Sociological studies have used them all in assessing the relationships between religion and success or failure of marriage. The assumption is that a positive relationship exists between church ties and marriage success.

Critical analysis may well challenge the casual relationship, thus robbing religion of its claim to making better people. Certainly the church either draws better people, or helps make them. Every church–religious index is associated with marriage success. The success index is not 100 percent, by any means, but it is higher for those with religious connections than those without. Here are the usual indices used: frequency of church attendance, marriage by religious ceremony, Sunday-school attendance, being devout, being a member of a religious body.

Even interfaith marriages are favorable compared to marriages of persons outside all faiths. The evidence will be surveyed in due course.

THE INTERFAITH MARRIAGE

Interfaith marriages are likely to increase very rapidly in our nation of mixed religious backgrounds, growing religious tolerance, increasing secular orientation, and the bringing together of more young people in large groups in school and college where the issue of religious differences is minimal. The church academy and church college were once most effective in seeing that young people married in the faith, even in the particular denomination. They no longer handle much of the total youth population; the school atmosphere is generally secular, and campus life is not much given to religious exercise. Even the sorority and fraternity houses are more tolerant and less exclusive in membership. Sororities have been the upper-class mother's greatest assurance of her daughter marrying into the "right" race, religion, and social class. It is true to a much lesser degree now.

While all of this means that the religious issue has become less significant in marriage, more people will be involved, even if their experience may be less serious than would have been true historically.

The Statistical Picture

In 1958 the Census Bureau published, for the first time, a nationwide picture of the extent of mixed marriages involving the three major religious groups in America—Protestant, Roman Catholic, and Jewish. Data are for all persons 14 years old and over, and cover 36,576,000 couples. Here is the situation as reported:

LIKE RELIGION		MIXED RELIGION	
Both Roman Catholic	8,361,000	Protestant–Roman Catholic	2,255,000
Both Protestant	24,604,000	Protestant–Jewish	57,000
Both Jewish	1,258,000	Roman Catholic–Jewish	41,000
	34,223,000		2,353,000

Proportionately, Catholics suffer most from interreligious marriages, over a fifth (21.2 percent) marry Protestants, and a few (0.4 percent) marry Jews. Of all marriages in the three major religious bodies, 6.4 percent were interfaith.

While these data suggest that the intermarriage problem is of significant dimensions, sample studies indicate that the actual number of persons crossing the major interfaith barriers in marriage is about twice as high as shown by the census data. Many abandon their church before or after the ceremony. Although they are of different faiths in background, the difference has vanished as a statistical fact. The authorities of the U.S. Census Bureau have expressed the view that census enumerators may have in some cases overlooked the fact that the husband and wife might be of different religions. Convincing studies have shown that the Jewish–Gentile marriages in the nation constitute about 13 percent of all marriages involving Jews (Rosenthal 1963). Sample studies suggest that those of Catholic background cross the line in 35–50 percent of marriages involving Catholics. Jesuit sociologist John L. Thomas (1956) of St. Louis University places the figures at almost half of all marriages, if the invalid (those not sanctioned by the church) are added to the valid interfaith Catholic marriages.

These data may accurately represent the approximate ratio of out-group marriages among the different major faiths, but in all cases, the number of these is approximately twice as high as shown. Babchuk and colleagues found that when couples change affiliations, they change to that of the mate with most education. Where the pair are equal in education, the shift is as likely to be toward the wife's as toward the husband's faith. Crockett, Babchuk, and

Ballweg (1969) find that religious homogeneity promotes family stability even when the homogeneity is achieved by one member changing faith after marriage.

Locke (1957) and his colleagues have proposed the thesis that, other things being equal, interfaith marriages will increase as the minority group decreases in ratio to the total population. But in this area other things are never equal. The Jewish group is the smaller ratio group but maintains an in-group loyalty unmatched by the Catholic group.

The smaller the minority group, the greater its exposure to the out-groups is likely to be, but the factor of more importance than this is the strength of the religious tradition. Another important variable, too, is the degree of difference in the religious faiths pairs have to bridge.

Weakening of the Religious Barrier

There are no legal barriers to marriage across religious lines, yet most church groups advise against it. Still, studies show that approximately half of college students would cross these major religious barriers in marriage if other aspects of the relationship were satisfactory. Gordon (1964) studied attitudes of 5407 college students in some 40 colleges and universities of the nation. He found 37 percent of non-Jews would marry Jews; 56 percent of non-Catholics would marry Catholics. In the total sample, half did not favor marriage to a person of another religion.

Almost half of the husbands in interfaith marriages studied by Prince (1962) would be willing for their children to enter such a marriage, and well over a third of the wives would be willing. Less than a fourth of the husbands and wives were negative on this subject. This would indicate that the effect of interfaith marriage is cumulative through the generations that do intermarry.

RELIGION AND MARRIAGE ADJUSTMENT

Judson T. Landis (1960b) found a very positive association between religiousness and success of marriage. Those reporting no faith showed a high rate of marriage failure. These findings are consistent with findings of sociologists over a period of some 30 years.

Rockwell Smith (1954), an astute churchman, has observed that religion is a very great socializing factor. During the dating period, young people are so completely wrapped up in each other and so completely satisfied emotionally that they tend to overlook the place of religion and church activities in their lives. However, when they settle down to the adjustments of marriage and community life, they wish to revive ties which have been most meaningful to them. Each then naturally turns to his own church and the church group he has found congenial.

If the couple are of the same religious faith, this building of the marriage into the larger fellowship of the church group is made easy and natural. If, however, they have different religious backgrounds, a great handicap faces

them as they try to build church relationships. Instead of being able to participate naturally in the same kind of religious exercise in the community, there is
a tendency to compete for church loyalty. The couple constantly finds a block
in the way of their joint participation in any kind of religious activity.

It is often only after marriage that the couple begins to realize, too, how
deeply embedded are the philosophies of life and standards of behavior that
form a part of any religious faith. A person who has had his life and goals
oriented around the goals and aspirations that are the essence of his faith finds
religion more significant in his life than he has realized. Often the person who
has been quite casual in his religious attitudes has more deep-seated religious
values than he is aware of until these values come into direct opposition to the
values of a person whose core of religious philosophy is quite different.

These facts are probably the basis of the findings of sociological research
which indicate that, where couples are not matched in religious background,
their church participation usually decreases after the marriage. Many couples
probably find this the only way to peace. Even though it may not bring satisfaction, it may at least help to reduce tensions. For example, Zimmerman and
Cervantes (1960) found that about half the Catholic men they studied who
were involved in interfaith marriages abandoned their faith.

The issue comes to a head when children enter the family and the question
arises as to whether or not to train them religiously, and if so, in what religion.
It is then, most frequently, that the problem of religious differences becomes
something besides a theoretical question between two individuals. How a
child's faith will be directed and his life values established are certain to be of
deep concern to parents. With this background, let us consider the findings of
research.

Persons with and Without Religious Connections

It was indicated that religious persons show evidence of greater success in
marriage. There are various measures of church and religious affiliation as
they relate to marriage. In 1967, Judson T. Landis related marriage survival to
being married in church. This study of 581 couples married an average of seven
years showed that 84 percent had been married in a church. Of a control group
taking counseling because of marriage difficulties only 41 percent were married in a church, and of a divorced group also compared, only 55 percent had
been married in a church. Even interfaith marriages have a better record than
those between persons without religious affiliation.

Zimmerman and Cervantes (1960) report that in marriages where one has
religious affiliation and the other does not, the divorce, desertion, and delinquency rate of children are generally twice as high as in marriages in which
both are affiliated with a religious group. Where both of the pair are without
religion, the chances of divorce, desertion, and of child delinquency are four
times as high as where there is religious affiliation.

Other studies have indicated that religious training makes a significant
contribution to marriage success and happiness. Both men and women with
strict religious training have been found to have higher happiness scores in

marriage than those whose training was rated "considerable to none" (Terman 1938). Those with many years of Sunday-school training also have been found to make a better adjustment to marriage than those with little or no training (Burgess and Cottrell 1939).

Whether or not a couple remains actively associated with some church organization is also statistically important. Even as early as the engagement period, church attendance has been found to be a factor in the success or failure of the relationship. One study (Burgess and Wallin 1953) found that more than half of the engagements in which the girl attended church more regularly than the boy were finally broken. This was also true of engagements in which neither had religious affiliations. Fewer engagements were broken among couples who attended church once a month or more.

This association with a church, which contributes to success in engagement, is equally significant in marriage. Higher marital happiness scores were registered by couples who, after marriage, continued attending church regularly. It has been found, too, that striking differences in marriage adjustment are associated with the circumstances under which a couple marries. Those who were married in a church or parsonage generally enjoyed a more successful marriage than those who took their vows outside a church before a civil officer. This, of course, does not mean that the ceremony and the minister in themselves exert a lasting influence upon the fate of the marriage. It is, rather, further evidence that those with serious religious connections are more marriageable than others, since those who take their religion seriously more often choose to be married with religious sanction.

At least in some measure, religion meets its promise to make family life better. Carol L. Stone (1954) studied 3810 high school students and 1469 college students, comparing those active and inactive in church affairs. She found that (1) those active in church had a more harmonious home life, (2) the church group was more active in school social life, (3) the church group had a larger circle of friends, (4) the church group was more satisfied with and had few criticisms of their home community, (5) the church group was more optimistic and less worried in outlook, and (6) the church group was more service-motivated, more interested in helping others. It is clear that association with religious institutions produces a better functioning family.

Religions vary greatly, however, in their contribution to marital happiness. The degree of authoritarianism in religion seems to have some relationship. Chesser's (1957) study in Great Britain of over 6000 marriages indicates that the highest proportion of happy childhoods and happy parental marriages were found among the nonconformists, that is, the Protestants, rather than in the Church of England group. The lowest degree of happiness was among those with no religion; Jews were a close second in producing the lowest proportion of happy marriages. Roman Catholics had the highest proportion of unhappy marriages and unhappy childhoods, and the highest rate of premarital intercourse.

The high rate of unhappiness among English Catholics is, in part, a reflection of their lower-class status. As in the United States, they are generally in a lower socioeconomic group due to their relatively more recent migration from southern and eastern Europe. But the prohibition against divorce itself consigns many couples and their children to a lifelong struggle.

For the religion–no religion pair, attendance at church may be a major issue. The husband's work week is time-structured, often to the extent of commanding some of his leisure time. This and community activities may schedule most of his weekdays. Sunday is his free day, and he feels he should have a right to do as he pleases. He may even feel that the free use of this day for relaxation and esthetic enjoyment is the essence of religion itself. To the wife, on the other hand, the Sunday routine of Sunday school and church represents the one certain time in the week when she can dress up, have social contacts outside the home with the family as a unit, and can be seen in the company of her husband. She is likely to find the church service relaxing and stimulating entirely aside from the religious context, since it is a marked variation from her regular weekday routine, and a part of the religious training of the children.

The church today is more vital to women in another nonreligious sense. Much of the social activity of the church is in women's groups, as is much of its service-directed activity, both local and worldwide. The church offers women many leadership roles—for many housewives their only such opportunity. Participation in church-going may be essential to obtaining and retaining leadership roles in many of these less formal activities of the church, and to many wives this is of great importance. They could go to church alone, but their position is strengthened if their husbands are beside them.

PROTESTANT–CATHOLIC MARRIAGES

Protestant and Catholic make up most of the interfaith marriage combinations, as shown by the census data. Many develop out of dating which was never meant to get serious. The couple becomes attached to each other before the religious issue takes on significance.

The Catholic group, in most communities, is in the minority and consequently under some pressure to cross religious lines in order to find suitable mates. In fact, more than a fourth of all Catholic youths in the United States have ecclesiastical marriages to non-Catholics (Thomas 1951). This takes no account of Catholics who forsake the church in marriage outside their religion. The highest rate of interfaith marriages is among those with higher education and with high socioeconomic status.

The Marriage Rite

Although all states require a license to wed, and most recognize the civil ceremony as being adequate, religious bodies require a religious ceremony. With Protestant denominations it is a ceremony with the benediction of the church. In the Catholic church, the wedding is a sacrament.

To have a sacramentally valid marriage, the non-Catholic must participate in this rite and be married by a priest. He must make vows regarding noninterference with the faith of the spouse and rearing of children. Most likely the couple has already agreed on their own solution to the birth control question, and one or both may have doubts about having children "baptized and educated solely in the Catholic religion."

Although the marriage must be Catholic to be valid, the Protestant member now has the right of repeating the ceremony in his own church, a right formerly denied.

The Indissolubility of Marriage   Since marriage in the Catholic Church is a holy sacrament, it may not be terminated except by death. While non-Catholics are undoubtedly very serious about the desire to make the union permanent, it is doubtful that many look upon it as indissoluble.

Margaret Mead (1968a) has suggested that an increasing number of Catholic mothers are advising their daughters not to marry in the church so they can get a divorce if they need one. For Catholics who do marry outside, this issue is resolved before marriage. For the faithful, it is a lifelong bond. Of course, if a mother does give a daughter such advice, it may well help ease the daughter's conscience in case she must leave the church for divorce.

It may well be that vows, seriously taken, help people tolerate marriage adjustments that would otherwise be very difficult. Yet marriage is such an intimate relationship, it is doubtful that vows as such smooth the way.

Birth Control   The birth control issue has been of serious consequence in Catholic and interfaith marriages. Practice ignores teaching with increasing frequency, and there are many dissenting voices among the church leaders and laity. In fact, no single issue has so much challenged the authority of the Pope in recent times.

The following is the July 29, 1968 statement of George N. Lindsay, Chairman of Planned Parenthood–World Population, in response to the pronouncement of Pope Paul VI about birth control:

> Pope Paul's pronouncement of birth control today marks a tragic turn in the history of the Catholic Church, and surely will be greeted with sorrow throughout the world. It is almost beyond belief that a man of Pope Paul's sensitivity, who has walked through the streets of Bombay and seen how over-population reduces human beings to misery and despair, can now feel compelled to limit the application of family planning. It must have been with great anguish that the Pope reached the decisions embodied in his statement, since he must know full well the burdens thus placed on Catholic families and on the world.
>
> His pronouncement may prove to be almost as futile as it is tragic for his Church. The number of Catholics who do indeed practice family planning, using effective medical methods, has steadily grown in recent years. The definitive Westoff–Ryder Study showed that in 1965, more than three-fourths of American Catholic wives practiced birth control, and more than two-thirds of these used forms of contraception other than the Church-approved rhythm.
>
> Surveys also show that most U.S. Catholics believe that birth control

A large committee of Catholic scientists and church leaders was appointed by the Pope to study the situation and make recommendations. They suggested that the rules be changed, but the recommendation was not followed. Yet there is increased violation of the rule. The National Fertility Study of 1970 showed that 70 percent of Catholic women were using birth control means not sanctioned by the church. This, of course, does not tell the whole story. How many do so only after having more children than they wanted, or could reasonably support? How many only after the mother's health or life were threatened, or after the marriage goes awry because of the overwhelming burden of too many children to care for? Should the Church ever change its position on birth control, a source of potential conflict, health risk, economic hardship, and sexual stress would be removed. Unwanted children have been one of the serious burdens of the Catholic marriage, whether intra- or interfaith.

Official discouragement of interfaith marriages has been described as a "battle for babies," since recruitment of members is largely through births of children to members. Vincent (1963) raised the question of whether a church would really be concerned with interfaith marriages if it could be proved that they added members to that particular religious body. He has not answered the question, but it has been answered by sample studies. Any particular church does lose members by interfaith marriages. Evidence is cited below.

There is a certain cynicism in these comments which may be unjustified. Most religious leaders are very humane persons. They have wide experience with the most vital aspects of interpersonal relationships. Even priests, handicapped as they are by living outside wedlock and in a cloistered masculine world, hear the intimate confessions of members and know the anguish of people in trouble. Most church leaders may object to interfaith marriages quite as much, if not more, because of the troubles people experience in them as from the business angle of adding members.

There is little question that the child-training issue is a major concern of the interfaith marriage. Baber (1937) was the first to point out that conflicts in Protestant–Catholic marriages centered around religious training of the child. He found that conflicts over the religious issue were about as numerous among couples who were both rather indifferent in religion as among the devout.

Since the training of the children is the greatest troublemaker in the cross-religion marriage, the Landis' (1973) research tried to find a statistical answer to child training and related questions by following out-group marriages into the second generation. It was found that among 4000 parents of the young college people studied, over a third of one religion or the other had forsaken their faith to follow the faith of the other spouse. This change of faith usually took place before marriage, although in some cases it came later. Among those who did not change their faith, it was found that half of the children had been reared in the Protestant faith, 45 percent in the Catholic faith, and 5 percent in no faith at all. Obviously the pledge taken by all Catholics to raise their children in the faith is not easily followed. Thomas

(1956) reports a loss to the Catholic group of 40 percent. The Church seems justified in being wary of the cross-religion marriage.

Landis showed further that in these homes young people are subjected to various religious training programs. In more than a third of the cases, the mother took all the responsibility. In most of the other cases, the child was exposed to both faiths, sometimes by one parent, sometimes by both. In a few cases, he actually was taken to both churches in turn. These college students, looking at the mixed marriages of their parents, were inclined to feel that in general it had been a serious handicap in their home lives.

Prince (1962), studying a small sample, found that the tendency was for the couple to raise the child in the faith of the mother. This tendency was much more pronounced when both husband and wife were from minority religious groups. Nationwide data for the Jewish group suggest that Judaism is losing about 70 percent of the children born to the mixed-faith couple. They may not be reared in the Protestant or the Catholic faith in many of these cases, but they are not reared in the Jewish faith (Rosenthal 1963).

Zimmerman and Cervantes (1960) indicate that in 9000 mixed marriages they studied, six out of ten children in the Catholic–Protestant mixed marriage end up rejecting all religion.

There are also scattered data which suggest that the birth rate of the mixed marriage may tend to run lower than that in the marriage of like faith. This seems particularly true in the case of the Jew. Whether it is the mixed marriage that is responsible or whether both the mixed marriage and the low birth rate are indicative of emancipation from tradition might well be asked.

A study by Christensen and Barber (1967) based on Indiana data found that interfaith marriages were of more secular pairs and that the pair tended to be older than average at the time of marriage. These factors would tend toward a lower birth rate.

It is apparent from widely scattered studies that the strong marriage pledge regarding rearing children in the Catholic faith is about as likely to be broken as kept. Pledges do not govern marriage behavior automatically. The amount of conflict that enters into violating the pledge is not known. It is likely that in many instances failure to keep it has involved stress between the couple themselves, with grandparents, in-laws, and perhaps church leaders.

JEWISH–GENTILE MARRIAGES

Berman (1968), discussing Jews and intermarriage, has concluded that the intermarriage difficulties are not so much those of religion as one of "feeling and family." There is great family loyalty among the Jews. The living generations are concerned about the marriage and the perpetuation of cultural traditions. The Jewish family carries over elements of the extended family, to which the gentile newcomer is a threat.

In recent years, great alarm has been expressed in the Jewish community, over the possibility of their disappearance as a people in the United States (Morgan 1964). Jews have a low birth rate, but the principal basis of the concern is intermarriage and the loss to the Jewish faith of children born to the mixed marriages. The loss has been placed at 70 percent. The Jews place a premium on learning, and since greater tolerance pervades the college campus, there is free mingling in dating regardless of religious heritage.

The religious issue is the preeminent one in the above consideration, but the sociological one is important because of the likelihood of clash of values, rituals, and conceptions of life.

An early study showed that comparatively few young people of Jewish origin dated outside their religious group—slightly more than a fourth of Jewish male and only 15 percent of Jewish female college students at the University of Minnesota. Jewish–Gentile marriages are not as frequent as Catholic–Protestant ones. This results in part from religious observances, but it probably also reflects an attitude of anti-Semitism, which in most communities is a live prejudice (Kirkpatrick & Caplow 1945).

About 13 percent of Jewish marriages are interfaith. Studies of Jewish–Gentile intermarriage show that in most cases the marriage is between a Jewish man and a Gentile woman; comparatively few are between Jewish women and Gentile men. When such marriages do take place, they are between reformed or liberal Jews. Orthodox Judaism does not permit Jewish–Gentile marriages except in cases where the Gentile has been converted to the Jewish religion. The more liberal and reformed Jewish group, which is now in the majority in the United States, has no absolute prohibition against intermarriage, but does discourage it. There is a very close family supervision of the dating of Jewish young people, particularly of the Jewish girl. Any dating between Jews and Gentiles is frowned upon by the Jewish community.

The real difficulty with the Jewish–Gentile marriage of the religiously emancipated Jew is that more differences than those of religion are involved. Judaism is a culture in and of itself, as is Christianity; it is not merely a religion. The Jewish world is a world of customs dating back through the centuries. Jews differ from Christians in observing a different day of rest, different religious holidays, different foods, and in numerous other ways. Not many young people reared in the Jewish culture can entirely forsake it, and few Gentiles reared outside this world can completely accept it.

One of the major handicaps in the Jewish–Gentile marriage has been that in approximately half the cases, one or the other or both families reject the new son or daughter. A second handicap is the prejudice against Jews exhibited in many circles. The Gentile in this marriage must face anti-Semitic prejudice against himself and his children.

It is often easy, when young people live far away from their own relatives, to forget how important religious differences can be when one joins two family lines in marriage. In these days of urban dating it is easy to forget that one marries, not only a person, but also a family. The Jewish family is a very closely knit group, and even though the Jewish young person may emancipate himself from his religion, he rarely emancipates himself completely from his family and its influences.

RISKS IN INTERFAITH MARRIAGE

Sociologists may have exaggerated the divorce problem of the interfaith marriage. Yet studies over a period of years do consistently show higher divorce

TABLE 12-1   Divorce Rates by Religion of Mates

MARRIAGE COMBINATION	STUDY I BELL (1938), MARYLAND 13,528 COUPLES	STUDY II WEEKS (1943), WASHINGTON 6548 COUPLES	STUDY III LANDIS (1949), MICHIGAN 4108 COUPLES
Both Catholic	6.4	3.8	4.4
Both Protestant	6.8	10.0	6.0
Mixed, Protestant–Catholic	15.2	17.4	14.1
Catholic husband–Protestant wife	—	—	20.6

rates than those of like faith, even engagements of those of different faiths are more fragile than those of like faith, according to studies of Burgess and Wallin (1953).

A report issued by the Department of Public Health in California, dealing with couples who had divorced or separated, shows that the break had come for interfaith pairs after a median duration of three to four years for the various religious combinations and after a median of six to eight years for those of like faith. Apparently, serious trouble develops more quickly between the mixed-faith pairs or they act more quickly in seeking separation as a solution to serious difficulties.

Divorce rates by religious affiliation of the married pair are shown in Table 12-1. Data are for different times and different locations. In interpreting his data on the Catholic husband–Protestant wife, Judson T. Landis suggests that the higher divorce rate of the Catholic husband–Protestant wife combination may be due to the initiative that Protestant wives generally take in the matter of divorce, an initiative which the Catholic wife cannot exercise in the other combination. It may, however, be more than a technical issue. There is reason to believe that such a combination could lead to a maximum number of marital problems. Child training, for example, is generally a wife's function, but when the father is the devout Catholic in a mixed marriage, the job of religious training falls largely upon his shoulders. When, as must often be the case, he has neither the time nor the ability to assume this function, serious family problems seem likely to result, particularly if he blames the wife for her failure to qualify as his substitute.

Zimmerman and Cervantes (1960), studying 40,000 urban families with children, found divorce rates three times as high in mixed Protestant–Catholic marriages as in those of like faith. They found the failure rate of the Jew–Gentile marriage highest of all interfaith combinations.

Vernon (1964) has rightly criticized such comparisons in tending to exaggerate failure. Because numbers are small, percentage differences are large. The same percentages applied to successes would be smaller. For example, if the divorce rate in intrafaith marriages were 5 percent and in interfaith marriages 10 percent, the rate would be double. Yet the success rate is 90 compared to 95 percent, a very small percentage difference.

SPOUSAL RELIGIOUS AFFILIATION TYPE	MARITAL SURVIVAL RATE
Homogamous Catholic	96.2
Presbyterian–non-Catholic	94.6
Homogamous Lutheran	94.1
Lutheran–non-Catholic	93.0
Methodist–non-Catholic	92.9
Homogamous Methodist	91.4
Homogamous Presbyterian	91.0
Catholic–Lutheran	90.5
Baptist–non-Catholic	90.0
Catholic–Presbyterian	89.8
Homogamous Baptist	89.8
Catholic–Methodist	83.8
Catholic–Baptist	81.6
Homogamous–unaffiliated Protestant	35.0
Catholic–unaffiliated Protestant	28.7

Source: Adapted from Burchinal and Chancellor (1962, Table 5, p. 758).

This kind of argument, however, does have a point. By this device sociologists may have overstressed negative aspects of the interfaith marriage. They may not have in terms of hidden meaning. Those close to it—counselors, ministers, parents, couples themselves—may well feel that divorce statistics do not begin to touch the problem.

The State of Iowa collects data on religious affiliation of marrying couples. These data, analyzed entensively by Burchinal and Chancellor (1962), are presented by survival rates rather than divorce rates. The studies show clearly that the mixed marriage has a shorter duration and also that the marriages of unaffiliated persons are much shorter in duration than those with church connections (see Table 12-2). Duration of marriages, they found, is also related to age and to social status; older age and higher social status lead to longer duration rates.

This study shows that the survival rates of certain interdenominational marriages are high, about as high as intradenominational marriages. Catholic–Protestant marriages show a high survival rate where marriage is with the more formal, liturgical denominations (Lutherans and Presbyterians). With the less formal, more evangelical denominations (Baptists and Methodists) survival rates drop to about 80 percent.

Numerically, Baptists and Methodists make up more than half of the Protestant population of the nation, with a combined membership of over 40 million. This being so, one would expect that most interfaith marriages of Catholics would be with Baptists and Methodists, where greater social contact exists. Regional distribution, however, is a factor. The Baptists are concentrated in the southern region of the nation where there are few Catholics. It is likely, too, that the evangelical denominations may less often cross the religious line than the more formal church adherents because a wider gulf of religious tradition is to be bridged.

For Catholics, divorce statistics are more significant than numbers would indicate. If one considers the stand of the Catholic Church against divorce, he can appreciate the greater inner turmoil and marital conflict to which any divorce testifies. A Catholic cannot get a divorce and remain Catholic. For every Catholic who resorts to divorce there are no doubt many more who will bear great difficulty rather than take the forbidden step.

Whether he suffers more in interfaith marriages than in Catholic marriages, where the rule of indissolubility is doubly binding is unknown. But the fact that more interfaith marriages terminate in divorce may mean that they do face greater religious problems. Most church leaders assume that they do, and consistently warn against such marriages. It is likely that the church's concern is in part an outgrowth of unfavorable experience with marriages of this type and not solely a concern for future church membership.

It is among the nominal (unaffiliated) Protestants that the survival rate of marriage is very low (Table 12–2). The rate of survival is lower in Catholic–Protestant unions where the Catholic member is the husband, as seen in the Landis study.

Burchinal and Chancellor (1962) have shown that the religious factor is less likely to terminate a marriage where husband and wife are older than average. High social class, too, lends to greater stability of the mixed marriage.

Christensen and Barber (1967) in their study of Indiana data, report that couples in interfaith marriages have certain characteristics that tend to differentiate them from like-faith marriages: older at the time of marriage, more of them are entering a second or subsequent marriage, more are pregnant at time of marriage, more are from high-status occupations, more have a civil ceremony, more live in urban centers.

The cross-faith group seems to be, as one might expect, a more secularized, liberated group. This in itself would help explain the higher divorce rate, although age and high social status should offset this factor. There is also a suggestion that there was a falling away from their religious affiliation prior to the marriage.

WEIGHING THE RELIGIOUS ISSUE IN ADVANCE

James R. Hine has published a unique device for helping young people face religious differences before marriage. Sixty-five pairs of cards list items of religious belief. Each looks at his set and sorts the cards into "agree" and "disagree" piles. When all cards have been sorted, they compare cards and discuss each statement representing a difference in agreement. The discussion of these beliefs makes them keenly aware of differences in fundamental attitudes in areas such as nature of God, creed, prayer, the Trinity, man's purpose in life, salvation, the Bible, eternal life, miracles, sacraments, giving, missions, religious rites in the family, and so on.

Here are some of the questions that are pertinent to a couple's future plans:

1　Can one of us adopt the other's church?
2　If not, can we be happy going to one church or the other, or will we each go alone to our own church?
3　Will one or both of us break with the church altogether?
4　If we agree to keep our church attachments, what will we do about birth control, observance of special religious days, or eating customs?
5　What about benevolences?
6　How will our parents and friends accept the match?
7　How will our children be reared? In which faith, or in no faith at all?
8　If in the Catholic faith, can the Protestant member fully accept church supervision of the training of his child?
9　Can we stand the pressure of devout parents or grandparents, or representatives of our churches, who will bring pressure to have the children reared in their own faith?
10　In case of emancipation from religious connections, are we strong enough to stand alone when the crises of life overtake us in marriage, or will we, as so many do, revert to the security, certainty, and faith of our childhood religion? This question is particularly pertinent for the Catholic-reared member.
11　If it is a Catholic–Protestant marriage, the Protestant member should ask, Can I tolerate Catholic direction of my marriage and Catholic religious training of my children?

INTERDENOMINATIONAL MARRIAGES

In our nation of such great complexity and of so many different sects and denominations, there is a wide range of devoutness and worldliness, entirely aside from increasing numbers who are totally against religion, promote atheism, or practice the arts of black magic and Devil worship. Sociologists have not measured adequately the significance to marriage of various extremes of worldliness and devoutness of the married pair. It may be quite difficult to do so except at extremes of the continuum. It is likely that the extremes seldom marry each other, but when they do it could be more significant to the marriage outcome than the marriage of, say, Protestant and Catholic.

Prince (1962), in his study of cross-religion marriages, included 52 marriages between different Protestant denominations. Although the sample is too small to justify wide generalization, two findings are strongly suggestive of outcome: (1) A very high percentage classed their marriage in the "entirely satisfied" or "very much satisfied" group compared to the interfaith marriages. (2) Only 19 percent retained their own separate denomination, compared to 55 percent of the interfaith group who retained their separate faith. In two-thirds of the cases the husband or wife adopted the other's faith. In 11.5 percent of the cases the couple adopted another denomination differing from the former loyalties of either.

If this research should receive further confirmation, one would be justified in the conclusion that interdenominational marriages usually do not terminate the couple's adherence to some Protestant body, and generally the religious difference is not a major barrier to the marriage.

Burchinal and Chancellor (1962) calculated survival rates of interdenominational marriages and found them generally quite high (refer again to Table 12–2). They were, however, dealing with the more standard denominations, rather than fringe revivalistic groups. It is probable that these groups do not too often marry into the more conservative denominations with large memberships. The highest rate of failure was among the nominal (unaffiliated) Protestants.

Such marriages may be very hard on church membership in particular denominations. Bossard and Letts (1956) have studied the problem of intermarriage by Lutherans, a rather conservative liturgically oriented group, through contacts with pastors. It was found that twice as many Lutheran women as men married outside their church. Although Lutherans are generally very loyal to their church, where they entered mixed marriages there was a loss of somewhere between 17 and 25 percent to the group.

One suspects that young people who are loyal to very orthodox or revivalistic religious groups would find themselves quite out of harmony with those who are members of the more formal or ritualistic churches. The formal and ritualistic group, too, is far different from the extremely modern fringe. Between such denominations, there is a vast difference in the level of religious appeal, esthetic appreciation, and emotional outlet.

While such differences may not be as great as Protestant–Catholic differences, for example, they are great enough to be grounds for caution. The dating period should be made to bring the couple, deliberately, into close relationships with the religious philosophy, the church, and the family of both young people. The liberal-minded person can generally feel little tolerance for the person who is extremely dogmatic or narrow in religious philosophy; it is often equally difficult for the one reared in a strict religious environment to liberalize his religion.

The sum of evidence to date would seem to be that interdenominational marriage probably leads to a considerable shifting of denominational allegiance, but does not seem to be a major handicap to marriage success or survival. Certainly the evidence is strong that church membership in and of itself is important to marriage success; that merely claiming to be Protestant or Catholic without practicing the faith is related to a high degree of marriage failure.

It is important that a young person who is a loyal member of a church think twice before marrying someone who has no interest in church and church affairs. The person with religious attitudes and church loyalties has had this slant toward life built into his or her personality for some 20 years before marriage. His particular values, attitudes, and aspirations are too deeply ingrained to be easily discarded or ignored. The Landis study (1949) previously cited makes it clear that marriages between those who are loyal to a religious system and those who are not, are relatively hazardous from the standpoint of success and permanence.

PROBLEMS

1   *Sociodrama:* A young man, religiously indifferent rather than agnostic or atheistic, has just proposed to a girl of serious religious faith. She refuses his

proposal. The play begins with her refusal. Bring out her explanations, present his arguments, and include in the play their final decision.

2 Name several attitudes characteristic of a religious person which would be assets to him in marriage adjustment.

3 Would you say that a Protestant minister who advises young people against marrying either Catholics or Jews is probably prejudiced and intolerant?

4 Think of the ways in which children born to a marriage magnify the problems of an interfaith marriage. How would you handle the religious training of a child of an interfaith marriage?

   a Let the father decide.

   b Let the mother decide.

   c Have some respected outsider decide.

   d Try to combine the dogma of both faiths.

   e Expose the child to both faiths and let him decide for himself when he is old enough.

   f Expose the child to neither faith and let him decide in later years.

   g Choose some other alternative.

5 In your opinion, what accounts for the greater degree of marriage failure among people without religious affiliation?

6 Catholic, Jewish, and Protestant faiths all share the same fundamental ethical codes. What, then, accounts for the many problems that confront marriages of mixed religion?

7 In most American homes is it the husband or the wife who assumes the religious leadership of the family? How would you explain this fact?

8 When individuals of different religious faiths decide to marry but maintain their separate beliefs, is there any justification for an intensive study by each of the faith of the other?

9 It has been said that the problems that arise out of interdenominational marriages often reflect differences in socioeconomic background rather than in religious belief. Does this statement make sense?

10 Is there anything that the churches could do to help make interfaith and interdenominational marriages more common and more successful? Do you believe that the churches should or should not make such an attempt? Why or why not?

11 Ask a marriage counselor, family relations counselor, minister, priest, or rabbi to describe one or more actual instances of interfaith or interdenominational marriages. Ask the speaker to note specifically the kinds of problems reported by the couple or couples, the solutions sought, and whether or not their problems were solved.

RACIAL AND
CULTURAL
DIFFERENCES

13

We are living in one of the most dynamic periods in history as measured by the breakdown of racial, ethnic, social status, and cultural barriers. Groups that once lived in a climate of social distance have become close associates. Vertical mobility has been rapid, and sympathy for the underdog has been expansive. No doubt this new climate has affected not only the marriage rate but also marriage outcome. In protest groups, youth quickly become closely associated with all those in the movement. Friendships ripen quickly and marriage may take place between those who lack a similar childhood and comparable body of tradition. Such pairs may find building a life together difficult or impossible. Some youth have, no doubt, unconsciously used an interracial marriage as their contribution to the solution of the race problem. It may improve the social image, but may not give them the kind of marriage that can endure.

Religion is a cultural barrier. Race is physical, but with significant cultural meaning. Religion is invisible. Couples may be mutually attracted and begin dating without knowledge of each others' religious inclinations and affiliations. Racial traits are always present. One usually does not become involved blindly. The exception is those blacks, who because they are dominantly white in genetic characteristics, have crossed the color line and "passed" as white. Studies of "passing" previous to the Civil Rights Act indicate that 10,000–15,000 blacks crossed the color line and became white each year. The rate may be much less since the emergence of racial pride among blacks.

THE RELATIVE WEIGHT OF RACIAL AND CULTURAL DIFFERENCES

Social distance is a psychological manifestation of the social structure. What society has established as social barriers become internalized in the individual during his socialization. He reacts accordingly, in expressing social distance. Bogardus (1968) early studies showed that the racial barrier is the most imposing one, that intermarriage is the social bond least acceptable to the white, and that distance is greatest in this area where the white marries a black. Gordon (1964) in his study of student attitudes in 40 colleges and universities, obtained the reaction of 5407 students to the question of intercultural and interracial marriage for themselves. Here is the way he classifies their answers:

DO NOT FAVOR MARRIAGE TO PERSON OF:	PERCENT
another color	91
another religion	50
another educational group	31
another nationality	16
a different economic class	13

WOULD FIND IT EASIEST TO MARRY A PERSON WITH:	PERCENT
economic differences	64
nationality differences	58
educational differences	39
religious differences	27
color differences	6

Clearly, color differences are still the greatest barrier between young people considering marriageability for themselves—far more serious than religion, education, and economic differences or nationality.

INTERRACIAL MARRIAGES

Arnold Toynbee (Moskin 1969a) sees intermarriage as the ultimate solution of racial problems, but recognizes that English-speaking peoples, along with some Western Europeans, have retained deep prejudices against it. They have not intermarried as have people in Latin America, in the Arab world, and in many other parts of the globe. Gunnar Myrdal, Swedish population authority, studying the American Negro, has stated that the greatest intensity of discrimination is in the intermarriage area. The militant white racist fears most that sooner or later some Negro boy will date his daughter. Then will come "mongrelization" of the white race.

The Statistical Trend   A press release of the U.S. Bureau of the Census (Feb. 1, 1973) gives the latest statistical picture of marriage between whites and nonwhites. During the 1960s there was a 63 percent increase, but the base from which increase was measured in 1960 was very small. Actually, the increase was from 0.44 percent in 1970 to 0.70 percent in 1970. During the decade there was a decline in the number of black men marrying white women—from 25,913 in 1960 to 23,566 in 1970. There was a great increase, however in the number of white men marrying black women—from 25,496 in 1960 to 41,223 in 1970.

By 1970 a third of American Indian males had white wives; of Filipino males, 24.4 percent; of Japanese males, 8.3 percent; of Chinese males, 8.3 percent; and of black males, 2.1 percent. During the decade the number of Japanese males marrying white wives rose from 3471 to 9872, and the number of American Indians with white wives rose from 12,044 to 40,039. (Paul Glick, of the Census Bureau, thinks that more complete census taking may be reflected in the large increase among Indians.)

Certainly, considering their ratios in the total American population, nonwhite groups other than blacks are further along the road toward amalgamation than are blacks. Although intermarriage is one index of amalgamation of the races, it is not the only one. Until recently many states barred intermarriage of blacks and whites. Historically, the crossing of white and black has been without benefit of marriage. White males from presidents and congressmen down through the social strata have sired children of their black servants. Racial intermixture has been so extensive that few pure blacks remain. Since the sexual contacts were between white man and black women, it was the black race that experienced "mongrelization." A child from the union would remain with his mother and be considered black. However, the racist fears contact between the black male and white female, for then there will be a greater attempt to have the child accepted into white society. So far the child of an interracial couple has had a place only in black society.

Much of the crossing between whites and American Indians has also been without benefit of marriage. In fact, wherever races meet, much crossing takes place outside marriage. Now that integration has at least theoretically come to the nation, it can be expected that a higher proportion of race crossing will be within marriage. In fact, once the process of integration and assimilation is well along, intermarriage is the logical next step. As with all cases of conflicts involved in social distance, once affairs reach the point where intermarriage is considered, the hostilities which create problems are already vanishing.

Race crossings will increase among the educated who work together on the college campus and fight together in the crusade for equality. The Peace Corps, too, creates many interracial contacts. These social forces will bring a respectability to interracial marriages they have not had previously. The general climate of opinion will also be more tolerant toward the children of the mixed marriages, so that this will no longer be so great an anxiety-provoking factor in the experience of those who brave the color line in marriage.

Those who are shocked to anticipate the increase in interracial marriages will do well to remember that throughout the course of human history the races have mixed. One need not travel widely to be convinced of this fact. The racial crossing between all branches of the human race is fertile.

College campuses are becoming more cosmopolitan yearly. Any observer of campus life is aware that the taboos against white girls dating boys of other races are breaking down, particularly when the dark-skinned male is from another country. Often marriages of this type mean marrying up into the aristocracy of the country from which the male student comes. This gives such marriages respectability. The next step is for dating and intermarriage to be less selective.

Special Problems of the Interracial Marriage

Dating across color lines is taking place more frequently. Current research can scarcely foresee the outcome of marriages and child-rearing in the cross-race situation. The best guide we have is what is known of cross-race marriages to date. Some of the same situations will be faced, even if with less intensity. The prognosis is not good for the immediate future. The data are worth pursuing for their prognosis on outcomes.

Knebel (1969) finds interracial marriage causing an identity crisis among black women who are rebelling against black men who prefer white women in dating and marriage. Through such means as The Miss Black America Contest black leaders are trying to elevate the status of black women and solve their identity problem.

Research Guides   R. Adams' (1937) early study of interracial marriage in Hawaii, where there is an indistinct caste-color line, and where two out of five marriages are racially mixed, showed that marriage problems were more a matter of cultural norms and sex roles than of social pressures affecting the marriage from the community standpoint. The native (Polynesian) Hawaiian woman marrying a Chinese or a white man of good character moved up in standard of living—and took pride in adopting the husband's way of life for herself and her children. In general these husbands were better providers than the native island males. The marriages in general did well.

In rare cases where the native male married a non-Polynesian female, marriages often turned out to be unsatisfactory. This male's standards of industry fell far below those of the Chinese or the white and the wife became intolerant of his easygoing ways and his lack of responsibility as a provider. These wives were, moreover, not willing to assume the customary tasks of the Polynesian wife.

Thus we have interracial–international marriages involving the same stresses turning out differently, depending on which combination of male and female are involved. The problem proves not to be racial, but rather one of subcultural differences, primarily in role expectations of male and female. This principie may well have wide applications in international and interracial cross-marriages everywhere.

One other principle discovered by Adams was that the degree of disorganization of the particular group or groups involved in marriages across race and nationality lines was a key factor in the divorce rate. Groups going through a period of rapid acculturation not only crossed the line in marriage more often, but also had very high divorce rates, both with in-race and cross-race marriages. This behavior was particularly characteristic of such groups of Filipinos, Koreans, and Puerto Ricans. Japanese and Chinese tended to remain loyal to their culture and to marry outside very little. Those who did break with their race and culture groups had a high divorce rate.

Since World War II there has been opportunity to observe intermarriage, both of nationality groups involving the same racial strain and of interracial groups. For example, in the year 1946 alone there were 1600 Air Force marriages to German girls, and thousands had married English girls. By the end of 1955, the American Embassy reported that there had been over 20,000 marriages of GIs to Japanese women. This was in spite of the fact that for a considerable part of the occupation period the Army forbade marriages with Japanese girls.

While comprehensive research is lacking, a few special studies throw some light on interracial marriage, particularly with the Japanese. Joseph Grant, writer for the Associated Press, reported an interview study of 224 wives from Europe and the Far East by University of Hawaii sociologist, Yukiko Kimura. All of these women had married Hawaiian men and lived in Hawaii for five years or more. Two out of ten considered themselves unhappy, wishing they had not come to Hawaii. Another three out of ten said they probably would not have married their husbands if they had it to do over again, thus making half who would not repeat their marriage. The largest percentage of unhappy women were Japanese who married "Nisei" husbands, that is, American men of Japanese ancestry.

The happiest marriages in this study were Japanese girls married to Caucasian husbands. The second group were Europeans married to "Nisei." Three-fourths of these European girls would marry their husbands again.

Apparently the main difficulty with the Japanese girl marrying the "Nisei" is with in-laws. The husband's family demands that the wife conform to Japanese old-world patterns. They expect her to work hard and be obedient. The modern Japanese girls do not wish to follow these patterns because most of them are from Japanese cities which have already been very much westernized.

It appears that the Japanese–American marriage in the United States since World War II has, for the most part, not fared too badly. The Schnepp and Yui (1955) study of 40 couples indicates that the marriages have on the whole done very well. Strauss' (1954) study in Chicago, based on interviews with 30 men and 15 women in American–Japanese marriages, indicates that in many respects marriage adjustment is eased by the combination of Japanese and American sex roles and marriage values.

In a very comprehensive analysis of the cultural and social interactional factors involved in the Japanese–American marriages, Strauss concludes that one cannot arrive at the easy conclusion that interracial marriages are necessarily doomed or even that they present unusually great problems of adjustment.

Such cultural values as the lack of vocational aspirations of the wife, the absence of strong institutional loyalties, even the lack of strong loyalty to the religious institutions of her nation, an attitude of acceptance of the American standard of living (which is far superior on every level to anything she has known), and the acceptance of the husband as he is, rather than pushing him to improve himself, all favor the Japanese wife. The Japanese philosophy of the girl shifting her allegiance to the husband's family when she leaves her home in marriage also helps her in making the adjustment to a new way of life.

Scoring happiness at 100 for very happy marriages, Baber's (1937) early study of 48 interracial marriages between whites and members of the black and yellow races rated their happiness at only 62, a score much lower than those of interfaith and mixed-nationality marriages. One-third of the couples had no children, although none of them had been married for less than three years, and the median period of marriage was ten years. Undoubtedly some of this group had refrained from having children because they did not want children born into an environment of discrimination and trouble. There was no way to know how large a proportion of such interracial marriages had already failed.

Pavela made a study of 95 black–white marriages in Indiana, where such intermarriages have been illegal since 1852 and where it has been illegal to perform rites for such couples. Of these, 69 were black men with white brides, 26 white men with black brides. He found couples more often entered marriage with a previous divorce and were older than average at the time of marriage. Most were middle class. Few were married in a religious ceremony.

Pavela (1958–1959) concludes, "It would appear that . . . interracial marriage occurs between persons who are, by and large, economically, educationally, and culturally equal and who have a strong emotional attachment, be it rationalization or real. The external pressures faced by the interracial couples are often great but certainly do not appear to be overwhelming."

He goes on to explain that with most couples, the children were still young and the real crisis of adjustment may have lain ahead.

Jessie Bernard (1966b) finds that racially mixed black–white marriages are about as homogamous as white–white marriages as to education. Wives of black men, regardless of color, tend to have more schooling than their husbands, because of the generally low level of schooling of black males.

Heer (1966) believes that black–white intermarriage will help reduce the status gap between the races. He finds that most black–white marriages since 1950 have been between black husbands and white wives, the high-status male trading class advantage for the caste advantage of a white wife. He finds that black–white marriages are on the increase but seen no likelihood of sufficient increase during the next 100 years to bring, in and of itself, full equality.

Some of the adjustments of the racially mixed marriage are inevitably due to the factor of race and reactions of families of the pair and of the community to them and their children. Some, however, may well have little relationship to the racial factor. Some of Barnett's (1963) findings suggest this. He finds that persons who have grown up in stressful parental families are more likely to marry those of other races or nationalities. We know that such a background is not conducive to marriage success under any circumstances. Also, those who undertake an interracial marriage have, on a greater-than-average ratio, been previously married. Such persons are higher marriage risks than those in their first marriage.

Interracial marriage, particularly where black and white are concerned, is still quite unconventional. Marriage is a very conventional institutional arrangement. Those who fit best are conventional people. All the community institutions which lend families support are conventional in attitudes and expectations.

The Child of Mixed Parentage   In the past, racially mixed pairs have accepted the fact that the child is classed as a member of the lower-status race. There is a long tradition for this in American society. It has been so with black–white offspring and American Indian–white offspring down to the sixteenth part. (Influencing this was a census definition, which was motivated by a desire to protect the child's share in tribal inheritance rights.)

Gordon (1964), after his comprehensive study of intermarriage, concludes that the chance of failure of an interracial marriage is greater than that of an interfaith marriage. Interracial marriages lack the social support which interfaith marriages have. Mass public opinion is opposed to the former. He goes on to comment about the fruit of such unions in these terms:

> The children born of Negro–white marriages in the United States are, I believe, among the most socially unfortunate persons in all the world if they seek or expect acceptance by the white community in America. . . . They must find their roots in the Negro community or remain unaccepted and unacceptable to the white community [pp. 333–34].

He finds unanimity of agreement among black–white parents that for their youngsters the teen-age years are the most trying of their lives because of the taboos on interdating. He then raises the question of whether a couple in love have any moral right to create such problems for their children. The long-term view, of course, is that such problems would vanish if complete tolerance prevailed; but Gordon is no doubt right in his appraisal of the current situation and that it will not soon vanish from our society.

Both the law and the weight of public opinion in American society stand in the way of intermarriage for certain groups. Yet crossing of ethnic and racial lines goes on. For some people there seems to be a fascination in unlike skin color which cultural taboos are insufficient to control. Stories are always afloat about the exotic flavor of interracial sexual ventures, and these encourage race crossing outside wedlock wherever peoples of different skin color inhabit the same territory.

There is no reason, from the hereditary standpoint, why race lines should not be crossed in marriage. There is even some indication that a kind of hybrid vigor results where pure strains are crossed, as is found in hybrid strains of plants and animals. In countries where race crossing is approved by custom there is no objection to intermarriage. Interracial marriages have taken on special significance in the United States only because of race prejudice, which expresses itself in segregation and discrimination. Prejudice is particularly severe against individuals crossing racial lines to marry, and the child of mixed blood is in many situations accepted by neither racial group. Color prejudice is a social reality and no amount of idealism or faith on the part of young people in love can make it possible for them to evade this fact. It may still be generations away from disappearing.

It must be expected, however, that while America plays a leading part in world leadership, her young men will have opportunities to marry girls of different racial and nationality strains when stationed abroad. Such marriages are often entered into from loneliness and during periods of great sex hunger. It is not likely that choices made at such times will be based on clear judgment and objectivity. There is often an inclination on the part of the youth to forget that his foreign wife will be expected to fit into a world entirely new and strange to her when he returns home. The transition is so great that few foreign women can be expected to make it without great difficulty and without considerable tolerance on the part of the husband and his family. The cultural differences here add to the racial difference.

THE EDUCATION FACTOR IN MARRIAGE ADJUSTMENT

Education is the most potent cure for American ills as well as those of the underdeveloped nations. We expect much of it in every area of human improvement. Marriage is no exception. By this we mean not courses in marriage specifically, although they are increasing, but amount of education in terms of years spent in school.

Numerous studies going back as far as the basic researches of Burgess and Cottrell (1939), and those of Lewis I. Terman (1938), have found a relationship between years of schooling and happiness and duration of marriage. The 1960 census shows a typical picture on a nationwide basis (see Table 13-1). More recently Luckey (1966) found marital satisfaction positively related to years of schooling.

There can be no doubt that the association between schooling and somewhat more favorable chances for success in marriage. The reason for the association is not well-understood. Several factors no doubt contribute. Those with higher levels of schooling marry later and have more maturity of

Proportion of Ever-Married White and Nonwhite Men Age 45-54 in Stable Marriages, 1960, By Years of Schooling TABLE 13-1

YEARS OF SCHOOLING	PROPORTION IN STABLE MARRIAGES	
	NONWHITE	WHITE
0–4	53.5	73.0
5–7	57.3	76.4
8	57.5	78.4
9–11	55.9	77.3
12	59.2	79.6
13–15	54.8	78.2
16	65.2	83.5
17+	71.3	85.7

Source: *United States Census of Population, 1960, Marital Status,* Table 4. pp. 77, 81. From Bernard, "Marital Stability and Patterns of Status Variables," *Journal of Marriage and the Family,* 28:421–439, November, (1966).

It will be observed that stable marriages within both white and nonwhite groups increase with level of education. (Stability is defined as a husband in his first marriage, living with a wife. In 89.9 percent of cases it was the wife's first marriage also.)

judgment, perhaps, in mate choice by virtue of more extensive dating and exposure to a wider range of choice. Schooling in itself is a maturing experience. Greater tolerance for others and greater ease in making adjustments may be acquired. Perhaps those with more education develop superior problem-solving techniques. Certainly the way a couple approaches problems in their marriage is of prime importance to its success. Whatever the reason, the relationship exists. Marriages of college-educated couples turn out far better than do average marriages. (For convincing data turn to Figure 14–3, which shows the probability of divorce by education, and to Figure 19–1, which graphs marriage happiness by occupation.)

Schooling is the gateway to stable income-producing occupations and professions. These give the kind of economic foundation associated with stable marriages. The college group moves into professional positions, and the marriage is protected by more social pressures such as reputation, respectability, and social expectation.

The problem of degree of difference in education which can be tolerated between mates is of concern to many in the late high school and college years. Should the young man in college forget the girl who did not wish to continue or was not able to do so? Should a wife "put hubby through" at the cost of her own schooling? Should she go to school while he is in the military? These are recurrent questions in the peer group.

It is a well-established fact that most marriages are between those of similar education and intelligence. This is to be expected in a country where everyone spends most of his dating years in school and associates for the most part with those of similar educational experience and achievement. High schools and colleges are sometimes humorously referred to as match factories.

Studies of college students indicate that girls prefer to marry men above themselves in education, while men generally prefer women their equals in education and intelligence. When it comes to actually selecting a mate, women come nearer to realizing their education ideal than do men. This is explained in part by the fact that more men than women reach the higher levels in education. It may also indicate that men attach much less significance to this qualification in their wives than do women in their husbands. In many instances, one suspects a young man actually in the marriage market discovers he does not want a wife who is his educational and intellectual equal.

Figure 13–1 shows the proportion of young college people marrying those who were educationally higher, equal to, and lower than themselves. Most college men married below themselves in educational status, but half the women succeeded in marrying educational equals. The further a young person went in college, the more likely he was to marry a person with some college training. Of those who graduated from college, 80 percent married persons with some college training.

The desire of women to marry up and the practice of men to marry down probably reflects basic differences in motivation in male selection. The male, who is by custom the breadwinner, is usually judged by a woman, at least in part, by his ability to offer security by constancy of income. Since education has a direct bearing on economic success, a good education has become an important selective factor by women's standards. The male has most to do with

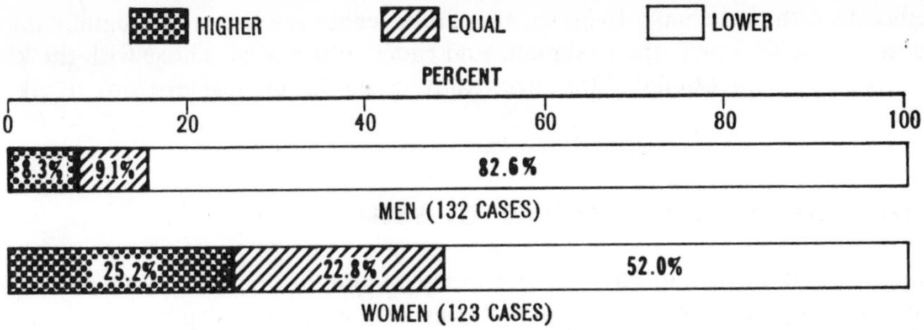

| HIGHER | | EQUAL | | LOWER | |

PERCENT

```
0        20        40        60        80       100
```

82.6%

MEN (132 CASES)

25.2%   22.8%   52.0%

WOMEN (123 CASES)

Educational level of mates selected by college youths. Most college men married below their level of education; very few married higher. Almost half of all college women married equal to or above their educational level—over a fourth above. Source: Paul H. Landis and Katherine H. Day, "Education as a Factor in Mate Selection," *American Sociological Review*, 10:558–60, August, 1954.

FIGURE 13-1

establishing and maintaining the general social status of the family, which is determined in our society by such factors as income, occupation, and standard of living. The young woman who can associate herself by marriage with a person of higher education and training is bargaining for a better standard of living than she could expect as a result of her own training and skills.

The man, on the other hand, in facing the problem of mate selection, is likely to consider criteria other than education of prime importance. Men are not particularly attracted to women with college diplomas or other evidence of intellectual prowess. Attractiveness and feminine charm rate higher in our culture, and their importance is constantly reaffirmed by pin-up girls, Miss America contests, and other symbols of the cult of beauty.

The belief in the intellectual superiority of the male has so long been a part of American thinking that few men, and for that matter few women, are comfortable in a relationship where the female is obviously the more outstanding. A marriage having this relationship frequently brings feelings of resentment, inadequacy, and frustration to the husband. Few men wish to have their position of authority in the family threatened by the superior educational qualifications of their wives. Popenoe believes the educated man wants a wife who will flatter his ego. Women reared in the popular tradition wish to feel that their husbands actually are superior persons to whom they may look up. Although one might think college women different in these attitudes, numerous class discussions with upper-division classes have convinced the writer that college women hold this view also.

That this pattern of assortative mating is deeply rooted is suggested by findings that women who marry above themselves in education are more likely to be happy in marriage than those who marry below themselves. In other words, the pattern is so well-established that acting contrary to it increases the danger of maladjustment in marriage.

In summary, the evidence favors the view that a similar amount of schooling is desirable for marriage partners, and that if there is a difference in the amount of education, it is better for the husband to be the one with more

RACIAL AND CULTURAL DIFFERENCES

education than the wife. Even so, these differences are much less significant to marriage adjustment than religious and racial differences. Those with the kind of extreme educational differences that could be critical are not likely to marry.

DIFFERENCES IN SOCIAL CLASS

Fiction and fairy tale have woven many a plot around the Cinderella-type prince-and-pauper marriage. Such stories have most meaning when they come out of a social system which is strongly stratified by class distinctions. The open-class system of the United States teaches that every man can be a king and attempts to ignore economic lines. This philosophy is encouraged by territorial mobility, which helps one shed one's past, and by the prevailing belief in social climbing, which tends to obliterate class lines.

The lower-class girl, class theorists find, is the victim of sexual exploitation by the upper-class boy when she is his date. If this is true, one might well ask whether the lower-class girl is in reality exploiting the boy's financial and status resources. Kinsey (1953) finds that lower-class girls are no more accessible sexually than upper- or middle-class girls. Each seems to participate in premarital intercourse in about the same proportion of cases. Kinsey does not, however, go into the matter of whether the joint participants in the sex acts are of the same social strata.

Although many studies have shown a tendency to date and marry within similar socioeconomic classes, lines are by no means rigidly drawn. Where differences in economic backgrounds are great, certain difficulties may logically be anticipated. Men and women alike who consider marriage into different social backgrounds or into families with very different ways of life must expect to overcome certain handicaps and make difficult adjustments in order to find happiness in marriage.

It is easier for a man to marry down the economic ladder than for a woman to do so. The man is not criticized so severely for picking a girl who comes from a lower social, economic, or educational level. If a woman is beautiful, he is excused, often envied, even though she falls short in many other qualities. At the same time, many social groups are critical of the woman who marries a socially, economically, or educationally inferior man. This is not particularly because she is giving up a higher standard of living. Actually, the criticism such a woman draws upon herself results from a complex of social attitudes and traditions. First, she is bucking custom—tradition says each woman should find someone to care for her and protect her, someone to give her all of the things she "deserves." It is popularly believed, too, that one's choice of a mate is a reflection upon oneself. The first question which is likely to enter the minds of her friends is, "Couldn't she do any better than that?" Finally, marrying "down" is generally taken as an admission of personal or social inadequacy.

The average girl can adjust more easily to a higher than to a lower standard of living. There is always some risk in marriage when the young wife is accustomed to a much higher level of living than her new mate can provide, although few girls should expect to start on the level their parents have attained by middle age. Only an unusual girl can face low-income living, even in her own home. The man who plans to marry under these circumstances owes it to his own future happiness, as well as to that of his fiancée, to make clear that he cannot hope to maintain the level of living to which she is accustomed.

If the wife, in order to maintain her past standard of living, begins to depend on her family as a source of income or to obtain accustomed luxuries and recreation, this becomes a source of embarrassment to her husband, whom society expects to provide for her. Sometimes the wife's family wants to save their daughter from hardships or presumed hardships. They cannot bear to have her going without things they themselves have, things she has been used to in her childhood home. In fact, they are even unwilling to have her go through the struggles that they themselves went through.

Scanzoni (1968) found that few marriages (less than a fourth) were dissolved where the husband's father had the same or higher status than the wife. Where the husband's father had a lower status than the wife, the rate of dissolution was above 60 percent. He also found the rate of dissolutions almost as high where the husband's education was lower than the wife's.

This kind of relationship between social class and marriage success is to be expected, for social class differences are a composite of education, income, and occupation, all of which relate to marriage success or failure. The social classes live in a different world: time of going to work, reading matter in the home, kinds of entertainment appreciated, ways of rearing children, esthetic appreciation, status symbols, erotic play, and many other behavior patterns differ. Generally, the lower-class home is not given much to reading or conversation. Action is characteristic. Deferring gratification for future gain is a middle-class value, not a lower-class one. This alone can create a host of problems in spending, in training children, etc.

PROBLEMS

1　*Sociodrama:* The honeymoon is over, figuratively as well as literally, and a wealthy, well-educated, young woman and her husband of humble background and little education are trying to plan their leisure hours together.

2　Charles and Katherine are graduate college students in a northern university. They have known each other since early high school days and are familiar with one another's values, ideals, and ambitions. They are both from wealthy families, both plan to be chemists, and both tend to be introverts with little interest in or need of outside friendships.

After five years of dating during which their attachment has steadily grown, Charles finally broached the subject of marriage, though none too courageously, for Charles is black and Katherine is Irish by descent. In your opinion should Katherine:

a　Refuse outright?
b　Talk the matter over with her parents and minister?
c　Consent?
d　Consent but plan to move to another country?
e　Consent but insist that they have no children?

f Delay her consent until she has discovered whether or not Charles would be accepted by her friends, parents, and community?

g Consent and plan to identify herself with his family and friends if they will accept her?

3 What might account for the attraction many girls feel for men 10–30 years their senior? What might be the advantages in such a marriage? What are the disadvantages?

4 If there is a foreign war bride in your community, ask her to describe some of the adjustments demanded by an international or interracial marriage.

5 "Marriage," they say, "is a private affair." Why, then, should an individual hesitate to marry someone of another race whom he sincerely loves?

6 In what way do children complicate the adjustments of interracial marriages?

7 Do you believe that encouraging interracial marriages among those who are unprejudiced would tend to reduce interracial hatred and intolerance in general?

8 Marie is from a patriotic French family. Otto was a German pilot in World War II. They both live in the United States now. They have lost their accents and few people could tell from looking at them that they are not of the same nationality. In what way, then, might nationality stand in the way of their achieving marital happiness?

9 What arguments can you think of in favor of marriages in which the wife is a few years older than her husband? What might the disadvantages be?

10 What age relationship between husband and wife do you consider ideal? Why?

11 A wealthy young man has proposed to a friend of yours from a lower-class home. Would your advice be:

a "Jump at the chance. This is every girl's dream."

b "His background of wealth doesn't make any difference in America, so don't let that influence you."

c "Don't marry him; you could never be happy together."

d Some other advice.

12 In our society, tradition favors a woman's marrying above rather than below her economic station in life. In your opinion, has the time come to do away with this practice as outmoded? Justify your answer.

13 What do you believe accounts for the fact that men generally prefer wives of equal or slightly less education than themselves?

14 Do you believe that the responsibilities of caring for a home, financial management, and child-rearing make a college-educated woman a better wife?

15 What educational relationship do you believe ideal for husband and wife? Why?

16 The Duke of Windsor's story (in his book, *A King's Story*) is one of the great romances of history involving those of very different background. Discuss and appraise the former king's choice.

AGE FOR MARRIAGE

14 Circumstances may have more to do with timing marriage than age in and of itself. There is the matter of having an eligible prospect. Having that, there are problems of schooling, military service obligations, special personal or family obligations, and unique personal goals to be realized prior to marriage, like extensive travel or achieving an income goal. Then there are reasons for hastening marriage, like pregnancy, desire to avoid a military draft, or desire to escape the restrictions and obligations of the parental home, which may be like jumping from the frying pan into the fire.

Readiness for marriage admittedly cannot be determined by chronological age alone. Yet it is difficult to acquire a mature perspective on life without attaining the experience which comes with the years. Success in marriage is, in part, a matter of readiness in the broad sense of having reached the age at which one can fit it into life plans, and accept and carry the obligations marriage involves. Levy and Munroe (1938) believe that emotional readiness for marriage is much more important than any particular personality trait. They believe that persons who have the proper mental attitude toward marriage can work out a way of life together and make a good adjustment, just as many people do in a field of work which may not be the most ideal from the standpoint of their interests and needs.

This view considers that "when to marry" is the real question and that this is answered in terms of one's own development. It holds that acceptance of the marriage relationship is of major importance—to be able honestly to practice the words, "to love, honor, and cherish, for better or for worse, until death do us part." It holds that a husband and wife can have a lot of conflicts and face many problems, but if they have this attitude of certainty toward their marriage, they can work problems out to a solution. They feel that an experimental approach to marriage is a sure signpost to Reno for divorce.

There is a finality about marriage, and only those persons should marry who have reached the time when marriage is more important to them than anything else. One's age at marriage, his preparation, the particular time in world affairs, the stage of one's career development, one's achieved state of social, emotional, and economic maturity—all have a bearing.

AGE FOR MARRIAGE

It is a commonly held belief that early marriages are likely to work out well, because of the adjustability of youth. The person who is older is pictured as habit-ridden and fixed in his ways. This notion may have had substance in the fixed relations of agrarian societies. In a rapidly changing society it is likely that the person who has lived a few more years and has gained a greater breadth of experience is more adjustable than the teen-ager with his limited horizon and circumscribed existence. The experiences of leaving home, changing communities, meeting and working with strangers, and planning one's life seldom come before the late teens or early 20s. These experiences might be expected to contribute appreciably to one's ability to adjust.

The Long-Term Statistical Trend

During this century, those who wish to marry have had an increased opportunity to do so. As a result of the great economic developments making early self-support possible, the chance comes earlier in life (see Figure 14–1). The long-term trend has been toward younger marriage; in the last decade young people have been delaying marriage somewhat.

The typical groom of 1890 was just over 26 years of age at the time of his first marriage, the typical bride was 22. Today the typical groom is just over 23 and the bride just under 21. In 1890, the average age difference between bride and groom was over 4 years, now it is about 2.4 years (see Figure 14–1).

Compare the prospects life offers young people in the United States, where economic circumstances and customs permit early marriage, with Ireland, where economic hardship and religious taboos against birth control cause more than a third of the women and almost two-thirds of the men to delay marriage past 30 years of age. Many there must postpone marriage until they have passed the childbearing age (Goode 1963).

In 1960 the United States census showed that only 7.2 percent of males had never married by age 45–49, 6.5 percent of females. In 1965, 64 percent of all women 55–64 were married and living with a husband (first or subsequent). According to predictions this figure will be 72 percent by 1980. Of women now 65–74 years of age, only 64 percent were married at age 25, now 93 percent of women age 25 are married; for men the figures are 42 percent and 72 percent, respectively.

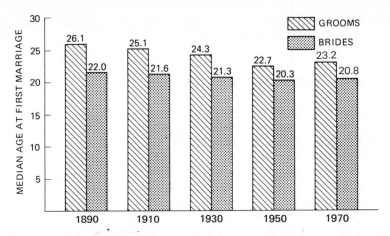

Median age for marriage. Note that the difference in age of bride and groom is also less than formerly—4 years in 1890 compared with 2.4 in 1970. Marriage age is decreasing throughout the world, but the average is higher—24 years for women, 27 for men—than in the United States (*Demographic Yearbook, UN*). Source: U.S. Department of Commerce, Bureau of the Census, "Population Characteristics," Series P-20, No. 122, March 22, 1963, (Table C) with 1970 data added.

FIGURE 14–1

In the United States, about 94 percent of all women are or have been married by the end of the childbearing age. This is the highest record in American history. Except for the sick and badly crippled, the deformed, the emotionally warped, and the mentally defective, almost everyone has an opportunity to marry. Even the handicapped often marry, thanks to social security, routine machine-powered jobs, and labor-saving devices in the home.

Teen-age Marriages

For many years there has been great concern over younger teen-age marriage and the problems it presents to parents, school systems, community welfare systems, and agencies working with young people. It is often disastrous when the young take on adult responsibilities and fail at them.

The number of marriages in the younger group has declined. There are fewer girls marrying under 18 years of age than 15–20 years ago (Parke and Glick 1967). Of women marrying 15 years ago, 23 percent were under 18; now only 15 percent are under 18. Not many young men ever did marry under 18, but the proportion doing so is less than 15 years ago, and the proportion marrying under 20 has also dropped substantially.

Still, far too many marry too soon, but a reversal of this trend has taken place. There are several possible reasons for this: More young people plan to have a college education, the military service creates a shortage of marriageable males at home, an awareness among young people that early marriages generally are headed for trouble (some have opportunity to observe this fact among their classmates who may be married and divorced), and the use of the pill and other sophisticated birth-control methods, warding off pregnancy and thus avoiding the forced marriage.

Success Record of Teen-Age Marriage

For 30 years students of the family have been examining the relationship between age at marriage and success or failure. One of the first such studies compared adjustments of individuals in various age groups of more than 500 upper-middle-class couples. It was found that the likelihood of good adjustment for women between the ages of 16 and 30 years increased steadily with later marriage. Among the cases studied, more than twice as many women nearing 30 were found to have made a good marital adjustment, as had women marrying under 18. Men who married before the age of 22 stood considerable chance of poor adjustment. Those who married between 28 and 30 took the least risk. However, men who married after 30 were found to make good adjustments less frequently. This probably indicates not that men become less marriageable as they pass 30, but merely that by this age those with the best potentialities have already been selected.

Divorce rates are much higher among marriages that occur at an early age. Burchinal and Chancellor (1962), studying marriages that ended in divorce, found that when both were 19 or under, the marriages lasted only half as long as when they were 20 or older. Where the husband was of low occupational status, duration of the marriage prior to divorce was also briefer than when he was of high occupational status. Age of marriage and occupational status are inevitably related since training is a prerequisite to high occupational status.

Glick (1957), studying census data, found divorce of those married before age 18 almost three times as high as those marrying between 22 and 24. He and Norton studied a nationwide sample in 1971, comparing marriage survival by age and certain social characteristics (Figure 14–2). Data are for white males in their first marriage. Note the high probability of divorce of those marrying under 20 and the very low probability for those marrying between the ages 25 and 29. The outlook for those marrying after 30 is much less favorable.

Christine H. Hillman (1954) analyzed inquiries to an advice column in a newspaper. She found that 66 percent of these inquiries came from married individuals, and that 72 percent of the inquiries of the people who were or had been married were from those who had married before they were 18. The median age of first marriages of these people was 16.8 years.

There are many reasons for the unhappiness and frequent failure of young teen-age marriages. No accurate statistics are available, but various studies and estimates suggest that 50–75 percent of all high school marriages are induced by pregnancy.

The forced marriage is unfortunate at any age and has even more counts against it with teen-agers. Many do not have the physical development to perform the normal functions of adult life, including work responsibilities and the biological functions of reproduction and child care. The human female is

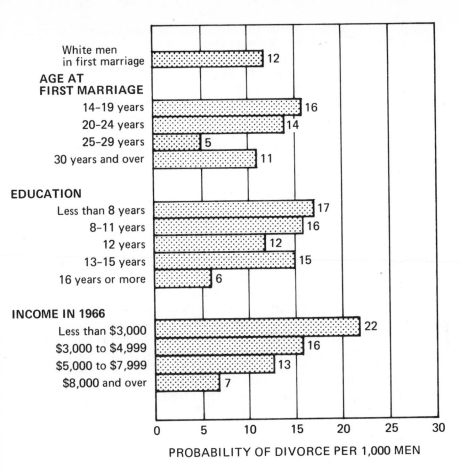

Average annual probability of divorce per 1000 white men in their first marriage less than 5 years, by selected characteristics, 1960–1966. Source: Paul C. Glick and Arthur J. Norton, "Frequency, Duration, and Probability of Marriage and Divorce," *Journal of Marriage and the Family*, 33: 314, May, 1971.

FIGURE 14–2

not fully ready for the reproductive function until long after puberty. Adolescent sterility has been noted by anthropologists observing primitives who have no taboos on sexual intercourse among adolescents. Full fertility and biological capability of producing sound offspring are not reached, on the average, until the early 20s. Montagu's (1958) studies show a high rate of infant and maternal mortality among adolescent mothers, and a high rate of premature births, miscarriages, and stillbirths.

Nesrin Bingol (1972), chief of pediatric genetics at New Medical College, finds that young teen-age mothers frequently bear children who have abnormally small heads by a year of age, and who are subnormal in intelligence. He also finds that children of mothers 17 years of age and younger have more congenital malformations, iron anemia deficiency, and other problems of prenatal development. Postnatally they more often suffer serious infections during the first year, and are more often "battered," reflecting the parents' lack of readiness emotionally to accept the responsibilities of child care. Other studies confirm that the children of young teen-age parents have an undue number of physical, social, and psychological problems due to their mothers' youth.

Young people may lack a good educational and vocational foundation to meet the economic demands that a family brings. Too often they are unready to give up teen-group activities and settle down; this is likely to be especially true of the male. Young couples are not old enough to win a respected place in the adult community; often not mature enough to stand the daily pressures and tensions that married living and children bring. These pressures are likely to be multiplied when the children are not wanted.

The comment of a young mother of three children, divorced at 21, may be typical of many. When asked if she had been too young at marriage, and if that was why it failed she replied, "I wasn't too young, but he was." She went on to explain that she made the adjustment, but that her husband found being tied down to the support of wife and children too much for him.

In some cases he may have been tied down involuntarily because of the girl's pregnancy, and he escapes his problem by terminating the marriage. This adds to her problems and to the social burden of the community supporting his children. Thus, the male economic role is transferred to the tax roll.

In some small communities a major problem of landlords is fending off applications for rentals by young divorced women with small children. In self-defense they often reject the women as unsuitable tenants, because their funds are at best limited, and alimony is undependable. The women are likely to entertain males in the home in a quest for new husbands and fathers, and they may marry and leave without notice.

Parental Influence on Early Marriage

Margaret Mead (1968a) concludes that today romance is less a factor in early marriage than 20 years ago. Now girls get married "to get away from their mothers." The small nuclear family has no place for two women in the household. Under the large family system this urgency did not exist.

But in marrying young many do not get away. A 1967 study by the U.S. Bureau of the Census shows that 19.2 percent of married couples in which the husband is under 20 were living with relatives, only 5.7 of those 20–24. Less than 2 percent of any other age group prior to retirement, lives with relatives. These data suggest that there is a high degree of dependence on parents and other relatives, and a risk of interference from relatives in the new marriage. Privacy is limited, and the chance for the couple to adjust to each other and maintain their own counsel is likely to be limited.

The young bride and groom are much more vulnerable to parental interference from both sides, and invite a real in-law problem. It is likely that parents on both sides feel freer to criticize a young couple and are inclined to feel it is their right if the couple is drawing support from them. The young are more likely to seek emotional support from the parents, and with it may come advice which one or the other of the pair resents.

The "Glick Effect"

Paul Glick (1957) first called attention to the fact that both high school and college women who drop out to marry have the highest rate of divorce in their respective age groups. Jessie Bernard (1966a) finds a similar relationship in her analysis of 1960 census data, and refers to the lower marital stability of the dropout group as the "Glick effect."

There has been considerable discussion as to whether factors in the background of the girl explain both her dropping out of school and her failure in marriage. A whole complex of disadvantages are involved in the failure of the marriage, some of them residual in the childhood environment, some induced by leaving school, and some by premature entry into marriage.

The very circumstances of entering marriage may also be a factor. Hungerford (1968) has pointed out that girls often enter into sex relations in the hope that this will lead to marriage. This brings the forced marriage. Since the boy was only interested in sex, he resents the responsibilities he is forced to assume.

Young marriages are for the most part among those of the lower socioeconomic classes where marriage problems and high divorce rates are problems of marriage at any age. In part, the high divorce rate of young married couples is a product of class itself, and as Udry, Bauman, and Chase (1971) point out, delaying age of marriage will not change one's class background (see also Bariz and Nye 1970). On the other hand, deferring marriage can increase one's economic security and chances for further education. These in themselves can improve one's chances of success, as can gaining the greater maturity that comes with age and experience.

MARRIAGE WHILE IN COLLEGE

There are two types of college marriage. The first is the student, already past the average marriage age, who marries and may begin his family while in college, or before coming to college. The other is the average-age student who marries before the rest of his peers consider marriage desirable. The problems of the two groups are considerably different.

The number of older married students increased sharply after World War II, when veterans flooded the campuses and married, requiring colleges and universities to face the problems of college housing and other aspects of the care of families and children.

Considerable sociological study of the veteran's group has been made, and findings are likely indicative of problems faced by today's veterans and older married students. Research has centered on relative success in school performance of married and unmarried couples, on their success in marriage itself, and on special problems the college marriage faces.

A Wisconsin study, for example, showed that even couples with children made better than average grades. The divorce rate during the first few years of college marriages is lower than among educated people generally. Judson T. Landis' study (1963a) of 544 couples at Michigan State College indicated that not only do these married students have a better grade average than the unmarried group, but that they have a greater sense of security and feel more settled. The men queried felt that a wife was a help rather than a hindrance in their college life. Of these couples, 95 percent gave themselves a rating of happy or very happy in appraising their marriage.

Some husbands were critical of the wife's interest in having more social life than the husband could take time for, but on the whole, college marriages were considered successful.

Lawrence L. Falk (1964) studied 40 married and 40 single students, comparing their grades and finding no difference. Those who married while in school kept the same grade level or improved. Christensen and Philbrick's (1952) study at Purdue University asked student couples whether or not, knowing what they knew now, they would marry again while in school. Three-fourths said they would marry while in college if they had it to do over again. A fourth of the group felt that the difficulties of making a living, finding housing, and doing satisfactory college work offered too great handicaps. The researchers, however, suggest the probability that some of these gave external factors as rationalizations, that in many of these instances the marriage itself was one which had little hope of surviving because of deep psychological problems. (Lower happiness ratings were in evidence in the group that would have deferred marriage because of college.)

It must be remembered that most of the marriages were government subsidized, so that economic worries were greatly reduced. While many sociologists, the author among them, believe that it would be wise social policy to subsidize the marriage of able and socially mature college students, such a program does not exist. This means that nonveterans are on their own when they marry, unless they can work out and willingly accept some sort of subsidy or loan from parents.

One of the possible eugenic benefits to the nation of college postwar marriages was that the birth rate of the college group increased. This, however, often created personal problems that college couples did not anticipate. The Michigan State study showed that two-thirds of the pregnancies among this group had not been planned; one-third admitted carelessness; the other third had done everything possible to avoid pregnancy. Clearly, a college couple must take into account the possibility, or even the probability, of having children (Landis 1963). Christensen and Philbrick found similar results in a study of student-couple pregnancies at Purdue involving 346 couples. Of course, birth control is more certain now than when these studies were made, but this will not take care of the carelessness factor. The Landis study further reports that children proved to be a serious handicap to college performance, taking time, making study difficult, requiring loss of sleep, and eventually wanting to play when the parents got home from school or work. Johannis (1956) reports that two-thirds of the parent couples he studied in Oregon felt that children brought difficult problems for the student marriage—crowding, high rent costs, problems of getting baby sitters and paying for them, and lack of play space for children. Medical care costs are also found burdensome.

There has been much criticism of the underclassman marriage, and considerable research into its special problems. Any teacher who has discussed the topic with college classes becomes aware of the disadvantages students see in marriages of the usual-age college student, particularly if he marries during the first years of college. He cuts himself off from much of the teen-age social life which is such a vital part of the college experience. His changes for leadership are undoubtedly greatly reduced, as well as his chance for developing special talents such as are demanded in the numerous extracurricular activities of the campus. He has a compensating social life among married young people which may replace some of these disadvantages. Yet class discussions in marriage problems courses lead one to think that the average young college person feels it would be a decided loss to have been married during the early years of college, entirely aside from the economic hardship that is likely to be faced. There is also, of course, the practical problem of the great risk of pregnancy before the educational career is terminated.

Margaret Mead (1960) has expressed concern over the trend toward early marriages which threatens intellectual development and makes earning a living take precedence over scholarly achievement. Unlike European society, where men of great ambition are encouraged to put off family responsibility, youth in our society are pushed into it. This, she believes, tends to deny them the chance to explore, challenge. She fears men can no longer be expected to strive for great achievement when they must give priority to earning a living and caring for babies. Babies have "engrossed women for a thousand years, and it now looks as if they were going to engross men, too." She goes on to ask the question whether anyone will have time for "statesmanship, art, science, exploration of outer space?"

No society can have both men and women devoting their time to infants. This makes for a "settled, security-loving, unadventurous people." This she views as serious in an age when countries like the Soviet Union and China have women as well as men striving for great achievement, feeling that the future belongs to them and is worth sacrificing for: "If we retire into a kind of fur-lined domesticity, in which everyone is concerned with his own little family and his own little house, I think it is going to curtail seriously the contribution that we can make as a nation to the development of civilization on this planet," comments Mead.

Kingsley Davis (1958), in a satirical vein, has commented on the early-marriage trend in the United States, with reference to the college group particularly. He points out that it tends to destroy the ambition of women, since they are becoming increasingly content to enter marriage and bear children without other significant contribution to society. Thus, they sacrifice professional and creative aspirations and fail to make a contribution to the labor force as, for example, they do in Russia where there are many women engineers and doctors.

The American girl seems too eager to enter into marriage as soon as she reaches approximate physical maturity. Many women sacrifice their future status as effective wives by cutting off their training while helping their husbands through school. Davis feels that often they cheat themselves out of the reward of high status in marriage and also risk their marriage, as the husband outgrows them in training and sophistication.

He suggests that the early-marriage rate tends to make young people, particularly girls, dawdle through school. They have little motivation to pursue academic interests seriously. He sees the young married generation becoming a generation of spongers, depending on parents to put up the money for school, a down-payment on a house, doctor and hospital bills when the baby comes, loans to buy an automobile or other luxuries.

Marshall and King (1966) have focused on the inadequacies of most of the research into college marriages and point out reasons for inconsistent results of the various studies. Such variables as age, social class, amount of government subsidy, economic background, and other socioeconomic factors affect marriage adjustments, as well as hardships the pair encounter, amount of leisure time, the difficulties of parenthood, whether the wife has to work, and whether the wife must drop out of school. All of these should be considered by researchers.

A study by Eshleman and Hunt (1967) suggests the social class variable may be a deciding factor in the couple's adjustment to both marriage and children. They find a higher ratio of marriages among those from lower-class backgrounds, and greater approval of the idea of marriage while in college. Husbands were less disturbed in their studies by having children in the home, perhaps from having grown up under more crowded conditions.

The authors feel that marriage may be made possible at an earlier age for the lower socioeconomic classes by college low-cost housing rentals, and opportunities for the wife to earn. Adjustments may be easier too, because the wife has lower educational aspirations than women in the higher socioeconomic classes. And the male may be less disturbed by the fact that grades do not usually improve over high school, since his educational background is often weak and he may have a lower level of scholastic aspirations.

Recurrent Problems of Campus Marriages

Although studies differ in many details of their findings, there are certain recurrent problems in college marriages. Many of them might exist outside the campus environment had these same people married at the same age, but our central question here is whether it is better to marry during one's schooling period or to wait. Economic hardship is a feature of campus marriages. In the Eshleman and Hunt study this was found to be true regardless of social class. According to all studies, three-fourths of the males and 60 percent of the wives were employed 40 or more hours a week. Veterans' subsidies, of course, help relieve this situation.

The education of the couple is threatened and may be terminated. There is a strong tendency for marriage to terminate the wife's schooling even if marriage and children permit the husband to struggle through.

Social life will be limited, as will extracurricular activities. The time and cost factors are significant here, as is living apart from group houses and dormitories. The wife's social life particularly will be limited, and even the simple home relaxations of radio and television will be restricted by the husband's need for quiet. Faced with such difficulties the older couple will tolerate them with greater equanimity than the younger couple.

However, the college marriage receives some social support not given marriages in the world off campus. Low-grade housing is less humiliating because most students are equal in this respect. There are many campus organizations catering to the married couple and to student wives, and there is an interest on the campus in children and their development. Nursery schools and child-care centers are likely to be more available than in the average community.

The college campus probably offers more protection from sideline romances than do work situations in the world outside. Yet a wife may gain a distinct impression that her husband considers the girls he associates with in the classroom and in the college student union building, very attractive. It is not unusual for him to roam during her pregnancy, and the campus offers ready opportunity. On the college campus there is likely to be more criticism of disloyalty than in the average industrial or other work situation, but extramarital ventures are not uncommon.

Whether advantageous or not, college couples have a basis for rationalizing their marital and family difficulties. They can justify their economic hardship, their bickering, their sacrifice of living standards, their denial of recreation, and their hardship for the children as a sacrifice of present pleasure for future gain. Even those in serious difficulty with marriage problems likely defer a decision regarding divorce, hoping that all will be well when they get out of college. But if they choose to seek it, they can more often find counseling help on the campus than they could outside.

Differential Rates of Growth of Mates

There is danger of the husband outgrowing the wife if she drops out of school to support him, or to become a homemaker, and thus isolates herself from many of the social experiences which would, for a single woman, bring a great deal of growth during these late teen years. The husband may outgrow the wife in training and sophistication, and he may reach the time in college or later when he feels the need for a more worldly (in the broadest sense) woman to share his role as a professional or businessman and to influence his career as the wife he has now outgrown never could.

Margaret Mead (1968a) sees an underlying psychological basis for the breakup of marriages after graduation from college or professional school. In putting her husband through, the wife takes over the role much like that of a parent. The husband feels little guilt in dropping her once he has reached his goal of schooling and has acquired his independence. She also may have pushed him to study and to finish school, much as a parent would, and may have even encouraged having children so that he could not leave her. As he would with a parent, the husband drifts away from his wife.

The problem of differential rates of growth, while exaggerated on the campus, is certainly not confined to campus marriages. Differential rates of growth and personality change explain many postwar divorces, when men return from worldwide travels with broadened experience and find the interests of wives or fiancées too limited. That women should have the same opportunities, and travel at public expense, is perhaps the strongest argument for drafting women, since most jobs in the military are clerical, administrative, and technological.

Differential growth rate is a lifelong problem for married couples in our day of rapid change, often taking the male into broader circles than the female. Whyte (1951), studying wives of management for *Fortune* magazine, learned that in the managerial hierarchy, industry does not object to a man getting a divorce, for it is felt he will choose a woman more compatible to the aims of the corporation when he chooses again. Industry recognizes that perhaps one of the main reasons why men on the climb get a divorce is because their wives did not climb with them.

THE OPTIMUM TIME FOR MARRIAGE

Marriage in the early 20s seems to offer the maximum advantages in contemporary American culture, although the late 20s would be better from the standpoints of adjustment and finances. But fears of not finding a mate, of being abnormal sexually or otherwise, a desire to fit the norm, pressures of parents and peers, and many other influences bear on personal decision. In addition, in times of military buildup there is a certain fatalism which makes some hasten to finalize relationships and build security.

College women who are not engaged or married by the last semester of the senior year seem anxious to marry and sometimes make a hasty choice. It appears that some men at this time reach a similar stage or at least a point of greater receptivity to marriage. However, a very strong career drive, requiring considerable training beyond college tends to delay marriage for both men and women, particularly for women.

The optimum time is in part the time when opportunity comes. Women are more aware of this than are men, and they should be. Their chances of finding a mate decline rapidly with age.

By the time a woman reaches 30, for example, her chances of marriage are little more than 50:50. After 45 the chances fall to 1:10 (see Figure 14–3).

The discipline and competitiveness that may characterize such a woman after a long period of schooling and business activity are in complete contradiction to those qualities most men regard as attractive in a mate. But there are several other handicaps, too. The young men she knew as a girl are already married. The professions into which women most often go—school teaching, social work, library work, and nursing—are, for the most part, female occupations offering few opportunities to meet marriageable men.

These women are further handicapped because men their own age are usually more attracted to younger women. When a man of 35 marries, he chooses not a woman of 32, but rather a woman in her late 20s. Likewise, a man in his late 20s is more likely to marry a girl in her middle or early 20s than one near his own age. This means that the professional woman in her late 20s must seek a partner among men approximately 35 years of age. Most men who are interested in or suited to family life are already married before they reach that age. A woman in her late 20s or early 30s is likely to find her best

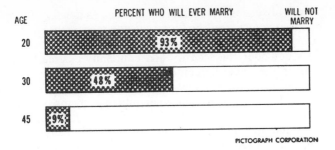

AGE | PERCENT WHO WILL EVER MARRY | WILL NOT MARRY

20 — 93%

30 — 48%

45 — 9%

PICTOGRAPH CORPORATION

Chances of marriage for single women. To remain single until 30 reduces chances for marriage by half, until 45, to about 1:10. Source: U.S. Department of Commerce, Bureau of the Census.

FIGURE 14–3

chance to marry among widowers and divorced men. There are some very desirable marriage partners among this group, but divorced men are a 50 percent greater risk, as far as marriage success is concerned, than men entering their first marriage.

One can argue that these figures simply reflect the fact that women who delay marriage until the later ages are a select group of the unmarriageable who choose careers as their only alternative. But if this argument is not the right one, then age must become a practical consideration in a woman's thoughts of marriage.

These facts are important not only to those young women who wish to delay marriage to pursue a business or professional career, but to those who for other personal reasons delay marriage until well into the 20s. Among this group are women who want to enjoy a relatively long period of freedom prior to settling down to the responsibilities of a home. Some want to earn enough to travel, thinking that after marriage they may never have an opportunity to satisfy this desire. Marriage seems so final to many girls; in fact, it means the end of many liberties that their education and experience have caused them to consider highly desirable. For a time at least the girl may place more value on these liberties than on marriage. In some cases in which the girl does not feel this way, her parents may.

Girls sometimes delay marriage primarily because they are cautious rather than because of a desire to achieve another goal in life. They want to be sure they have reached an age when they know what kind of husband they want. They may want the security of a career to fall back on if their marriage should fail or if untimely death should take their husband.

All of these are worthy motives and each must decide for herself whether the goals she seeks to realize before marriage are important enough to justify the risk of finding herself at an age and in a work situation where establishing close friendships with the opposite sex is difficult.

With all the advancement in work opportunities, the desire to marry has remained uppermost in the plans of most women. Whether the "new feminism" will prompt an increasing number of capable women to undertake careers that require years of preparation and involve the likelihood of giving up marriage and motherhood remains to be seen.

AGE FOR MARRIAGE

The growth of singles' clubs and the increase in housing and recreational facilities for the single person are factors in the movement toward single life. Today spinsterhood does not necessarily mean sex denial, although sex outside marriage does not offer the security and continuity desired by most people. The sentiment in the scientific community that in a world rapidly becoming overcrowded the single state should be encouraged for increasing numbers of women may also lessen the value placed on marriage by most women.

The college man at the close of his education has to face certain problems with respect to the time he wishes to marry. Although he is already well past the age when he might reasonably marry, he is likely to endure economic hardship if he marries immediately. If he is entering a profession, he will have a relatively low income for a period of several years. He may, in the face of these economic handicaps, choose to delay marriage. If he delays marriage itself but becomes engaged, there is the difficult problem of living as an engaged person for a long period of time. He may, on the other hand, decide to remain a bachelor, delaying any serious interest in engagement and marriage until he becomes established in his profession and has sufficient income to support the home and family that he desires. There is some danger in this case that he may lose all interest in romantic attachments and fail to marry.

AGE DIFFERENCE OF MARRIAGE MATES

Few problems have been more thoroughly researched over the last 30 years than the possible effect of age difference on marriage success. With the shortage of marriageable males in the population, and the necessity for many young women to marry older men, the question takes on new significance.

Most couples are similar in age, with the male slightly older. This is true in part because girls mature somewhat earlier and wish to marry sooner than men do, and also because the male is still the principal bread winner and must think in terms of earning capacity.

As women have come to earn, the age differential of males has declined. The age difference was 6 years in 1890, when census data were first assembled, now it is 2.6 years. In Europe there has been a wide gap in age of husbands and wives historically for economic reasons. The age difference is still greater there than in the United States, but it is declining as prosperity spreads.

Age difference of the pair is one of the least significant variables studied. As far as getting along together, whether the couple is equal in age or far apart seem not to be measurably important. We have already pointed out that if both are young, there is little chance of a successful marriage. Perhaps if one partner had married an older mate, he might have succeeded.

When marriage age differs by eight to ten years or more, the relationship frequently takes on the character of a father–daughter relationship when the man is older, and a mother–son relationship when the woman is older. Some such marriages do achieve great happiness, but it is possible that they are entered into only when the persons involved prefer the parent–child relationship to one of equality. That is, such marriages may be selective according to particular personality types.

Certain obvious difficulties are inherent in these marriages. If the wife is

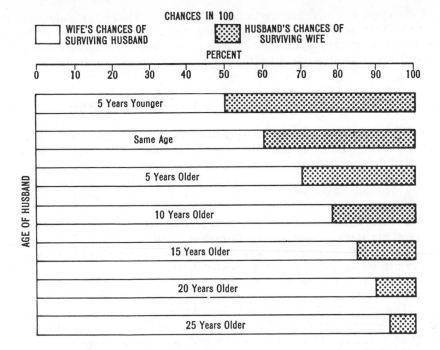

Chances of mate survival by age differences. The longer life span of women, and the fact that they are usually the younger member of the pair means from few to many years of widowhood for the wife in the average marriage. The May–December marriage, where the male is older, greatly increases the likelihood of a long period of widowhood. Source: Metropolitan Life Insurance Company, *Statistical Bulletin*, September, (1953b).

FIGURE 14–4

considerably older, the couple's ability to have children may be greatly decreased; if the husband is decidedly older, the wife is almost certain of a long period of widowhood. If the husband is older by a period of many years, this widowhood may well come while she still has dependent children (see Figure 14–4).

Sex powers of the older person may wane, particularly the male, opening the way for jealousy and suspicion of the younger wife's behavior. The problem is likely more his than hers; many women are quite content with less sexual attention of a man whom they greatly respect and who can provide well for their needs and those of the children. The marriage of the young girl to the older man usually involves marrying up economically and guaranteed financial security.

Time devoted its essay of February 21, 1969, to the theme "In Praise of the May–December Marriages" and made a strong case for them when the male is the older.

The article pointed out how much more common such marriages were in our society in an earlier day, when so many wives died in childbearing, and also how much more usual they have been in Europe than here. *Time* predicts that with the increased length of life, and the number of divorces in the later years of marriage, now that marriages last so long, May–December marriages are sure to increase. They quote the old saying that "it is better to be an old man's darling than become a young man's slave," and add that "it may sometimes be better to be a young woman's darling than an old woman's curmudgeon."

MARRYING THE WIDOWED OR DIVORCED PERSON

The widowed may have had a successful marriage which can be a good credential for a future spouse. This is not so true of the divorced, who make up most of the eligibles in the older group. Second marriages are more risky than first marriages, and remarriage of the divorced woman is somewhat more risky than that of the divorced man, as far as likelihood of another divorce is concerned.

Judson T. Landis (1963a) finds that persons entering their second or subsequent marriage do so with fewer formalities such as formal weddings and engagement rings, and there is less often parental approval. They have more often had sexual intercourse with others than a spouse, and in 75 percent of cases have had premarital coitus before consummating the second or subsequent marriage.

The woman in the city is particularly likely to face this question of marrying a divorced man, for of the men approaching 30—the group to which she is most attracted—there are few single ones who are marriageable. Many in this group have faced repeated rejection and so a widower or divorced man may seem to be a much better marriage prospect. Even college students are not as strongly opposed to marrying divorced persons as some might expect. Judson T. Landis (1968) has asked large numbers of college students in 12 universities, and at two different periods of time, the question, "All other factors being satisfactory, would you marry a person who has been divorced?" In both studies, it was found that 48 percent of the college women would do so; 54 and 56 percent, respectively, of the college men.

Census data show that the rate of failure in second and subsequent marriages is much higher than in the first marriage. The divorced man is a 50 percent higher risk than the single man, and the divorced woman is a somewhat higher risk still. Divorce rates increase with increase in the number of remarriages. Thomas P. Monahan (1958), studying divorce statistics for Iowa during the years 1953–1955, found the rate to be 16.6 per 100 marriages for those in their first marriage. Where one had been divorced, the rate jumped to 36.6 per 100 marriages.

Most marriages in the older age group are of persons previously married; in fact, 23 percent of all marriages are second or subsequent marriages.

PROBLEMS

1   In the light of evidence studied so far in this course, do you feel it is better for a girl to marry a little too young rather than take the risk of not having a chance to marry when she is older?

2 What are your views on the desirability or undesirability of college marriages? Consider your answer from the following standpoints: economics (for example, would you feel it right for the wife to carry the economic burden until the husband is through school?), parenthood, the change in recreational life and freedom involved, studies, risk to completing education, and other problems you foresee. Would you be willing to marry while in college?

3 Beth and Keith are juniors in college. They have dated since their freshman year and have been engaged for over a year and a half. They are quite certain of their compatibility but have serious doubts about advisability of marriage. Beth has one more year to complete her education and Keith must continue for at least another six years before he is prepared for his vocation. He cannot hope to support a wife and home until his education is completed, and since his family is already contributing to his education he can expect little more financial aid from them. Beth feels that is would be a mistake to delay marriage for six years, at which time both would be 26 years old. What would be your advice?

    a Wait the full six years?

    b Marry now and get as much financial help from both families as possible?

    c Marry now but delay parenthood for the six years?

    d Postpone marriage until Beth's graduation and plan to have her support the family?

    e Other advice?

4 *Sociodrama:* A high school senior girl is wondering about the desirability of marrying her 20-year-old fiancé before he is drafted. She discusses the problem with an older girl whose husband is overseas.

5 Which area or areas of maturity do you consider most essential as prerequisites to marriage?

    a Physical maturity—a fully developed body.

    b Intellectual maturity—a fully developed mind.

    c Emotional maturity—understanding and perspective with reference to your own feelings.

    d Vocational maturity—definite vocational goals.

    e Philosophical maturity—a fully developed and satisfying philosophy of life.

6 Discuss the importance of these kinds of maturity and decide which is most essential. Here are three individuals, *A, B,* and *C,* from whom you are to select a marriage partner. None of them is ideal. Choose the one with that combination of traits you consider most important.

    A is—
    physically immature
    intellectually very mature
    emotionally immature

    B is—
    physically very mature
    intellectually immature
    vocationally mature
    emotionally mature

    C is—
    physically mature

intellectually immature
vocationally immature
emotionally very mature

7   Discuss the experiences you have had since high school graduation which have affected your values and tastes in mate selection. Answer such questions as:

    a   Is your "ideal" mate today different from the ideal you held during high school days?

    b   Has your attitude toward having children changed?

    c   What specific experiences have contributed most to any change or maturation you observe?

8   *Research exercise:* Poll the class on the ideal age at which a man and a woman should marry. Tabulate results and make a four-way comparison: men's view of ideal age for man and for woman, women's view of ideal age for woman and for man. If differences are found, try to explain them in terms of (*a*) economic factors, (*b*) customs, (*c*) sex interests, (*d*) maturity, and any other factors that may seem important.

9   *Sociodrama:* A mother tries to discourage her 19-year-old daughter from marrying a man 20 years her senior.

ENGAGEMENT

15 The marriage commitment is legal, and meant to be final. There are many steps in emotional and semicontractual commitment between the beginning of serious intentions and the marriage license. None of them need be taken. The expression of commitment depends on the social class of the couple, local customs, whether they are in school, and other such factors. In the high school and college community, exchanging tokens—class rings or pins, sorority or fraternity insignia, athletic sweaters, charm bracelets, love beads, medallions, or other symbols—precedes the more serious pledge of engagement, usually accompanied by the engagement rings.

Research suggests that these various stages leading up to the engagement are taken more seriously by girls than boys, as perhaps they should be. Girls tend to be more marriage-oriented than boys, and winning in a competition in which they have to play the passive role is more of an achievement. With engagement the relationship passes beyond the recreational level of association to the more serious roles involved with life planning and adult decision-making. Involvements become more than emotional; they become practical also. Decisions must be made, life choices intrude themselves, values and goals must be compared, and certain differences must be reconciled or accepted.

IMPORTANCE OF THE ENGAGEMENT CONTRACT

In all cultures, marriage tends to be formalized by custom, as societies assume that they have a stake in new family formations. In our culture, engagement is a step toward formalizing relationships in the community. Today it does not constitute an irrevocable commitment. The contract is oral and personal, rather than institutionalized. It can be broken by personal choice without the penalties of law or the threat of breach of promise litigation.

Students of marriage find engagement a desirable intermediary step. Elopements, most of which involve no engagement, or a short one at best, are one test of marriage without engagement. Popenoe's (1938) study of 738 elopements shows that in nearly half of them, there was parental objection to the marriage, and that less than half led to happy marriages. When the motive was economic, or the wish to avoid publicity, over half were happy, but when the reason for elopement was pregnancy, only a third were happy.

Landis and Landis' (1973) follow-up study of 581 couples who had eloped and been married an average of seven years, comparing them with 155 couples in the California Court of Conciliation and with 164 divorced persons, shows that 88 percent of the first group had been formally engaged, while only 37 percent of the group seeking counseling and only 57 of the divorced persons had been formally engaged.

Significant as such data are in forecasting the probable outcome of marriages following elopements, lack of engagement is not likely to be the main determining factor. All cultures permit elopements to allow evasion of the formal customs centering around marriage. The writer has hunted with an African tribesman who took his bride into the bush and hunted for survival rather than pay the bride price of cattle or goats. The conditions which surround the elopement are more likely predictive of the outcome of the marriage than the fact of elopement itself.

LENGTH OF ENGAGEMENT

Early studies show a positive relationship between long engagements and success in marriage; those of two or more years have a high ratio of success, whereas those under six months show a high rate of marriage failure, with few leading to good marriage adjustment. Whether these findings still have validity is open to some question. As far as the college generation is concerned, they do not consider long engagements necessary or wise. The writer's classes, almost without exception, unanimously favor engagements of not more than four to six months.

Their reasoning is based on the fact that there are so many preliminary steps preceding formal engagement that many of the issues once deferred to the engagement period are now resolved prior to the engagement. Also, many of the intimacies, confidences, and plans once deferred to engagement are shared prior to the engagement. They seem to feel also that during this preannouncement stage many relationships that would not have weathered the formal engagement period end, and with less public exposure. To the extent that this is true, the length of the engagement ceases to be a primary criterion of the degree of understanding and adjustment.

Today, when young people associate so closely and when considerable physical contact is customary, many authorities are inclined to look upon an engagement of more than a year as producing too much sex tension to be justified, although viewpoints differ on this subject.

Burgess and Cottrell's (1939) study of over 500 married couples showed that only a fourth of those married after an engagement of less than three months made good adjustments in marriage; half of them made poor adjustments, the rest only fair. Those who had no engagement also showed a high proportion of maladjustments. With an engagement period of up to two years or over, the proportion of happy marriages greatly increased. In fact, of those who were engaged two years or more, only 10 percent were characterized by poor marital adjustment. Other studies have shown similar results.

It is open to argument whether length of engagement is the primary factor, or whether people of more steady temperament tend to prolong their engagement; but one thing is certain: A fairly long engagement eliminates many romances that could not have succeeded in marriage.

It is likely that a long acquaintance before engagement is more significant than the long engagement itself. Burgess and Cottrell's early research showed that long acquaintance was associated with good marriage adjustment. Landis and Landis' (1973) study of 581 couples (mentioned above) shows that over 40 percent of each of the two latter groups had known each other less than a year before marrying, whereas only 16 percent of the couples still outside divorce or counseling groups had been so hasty in entering marriage.

If a couple has known each other for a long time and has had a long period of going steady, a lengthy engagement may be less important than if each has known little about the other's background and if they have gone together only a few months before engagement. The really important thing is not how long the engagement is but what is accomplished during the period. Getting really well-acquainted is the most valuable outcome of any engagement, and in nearly all cases getting acquainted takes time.

It is important, too, that a couple be engaged long enough to see whether they can work out patterns of adjustment which will assure the continuing development of an ongoing companionable relationship. A long engagement, however, can do nothing for the couple who are not going in the right direction in their adjustment to each other. They should learn that they never can develop a satisfactory relationship. But a long engagement can give those who are moving in the right direction the opportunity to learn what kinds of adjustment techniques work for them. Both results are equally important—the one in blocking unwise marriages; the other in building assurance that the pair relationship has qualities that will endure in marriage.

Some young people are inclined to feel that marriage can be speeded up. Such a philosophy is particularly prevalent in wartime, and probably explains the high rate of failure of war and postwar marriages. Getting acquainted is deferred until after marriage and then the couple finds that each had married a strange and incompatible person.

Today, the period of serious association is probably no shorter than in an earlier day. Koller (1951) followed the length of going together through three generations, and in all three the serious period of going together covered a median period of a year and a half. The real difference was that in the earlier generations it was not unusual for the couple to have known each other for a lifetime. Today, a couple must spend a great deal of time merely getting acquainted with each other's background, personality, and aspirations. This makes time all the more important in preparing the way for a successful marriage.

In his 1967 study of thousands of college students in a number of universities, Judson T. Landis found that the time between first date and engagement is about the same as it was 25 years ago. The route from first date to marriage takes about three years for the college group. The buildup to a close relationship is slow: the typical pattern is casual dating five months, steady dating eight months (during which time they have an "understanding"), and six months of formal engagement.

This cautious pattern may well explain why college marriages turn out well in a larger proportion of cases. There are the factors of added age and the maturing effect of the educational experience.

DISAGREEMENTS DURING ENGAGEMENT

There is considerable evidence that engagements are seldom calm periods of perfect happiness. With growing intimacy and understanding, and with more frequent and less formal contacts, disagreements are common, and actual quarreling may being. Burgess and Wallin's (1953) study of 1000 engaged couples was focused upon discovering exactly what does happen during the modern engagement. They found that, among the couples studied, agreement on most issues was the rule. On every topic the study covered, some couple disagreed, though the proportion of disagreement varied greatly on different items. As many as one couple in four experienced disagreement on some issues.

The one area in which there was most agreement dealt with dating. Since engagement is primarily a matter of association during dates, this perhaps would be expected. The next highest area of agreement dealt with demonstration of affection. The third was arrangements for marriage. The areas of most frequent disagreement were questions of conventionality, friends, philosophy of life, and ways of dealing with each other's families. This latter indicates that in-law problems actually begin before marriage for at least a fourth of the couples. A more detailed analysis of replies showed that only 17 couples out of the 1000 always agreed in all areas of their relationship. Only 185 always or almost always agreed in all areas of their relationship. Concluding their analysis of the experience of engaged couples, Burgess and Wallin indicated that about two-thirds of the couples experience some strain. They described the engagement period as one in which the couple attempts to adjust "conflicting differences in the interest of the survival of their relationship."

These researchers also asked whether the couples experienced jealousy often, occasionally, or never. Men are the more jealous sex. Their answers were: often, 16.4 percent; occasionally, 55.1 percent; never, 28.5 percent. Forty percent of the women were never jealous; 49.5 percent, occasionally; only 10.5 percent, often. This analysis shows that some insecurity is present during most engagements because of previous dating of the partner, or because of lack of mutual trust, the one doubting the affection of the other. Men seem to suffer from a greater sense of doubt regarding loyalty in the engagement relationship than do women. The authors conclude the young people should not expect the engagement period to be "one of continuous bliss and ecstasy."

The disagreements which arise during the engagement period may conclude in a variety of ways. Frequently they are resolved and the relationship is strengthened for having weathered conflicts. In other cases, the disagreements as they increase in number begin to create serious doubt in the minds of one or both about the desirability of marriage. It was found, in fact, that about half of the men and women studied felt hesitant about the marriage at some time during the engagement period. A fourth of the women and a fifth of the men wished they had never become engaged, and about as many at some time seriously contemplated breaking the engagement.

At such times it is very common for young college people to discuss the advisability of marriage with those in whom they have confidence. Approximately two-thirds of the men and women discussed the advisability of marriage with their respective mothers; over a third, with their respective fathers; a fourth, with friends; and a smaller percentage, with other relatives, with doctors, etc. Almost half of both men and women at some time during the engagement felt hesitant about marrying the person to whom they were engaged. About one in four engaged couples, at some time during the relationship, broke off temporarily. Moreover, 16 percent of the men and 23 percent of the women had had previous engagements, and 15 percent of the couples studied, later broke their engagements.

These data indicate quite clearly that among college engagements, at least, there are frequently serious doubts and uncertainties about the desirability of following through to marriage. Burgess and Wallin conclude that the love relationship desired in the American marriage could scarcely be realized without considerable association between men and women before marriage; that there is reason to believe "that various combinations of men and women differ considerably in their probabilities of developing into more or less durable love relationships." Trial and error, they feel, is necessary in order to ensure the maximum number of desirable combinations. Often the relationship proves to be inadequate.

Burgess and Wallin also conclude that one of the serious weaknesses of the engagement period is that it is too often carried on exclusively in an atmosphere of recreation and play, giving an unrealistic picture of what marriage will be like.

ENGAGEMENT CONFESSIONS

Mark Twain is reputed to have said, "Confession is good for the soul, but bad for the reputation." The very real feeling of interrelatedness of those deeply in love often induces a mood of confession and repentance. During the engagement period, or even before, young people frequently feel a strong urge to confess all their past sins to each other, the girl to test his love, the boy to shed his guilt.

This seems to be a normal phase in the development of love, particularly for the male. Sometimes this way of relieving guilt feelings for past misconduct is an asset, not only to the individual, but to the couple. It may be an indication that the couple has become intimate enough to want to share with each other secrets known to no other. It may also indicate a strong sense of mutual need and trust.

The question of the desirability of confession at such a time is not so simple, however, as it initially appears. One might well ask himself, "Will the other person have the background to absorb these confessions with understanding, or will it only raise doubts and uncertainty about the advisability of marriage?"

Of course, it all depends upon the kind of thing being confessed and whether or not it has a bearing on the marriage. Certainly if there are factors in one's background that might have a direct or serious bearing on the marriage, the person one intends to marry should know about them.

Landis and Landis (1973) found that all engaged students they studied of both sexes confessed nervous breakdowns, suspected bad hereditary traits, previous marriage, and having a child out of wedlock, although, of course, few had such serious issues in their background. Almost three-fourths of boys who had had sex experience with another girl confessed it; two-thirds of girls with previous sex experience confessed it. Petting experiences were confessed in approximately 60 percent of cases; a higher proportion of boys with experience than of girls with experience confessed.

Later studies (Landis and Landis 1973) found that almost all students do confess their past necking and petting experiences, and most of those having had premarital sexual intercoruse confess (91 percent of men and 86 percent of women). Those who have had serious family problems also reveal them.

If one is in doubt as to whether it is the kind of confession that might help or hinder the marriage and whether it actually needs to be made, it is often better to talk to a physician, counselor, minister, or other confidant first. It is useful to get the advice of a third party before taking the risk of revealing matters which may have no significance whatever to the marriage and may actually create mistrust. It is not wise to confess matters which are of no consequence to the marriage and which may be held against one later.

THE PREMARITAL EXAMINATION

A premarital physical examination is required in many states. Often it is only to check for venereal disease. Sometimes it includes other possible problem areas but, in general, it should be more extensive than it is. The examination is usually sought immediately before the marriage. A much better practice, for the girl, is for her to visit a doctor, marriage clinic, or specialist in women's problems three months before marriage so that she may benefit by a long period of counsel. In cases where the hymen has to be stretched, or special treatment given, this can be carried on for a period of time before marriage. There is also the advantage of gaining confidence and understanding by discussing the sexual aspect of marriage with someone who is objective and understanding. This has great value for women who have strong taboos regarding sex teachings and behavior. During this period, there is time for the woman to acquire knowledge of contraception from her doctor, be fitted with a contraceptive device and learn how to use it, or build pregnancy immunity with "the pill."

By starting early the couple will also have time to investigate with a specialist their hereditary backgrounds, possible defects of organic development, and other factors that might have a bearing on successful adjustment in marriage and the rearing of children. Couples should be able to discuss sex matters and attitudes together and with the doctor. They should not hesitate to discuss with a doctor or marriage counselor the psychological as well as the physical aspects of sexual adjustment. They should read books which will give them information as to techniques and attitudes appropriate to the sexual relationship in marriage.

The latter part of the engagement period should, of course, be a period in which the young people enter into a serious discussion of aspirations with regard to children and family. This is the time to understand fully each other's attitudes and interests in children. Some states grant an annulment if one party can prove that the other had decided prior to the marriage not to have children. Although most young people plan to have children, not all do so. The prospective mate has a right to know this beforehand.

A study of two generations (Paul Landis 1951) shows that 90.8 percent of the present generation of married college women and wives of college students discussed children with their prospective husbands before marriage and 55 percent sought premarital advice, as compared to 50.4 percent and 25.2 percent, respectively, of the previous generation.

PREMARITAL COUNSELING

A comparison of two generations (Paul Landis 1951) on the source of premarital advice showed that of the mother's generation only a fourth sought premarital advice; of the married daughters, 55 percent did. Among mothers, few sought advice from anyone but relatives and friends. Three-fourths of the daughters who sought advice consulted a doctor. None in the parent's generation sought the advice of a minister or teacher. One in ten daughters consulted a minister; one in 35, a teacher. Intelligent young people with access to marriage clinics should not hesitate to seek advice and to put their love under critical examination by counselors experienced in the complexities of human relationships. The counselor is the best person to consult about the biological and psychological aspects of marriage, and he can advise on conflicts and differences that may have led to doubt in the relationship, and on any other problems that may seem important. A counsel does not moralize or condemn. His business is to see the client's problems from the client's viewpoint, help the client view them objectively, and assist, when necessary, in working out mutually satisfying solutions. The counselor can also give advice on practical matters dealing with marriage itself: legal steps in obtaining a license, how much to pay the preacher, etc. In the well-developed marriage clinic, too, there is a medical specialist who gives full time to pelvic examinations, problems of birth control and sterility, and various other psychosexual aspects of the marriage relationship.

The oldest marriage clinic in America, the American Institute of Family Relations at Los Angeles, has for many years given premarital emotional maturity tests to couples coming for advice previous to marriage. These tests, combined with a thorough physical examination, make up a major part of the premarital counseling. Couples who go through the clinic and who are reassured of their suitability for one another show a high rate of success in marriage.

Paul Popenoe says that not one divorce occurred among couples who came to the institute for premarital assistance during the first eight years of its existence. This record is outstanding, for the clinic is in the city of Los Angeles where the divorce rate is high. Marriage fitness tests have been used extensively in the marriage clinic at Pennsylvania State University. Writing a few years after it was established, Clifford Adams, psychologist and director of the marriage clinic, stated (Adams and Packard 1946, Preface):

> . . . hundreds of couples who were tested before marriage at the Marriage Counseling Service are checked periodically after marriage to find how they are making out. Of all the marriages which the service predicted would be successful, not one has yet ended in divorce or separation. Most of the people who went ahead despite the clinic's cautions are already in serious trouble or have been divorced.

While this testimony is convincing, it does not necessarily mean that all divorces would be done away with if all young people would go to a premarital clinic for counsel and heed its advice. Since the marriage clinic is a new institution, it is to be expected that most of those who have used it have been the intelligent and serious persons who are willing to face facts and follow wise counsel. This may mean that most young people who have used the clinic would have been successful in marriage anyway. There can be no doubt that specialists in counseling can be most helpful to any prospective marriage.

That counseling should be on a broad scale is suggested by David Mace (1972), who says that a common complaint of those having trouble in marriage is "Why didn't someone tell me *that* before I married?" "That" unknown covers many things. Certainly one of the most important unknowns is the extent to which the young child confines the young mother and restricts the social and recreational activities of the couple.

"That" may involve hereditary defects in offspring which could have been avoided had the couple sought genetic counseling prior to marriage and learned what recessive traits they each carried. "That" may be the discovery that the mate has a philosophy of child training that is entirely incompatible and from one's viewpoint intolerable to live with. Good counseling sessions will bring such differences into the open where they can be discussed. If no reconciliation of viewpoints is possible, seeking a mate with a more suitable background or genetic quality may be the only solution to the couple's problem.

TIME TO GET ACQUAINTED—
AN INDISPENSABLE PRECAUTION

Of all the simple precautions to ensure marriage happiness, the most obvious and readily accessible one is time—enough to know that the match is a suitable one. Most marriage failures are courtship failures. This point cannot be over-stressed.

The key to success seems to be through acquaintance—being together enough before marriage to know whether there is a basis for compatibility. Marriage, in order to last, must be based on lasting qualities, which cannot be tested in whirlwind romances ending in premature marriages. Of course, almost everyone knows of a marriage like this that has succeeded, but research evidence suggests that such marriages are among those lucky accidents in life. Most marriages hastily contracted do not survive.

Figure 15–1, dealing with 526 married couples, gives a characteristic picture of research on this subject. It indicates that less than a fourth of the "under six months" couples made a good adjustment. (Remember that the couples who divorced quickly have been eliminated, since this is a study of married couples.) Half of these survivors in marriage considered their marriage adjustment poor. The proportion of good adjustments increased with increased length of acquaintance.

Whether people with short get-acquainted periods represent a type of

Relationship of marital happiness to length of acquaintance. Short acquaintance before marriage means great risk. Source: Based on data from Ernest W. Burgess and Leonard S. Cottrell, *Predicting Success or Failure in Marriage* (Copyright 1939 by Prentice-Hall, Inc., New York). Reproduced by permission of the publisher.   **FIGURE 15–1**

LENGTH OF FRIENDSHIP BEFORE MARRIAGE	POOR ADJUSTMENT	FAIR ADJUSTMENT	GOOD ADJUSTMENT
Under 6 months	46%	31%	23%
6–23 months	38%	22%	40%
2–4 years	28%	28%	44%
5 years and more	5%	38%	47%

temperament that fails in marriage, or whether these same people, had they prolonged their dating and engagement, would have broken up their relationship, we can only guess. It seems reasonable to suppose that the length of the period is not in itself the only reason for unsuccessful marriages, although it could be an important factor. The early stages of dating are often very romantic; marriage at this time might lead a person to expect more than any marriage can realize. A lengthened, steady-dating period usually brings about a more reasonable understanding of the person, and diffuses the halo effect of early romance.

Warning Signals

Length of acquaintance alone will not guarantee a successful marriage. Many people marry who know each other so well already that they have serious misgivings about their compatibility, and yet move ahead toward marriage and later regret. So this rule must be added: "Heed the danger signals!"

A case comes to mind of a minister's wife who, after 15 years, had to end her marriage. There were two children, a boy and a girl. When she left her husband to prepare for teaching, she took the boy with her and left the daughter with the husband. In leaving the church, she faced great opposition. There was a serious threat to her husband's position in the church as well as great pressure from the bishop to get her to stay merely to put on a proper front. She finally told him that even if it wrecked the whole church she could tolerate the marriage no longer; it was a question of breaking up the marriage or going to a mental institution. She admitted she had no one to blame but herself for the 15 years of misery she had endured. During the eight years they were going together his intolerance, tendency to dominate her, refusal to genuinely accept her as an equal, and coldness, had all troubled her greatly. But, he was a good man, a Christian, and a minister. She felt that there must be something wrong with her. The prestige of his work, her desire to share in it, and the service it represented, made a great appeal to her. She said that she hoped that, by some magic, marriage would change the situation with regard to their interpersonal relations; she went ahead into a marriage which almost destroyed her.

A Canadian girl wrote and asked whether she should marry a person she had been going with for some years. She described him and her many reactions to him. Among her comments was, "He has a way of talking which I find rather obnoxious."

Why should a young lady need advice as to whether to marry under these circumstances? If she finds certain traits very obnoxious on an occasional date, how is she going to tolerate this man across the table three times a day?

Landis and Landis' (1973) follow-up study of 581 married couples, mentioned earlier, shows that only 29 percent of the first group had considered breaking their engagement, 44 percent of the group in counseling, 50 percent of the divorced persons. The successful group had only 9 percent who had temporarily broken their engagement, the others 26 and 22 percent, respectively. Of the successful group 90 percent had felt confident the marriage would be happy, 83 percent in the counseling group and only 71 percent of the divorced persons. This would seem to indicate that seriousness of adjustment problems is somewhat predictive of marriage difficulties and outcome, and that their own expectations for the marriage had some predictive value. It appears there was considerable unwarranted optimism.

In this same Landis study, parents' approval or disapproval was a more predictive factor as to wisdom of the marriage than the couple's own faith as to outcome. Of the successful couples, 84 percent had approval of the marriage from both sets of parents, while only 58 percent of the groups in serious difficulty had approval.

ENGAGEMENT FAILURE

Various studies place the rate of failure of engagements at from one-third to one-half. Even so, some students of marriage feel that more should be broken, basing their opinion on the number of marriages which fail after a short time.

Reasons for failure in serious affairs was investigated extensively among college students at the University of Minnesota some years ago (Kirkpatrick and Caplow 1945). The causes of conflict in serious affairs involving college students were (most common first): jealousy, possessiveness, criticism, irritability arising from emotional tension, dislike of friends, accusations of loss of interest, disagreement about the future, dominance, dependence, exploitation. While these issues cause much grief in serious affairs, these specific reasons were not given as the ones responsible for the breaking up of love affairs. The 71 men in this study who reported broken love affairs had broken 230 affairs in all; the 121 women interviewed accounted for a total of 414 unsuccessful affairs. The reasons given were (most frequent first): mutual loss of interest, subject's interest in another person, partner's interest in another person, parents, friends.

Much of the dissimilarity between these two lists can probably be accounted for on the basis of specificity. Loss of interest, and interest in another by one or the other or both, which accounts for the termination of about 90 percent of the affairs in the second list are, without doubt, the result of such factors as jealousy, possessiveness, criticism, etc., that rank high in the first list.

Affairs where both lose interest are the easiest to terminate. There is little explaining or rationalizing to do and presumably no one is seriously hurt. Where one causes the breakup because he or she has found another, it is a different matter. Here there is the possibility of the deserted partner suffering jealousy, defeat, humiliation, and other feelings which the love relationship is capable of producing.

Parental influence is often a factor in the girl's reasons, perhaps indicating that parents watch the mate-selection process of the girl more than that of the boy. Would these same types of conflict issues be equally operative in the breakup of noncollege couples or in the breaking of engagements? There has been little attempt to study the noncollege population. Undoubtedly parental influence is often a factor in the termination of affairs among younger teenagers and is likely to be exerted before engagements take place.

What proportion of serious college affairs break up? The study above shows that 71 percent of the serious love affairs of the girls had been broken; 73 percent of those of the men. The median age of the group at the time of the study was 22 years.

About what proportion of couples make a go of their affairs up to engagement? Burgess and Wallin's (1953) study of 1000 engagements showed that only 20–30 percent of young people have never gone steadily with anyone except their future spouse. Most college students have gone with two or more persons before becoming engaged.

The average engagement is not without its periods of doubts and conflicts. These alone cannot be reason enough for breaking an engagement. Are there any clues to indicate when a couple should cease their attempts at adjustment and turn instead to new relationships? In any serious affair, whether it involves a ring, a pin, or a promise, the following situations should be considered definite indications that the relationship holds little promise of future success:

1 *When many reforms in the partner are planned for after marriage:* Changing one's ways—habits, ideas, and values—is a difficult job, one that takes time and effort. It always seems easier to try to change the other person to fit one's own way of life than to make fundamental changes in oneself.

This reluctance to change one's own ways, coupled with the desire to erase the annoying or distasteful habits, attitudes, and manners in the prospective mate, is the cause of many major difficulties in marriage. When one marries, he or she is taking a "person" with a fully developed personality, not a piece of clay that can be molded into any desired form. The man or woman who marries with the expectation of remaking the new spouse into a more desirable person is in for a rude awakening.

Everyone carries into marriage the same ways of meeting problems that were used before marriage. The woman who escapes into illness rather than meet the unpleasant issues of life will likely resort to this same escape in marriage, where there are even more issues to be faced. The man who thinks this technique of adjustment will be changed by marriage is fooling himself. The man who has used drinking as an escape from problems before marriage will find even more worries to escape after marriage. In times of crisis he is likely to resort again to drinking rather than face and attempt to solve his problems. A woman who thinks she will change this is usually kidding herself.

Irritability, intolerance, moodiness, lack of respect and consideration, placing blame on others rather than shouldering it oneself—these and many other such traits are likely to be magnified rather than cured by marriage.

The writer once conferred with a college couple who failed in part because the husband tried to correct the way his wife walked. His nagging became intolerable. Another couple failed in marriage when the husband kept trying to get his wife to correct a slight lisp in her speech which dated back to her childhood and which she probably could not correct. Why should these men have married these girls if they found such traits obnoxious? Why didn't they choose girls they would not have to remake? Many other men would have had no objection to these traits.

One suspects it was not until after marriage that they realized these traits might reflect unfavorably on them in professional circles. Maybe they did object to the traits before marriage and sincerely thought they could change them. It may be that these traits became the object of attack, when more basic matters were involved.

Mutual respect is an essential of the marriage relationship. If one finds himself losing it during engagement because of traits that seem obnoxious, prove embarrassing in social relationships, or threaten to reflect unfavorably on one's work, conventions, or reputation, it is time to be wary.

There are young marriageable people whom one will not need to reform, if one is realistic. If one's standards are so impossibly high that everyone of the opposite sex seems to have many annoying traits, then successful marriage is out of the question anyway. If one must do a lot of reforming, it is better to attempt to do it before marriage. Then, the chances are that the marriage will not take place and both will be saved much trouble.

2 *When the couple recognizes failure in adjusting toward a compatible relationship:* The patterns of adjustment that are established during the serious stage of dating will be the ones carried over into marriage. If roles of dominance and submission are evident then, they will characterize the marriage. If equality is the pattern established, this will likely continue into marriage. If quarreling is the method of adjustment, rather than discussion and working out of solutions to problems, this will probably carry over into marriage. If one or the other of the pair puts parents, brothers, or sisters first in his emotional attachments, marriage will not cure this. An objective appraisal of the relationship by oneself, or better still by fair-minded friends and relatives who observe the match, will tell a great deal about what the marriage is to be. So, also, will an objective analysis by a marriage counselor or other professional person of wide experience. Such case-history observations are valid measures of the potential marriage, allowing for the margin of error that enters into all such human judgments.

The most extensive study of serious love relationships to date, that by Burgess and Wallin (1953), has related engagement success to later marriage success. The authors work on the assumption that the type of interpersonal relationships begun during the period of going steady and being engaged, will not be radically altered in marriage, and that, therefore, the adjustment made during the engagement is predictive of the kind of adjustment that will be made in the marriage.

Among the engagement factors found to offer a basis for forecasting the success of the marriage are: (*a*) the nature and degree of love of the couple; (*b*) their temperamental compatibility; (*c*) their emotional interdependence, dependence, and independence; (*d*) their common interests, including their attitude toward children; (*e*) their method of making decisions and the locus of their authority; (*f*) their adaptability; (*g*) their vulnerability to adverse factors such as interference by relatives and friends, economic difficulties, etc. This research suggests that the adjustment level reached during engagement sets a couple's pattern for the marriage and offers a basis for forecasting its success.

On a statistical basis, this study reports a correlation of 0.50 between engagement history and other engagement factors, and marriage success. The researchers explain the lack of a higher correlation by such factors as the inadequacy of tests of success of engagement and inadequacy of measures of success in marriage, and by dynamic factors which enter into the relationship in marriage that were not foreseen.

3 *When one or both lost interest:* Loss of interest is one of the most frequently given reasons for the termination of an engagement or serious affair. This is actually only a simple way of indicating any one of a number of things. Dissimilarity of backgrounds, interests, and values generally lead to gradual loss of attraction, as may the more or less serious personality deficiencies or unpleasant personal traits in one or the other—traits which were not discernible or were easily forgiven early in the affair. Loss of interest may merely indicate that the relationship was never intended to lead to marriage—that it was, in fact, only a "grown-up" version of going steady. Many such casual affairs do become serious without the couple's giving up their intention to refrain from marriage. This is often true of young people in school or professional training. When the motivation of marriage is lacking, attraction generally eventually dies of its own accord. When the attraction gets out of control and problems of deeper involvement, particularly of a sexual nature, begin to threaten, such couples usually change their plans in favor of marriage or they break up.

The common expression for the undesirable deep emotional involvement is "getting too serious," by which women mean that the male has begun to demand a sexual relationship, and by which men mean that the female wants to get married.

Breaking Up

Occasionally, a couple feel trapped in their relationship with each other. When they say this, they may mean several things—emotional involvement that they find difficult to break, physical attachment where a complete sexual relationship has been established, social responsibility in the cases of pregnancy, or involvement of family and friends and possessions. Men more often feel trapped in the serious relationship than do women. Where sexual intercourse is involved, men more often feel trapped than do women, since they may believe it unfair to terminate the relationship. If an affair has been of long duration the man may feel, too, that it is unjust to drop the woman after having kept her restricted for so long.

The emotional damage of the breakup is, of course, the important thing from the standpoint of facing the future. Unless the relationship terminates by mutual agreement and on the basis of loss of interest, there are likely to be severe readjustment problems for at least one of the mates. Most student reactions indicate that there is considerable emotional turmoil in the breakup of a serious affair. In fact, one suspects that the breakup of love affairs is responsible for the most serious emotional crises facing young people today.

In the background of the breakup are such factors as repeated misunderstandings, conflicts, and a growing awareness of differences in background, aspirations, values, and life plans. There may be opposition of parents or of other relatives and friends, coldness due to separations or to a growing recognition of undesirable personality traits, and an awareness of cultural, economic, religious, or other differences that foreshadow trouble.

Assuming this kind of background in the couple's love development, there are five steps through which the breakup goes, according to the most extensive study made to date (Burgess and Wallin 1953): (1) difficulties involving misunderstandings and quarrels; (2) the actual breaking of the engagement, which may be an abrupt act or a tapering-off process; (3) the emotional crisis, the severity of which depends somewhat upon the extent to which it has been expected by both parties; (4) the rebound experience which often leads to a new emotional involvement with someone else; (5) a reappraisal of the engagement experience in terms of future behavior. This study finds that the person is often more cautious in making a new commitment, sometimes even cynical concerning the fidelity of the opposite sex.

The period of time required "to get over it" varies little between broken engagements and other serious affairs. In both cases the range is from one or two weeks to over two years (Landis and Landis 1973).

College students studied at the University of Minnesota (Kirkpatrick and Caplow 1945) were asked about various "adaptive reactions" in an attempt to get some insight into the emotions and problems that followed the breakup of serious affairs. The reactions reported were (most frequent first): remembering only pleasant things, dreaming about partner, day-dreaming, frequenting places with common associations, preserving keepsakes, reading over old letters, imagining recognition, liking or disliking people because of resemblance, attempting meetings, avoiding meetings, avoiding places with common associations, remembering only unpleasant things, imitating mannerisms. There is considerable evidence of day-dreaming and of thinking about pleasant bygone dating days. About half of the group got over the affair immediately, but a third of the men and a fifth of the women said it took them several weeks. Another fifth of the women and 7.7 percent of the men said it took them several months. Five percent of the men and 5.3 percent of the women said it took a year. The real sufferers, 5.3 percent of women and 2.3 percent of the men said it took several years. One may well suppose that some of this group will never get over the broken affair to the point of being able to love and marry.

Getting over an engagement is similar. The time required may range all the way from a week or two to over two years. Landis and Landis (1973) indicate that over two-thirds of young college people get over the emotional effects of a broken engagement in less than six months, and only 12 percent suffer ill effects after a period of two years.

The Landis study of 1059 students in 11 colleges showed that the typical reaction of the young college person to the breakup of love affairs is to remember the association as a pleasant one. About two-thirds have this reaction. Almost as many soon begin dating somebody else as an aftereffect of the breakup of the engagement. More than a fourth continue to day-dream about the lost lover.

Almost a third of the girls preserve keepsakes from the previous love affair; few boys do this. Half of the young people report trying to avoid meeting him or her afterward. About an equal number attempt to meet him or her. Girls are more likely to reread old letters, to remember pleasant associations, frequent places where the couple have been together, day-dream, and so forth. It is only rarely that one or the other thinks of suicide.

No doubt the kind of emotional reaction that follows a broken love affair depends somewhat on the way the break is made. There are mean ways to break up. If the couple discusses the situation reasonably and tries to face a solution together, the aftereffects should not be too serious. The most tragic affairs, no doubt, are those in which one person is still very deeply attached and wishes to continue the relationship to marriage and the other, seeing no possible future in the situation, breaks it abruptly without discussing the matter with the partner. This is particularly serious for the individual who is left with the feeling that something is seriously wrong with him or her.

The broken affair or engagement becomes a serious threat to future marriage prospects if the lost partner was idealized to the point that all future affairs pale. The "phantom lover" experience is less common today, when most young people have dated enough to know they have another chance. The seriousness with which most breakups are taken may be more an indication of lack of previous experience than it is a measure of love. One who has dated widely before becoming serious can probably face the future with optimism; those with little or no previous dating experience would be more likely to suffer bereavement on an involuntary termination.

PROBLEMS

1 After an engagement of 16 months which of the following discoveries would probably lead you to break your engagement?

 a He or she has an uncle in a mental institution.
 b He or she confesses to having sexual relations with another person at the age of 13.
 c He or she refuses to join your church.
 d He or she suggests not inviting a certain old friend to the wedding because "he wears such odd clothes people would laugh."
 e He or she refuses to establish a home in another community because of parental wishes.
 f He or she still enjoys flirting with casual acquaintances.
 g He or she shows slight tendencies toward characteristics of the other sex.
 h He or she looks down upon the social and economic status of your family.
 i He or she keeps asking questions about your past instead of reassuring you of unqualified devotion.
 j He or she suddenly suggests that you extend your engagement for another six months and that three of these months be spent in separation to test the love.

2 Your close friend is brokenhearted because his girl has just returned their engagement ring. What would your advice to him be?

 a Forget her and start dating Jean who thinks you are attractive.
 b Ask her to give you one more chance.
 c Try to make her jealous by dating other girls.
 d Talk it over with her parents.
 e Spend most of your free time on something else for a little while—reading, outdoor life, traveling.
 f Make sure that some of the other girls know that breaking up was her decision.
 g Decide once and for all that is is better to date than to ever get serious.

3   Do you believe that if a young man begins to tire of his fiancée he should:

     a   Tell her outright and break the engagement.

     b   Gradually show his loss of interest.

     c   Ask a friend to tell her.

     d   Be seen with someone else.

     e   Wait for her to break the engagement no matter how long it takes.

     f   Initiate the subject deviously even if it takes several weeks to make the point.

   Do the views of the boys and girls in the class tend to differ in their choice of alternatives and the arguments by which they support them?

4   List the advantages of a broken engagement over a broken marriage.

5   Bob and Marcy are physically very much attracted to one another. They enjoy the same books and sports, they agree on family size and politics; but Marcy suggests breaking the engagement when she discovers how different are their codes of ethics. Think of a number of situations in which ethics might seriously endanger a marriage.

6   *Sociodrama:* Jim and Kay thought they were "made for each other," but now Kay is suggesting they break their engagement. Let their friendly but serious discussion touch upon some of the situations or discoveries that have brought them to the point of breakup.

7   *Sociodrama:* The wedding is a week away. Most of the gifts have arrived; the wedding gown in finished, the wedding invitations have been sent out, and reservations have been made for a honeymoon. The young bride-to-be has just admitted to herself what she has subconsciously known for a long time, that she has been in love with love, not with her fiance. In a burst of fear and uncertainty she rushes to her parents for advice and comfort.

   The drama pictures the attitudes of a level-headed father, the excited mother, and the very upset daughter.

8   Should a couple refrain from breaking their engagement because of the embarrassment it would cause and the talk it would create?

9   *Sociodrama:* A young woman visits a marriage counselor and, among other things, brags that she and her fiance "never disagree on anything." The counselor is dismayed. Continue the discussion emphasizing the questions the counselor might ask.

10   Study the following list of items about which an engaged couple might find themselves in disagreement. Be ready to discuss areas where disagreement would cause you to question the desirability of marriage.

     a   Whether to have a large formal wedding ceremony.

     b   Number of children desired.

     c   Whether to have children.

     d   Politics.

     e   Religion.

     f   Whether "the man runs the family."

     g   What is "good" in music and art.

     h   How children should be disciplined.

     i   Whether to buy a home or spend the money on a long trip.

     j   Leisure time interests.

11   An engaged couple who are deeply in love ran across a "marriage success" test in a popular magazine. The test, composed by an outstanding man in the field, indicated that their chances for marriage success were very slim. What would your advice to this couple be?

12   Clifford and Madelaine were engaged. While Clifford was stationed overseas he had a brief affair with an English girl. Should he:

a   Describe the whole affair to his prospective wife?

b   Let her know there was such an affair?

c   Say nothing about it?

13   Are there psychological as well as physical reasons for the premarital physical examination?

14   What are your reactions to the idea that couples who are in love can take tests which will tell them whether they can succeed in marriage with one another?

15   Under what circumstances would it be unwise for an individual to confide all his past history to his prospective mate, or do you feel each should tell everything about his past?

THE RESEARCH SCORE ON PREMARITAL SEXUAL EXPERIENCE

16 Throughout civilizations chastity has seldom been a significant norm. It has little if any survival value. The problem of man, until recently, has been one of providing enough offspring for the race to survive the slaughter of disease, pestilence, famine, and war. As civilizations advance, chastity becomes important to the maintenance of family position among the upper classes. Such families have much to lose should their young become bound to those who do not represent the same level of affluence and wealth.

The increase in premarital sexual activity on the college campus is in part a reflection of the entrance to college of increasing numbers of the lower middle class and the upper lower class. These classes have never had strict rules concerning chastity, because they have not had a social position to guard. The climate of the times is, of course, a pervading influence.

TRENDS IN PREMARITAL SEXUAL BEHAVIOR

The press is generous with words about the "sexual revolution" on the campus, and at times implies that it has reached the level of promiscuity. Careful studies of student attitudes and behavior are more temperate in findings. Of course, it must be assumed that the more permissive the culture from which young acquire their norms, the more sexual activity there will be. So far there has been much less alteration of behavior than of conversation and attitudes. For most young people, guilt feelings are still a part of violating the moral code in the sexual area. The proportion of college women who engage in premarital coitus has increased, particularly among juniors and seniors. Even so, violators of the moral code suffer a great deal of anxiety. It is believed that the proportion of males having premarital sexual relationships has been relatively constant. Even those who restrict themselves are reluctant to condemn another for sexual relationships with an engaged partner. A common statement runs something like this: "I could not have sexual relationships until I marry, but I do not blame those who can and do."

Landis and Landis (1973) conducted a study of 1005 men and 2184 women in 18 colleges and universities, and compared attitudes toward premarital sexual relations with a similar study they made in 1952 and a Cornell study in 1940. More permissive attitudes are reflected. In 1967, more than three times as many males as in 1940 believed sexual relationships were proper for both (15 percent compared to 47 percent). The proportion of women holding this view had risen from 6 percent to 21 percent. Only 24 percent of men and 39 percent of women felt both should be chaste.

Kanin and Howard (1958), studying 177 wives of college students in a midwest university, found that 43.5 percent had had sexual intercourse prior to marriage. This study confirms other studies which show that social class and religion are factors in frequency: the lower the social class of the wife, the more likely she is to have permitted sexual intercourse before marriage, particularly if engaged to an upper-class male. Seriousness about religion is a great deterrent to premarital sexual intercourse. Concerning social class, Kanin and Howard suggest that more than differences in class mores are in operation; the upper-class male is probably exploitive of the lower-class female in a way he is not with one of his own status or above; the lower-class female, lacking other devices of attraction, uses sex to the maximum advantage in winning her man.

The Landis (1958) study of students in 18 colleges and universities found 1 percent of women and 4 percent of men had sexual relations during casual dating; during steady dating it rose to 29 percent of men and 12 percent of women; during formal engagement 48 and 45 percent respectively. Packard (1968) reports that 43 percent of college-educated women had had coitus before they married, compared to 27 percent reported earlier by Kinsey. The trend is in the direction of permissiveness with affection, and even greater permissiveness with engagement commitment.

Coombs (1971) polled 54 physicians and 78 marriage counselors, professional people closest to the behavior of young people in the current moral-sex scene. Slightly over a fourth of physicians and about a third of the marriage counselors see a "flamboyant sexual revolt" taking place. Numbers were even lower on the "new morality" issue.

Various surveys made currently suggest that the proportion of males having coitus during college has increased from around 55 percent at the beginning of the century to perhaps as many as 75 percent today. The increase for college women seems to be from around a fourth at the beginning of the century to perhaps around half today. The greatest incidence is during the junior and senior years, when many are engaged (Packard 1968; *Time,* 1974).

In a 1969 survey for *Time,* the Louis Harris Poll studied changing American morals. Marked changes in sexual morality were evidenced among professionals, college graduates, prosperous citizens of suburbia, and those under 30. Those over 50, the less educated, and less prosperous still clung to traditional sexual morality.

There is a growing tendency to evaluate sex, not in terms of right and wrong, but of whether it is a genuine expression of affection. The test becomes a psychological rather than a moral one. The question has changed from "Is it right?" to "Is it right under the circumstances which exist between us?"

While there can be little doubt that a large proportion of college girls live by traditional codes, an increasing number are willing to grant others the right to live according to their own conscience. Perhaps the greatest risk in this kind of atmosphere is that many girls, who have a built-in conscience clearly defining right for themselves, try to embrace the other code and find themselves inflicted with deep psychological wounds. Their rationalizations, their reading of supporting literature from "experts," their discussion with peers, do not quiet their conscience.

This is by no means a female problem only. The male is more immune from restrictions of morality because few families instill in the male so strict a code, yet there are college men who suffer deeply from having reached beyond the bounds of their internalized moral values. There are also more college men who live by a strict moral code than the popular magazines would lead one to believe.

A BROAD VIEW OF PREMARITAL SEXUAL EXPERIENCE

An anthropological study by Murdock (1950) of 250 societies throughout the world shows that 70 percent permit sexual experimentation before marriage. Even among the 30 percent which place a taboo upon premarital sexual relations, the taboo most often applies only to girls. In many of these societies, marriage comes soon after puberty. The prohibition against premarital intercourse is actually a prohibition against prepubertal intercourse. In most societies also the taboo is upper class only.

This study concludes that there is nothing in human societies generally to indicate that a taboo on premarital sexual relations has any value to survival of the group. In most societies it is assumed that premarital intercourse has no relationship to postmarital fidelity (all societies seek postmarital fidelity); in other words, it does not seem to interfere with the function of the family institution, once marriage has been entered into. (Evidence that it increases marital infidelity in our society is presented later in this chapter.)

Where premarital sexual relations are sanctioned, intercourse usually is not extensive or promiscuous. The society recognizes it as a means of preparing for marriage, rather than as a means of indulging in sexual excitement as such.

So much for human experience in the broader perspective. Are there reasons why our society should differ in this matter from the general norm? Does it actually differ?

REASONS FOR AND AGAINST PREMARITAL COITUS

The question of premarital coitus is one of the most important issues facing couples today from the beginning of their casual contacts through the engagement period. Numerous reasons for and against premarital coitus are advanced. Kinsey (1953) has summarized these arguments as found in the marriage manuals:

REASONS FOR PREMARITAL INTERCOURSE

1   It may satisfy a physiological need for a sexual outlet.
2   It may become a source of immediate physical and psychological satisfaction.
3   If there is no guilt, it may increase one's ability to function more effectively in other, nonsexual fields.
4   It is more valuable than solitary sexual activity for developing one's capacity to make emotional adjustments with other persons.
5   It may develop one's capacity to make the particular sorts of emotional adjustments which are needed in marital relationships.
6   It may provide training in the sorts of physical techniques that may be involved in marital coitus.
7   It may test the capacities of two persons to make satisfactory sexual adjustments after marriage.
8   It is easier to learn to make emotional and physical adjustments at an earlier age; they are learned with greater difficulty after marriage.
9   Failure in a premarital relationship is socially less disastrous than failure after marriage.
10   Heterosexual experience may prevent the development of a homosexual pattern of behavior.
11   Premarital coitus may lead to marriage.
12   In at least some social groups, an individual may acquire status by fitting into the group pattern for behavior.

REASONS AGAINST PREMARITAL INTERCOURSE

1   The danger for the female of pregnancy.
2   The danger if abortion is used to terminate a pregnancy.
3   The possibility of contracting a venereal disease.
4   The undesirability of a marriage which is forced by a premarital pregnancy.
5   The traumatic effects of coitus which is had under the inadequate circumstances which are supposed to attend most premarital relations.
6   The damage done by the participant's guilt over the infringement of the moral law.
7   The guilt at the loss of virginity, and its subsequent effect on marriage.
8   The fear that males lose respect for and will not marry a female with whom they have had coitus.

9   The damage done when guilt feelings are reawakened after marriage.

10   The guilt resulting from fear of public disapproval.

11   The risk and fear of social difficulties that may follow discovery of the relationship.

12   The risk and fear of legal difficulties that may follow any discovery of the relationship.

13   The possibility that premarital coitus which is satisfactory may delay or prevent altogether the individual from marrying.

14   The possibility that the coitus may make one feel obligated to marry the sexual partner.

15   The possibility that guilt over the coitus may break up an otherwise desirable friendship with the sexual partner.

16   The overemphasis which premarital experience may place on the physical aspects of friendship and marriage.

17   The likelihood that premarital irregularities will lead to later extramarital infidelities, with consequent damage to the marriage.

18   The possibility that the female will be less capable of responding satisfactorily in her marital coitus because of the traumatic effects of premarital experience.

19   The fact that premarital coitus is morally wrong.

20   The principle that abstinence from such activities may develop one's will power.

THE WEAKENING OF SOCIAL CONTROLS

The sex drive is a strong one and all cultures check it to a greater or lesser degree. Civilization requires this. The control of the sex drive prior to marriage has a long history in our culture, going back at least to Victorian England. To control young people, who are throbbing with hormones (the male particularly in the peak period of drive in the midteens), takes a great deal of internalization of standards. In addition, there must be external constraints. Even then there is certain to be considerable violation, and there has been, as Kinsey's research showed.

One reason adults are so sure that the sexual revolution has swept all young people along in a tide of licentiousness is that they observe the disintegration of the external controls. They know also that religion and moral suasions have weakened the built-in controls.

Weakening of the Sex–Sin Norm

Earlier studies by sociologists and by the Kinsey Institute of Sex Research left little doubt that the sin conception of sex out of wedlock was a very strong element in social control. The deepest form of guilt from days prior to Hawthorne's *Scarlet Letter,* was sex guilt. The sin concept of sex has weakened and with it, social control. Young people who are serious about finding a positive answer to their doubts and queries even find a church atmosphere in which positive assurances are less often given. Where there was certainty in the church leadership as to what the moral code in the sexual area should be, there is now debate by the clergy and less moralizing about sexual matters. Where there was prohibition, there is now a tendency to be permissive or silent. Those who wish an answer may seek in vain for an authoritative guide.

As Packard (1968) points out, some ministers and religious journals have been arguing seriously about the *Playboy* philosophy, rather than rejecting it outright. While some parents when faced with religious leaders who fail to take stands may feel less guilt and anxiety about their children, it is Packard's opinion that others seek a church where their children will have the guidance of a minister who "preaches what is right." Women's Liberation leaders may be more seriously concerned now than ministers about premarital sex, not because of moral prohibitions, but because women so often get the worst of the deal.

Even with the weakening of religious controls, they are still among the strongest in our culture. Landis' 1967 study of 3189 students in 18 colleges and universities sought to learn reasons for refraining from premarital sexual intercourse of 44 percent of men and 75 precent of women who wanted to wait until marriage. Family training and religion were strong motivating factors, although about a third of both sexes feared pregnancy.

Conflicting Professional Opinion

Certainly morals and social norms seldom originate in professional opinion. They have much deeper roots. By the same token, professional opinion does not readily change the mores. But professional opinion is not without influence, particularly on the college campus, where youth seek guidance and consider the intellectual a prestigious guide. If this were not so, the whole college experience would be a farce.

A few counselors have long taken a strong position in favor of premarital sexual experience. Walter Stokes (1953), for example, holds that the best sexual development is possible through premarital sexual experience under emotionally favorable conditions. He believes that in women there is a relationship between the sex response and the development of vaginal musculature. He takes no stock in the idea that we should teach sex is beautiful and proper, but there should be no experience with it until after marriage. He bases his argument largely on clinical evidence, finding that the young male who comes for counsel previous to marriage boasting that he has never masturbated, or had any sex experience, offers almost hopeless prospects for success in marriage. He goes so far as to say that all of the chaste young men turn out to be impotent to the degree of requiring extensive psychiatric treatment. Stokes finds also that girls who have had no sex experience are more likely to faint during vaginal examination and to otherwise exhibit the tenseness and fear that grow out of lack of sex training and experience.

The unanswered question is, of course, would these same types have been any different had they attempted premarital sexual intercourse? Or would the conditioning which led to these negative attitudes toward sex have been intensified by failure and guilt had they attempted intimate forms of sexual experience.

He does present limited positive evidence for his position. He indicates that he has worked experimentally with a group of patients who came to him some years ago at the time of their marriage. He has helped these patients train their children without the usual sex inhibitions, and reports that when these youngsters are ready for marriage, he finds an amazing zest for sex enjoyment, greater maturity, and greater sense of responsibility than is usual in young people of their age.

Albert Ellis, clinical psychologist and counselor in New York City, likewise takes the position that virginity and chastity represent cultural lags in our thinking about marriage preparation. He believes that extreme sexual difficulties in his clients are directly attributable to taboos against premarital sexual relations and masturbation.

Sociologically, this view has a certain weakness. Social systems have always operated on the assumption that maximum physical satisfaction is rarely or never possible in human relationships—that only through restraint on biological appetite, by restricting it to customary channels of expression, can human society as such exist. The sex impulse is, therefore, always regulated in relation to the goals and objectives of the family itself. Societies are concerned not with maximum satisfaction of the individual from the sexual act, but with establishing controls which act as a bulwark to the family system.

Many counselors and researchers are firmly convinced that conventions must be given a place in appraising premarital sexual behavior, and they feel just as certain that, conventions being what they are, premarital chastity is desirable. Among counselors and authors who are strong in their support of the mores and David Mace, Harold T. Christensen, Abraham Stone, and Emily Mudd.

Coed Living

There are external symbols of sexual laxity in many aspects of behavior which lend credence to the elder generation's fear of promiscuity among the young: greater exposure of the body in conventional dress, bikinis, and nude bars, and nude photographs in respectable magazines. Perhaps most ominous is the freedom with which young people associate without the least token of chaperonage.

Living in the same dormitories, removal of restrictions on visiting in rooms of dormitories, living in off-campus apartments, and unmarried couples actually living together without interference or discipline from university authorities have added to the viewpoint of "universal laxity." Option and choice are different matters. Most college young people do not choose to live together outside marriage. Their internal restraints are too strong. In fact, such behavior is not universally approved even among the younger generation. Perhaps some are mature enough to see that "Sex for fun cannot be serious; it cannot be a lifelong commitment; it implies no responsibility..." (Bernard 1972, p. 305).

The full effects are as yet unpredictable. Closer association may even alter relationships and attitudes of men and women toward each other. Joseph Katz (1968) studied coed housing in Stanford and found not only that 95 percent of the students favor it, but also that it has led to "at least a partial moratorium on sex." Shared dining and classes avoids overidealization, reduces "mutual teasing and destructive behavior characteristic of campus dating, leads students to regard each other more like brothers and sisters." He concludes that it may modify sex relationships and strengthen marriage. *Time* (1974) summarizes several research findings on coed dorm living which show that such living makes for more normal relationships not only between men and women, in that there is less idealization, but also between women themselves. Women are less "competitive and irritable" than when living isolated with women. Many sex stereotypes as to what is masculine and what is feminine disappear with shared dorms, with shared dining. Studies find casual sex no more common than with segregated living arrangements.

THE PRINCIPLE OF LEGITIMACY

Fear of pregnancy is less a force in controlling premarital coitus, since risks have largely been eliminated, however, the illegitimate birth rate is rapidly increasing. Why? Either (1) contraception as used by the unmarried is most risky; (2) it is not used; (3) one party or both seeks pregnancy; (4) girls are more inclined to see pregnancy through rather than seek an abortion. Illegitimate birth rates in the United States rose from 7.1 percent of all births in 1940 to 23.3 percent in 1969 for all races combined. For whites the figure rose from 3.9 to 13 births per 1000 unmarried women, for the nonwhites from 39.1 to 83 (see Table 16-1). The National Center for Health Statistics placed births out of wedlock at 300,000 for the year 1967.

Katherine Brownell Ottinger (1969), of the Childrens' Bureau, estimates

TABLE 16-1   Adjusted Age-Specific Illegitimacy Rates, All Women, by Color: United States, 1940, 1960, and 1968.

AGE (YEARS)	1968	1960	1940
WHITE			
15–44	13.0	9.3	3.9
15–19	9.9	6.9	3.6
20–24	22.6	18.5	6.0
25–29	21.5	17.1	4.3
30–34	14.8	10.8	2.6
35–44	4.7	3.9	1.3
NONWHITE			
15–44	83.0	90.2	39.1
15–19	86.5	78.5	48.4
20–24	109.0	147.1	52.2
25–29	96.6	137.4	36.7
30–34	75.1	97.3	26.5
35–44	24.2	31.9	10.9

Data from Westoff and Parke, 1972.

that 44 percent of babies born out of wedlock are born to mothers 13–19 years of age, and that in 1969 there were 74,000 babies born to school-age girls 17 or younger.

Table 16–1 shows the distribution of births by age groups. We can see that the ratios are highest, not among the young and ignorant, but among the older group who should know most about contraception. The illegitimacy rate is 21.5 per 1000 among unmarried white women 25–29 years of age. Obviously contraception is not the full answer. We are dealing here with very complex motives.

The difference in the figures for whites and nonwhites is due to two or more factors. Nonwhites are less likely to seek an abortion, and are also less likely to marry soon after discovering pregnancy, often waiting until a child or two is born before marrying. The child born out of wedlock is more accepted in the nonwhite family and nonwhite community, and there too, the lower-class black male feels less responsibility for the economic liabilities of parenthood. Black women are more often the support of the family than are white women.

As more is understood about the poor, it is increasingly evident that those in this subculture have very different family and marriage values from the middle class. Among the poor, consensual unions without ceremony are the rule and preferred by women as well as men. Men show little promise of being able to offer the family steady support or inheritance. They do not want the legal entanglements which marriage and divorce imply. Women prefer not to be tied down to men who feel superior to women and are "immature, punishing, and generally unreliable." Without marriage, women have some of the freedom always claimed by men and retain full right to the children if they choose to leave the man or are abandoned by him. The house and any other property belong to the woman if she forces the man to leave.

In the United States, the consensual union is most common among nonwhites where poverty is concentrated. This subculture has a definite bearing on the illegitimacy statistics of nonwhites.

One can speculate at length about the reasons for the increase in illegitimacy rates in the "Pill Age," but the seriousness of the consequences to society cannot be denied. In addition to the unfair burden on the mother and the unprotected child, society must take over the task that belongs to the responsible adult male—the support and training of his offspring.

The Economic Problem Aside from the question of morality, society has great economic stakes involved. More than a fifth of all these children are cared for on welfare rolls. Where there is no father to assume the economic burden, parents, other relatives, persons who adopt, or welfare agencies must bear it. One need only compare the number of illegitimate children in this country with that in the Latin American cultures to realize how serious the problem can become. In this respect northwestern European culture and that of Scandinavian countries are in striking contrast. In Scandinavia, the state is custodian of the child, through welfare guardians (Linner 1972). It is the responsibility of the state to locate the father and give the child his name. The law provides that the child will have equal rights to inheritance with the child of any marriage the father may have. There is no compulsion to marry, but the father assumes the same financial responsibility of parenthood that he would assume if he were married. The child has all the rights he would have if the couple married. The mother has the regular protections of social security available to all mothers in addition to certain benefits. This situation permits the equal freedom of men and women to participate in the sex act, both before marriage and in extramarital sexual relationships—a basic necessity in sex equality.

We are moving toward giving the unmarried mother and child greater protection. Zetterberg's (1969) study shows that 93 percent of Swedish people interviewed approve sexual intercourse for the engaged or those going steady, 99 percent feel that children of unwed parents should have the same rights as children born in wedlock, and 98 percent feel that unwed mothers should have all the rights of the married. The terms *illegitimate* and *bastard* have long been replaced by the term *children of unmarried mothers.*

The principle of legitimacy involves much more than economic support and protection of inheritance rights for the child. The matter of social support is very important. Obviously, Sweden gives far more social support in terms of attitudes and acceptance and imposes less condemnation on the innocent child and mother. This is perhaps the real test of moral norms. Our culture still does not fully meet the test. The child, under our moral norms, deserves a name, and the name with full respectability is that of the father. Legitimacy is established when the child is born to parents married to each other. This assures him his legal rights, economic rights, and rights to full social acceptance. It will take a great alteration of the mores before this situation changes substantially.

The Socialization Problem   Robert Sack, of the gynecology department at the University of Southern California School of Medicine, in a press statement, commented on the eight-fold increase in teen-age pregnancies over a period of 25 years:

> "It staggers my imagination to think what's going to happen to those hundreds of thousands of babies when they grow up. To keep and raise all these children out of wedlock is going to change the whole complexion of our society," he said. "Sooner or later, the baby being kept and raised by a child-mother is going to become a social problem."

He placed the school-age pregnancies at a current rate of 197,000 per year in California.

The girl in the black ghetto is often caught in a vicious cycle. The eldest daughter is likely to be born while her mother is barely beyond childhood. This girl is then given the burden of caring for the younger children. When she is a young teenager she may have a child of her own.

FACTORS IN THE HIGH PREGNANCY RATE

Some males regard having sexual relations with a girl as a proof of masculinity, and have no concern for the consequences to the girl of a possible child. For many women, pregnancy proves their femininity, and some actually want to have a child of their own regardless of other consequences. Some girls get pregnant to spite parents, or to trap a mate, while others feel that any preparation spoils the spontaneity of the sex act. Many who are troubled in conscience could not consider preparation including the pill, which takes much foresight. Most girls will not take the pill in advance because of guilt they feel about what they might do. Perhaps psychologically it represents a form of aggressive behavior which they cannot accept for themselves.

McCandless (1968) gives a motive for pregnancy among the lower working class which it will be difficult for the average college student to understand. For them the only "genuine creation" may be the "production of something perfect"—the bringing into the world of a baby.

Vincent (1969) says middle-class girls are more ego involved that lower-class girls. They must be sure that sex becomes a means for self-enhancement, they want intense emotional involvement as a proof that they, not just sex favors, are meaningful to the male. Lower-class girls are interested in winning the boy through sex, and use it as a way of gaining affection.

In addition, there is much ignorance about sex and carelessness. Some consider the forms of contraception they know unsanitary; some trust unreliable methods. Other couples fail to communicate with each other and assume the other has taken the necessary precautions.

Universal and honest contraceptive information given to all prior to puberty would help alleviate the problem, but as a society, we are far from accepting this goal. Long-term immunity to pregnancy would be another approach, but it would require parental consent, or else radical modification of law regarding treatment of those under age by the physician. Neither of these goals are readily attainable now. The morning after pill is here and can help if used.

Judson T. Landis reports in his 1967 study that 50 percent of college students studied who had broken an engagement had had sexual intercourse with the partner without having taken reliable contraceptive precautions. College students could be expected to practice more than average restraint, and to have fair knowledge of contraception and access to contraceptive devices. Apparently, accessibility to contraception is not enough to avoid pregnancy.

The Scandinavian experience indicates that the goal of security for children within marriage in a society which sanctions premarital sexual intercourse is not attainable. With extensive contraceptive knowledge and widespread trial marriage, which implies no compulsion to marry even when the girl is pregnant, about half of brides in Sweden are pregnant at their wedding and approximately 10 percent of children are born out of wedlock (Zetterberg 1969).

Scandinavian societies have had to develop a system of social institutions and mores to supplement the family in order to meet the needs of unmarried mothers and their children. We have much less adequate social institutional support for mother and child.

The fact is that the widest possible access to contraception by all will not provide immunity from pregnancy. Some men will still think that getting a girl pregnant is a test of masculinity. At times, women have a deep conscious or unconscious desire to get pregnant. Both sexes, when autonomic biological drives take over during extreme periods of sexual excitement, lose perspective. This is true both within marriage and outside marriage. Downs and Clayson (*Time,* May 29, 1972, p. 28) psychiatrist and psychologist, respectively, of Cornell University, challenge the concept of "unwanted pregnancy," presenting evidence that it is more wanted than unwanted. They studied the personalities of 108 patients wanting an abortion, applying tests of emotional health. (Most of the sample were well-informed about birth control and had practiced it previously.) They found that in 85 percent of cases the pregnancy was preceded by emotional shock like death of a relative or loss of a long-standing love relationship. The conception took place during a period of extreme emotional stress. They suggest that pregnancies do not take place by chance, but to repair "a threatened or damaged psyche;" the person needs to prove something to himself at the time (p. 88).

Downs and Clayson's position may be extreme, and their data insufficient for broad generalization, but it is suggestive that emotional factors may override rational considerations in the practice of contraception even among those who know the risks.

EFFECT OF PREMARITAL SEXUAL EXPERIENCE ON ENGAGEMENT

The sharing of sexual experiences, providing they are mutually sought and satisfying, does much to strengthen the close relationship of husband and wife. When intercourse takes place during the engagement period it can be assumed that it does so by mutual agreement. It may be mutual only in the sense that the female yielded to a great deal of pressure from the male. The decision to refrain may be by mutual agreement or by female denial. Do mutually sought sexual relations at this time have the same beneficial effects upon the engagement as they have upon a marriage relationship?

In studying couples during the period of their engagement, the most authoritative study (Burgess and Wallin 1953) to date asked 81 engaged men and 74 engaged women the effect of premarital intercourse on their relationship. Over 90 percent of each group said they thought it strengthened the relationship. Slightly over 5 percent of the women thought it had a weakening effect, but only 1 percent of the men thought so. The others thought that it had no effect at all on their relationship.

These reactions, of course, must be weighed in light of the long-term effects on engagement and marriage; the temporary effect may be to strengthen the relationship, but the long-term effects may be quite different. It is possible, too, that couples at the time of the interview might have been rationalizing considerably. In any case, it was found that engagement adjustment scores were somewhat higher for the group that was not having intercourse. On the question of whether engaged men and women had had sexual relations with persons other than the affianced, adjustment scores were slightly higher for those who had had no such relations, but there was no significant difference between those who had had sexual relations with the affianced only and with the affianced and others. Nor did frequency of intercourse with the affianced or with others seem to have any relationship to the problem of adjustment. Whether they had intercourse at all seems to have been the significant factor.

This study shows further that more couples who had had intercourse than those who had not had intercourse broke their engagements. Although the sample dealing with broken engagements is small (31 cases), it lends support to the view of some doctors and counselors that the male's desire for marriage is lessened when his sex needs are being regularly satisfied outside marriage. The need for regular sexual intercourse is generally one of the most powerful incentives of the male to marry.

Among the reactions most often reported by couples engaging in intercourse were relief of physical tension and confidence that they were going to be married. Among unfavorable feelings most frequently reported were fear of social disapproval, which was mentioned by more than a fifth of both men and women, and fear of pregnancy, which was mentioned by about a fourth of men and women. Sixteen percent of women also reported feelings of guilt. The guilt factor has no doubt decreased since this study was made.

The researchers consider it significant that none of the group, in reporting feelings or justifications that accompanied premarital sexual relations, mentioned sexual experience as a test of sexual compatibility. They conclude that premarital sexual relationships, therefore, are not entered into as a guide to physical compatibility; rather they occur, not with any long-time definite purpose in mind, but as a relief for "frequent and intensive erotic stimulation."

Kirkendall's (1956; 1961) study has accumulated the case histories of 250 premarital relationships of college students, focusing interest on the quality of the interpersonal relationship which is associated with premarital intercourse. He concludes that "practically all the premarital coitus in the preengagement period takes place under conditions which, in both the short and long run, result in more suspicion, distrust, and less ability to set up a good relationship later." Some engaged couples are drawn closer together by coitus during the engagement period, but this study reports other cases where the couple was also drawn closer together by a decision not to have intercourse, indicating that an intimate level of communication may be the main factor in drawing them closer together. Kirkendall concludes that sexual intercourse usually weakens the relationship, and often terminates it.

He finds that motives of men and women differ, and this often leads to misunderstanding. The man usually enters into a sexual relationship merely for the physical thrill, to make himself feel a man, or to accomplish what some of his friends boast about accomplishing. A woman is more likely to enter the relationship to hold the man, or to push him into marriage. After the sexual relationship she may become possessive, show great anxiety to make the relationship permanent, and talk a great deal about marriage. The boastful man begins to feel more sober and senses that he is being trapped. Men in this situation are generally much less interested in marriage than are women. This situation arises frequently as increasing numbers of the unmarried who are living together seek counseling help (see chapter 29). Such commitments lead to many of the complications of marriage without the assurances which marriage brings.

Women generally sense more guilt than do men when they break the moral codes. This also leads them to encourage the marriage idea. With the loss of virginity, marriageability has been somewhat weakened as far as other prospective mates are concerned. If her violation of the code is discovered, she is much more exposed to shame and social censure than is the man, so she feels much less safe. Often the greatest threat to her reputation comes from the man, who may be very indiscreet in boasting about his conquest to friends. This not only threatens the woman's reputation, but makes it more likely that other men will expect sex favors if the pair breaks up.

Men are not undamaged by casual sexual experience. Many find it hard to settle down when the time comes to marry. Some are forced into marriage before they are ready by a sense of guilt, because the girl with whom they have had intercourse becomes pregnant, or fears she is pregnant, or merely claims to be to force marriage.

LeMasters (1957a) feels that coitus tends to gloss over serious differences between couples so that these do not appear until after marriage. He believes many couples "neck their way out" of problems before marriage, rather than facing them. Sex thus becomes a confusing force during mate choice.

In talking with engaged couples one frequently hears a young woman say, "My fiancé is always tense and cross before a weekend is over, but I'm sure the problem is sex tensions." This may well be. It may be desirable, however, to take a second look at the relationships, and make sure that even the restrained sex play entered into is not an effort to keep from facing the real issues, or a device for forcing complete sex relations.

Refraining from sexual intercourse during the engagement period is, of course, often extremely difficult, especially today when close physical contacts are customary. Sexual intercourse, Burgess and Wallin (1953) found, is more often entered into by those who have prolonged their engagement 16 months or more. Kinsey (1953) finds, too, that the incidence of premarital coitus increases with delayed marriage. The likelihood of women having an orgasm in premarital intercourse also increases with age. In other words, delay of marriage increases both the incidence of premarital coitus and of orgasmic experience. He also finds that females who begin coitus early, marry early. Those who attain higher levels of education are more likely to have had premarital coitus by the time of their marriage because of later age of marriage.

Some feel that petting to the point of orgasm may be a part of the natural psychosexual development of this period, a satisfactory substitute for coitus, and a desirable preparation for marriage. It does permit the cultivation of sublimated forms of sexual expression in the male and thus prepares him for the more complex and sympathetic part he is often expected to play in the sexual life of the modern married couple. It has the advantage of deferring pregnancy until marriage in cases where couples find it necessary to reduce sexual tension. Use of this outlet depends upon the extent to which intimate petting can be engaged in without guilt, perhaps more than on actual physical factors.

It must be recognized, too, that most young people have difficulty in petting to the point of orgasm without running considerable risk of actual intercourse. For many couples intercourse occurs, not after mutual agreement, but after mutual stimulation has erased their combined self-control. There are other possible disadvantages to this solution. It frequently brings satisfaction

EFFECT OF PREMARITAL SEXUAL EXPERIENCE ON SEXUAL ADJUSTMENT IN MARRIAGE

A rationalization frequently used by young people to justify premarital sexual relations is the wish to prove their adequacy for the sexual aspects of marriage, and also to prove that they are "physically mated." It is likely that some adolescent girls yield to this argument of the male because although they have no real sex interest they feel they should have. They may be told that they are frigid and cold because they do not feel a sex drive comparable to that of their male partner.

There is abundant evidence that the average woman, especially in her teens or even in her early 20s, has less capacity to respond sexually than she will have later (evidence is presented in Chapter 20). It is not too likely that the average girl, during a short period of premarital sexual experimentation, will develop the capacity to experience orgasm. Her failure to respond may create anxiety concerning her ability to respond when there is no real reason for such anxiety.

To learn whether premarital sexual intercourse affects sexual adequacy in marriage, Burgess and Wallin (1953) interviewed couples during engagement and again after several years of marriage. This study shows that orgasmic adequacy in marriage is favorably related to premarital sexual experience—the more sexual experience the wife has had, the more likely she was to experience a full orgasm in her marital relations. This generalization held true both for women who had had sexual relations only with their future spouse and those who had had sexual experience with other men as well. These findings correspond to those reported by Terman (1938) and Kinsey (1953).

Confirming support for this view is found by Kanin and Howard (1958) in studying the degree of sex satisfaction on the wedding night and during the honeymoon of 177 wives of married students on a college campus in a midwest university (Kanin 1960). The more complete their sexual activity before marriage, the greater likelihood of satisfaction. Far more of the wives with premarital sexual experience, however, had sex difficulties during the early days of marriage, and of the 14 women who reported long-time difficulties beginning during the first two weeks of their marriage, all had had premarital sexual intercourse. Five of these women reported that they felt like "sex servants." This suggests that the woman who engages in sexual relations before marriage may have no argument in restraining her husband after marriage.

In further study of this group, Kanin reports that the upper-class girls reported least frequency of premarital coitus; the middle-class girls, next; and the lower-class girls, greatest frequency. He found that premarital coitus was associated with avoidance of a honeymoon, abbreviated dating histories (couples tended to move quickly into marriage), decrease in the use of premarital counseling, and a decrease in the usual psychological disturbances of the wedding day.

The American Institute of Family Relations collected some 2000 questionnaires, predominately from among college graduates in the United States. The initial orgasmic response of women who were virgins at marriage was 28 percent, compared to 39 percent of those who had had experiences of premarital intercourse. The differences vanish quickly with sexual experience in marriage. At the end of the first year, the following results were reported:

	PERCENT HAVING ORGASM	
	VIRGINS	NONVIRGINS
Younger wives	67	63
Wives over 30	63	59

These data suggest that even with marriage greatly delayed (into the thirties) orgasmic response is not dependent on the cultivation of early response through premarital sex activity. Popenoe (1961) believes that there is evidence here, and in clinical observation as well, that a large part of "premarital sexual experience of young women is neurotic rather than normal." Confirming this view are Reevy's (1959) findings concerning premarital petting and other forms of sexual activity, including sexual intercourse and marriage predictability scores. He summarizes his conclusions thus, "The group with unfavorable marital predictions can be characterized as being more active sexually than the group with favorable marital predictions." Shope and Broderick (1967) compared the marriage adjustment of 80 virgins with 40 women who had experienced orgasm during sexual intercourse prior to marriage and 40 who had had sexual intercourse without orgasm. The virgins made better overall sexual adjustment, although differences were not greatly in their favor. The girls who had had orgasm did not differ in marital happiness or sexual adjustment from those who had not.

Kinsey (1953) makes a strong case for the biological desirability of premarital sex experience, holding that long abstinence, restraint, and avoidance of physical contacts and emotional responses before marriage may well lead to the building of inhibitions which damage the capacity of the organism to respond sexually in marriage. Petting to orgasm, intercourse to orgasm, or even masturbation to orgasm, he believes, help prepare the organism to react physiologically. Those who masturbate extensively prior to marriage are more likely than others to have orgasm in marriage, and there is a close relationship between the experience of intercourse to the point of orgasm prior to marriage and ability to reach it during the first year of marriage. These findings, of course, may only mean that the highly sexed female is the one who engages in various kinds of sex stimulation prior to marriage.

One of the great faults of the Kinsey work was that he interpreted findings from the standpoint of biology. Sociologists have to recognize that moral reality is quite as binding on human beings as are biological impulses. In fact, moral suasion has precedence over biological impulse in societies everywhere. Man cannot satisfy his sexual desires in defiance of moral codes and go unblemished either in self-conception or reputation.

Sociologists have pursued their study beyond the point of simple physiological response. In a study of the total sexual adjustment scores of 600 men and women in marriage, no relationship, favorable or unfavorable, was found between sexual adjustments scores of husbands and wives and premarital intercourse. (Burgess & Wallin, 1953) It was found, however, that there was a slight favorable relationship to good adjustment where each had had sexual experience with both the future spouse and others. (The sexual adjustment score was based on answers to questions relating to various aspects of the sexual relationship with the marriage partner.) Clearly, ability to achieve an orgasm is not a complete test of the adequacy of the sexual relationship.

On the other hand, even this sociological study concludes that there is no statistical foundation for the belief that premarital intercourse is unfavorable to sexual adjustment in marriage. It recognizes, however, that people who are most likely to suffer from fear, or guilt, and anxiety because of premarital intercourse do not engage in it.

This research carried the investigation one step further in an attempt to relate premarital sex experience to total adjustment in marriage as measured by (1) marital happiness, (2) general marital satisfaction, (3) love, and (4) marriage permanence. The findings in general agree with those of Terman, (1938) Davis, (1929) Popenoe, (1961) and Locke, (1951) that virginity prior to marriage is most favorable to total marriage success.

This suggests that the total pattern of marriage adjustment is something quite different from sexual adjustment alone. It may well be that secondary reactions to the premarital sexual experience are the decisive ones rather than sexual adjustment as such. Guilt and anxiety, a lack of mutual confidence, a suspicion that a pattern of disloyalty has been established which may lead to extramarital coitus—such feelings may be lurking in the background.

Kinsey finds striking proof that those having had premarital coitus are more likely than others to have premarital coitus again, and also that those having had premarital coitus are much more likely than others to have extramarital relations (see Figure 16–1).

Intent to have premarital coitus. Source: Alfred C. Kinsey and others, *Sexual Behavior in the Human Female* (Philadelphia: W. B. Saunders Co., 1953). Reproduced by permission of Dr. Kinsey. Females without premarital coital experience generally are positive that they will not engage in it. Almost half of those who have had premarital coitus intend to repeat it. The Kinsey research shows that experience in premarital coitus also increases the likelihood of extramarital coitus.   **FIGURE 16–1**

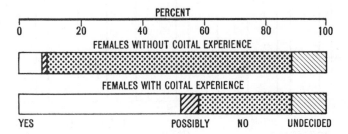

Data relating premarital to extramarital coitus of women show, for example, that those who had had premarital coitus are twice as likely as others to have extramarital coitus. Moreover, a greater proportion of those who had had extramarital coitus than those who had not, thought they would do the same again. This would seem to give some justification to the fear of disloyalty although change of custom and morality may well lead to greater stability in time. Zetterberg (1969) finds no evidence of increased marital disloyalty among the Swedes with their greater permissiveness and experience with sex prior to marriage.

On the moral issue, however, there is not too much evidence of a carryover of guilt in Kinsey's data. Only about 31 percent of the unmarried females who had had premarital coitus regretted it afterward. Only 23 percent of the married females regretted it. The incidence of regret was not even particularly high among females who had experienced premarital pregnancy. As would be expected, knowing the nature of the human conscience, those who had experienced the greatest amount of coitus over the greatest period of time were least likely to have regrets. Those without religion were less subject to regret than those who were devout (see Figure 16–2).

FIGURE 16–2   Relationship between regret after premarital coitus and religious background. Source: Alfred C. Kinsey and others, *Sexual Behavior in the Human Female* (Philadelphia: W. B. Saunders Co., 1953). Reproduced by permission of the publisher. The more devout the woman, the greater the likelihood of regret following premarital coitus. Intermediate shading indicates some lesser degree of regret. Devout Catholics most ofter suffer regret.

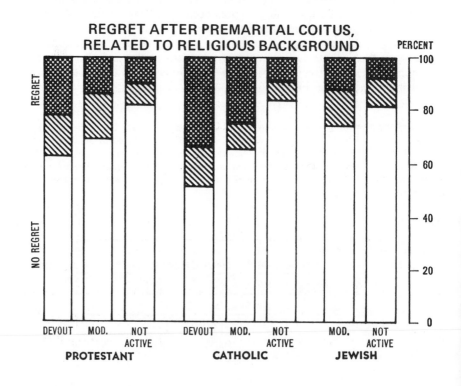

REGRET AFTER PREMARITAL COITUS, RELATED TO RELIGIOUS BACKGROUND

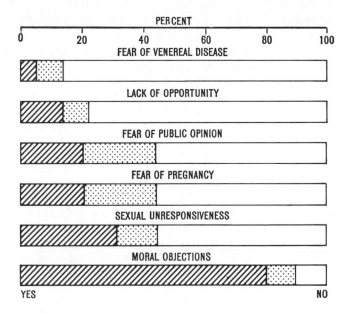

PERCENT

FEAR OF VENEREAL DISEASE

LACK OF OPPORTUNITY

FEAR OF PUBLIC OPINION

FEAR OF PREGNANCY

SEXUAL UNRESPONSIVENESS

MORAL OBJECTIONS

YES   NO

Factors restricting premarital coitus given by women. Source: Alfred C. Kinsey and others, **FIGURE 16–3**
Sexual Behavior in the Human Female (Philadelphia: W. B. Saunders Co., 1953). Reproduced
by permission of Dr. Kinsey. Moral factors are the major control against premarital coitus, and
sexual unresponsiveness the second. Black shading indicates replies falling between yes and
no, including data from females with and without coital experience. Judson T. Landis currently finds family and religious restraints the more effective ones (*Op. cit.,* Table III, p. 169).

Again, of course, one is dealing with the group who do have sexual relations, and with their after-adjustments. This is the morally liberated group.
Average reactions of all persons to premarital sex experience would undoubtedly be quite different.

These findings may be challenged too on the ground that an expression of
"no regret" may not tell the whole story. In fact, Lester Kirkendall (1956)
teacher and marriage counselor, in his study of 250 college couples having
sexual intercourse shows that many who claim no regret, at the same time tell
of experiences of hurt feelings, recriminations, bitterness, distrust, etc. Some
boys who report no regret also tell of girls trying to "trap" them into marriage. Even in cases where there is no sense of guilt, there is often a sense of
distrust, suspicion, and disrespect, which indicates that the human relationship
involved has degenerated because of the sex experience.

Studies by Hillman (1954) of inquiries to an advice column of a metropolitan paper indicate that premarital sexual intercourse had brought more
problems to the column than any other single factor; 3371 letters dealt with
problems arising from this source. The second most frequent problem arose
out of unfaithfulness on the part of the other party. This type of inquiry
brought 1887 letters. Alcoholism was third, with almost as many inquiries.

In the final analysis, the question of premarital sexual relations must be

THE RESEARCH SCORE ON PREMARITAL SEXUAL EXPERIENCE

weighed in terms of morality and notions of propriety rather than of biology alone.

Religious and moral convictions are the strong controls on sexual behavior. One may well suspect that when persons who hold these convictions violate sexual mores, they suffer most. Kinsey finds religion the most powerful influence among both men and women in deferring sexual relationships until after marriage (see Figure 16–3). Judson T. Landis (1963) found that more than a third of the men in the 11 colleges studied in 1952 gave this as a reason for refraining, and 31 percent of the women concurred. In the Cornell 1940 study, 21 percent of the total group refrained for religious reasons. (Both of these groups placed family training far above religious beliefs as a reason for refraining, and more also gave as a reason simply wanting to refrain until after marriage.)

Dedman found religion a strong deterrent to premarital sexual relations, as did also Kanin and Howard (1958). Of engaged couples who were both regular in church attendance, in the latter study only 28 percent had premarital sexual intercourse; of the couples with one regular attender and one nonregular, 48 percent; of the nonregular attenders, 61 percent.

In their nation-wide sample of girls in the United States, Kantner and Zelnik found (1972) that religious affiliation makes little difference in proportions engaging in premarital sexual intercourse, except that the incidence was low among fundamentalist protestants. Faithful church attendance does, however, hold down the incidence, particularly among those attending church four times a month or oftener (Table 16–2).

Although American data show very clearly that religion is a great restraint on premarital and extramarital sexual activity, there is no doubt a great difference related to the particular church attended. Chesser's (1957) study of over 6000 marriages in England shows that almost half of the Roman Catholic women had had sexual intercourse before marriage, by far the highest

TABLE 16–2 Percent of Unmarried Young Women Aged 15–19 Who Have Ever Had Intercourse, by Race and Number of Times They Attended Church in Month Prior to Interview

	BLACK TIMES ATTENDED PER MONTH			WHITE TIMES ATTENDED PER MONTH			TOTAL TIMES ATTENDED PER MONTH		
RELIGION	LESS THAN 3	3-4	4 OR MORE	LESS THAN 3	3-4	4 OR MORE	LESS THAN 3	3-4	4 OR MORE
Catholic	68.4	27.6	[a]	29.8	19.0	8.9	32.1	19.2	9.3
Jewish				16.2	27.2	8.9	16.2	27.2	8.9
Mormon				10.4	[a]	9.1	10.4	[a]	9.1
Fundamentalist	66.4	41.0	27.0	32.3	31.8	11.9	38.6	34.4	14.2
Other Protestant	62.2	50.7	45.2	32.8	17.5	12.2	37.3	26.1	17.7
None	63.3	[a]	[a]	44.2	[a]	[a]	47.0	[a]	[a]

Source: John F. Kantner and Melvin Zelnik, "Sexual Experience of Young Unmarried Women in the U.S.," *Family Planning Perspectives*, 4:9–18, October, 1972.
[a] Unweighted N = < 20.

MATE CHOICE

proportion of any religious group studied. Only one-fourth of the Protestant group had had sexual intercourse before marriage, and only one-fifth of the Jewish women.

It is apparently on the grounds of religion, morals, parental attitudes, and their own conception of their future that most young people refrain from premarital sexual intercourse rather than on the basis of biological considerations. As one girl expressed it in her term paper "I want to have a honeymoon that means something new to me. I don't want it compared with another place, another man. And I never want a husband who could throw it back to me that I was pregnant, that he had to marry me."

MENTAL HEALTH AND PREMARITAL SEXUAL RELATIONS

Mead (1968a) suggests that young people are moving away from the position of feeling guilty about sleeping with someone, to feeling guilty if they are not sleeping with someone. This statement may be good journalism, but there is no support for it in the researches known to the writer. Undoubtedly there is more pressure to sleep with someone, although not just anyone, simply because it is less taboo; but the pressure is not the result of feeling guilty because one does not sleep with someone. There may be cliques which regard such behavior as a mark of belonging, and it is a male status symbol, but researches show clearly that it is the sleeping with someone to whom one is not married, not refraining from it, that brings a sense of guilt to some males and to many females.

Reiss (1967; 1971) reports that guilt exists to an extent with the practice of all levels of sexual intimacy—kissing, petting, and coitus—among the college group, even when the participant does not exceed his standard; but those who exceed their standard, experience most guilt. He interprets this to mean that intellectual standards are not equivalent to emotional standards. His researches show that males suffer less guilt at all levels of intimacy. He concludes that fear of consequences of intimacy may be a part of guilt feelings.

A part of the problem may be that of all forms of self-indulgence. It is usually not until afterward that the participant becomes fully aware of social consequences. In the excitement of the moment, the person yields to deep animal autonomic reflexes. Later assessment often involves a realization that one has betrayed oneself and one's mate. This is probably most true when there is an awareness that the whole affair was without genuine emotional commitment. Of course, the degree of guilt depends on the degree to which the conscience has been dulled by repetition of such behavior.

Indications are that in time the guilt feelings subside, as they do with any repeated violation of conscience, but whether they are suppressed and later surface to cause guilt and become a factor in neurosis can scarcely be revealed by studies.

Evidence is far too meager to indicate what lasting influence premarital sexual relations have on the personality and mental health of the individuals involved. We do know this—most young people in the United States develop, as they mature, a rather exacting code of right and wrong on sexual matters.

These codes are generally centered about religious teachings, but whether they are or not, religious ethics act as nearly inflexible yardsticks by which persons judge their own behavior and that of others. When one allows himself to act contrary to these codes, society seldom has to punish him; conscience does.

In this area there is little or no statistical evidence available. Clinical data is available, however, indicating the results of self-betrayal. An illustrative case from a counselor's experience is described below.

> Virginia, daughter of a small-town minister, migrated from her home in Tennessee to a large northern city shortly after her graduation from high school. She lived in a furnished room with a girl friend, became active in church affairs, and obtained steady employment in a clothing store.

> George, one of her co-workers, was attracted to Virginia and they dated one another irregularly for a year and a half. There followed a period of six months when they dated one another exclusively, spoke often of marriage, and after considerable urging on George's part had sexual intercourse more or less regularly.

> Even though they used a contraceptive device, Virginia became pregnant. After two unsuccessful attempts at abortion by pills, she confided in George who willingly agreed upon an early date for their marriage.

> The marriage itself proved to be a generally happy and successful one. When Virginia occasionally became depressed concerning the circumstances of their marriage, George reassured her. None of their friends or acquaintances learned of the untimely conception.

> After the birth of the first child, however, Virginia's periods of depression became more numerous and lasting. The climax came when she attempted to enter the date of her marriage and of the birth of her child in her Bible. She found herself incapable of writing the birth, or of inscribing false dates. She began to dwell constantly upon the matter, feeling a deep sense of guilt and unworthiness. She could no longer go to church, associate with her friends, or even feel at ease with her husband.

> In the end, a period of intensive professional counseling was necessary merely to enable her to continue even somewhat effectively in her roles as wife and mother. At this time, three years after the birth of her first child, she still experiences periods of dangerous depression in which suicide plans figure vaguely, but persistently.

Not all such cases reach the attention of professional counselors. It is safe to say that, though the percentage of persons so haunted may not be great, the pain and guilt they suffer make their cases highly significant. For every young person who takes lightly the risks involved in premarital sexual intercourse—and the temptation to do so will increase as contraception becomes more dependable—there remains one basic question, "What will the experience mean relative to my own self-respect and mental health?"

Until the moral teachings of most American families undergo very fundamental changes, there will be many young people who suffer as much or more from psychological repercussions as from the potential social consequences of intercourse prior to marriage. Parents' two great concerns about their children still are their sexual behavior and spending habits. Most adults have not accepted or taught their children permissive sex attitudes.

The basic moral development of the child begins very early in the family. It becomes relatively fixed at an early age, and does not change with rationalizations that "other people do, why can't I?" This is the conclusion of Peck (1960) and his colleagues after a 16 year study of a group of children. They reported: "It appears, in summary, that the basic qualities of personality structure and interpersonal attitude are predominantly created by the child's experiences with his parents."

RISKS OF EXPOSURE

In a Kinsey (1953) sample of 2094 single white females, ranging in age from adolescence to 40 years, who had had premarital coitus, 476 or 18 percent had become pregnant—almost one in five. Many of this group were not yet married, so the likelihood of even a greater proportion becoming pregnant prior to marriage is, of course, to be taken for granted.

Fifteen percent of those who had become pregnant had been pregnant more than once. While this seems like a high proportion of pregnancies, Kinsey finds that for any given act of intercourse among this group the average is only one pregnancy for each 1000 single acts of intercourse. Such statistics are, of course, deceptive. The individual who is highly susceptible to pregnancy is vulnerable, whereas a sterile couple, or near-sterile one, is not at all.

There is no doubt that the Kinsey sample was of women who were abnormally sexually active and exposed to pregnancy. Yet the risk is always there. No matter how effective birth control becomes, it will not eliminate premarital pregnancy.

The "contraceptive society," as Zetterberg (1969) has labeled modern society, particularly referring to Sweden, has succeeded to a remarkable degree in separating sexual intercourse from procreation. His study of Swedish couples shows that there are 1100 acts of sexual intercourse for each birth. Contraceptive knowledge is more available to the unmarried in Sweden than in the United States, contraceptive devices are more accessible, and moral codes are less condemnatory than here.

HANDLING PREMARITAL PREGNANCY

One must assume that in American society premarital pregnancy is seldom consciously sought by the middle-class girl, and particularly not by the college girl. When it occurs there are three alternatives—marriage, abortion, or unmarried motherhood. The third has been discussed; the other two merit consideration.

Marriage is the ideal solution if the couple are ready for marriage and have favorable attitudes toward life together and parenthood, which is unlikely when there has been no period of close association prior to pregnancy. Even where there has been, the very fact of being forced to marry sooner than the couple had expected may be a handicap, and if problems arise about the marriage, one partner may be quick to accuse the other of responsibility for the pregnancy. Both have been hurt by the obligation to terminate other plans in order to settle down to the responsibilities of homemaking and parenthood; both have suffered some sense of shame and humiliation in being "caught." They may have a feeling of guilt, too. And they may, in fact, because of all these unfavorable factors, actually have lost their love and respect for each other before they enter into the marriage.

Christensen and Rubinstein (1956) have studied the problem of premarital sexual intercourse primarily from the standpoint of the effect of pregnancy on later success in marriage. These studies leave no doubt that premarital pregnancy is a hazard to successful marriage. Premarital pregnancy is associated with an abnormally high divorce rate (see Figure 16–4). They suggest that it may be associated with other unfavorable factors like venereal disease, incurring anxiety and guilt, and inciting social condemnation. Locke's (1951) study, which compared backgrounds of divorced and happily married couples, showed a fairly high number of pregnancies previous to marriage among the divorced.

Landis and Landis' (1968) study of 581 couples, married an average of seven years, comparing them with 155 couples in the California Court of Conciliation and with 164 divorced persons, shows a much higher incidence of premarital sexual relationships with the spouse and of premarital pregnancy for the two problem groups.

Swedish social workers reported to the 1953 European Study Tour on Marriage and Family, of which the writer was leader, that many divorces are caused there by marriage having been entered into because of premarital

FIGURE 16–4   Relationship between premarital pregnancy and divorce. Source: Harold T. Christensen, O. P. Bowden, and H. H. Meissner, "Studies in Child Spacing: III—Premarital Pregnancy as a Factor in Divorce." *American Sociological Review,* 18:641–44, December, 1953.

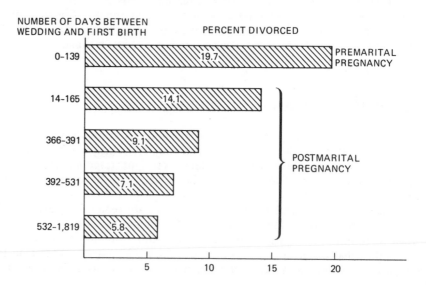

Percent[a] of Wives Who Approve Different Reasons for Abortion, 1965 and 1970   TABLE 16–3

REASON FOR ABORTION AND YEAR OF SURVEY	TOTAL[b]	WHITE	BLACK	WHITE, NON-CATHOLIC	WHITE, CATHOLIC
Mother's health endangered					
1965	89	89	89	93	77
1970	90	90	86	93	82
Pregnancy result of rape					
1965	53	54	43	58	43
1970	71	72	64	75	63
Probable deformity of child					
1965	51	52	37	58	40
1970	69	71	60	74	59
Mother unmarried					
1965	12	13	10	14	9
1970	32	33	27	36	22
Couple cannot afford child					
1965	11	11	13	12	8
1970	25	25	29	28	16
Couple do not want child					
1965	7	7	8	8	5
1970	22	22	24	24	14
Minimum number of women[c]					
1965	4,529	3,537	928	2,494	1,043
1970	5,623	4,729	766	3,516	1,194

Source: Richard Pomeroy and Lynn C. Landman, "Effective Abortion and Birth Control Services to Teenagers," *Family Planning Perspectives*, 4:44–55, Oct., (1972), Table 5). Data for it are credited by these authors to E. Jones and C. F. Westoff, "Attitudes toward Abortion in the United States in 1970 and the Trend Since 1965," in C. F. Westoff and R. Parke, Jr., eds., *Demographic and Social Aspects of Population Growth*, GPO, (1972).

[a] "Other" responses omitted from percentage bases.
[b] Percentages weighted; number of women unweighted. Total includes other nonwhites.
[c] The number of women varies slightly for each question due to the omission of those giving "other" responses. The number given represents the smallest number in that category used as a percentage base.

pregnancies. Yet in Sweden there is no pressure whatever from social workers or public agencies to encourage marriage if the couple involved in the pregnancy do not wish it. This suggests that even where all conditions in the society favor premarital pregnancy, it seems to work to the disadvantage of marriage. In our culture, even with the strong taboos against illegitimacy, marriage counselors do not recommend marriage if the young couple involved are no longer interested in each other.

Abortion is now legally available throughout the nation. It is one of the rights women have won for themselves via the Supreme Court. This is a way of terminating pregnancy for those whose moral and religious values permit. It is unfortunate that many young girls least able to nurture a child properly, least often seek abortion. They want to keep the child as though it were a pet, having no conception of their inability to rear a child properly and to socialize it adequately. Among the lower classes, the whole family may take over much of the task so that it is not too badly done. In the commune it also becomes a group process. Evidence to date suggests that the commune does a fair job with the baby and small child, but as the child grows older, he becomes an increasing problem; older children need regular schooling, an established routine, and responsible adult counsel and example, which are often lacking.

Historically, the typical abortion case was the married woman who already had as many children as she wanted. Now the typical case is said to be the single, white, unmarried girl in her early 20s. It is too early to tell what the recent removal of abortion from the area of legal prohibition will do to the abortion rate and to the characteristics of women who seek abortion. In Japan, abortion tends to be a substitute for birth control. Presumably here, where access to birth control devices of a high degree of effectiveness are more available, this will not be the case. Under the best circumstances, abortion in our culture, because of moral norms, is far from being as psychologically acceptable as birth control. Our religious philosophy claims concepts of the immortal soul and eternal life; the religions of Japan do not. Abortion is not as safe anatomically as is birth control. Dr. William J. Sweeney states, "I don't like doing abortions, although I perform them. . . . Abortion is certainly not the simple process people have been led to believe" (Sweeney and Stern, 1973).

The Supreme Court ruling is being challenged on moral and religious grounds, yet there is a growing demand for the right of choice in abortion among whites, blacks, and among Catholics as well as non-Catholics (Table 16–3).

EXTENDING BIRTH CONTROL AS A PREVENTATIVE MEASURE

There is increasing public support for extending birth control to sexually active teen-agers. Several colleges and universities now provide birth-control counseling and contraceptive information and devices as a part of their normal health service procedures. Public support of birth-control services to sexually active teen-agers is strong. In June 1972, Gallup's survey showed that 73 percent of whites and 63 percent of blacks support such a program. The survey cautions that the black sample is small, but that other samples show little difference in attitudes of blacks and whites. The West Coast is more emphatic in support than other sections of the country. The more affluent in terms of education and income and the younger generation are more supportive than other groups (Table 16–4).

PROBLEMS

1   *Research exercise:* Poll the class or some other student group on the questions, "Do you believe in premarital sexual relations? Why?" According to tabulations:

    a   Does most of of your class favor or oppose premarital sexual relations?

    b   Does favorableness to premarital relations tend to be associated with one or the other sex in your group?

    c   What reason is most often given in favor of premarital relations?

    d   What argument is most often given against it?

2   Discuss the institutional changes that would be required if premarital sexual relations were condoned in the United States?

TABLE 16-4 Percent Response to the Question: "To What Extent Do You Agree or Disagree with the Following Statement: 'Professional Birth Control Information, Services, and Counseling Should Be Made Available to Unmarried Teen-agers Who Are Sexually Active'," by Education and by Age

RESPONSE	18-29			30-44			45+		
	NOT HIGH SCHOOL GRADUATE (N=62)	HIGH SCHOOL GRADUATE (N=161)	COLLEGE (N=173)	NOT HIGH SCHOOL GRADUATE (N=90)	HIGH SCHOOL GRADUATE (N=184)	COLLEGE (N=112)	NOT HIGH SCHOOL GRADUATE (N=349)	HIGH SCHOOL GRADUATE (N=237)	COLLEGE (N=161)
Total Pro	69	80	90	60	82	86	55	70	83
Strongly Agree	45	45	60	25	32	47	19	32	40
Agree	24	35	30	35	50	39	36	38	43
Total Con	24	19	8	39	18	12	35	25	14
Disagree	21	9	5	20	9	11	18	14	6
Strongly Disagree	3	10	3	19	9	1	17	11	8

Source: Richard Pomeroy and Lynn C. Landman, "Public Opinion Trends: Effective Abortion and Birth Control Services to Teenagers." *Family Planning Perspectives*, 4:44–55. *Oct*. (1972. Table 9).

273

3 In the long run would premarital sexual relations tend to increase or decrease the freedom of young people?

4 As a group do you feel that sexual relations are less objectionable during an engagement than before an engagement?

5 Your friend's fiancée has become pregnant but both agree that had it not happened they would have broken their engagement. What would your advice to him be?

   a Get out of town.
   b Take her to an abortionist.
   c Marry her and try to make it work.
   d Marry her with the understanding that you will get a divorce when the child is one year old.
   e Take her to an institution for unwed mothers and put the child up for adoption.

6 A very religious girl, in a moment of excitement, consents to sexual relations with her fiance and discovers two months later that she is pregnant. List the possible social and psychological consequences if:

   a They marry after her third month of pregnancy.
   b They decide not to marry at all.

7 In your opinion how might parents and institutions, such as church and school, best help young people to avoid the dangers of premarital sexual relations?

8 Discuss the statement, "The chief danger of premarital sexual relations is to one's mental health rather than physical well-being."

PART V

MARRIAGE ADJUSTMENT

MARRIAGE
ADJUSTMENT

17 In the novel *Elizabeth and Her German Garden*, Countess Russell describes the husband as "quite a nice, harmless little man, pleasant to talk to, good tempered, and full of fun; but he has that horror of being made better by his wife that distinguishes so many men." The wife, in turn, sees in his refusal to rise when she enters the room and to open doors for her, evidence that her marriage is a failure.

Marriage involves a whole new system of reciprocal roles. It can function in no other way. It also involves role conceptions, which in the above instance do not harmonize. The husband and wife are each convinced that "I am right; you are wrong." Involved in the role conflict is a threat to the self-image of each.

Cultures which rigidly prescribe roles for both husband and wife minimize role conflicts. Each sex is reared from childhood to anticipate its sex roles and is trained to carry them out in marriage. Cultures which fail to maintain role definitions necessitate numerous adjustments, as individual couples must work out reciprocal roles with a minimum of help from tradition.

In the tradition-oriented joint family systems operating in such countries as India and Pakistan, role definitions are provided for both man and wife so that very little attention must be given to problems of marriage adjustment. In East Africa, an Indian wife, on learning that the writer authored books in marriage–family problems, asked quite seriously, "But what could there be to write about?" In a family system rooted in tradition which still outlines a rigid framework of roles, authorities, and values for the man-and-wife relationship as in India, there is little to write about. What happens is taken for granted; defined institutional relationships are not viewed as individual problems or subjects for analysis.

THE HONEYMOON

The early days and months of marriage involve a subtle series of interactions by which each partner is trying to reshape the other in his or her own image of what a mate should be. True, this is not always subtle, and it does not necessarily begin after marriage. If the marriage lasts, it will continue and take a decidedly different turn when children are born. The honeymoon is a special adjustment period. Popularly looked upon as a time of supreme bliss, it may actually be one of the most strenuous of adjustment periods. There is some truth in novelist Philip Wylie's contention that "Honeymoons Are Hell." Others have spoken of postmarriage depression.

The honeymoon at its best, however, can be an enjoyable and not too strenuous event. Understanding the significance of the honeymoon can save a couple months of more difficult adjustment. When the honeymoon is unrealistically planned, however, it can actually become a liability rather than an asset to the new marriage.

The least successful honeymoons, from the standpoint of marital happiness, are those that seek to cram into a week or two all of the activity, adventure, and travel which the couple should not expect to afford for another five or ten years. Parents are often guilty of encouraging couples to undertake too much. Since the length of the honeymoon trip, and the people and places one visits, are frequently reported in the hometown paper, the honeymoon is often used as a testimony to one's social and economic status rather than one's good sense.

The most desirable honeymoons from the standpoint of all-around happiness are those which are planned for rest, being alone, and spending time with others and group activity.

Time for Rest   The commercialization of the wedding has been called a "national scandal" almost equal to the funeral scandal. The wedding industry is a seven billion dollar enterprise, with caterers, florists, dressmakers, photographers, printers, musicians, jewelers all making a profit. The public wedding takes on many elements of conspicuous consumption, rather than of a solemn religious occasion.

The bride particularly enters the honeymoon in a state of extreme fatigue. In this condition of nervous and emotional exhaustion, the couple begin their life together. Regardless of how well-acquainted they have become during their engagement period, marriage is bound to raise new situations requiring thought, sensitivity, and tact. Nervous and physical exhaustion make it doubly difficult for the young couple to meet these inevitable circumstances with wisdom and patience. The awkwardness which frequently accompanies this period of initial intimacy is easily exaggerated by fatigue, until the loved one—so familiar only yesterday—may begin to seem strange and more than a little frightening. Research suggests that not more than half of couples can expect early sexual adjustment. (Data are presented in Chapter 20.)

The couple's first venture into sexual relations is likely to be discouraging. Strain, fatigue, and awkwardness often make intercourse difficult or unpleasant for the new wife. The long-awaited experience often turns out to be frightening and completely disillusioning. As one young woman commented about her honeymoon, "If I ever see that doctor again, I'm going to give him a piece of my mind for the buildup on sex he gave me." She indicated how awkward and embarrassed she was about sexual intercourse even though she was informed and knew what was expected of her. She concluded with, "It was not till weeks later that the wonder of it came to me."

Time for Being Alone   Dating and engagement activities normally lead a couple along a path of steadily growing intimacy. By the time they begin to consider marriage seriously, sexual attraction and desire have begun to loom as significant factors in their relationship. By the day of the ceremony, this desire for complete fulfillment has generally reached its peak. Yet, sexual fulfillment for the new wife usually is not a simple matter of sexual intercourse. Her greatest satisfaction and happiness may come primarily from the hours of intimate companionship, wooing, and the gradually increasing sexual play that precede intercourse.

When a couple spend their honeymoon in an atmosphere of hectic social activity their opportunities for these periods of gradual sexual preparation are lost. Not only does the sex act itself fall short of expectations, but also the full meaning of emotional oneness is seldom realized.

Sexual adjustment is not the only justification for planning time to be alone. During engagement couples oversell themselves to be sure of winning the mate. Now, during the early days of marriage, this idealized mate becomes more and more a real person, both actually and in the eyes of the spouse. The honeymoon should be a time of getting reacquainted. The new person who emerges from a period of continuous intimacy is likely to be very different in many respects from what was expected. Problems and uncertainties may even be aroused in the process of this awakening, and they can seldom be met and solved in a crowd or among relatives and friends.

Time to Be with Others and for Doing Things in a Group   Before marriage many couples find it difficult to be apart for a single moment. They feel that they want to spend every moment of the rest of their lives alone together. Yet, experience shows that honeymoons spent in complete isolation from other people and from all group activities are more than most young people can take.

Many hotels, lodges, and resorts cater especially to honeymoon couples. They provide lengthy meal periods and a variety of activities from which couples may choose and thus live at whatever pace they desire. Such institutions assure the couple the companionship of their age group.

Whether a couple select an institution or prefer to make their own arrangements, it is important that they consider a number of factors in making the decision: (1) amount of money to be spent; (2) length of honeymoon; (3) activities both would enjoy; (4) amount of travel involved; (5) opportunities for rest as well as recreation.

ALL MAKE ADJUSTMENTS

The first days of marriage, if all goes well, involve erotic pleasure and a degree of ecstacy. This level of emotion cannot be sustained, and in any case it would hinder the adjustment to demands of new relationships and practical problems which arise. The role of homemaker is thrust rather abruptly on the young bride. She has little preparation for its demands and even less advance opportunity for making this role significant to herself, and fitting it into her scheme of values (Lopata 1966). The degree of adjustment that takes place in marriage is determined in considerable part by adjustments made previous to marriage. Some couples work out techniques of adjustment during the days preceding marriage and carry the same patterns over. Some couples, it may be supposed, never had major adjustment problems in their relationship before marriage and do not have them once they are married. There are others who have many problems of adjustment because they should never have married in the first place.

Burgess and Wallin's (1953) study of married couples whose engagement periods had been studied when they were in college showed that more than half of husbands and wives were aware of no major adjustment in marriage. These were for the most part couples who made their adjustments during the engagement.

Adjustment problems in marital relationships may arise over such factors as sex, social life, religion, economic problems, in-laws, friends, or recreation. They may also develop about problems of temperament, adaptability, and children. All such issues may be solved if the couple approach them cooperatively and with a will to succeed.

Burgess and Wallin find that a person's adaptability has the most to do with successfully fitting into the marriage relationship. Adaptability is defined as "the person's capacity to change his roles, his attitudes, and his behavior in order to adjust to those of the other person or to a new or modified situation."

Adaptability, it is believed, is determined by the person's "empathy, flexibility, command of appropriate attitudes and roles, and motivation to adjust." By empathy is meant understanding of the other person to the point of recognizing and appreciating his motives. This trait in the marriage relationship, research shows, is dependent to a great extent upon the husband's and wife's ability to communicate with each other, for understanding to the point of empathy is possible only as they confide, talk, and discuss issues fully.

Flexibility, the study shows, is partly psychogenic, that is, determined by the early years of conditioning. It consists essentially in being able to vary one's responses within a situation. On the matter of motivation to adapt, findings indicate that the couples most in love are most willing to adapt to each other. New situations, crises, and a will to succeed all have a bearing on the person's motive to adapt. It is also reported that associating with an intimate group with similar motives is a strong factor in motivating the individual toward particular kinds of adjustment. For example, the young wife who does not want children may readily and almost unconsciously change her motivation by association with a young married group with babies and an interest in them.

There are at least three types of decision-making in the marriage relationship: (1) the authoritarian type, in which the decision is handed down by the spouse who assumes the superior role; (2) verbal coercion, whereby one mate forces his opinion upon the other after strong argument; and (3) the democratic type, in which there is mutual discussion between husband and wife.

Various researches extending over a period of more than 35 years show that the democratic partnerships are the happiest. This, of course, does not mean that other kinds of relationships cannot and do not succeed. Rather, the democratic partnership, probably the hardest of all to practice, brings great rewards to those who succeed with it. However, the highest middle-class divorce rate is found among those who try it and fail. Highly individualistic men and women often can settle for nothing short of the ideal.

WIVES ADJUST MORE THAN HUSBANDS

Definitions of equality have changed much during the last few years, for they are prefaced on role expectations. What was once considered equal and appropriate, is no longer considered so in many households, especially those strongly influenced by the more radical fringe of Women's Liberation. They see every tradition which assigned men and women different roles as symbolic of inequality. Others do not view them so.

Past research indicates that the ideal of democratic cooperation on the basis of mutuality is seldom fully realized, although it is probable that each generation is nearer to it. There is no precise way of knowing how close the average marriage comes to approximating genuine equality.

A study (Burgess and Cottrell 1939) of over 500 marriages showed that in the American marriage at that time the wife was doing the major part of the adjusting. Burgess and Wallin's (1953) later study of college-educated couples reported that either husband or wife may make most of the adjustments in marriage, or they may adjust equally, but more often both husband and wife agree that the wife has made the greater adjustment.

It may be inevitable that women will adjust somewhat more than men because of the demands of marriage itself. A man rarely changes his vocation or place of residence for the sake of his marriage. A woman must often drop out of the work world entirely and move to the location in which the husband is employed. This puts the major burden of vocational adjustment on her. The woman who has been gainfully employed must shift the entire routine of her life in taking over the management of her home, even though she may continue to work. Where she formerly had independence and directed her life to suit her own convenience, she is now required to consider the interests and work activities of the husband.

When children come into the family the wife faces the most difficult adjustments of all. The man's role is little affected. In our nuclear family, being a mother is the most demanding, exacting, and time-consuming task the modern woman faces during her lifetime. To be constantly tied down by the helplessness of the small child is a nerve-testing, exacting routine for women, particularly those who face it with an attitude of frustration, rather than one of pleasure and pride.

Throughout the entire period of child-rearing, the demands on the mother are much more rigorous than those on the father, and come from various sources—children, husband, and groups in which the children participate. In a real sense, there is a long period in the life of the mother when there is little opportunity to think in terms other than family needs. Too few come to motherhood prepared for the transition.

This fact makes for more difficult adjustments in the later years, too, when the children leave home and she must develop new interests for herself. The husband continues in his chosen work throughout his lifetime and faces no adjustment crises in his routine until retirement. The whole lifetime of the married woman is almost inevitably one of continuous adjustment.

TIME VERSUS TECHNIQUE

Judson T. Landis (1946) studied the time it took couples to reach a satisfactory state in six general areas of adjustment—sex, money matters, social activities, in-law relations, religious activities, and mutual friends. Except for the first two areas, which will be discussed in separate chapters, adjustment was satisfactory for two-thirds to three-fourths of the couples from the very beginning. The marriages analyzed had lasted for an average of well over 20 years at the time of the study. A third to a half of those who had not made an early satisfactory adjustment in these four areas never did, and were still maladjusted.

In about 10 percent of the cases, the adjustment was satisfactory for one spouse, but not for the other at the beginning of their marriage. This, no doubt, reflects differences in values and expectations of men and women as to what the marriage should be.

Does time bring the necessary adjustment? Landis implies that it does for a certain proportion of couples. Burgess and Wallin (1953) are positive that time has nothing to do with adjustment:

> The point needs to be made that the passage of time in itself does nothing. Of course, a spouse having endured an unsatisfactory condition may at last come to accept it. But any emphasis on time as a curative factor may result in a laissez-faire attitude toward dealing with an adjustment. . . .
>
> Our review of the interviews of adjustment made in the first three to five years of marriage suggests that adjustments do not happen with the passage of time. They are either made or they are not made (617–18).

The decisive factor is whether husband, or wife, or both are adaptable. According to this view, then, technique is all-important. Either during the engagement or in early marriage a couple adopts techniques which lead to a satisfactory working relationship or else they are likely to remain at odds.

The truth probably lies somewhere between these positions. There is no doubt that some couples mature in marriage and become more considerate and understanding in their relationship to the mate. An in-law problem may be cured by time, through death or migration, for example. Time is an important factor in the pair relationship both before and after marriage. Many, no doubt, follow an arbitrary and unyielding pattern after marriage which was already apparent during the engagement. Accommodation or failure are the only alternatives for these people. Time alone will only fix the already established relationship.

THE IMPORTANCE OF EARLY ADJUSTMENT

Whether adjustments are made prior to or early in marriage, the earlier the better the chances for the couple. First, during engagement and early marriage most couples are more eager to make their relationship succeed; there is greater motivation to success. Second, they are at a period in life when adjustments come more naturally than they will later. Third, and perhaps most important, is the fact that marriage habits have not yet developed. A new relationship is flexible. As the marriage pattern becomes increasingly crystallized around certain ways of acting and reacting, the problems involved in changing become increasingly complex.

The important thing is not just reaching a verbal agreement, but mutually practicing insofar as possible the agreed-upon behavior. A young man, for example, may be talked into agreeing that his wife rather than his mother should decide questions about his new home, but unless he is willing to act accordingly from the very beginning, there is little hope that he has really been convinced.

In the matter of general marital adjustment, the following rules are practical ones to follow:

1   Work out mutually satisfactory solutions to major differences before marriage.
2   Problems (such as those that might grow out of sexual relations) which cannot be met before marriage should be solved as early in the relationship as possible.
3   Throughout married life, problems and differences should be met and solved as they arise. The longer an unsatisfactory marriage situation is allowed to persist, the greater the problems involved in changing it.

The scriptural admonition, "Let not the sun go down upon your wrath," is an excellent guide in marriage.

ADJUSTING TO THE KINSHIP STRUCTURE

With marriage, families are joined. Life will never be quite the same for any concerned parties. A new dimension is added to family life that will continue through the life of the married pair. In our highly individuated society there are few traditional guides that are adequate for dealing with kin, but scarcely can one cut them completely off. The degree of desired and necessary involvement differ from couple to couple. Financial involvement is usual minimal. It is seldom necessary to share living quarters. Special occasions do often involve family members, and when children are born, the interest of kin greatly increases.

IN-LAWS

Throughout history mothers-in-law have been considered troublesome. Most societies have inflicted severe penalties on a man if he and his mother-in-law meet (Shlien 1965). In Northern Australia, a man who speaks with her must be put to death, and among another group in the South Pacific, both parties would commit suicide if they should meet. In Yucatan, a man believes he will be made sterile for life if he meets his mother-in-law face to face. Since Navaho men believe they will go blind if they see their mother-in-law, she may not attend the wedding.

Apparently, fear of seduction of the young husband by the mother-in-law, or some such incest taboo, is present in many of these restrictions. Little is feared from the intrusion of the husband's mother into the marriage.

In parts of India, where the joint-family system of the Asian world is meeting the individualistic nuclear family of the Western World, social workers report that suicides are greatly on the increase among young wives. The bride who has learned Western ways is not happy to become a servant in her husband's parents' household, and be ordered, persecuted, and outrivaled for her husband's affection by the husband's mother and sisters. An ex-governor of Bombay felt the situation was so serious that he proposed a law providing punishment for such in-law persecution. All over India the mother-in-law is proverbially considered a devil. With the joint-family system, and patri-local residence of the young couple, such a concept of the husband's mother is not surprising.

In the United States, the in-law crisis, if it does not come before marriage, reaches its worst proportions soon after. Each family is appraising the new addition. Parents have a hard time letting go and continue to hope to direct the lives of their children in a proper and helpful way.

The in-law conflict in the United States is unpredictable since it is a matter of interpersonal relationships and not an institutional arrangement. This is very unlike most cultures where the relationship of in-laws is explicitly institutionalized; the culture defines the claim that parent family and the adopted family will have on the new members. Usually in the joint-family system, particularly if it is patri-local, the son's mother has comprehensive claims on the new daughter. Until she has borne a son, the young wife is expected to have a rating quite like that of the servants in the household, and to be subject to the mother-in-law's command.

As American marriages get established, parents are somewhat less likely to interfere. They learn that advice is not wanted and will be ignored, or they come to see that the new pair is capable of handling its own affairs. Also, the longer a marriage has existed, the greater likelihood that parents will have died and, therefore, have been removed from the possibility of interference. This, of course, is not by any means always the case. Sometimes when one parent dies the other moves in with the young couple, adding to the problems of adjustment.

In a very real sense every family has its own distinctive way of life. Marriage adjustments are often intensified because each member of the pair tries to reestablish the way of life of his own childhood family. For this reason, in-laws may get blamed for problems they are only indirectly responsible for causing.

On the other hand, both parental families are judging the new in-law addition by their own standards. It is particularly true that the husband's family is likely to be looking the new daughter-in-law over very carefully, trying to form a judgment as to whether she is going to be able to fit their family pattern. The son's relatives are often guilty of trying to make his wife over to fit their pattern. Their ideas of her duties as a wife may be quite different from her own, and, in fact, quite different from what her responsibilities as a wife should be. If they start out to reform her, she may soon find her husband and all his family in agreement as to what she should become to be the good wife.

Actually, the new marriage may require quite a different marriage relationship than that which has been made by either set of parents. Yet it is not unusual for the new wife to find herself hemmed in by their expectations, being gradually forced to conform to their family customs. Undoubtedly, the extent to which the wife is subjected to scrutiny depends on the degree to which premarital acquaintance has been thorough and carried on in close contact with the husband's parents. In such cases much of this adjustment has been made in advance.

Yet there are those who marry knowing there is going to be trouble. Judson T. Landis in 1967 studied 581 marriages. Of those who reported an in-law problems, 41 percent indicated they had been aware of it before they married.

Husband's Mother More Often Intrudes   Folklore holds that there are times when any young wife may find it comforting to run home to her mother, instead of establishing from the outset the habit of talking over her problems with her husband. The fact is, however, that the husband's mother is most often the problem in-law in the modern marriage. The attachment between mother and daughter is a very strong one, but mothers cling even more tenaciously to a son and become a greater nuisance in a son's than in a daughter's marriage.

One might, of course, expect young women to feel that their husbands' mothers were the greater problem since they would naturally be more tolerant of their own mothers than of the husbands'. But these young women had discovered what research also shows regarding the in-law problem in contemporary marriages. The husband's mother has much more difficulty in letting go than does the wife's mother.

This, perhaps, is not the only factor. The husband's mother identifies the wife's role in marriage with her own and, therefore, is likely to be extremely critical. The wife's mother is less likely to be critical of her own daughter, since she follows housekeeping and marriage patterns which the mother has instilled. The wife's mother is not likely, either, to interfere so much with the young husband's role, since she has no close identification with the male role.

Judson T. Landis (1973), studying in-law-relationships of 544 student couples, found the mother-in-law was the cause if a problem did exist. For the wife, the mother-in-law was causing friction in half the cases, for the husbands in 42 percent of the incidents. The next most troublesome person was the sister-in-law, who caused friction for 16 percent of husbands and 13 percent of wives.

Blood and Wolfe (1960) find, as did the Landis', that the younger the couple, the more difficulty there was with in-laws. It is apparent that parents feel more free to interfere with the youthful couple. Parents undoubtedly see more mistakes, more often mistrust judgment of the young bride or groom, and the young more often solicit advice and financial help. The young have more often married against parental advice, for reasons of pregnancy, and consequently lay themselves open to criticism.

A study by the U.S. Bureau of the Census (1968, Table B, p. 2) shows that 19.2 percent of marriages in which the husband is under 20 were living with relatives, only 5.7 of those aged 20–24. Less than 2 percent of any other age group prior to retirement lives with relatives.

Duvall (1954) analyzed case-history documents of over 1800 in-law relationships. She found the husband's mother (the wife's mother-in-law) the most trouble-causing personality. Next was the wife's mother, with the husband's sister a close third.

The in-law adjustment is twofold. Newlyweds must reckon with the impact of relatives on the family, and also with their own ties to parents and relatives as they affect the new marriage. Although parental ties are supposed to be fairly well-broken by attachment to the new mate prior to marriage, and fully severed in an intimate sense when the marriage is consummated, the break is not always so complete.

Winch (1952) found, in a study of the carryover of attachments, that the mother is the preferred parent of both husband and wife; that the son is the preferred child; and that the mother–son relationship is the strongest family relationship. He believes that the strong attachment of the son to the mother impedes his mate choice and also his adjustment in marriage. Burgess and Wallin (1953), in their study of engaged and married couples, find that both son and daughter carry over strongest attachments to their mothers.

These and other authorities seem to agree that though both son and daughter carry over close attachments to the mother, the son having been away from home more has emancipated himself more completely from attachments to his mother prior to his marriage. Even though his mother may cling to him more than the wife's mother to her, his prior independence from her and the cultural expectation that he be independent may make his emancipation from his mother as easy, if not easier, than that of the daughter from her mother.

Time and Distance Factors   About one in ten couples, according to Judson T. Landis' (1946) study, had not worked out a satisfactory adjustment with relatives after more than 20 years of marriage; another 7 percent had taken one to 20 years to do so. If this group is typical, the in-law problem is a difficulty of considerable importance over a long period in one of every five or six marriages. The study does not indicate whether parents are responsible, the clinging of the husband or wife to a parent, or whether both situations are responsible. It is probable that in many cases the strong attachment to a parent on the part of one of the mates is a two-way attachment and that the difficulty in the marriage is ultimately resolved only by the death of the parent.

Actually, the in-law problem may not now be as serious as it once was. In our mobile society young people often live in a separate community from their parents. Moreover, Social Security has helped remove the necessity of children caring for the widowed parent in their own home.

Positive Contribution of In-Laws   The in-law relationship has been discussed as a problem. It is not always so. Many married couples do not have in-law problems at all. Duvall's (1954) case histories show that in many cases the young wife appreciates the husband's mother as a second mother, loves her, and finds her helpful. The husband sometimes finds the wife's mother a substitute for his real mother who has died, or a second mother if his mother still lives. Many times the in-laws help with the children, take the wife in while the husband is away in military service, and care for her and her children in case of his death or their divorce.

Duvall's study also shows that the in-laws sometimes suffer from the neglect or inconsiderateness of children. They do not know quite what role to play with their married children, and later, with the grandchildren. This is a new situation and unique to our type of marriage–family system. Such role relationships are never left in doubt in the ancient cultures of the world. In the in-law area, as in so many relationships of the married pair in urban industrial society, roles must be worked out through the adjustment process because they are no longer defined by custom.

Schlesinger's (1969) in-depth study of 84 successful remarriages of Canadian couples—middle-class, somewhat superior in intelligence and schooling, and still fairly young, who had made a success of their marriage—suggests that in-law relationships was a major area of adjustment for them.

It is undoubtedly true that during the divorced period spouses have "returned to mother," in a certain degree, reviving the parent tie. Parents may have a difficult time releasing the child a second time. Often in the case of divorce, there are children, usually left with the mother. Here, too, the daughter is often required to reestablish parental ties. This may make it doubly hard for grandparents to release her and their grandchildren to a new husband who is not the father of their grandchildren.

DISILLUSIONMENT WITH MARRIAGE

Marriage is a demanding contractual arrangement, designed to make the world safe for the rearing of children. It imposes numerous new roles, and many obligations not only to the mate but to the mate's family and the community. Perhaps no human relationship demands so much bargaining, so much struggle for ego satisfaction and power, and so many compromises. There is little prior preparation of attitudes and expectations in our romantically oriented culture, where youth move from a world of games to the stern realities of adulthood which come with marriage.

One of the more significant of all early adjustments is the discovery that marriage is, after all, primarily a routine way of living. During the early days of marriage there is a preoccupation with the personal feelings and responses of the mate. This is gradually lessened as a living routine is established. Men suffer more from disillusionment than women. Loss of freedom, new household obligations, and economic responsibilites are a part of the normal cost of marriage. Romance decreases in reality.

Hobart (1958) finds some evidence of postmarital disillusionment in both men and women. The disillusionment shows up most in the areas of personal freedom, marital roles, having children, in-law relationships, values of neatness, values on control of money, and attitudes toward divorce. He believes his data show some evidence of a relationship between degree of romanticism prior to marriage and disillusionment.

In marriage the sexual tension of the chaste engagement eases in the satisfying release of sexual relations. The "put on" self of the engagement period becomes the more routine self, with ups and downs of moods and tempers. "Woe unto him or her who cannot understand and accept this 'disillusionment' of marriage," say Levy and Munroe (1938), "The person who must have glamour, who cannot take the disillusionment of settling down, is not ready for marriage." This kind of person, even though he resorts to divorce, will find that a new marriage will not help. He has not yet come to accept himself or to know what his own needs are. He will not find them in marriage. "Glamour in marriage cannot be continuous, but it needn't be absent." All human beings must learn sooner or later that man is not capable of living at a high pitch of glamorous excitement.

If dating has carried the couple well beyond the first excited stage of love, considerable realism should have entered the relationship before marriage. In such cases disillusionment should not be great. Marriages entered into hastily, and in the overly excited first stages of the pair relationship, may be in for a most painful period of disillusionment.

Some couples sense this risk. During World War II, a young woman who had married the day before her new husband, a young man she had known only briefly, had left for a foreign post with the military, expressed her anxiety over the fact that her husband was writing her an average of 35 letters a week. They were long letters in which he was pouring out his heart in an overromanticized love.

She was still working in her home country as a home economist, was of a more practical nature, and still felt herself a part of real life. She feared the reality he would have to face when they were able to live together as husband and wife. "I'm no angel," she said. "In his dreams now I seem to be. I'm not sure whether he can accept the discovery or not."

For some, the disillusionment of marriage comes quickly, and the relationship is on its way to early termination from the outset. This is not surprising, for many marry who are not suited to marriage. Some never will be, others will be only after disillusionment which shocks them into a greater sense of reality about the marriage relationship.

Others marry for the wrong reasons, or for no conscious reason at all. It may well be that most people marry for wrong reasons, but are adjustable enough to reappraise the situation and work out a marriage of reality. Men particularly are at a loss to give a reason for marriage. Ask the question of them unexpectedly and they are likely to falter. A woman is more likely to answer in terms of the fine qualities of the man she married.

The underlying motives for marriage are, of course, often very complex. The insecure seek an anchor, the sex-hungry seek a partner, and the pregnant seek respectability and relief from guilt. Those from troubled families seek to escape them, some marry to spite another, and others marry on the rebound. Some marry because they fear time is running out for them. The supply of eligibles they depended on is dwindling. Some seek social status in their marriage. Some wish to escape the pressure to marry exerted by family and friends.

Little wonder that some become disillusioned.

PROBLEMS

1   Ralph and Evelyn are trying to decide how and where to spend their honeymoon. They are young, out-going, and companionable, but neither has a serious hobby. Their list of possible choices has been narrowed down to six. Which of the six would you oppose and why?

   a   Visit Evelyn's aging but lovable grandparents on their little Iowa farm.

   b   Visit Ralph's uncle who owns a dude ranch in New Mexico.

   c   Rent a secluded little island hide-a-way off the Florida coast.

   d   Spend a week in New York City seeing the current plays, buying clothes, seeing all the sights, and if possible, landing a job for Ralph.

   e   Join two other honeymoon couples who are going from Florida to South America on a small yacht.

   f   Spend a more-or-less unscheduled week in Miami.

2   Couples who are happy and report that no adjustments have been necessary are probably:

   a   Well-mated.

   b   Lying.

   c   Delaying the adjustments until a more appropriate time.

   d   So used to adjusting that they are unconscious of doing it.

   e   Unusually successful in their sexual adjustment.

3   In the marriage of your parents or acquaintances, is there any evidence that adjustments are still taking place? Without giving names, describe a situation in which you have observed an adjustment in a marriage that has lasted over five years.

4   List the circumstances under which you would agree to have either your father-in-law or mother-in-law share your home.

5   Married students in the class describe your early relationships with your in-laws. In what areas did problems most often arise?

6   *Research exercise:* Poll the class or some other student group on the question, "In what areas do you anticipate the most numerous adjustments in the early weeks of marriage?"

a   Diversity of ethical codes.

b   Recreational interests.

c   Sexual relations.

d   Little things such as habits of daily living.

e   Religious beliefs.

f   Home management.

g   Life philosophies.

h   In-law relationships.

Tabulate results. Does the class tend to agree on areas of greatest likelihood of difficulty? Do the areas of anticipated adjustment differ according to sex?

7   Do you believe that women usually have to do more adjusting in marriage than do men? That marriage changes their way of life more completely than that of men?

8   *Sociodrama:*

a   A doting mother whose only son has recently married visits the young couple regularly and explains, "I only want to help out; I know how much a young bride has to do and how many things she has to learn." Tension mounts with each visit and the play opens with the young bride finally telling her mother-in-law how she feels about the situation.

b   A young bride, after a month of marriage, discusses with an older married sister, her disillusionment with marriage.

PATTERNS OF
ADJUSTMENT

18

"Husband power" was once assumed, and socially supported. Now there is much talk of "woman power, wife power," and increasing concern about "couple power." In any kind of close living or working arrangement between human beings, some way of getting along together must be worked out if the association is to last. Business partners must divide privileges, responsibilities, and work, as well as profits. Roommates in a dormitory must each modify some of their ways if they are to spend a year together. Single women sharing an apartment must agree on many things, or agree to disagree—on hours for doing certain things, food, and furniture. This necessity is even greater with married couples, for the possible areas of conflict are more numerous than in any of the other pair relationships mentioned.

In all human relationships, whether of individuals or groups, certain interaction processes and adjustment devices are characteristic. The simplest of these is *dominance* and *submission*. This pattern is seen everywhere—in the chicken yard, where psychologists have spotted the dominant hen by her ability to outpeck all the others and make them bow to her demands; among the forest animals, where the most powerful male wins the female after defeating all comers; among children in their play; among adults in many work and social situations. Once the relationship of dominance and submission has been established, quarreling and conflict cease. The superior need no longer fight to hold his own, for the inferior has already been cowed.

Conflict is another common interaction pattern between persons. At its worst, it aims at annihilating the enemy. In its more gentle forms, it is expressed in quarreling, which is an attempt to annihilate the opponent on the ego level. Where conflict exists, adjustment has not been reached. In fact, conflict is one of the common ways of striving for an adjustment. The difficulty with this device is that someone always has to lose before there can be peace, unless there is compromise and both can be content to call it a draw.

Accommodation is a sociological term which means about what is meant by the common phrase "agree to disagree." It is settling issues by permanent compromise of differences. Conflict is tiring, even in the form of quarreling. There comes a time to call a halt and stake out neutral territory if there is to be any getting along at all.

Competition is a common pattern of American life. It aims at outdoing the other person by superior performance. Modern business is geared to perpetual competition. Success in modern education for the most part is measured by one's ability to outdo one's classmates—by landing a little higher toward the "A" side of the normal curve. Men live in a competitive world throughout a lifetime. Women live competitively in school and college.

Cooperation is the goal of adjustment. Instead of a couple's outdoing each other, their mutual aid and mutual sharing are the pattern of cooperation. It gives to each the other's strength. The cooperative couple is the adjusted couple.

Each of the above processes appears in some form in every marriage. The device employed most often and the kind of adjustment arrived at determines the happiness of the marriage.

DOMINANCE AND SUBMISSION

The story is told of a strapping big lieutenant who married a girl of small stature inclined toward bossiness. After carrying her across the threshold, he took off his pants, handed them to her, and commanded her to put them on. She put them on, then protested, "Why, Bill, they're three times too big for me."

His reply was, "Don't forget that."

In the relationships of husbands and wives, dominance and submission have been the most important characteristics of man–wife relationships, with the male historically more often assuming the dominant role. This solution to the problems of the marriage can be simple, clear-cut, and remarkably effective if each member of the pair can accept it. There is little quibbling over issues and little time spent in family councils.

Many of the peaceful marriages in which there were never any real quarrels are explained by this clear distinction in the authority of man and wife. If Grandpa was the patriarch that most men in his time were, he blew off steam and his wife humbly took it, slipping off into the bedroom to cry rather than fighting back. Other women had their way by subterfuge. They had to recognize the superior physical strength of the husband, but resorted to their wits to outmaneuver him. *Life with Father* depicts the strong male figure well and also the wife who knew how to get her way in a situation where open conflict would have been futile.

Rainwater's (1965) study of authority patterns by social class suggests that equality in decision-making is most likely to be found among middle-class couples. At the working-class level, particularly among blacks, but also to a certain extent among whites, the wife is most likely to dominate in decision-making.

Landis and Landis (1968) studied the marital happiness of 3000 marriages of parents of their students. He found the democratic marriages far more often happy than those in which either husband or wife were definitely dominant. Strong wife dominance was least often related to happiness. A tendency toward male dominance was quite favorable to happiness but not equal to the 50–50 pattern.

Among couples in trouble to the point of seeking counseling help, the Landis' found the husband dominant in half, the wife dominant in 31 percent, and in only 29 percent 50–50 dominance.

A survey covering 2596 well-educated families attempted to learn not only who was boss but also whether the couple was happy with the arrangement. Students in three colleges—the University of California, Oklahoma Agriculture and Mechanical College, and Columbia University—were asked by Paul Popenoe to rate couples with whom they were well-acquainted and who had been married at least five years as to (1) who was boss in the family and (2) happiness of the marriage. It was found that men were dominant in 35 percent of the cases and women in 28 percent; in 37 percent there was a democratic partnership. Of the democratic partnerships, almost nine out of ten were found to be happy; of the male-dominated couples almost two-thirds were happy; of the wife-dominated marriages, less than half.

Christensen and Johnsen (1971) found a strong trend toward the traditional authority pattern among college students, who were asked in 1951 and again in 1967 which authority pattern they favored in their marriage. The study found that in 1951 32 percent of males and in 1967 74 percent favored the male as head of the family. Of the college women, in 1951 41 percent favored the male as head, and in 1967, 72 percent. "Neither as head" obtained favorable responses in 1951 from 42 percent of males, and in 1967, 17 percent. In 1951 56 percent of the women favored "neither as head," and in 1967, only 23 percent. It would be interesting to learn whether Women's Liberation has radically influenced this trend in college student norms since 1967.

David Mace (1953) emphasizes the point that there are many patterns of marriage which can succeed. He believes that the marriage in which dominance and submission are the characteristic pattern often has a place, concluding that "there are people who want to be dominated—and not all of them are women."

The democratic ideal, while it is a norm for the urban–industrial marriage, certainly need not be attained by all persons in order for them to be happy. Many couples can and do live together very successfully in a relationship of dominance and submission. It is when one insists on this kind of relationship and the other finds it incompatible that trouble begins.

It is an unusual couple who have not had some very serious quarrels during their engagement period. Those who do not are probably not well enough acquainted or have failed to be together in enough different situations to learn some of their real differences.

For those who have no misunderstandings before marriage, the first real clash after marriage is likely to be unusually disturbing. The chances are that the young couple will wonder how two people so much in love could possibly quarrel so.

Quarreling Is Near Universal   The American Institute of Public Opinion, in one of its national surveys, asked couples whether they had marital disputes. Four out of five couples admitted that they did. The researchers in interpreting these data suggested that they suspected the other fifth either had had some pretty serious marital disputes, or else were still honeymooners, or were people who had passed their golden anniversary and forgotten a great deal.

> Absence of quarrels is too often regarded as a criterion of successful marriage. Usually it means little more than indifference—a superficial placidity attained by shallow people or those whose real interests lie outside the home, or those who, with or without a day of reckoning, habitually bury their antagonism under the thick cotton pad of polite behavior (Levy and Munroe 1938, p. 76).

Quarreling in marriage is one indication that husband and wife both recognize their equal status in the marriage. The way a young couple handle a quarrel is the thing that tells whether they will build a cooperative union. The issues about which a couple quarrel indicate areas where adjustments have to be made.

Judson T. Landis 1967 study of 581 married couples showed that discussion and compromise is the effective way to get along. Arguing and quarreling led to negative reactions, yet more than two-thirds engaged in this kind of behavior. Over half at times refused to talk to each other. Avoidance in the area of difference was reported as behavior practiced by about two-thirds; 62 percent of husbands reported that wives cried at times, and 48 percent that she denied him sex relations.

The most extreme reaction reported was becoming physically ill from encountering differences. This reaction was reported by 16 percent of husbands as a reaction of their wives and by 7 percent of wives as a reaction of their husbands.

Mace (1953) states that although a couple are drawn together by such affinities as a need for sexual fulfillment, the need for comradeship—that is, to share a common destiny and to avoid loneliness—and the need for a sense of belonging, it is just as certain that at some point in their relationship, hostilities must appear to protect the ego of the individual against too great an encroachment by the other party. This is the only way, he believes, that the personality can avoid destruction. Couples must learn where the point of equilibrium is.

Searles (1959, p. 73) has concluded that people become schizophrenic partly by reason of "a long continued . . . unconscious effort on the part of some person or persons . . . to drive him crazy." This can be a family conspiracy, even though unconscious. Better to tell another member of the family "you're crazy" now and then than to let matters fester to the point where there develops the "unconscious need to drive somebody else crazy so that an unhealthy state of mutual dependence can continue despite anxieties and frustrations."

Mace believes that because of this inevitable hostility, quarreling has a proper and useful place in marriage in that it lets off emotional steam, whereas intellectual interchange on the discussion basis fails to do so. He feels that the couple needs at some time to feel the heat of each other's points of view and needs. To quarrel without either partner giving ground, until emotion is dissipated and they are drawn together by some affinity, most likely sexual need, is likely to be disastrous. No equilibrium is reached, and the marriage simply fluctuates back and forth between hostility and attraction. Also, for one partner to give in for the sake of peace is not good. In this case, one member becomes the tyrant and the other submits.

Discussion of issues is a rational substitute for quarreling and argument. Quarreling is a direct attack on an opponent. It is an attempt to in some measure destroy him. Discussion, by contrast, is an attack on issues to be settled. The one is personal; the other is impersonal. The one leads to chronic nagging; the other brings out issues on which the couple differ, airs them, and tries to work out an intelligent solution. But discussion does not vent hostilities and is not an adequate substitute if there are deep hostilities.

Physical Combat

At the far extreme of marital conflict is physical combat. Most husbands are stronger than their wives and can dominate them by force. One of the best indices of the extent of physical combat in families is the police record. New York City Police Department figures show that 40 percent of injuries to officers result from trying to settle disputes within families. Social workers, who might be expected to be called in for help, are not on duty 24 hours a day, seven days a week, as police are. In economically depressed areas, where tensions build up from congested living, fights are most frequent at night and on weekends when the husband is home. The police are called in to help settle conflicts as best they can (*Family Life* 1972).

In such a social climate, the four day work week may well bring more family problems than it solves. With little money for outside recreation, more time for a weekend drunk, the male underfoot for a longer stretch, problems of family conflict can multiply.

Quarreling Versus Other Reactions to Marriage Frustration

Psychologists and counselors recognize the need to vent hostilities in the average marriage to the extent that various counseling techniques have been developed which encourage domestic battle, often in group situations. Bach and Wyden (1969), in their book, *The Intimate Enemy,* stress the virtues of quarreling, and set forth fair rules for it. They stress the motto "Couples who fight together, stay together," and "A fight a day keeps the doctor away." The fight must be a fair fight. Bach claims that couples he has taught his "fight-training" are living more satisfying lives than before. He has trained many in his marathon group sessions.

Whether results are from his unique genius in working with people or could generally be used by others it is too soon to know. And whether all couples could benefit from intensive, often violent, fighting therapy, is seriously to be doubted. There may well be many types who would be destroyed by it.

Quarreling, like many adjustment devices, though never a constructive means is often a better alternative than many others that are likely to be needed if provoking circumstances exist. Situations can reach the point where some kind of action has to be taken, or the inner disturbance will cost more than venting the emotion externally. The intimate husband-and-wife relationship requires so much encroachment on the private domain of the other's ego that an explosion may be needed to release tension and establish balance. The explosion clears the air for discussion by venting the emotional pressure. It may open the way for the couple to work out a more clear and understanding relationship, and thus strengthen their relationship with each other.

In the violent quarrel, the real issues are more likely to come out than they are under other circumstances. The making-up process often leads to a deeper level of intimacy than existed before, for the sequel is often a confession or admission of mutual guilt and responsibility. People who can quarrel are much less likely to get involved in serious psychological problems than are those whose recourse is sulking or avoidance. Quarreling is a better adjustment device than brooding, walking out, or running home to mother or to a neighbor. It is better than the neuroses which may develop from constantly ignoring or repressing hostility issues. It is better than escaping in drink, desertion, or a romance outside the marriage. It is even better, although some authorities disagree, than quietly and passively engrossing oneself in religion as an antidote for adjustment.

This is not to say that a couple who can live without a quarrel is not a happier or more perfect pair. There is no doubt that they are. But most couples cannot, at least in the early stages of their marriage, expect to live at this level of perfection. The problems to be worked out are usually too numerous. Quarrels begin with trivialities, but they uncover much more. The triviality is the trigger. The built-up hostilities, frustrations, and aggravations are the background for the explosion. As the emotionally charged quarrel breaks loose and the destructive impulses of one mate are vented on the other, the real issues of the quarrel are likely to be exposed. As the heat of wrath grows, that standard phrase comes forth, "And another thing," and with it an exposure of the vital issues. The issues are no longer trivial; they are the very issues that determine marriage survival or failure.

Compromise Not Enough   Whether the quarrel leads toward adjustment or carries the marriage toward disaster will depend on the outcome. Of these there are several possibilities. Compromise is a more logical outcome perhaps than one would expect in a really heated quarrel. Genuine contrition allows the couple to each recognize his faults and ask forgiveness for them. This may bring the partners to a deeper level in understanding of each other's needs and thus may result in a more perfect love. People who have never had issues to overcome perhaps cannot understand how this can be. This kind of outcome leads to the building of closer marriage relationships and decreased hostilities. It leads to mutual acceptance and increased mutual respect. This is perhaps the finest outcome possible in any kind of human conflict, for it is not merely the peace of compromise that points the way to accommodation (discussed in the next section) but it is also a genuine approach to mutual identification and to becoming one in spirit and in aims as well as in flesh. Genuine compromise is, of course, a step forward. And in some marriages, compromise of a purely rational character is necessary. Compromise is not enough, however, where it proves only to be a truce in a cold war. The same hostilities are there if the issues over which the quarrel took place are still there.

If each continues to feel that the other is wrong, that the other is to blame, that the other person is the one who must change, the truce cannot last. It will revive again and continue, and perhaps with each battle the road back to genuine mutual understanding will be made more difficult.

If the result is a draw and each recognizes and respects the other person, then the ground is laid for an accommodative relationship in the particular areas of tension.

The quarrel may end in one party or the other being completely cowed. Such a marriage can last. It may be that the wife can recognize and respect her husband and be willing to be subservient to his demands and needs. She may be able psychologically to accept this without neurosis. She (or he) can, however, in being cowed, be put on the way toward the development of psychosomatic illness which are the ego's way of expressing frustration.

In an earlier day, many women, when they had lost all hope of being treated fairly in their marriage, found solace in religion, sufficient solace to retain their sanity. Many today, with less faith but with equal provocation, end up in a mental institution. Mary Marker (1956) published the account of a woman who found solace in prayer and faith in a marriage where many years of crying had brought no solution:

> I never express my needs to my companion but rather to my Heavenly Father. He is our friend and will fill our needs if we trust Him. I have had many things I have wanted badly. Because I knew my husband would be cross and angry if I mentioned them to him, I asked only my Heavenly Father. Many of them came slowly but surely.
>
> Early in my marriage I learned that for peace there had to be a 100 percent husband marriage. So for peace, here I have had to take the mental attitude that I am the hired girl working in his home with no more rights than a hired girl. I talk of only things he is interested in, and when I am with him, I do the things he likes to do.
>
> With this attitude, I can be grateful for all the crumbs he shares with me. To me, the house, furniture, money, children—all things are his and I am fortunate to be able to be in his home that I might care for and be with his children.

One suspects that few psychiatrists would agree with this woman's solution. In fact, it is doubtful that many moderns could accept it for themselves without being victimized by their frustrations to the point of emotional collapse.

In quarreling there is always such a thing as victory without a solution. Certainly the situation that tends to neurotic symptoms proves to be of this character. There may be victories where neither is left cowed but where one is left rebellious, even though silent—more hostile and more deeply determined that in the end he or she must win, must destroy the other or the marriage. If this is the solution, the divorce will take place in the atmosphere of vengeance.

Human nature is complicated, and it is most difficult to spell out all types of situations, the hurts, and the solutions that couples arrive at through venting antagonisms. The list of outcomes mentioned must be considered only as suggestions.

Vicarious Relief   Critics may well say that mature persons do not use quarreling in the marriage relationship to vent frustrations. But where is one to find a world of such human beings? True, the more mature person learns vicarious ways of venting hostilities undamaging to others. All can practice in this direction.

The old-fashioned butter churn offered many a mother and grandmother a wonderful relief from the aggravations and frustrations of a dominant and contrary husband. They gritted their teeth and slammed the plunger down. The vigor depended on the extent of their hostility and the depth of their feelings of aggression, which they dared not vent directly on the husband. The result was good—the butter came more quickly, and their feelings were relieved without being taken out on their children.

Some vent hostilities in driving an automobile. A psychiatrist living in the outskirts of Los Angeles indicated that he enjoyed the long drive to work through the Los Angeles traffic very much. "It vents my hostilities," he said. Drivers are dangerous when venting their hostilities while in heavy traffic; many seem to get the thrill of combat in dodging traffic, or in speeding, or in outwitting the traffic patrol. This is not a recommended way of relieving one's emotions.

The batting of a ball, the playing of handball, any vigorous physical activity, is for many a wonderful way of easing the spirit of tension and aggression. Perhaps one of the great psychological benefits of hunting and fishing, mountain climbing, and the conquest of nature lies here. The revival of interest in these activities in our day, when so many live under heavy social pressure, lies in part in the fact that conquest of nature restores the ego.

Every person needs to learn how to vent hostilities in vicarious, harmless ways, whether this be by pounding the piano keys or by throwing darts. Thus it is possible to restore one's own ego without destroying another person.

When children enter the marriage, quarreling or even arguing vigorously often gives the children a disquieting sense that there is deep trouble in the family. Couples who must continue to do a certain amount of quarreling and arguing should be particularly careful that it is done in such a way, or at such a time, as not to give the children a sense of insecurity.

Barbara Steel, in a popular article, reports asking a friend the secret of her long and happy marriage. The reply was that she and her husband discovered early in their marriage "that there was no subject on which we could reach an agreement. And so ... we've never tried." Hannah Lees (1957) wrote an article entitled "How to Be Happy though Incompatible" and made a very strong case for her thesis. She declared that men give no thought to the problem of compatibility. Wives may as well face the fact, and a lot of emotional probing will not improve matters at all. She feels that few men give wives the attentions they feel they need because husbands are preoccupied with other things and take marriage for granted. Almost every marriage, she concludes, has many areas of incompatibility. It is to be expected.

There is much sense in this. Of course, the crux of the matter is: How many areas of incompatibility can be tolerated? And, how serious is the incompatibility to those aspects of the relationship which are most vital?

If the husband is inclined to direct or correct all the wife's moves when she goes bowling or when they sit at the bridge table, they may find it essential to seek their recreation separately.

The wife may not like the fact that the husband wants an occasional weekend to hunt with the boys, but she comes to recognize that escape into the male subculture provides a type of recreation he needs and likes; and so she accepts it, even though it means that she has to be alone sometimes. At first she may quarrel about this; then she probably realizes that there is no use quarreling about it the rest of her married life. Such weekends are important to him, and she recognizes this fact, even though she would like to have it otherwise.

The husband may not like the fact that his wife—say she is a former teacher—takes occasional work as a substitute teacher. Her working inconveniences him. He storms about it at first because his meals are not ready on the days she teaches. She explains that she needs to get out of the home and keep in touch with people and activities that she likes. He grumbles for a while but learns to step aside and let his wife work out this part of her life to suit herself rather than him.

The petty irritations of living are often the worst irritations of all. Kirkendall tells of a young wife in one of his classes who was irritated almost beyond endurance by the fact that her husband left his socks on the floor. Kirkendall asked the class of young women what they would do.

"Nail them to the floor," one said. "Put them on his desk," another suggested. And so the answers came—a dozen or more—all of them solutions which would have increased the tension between husband and wife.

Finally one girl, registering a tone of disgust at her classmates' answers, said "They're not very heavy. Pick them up!"

"But," the wife protested, "he's got *no right* to expect me to pick things up!"

A marriage is in for difficulties when either husband or wife insists on living by rights. There are many instances in any human relationship where someone must go the second mile, and there are many second miles to be walked in a successful marriage. It will sometimes be the husband who walks them and sometimes the wife. When both are willing to do this, there is a kind of sharing that raises the marriage relationship to the highest level of happiness.

How much one can give and take very often depends on what the issue symbolizes for him or for her, as the example of the socks so well illustrates. Many women can pick up the socks day after day, and, though they dislike it, they take it as part of their work routine and come to accept it. But the wife who protests "He's got no right to expect," "It's not democratic," etc., has much more at stake than household routine. Ego and status values of great depth are apparently at stake in her case. She no doubt feels herself in servile status picking up socks. If this is so, the giving will probably have to be on the husband's part.

Without doubt, the greater the number of areas of accommodation, the less likelihood there will be of a completely happy marriage. Yet in most marriages there must be some acceptance of the mate in spite of certain incompatibilities. Topics on which the couple can never agree are not discussed. A "Keep off" sign is posted over these topics. It is far better simply to let them lie. There are certain fields of activity which the couple must avoid altogether.

Avoidance may not meet the ideal of the romantic marriage, yet if couples, by avoiding certain subjects, issues, places, or even each other completely for periodic separate vacations or other breaks, can thus keep the peace, they may find this the most satisfactory way of marriage for them. Many cannot submerge their personalities fully in marriage. There are vital zones of overlapping, but this is all there ever can be. Those who learn this about themselves and their mate may well find their marriage quite satisfactory, in fact, as satisfactory as any marriage could be for them.

COMPETITION VERSUS ADJUSTMENT

The ego and the love motives in human personality are forever at odds, yet the ego must be preserved from extinction even in marriage. In a society where the game of competition has become the most engrossing activity of life, love is always threatened. In love, one cannot count marks and scores, dollars and cents, honors and distinctions, prizes and awards. These are part of the ego-expressing game. Love cannot be measured in the balance of fair exchange. It gives without asking in return.

The educational and occupational worlds are worlds of competition for survival. Success and status are dependent upon the development of this trait in the personality. In most relationships of adult life in American society, equality assumes competition. Competition involves rivalry—the spirit of excelling and outdoing. This spirit has come to characterize the lives, not only of men but also of women. It is the predominating pattern of school activities from earliest childhood through the college years.

Work relationships in industry and in offices and the vying for social position and standard of living also show this pattern. Admittedly, competition is an invigorating characteristic of a society which has always preached the doctrine of social climbing—a faith of a people who believe that there is room at the top.

Marriage, by contrast, is an institution of close complementary cooperation. Its success or failure depends upon the couple's ability to work together as a team and to get along. Among young people today, each of whom has gone to college and competed both educationally and in the work world, the competitive habit often brings great difficulty to marriage because it is hard not to carry over the competitive spirit into the marriage relationship.

If both continue to work, they may feel they are competing with each other in the amount of income they earn, in the type of expenditures they are able to afford, and in many other aspects of their personal relationship. This is one of the great difficulties faced by the emancipated couple in this age. Instead of being able to bolster each other and strengthen each other's roles in the community and work world, each finds himself trying to detract and run down the mate as a way of maintaining or building up his own status. The wife may envy the husband in his work if she is confined to the home; if both work, they may feel competitive in seeking status, just as couples who are friendly in school sometimes feel competitive over athletic or social success or grades. This competition destroys the couple's feeling of security in each other. The wife feels humiliated by the husband's success, or the husband feels outdone by the wife's achievements, whether they are in social life or the work world.

Rather than being able to share the joy of the partner's achievement, the mate then is likely to suffer from inferiority feelings. Rather than push the mate forward to further success, each tries to draw the other down to his own level. Rather than bolstering the husband's or wife's feeling of self-importance, the mate tries to "cut him down to size." Rather than the marriage being a cooperative sharing, it is subjected to the same strain as business and social life outside the family, where rivalry for position and influence replaces a genial spirit of working together. This is one of the important reasons that every marriage for the well-informed modern couple is a marriage of constant adjustment.

This problem is often presented as one peculiar to the modern wife. It is so only because men have by custom so long been granted authority that the wife gets blamed for her attempt to realize equality in the marriage. Something has to give in such marriages, for affection evaporates and the marriage becomes comparable to a business relationship, with the same ruthless driving for success, the same quest for recognition. As love dies, the craving for status and recognition become more desperate. Human nature is so constituted that if one has a full and understanding love, his ego requires little satisfaction in the marriage relationship; without love the ego makes great demands. If the love relationship is lost in marriage, the ego becomes immense, demanding satisfactions and recognitions that are entirely beyond reasonable expectations.

Popenoe says that the American male wants a woman who will bolster his ego—give him sympathy, warmth, and security—not outdo him. In writing to college-trained women, he has warned that even in our sophisticated age, men are not interested primarily in women with college degrees. They want a woman in marriage to satisfy emotional needs that cannot be met in the competitive activities of work life. This is no doubt the great appeal of the foreign girl to the American male. (For research bearing on this, see Chapter 13.)

Women, too, in marriage are, in the final analysis, looking for the emotional security that comes from being wanted, loved, and cared for. They crave a sense of belonging. They want this without paying the price of sacrificing their right to be individuals.

The American marriage today sets before men and women the highest ideal of which man has ever dreamed—that of sharing on the basis of complete equality, or recognizing each other as full, complete, and self-sufficient individuals, with rights, privileges, and aspirations to be satisfied both within and outside the marriage. This type of marriage is a much finer relationship than one based on dominance and submission, and yet it is one which is increasingly difficult to attain. This is not because men and women do not realize its merits, but because they are built for a competitive relationship and cannot meet the demands of such a marriage. Consequently, most marriages are a compromise.

The secret of a happy marriage, like a happy romance, is cooperative, self-sacrificing sharing. It is the part of each spouse to bolster, support, and build up the ego of the other. Both men and women seek to satisfy their wish for emotional security in marriage. Both must also find success and recognition to be happy.

REALISM IN EXPECTATIONS

Marriage, in its interpersonal relationships, is not a highly standardized institution. It is, rather, highly individuated, and a pattern satisfactory for one couple would not be good for another. For the most part, research to date has been drawn from the middle and upper-middle classes. There is no doubt that family patterns of the lower classes differ considerably in many respects and that the kinds of adjustment described in many situations in the preceding pages would not be satisfactory for certain couples.

The ideal marriage relationship has been outlined. One should not be discouraged if he does not fully realize the ideal of cooperation. One meets couples who seem to be happiest together after a good spat. They have let off steam and seem closer for it. And there are some wives who seem sure of their husband's love only after he has given them a good beating.

Most such marriages are among couples from cultures where the expression of violent emotions is sanctioned by customs and where male dominance is still accepted. The book and film, *The Quiet Man*, depicted a marriage relationship in which the American male failed to conform to the expectations of Irish culture and lost the respect of both his wife and the community. Only when he became his wife's master did he regain a place of respect.

If a couple has found a satisfactory life together along these embattled lines, who is to say that their roles should be revised for the sake of an ideal? Such couples might find a peaceful life a monotony. Often the wife who requires such treatment of a husband in order to love him has been punished or severely dominated by her father during her upbringing.

But in the genuinely democratic marriage of sharing and cooperation—the ideal of the American family system today—adjustment rather than conflict is the accepted goal. This is for most couples the road to understanding. In general, it is assumed that such a philosophy of adjustment offers a far superior type of human relationship to that which is sometimes attained by means of a struggle for mutual acceptance.

In a definite sense, every family pattern in the United States is different. In fact, some authors talk about family culture, referring to the unique characteristics of each individual household. One should not be anxious about his future if his pattern of life does not exactly fit the norm which this or any other book presents. The important thing is that the pattern of life established create a mutually satisfying family environment and provide a home in which children feel secure.

Successful marriage adjustment is not for the perfectionistic, nor is it for the callous and inconsiderate. The democratic marriage offers a sharing between human beings of their strengths and weaknesses and their troubles and anxieties. Husbands and wives cannot, in all situations, see eye to eye, and most marriages would be monotonous affairs if they did. Adjustment, after all, is a relative thing. It assumes a working relationship which is satisfactory in most respects for the persons involved in it. It need not satisfy neighbors, friends, even relatives, and it need not satisfy every criteria of research or of marriage books.

Young couples must avoid constantly taking their marital temperature and worrying about the state of their relationship together. They must be realistic and practical about the marriage and recognize what it can and cannot do. Within the family, as in other institutions, there is always the tendency of the individual to want to have life ordered to suit him. However, the institution itself survives only as life is ordered to suit the group. The struggle between these two forces has always gone on in every marriage. It is particularly active today with the recognized equal status of family members; the struggle between individual interests and group interests becomes more evident.

If the central purpose of the couple is to maintain a working relationship and to face life's issues together, most of the minor differences will be submerged in the longer and more distant goal. Much divorce today takes place over petty issues because the couple have not decided in their own minds that their marriage is going to be a success, that it has a future, and that its central purpose will be fulfilled regardless of the many fringe adjustments which must be made in the relationship.

PROBLEMS

1   If one or the other spouse tends toward dominance in marriage, do you think it should be the husband or the wife, or does it matter? Upon what grounds would you justify your position:

    a   Tradition.
    b   Pattern of your parental home.
    c   Family well-being.
    d   Natural law.
    e   Economic factors.
    f   Intellectual differences.
    g   Other factors.

Do the men and women of the class agree? What is the most common justification offered?

2　List several areas of a marriage in which accommodation rather than adjustment is likely to occur.

3　Mary and Jarvis are both college graduates with responsible and well-paying jobs in a large, highly competitive advertising agency. Their jobs rest on their ability to think up schemes for outdoing other firms and outselling other products. They even compete with one another at their jobs, since their salary and prestige depend upon the number and quality of ideas that each submits. How might they guard their private lives from the competitiveness they must feel while on the job?

4　List several situations or personal qualities to which you would refuse to adjust, or even to accommodate, in marriage. Does there tend to be consensus among class members on any of these adjustment limitations? Do men's and women's views differ?

5　Describe a situation in which a quarrel might serve as a desirable adjustment device.

6　*Research exercise:* Poll the class or some other student group on the question, "In your own home what pattern of adjustment seemed to prevail?" Tabulate results by sex. What patterns of adjustment are most often found? Do men and women have a different conception of adjustment patterns in their homes?

7　Do you believe that some men, as well as some women, are happier in marriage when they have a mate to dominate them and make decisions for them? If so, how do you explain such personalities?

8　Do you believe that an occasional quarrel is as necessary to a marriage as a pressure valve is to a pressure cooker, that both provide means for letting off steam and keeping the lid from blowing off?

9　Do you believe that competitiveness is on the increase or gradually being reduced in the relationship of the sexes before marriage? After marriage?

10　*Sociodrama:* Stage a quarrel between husband and wife over some common problem such as money, recreation, friends, or religion. At the end, let the group discuss the quarrel as an adjustment device. Would another pattern have produced better results?

11　What is your opinion of "fight-training" for marriage partners?

MARRIAGE
HAPPINESS

19 In our culture the "happiness" measure is applied to marriage more than to any other relationship. Happiness is, in fact, considered *the* measure of success as perhaps in no other society on earth. Yet there are no precise measures for it. A Gallup poll published in 1969 found that one in four American wives would pick a different husband if they could start again. That is certainly one index of some degree of dissatisfaction, and probably unhappiness, with their present spouse. The same poll found one in ten husbands would pick a different wife, which suggests that men get a better deal in marriage from their point of view than do women. A Louis Harris Associates poll in 1972 reported married women to be twice as happy as those divorced or separated. Getting rid of the husband apparently is no sure way to greater happiness for those who seek this solution to their marital woes. Divorce is not the cure-all for husbands either. Numerous studies report the highest suicide rate in the population among divorced men.

Happiness is an elusive quality, perhaps more often found by those who do not seek it directly than by those who do. In marriage it is in part a by-product of assuming responsibility. It is also affected by temperament. Some are more gloomy and pessimistic than others. General health and energy affect it, and certainly basic to it is conditioning by the childhood home. Unhappy homes produce unhappy children, who become unhappy adults.

Happiness is in part a matter of perspective. We have spoken of the disillusionment of early marriage. The perspective here is that of young people who have not quite forgotten the romantic dreams of the courtship period. But old people, looking back over the years, choose as happiest, not the so-called carefree years of youth but the busy years of family rearing. Concepts change with time and experience. Certainly factors in marital unhappiness today are misconceptions of the more radical followers of Women's Liberation about the bondage of marriage and child-rearing. "Bondage" or "fulfillment" are in part matters of perspective.

PROPORTION OF MARRIAGES ATTAINING HAPPINESS

Intangible and elusive as the quality "happiness" may be, most husbands and wives recognize it once it has been attained. It has been found that husbands and wives usually agree in their estimates of their marital happiness and also that outsiders who know the couple well generally agree with them in estimating the degree of their happiness. Research spanning a period of more than 40 years has also shown that the happiness ratings of a couple do not change much over short periods of time.

Burgess and Cottrell (1939) had 526 couples rate their marriages as to happiness. These are their replies:

HAPPINESS RATING	NUMBER	PERCENT
Very happy	224	42.6
Happy	108	20.5
Average	76	14.4
Unhappy	71	13.5
Very unhappy	42	8.0
No reply	5	1.0
Total	526	100.0

It will be seen that over 63 percent classified their marriages as either happy or very happy and that only 21.5 percent classified them as unhappy or very unhappy.

Judson T. Landis studying 3189 marriages in 1967 (see Landis and Landis 1973) found that about the same proportions of marriages were happy or very happy, average, unhappy, or very unhappy.

Life, on April 28, 1972, sent out a questionnaire asking respondents to rate their marriages as to happiness; they received 62,000 replies. Of those responding, 80 percent rated their marriage as "happy" or "very happy."

These studies are fairly consistent in showing that approximately 60 percent or more of marriages are considered very happy or happy by the couples themselves, and that 15–20 percent are considered unhappy or very unhappy. Apparently, then, a fairly high proportion of marriages that last do lead to happiness. It is possible also that some of the couples who at the time of questioning were unhappy may have been happy earlier in their marriage.

These studies probably give a little brighter picture of marriage than actually exists if all marriages are taken into account. Presumably the most unhappy marriages end in divorce. These studies excluded divorced individuals.

Self-ratings of happiness are indicative of how one feels about one's own marriage. Observations of the marriage by others might presumably be different. Among the historic studies are two which have ratings by others. Richard Lang (1939) obtained ratings by close friends of couples and reported the following:

RATING	NUMBER	PERCENT
Very happy or happy	10,798	61.6
Average	3,322	18.9
Unhappy, very unhappy, or divorced	3,413	19.5
Total	17,533	100.0

At the University of Southern California, a study of 2080 married men showed that 58 percent were happy; 15 percent doubtful; 27 percent unhappy; and that of 2176 married women, 58 percent were happy, 15 percent doubtful, and 27 percent unhappy (Popenoe and Wicks 1937). The ratings were by graduate students and were made for educated couples of their acquaintance.

Chesser's (1957) study in Great Britain, dealing with over 6000 women, shows that happy marriages are closely related to happy childhood there, as they are in the United States. Childhood happiness is, of course, dependent largely upon the happiness of the parents' marriage. Happily married women, Chesser found, are as much in love with their husbands after marriage as before. They do not regret their marriages and would marry again. The unhappy women's love has diminished since engagement and the first year of marriage. Three-fifths of them would marry different men if they married again, and a third, if they had their choice, would not marry at all. Three-fourths of these women found after marriage that their husbands were not the sort of people they thought they were before marriage. Most of those who were happy found their husbands as they thought they were prior to marriage.

It is evident from such research that women tend more toward extremes in their expressions of happiness or unhappiness than do men. It is likely that a wife's happiness is more completely dependent on the marriage than that of her husband. She lives much of her life in the family environment, and female subculture leads her to believe that much of her fulfillment is to be in marriage.

Many years ago sociologist Hornell Hart (1940) developed a scale for measuring happiness called the "euphorimeter." Zero was the point between happiness and unhappiness. He found that young people who are unmarried scored 75 points on the happiness side, those engaged to be married, 173 points; married people who had never considered divorce, 200 points on the happiness side; those on the verge of divorce, 160 points below zero. Prisoners under guard on a chain gang scored 150 points below zero. If this scale is a valid measure, the obvious conclusion is that marital tensions can produce great misery.

The Feminist Revolt Element

There is little doubt that the feminist crusade has introduced a new element into the domestic scene. At the extreme fringe are those who see most of the values of female subculture as degrading. Denigrating attitudes are built into the mental and emotional set of the female from the initial socialization to adulthood—willingness to be compliant, to be subservient, to accept the male as dominant, etc. The marriage contract is seen to be loaded in favor of the male. Even the change of name to that of the male is symbolic of subservience. The woman is to be the man's vassal. He wields economic and social power, particularly if he has more education. And among the lower classes with less education, the male is still a patriarch. Physical coercion makes him dominant and he uses it at times. In suburbia, the male has the advantageous position, as the female depends on him for a living, and is more shut off from a variety of social contacts than he. His power increases as the wife is confined to the home with childbearing and child care. She feels herself in eclipse while he gains in occupational and social stature (Gillespie 1971).

"The Drop Out Wife" (*Life* 1972), who abandons husband and children for the glories of the feminist crusade, is certainly the exception to what even most feminists want, but she does set many wives to thinking of alternatives to the dull routine of family life. *The Female Eunuch* (1971) does not plot a suitable path for most young women, if marriage statistics are any index of women's wishes. But certainly it has become easier for a woman to think of a single life without stigma, and for all women to realize that there are ways to get along without the male.

One could cite many examples of new norms emerging in the female subculture. It is becoming easier to conceive of other ways to happiness and fulfillment than marital bliss alone.

QUALITIES OF HAPPY MATES

Terman (1938) tried to determine the principal traits that characterize the happy and the unhappy husband and wife. Here are the traits he found most indicative:

HAPPY WIVES	UNHAPPY WIVES
Have kindly attitude toward others	Often have feelings of inferiority
Like to help underdogs	Tend to be defensive or aggressive
Tend to be conventional	Are easily annoyed, irritated
Are cooperative	Often join clubs only to get an office or recognition in them
Have strong urge to save money	
Are optimistic about life	Are extreme in their views
Do not take offense easily	Are more likely to be neurotic
Are less interested in social activities such as dances	Lose tempers easily
	Are impressed by thrilling situations
Like to teach children	Seek spectacular activities
Put less importance on clothes	Want to be on the move; are romance seekers
Are systematic homemakers	
Do less day-dreaming	Show little interest in others

HAPPY HUSBANDS	UNHAPPY HUSBANDS
Have greater stability	Often have feelings of inferiority
Are cooperative	Compensate by browbeating wife and
Get along well with business associates	subordinates
Are somewhat extroverted	Dislike details
Are conservative in attitudes	Are more radical about sex morality
Are willing to take initiative	Are inclined to be moody
Take responsibility easily	Are argumentative
Do not get rattled easily	Like recreations that take them away
	from home
	Are likely to be careless about money

Clearly, many of the attitudes and behavior traits mentioned in these lists are rooted in early training. Some of these factors may, of course, relate to the character of the marriage itself. For example, whether a husband likes recreation outside the home may depend a great deal on the kind of home his wife provides. The unhappy wife's restlessness, too, may depend on the kind of security and ego satisfaction the husband provides.

In one of its series of polls, the American Institute of Public Opinion asked respondents what they considered the most important qualities of husbands and wives. The question was worded thus: "What would you say is the most important quality in a good husband (wife)?" Here are the five most frequently given answers:

QUALITIES MEN WANT IN A WIFE	MARRIED MEN (PERCENT)	SINGLE MEN (PERCENT)
Good homemaker, good housekeeper, etc.	47	28
Agreeable, good company, pleasant disposition	18	21
Faithfulness, loyalty	15	16
Cooperative, a partner	13	8
Patience, understanding	11	9

QUALITIES WOMEN WANT IN A HUSBAND	MARRIED WOMEN (PERCENT)	SINGLE WOMEN (PERCENT)
Good provider	42	28
Faithfulness, steadiness	22	24
Kindness, consideration	20	13
Agreeable, good company	14	16
Cooperative, a partner	55	1

In a day of restaurants, delicatessens, and laundries, it is a little surprising to find that almost half the married men mentioned the old-fashioned quality of being a good homemaker and housekeeper. This, along with good cooking, is about the same standard that their great-grandparents probably would have set. In fact, it is the trait Solomon emphasized centuries ago in his description of the good wife:

> She seeketh wool, and flax, and worketh willing with her hands. She is like the merchants' ships; she bringeth her food from afar. She riseth also while it is yet night, and giveth meat to her household. . . . She perceiveth that her merchandise is good: the candle goeth not out. She layeth her hands to the spindle, and her hands hold the distaff. She is not afraid of the snow for her household; for all her household are clothed. . . . She looketh well to the ways of her household, and eateth not the bread of idleness (*Proverbs* 31:13).

Even with our great stress on companionability and compatibility, only a small portion of men mention these traits. Married women are quite old-fashioned, too, in one respect. Almost half of them want the husband to be a good provider, but with them the cooperative partner is even more important. This latter attitude suggests that women hold the new concept of marriage in much higher regard than men.

When one compares the standards of single and married men and women, one sees why some adjustment in marriage is necessary. Little more than a fourth of the single men thought of housekeeping and homemaking as of great importance, but almost half of the men with experience in marriage considered it of great importance. Similarly, single women were much less often concerned about marrying a good provider than were married women.

Some 19 percent of both single men and women did not know what qualities they wanted in a mate. This group perhaps will have few adjustment problems. More likely, they will know what they want if they fail to find it in the person whom they marry.

HAPPINESS DURING THE MARRIED LIFE CYCLE

Adjustment to marriage and family life is a progressive thing. Better or worse rather than stationary relationships are likely to characterize most human associations. Into every family, factors intrude from the outside. There are relatives, social activities, clubs of one member or the other, friends, children and their problems, obligations to city, church, and school. There are always various influences that infringe upon the family to affect its relationships—economic hazards for which the couple is in no sense responsible, health difficulties of relatives or of the members of the family, tragedy due to the death of near relatives or death within the family, tragedy due to sideline romances. All these factors—in fact, everything which enters into the experience of one or both members of the pair—affect the marriage relationship in one way or another.

Some of these factors make for greater solidarity. Many couples, as they share an increasing number of experiences together, grow closer to each other in understanding, sympathy, and mutual dependence. In other cases, experiences divide the family and force members further apart, so that in every marriage there tends to be greater or lesser satisfaction with the marriage partner as time goes on.

Even marriage conflict and divorce are seldom events that happen suddenly. There is usually a long period of increasing friction and conflict prior to the divorce (see Chapter 28), and even in the best-adjusted families there is often a long history of adjustments, some of which were not wholly pleasant. Marriage, like other relationships, is not always ideal; in fact, it is doubtful whether it is ever ideal. The storybook concept of a couple marrying and living "happily ever after" is a beautiful illusion. Marriage, like every other human relationship, is a developing, growing, changing affair. The degree of its satisfaction depends upon many factors, not the least of which is the ability of people to find in personal relationships the kinds of responses which satisfy them.

In our day of intimate interpersonal relationships, most marriages face the supreme test at some time. Even happy marriages may approach the point of divorce when certain forces impinge upon the relationship: disloyalty of one mate, financial crisis, in-law crisis.

Burgess and Cottrell's (1938) study of happiness in marriage according to years of marriage shows that happiness scores are higher during the first year of marriage. They drop about 10 points during the first six or eight years. After many years of marriage they seem to be somewhat higher again but not so high on the average as at the beginning.

Lang's (1939) study of the happiness of 7393 couples, as reported by friends rather than by the couples themselves, finds more couples happy and fewer unhappy during the first two years of marriage than during the later years of marriage. The number of discontented couples, according to the study, slowly increases with the number of years married.

Cuber and Harroff (1965) studied the marriages of persons of the upper middle class in the age group 35–55, all stable (married for at least a decade), and rated them in terms of relationship that seemed to prevail. Categories were "conflict-habituated," "devitalized," "passive-congenial," "vital," and "total."

The authors conclude that there are very few good marriage relationships, i.e., "deeply satisfying," as appraised by themselves. Couples reported that more vital relationships were often found outside the marriage but that the marriage continued out of "habit, tradition, and austere social sanctions." The researchers conclude that at this stage in life "the good man–woman relationship in marriage is the exception rather than the rule."

DeBurger's (1967) analysis of letters addressed to the American Association of Marriage Counselors for help shows that problems connected with "affectional relations tend to increase as length of marriage increases." Not so with the sexual relationship of the husband. His problems decrease with length of marriage. The wife's sexual problems, though less often present, persist.

Luckey (1966) found that couples married for approximately eight years saw less favorable personality qualities in their mates, the longer they were married. This was true of both those who were satisfied with their marriage and those who were not.

Counselors are aware of a late "middle-age slump" in many marriages. Clinton E. Phillips (1968), director of the Department of Counseling of the American Institute of Family Relations, lists it in his outline of marriage phases as: "Disenchantment (threats of divorce) process"—children are leaving home; the couple may already be grandparents at age 45 or soon after; they are beginning to look forward to 30–50 years together in the empty nest; they need new meaning in their lives.

The wife may be absorbed in the emotional adjustments of menopause or consumed with loneliness over the children's departure from home and community. She neglects the husband or is callous to his feelings of loss and loneliness, which may be as strong as her own. The husband at this time is particularly susceptible to the romantic lure of a younger woman, who may seem to promise him his lost youth and a new lease on life. He may even plunge into an adolescent love affair with all the violence and emotional turmoil of a 16-year old in his first throes of puppy love in compensation for his first awareness that youth is past, much opportunity is gone, and ambition is unfulfilled. If he has been successful, he may wonder now about the purpose of it, with the children gone and security already built for the future.

This experience of middle age provokes the saying "There's no fool like an old fool." Unless the wife shows unusual wisdom or unless social restraints of the community are strong, this affair of the late 40s or early 50s may actually break the marriage, for in some cases the husband learns too late that he is not so young as he thought he was. For the ventures of a new sex experience, of which he may tire quickly, he has sacrificed a companion who could share the wisdom and understanding of his years. With that sacrifice he has lost the lifetime continuity of experience which they share in each other and in their families.

This is the time for the couple to find outside interests, hobbies, companionship, and all the other things they have dreamed of during the busy days of hard work and family rearing. Now comes the time to enjoy their postponed travel and leisure.

Gradually, the grandchildren will become the focus of attention and a new emotional outlet. They will give the aging couple a grasp on the future and revive a close family bond.

Plotting the Happiness Cycle

There have been various attempts to chart the happiness cycle. Although the response may vary with the nature of the questions asked and the respondant's time of life, there is some merit in the happiness profile. The Rollins and Feldman (1970) study is presented as an example of the happiness profile of husbands and wives in Figure 19–1. Note that wives start at a higher peak than husbands, but that the curve of happiness also drops more rapidly until by stage IV it is below that of the husband. It never equals the husband again, but both find renewed happiness as they enter retirement and have life to themselves again.

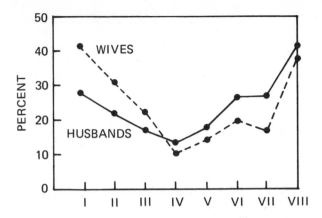

Stages in marriage life cycle. Source: Boyd C. Rollins and Harold Feldman, "Marital Satisfaction over the Family Life Cycle," *Journal of Marriage and the Family,* 32:20–28, Feb. (1970).

FIGURE 19–1

Occupation and Happiness

Elliott L. Richardson (1972) released a report of a special research task force on the relationship between the job and social unrest. It found that many of the nation's 82 million workers hate their jobs, and that their unhappiness is a factor in many social ills. The report concludes:

> Worker discontent is measured by declines in physical and mental health, family stability and community participation, and an increase in social and political alienation, aggression, delinquency and drug and alcohol addiction.

Obviously, all of these social ills affect the happiness of the marriage and its climate as a place for the upbringing of children. Occupations differ greatly in the satisfaction they yield to the worker, and consequently in their effect on marriage and family relationships. Sociological studies, although not abundant in this field, do give some measure of the correlation between particular occupations and marital happiness.

Lang's (1939) extensive study dealt with this problem, classifying the happiness of over 17,500 couples according to the husband's occupation; ratings were made by friends of the couple. Marked variations are observed. Whether these statistics mean that occupation is in part responsible for marital happiness or whether marital happiness is primarily a value of the upper and middle classes is uncertain. Whatever the meaning one assigns to the differences, they are striking (see Figure 19–2).

A third to almost a half of the marriages in the occupational groups at the top were rated "unhappy" by friends who knew them well, and only 10–15 percent of those at the bottom were rated "unhappy." Lang advanced the theory in explanation that (1) occupational groups that are mobile are less happy and (2) groups over which the community exercises less control are less happy. The

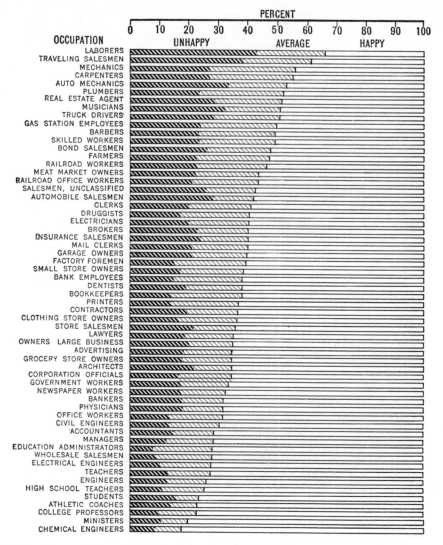

FIGURE 19–2 Husband's occupation as a factor in marital happiness. The results of ratings made by friends of 17,533 marriages, in which the husbands were engaged in the occupations listed in this chart, seem to show that professional men have the happiest marriages. Those in the occupations requiring mobility have more unhappy marriages. Source: Richard O. Lang in Ernest W. Burgess and Leonard S. Cottrell, *Predicting Success or Failure in Marriage* (Copyright 1939). Prentice Hall, Inc., New York). Reproduced by permission of the publisher.

latter point reminds one of the comment of an early Greek philosopher, who observed that a man's troubles begin when he is free to do as he pleases. It will be seen that most of the group shown at the top of the chart move about from place to place a great deal in their occupations, and the communities in which they live exercise little control over them. The traveling salesman is the folklore stereotype of the worker who escapes community control.

At the bottom of the chart are occupational groups which require little migration and over which the community exercises strict control—ministers, college and high school teachers, and students and administrators.

Popenoe's (1947) study of 3528 marriages, in broad occupational groups, showed that farm marriages were the happiest of all occupational groups, over two-thirds of them being happy. At the other extreme were the marriages of unskilled laborers, less than half of which (only 42 percent) were happy. Professional groups ranked next to farmers in happy marriages, semiskilled groups ranked next to the bottom, and business groups fell in the middle. The happiness ratings in the study were made by students at the University of California and at Colorado State College of Education. They rated only marriages that they knew well and had lasted five years or more.

Burchinal and Chancellor (1962), studying the duration of marriages in Iowa, found that among those who divorced, the couples having high economic status stayed together longer than did those having low economic status. In general, those of low economic status marry earlier, too. Their study further showed an early dissolution of marriages in which both partners were 19 or under.

Jessie Bernard (1966a), using 1960 census data, measured marriage stability (defined as men from 45 to 55 in their first marriage living with a wife, not necessarily a first wife—90 percent were the wife's first marriage). Table 19-1 shows that stability of marriage as so defined is lowest for those at the lower end of the scale of occupations and highest for the more stable and better-paid occupations.

The evidence of such studies suggests that finding happiness consists in part of finding an occupation in which people either place a value on happiness and find it as a consequence, or in which happiness is more nearly an inherent part of the total life pattern. At least it is quite evident that happiness in family life is related to occupation.

Proportion of Ever-Married White and Nonwhite Men Age 49-54 in Stable Marriages, 1960, by Occupation TABLE 19-1

OCCUPATION	PROPORTION IN STABLE MARRIAGES[a]	
	NONWHITE	WHITE
Professional and technical workers	69.1	84.2
Managers, officials, proprietors	63.2	82.0
Clerical workers	64.6	81.1
Sales workers	64.9	79.8
Craftsmen, foremen	61.2	79.5
Operatives	60.5	78.8
Service Workers	54.2	73.6
Laborers	58.6	77.2

Source: Bernard (1966a). Data from U.S. Bureau of the Census (1960, Table 7, pp. 96, 99).

[b] Note that marriages are more stable for white than nonwhite, and within each racial group, for those in occupations which provide regular income and offer higher status.

Rosow and Rose (1972) studied "initial complaints" of professional persons filed in California during the first six months of 1968 (90 percent of such complaints lead to divorce). They were particularly interested in comparing the rate for doctors with that of other professions. The folk myth that doctors have a high divorce rate is not supported by this study of 3408 high-level professional people, 267 of whom were physicians. The complaint rate shows that physicians were among the lowest of the professions, as is seen in Table 19–2. Lang's data on marriage happiness also showed that physicians were near the top in marriage happiness (refer again to Figure 19–2).

INCOME AND MARRIAGE STABILITY

Happiness of marriage and its duration are probably related. There is considerable evidence that certainty and regularity of income are favorably related to success in marriage and have been for many years. Burgess and Cottrell (1938) first reported the relationship. Parke and Glick (1967) cite the elimination of poverty as one of the two factors which will probably reduce the divorce rate of the future, for they found stability of marriage related to stability and amount of income.

Bernard's (1966a) study related income to marriage stability (stability defined as explained above). It will be observed in Table 19–3 that nonwhites and whites alike show greater stability with greater income.

Economic problems pile up in the lower socioeconomic classes and bring with them problems in the marital relationship (Rainwater 1965). This is, of

TABLE 19-2   Comparative Divorce Rate of Selected Professions

PROFESSIONS	ANNUAL COMPLAINT RATE PER 1000
Authors (nec)[a]	29.3
Social scientists	28.4
Architects	26.7
College Faculty, administration (nec)	20.2
Lawyers, judges	19.5
Engineers	18.5
Chemists	17.2
Editors, reporters	16.7
Accountants, auditors	16.5
Dentists	16.5
PHYSICIANS	16.4
Natural scientists (nec)	16.1
Totals	18.3

Source: I. Rosow and K. D. Rose, "Divorce Among Doctors," *Journal of Marriage and the Family*, 34:587–98, Nov. (1972).
[a] (nec): not elsewhere classified.

Proportion of Ever-Married White and Nonwhite Men Age 45-54 in Stable Marriages, 1960, by Income   TABLE 19-3

| INCOME 1959 | PROPORTION IN STABLE MARRIAGES[a] | |
	NONWHITE	WHITE
No income	38.5	57.9
$1–999 or less	49.9	64.8
$1,000–2,999	55.6	73.7
$3,000–4,999	58.2	78.0
$5,000–6,999	62.8	80.5
$7,000–9,999	68.0	82.0
$10,000 and over	69.0	84.7
Median income	$3,079	$5,613

Source: Bernard (1966a). Data from U.S. Bureau of the Census (1960, Table 6, pp. 113, 116).

[a] Marriage stability increases for both white and nonwhite with increase in income. Stable marriages refer to marriages in which men have been married only once and wife is present. In 90 percent of the cases it was also the wife's first marriage.

course, inevitable in a society where so much in the way of escape from monotony is dependent on cash expenditures. Cutright (1971) relates marital stability to income, with education and occupation controlled as variables. He finds high earnings related to mutual respect of the couple, and to a higher evaluation of the husband's role. There is greater job satisfaction and a bond of material possessions which couples do not wish to fragment.

Table 19-4 presents census summaries of the ratios of various race and income groups who have remained married for different age groups. It will be seen that the lower the income the less is the likelihood of the spouse of the first marriage still being present.

Percent of Ever-Married Males who were Neither Divorced nor "Separated" from their Spouse: By Husband's Age, 1959 Income, and Color, United States, 1960   TABLE 19-4

| HUSBAND'S 1959 INCOME | PERCENT OF HUSBANDS | | | | | |
| | 25–34 | | 35–44 | | 45–54 | |
	WHITE	NONWHITE	WHITE	NONWHITE	WHITE	NONWHITE
None	81	69	82	70	84	76
$1,999	87	82	85	80	86	82
$1,000–2,999	94	89	92	86	83	88
$3,000–4,999	97	91	96	90	96	89
$5,000–6,999	98	94	97	92	97	92
$7,000–9,999	98	94	98	94	98	95
$10,000 or more	98	92	98	95	98	94
Total	96	89	96	87	96	87
Gross color difference	7		9		9	

Source: Phillips Cutright, "Income and Family Events." *Journal of Marriage and the Family*, 33:291–306, May, (1971). U.S. Bureau of the Census (1966, Table 6).

PROBLEM AREAS ON WHICH HAPPINESS MAY HINGE

Certain cultural conceptions have much to do with determining differences, the resolving of which husbands and wives consider essential to their happiness and success in marriage. In order to get some idea of what these basic issues are considered to be, the writer asked over 1100 women—college girls, wives of college students, and the mothers of these two groups—what the five most important things were in making happy and unhappy marriages.* This gave a picture of the views of women through two generations and of both single and married women in the present generation. The answers of these groups were not far different, indicating that the same problems persist and are recognized now, as in the mother generation, and by single as well as by married women. In Table 19–5, the percentages of women who named the items listed as one of the five most important in marriage are given.

The most striking fact is that economic and financial problems take first

TABLE 19-5   Conceptions of Two Generations of Women as to Factors Producing Marital Happiness and Unhappiness

FACTORS PRODUCING UNHAPPINESS IN MARRIAGE	PERCENT OF 1138 WOMEN OF TWO GENERATIONS LISTING FACTOR	FACTORS PRODUCING HAPPINESS IN MARRIAGE	PERCENT OF 1071 WOMEN OF TWO GENERATIONS LISTING FACTOR
Financial and economic problems	51.9	Lack of financial problems	48.5
Infidelity, unfaithfulness	35.3	Similar social interests	41.7
Personality clashes	34.5	Understanding and	
Vices (drinking gambling)	32.6	consideration	40.5
Religious differences		Children	40.1
(no religion)	28.4	Affection, love, devotion	30.9
Sexual incompatibility	21.3	Agreement on religion	24.7
Lack of understanding		Sexual compatibility	18.2
and consideration	19.3	Lack of personality clashes	16.5
Different social interests	18.9	Confidence and faith	
Selfishness, wanting		(trust)	14.4
own way	16.7	Unselfishness	13.6
Lack of confidence		Similar education	
(jealousy)	16.1	and ability	12.7
Childishness	15.2	Lack of vices	4.0
In-law trouble (relatives		Lack of interference	
interfering)	14.6	of relatives	3.1
Differences in education		Others	68.6
and ability	10.6		
Lack of affection	7.2		
Others	59.4		

Source: Paul H. Landis (1951).

*This was not a checklist. Women wrote in a blank space the items they considered important.

place in the opinions of women, in both their lists of factors causing happy and unhappy marriages. Separate chapters in this book are devoted to adjustment to money problems of marriage.

The next most important field has to do with fidelity, general sexual compatibility, affection, and love. If one combines these items in the list, this area of adjustment is mentioned by more women than any other. Asked to mention the one thing most disastrous to marriage, more women listed the problem of infidelity than any other. A separate chapter will be devoted to the area of psychosexual adjustment.

Trouble Areas

A second approach to this question of happiness or misery in marriage is to study areas of trouble among those actually seeking help. DeBurger (1967) has made a tabulation of "help-request" letters received by the American Association of Marriage Counselors. It will be seen that the affectional aspect of marriage problems is uppermost in the wives' lists, the sexual in the husbands' (see Table 19–6). It may well be that they are talking about the same problem viewed from the perspective of female and male subcultures. At least the two areas have some relation. Personality relations are another area of considerable trouble. Money problems do not show up in this study, probably because most couples do not seek financial help from this source.

Alcoholism   The prominence of alcoholism in contemporary society and its disastrous effect on marriage and family life make some understanding of it of more than incidental importance (see Figure 19–3). There are more than nine million alcoholics in the United States. In fact, we have one of the highest rates of alcoholism in the world; and alcoholism, and the excessive use of alcohol short of the disease, may well be one of the major problems of marriage adjustment today. For alcoholism is not only a problem in and of itself but also brings with it many concomitant problems: nonsupport, infidelity, abuse, lack of companionship, and loss of status.*

Alcoholism is basically due to an inadequate psychological constitution, to feelings of inadequacy. Studies of marriage combinations where alcoholism is involved indicate that the spouse is not always blameless. Research suggests that the wife of the alcoholic husband is often a very difficult person, that there is considerable sense in the expression "she drove him to drink."

There is also evidence that the wife of the alcoholic often gets some kind of deep satisfaction out of his plight. It may be a way of expressing her superiority, or it may be that she gets pleasure in punishing him. Clinicians find that sometimes, even though the alcoholic is cured, the wife is not happy until she creates pressures that make him an alcoholic again. She seems to like his dependence.

*John L. Thomas (1956) has stressed such factors in relationship to the problem of alcoholism in the Catholic family. He finds it is not unhappiness that drives the mate to drink. The drinking habit is in itself dangerous for many. See also Gordon (1964, Ch. 4).

TABLE 19-6   Major Problems Revealed by Husbands and Wives in 1412 Help-Request Letters[a]

CATEGORY	HUSBAND (PERCENT)	WIFE (PERCENT)	TOTAL (PERCENT)
Affectional Relations	11.5	31.0	27.6
Spouse cold, unaffectionate			
Spouse in love with another			
Have no love feelings for spouse			
Spouse is not in love with me			
Spouse attracted to others, flirts			
Excessive, "insane" jealousy			
Sexual Relations	42.1	20.6	24.4
Sexual relations "unsatisfactory"			
Orgasm inability; frigidity, impotence			
Sex deprivation; insufficient coitus			
Spouse wants "unnatural" sex relations			
Role Tasks–Responsibilities	0.0	6.0	4.9
Disagreement over 'who should do what'			
Spouse's failure to meet material needs			
Parental-Role Relations	0.0	1.7	1.4
Conflict on child discipline			
Parent–child conflict			
Intercultural Relations	11.5	11.4	11.4
In-law relations troublesome			
Religion and religious behavior			
Situational Conditions	4.0	3.4	3.5
Financial difficulties; income lack			
Physical illness, spouse or self			
Deviant Behavior	7.5	8.7	8.5
Heavy drinking; alcoholism of mate			
Own heavy drinking or alcoholism			
Spouse's "loose" sex behavior			
Own illicit sex behavior			
Compulsive gambling			
Personality Relations	23.4	17.2	18.3
Spouse domineering, selfish			
Own "poor" personality; instability			
Clash of personalities; incompatible			
Spouse's violent temper tantrums			
Spouse withdrawn, moody, "neurotic"			
Spouse quarrelsome, bickering, nagging			
Spouse irresponsible, undependable			
Total	100.0	100.0	100.0
	$n = 252$	$n = 1160$	$N = 1412$

Source: James E. DeBurger, "Marital Problems, Help-Seeking, and Emotional Orientation as Revealed in Help-Request Letters," *Journal of Marriage and the Family*, 29:712–721, November, (1967).

[a]Chi-square = 91.80; $P < 0.001$ (eight categories × husband–wife status).

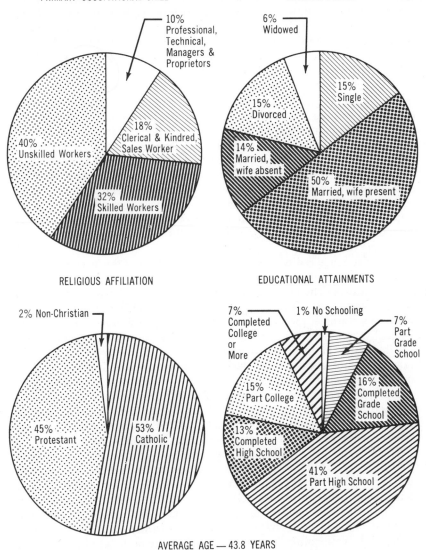

PRIMARY OCCUPATIONAL SKILL

10% Professional, Technical, Managers & Proprietors

18% Clerical & Kindred, Sales Worker

40% Unskilled Workers

32% Skilled Workers

MARITAL STATUS

6% Widowed

15% Single

15% Divorced

14% Married, wife absent

50% Married, wife present

RELIGIOUS AFFILIATION

2% Non-Christian

45% Protestant

53% Catholic

EDUCATIONAL ATTAINMENTS

7% Completed College or More

1% No Schooling

7% Part Grade School

15% Part College

16% Completed Grade School

13% Completed High School

41% Part High School

AVERAGE AGE — 43.8 YEARS

The typical alcoholic (average age 43.8 years) as found among patients of the Chicago Alcoholic Treatment Center. Alcoholism disrupts the lives of all family members. Source: *Chicago's Alcoholic Treatment Center News*, 1:2, September (1964). By permission of Chicago's Alcoholic Treatment Center.

FIGURE 19–3

One of the tragic effects of alcoholism is on the children. It is particularly likely to build hostilities between the father and the adolescent son (Kalashian 1959).

Joan K. Jackson (1956) has outlined seven stages in the cumulative pattern of alcoholism. First, there is the stage in which the victim denies the disease. After each drinking bout, there is an attempt to define it as normal. The main anxiety at this time is the social risk of drinking behavior. Both husband and wife feel that if it becomes widely known, the status of the family will be threatened. This proves to be of greater anxiety to the wife than to the husband. Normal behavior is rationalized by attempting to compare the husband's behavior with that of friends.

The second stage involves an attempt to eliminate the problem. This is done by becoming more isolated socially as the family becomes consciously more drink-centered. Drinking tends to become the symbol for all the conflicts between the spouses as well as between parents and children. The children are shielded from the father's behavior, and attempts are made to hide it from the employer by lying. Alienation between spouses increases. The more the wife expresses her hostility, the more the husband drinks. Discussions as to what the cause of the problem is and how it can be solved seem to be increasingly unproductive. The wife feels inadequate as a wife, as a mother, and as a woman. She begins to feel that she is inadequate to meet her husband's needs. She tends to devaluate herself. In spite of all the attempts to reorient values, the drinking continues.

The third stage is disorganization. The attempts of the husband to control his drinking are more sporadic or are given up entirely. The wife adopts a fatalistic attitude. The family shows increasing demoralization. It is no longer possible to conceal the father's behavior from the children. The father has lost much of his status in the family. The sexual relationship between the spouses has usually been severely disturbed. In fact, to quote Shakespeare, "it provokes the desire, but it takes away performance." Recent research shows that although alcohol does not kill desire, it does reduce ability to perform for many alcoholic males. The family resorts now to public agencies for support, a procedure which damages self-respect. The wife may begin to worry about her sanity and find herself engaging in behavior which is often random and senseless as she becomes more anxious and hostile. She finds that she has deviated widely from her former self and feels that she is no longer "the real me."

Stage four is usually produced by some subsidiary crisis like an accident or arrest. It requires that some decisive action be taken if the family is to survive. The wife takes over the husband's role; the husband comes to be ignored and is assigned the status of a delinquent child. The wife begins to recognize her obligations to her children as parallel to her obligations to her husband. As feelings of pity and protectiveness arise, the hostility tends to decrease. The wife begins to rationalize the situation so that she no longer has to relate his drinking to herself or to other family members. She assumes control of the family, regains a sense of worth, worries less about her sanity, and begins to plan long-time goals for the family. She may be helped in this by numerous agencies. Her shame decreases. If she happens to contact Alcoholics Anonymous, she gets a new perspective on the drinking problem and therefore loses her sense of shame and comes to see the problem as an illness. She begins to renew extrafamily social contacts among people who are not disturbed by her husband's drinking problem.

Now comes a period of unemployment, imprisonment, or hospitalization. Other women have usually come into the life of the husband. He may not even hesitate to bring them to his own home. Finally the husband recognizes that he needs help with his problem. The family begins to mobilize itself, to try to reinstate him, and to help him get into contact with agencies which may offer a cure. Roles are reshuffled as an attempt at attitude change is made. Then there follows bitter disappointment if treatment fails.

In stage five comes an effort to escape the problem by separation. This usually means legal separation or divorce for the wife. The husband may accept it passively or resist. In this stage, the family may be threatened by physical violence or actually experience it. The husband may give up drinking for a short time. This action often leaves the wife confused as to what course to pursue. It is hard for her seemingly to desert him in an hour of crisis. She may resort to help from public agencies to ease her conscience or to make it possible for her to live alone.

Stage six brings the reorganization of family life into separate households. The wife must reshuffle her roles, adjust her emotional reactions, work out her feeling of bereavement, and go through the other crises of any divorce action. There is the added problem, however, that the alcoholic may feel that he has to get even with the family for deserting him.

Stage seven is defined as the stage of reorganization of the whole family as a unit if the husband achieves sobriety, with or without separation. Even if there is a complete cure and the restored marriage lasts, there are many role adjustments—the mother has long been accustomed to managing for the family, to assuming the father and manager role. There are also the numerous debts and other obligations that have to be met along with current needs. Children may be unable to accept the father in his restored role. They may carry over deep hostilities or distrust. They may refuse to accept his judgment. The wife therefore hesitates to relinquish control in her role as the decision-maker. It is very hard for any member of the family to forget the past. The father himself may be more demanding than is justified. He may feel superior because he has overcome his difficulties.

Gradually the memories of the drinking problem fade into the past; its influence remains, however. Whether the wife will be allowed to drink at parties or whether the children will be allowed to drink are problems of unusual significance, for here is a husband who knows that to drink again is to again become a victim. If the husband has been restored through Alcoholics Anonymous, he often throws himself so fully into activities associated with them that he neglects his wife and family. Even though the wife is free from alcoholism within her own family, she is not free from alcoholics, since the husband may keep the house full of men he is helping.

Haberman (1966) finds that children of alcoholic parents have many more symptoms of maladjustments than those of a control group of nonalcoholics and a control group of parents with stomach trouble. Of the eight problem symptoms compared, all were more common in children of alcoholic parents; the most difference was found in the area of temper tantrums, fighting with peers, and trouble in school. Children of alcoholic families were also more often known to correctional and school authorities as troublesome.

This analysis has dealt with the sequence of steps followed by the male alcoholic. Alcoholism in the United States is no longer a male problem, although men are still much in the majority. Women alcoholics number over two million. The results are no less tragic. The personality decline may be less public, as the wife can remain secluded in the home as she progresses to the lower stages. The essential difference in the pattern of addiction is that male alcoholics usually start heavy drinking in their 20s; the female usually does not start heavy drinking until she is in her 30s.

Gambling   Compulsive gambling is destructive to family life. Like alcoholism, it is considered a disease, and a most difficult one to cure. It, too, has its roots in a disturbed childhood environment and feelings of rejection. The gambler uses money to buy love and borrows money to support his gambling.

Compulsive gambling leads to the neglect of wives and children and, at times, to their support by relatives. It often leads to bankruptcy, yet the compulsive gambler returns to his betting again and again.

It is believed that compulsive gamblers may be as numerous as compulsive drinkers. A Gambler's Anonymous, patterned after Alcoholics Anonymous, founded some ten years ago, has a following of thousands.

Drug Addiction   Until recently, our nation has been relatively free of drug addiction. The more frequent use of drugs—for "kicks," for emotional release, and because it is the thing to do in many circles—undoubtedly means that many families have to reckon with this problem. There are always those who will come to depend on drugs and for whom one drug leads to a more potent one. In time these insecure persons' lives become absorbed in a quest to satisfy the drug hunger to the neglect of their wives and families.

PROBLEMS

1   After interviewing the community's oldest couple on their golden wedding anniversary, the newspaper reporter cheerfully asked, "Does all this publicity thrill you? Tell me, are you as happy together today as when you were courting?" The old lady snapped back, "Listen young fellow. We're a dozen times happer today than we were when we were young, but it isn't the publicity that makes us so. You'd have to be married fifty years before you could understand just how happy we really are and why!"

What are some of the things that might account for increasing marital happiness with the passage of time?

2   Betty is neither pretty nor witty. She wanted to marry young but she was almost 30 before someone finally proposed. Now she is determined to make her marriage a success by making it happy.

Her plan is that Bob's income should take care of their everyday needs. Her own income—for she expects to continue working—she calls the "fun fund." It will provide them with two vacations a year, a new car every second year, a show or theater three evenings a week, and funds for entertaining every weekend.

Betty feels sure that in their old age they will look back upon an unusually happy marriage. What is the logic of Betty's reasoning? What important factors has she failed to consider?

3 Aside from the actual size of their incomes, compare the way of life of a judge with that of a man who goes from one selling job to another. What circumstances suggest that the judge's family has a greater chance of realizing a happy life? (Consider status in community, self-appraisal, security, leisure time, companions, social controls surrounding each, etc.)

4 American wives are frequently criticized for their "refusal to grow up and grow old gracefully." Is this criticism justified in your opinion? What indications are there of its validity or inaccuracy? If true, does it have a bearing on realizing lasting marriage happiness?

5 Which of the factors below would you consider least important to marriage happiness?

a Size of income.

b Stability of income.

c Vocational adventure.

d Health.

e Community satisfaction.

f Job security.

6 Do the older childless couples of your acquaintance seem:

a Less happy?

b More happy?

c Just as happy as those with families?

7 Most writers in the field of marriage relations argue that conscious effort and planning are more conducive to marriage success than the attitude "If we love one another, we're bound to succeed." Does this mean that couples are more likely to be happy if they make happiness an end in itself and keep this goal constantly in mind?

8 Discuss the statement, "Happiness is the by-product of a productive way of life."

9 Much is written about divorce, separation, and marital discord. Has America reached the point where most marriages fail to achieve happiness?

10 A young student in a preparation for marriage course voiced the following opinion: "Couples should probably postpone parenthood for at least five years, for it is only in early marriage that couples may be said to be happy. After they have the responsibility of children, they have to forget about themselves and dedicate their lives to child-rearing."

  Do you agree that happiness is bound to fade with the passing years? What does the evidence suggest?

11 How do you explain the fact that stability in occupations is associated with marital happiness?

12 What factors probably account for the apparently high rate of failure and unhappiness among Hollywood marriages?

a Instability of income.

b Temperament of actors.

c Neurosis.

d Cultural standards unlike those of United States in general.

MARRIAGE HAPPINESS

   e Competition to get to the top.

   f Marriages for publicity only.

   g Marriage failures are not numerous, just overly publicized.

13 *Sociodrama:* Two young wives discuss the marriage of a mutual acquaintance in such a way as to reveal the grounds upon which a marriage is rated as either happy or unhappy.

14 *Sociodrama:* A mother criticizes her married daughter's decision to postpone parenthood in order to maintain a "happy marriage."

SEXUAL ADJUSTMENT

20 The ability to separate sex from procreation has been achieved, and all social layers of the population share this ability in increasing proportions. For most, the moral right has been asserted even where church pronouncements may still forbid. No single development has done so much to give women real freedom from the bondage of unwanted pregnancy. The ability of man to control population marks a great step forward in his control over his social and economic destiny.

The personal problem for the individual couple remains—that of adjusting their own interpersonal relationships in the area of sex and reproduction. Letters to the American Association of Marriage Counselors seeking help are heavily concentrated about sexual problems (refer to Chapter 19).

CONTINUITY OF THE SEXUAL BOND

In nature, sexual adjustment is not a problem. Generally, there is no continuity of relationship between mates, although there are exceptions. Some birds and a few animals pair for life. In general, animals do not. Even those birds which mate for life, confine their sex life to the rhythm of the biological season. Their interest in the opposite sex is momentary, when nature calls for sexual expression. Beyond that, the male's responsibility usually ceases, and the female's maternal instincts take over the problem of nurturing the young.

It is not so with human beings. Society demands a continuity in the relationship between male and female that is institutionalized everywhere in the world in some form of marriage–family relationship, as are social pressures for providing this continuity. And there are numerous rules to hinder termination of the pair relationship. Not all pairings of mates can last, but the assumption of all societies is that in adulthood there will be a continuity in the male–female relationship. This is usually a paired relationship, although it may involve multiple mates. Whatever the sanctioned relationship, it is certainly far more than a sexual relationship. In fact, the sexual relationship is made subservient to economic and status relationships. It is also made subservient to the marriage rules of the culture and its sex taboos. The institutional aspects of the man–woman relationships are so elaborate in all cultures that the sexual aspects become a relatively incidental matter. For man, sex is not merely a biological fact; it is one of the most significant sociological, psychological, and emotional facts of existence. Culture makes sex more than a biological act. For man, there is no such thing as mating without emotional connotations.

One of the unique facts about the human biological mechanism is that both male and female seem to be without a conspicuous seasonal period such as one finds throughout animal life, where the coming into heat of the female, or of rut in the male, causes each to aggressively seek to copulate. There is no specific period of rut in the human male, and there is serious doubt whether there is a period of heat in the human female. (Evidence pro and con is presented later.) The sex act is primarily a factor of social, psychological, and emotional, rather than biological motivation. This is the basis for a continuing sexual relationship between male and female, a relationship which need not and does not in most of its functioning have any relationship to procreation at all. After a woman comes to share bed and board, the provider expects to have sexual access, subject to whatever codes and taboos exist in the culture. By virtue of customary regulations of the marriage system, it is assumed that the husband has this right as part of his bargain to support a family. The wife must therefore give his needs priority over her own feelings. This tradition, incorporated into many state laws, which gives the husband the right to sexual intercourse even against the wife's will, because he supports her, is certainly a legitimate point of attack of the current feminist crusade.

The male is capable of copulating with an unaroused and even uninterested female. In some marriages the sex act is performed without the female's interest. Its timing is determined primarily by the male's readiness, as is its consummation by the male's period of response. This pattern is not found elsewhere in nature but is established in the adjustment of the human male and female in the institution of marriage, where romantic love, economic interests, mutual aid, and many other such values become blended with sexual drives into a highly complex system of motivations.

The human female's accessibility in marriage is to quite an extent a matter of logic rather than desire. In marriage, coitus is expected and customarily sanctioned. The husband, though his desires are not periodic, does have regular sexual needs because of the build-up of semen in the glands. Only as he is taught to go through the courting period, to be considerate of the female's feelings, to recognize that her arousal is a part of his obligation, does he sense any need to regard her feelings in the matter at all.

In our culture, where the wife is not only mother but mistress, she is given few of the customary protections by which she may be relieved temporarily from the sexual advances of her husband. Many cultures taboo intercourse during pregnancy, during menstruation, and when the mother is nursing her young—with primitive peoples this may be two or more years—and some taboo it during periods of activities demanding the concentrated expenditure of male energy—in periods of battle, when the hunt is on, when fish are to be caught, when artistic products are to be made, when praying needs to be done.

If the female is taught by the culture to be sexually passive, her rewards are not considered important. It is enough that she have children. If she is taught to be assertive, then the male's courting gestures, his ability to arouse and inspire and finally to satisfy, put him to a sexual test. It is under this latter type of marriage philosophy, current in the United States, that the concept of sexual adjustment has become a serious consideration.

NO ESTRUS PHASE IN THE HUMAN FEMALE

The period of heat is marked in apes and baboons by swelling of the vaginal area and changes in behavior. In the wild baboon troop, the female in estrus seeks out males of her choice to satisfy her desire, beginning usually with one of lower status and working up in status until her needs have been fully met.

Research among both single and married women fails to show any of the psychological characteristics of an estrus period. That there is a rise in body temperature of a fraction of a degree near the time of ovulation (most often falling between the eleventh and fourteenth day from the beginning of menstruation, see Chapter 24) is a well-established biological fact. Benedek (1952) finds endocrine and dream reactions at ovulation that give some evidence of an estrus period. But if this is a physiological estrus, overt behavior does not betray it.

Most research shows a slight shift in intensity of sexual desire at certain times of the month, but in any particular study the rise in the curve is slight, and the research of different workers with different groups leaves the whole matter open to question. It is likely that slight statistical differences at different periods in the month are social rather than biological. Research suggests that the time of greatest desire is just before or immediately after menstruation, the least likely times for pregnancy to occur.

Judson T. Landis (1957), studying a sample of 181 college girls, found that more report increased sexual desire directly before menstruation than at any other time. The second peak is after menstruation. The data do not show an increase in sexual desire at the time of ovulation, as might logically be expected if nature provides an estrus in the human female. Margaret Mead (1949), from her knowledge of numerous cultures (many of them permitting premarital sexual experience), concludes that prior to marriage the female controls the timing of the sex act, after marriage, the male does. This change would not take place if the female were approachable only in times of heat, or if the male were potent only seasonally. Nonbiological factors are operative.

It appears that sexual desire among modern women is largely a function of the psychological climate produced by contact with the male, both before and after marriage. In marriage, frequency of the male's demands may well determine whether the wife has any desire at all. If she has, in most instances it will likely be after menstruation, since with most young couples menstruation is the longest period of abstinence. Because this is the period of estrogen pickup, many have renewed energy, which may also be a factor. Others who suffer considerable discomfort and depression prior to menstruation may well seek the comfort and loving which sex involves, not from physical desire as such but for the secondary reasons which are most important at this time. There is, however, a pickup in energy due to an increased metabolic rate just before menstruation, which is undoubtedly a factor. Finally, premenstrual desire may be in part a rational and planned matter. The wife, if she enjoys the sexual relationship, is interested in intercourse as a means of abbreviating the period of continence ahead. Her awareness of her husband's needs may also be a factor in her encouraging his advances and courting; or he may, if he is aware of the coming period of continence, be more aggressive than usual, stimulating both her interest and his own.

This kind of speculation illustrates how complicated by conscious, psychological, and biological factors the human sex urge is and how far it can be removed from a rhythm of nature, if such exists.

The highly socialized character of the sexual experience, its romantic connotations in our culture, and its diversity of meaning in the interactions of individuated men and women have apparently largely removed it, for the female, from the level of physical desire and made it secondary to the whole area of sociality and generalized feeling. The lack of an estrus period in the female and a period of rut in the male and his frequent readiness are undoubtedly important factors in this trend of the psychosexual orientation of the female.

SEXUAL ADJUSTMENT AS A GOAL

Every society faces the problem of resolving the strain involved in the different biological natures and sexual proclivities of male and female. Many societies have solved the problem by denying female sexuality and leaving not only initiative but satisfaction to the male alone. Polygynous societies try to balance male sexual needs for the more prosperous classes with those of the female by providing sufficient wives so that when one is incapacitated by sickness, pregnancy, childbirth, or lactation, another will be accessible. The mistress system, where sanctioned by custom, permits a similar male outlet, as does concubinage. The monogamous systems of the world have historically sanctioned prostitution as a device for balancing out the male's presumed greater needs for sexual expression.

In polygynous societies, males complain of too many demands from their wives, as each tries to tempt the husband to her bed. In monogamous societies, generally, the male is perpetually unsatisfied because of deprivation or because of the monotony of one wife.

The romantic marriage in America has perhaps put a greater strain on both men and women in sexual adjustment than has any other system. The wife plays the role of both mistress and wife, attempting to meet the husband's sexual needs fully. The pledge of romantic loyalty compels the husband to confine his advances to the marriage bed. This means that he must make adjustments to incapacities of the wife and deny himself sexual expression at times for the sake of the romantic bond. The wife is expected to accommodate the husband's sexual needs when incapacitated to a degree by pregnancy, lactation, and other indispositions. And in this day of female assertiveness, she may find her husband unable to rise to all her challenges.

THE MEANING OF SEXUAL ADJUSTMENT

Sexual adjustment is not synonymous with equality of the couple's sexual desire or frequency of the orgasmic response. Neither does the concept of sexual adjustment involve the regular subordination of one mate's interests to those of the other. Adjustment is a matter of the satisfaction of both. One couple may be spoken of as sexually better adjusted than another. The difference between them is not a matter of frequency or intensity of the sex act but of the differing degrees to which each couple obtains satisfaction and happiness from whatever relationship they have. Complete satisfaction comes from the unrestrained sharing of these moments of greatest marital intimacy.

This does not mean, however, that both partners must experience similar responses to the sex act. For the male, intercourse brings orgasm and accompanying tension release; for the wife it may bring no physical climax at all but only a feeling of being loved and needed. As long as each partner is satisfied with what he or she obtains from the act, their adjustment may be said to be a good one.

When there are marked differences in the desire of the two mates, adjustment is difficult. Whether they want intercourse only once a month or several times a day is not the point. The significant consideration is whether the frequency of desire in one mate is compatible with the desire of the other or whether a mutually acceptable compromise can be worked out.

The desire of the husband—particularly in the early years of marriage—tends to exceed that of the average wife. Good adjustment generally requires that each make some concessions to the needs of the other. The husband withholds his advances when the wife seems genuinely uninterested. The wife must occasionally participate when she does not really desire satisfaction herself.

Equality of orgasmic response seems to have even less bearing on sexual adjustment, providing both mates accept the difference as a relatively unimportant one. Males experience an orgasm as an inherent part of semen discharge. Wives vary greatly, but it has been found that in the average marriage considerably less than half of the women can expect always to have an orgasm, and during the early months of marriage as many as half of wives experience few if any orgasmic responses at all.

The wife should, and usually does, expect satisfaction in the sexual relationship. Unless she has been hemmed in by taboos and irrational fears in her sex education, has suffered trauma from sexual attack, or is overwhelmed with guilt from premarital sexual indiscretions which violated her conscience, she is in most instances capable of as deep a physical and emotional satisfaction in coitus as is her husband, although frequently these reactions are of a different kind. All modern scientific study shows that the sexual relationship is normal and beneficial to both male and female.

Healthy Sex Attitudes

Inability to perform or respond sexually is in most cases psychological rather than physical. This concept brings up the important problems of acquired attitudes as fundamental factors in conditioning.

Current conceptions of sex are varied, even within the confines of an average American community. To a few sex is sin. To others it is an activity to be indulged in for procreation only. To some its primary purpose is pleasure. For still others it represents the highest form of human sharing. Even in marriage, sex can mean different things at different times, depending on the total relationship of the pair. Instead of being an experience in sharing and affectional expression, it may turn out to be an experience in male conquest, domination, or exploitation.

There has been a great deal of speculation on the degree to which a child's early conditioning affects his later capacity to give affection and to respond to sexual stimuli. Freudian-oriented literature assumes that the child's relationship with the parent of the opposite sex has decided influence on psychosexual development. More likely it is the total family pattern which conditions one's attitude toward members of his own sex, toward the opposite sex, and toward marriage, rather than one's particular relationship with a member of the opposite sex within the family. This total influence is so complex that simple generalizations regarding a unilateral factor in determining psychosexual development are likely to lead to more error than insight. Of this much we can be sure—fundamental attitudes as well as actual behavior patterns basic to a development of the capacity for affection are learned in the family and have much to do with a person's psychosexual development. This point was stressed in Chapter 8 and need not be dwelt on at length here.

Tenderness, ability to show affection, and responsiveness are developed in the child by his relationship with the parent. In loving a responsive parent, the child develops a capacity to love others. With expanding contacts, the child develops ability to show affection to others as others show affection to him. In normal development, the mother and other love objects recede into the background as heterosexual love emerges.

The child born in a home without affection is likely to develop without any real capacity for it or any means for expressing it. If he has constantly been rebuffed by his mother and rarely shown affection, he keeps what feelings he has to himself and rarely can relax in the presence of affection. By such a simple process of conditioning, the capacity to love is limited. The child's relationship with the parents is therefore the critical experience in the development of capacity to give and respond to affection in later years.

The attitudes expressed in a child's home are also important in determining his later adjustment in marriage. Even in families where affection and warmth are openly exhibited, sex itself often remains an unmentionable subject, surrounded with mysteries that are suggestive of sin and immorality. It is not enough to shield a child from undesirable or frightening sexual experiences. To assure him of healthy attitudes some positive sex education is necessary. Complete silence is not really neutral. To a child's inquiring mind, this is influence in a negative direction.

Thus, it is not uncommon for a young person (usually the girl) from an otherwise conscientious home to enter marriage with fears and misgivings about the sexual side of the relationship. Such fears are not easily overcome. While they are probably not so common today as in earlier times, it is true that marriage ceremonies do not have the magic power to redraw mental pictures and attitudes concerning sex which have been built up during childhood and adolescence. The marriage ceremony removes only the legal and moral restrictions.

Below is a listing of some of the most common attitudes that are conducive or detrimental to sound and early sexual adjustment in marriage.

ATTITUDES CONDUCIVE TO SEXUAL ADJUSTMENT EARLY IN MARRIAGE

1   Coitus is a normal, right, and recreative experience as well as a creative experience.

2   Both husband and wife are capable of sexual gratification.

3   Both husband and wife should be considerate, sympathetic, and patient in sexual relations.

4   Sexual expression is usually a more direct urge in the male, and while he can cultivate some sublimative arts, the male is not to be criticized for his greater preoccupation with coitus as a purely physical act.

5   Consistent with physical well-being and mutual interest, there are no restrictions that need be placed upon the sexual expressions of a couple, either upon the method, frequency, intensity, or duration of expression throughout the couple's lifetime.

6   Coitus can serve different functions at different times. It can be for pleasure, for comfort, to express love, for relief from tension, for the serious intent of having children, or for rejuvenating a tired body or spirit. It is the closest form of human sharing.

ATTITUDES DETRIMENTAL TO SEXUAL ADJUSTMENT EARLY IN MARRIAGE

1   When a husband really loves his wife, pleasant conversation and intimacy become much more satisfying to him than coitus.

2   Men are like animals in that coitus can never acquire any spiritual meaning for them.

3   Women can never get the pleasure from coitus that men do; they should accept it, therefore, simply as one of their duties as wives.

4   Nice girls, because of their higher values and ideals, do not lose themselves in

sexual play; they remain patient and reserved and do not show a great interest in the matter.

5   Only a very vulgar or degenerate man is pleased by experimentation in sex play outside the common pattern.

6   Sexual intercourse is inevitable in marriage, but talking about it before or after is bound to be embarrassing and detracts from its spiritual quality.

7   In a marriage between modern, enlightened people, the wife who cannot equal her husband in desire or response should consider psychiatric or medical attention, for she must be either physically or emotionally defective.

8   It is a husband's duty to woo his wife from reluctance to eager anticipation before each sex act. The husband who does not or cannot accomplish this, who sometimes becomes impatient, is inadequate and failing in his function, for no wife can become interested otherwise.

9   Coitus is a private affair. To seek outside help, to get books from the library on the subject, or to talk about what's wrong with one's mate is an admission of failure.

10   Once a man has saddled his wife with a house and children he has no right to complain if she loses her interest in coitus.

VARIETY IN THE MONOGAMOUS MARRIAGE

The sexual relationship of the happily married couple can represent one of the most creative and distinctively individualistic and rejuvenating aspects of their life together. In most instances, the husband is the aggressor. Yet many couples find mutual satisfaction in the wife's occasionally reversing the roles. This is but one of the many variations they develop to add to the freshness and adventure of their sex life.

Frequency of coitus, positions during sexual intercourse, the amount and nature of the foreplay, and the degree to which the couple speak of the relationship varies from time to time. Levy and Munroe (1938) suggest the variety of uninhibited married sex life:

Study of the sex activity of relatively uninhibited happily married couples demonstrates very beautifully both the unorthodox nature of their impulses and the ease with which they are integrated into a "normal" heterosexual pattern. Sometimes the pair will be close and affectionate. Tenderness will pass into a rather solemn passion, a confirmation of their abiding love for each other. At other times their mood will be wholly frivolous. Intercourse then will be just a rattling good time without deeper implications. Or the husband will seek protection and cuddling at his wife's breast. Or he will lie like a girl while she takes possession of his body. At times he will vulgarize the act with smutty words or take a fine pleasure of hurting his wife and forcing her to his will. Or the couple may play at an illicit relationship, acting out a little seduction farce for their own benefit. They will try out odd positions and experiment with unusual parts of the body. Often, too, intercourse will be a routine satisfaction of a bodily need about as romantic as orange juice, toast and coffee for breakfast. Our uninhibited happily married couples will take all of these variations and find them good (p. 129).

335

The limits within which variations should be practiced are few and simple. They should bring neither physical nor emotional harm to either mate. They should be indulged in only by mutual inclination, for atypical behavior can bring disastrous consequences if not understood or appreciated as normal and legitimate by the mate.

This does not mean that the couple must share similar views of this matter from the outset. Very few do. It is important, however, that the individual who initiates a typical behavior does so only gradually and with utmost care in observing responses. In this, as in all sexual development, the male usually is the teacher.

SPECIAL PROBLEMS IN THE SEXUAL RELATIONSHIP

Humans are highly variable in sexual potency and receptivity. They also may develop sexual inclinations in the course of their development which are not conducive to the successful functioning of coitus in marriage.

Frigidity

Too little understood but much talked about are frigidity in the female and impotence in the male. A woman is not frigid simply because she may not experience an orgasm in sexual relationships or does so only on rare occasions. If she is capable of affection and of sharing the sexual relationship without a feeling that it is obnoxious and repulsive, she is not frigid. Frigidity rightly refers only to the few cases in which the psychological and emotional block is such that the woman cannot accept the sexual relationship and its affectional expressions. Such feelings of repulsion are due to deep-seated psychological problems, sometimes to tragedy, shock, or faulty upbringing, and are problems which require mental therapy.

Impotence

Impotence in the male likewise is a condition of emotional blocks which make it impossible for him to participate in the sex act. In cases where it exists, it is rooted in the emotions and can be cured only by psychological therapy. Seldom is it biological in origin. Freud (1960) described it as the ailment the practicing psychiatrist was most often called upon to treat. He spoke of psychological impotence as "the most prevalent form of degradation of erotic life." He says further,

This strange disorder affects men of a strongly libidinous nature, and is manifest by a refusal on the part of the sexual organs to execute the sexual act, although both before and after the attempt they can show themselves intact and competent to do so, and although a strong mental inclination to carry out the act is present.

It often applies to only certain sexual objects or to certain women. Needless fear is sometimes a predisposing condition. For example, many males worry about the size of the penis or if it is not straight when in erection, and about its difference from other males' in these respects. These are matters in which there is great individual variation, and they have no bearing on the ability of the male to satisfy a mate, any more than does the size of the vagina have a bearing on satisfaction of the male.

Female aggression is an increasing factor in male impotency, as viewed by practicing psychiatrists and counselors. Masculinity is closely associated with self-conceptions of masculinity. A threat to sexual prowess can be devastating to the male ego. This is no doubt one reason why masculine-dominated societies have so often negated female sexuality.

Homosexuality

Homosexual tendencies represent a common type of sexual abnormality and in some instances affect marriage relationships. It is fairly well-established that such tendencies are not inborn but are due to conditioning. Just as man is born to hunger but without any definite notion as to what is fit to eat, so he is born with sex drives. His social experience tells him how they can be satisfied.

Some cultures have elevated homosexual experience to a position far above the heterosexual. The Greeks in the period of their historic glory did so, considering marriage a practical child-rearing arrangement but homosexual love the true romantic love. Women in the Isle of Lesbos, which lies between Greece and Turkey, elevated love between women to the supreme level. This is the origin of our word *lesbian* for female homosexuals. Our culture abhors homosexual behavior and condemns it both by law and custom. The most effective approach to the cure of homosexual tendencies is through some form of psychological therapy.

Confirmed homosexuals usually do not marry; some fear to test their sexual adequacy with members of the opposite sex. But many married males seek homosexual outlets during periods of separation from their wives for long periods of time, as in the military and in prison. They also seek outlets for variety and for other personal reasons. A serious problem here, in addition to the break that homosexual activity may cause if the wife should learn of it, is that it can lead to public disgrace of the family, the man's loss of position, or his being blackmailed.

The lesbian wife's problem is not likely to lead to public exposure or blackmail, for it is of less social concern. It will more likely express itself in denying coitus to the husband and in forming close ties with another woman or women to the neglect of the marriage affectional bond. This can be a real challenge to the husband's sense of masculinity.

Few cultures have confined sexual relations strictly to marriage; prostitution, the mistress system, concubinage, secret liaisons, and special occasions like festivals and initiation rites allow the satisfaction of erotic interests without threat to the marriage relationship because they are sanctioned by custom.

Infidelity is seldom found to accompany happiness or adequate sexual adjustment in our romantic marriage. The crucial question is, however, whether infidelity or unhappiness in marriage comes first, and which tends more frequently to cause the other? It is easy to understand how one who discovers infidelity in his or her mate is likely to feel bitter and unloved and thus to lose whatever pleasure he or she might have found in coitus. Thus, infidelity might logically be said to cause sexual maladjustment. On the other hand, the husband or wife who charges that the mate's infidelity has ruined the marriage may be ignoring an important fact—the mate may have been unhappy with the marriage before an illicit affair could appeal.

Until recently laws forbade adultery, but never penalized it. Nor have laws attempted to control extramarital relations except where it made them grounds for divorce. In this as in most other areas of marital adjustment, the crucial consideration is not an arbitrary rule but an analysis of how the mates involved view the infidelity. In some marriages, a husband's obligations are considered to center around providing and caring for his wife and family. Companionship, love, and faithfulness, while desirable, are not considered the crucial demands of marriage. At the other extreme, unfaithfulness may be taken lightly because marriage itself is taken lightly. There are apparently some happily married couples who consider extramarital relations of no importance to the marriage itself. Some liberated young people claim to consider such ventures helpful to the marriage.

The marriage vows, which most take seriously, reflect the traditional American view that when two individuals marry it is for better or worse and for a lifetime. Sexual fidelity is considered not only desirable but obligatory. One does not run out on a mate because of financial problems, sickness, or disability; neither does one break his vow because of disappointment over their sexual life together. The relationship is assumed to be a binding one, and the interests of the family are considered to far outweigh those of the individual.*

Many of these traditional views are justified on religious grounds as well as personal ones, and the general welfare of society lends additional argument to their continuance. Where the individual family rather than any other institutional agency is held responsible for the care and upbringing of children, there is considerable logic in the widespread rejection of extramarital relations. A more stable family and consequently a more stable society are thought to result from the expectations and demands for fidelity placed upon both husbands and wives. Husbands like to feel that the children they support are their own. This may be the basic reason that adultery is so widely forbidden in human society.

*A worldwide survey of 250 societies found that in only five (2 percent) are adulterous relationships sanctioned; see Murdock (1950).

The Kinsey (1953) research group found that of people studied, approximately 26 percent of women and half the men had had extramarital sexual relations. Forty-one percent of the sexually unfaithful wives had had sexual experience with only one partner. For almost a third of wives who were unfaithful, the act of unfaithfulness had occurred only a few times, often only once. This experience was for many unpremeditated.

The attitude of the younger generation toward extramarital intercourse under special circumstances seems to be more or less one of toleration. A study of the attitudes of 223 engaged men and 215 engaged women toward extramarital relationships showed that approximately half of both men and women would justify extramarital relationships for both men and women under certain circumstances. Women were less tolerant toward infidelity for women than were men.

Over half the men would justify infidelity on the part of the husband in case of frigidity in the wife. A fourth of women would justify their infidelity in case of unsatisfacory response from the husband. Twenty percent of men and 16 percent of women would justify it in cases of general dissatisfaction with the spouse. Twenty-three percent of women and 18 percent of men would justify it in case of strong attraction for another person. Almost half thought it would be justified in case of repeated unfaithfulness of the spouse.

The romantic marriage is based on sexual loyalty. It is interesting to observe that most of the reasons recognized as adequate for unfaithfulness are those which indicate that mutual sexual responsiveness is not present in the marriage.

A *Time*—Louis Harris (1969) poll reports a striking increase in marital infidelity during the years 1964–1969, with the changing moral standard most pronounced among the upper-socioeconomic, upper-educated, suburban population, and among young people under 30. Conventional standards are still strong among the lower-income, less well-educated population, particularly those who live in small towns. The poll thus finds two American attitudes in regard to moral standards.

In cases of marital infidelity where there has been public exposure, one of the difficulties in restoring confidence between mates is that the offended party feels disgraced in the eyes of the community. He is made to feel that he is doing less than his duty (more often her duty) if the spouse's offense is tolerated. If tolerated, it may also require tolerating the lying and deception that is used to cover it up. In many circles, it is more or less expected that the innocent spouse divorce the disloyal one, thus exacting the ultimate penalty.

From the standpoint of reconciliation of the pair, it may be important to analyze reasons for the adultery. Was it momentary sex hunger during a period of absence? Was it a means of defying the mate? Was it an escape from some frustration or defeat? Was it venturing in quest of variety? Does the offending person still love the mate and wish to continue the marriage?

Often the husband and wife themselves do not know the answer to these questions. By visiting a marriage counselor or psychiatrist or by discussing the problem with a person who approaches the situation not as one of guilt, but as one in human relationships, they may be able to maintain a marriage relationship which is vital to both and to their children.

We have discussed briefly many new conceptions of the pair relationships which have emerged. The extent to which they will loosen the sexual tie of mates without breaking the marriage is yet to be seen. It is doubtful that jealousy for the love object and the need for security which loyalty and trust bring has been eradicated from personality. And it seems likely that most husbands will want full assurance that the child they are to support is their own.

PROBLEMS

1 Helen and Tom are the pride of their community—happy and very much in love after six years of marriage. Tom is called the perfect husband—thoughtful, considerate, and proud of his wife. And who could want a better wife than Helen? She is pretty, efficient, and devoted. Only her closest friends know that sexual relations have never given her pleasure, and they admire her for never having hurt Tom by mentioning this fact. What would you say about Helen?

   a   She has shown more realism in her sexual expectations than most women.
   b   She is reasonable and has therefore made a satisfactory sexual adjustment.
   c   She has cheated herself and her husband by not telling him of her problem.
   d   Her sexual life could probably be improved.

2 What relationship do you believe exists between a happy marriage and sexual adjustment? Would you say that happiness in marriage:

   a   Is the result of satisfactory sexual adjustment?
   b   Produces satisfactory sexual adjustment?
   c   Is not closely related to satisfactory sexual adjustment?
   d   Is neither cause nor effect, but is generally associated with satisfactory sexual adjustment?
   e   Is primarily a matter of attitude rather than of physical satisfaction as such?

3 In a popular book which promises to each its readers *How to Achieve Sex Happiness in Marriage,* approximately three-fourths of the writing is devoted to discussions of techniques in sex. About one-fourth of it is devoted to helping the reader form healthy general attitudes toward sex in marriage. In your opinion, which of the two areas, technique or attitudes, is responsible for most of the problems that trouble sexually unadjusted couples?

4 In almost every American city one may see motion picture theaters crowded with men enjoying sexually suggestive skits and jokes and seminude female performers. Are these audience made up mostly of:

   a   Sexually abnormal men?
   b   Sexually immature men?
   c   Sex-starved men?
   d   Men who are probably normal?

   Upon what grounds do you base your opinion?

5 A happily married woman who feels that the sexual adjustment she and her husband have made is a good one suddenly notices her husband reading books on sex techniques. Later he begins to initiate certain new and somewhat unconventional sexual practices into their relationship. In your opinion should she:

   a   Talk about it with a psychiatrist?
   b   Let her husband know she is worried about him?

SEXUAL ADJUSTMENT

c   Read the books with her husband?

d   Reexamine his background for a hint of some sexual abnormality?

e   Accept his behavior as natural?

6   For what specific reasons is sexual fidelity generally considered basic to sexual adjustment?

7   Are there any circumstances under which you consider sexual infidelity justifiable in a happy marriage?

8   *Sociodrama:* Two mothers discuss the attitudes toward sex that their 15-year-old daughters are learning from their high school course in preparation for marriage. One mother favors the course; the other is shocked by it.

9   What do you know about the nature and extent of homosexuality? As a class, or through a committee, study this problem in the United States today. Discuss it along the following lines:

a   What are believed to be its causes?

b   Is there a cure?

c   What is our legal and social treatment for the homosexual?

d   Is a slight homosexual tendency dangerous?

e   What better program and/or attitude might be adopted with reference to homosexuals?

10   In your opinion, if a couple begins to talk together and joke about their sexual relations, are they apt to detract from its spiritual quality and reduce it to a mere physical act?

SEX EXPECTATIONS

21 Our romantic culture carries with it latent sex expectations which may have little basis in realism. Although our culture is one in which sex is more talked about, and used more extensively in entertainment and advertising than in almost any other part of the world, sex ignorance is appalling. The masses do not have a scientific sex vocabulary. Otherwise informed leaders are often grossly ignorant of the facts of human biology and psychology where sex is concerned. For example, McHugh and Moskin (1958) studied the attitudes and information of ministers in the area of sex. They found most of them grossly ignorant, uninformed, and incompetent as counselors. Less than 15 percent were actually competent to counsel, and 50 percent preached that sex is evil. Their study of 451 young ministers concerning their information about reproduction showed that 35 percent did not know the period of greatest likelihood of pregnancy and almost half thought menstruation cleared the womb of the unfertilized ovum. Almost three-fourths considered a woman slightly ill when menstruating. Forty percent thought a woman's sex interest ceased at menopause.

It is very likely that many doctors would not score much higher on some of the psychological and emotional aspects of sex as it affects the marriage relationship.

Preparation   The male is responsive to a wide range of psychic and physical stimuli. The female may require considerable love play, called "foreplay" in counseling literature. In this the male is normally the aggressor; the female the pursued. Love play in marriage is likely to be bypassed by the husband. If it is, he need not be surprised that his wife often cannot share the sexual act to the fullest. Mutual sexual enjoyment usually requires that the act of courting be maintained in marriage. The courting consists of stimulating the more sensitive zones of the female's body. This brings about a flow of lubricating fluids in the vaginal tract, preparing her for the sex act. It also stimulates lubricating fluids in the male. This, with the psychological readiness, is complete readiness for the sex act.

The Sex Act   The sex act involves stimulating with increasing ecstasy until one or both reach an orgasm, which is a series of spasmodic muscular contractions. In the male, climax is accompanied by the discharge of a tablespoon or two of seminal fluids carrying the sperm. In the female, there is no such discharge with the spasmodic contractions, but there may be a sucking motion in the uterus which can help draw the sperm up through the opening of the cervix, thus increasing the likelihood that the sperm will reach the fallopian tubes and meet the egg cell. To reach an orgasm usually requires that both participate in spontaneous rhythmic motions. For the male the glans penis is the principal area of stimulation; for the female the clitoris is the focus of stimulation.

Any form of foreplay or stimulation which proves exciting and any physical position for the sexual act that they wish to assume are proper. The usual face-to-face position, with the male surmounting the female is not the universal position as human cultures go. Mutual enjoyment should be the determining factor in the position or positions assumed, although what is customary in the local culture will seem more natural. Personal inhibitions of the mate cannot safely be ignored.

Afterplay   The male is usually relaxed and ready for sleep on concluding the sex act. The female usually desires further courting play, in an atmosphere of "delicious langour" in which she senses great tenderness for the male. This is a time for strengthening the love bond and often for close confessions of differences and for patching up difficulties that have entered their lives. This is called the period of afterplay.

The Importance of Spontaneity

Margaret Mead (1949) has stated as a principle that the more a creature thinks, "the less he may copulate, unless copulation and thought are skillfully integrated at each level." She goes on to elaborate this view, indicating that in cultures where goods are considered to be limited, the expenditure of energy in sexual activity is likely to be conceived as a loss from productivity.

She believes that the sexual functioning of the male is most effective when it is most automatic, a response to simple signals such as the exposure of the female and her gestures, and that conceptions of romance, moral qualms, and other abstractions complicate the sexual functioning of the particular group or social class involved.

She finds that in the upper-class groups these inhibitions are likely to be most common and that numerous indirect culturally conditioned practices for stimulating the male are invented. Among the lower classes such stimulations are not found and are not needed. The male's approach to sex is direct, uninhibited, and automatic. Research shows that in the lower social classes females much less often experience pleasure from sexual intercourse. Rainwater (1965) compared wives' gratification by social class; lower-class wives received "very positive" responses in only 20 percent of cases, "positive" in 26 percent, "negative" in 54 percent. The middle class reported "very positive" in 50 percent of cases, "positive" in 36 percent, and "negative" in only 14 percent of cases. To some extent at least the differences in satisfaction reflect the importance of foreplay and cultural symbolism in the creation of interest in the wife.

LENGTH OF TIME REQUIRED FOR SEXUAL ADJUSTMENT

Among those whose expectations need to be deflated are the "enlightened youth" who feel sure that they have a head start toward sexual adjustment because they recognize that such an adjustment will be necessary. As one young man explained to his friend, "Marian and I have taken all the courses and read all the books. We know just what kind of things have to be worked out, so it's not likely to take us more than a week or two to overcome any of the problems we're likely to experience."

This young man may have been correct. For a few the adjustment does come easily, and certainly being well-informed is an asset. But sexual adjustment is much more than knowing the right answers. It involves one's most deeply rooted attitudes, habits, and values; and when everything else is normal, it may require time, practice, and patience. Judson T. Landis (1946) found that sex is the one area in which couples least often experience mutual satisfaction from the beginning. (Other areas studied were spending, social activity, in-law relations, mutual friends, and religion). The study dealt with 409 couples who were the parents of college students at Michigan State, and compares the periods of time they required to make adjustments in their sexual relationship. Few more than half agreed that sexual relations had been satisfactory from the beginning; in another 12 percent of cases, one member had thought the relationship unsatisfactory. At the far extreme are 12.5 percent who never made an adjustment in sexual relations, and yet they were still married at the time of the study.

His 1967 study of length of time it took 215 wives to achieve orgasm shows that there is still a time lag after marriage. Only 58 percent experienced

TABLE 21-1   Percentage of Two Generations Listing Sexual Compatibility or Incompatibility as One of Five Factors Which Most Affects Marriage Happiness or Unhappiness

| | SEXUAL COMPATIBILITY | | SEXUAL INCOMPATIBILITY | |
	NUMBER	PERCENT	NUMBER	PERCENT
Mothers	83	16.1	90	16.7
Single daughters	74	16.6	113	23.2
Married daughters	38	35.2	39	35.1

Source: Paul H. Landis (1951).

orgasm during the first four weeks of marriage, 22 percent took a month to a year, 7 percent more than a year, and 13 percent had never experienced an orgasm.

Kinsey (1953) reported that adjustment problems appeared at some time during the marriage in two-thirds of the relationships he studied. The writer's study of marital happiness of two generations indicates that more young married women than their mothers considered sex adjustment an important factor in happiness (see Table 21–1). While we have no way of knowing the extent to which this view reflects difficulties in the younger generation's own experience, we assume that it probably does.

Sex education, at the college level particularly, has led the new generation of women to expect completeness in their sexual life. Literature given to newlyweds also stresses the possibility of women's full participation in sex experience. This literature often gives rather elaborate information of physical positions to be taken in sex relations and other intimate details of sex functions. It is possible that the new generation, in their conscious effort to achieve completeness in sex relations in marriage, may hinder rather than help sexual adjustment.

The overemphasis on sex in modern marriage may be another factor. Because of women's great hopes for complete sexual relations, many are dissatisfied with the adjustment they are able to make. It is possible that many seek divorce on grounds of sexual incompatibility who in another generation would have been content because their expectations were more modest. It is possible also that some daughters were still so recently married as to be in the early stages of sexual adjustment. It may be, too, that some were facing difficulties imposed by different sexual patterns introduced into their marriage that their husbands learned in their military experience abroad. Whatever the cause, the problem of sexual adjustment seems to be one that unduly preoccupied the thinking of the newly married group here compared with the other two groups studied.

Those who do not achieve sexual adjustment after a few months of marriage should seek the advice of a family clinic or of an understanding physician. To enjoy the sexual relationship in marriage is a desirable goal for both men and women. Those who are lacking in health, have been shocked by punishment when young for exploring sex organs, have thwarting attitudes, are emotionally too deeply attached to parents, or are lacking the basic knowledge of how to participate in the physical act—these may fail to achieve it. There is a cure for many of these cases.

Unrealistic expectations concerning the length of time adjustment may require are very serious but probably not so common as other types of misconceptions that may affect the adjustment process. Many young people enter marriage with no ideas, or only false ideas, about what the physical and psychological responses of each mate are likely to be. What is a realistic expectation?

ORGASMIC REACTION

In only half of the marriages of young couples can it be expected that the wife will experience an orgasm during the honeymoon and the first four weeks of marriage. In a fourth of the cases, it will take from a month to a year. Whether biology alone is responsible for the fairly high proportion of married women in our culture who are slow to experience an orgasm is, of course, an unsettled question. It is known that the female has a much less localized sex interest than the male (see Fig. 21-1). Most virgins have little or no localized sex desire, and most women who achieve it do so only after experience in marriage. Sex feeling is much more diffused throughout the body of the female and more closely related to affection and general emotional satisfaction.

With the male, sex can often be isolated from love feelings. No doubt the same thing is possible for many females, but as the female is trained in the middle and upper classes of our society, affectional factors are highly important to sexual responsiveness.

Total sexual outlet in males and females. Striking differences in sex activity are indicated at all ages. (Lines show median frequency of orgasm in total sexual outlet. Dotted lines represent estimates for the prepubertal period.) Source: Alfred C. Kinsey, and others, *Sexual Behavior in the Human Female* (Philadelphia: W. B. Saunders Co., 1953). Reproduced by permission of Dr. Kinsey.

FIGURE 21-1

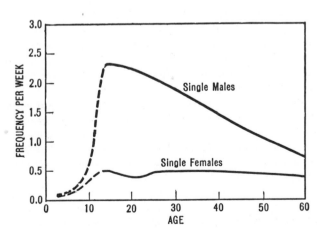

Some authorities believe that practically all women could develop orgasmic adequacy if training from childhood were adequate and there were no shocks or other developmental factors to interfere with normal maturation. They are inclined to blame sexual maladjustment almost exclusively upon psychic factors, which have deep roots in childhood development or which grow out of the ignorant blundering of the male during the early period of marriage. Some counselors believe that skillful counseling and direction can cure most of these cases. In this age of counseling and optimism concerning female sexual adequacy, it is probable that these views overstate the case.

Kinsey (1953) and his co-workers found that about 50 percent of wives experience an orgasm at least once during the first month of marriage and that about 75 percent do so by the end of the first year. This rises to above 80 percent by the fifth year and to a peak of almost 90 percent by the fifteenth year of marriage. These data refer not to regular orgasm but to having had the experience at least once.

There is, of course, great variation. Some wives have multiple orgasms during a single act of intercourse; others have an orgasm only once or a few times in a lifetime. Approximately 10 percent of married females in Kinsey's sample had never reached an orgasm at any time in their marital coitus. About 75 percent had responded at least once in the first five years of their marriage. Generally speaking, the older a woman (up to age 40), the greater the likelihood of her having an orgasm. The peak period in women's experience seems to be age 31–40. Lack of orgasm is very common in the younger marriage group. For example, between the ages of 31 and 40, 90 percent of the females had reached an orgasm at least once, whereas, among the married females 16–21 years of age, only 71 percent had done so. After 40, the incidence declined somewhat.

The Kinsey researchers found that 70–77 percent of coital experiences in marriage produce an orgasm for the wife. The incidence is much less in the early years of marriage than in the later years, ranging from an average of only 63 percent in the first year of marriage to 85 percent in the twentieth year of marriage. The figures need some interpretation. During the early years of marriage, coitus is more frequent and is often engaged in for the sake of the husband, whether or not it brings satisfaction to the wife. These are his most active years, sexually speaking, while at the same time the wife is most heavily burdened by pregnancy and the care of small children. In the later years of marriage, the husband's sexual needs have diminished and more nearly equal those of the wife. The wife loses her fear of unwanted pregnancy and may participate in sexual activity without this inhibiting fear. Also, she is in a period of life when family burdens are light.

In the average marriage, somewhat less than 40 percent of women can expect always to have an orgasm. The proportion will be considerably lower than this for those with lower education levels and considerably higher for those with higher education levels. The proportion will be somewhat less during the early years of marriage and somewhat higher in the later years, according to the Kinsey findings.*

*Judson T. Landis (1954) finds that the Kinsey sample of women was probably a very highly sexed group and that therefore norms for women in general would be much lower.

MARRIAGE ADJUSTMENT

It cannot be emphasized too often that orgasms cannot be taken as the sole criterion for determining the degree of satisfaction which a female may derive from sexual activity. Considerable pleasure may be found in sexual arousal which does not proceed to the point of orgasm, and in the social aspects of a sexual relationship. Whether or not she herself reaches orgasm, many a female finds satisfaction in knowing that her husband or other sexual partner has enjoyed the contact, and in realizing that she has contributed to the male's pleasure. We have histories of persons who have been married for a great many years, in the course of which the wife never responded to the point of orgasm, but the marriage had been maintained because of the high quality of the other adjustments in the home (Kinsey, et al. 1953).

So Kinsey and colleagues conclude from their studies. Whether one is concerned with general marital adjustment or with sexual adjustment alone, the facts seem to indicate that the purely physical aspect of sex is being greatly overemphasized today.

No two women will respond exactly alike. For some the orgasm is a muscular spasm of almost epileptic proportions; for others it is nothing more than a relaxing sigh. For still others it does not exist at all, and yet they enjoy the close contact of the sexual embrace and feel content in helping the husband satisfy his needs.

The ability to respond is more often a matter of psychology than physiology. In women, sexual response is likely to be identified with a whole complex of attitudes centering about genital functions. The woman who dreads menstruation and who dreads pregnancy may also find sexual response difficult. The woman who has welcomed menstruation as a normal function and who is eager for childbearing and motherhood is more likely to make a good sexual adjustment.

The male usually experiences an ejaculation and the accompanying orgasm in sexual intercourse. There is no evidence to indicate that all women can reach an explosive climax. The female has no organ of sexual sensation fully comparable in importance to the male organ. In many women, there is no developed clitoris and even in those who have a developed clitoris, the organ in no way corresponds in size and area of sensitivity to that of the male. Generally speaking, the woman's sensation awaits development by the male sex organ.

In many societies all that is expected of women is that they be passively receptive. Whole societies can ignore the climax as a part of female response, Mead (1930, 1939) finds. She also finds that in some societies, as in Samoa, where males have an elaborate repertoire for stimulating the female, some women cannot respond to sexual stimulation. Mead states the probability that an undeveloped clitoris, lack of tone in vaginal muscles, poor general health, or other weaknesses may be factors. Even though the female probably has more sensitive erogenous zones capable of sexual stimulation and orgasm than the male, sexual response is less universal than among males. Responsive sexuality in the female is a learned reaction.

The female clitoris, the organ of sensation, is above the entrance to the vagina and can experience friction only as the vaginal muscles draw it down under sexual stimulation. In many women it is too high up to be stimulated at all by the penis and the wife experiences orgasm only as manual friction by the husband accompanies sexual intercourse. A lack of understanding or inhibitions for such couples may be critical factors.

The American Institute of Family Relations has found, among wives coming to the clinic for help, that a lack of tonus in the pubococcygeus muscle is a key factor in lack of female response. By strengthening this muscle through exercise, which consists essentially in flexing the muscle as in shutting off urination, they are able to improve response in many instances. Maxine Davis, in her book, *Sexual Responsibility in Marriage,* claims that "orgasm adequacy" is less rare than once thought, if women can be taught to use the "magic muscle." Even she, however, recognizes that too much emphasis has been placed on the orgasm, leaving "everybody expecting too much." She recognizes that for some women the orgasm is very mild, while for some, it is almost as intense as labor pains.

The Masters and Johnson (1966 and 1970) clinical approach to problems of sexual functioning involves a series of steps beginning with a male-female therapy team who explain anatomy and sexual functioning generally. They find that sexual problems are more often caused by ignorance and poor conditioning than by deep-seated neuroses. Later the couple is encouraged to develop communication and sensate feelings by sensual contacts short of sexual intercourse in the privacy of their own quarters. Theirs and other clinical approaches are briefly discussed by Ellen Switzer (1974).

In the current popular conception of sex, the test of marriage seems to be the ability of husband and wife to realize a mutually satisfying physical climax in their sexual relationship. The suggestion that such coordination is not always necessary and often even impossible is difficult for most young couples to believe at a time when so many doctors, psychiatrists, counselors, and writers have emphasized the physical aspects of sex.

Orgasm Not the Only Test of Sexual Adjustment

Coitus, as an expression of love and mutual regard in marriage, as a thing which encompasses the personalities of husband and wife, is a symbol of their oneness. As a mechanical process to be judged by the intensity and coordination of physical release alone, it is no more significant than such release among creatures of the barnyard. By making the perfection of this mechanical process the goal of sexual life in marriage, many marriages are found wanting. Yet it is known that there are, and always have been, happy and otherwise successful marriages that have failed to reach this physical goal, just as there have been many sexually satisfying marriages that have ended in the divorce court.

Because of the current narrow and unrealistic concept of sex, some men and women fear to marry. Others go through married life with unnecessary feelings of personal guilt, frustration, and failure. Kavinoky (1943) a gynecologist and past president of the National Council on Family Relations, believes that the fear of inability to measure up to this standard has given us frigidity, impotence, and many other marriage problems. Strecker (1952), a psychiatrist, agrees. He believes that the physical rewards of the perfect sexual relationship have been too greatly emphasized by his own profession as well as in fiction and so-called scientific literature.

Much of this current misconception of what sex in marriage should be is centered on the kind of sexual satisfaction a woman should receive. It is popularly believed that she or her husband is inadquate if she fails regularly to achieve an explosive physical climax. This belief persists in spite of the contradictory nature of the facts concerning orgasmic response which were presented above.

Realistic expectations are important to marital adjustment, for a marriage cannot long survive in an atmosphere of failure and frustration. Too many marriages crumble under the weight of sexual disappointment that would have been unnecessary had the couple but known the facts.

A young divorcée still thinks with tenderness about a marriage that broke up because of this striving to reach an impossible goal. She confided to the author:

> We would have been the happiest couple in the world if, somehow, we could have forgotten all the "stuff" we ever heard or read on the subject of sex. My happiest moments were when we were together. I loved to feel his nearness and wanted nothing more than to satisfy his every wish. But he was sure that I should get the same excitement out of sex that he did. We never relaxed and enjoyed the intimate life that could have been ours; instead we searched for a kind of mutual ecstacy that was forever out of reach. Our sex life became a time of tension and awkward experimentation that left us more and more upset and dissatisfied. After a while, I lost the simple but deep happiness I had known in our intimate life, and from there on our marriage seemed of little value or meaning to either of us.

While very different from the explosive climax promised in most books, this couple might have been content with their sex life had they not expected so much from the physical side alone. The pleasure the wife received from mere intimacy with her husband was amply rewarding. Many happily married wives share this woman's feeling of joy in sharing themselves with their husbands, a joy which often fully compensates for their own lack of physical excitement. Many wives do not need peaks of sexual excitement. They are quite content with simple intimacies—the nearness of a husband, the protectiveness and security of his body, the touch of his hand, a kiss.

The woman who has not expected too much and who is not guilt-ridden and frustrated by her inability to match her husband's sexual desire can nevertheless establish a completely happy marriage which leaves none of her husband's needs unsatisfied.

Kavinoky believes that the pendulum in sex teaching has swung to the extreme of a "narrow physical concept of the act." It is time we consider sex "in its relationship to the entire life of the two people concerned." She is less concerned about a specific reaction to the sexual relationship than that the couple find in it adventure, excitement, release from tension, contentment, unity and spiritual oneness, and, in times of sorrow or trouble, even comfort and consolation.

If this concept of sex is accepted, young people can be less concerned over their failure consciously to attain certain reactions. In removing anxiety, it is possible to relax and find genuine physical satisfaction. This also permits those who fail to do so to live happily without guilt.

Technique Is Not Enough

This does not mean that physical techniques are never important. They are, and couples should try to adjust to each other's needs by discussing them frankly and, when necessary, even seeking help from a doctor or counselor. But the first criterion of success should always be whether the two people themselves are happy in their sexual life. If the wife finds that a physical climax in some sort of complete and explosive form is necessary to her satisfaction and her husband is, through faulty timing or techniques, unable to achieve this condition, she may be frustrated and unhappy. A good marriage counselor or doctor can sometimes offer help to the couple in attuning their responses. The importance of such an adjustment cannot be dismissed lightly. Often it is only a matter of faulty sex education that is to blame. The husband may not realize that courting prior to the sex act is often essential to her response. Or the wife may not understand her own sensitivities and her powers of bringing the greatest degree of pleasure to both her husband and herself.

Techniques are not of first importance. More often what may be required for harmony is not refinement of technique, but rather, "a mutual generosity of body and soul" (de Beauvoir 1953, p. 402). Many will obtain the explosive reaction by preliminary love play and improved timing; others, with the best love play, will never reach it, but with proper attitudes can find pleasure in the intimacy and sharing that can come to all happily married people. Love and trust constantly expressed are great satisfactions in themselves. Despite Hemingway's classic description, the earth need not always move in the ecstasy of sexual love.

Two final facts should be mentioned in connection with sexual adjustment and the orgasmic response of the female. First, such an ability has no necessary connection with her capacity for becoming pregnant.* Second, neither is the capacity to respond with orgasm affected by menopause and cessation of capacity to reproduce, as many generally well-informed people suppose it to be.

Chesser's (1957) study of sexual adjustment among English women and their happiness in marriage showed that one-half of the happiest women had a great deal of satisfaction in sexual intercourse; only one-tenth of the unhappy women did. On the other hand, it must be pointed out that half of the happily married women did not get a great deal of satisfaction out of the sexual relationship as such.

Burgess and Wallin (1953) report guilt feelings among men whose wives did not respond to orgasm. This they suspected was a middle-class norm which had not yet affected the lower classes. Bettelheim (1962) states that "today the

---

*Orgasm may set up a sucking motion in the uterus and aid in pregnancy, but this action is not necessary to pregnancy.

boy wants his girl to prove him a man by her 'orgastic experience.' " In trying to have one for him, she becomes anxious and often ends up pretending.

Ruth Cavan (1969) has stressed the fact that "anxiety and intense effort to achieve only add to difficulty" and goes on to state that the "great concern with . . . lack of orgasm . . . is not limited to the wife's feelings of deprivation, but may become a contentious subject leading to lack of satisfaction . . . for both husband and wife."

Bettelheim blames the "alarming rise in homosexuality" to such factors in the relationships of husbands and wives.

RELIGION AND SEXUAL ACTIVITY IN MARRIAGE

Wallin (1957) studied the degree of religiosity as it relates to sexual gratification. He found that religion apparently is a sublimating factor in women's sex–marriage relationships, for low sexual gratification scores of religious women depreciate their overall marital satisfaction scores less than do low sexual gratification scores of the nonreligious. This relationship is not clear in the case of men.

FREQUENCY OF COITUS

Two major variables affect frequency of sexual intercourse: (1) the sexual conceptions of the culture pattern and (2) sexual energy of the pair. The first area sets out for every man and woman the pattern of expectations for both self and mate. The second accounts for the wide range of variations from couple to couple.

There are cultures which hold norms that by our standards would represent great excess. Sexual intercourse several times a night is expected. Other cultures aim at the goal of eliminating sex from the marriage. We have cited the Manus tribe, who consider seminal discharge a form of excretion. In Hindu culture, around age 40 a man enters the age of contemplation and is expected gradually to merge sexual energies in philosophical contemplation.

Our culture falls between such extremes. Norms differ with length of marriage, age of the couple, and perhaps much more between social classes than we know from research. But we do have sort of a general norm from sample studies. And we have norms for husbands and wives. These do not reflect the range of individual variation. Some males rarely want sexual intercourse, and quite a percentage of women rarely or never experience orgasm, yet there are couples who have sexual intercourse nightly or even more frequently. Kinsey notes a case of a woman who reported 70 orgasms weekly.

Terman (1938) studying psychological factors in marital happiness of 792 couples, found that husbands on the average wanted coitus somewhat more frequently than wives (see Figure 21-2). To summarize briefly Terman's findings according to the way his married couples matched up sexually, the following table is given, showing the proportion of wives and husbands who were satisfied with the frequency of their sexual relations:

	WIVES (PERCENT)	HUSBANDS (PERCENT)
Too frequent intercourse	24	3
Just the right amount	53	54
Too little intercourse	22	44

Frequency is largely determined by the biological rhythms of the couple, particularly of the male. The buildup of seminal fluids, along with psychological stimulation operate here. Sexual appetite is, of course, variable with amount of activity and with degree of restraint and self-control. Frequency is not a matter of morals in the view of most married people. It is a recreative activity without being an intentional act of procreation, except on rare occasions. The norm of younger people is two to three times weekly, but variations up and down from this norm are to be expected.

The degree of resulting stimulation—the extent to which the couple feel tired and irritated or rejuvenated and more energetic—is the practical measure of desired frequency. Usually the husband is more eager and must temper his demands to the wife's tolerance; otherwise she becomes fatigued, irritable, and may in time dread his approaches. If the wife is the more eager, too great demands may lead the husband to the point of impotence.

It is very likely that the degree of sexual satisfaction in coitus will depend on the degree of mutuality. In this there appears to have been some improvement in recent generations, possibly due in part to the male's increased recognition of the need for restraint in order to meet the wife's norm. Of wives in the Kinsey (1953) research born before 1900, marital coitus had a frequency

FIGURE 21–2   Preferred frequency of intercourse. At all ages, the wife's preferred frequency averaged less than the husband's. Such averages, of course, do not depict the wide range of individual differences in both men and women. (Data are for 792 married couples.) Source: By permission from Lewis M. Terman. *Psychological Factors in Marital Happiness* (Copyright 1938, McGraw-Hill Book Co.).

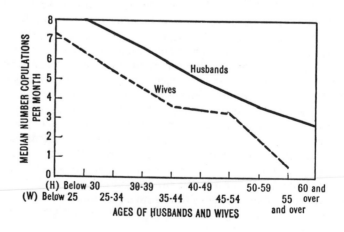

of 3.2 per week; of those born after 1900, the frequency was 2.6. This research also finds a greater variety of techniques and more foreplay among couples at the later period; also that more wives responded to orgasm—37 percent of those born prior to 1900 and 42 percent of those born later.

All these findings would seem to point toward greater mutuality in the sexual aspect of marriage and to greater satisfaction of sexual needs.

Happy is the person who is married to a mate with similar desire frequency. The average for couples in the United States seems to range between 10 and 15 times a month. In other words, the cycle of the usual marriage is one to three times a week. Figure 21-2 shows the average difference in desire for intercourse of couples of different ages. It will be seen that the men at all ages feel the need for coitus more often than the wives. These data are, of course, averages. In some couples the wife is more strongly sexed. Kinsey's data show the range of extremes more variable in women than in men.

At the beginning of marriage, daily intercourse is not unusual, with a gradual tapering off as the novelty of it passes, until the couple adjusts to their normal cycle of needs. After this point there is a slow decline in frequency until the late 50s. From then on coitus may continue until old age with declining frequency, depending on the physical energy and psychological outlook of the pair.

Studies of the great biologist Raymond Pearl and some later studies suggest that sexual intercourse is most frequent among farmers, second among people in the business classes, and least frequent among those in the professions. Such differences might be explained in terms of diversity of interest, habits of living, physical energy, variety of other recreational outlets, and psychic stimulation outside the marriage, rather than by differences in biological drives.

SEXUAL DENIAL IN MARRIAGE BARGAINING

The most extensive commercialization of sex is found in prostitution. But it is used extensively in bargaining in dating, particularly where the male pays the bill for dates. We have cited Margaret Mead's statement that prior to marriage it is customary everywhere for women to determine when and whether the sex act takes place. In marriage the male makes these decisions.

No doubt this broad statement has quite general application, but there are times in the marriage relationship when wives use sex for bargaining. Perhaps they always have. Herodotus describes the affiliation of Greek wives, intent on stopping war. They were to put on fine garments, allure their husbands, and excite them sexually, then deny them sexual relations unless they agreed to stop warfare.

Wives have no doubt always used their sexual bargaining powers even if with less altruistic motives. Males are much less likely to do so. Wives may also use denial more often than husbands as a penalty for disagreement and tensions in the marriage.

In 1967, Judson T. Landis surveyed 581 couples, of whom one member of each had been in his marriage classes at a previous time (average for all, seven years previously). His data show that 48 percent of the husbands reported that their wives at times denied them sex relations as a reaction to marital differences; 40 percent of wives admitted denial. Only 24 percent of wives reported husbands refusing to have sex relations.

SEXUAL ACTIVITY THROUGHOUT THE LIFE CYCLE

Many young people are inclined to think that sexual attraction and sexual drives are characteristic phenomena of youth but have no significance in the later years of married life. This notion is very persistent, and it is also completely inaccurate. Although youth is the more highly romantic age, and although, for the young male particularly, sexual drives may seem overwhelming, sexual attraction and interest in sexual intercourse persist throughout most of the years of married life.

Kinsey's data deal with large samples of both males and females in the later years of life. The young male reaches his maximum capacity during the teens, having on the average an orgasm approximating two and a half times per week. His sex activities decline consistently thereafter. But at 60, only 5 percent of males, he finds, are inactive; at 70, only 30 percent. Some are still active at 80 or older.

The average female during the early teens has little capacity for sexual responsiveness. Even at 20, her medium orgasm is about one every three weeks. She reaches her peak of orgasmic response—about one every two weeks—at around 30 years of age, and remains near this level until she is past 50. At age 60 her capacity to respond by orgasm remains almost as high as it was at age 20.

GENITAL STRUCTURE

This is not the place for an extensive discussion of human physiology. Presumably most young people will have made some study of human physiology before they study this book. On the other hand, there are always those who have had no training even in the fundamentals of reproduction. To enter marriage in such a state of ignorance can bring serious consequences in the fields of sexual and general adjustment.

Figure 21–3 gives a detailed frontal view of the female reproductive system, with a cross-sectional view in the lower part of the diagram. The point of deposit of semen by the male is in the vaginal tract near the cervix. The sperm must be sucked in or swim through the cervical opening and travel up through the uterus to the fallopian tube to reach the ovum. The ovum, or egg, and sperm can meet only during a short period of the month, usually seven or eight hours.

Figure 21–4 shows the male reproductive organs. Millions of sperm are manufactured daily in the testicles, which lie outside the body in the scrotum,*

---

*Sperm require storage in a temperature lower than normal body temperature.

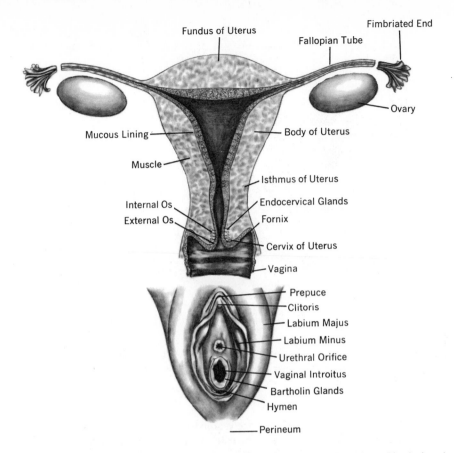

Diagrammatic view of female reproductive system. Source: C. L. Anderson, *Physical and Emotional Aspects of Marriage* (St. Louis: C. V. Mosby Co., 1953). Reproduced by permission of the publisher and Dr. Anderson.

FIGURE 21-3

are stored in the seminiferous tubules and are discharged through the penis at the time of the male orgasm in sexual intercourse. In normal sexual intercourse millions are deposited, along with fluids from Cowper's gland and the prostate gland, in the upper end of the vaginal vestibule of the female.

PROBLEMS

1   It has been stated that, with reference to their sexual expectations, "American women have gone from one extreme to another. They used to expect nothing; now they expect everything. Of the two extremes, today's is probably the more dangerous." Discuss.

2   What are your reactions to the proposal that it would be desirable for each young

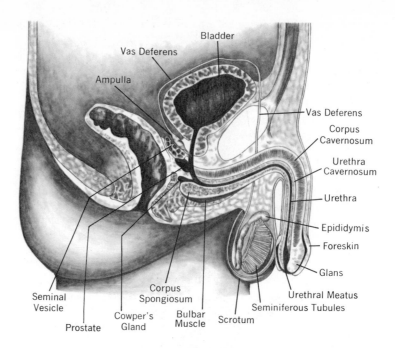

FIGURE 21–4   Diagrammatic view of male reproductive system. Source: C. L. Anderson, *Physical and Emotional Aspects of Marriage* (St. Louis: C. V. Mosby Co., 1953). Reproduced by permission of the publisher and Dr. Anderson.

couple to set a time limit of, say, one year in which to achieve sexual adjustment? During the year they would read about sex, patiently experiment, and seek help if necessary. At the end of the period they might reasonably say that they had done everything possible, and, if they still feel dissatisfied, they should seek a divorce.

3   What would your advice be to a women who has experienced no orgasm by her third year of marriage?

    a   Visit her doctor.

    b   Visit a psychiatrist.

    c   Keep trying.

    d   Discuss the matter with her husband.

    e   Accept the fact gracefully and recognize that she need not match her husband in orgasmic response.

    f   Some other alternative.

    Defend your choice.

4   Most couples with children believe that their marriage is a happer one than it would have been had they remained childless. Why then is some form of birth control often considered important to marital happiness?

5   What stand does the Catholic Church take on birth control?

6   Sexual relations, even in happy marriages, are thought by most young people to cease by middle age. It is difficult for many to realize that older people could find

one another sexually interesting and attractive. In general, what are the facts concerning duration and frequency of sexual activity among older couples?

7   While no class is a typical cross-section of young people, your class nevertheless represents various levels of opinion and knowledge. Poll the class on their sex knowledge as it was prior to reading this chapter with the statements below.
Before reading this chapter I believed that:

a   Sexual adjustment was generally a matter of (1) hours, (2) days, (3) weeks, (4) several months, (5) a year or so, (6) a lifetime.

b   Most women experience an orgasm (1) generally, as do men, (2) almost always, (3) about half the time, (4) occasionally, (5) very seldom.

c   In order for both mates to be happy, the wife (1) must experience an orgasm, (2) should experience an orgasm occasionally, (3) need never experience an orgasm.

d   The average young couple engages in sexual relations (1) nightly, (2) almost every night, (3) about once a week, (4) infrequently.

e   That sexual relations between couples tend to cease (1) after the first five years of marriage, (2) after about 12 years, (3) in middle age, (4) after menopause, (5) when the couple become very old.

In analyzing the results of this poll, consider the degree to which the answers agree with the facts in the chapter and differ by sex.

ECONOMIC VALUES IN MARRIAGE INTERACTION

22 The hippies have created a contracul-
ture in which economic values are depreciated. Although their style of life is
too lacking in cleanliness, sanitation, and aesthetic qualities to appeal to the
majority of youth, their rebellion against material affluence has proved conta-
gious among the masses. Many middle- and upper-class youth have come to
question their possession of comforts and luxury in such abundance. Many
have rebelled in some measure, and the alienated few have joined the
contraculture. Those more positively oriented, in denying affluence, have
joined social crusades where humanitarian motives can be given expression.
Action, Peace Corps, Youth Corps, Head Start, VISTA, and many such ventures have become for a time "their thing."

For most, when the time comes to marry and raise children, the more
mundane values must take over. Family formation requires money, and if history is any guide, money problems are parallel to sex problems in marriage.
Most couples experience both.

SYMBOLIC MEANINGS

Thorstein Veblen, the brilliant iconoclastic economist, saw material goods as a
means to status. He enlarges upon this theory in one of the most cutting
satires in social science literature, *Theory of the Leisure Class*. Leisure itself is
the key to social status—it testifies that here is a man who lives with little

work; he has plenty. His wealth is spent in costly publicity-gaining activities—at the races, golfing, hunting, gambling, and in lavish entertainment of the "right" people. Conspicuous consumption (lavish spending in ways that are obvious to others) is another device of status seeking, as is conspicuous philanthropy.

Veblen saw this pattern as affecting not only the wealthy but all who imitate them, or nearly everyone in our culture. He saw deeply into the mainsprings of human nature in the area of economic motivation. However, the motivations he saw operating in our economic life seem to be more typical of nonindustrial civilizations, where there is no middle class, than of modern American society. The American, in spite of his supposed greed and moneymindedness, is less driven to conspicuous consumption than are many peoples of the world. Yet the use of goods for status does operate here and it is a factor in the relationships of men and women. The Veblen views point up the fact that the adjustment struggle centering about money in marriage is of much deeper significance than monetary values as such. Money is at the roots of status seeking in the value systems of men and women, and what money means to a particular individual must be understood in this broader framework.

ECONOMIC ADJUSTMENTS AFTER MARRIAGE RATHER THAN BEFORE

The property problem in the institutional marriage systems of the world is negotiated in advance of marriage by the families concerned. Economic values, as we have seen, are critical in mate choice where elders are in control of matchmaking. Property and family status are the criteria of appropriate mate choice, not personal characteristics of bride or groom. In our propertyless concept of mate choice, however, love and companionability are what count. Property matters are considered later.

Money, or, more broadly, economic values, have become the symbol of innumerable needs and satisfactions; and because they have, money values become the supreme issues in many aspects of husband–wife adjustment in the marriage. The real problem of the modern marriage is not merely how money shall be earned or how it shall be spent, but rather the kind of values in life which the couple seek to obtain through its use. Differences in ideas concerning the use of money in the marriage are symbolic of basic differences in personal values and aspirations, for money actually has a place in the personal values of everyone, and the ends the individual pursues with money are symbolic of his total value system.

The person with a background of thrift and practicality may, for example, experience real satisfaction and boast at length about the bargain-counter purchase of a dress at a fourth of its regular price. In this person's scheme of values, such a purchase represents a shrewd and wise way of overcoming economic limitations and of actually achieving success and status. Those reared in a luxurious environment and those who aspire to a higher social status are likely, by contrast, to achieve satisfaction through buying a garment that is conspicuously expensive or that bears the label of the most exclusive shop.

A *Fortune* poll asked men and women to indicate which sex they thought was the more extravagant. A majority of both men and women felt that women are the more extravagant. Undoubtedly, this feeling is the basis of much of the conflict between husband and wife over economic values. Probably the reason women have gained the reputation of being more extravagant is that they do such a high proportion of the spending. It usually falls to the wife to do most of the day-to-day shopping.

Far too often the male role becomes that of supercritic of all the purchases. Frequently, he does not mean to be a critic; he just wants to know what is going on. When he notices new drapes at the living room windows, he asks, "Where did these come from?" The wife, if she is sensitive, may anticipate the next question, "What did they cost?" When steak appears on his table, the husband asks, "Where did you get this steak?" perhaps meaning, "It's a fine piece of meat. Go there more often." Or he may mean, "We're buying more steak than we can afford," or "Steak like this costs more than we can afford." In either case, the wife has the feeling he is questioning her judgment. If the steak happens to be a tough one, he may growl, "Where'd you get this piece of leather?" Immediately he implies that her judgment in purchasing meat is not to be trusted.

So the interactions centering about the wife's role as purchasing agent in the marriage go on. In this role she is inclined to receive little praise and a great deal of blame.

When it comes to the large purchases, like the family car, a house, life insurance, or investments, the husband acts. Women's judgment is not appreciated in such circumstances. They supposedly do not know the business world. When the husband makes an investment error, which he is as likely to do as not, he prefers to live above censure, but if called upon to justify his move, he rationalizes that one must, in investment ventures, expect to make some mistakes, that the man who does not venture never has anything.

At the nonthrifty extreme are those husbands who are always out for a quick deal which promises to bring the family immediately to the luxury plane. It may be the horses that fascinate them, the stock market, the long shot in a business venture, or any one of the thousands of deals that bait the speculation-minded with a gambler's hope of quick success. Certainly, some wives are guilty of this, too, but generally speaking the husband is the culprit, while the patient, or impatient, wife protests, guided by the sound evidence of past example.

It is difficult for men to recognize that one of the most influential newspaper financial columnists and authors on income tax matters today is a woman (Sylvia Porter)—a married woman. For years she used only her initials to hide the fact that she is a woman. It was feared that she would have no readers if her sex were known.

Women, the Bargain Hunters   Wives, much more than husbands, are bargain hunters when it comes to buying. Considering their time of little value, they are inclined to do a great deal of footwork and sometimes drive the family automobile a considerable distance to save a little money. They work on the philosophy that anyone can get an article at the full price but that it takes a shrewd woman indeed to find a bargain. At some social levels, there is prestige as well as personal satisfaction in such achievement, particularly if it is learned that some unwitting friend or neighbor paid more for the same article. In certain instances, bargain hunting becomes such a fascinating game that sale items are bought in excess and the total outlay far exceeds the savings. If purchases are confined to the actual need, however, there is a saving.

Men, the Discount Seekers   There are many exceptions, but generally women do not believe in arguing the seller down in price. They feel guilty in trying to do so. Perhaps they feel it is giving the impression they cannot afford the article. Verbal bargaining is where the male shines. He wants to do his shopping in a hurry and without unnecessary footwork. He is aware that nothing is saved by driving the car about hunting for the cheapest article in town, but he likes the game of beating the seller down. He will argue that the markup is for time customers, to cover worthless trade-ins, that such items are not moving any more—anything to bring the seller to his terms. And he is always ready for a chance to gloat about his bargain and to strut his success before his less brazen neighbor who was sucker enough to pay the full price. Buying wholesale, too, has become a great American game.

Merging Roles   With the entry of women into the work world, the traditional clashes between husbands and wives over economic values have been modified. Where both work, both often shop together in the supermarket. While the wife is filling her shopping cart with canned goods, the husband is over at the meat counter selecting the steak or roast that strikes his fancy or his purse. And where both earn, they are more likely to talk over investments and plan them together.

The wife who has had experience in earning also may realize as clearly as does the man how much labor goes into earning the money for a particular expenditure. Such wives' standards of value may in time become similar to those of the husband in spite of different values dominating the childhood training of boy and girl.

The old division of labor within the household tends to break down, too, as sex roles become modified to fit modern economic roles. Where both husband and wife work for wages, the hard-and-fast line no longer exists in their division of labor in the home. While it is assumed that this has increased the cooperative spirit of the household, all is not peace. The very fact that roles are no longer strictly defined, and the division of labor is no longer clear, is the basis for many a family argument. Where division of labor is fixed, each accepts his place and carries out his appointed task. Where there is no real division of labor, the couple must define each new work situation for itself. This calls for the maximum of tolerance, good humor, and cooperation. It also calls for a great deal of good sense.

So the problem is ramified into hundreds of struggles between husbands and wives in their attempts to define a satisfactory division of labor and a compatible scheme of economic values. Maximum adjustability is required if marriage is to be a truly cooperative economic venture.

PROPERTY OWNERSHIP VERSUS COMFORTS

In the rural economy of an earlier day—and some of those values still survive—the accumulation of possessions was symbolic of a person's accomplishments. The contrasting urban value is to "live well" whether one actually owns anything in the way of tangible assets or not. There is a world of difference in the two approaches to life, and where the two meet in marriage, as they often do, a major compromise is required.

The roots of the first series of values, so deeply imbedded in history, persist and merit a brief examination. In an agricultural economy a man's character and accomplishments were measured by the time he went into the field in the morning, the acres of fertile land he acquired, the success of his crops, and the size of his flocks and herds. Woman was a helpmate in these achievements and shared a sense of accomplishment and respect in them. She also acquired success and respect in a domain of her own. The successful agrarian housewife was respected for the good bread she baked, her pies, cakes, doughnuts, or noodles, or for some other specific art in which she excelled her neighbors. For her homemaking and general ability to carry her share of the farm load, she received unspoken but deeply felt gratitude from her husband and respect from her neighbors.

The new world of wages and salaries and the new setting of urban industrial civilization have shifted emphasis from the desire to accumulate possessions or to achieve in domestic spheres where accomplishment was once significant. The values of the ordinary person now center about earning in order to spend for a higher level of living. This means greater comfort, greater leisure, even greater luxury. The quest for security in land, house, and other real property has receded. Women's domestic arts now have to compete with the processed products of the great factory, with its packaged cake mix, pie crust, and frozen foods.

The economic world is no longer family-centered, nor are economic values so clear-cut in the personalities of either man or wife. The comfort-minded and the possessions-minded are merely two points of view among many contrasting types of value systems around which personalities are oriented.

INVESTMENTS IN MALE AND FEMALE SUBCULTURES

Gain made by investment of money for long-term goals of family security has been largely in the area of the male subculture. Many wives think that when they spend money for something they want, they are making an investment; some even consider this saving. These ideas shock the investment-minded husband. Such subculture value differences may bring arguments and misunderstanding in early married life and can be serious indeed in later life if the wife is left with property which must be managed if she is to remain independent and live in the comfort which her husband's management of money may have provided.

Because women live longer, they inherit much of the wealth in houses, farms, livestock, lands, stocks, bonds, life insurance, and cash. It has usually been the husband's money management which has led to whatever estate has been accumulated. Suddenly, usually without prior training on the part of the wife for the responsibility, it is hers to use, to manage, and, if she has the capacity, to multiply until such time as it is passed on to the children and grandchildren or to whatever charity she may choose as an alternative to passing on the inheritance to her descendants.

Albert E. Schwabacher, Jr., (1963) has commented with the wisdom of the wide experience of an investment banker, on the weakness of widows. He expresses the view that women probably own half the property in the country but control only about 20 percent, since most husbands and estate planners leave it in such a form that control is provided for through pensions and other plans. But when they are left free to control their money, they usually turn to professional managers, most of whom are men.

As a manager of money, Schwabacher has found that women with understanding of money and property management are rare. Only a few are informed, intelligent, and competent in this area of operation. He finds that with many, discussing business is a waste of time. Often he finds that women appraise investment situations strictly in personal terms and by impulse. "Buy Aunt Sally Candy Company stock!" Ask her why, and her answer is "I like candy." The fact that the stock earns no money makes no difference. "Don't buy any Safeway stock." Ask her why: "A Safeway clerk was rude to me."

He finds that many want to sell a good stock—one that should be kept—on impulse, while others want to keep a stock that has no future "because my departed husband bought it."

As a manager of money, he feels that the female subculture is weak. Women are not taught the principle of risk involved in investment—to invest in a capitalist economy means risk, the possibility of losing. A capitalist society is always short of risk capital, and women tend to hoard wealth or have it managed too conservatively, so that much of it is of little use in expanding the economy.

SATISFACTIONS OF PRODUCTIVITY

Except among the contraculture group, one of the principal roads to personal satisfaction and high social standing in our culture is still through productivity. The wealthy in America have failed to fit Thorstein Veblen's picture of the leisure class. They have not, in fact, been a leisure class; they have been among the most productive individuals in the economic system, for here a man's measure is still, in part, his ability to contribute something worthwhile to monetary wealth.

Being productive brings a feeling of importance and the admiration of others. The desire to feel important and to be admired explains in large part the acquisition of wealth and property throughout history. The flocks and herds, apartment houses and factories, finery and gadgets, and particularly the material comforts and luxuries, are means. Possession shows the world that this man or woman, or this man and woman together, have been able to get ahead in the highly competitive struggle for financial success.

The urban worker employed by others, particularly the salaried worker, has found it difficult to find as much satisfaction in productivity as the self-employed man. In fact, the tendency of the labor union movement and of labor union philosophy has been to play down production and play up income received for production. Slowdown and other devices have tended to make the worker feel that to produce more than the man working at his elbow is disloyal to labor and tends, in the long run, to reduce the number of jobs available for workers. This value, of course, is in direct contrast to the old rural value under which a man's productive effort was a measure of his character—almost of his religion.

This need to feel productive is still to some extent characteristic of the great majority of Americans, but there is evidence that it varies greatly among individuals and can be cultivated or largely destroyed by early training. The average male exhibits it more consistently than does the average female. In most communities, however, as has been stressed, a man is still judged and judges himself primarily in terms of his productivity, not by his success as a father, husband, or human being. He may be happy and well-adjusted, but until he makes his business a prosperous one, he is likely to remain a failure in the eyes of his neighbors. He may have ulcers or suffer from high blood pressure and constant worry, but among his acquaintances he is known as a "go-getter," because he has put himself—his time, money, energy, and perhaps his health—into achieving vocational success.

This difference in values, or in the emphasis upon values, is not a serious problem on a national or even community-wide basis. Such differences, in fact, tend to complement one another, and both extremes can find satisfaction in our culture as well as in our economy. A real problem does arise, however, when such differences clash head-on in marriage. Clashes of this kind are not uncommon, since the value of personal productivity is much more strongly emphasized in the rearing of boys than of girls.

Women judge themselves and one another more consistently in terms of consumption. The location of one's residence, the conversation pieces, and the number of one's labor-saving devices rather than what one can produce determine one's success and status in the community.

In many marriages, then, the husband is largely production-oriented, while the wife is consumption-oriented. When an adjustment is not reached or when funds do not allow for the satisfaction of both, a clash almost inevitably results.

Overemphasis on Productivity   The well-known practice of the farmer building a good barn before considering a new house for the family is often ridiculed, but the farmer is production-minded. He makes his living from the barn. Without it he feels he cannot afford the new house, the running water, or the bathtub. It takes a rurally reared woman of the old school to have sympathy with such standards, and if one is to read meaning into the extensive migration of girls from farming areas immediately after high school, one must surmise that a decreasing proportion of farm girls are willing to sacrifice their comfort to a production philosophy of farm living.

It is characteristic of the older generation of farm families to become so production-minded that even when they can afford the higher level of consumption that would spell comfort for parents and children, they continue to draw all their satisfaction from producing, living on in the same old, inconvenient way. This is often a point of conflict between parents and teen-agers in the farm family. The teen-ager becomes ashamed of his home and living conditions and tries to make his voice heard in getting the house improved so that he will not feel embarrassed when bringing his friends there.

The vice of undue production-mindedness is not entirely one of the rural male. The struggling small-town or urban businessman, particularly in the eyes of a consumption-minded wife, may also be guilty of wanting to plow everything back into the business. He justifies this in terms of greater comfort and wealth in the future. The wife often wants her comfort now.

Then there is the aspiring professional man who feels disposed to plow all family surplus into his further training rather than permit the wife to raise the level of family living. Legitimate as such a goal is, wives and husbands may not see eye to eye, and, of course, there are many husbands who are too willing to sacrifice the interests of the marriage to their own ambitions. At least there are often legitimate points of difference between husbands and wives centering on the philosophy of the utilization of money as an investment in future productivity rather than as an investment to improve the family level of living.

In thinking of production-mindedness and consumption-mindedness, one finds striking examples of types in the movie colony. John Barrymore made millions but lived it up in "wine, women, and song" and ended up in debt, with even his household goods confiscated by creditors. That is consumption to the limit. Walt Disney's daughter, in writing about his distinguished father, told how at home there was never much ready cash. Beyond the necessities for living, everything went into her father's latest project: a new cartoon series, Disneyland, etc. Production-mindedness is in evidence here.

Woman's Need for Productive Outlets

Much is written today of the failure of competent women to live up to their promise, of their great readiness to settle down into an early marriage, childbearing, and domesticity. Much is written also of the fact that many find later in life that they settled for too little. They find life boring, domesticity less satisfying than they had hoped, and themselves unprepared for the kind of work roles they might have found satisfying had they pursued education to its conclusion. They awake too late to the fact that the last 30–40 years, after children are no longer dependent, are important ones.

Betty Friedan (1964) declares, "If women do not put forth, finally, that effort to become all that they have in them to become, they will forfeit their own humanity." She discovered after writing the *Feminine Mystique* that a surprising number of women have found a new "fourth dimension" of productivity that makes their lives complete.

The woman's need for productive outlets is one which many husbands, busy in their own work or creative hobbies, fail to appreciate when their wives insist on working outside the family. For many women housework alone does not provide sufficient recognition and creative satisfaction to justify their existence to themselves. To live the full and complete lives they desire, and to avoid the neurotic developments which come from a feeling of uselessness, they must seek activity in outside employment. This explains why women, by and large, are more willing to engage in gainful employment than men are to have them do so. Polls of young people show that many more girls than boys think girls should work before marriage and also after marriage. This difference in viewpoint can become an issue in marriage and is an area where an adjustment must definitely be worked out.

For some women the home alone is not enough and cannot be. The job means a great deal as an escape from the monotony of home and as a way of expressing the need to achieve and create. Previous to the time that children are born, particularly, the average young wife can escape loneliness and monotony only by being given an opportunity to work and to secure the recognition that comes with earning. The husband who blocks his wife in her work endeavor is inviting trouble for himself, his wife, and the whole family. Research confirms this view.

Women who are able to find a sense of productivity in household activities alone and in the rearing of their families are happy indeed. The ability of a woman to do so depends, no doubt, on a number of factors. The conception of what a wife should be, what she may do, and how she may act is usually learned in early life as she observes her mother and absorbs her mother's attitudes concerning a wife's role. These early impressions are very strong and frequently account entirely for the later attitudes and behavior of the grown girl. They are not incapable of modification, however. Other women whom the child admires, a school curriculum emphasizing career training rather than preparation for a domestic life, or a husband who gives little credit and recognition for housework—any or all of these help account for the overwhelming personal need of many wives and mothers to find work outside the home.

In the end, a large proportion of women must find a place outside the home to feel content. Family-rearing is a transient experience, largely over by age 40. Then, if not sooner, most women need new outlets. For the woman who completed school early and is inadequately trained, this offers serious problems. Most women may have to return to school to brush up or to improve work skills. These necessary adjustments also require the sympathy and understanding of the husband. Such adjustments cannot be appraised primarily in terms of increased earning power but rather in terms of increased self-esteem for the wife who may no longer feel useful.

Husband's Appreciation Needed   At all stages of their married life, appreciation by the husband is needed. The appreciation he gives the wife in her domestic roles is frequently the deciding factor, as well as his recognition of the savings to the household from the labor contribution she makes. Often, in fact, the husband is far too little aware of her very great economic contribution and is quick to criticize and slow to praise her for her part in making the family an economic success. In today's labor market, the wife and mother probably contributes around $10,000 to the family income by her labors. It varies with the level of living of the family, the number of children, her skill in creating and in saving, and many other variables. Of course, the value of a good mother cannot be measured in monetary terms primarily. Who can put a value on the importance of adequately socializing the young child and giving him a sense of security?

In the early years of marriage, husbands and wives alike generally exert considerable influence over the role attitudes of their mates. The man who marries a working girl and takes her out of her earning role, for example, can do much to make her transition to housewife and mother an easy and unregretted one if he greets each of her domestic efforts with praise and real appreciation. The young wife, wanting very much the recognition of her husband, generally enjoys the cultivation of qualities and abilities which he admires. If, on the other hand, he challenges every expenditure, asks her to justify every bill, and rarely if ever expresses any appreciation for her thrift and saving or her long hours of regular work in providing for a comfortable home, she can take little pleasure or pride in her new wife–homemaker role.

The need for recognition of the homemaker role is particularly acute in urban homes, in cases where the wife does not continue in gainful employment. Farm women still take great pride in their productive activity within the household, recounting at every opportunity the number of quarts of this and that they have canned, the glasses of jelly made, the pickles and preserves, and the jars of sauerkraut and pickles in their basements. One reason they can do so is that their husbands and their communities rate this productive role favorably.

THE STRAIN OF OVERCONSUMPTION

The average urban housewife takes comparatively little pride in the kind of productive activity that goes on in the home. Her satisfactions, therefore, have to be derived largely from the kind of consumption in which the family can engage. The well-furnished home and well-dressed children are a means to a feeling of recognition and importance for her. To the extent that this is true, her personal satisfactions among her neighbors and relatives is dependent on the amount of money she can spend for the improvement of the level of living in the family. It is her source of pride and personal satisfaction. What the husband considers extravagant may be necessity for her, basic to satisfying her need for feeling important.

This all goes to say that the expenditure of money is not always the same to the man as to the woman, and one has difficulty in understanding the other unless he tries to appreciate what the motivation may be. The motivation may not be too evident. In fact, one must assume that the economic activities of both men and women are deeply fraught with significance in terms of the recognition they bring to the personalities of the individuals involved.

One hears less today about the underworked and overshopping housewife, but no doubt she is still present in many circles, making marriage adjustment quite difficult, particularly for husbands whose training has built into them a wide streak of thrift. Such husbands must recognize that the cure for such a wife is some other outlet for personal recognition.

Actually, the current pressure on all sides is to encourage the new couple to overstrain their economic resources in an effort to match the pace of friends, fellow workers, or neighbors. The luxury goal of living is evidenced in the whole trend of American invention. Once a particular invention has reached a stage of relative mechanical perfection, the manufacturers compete in terms of beauty and ornamentation. In fact, this becomes the final level of appeal in modern advertising, for here there is no satiation point. There is a limit, for example, to the amount of horsepower that is desirable in an automobile engine. That limit may have been reached or even exceeded in the present state of highway development. But when the automobile market becomes highly competitive, the major emphasis shifts to styling and design. In this there is no limit to the creative imagination of man. One new model can follow another year after year by a change in style. This keeps up the hunger to buy and puts competition of new-car ownership strictly on the basis of prestige rather than utility. If only automobiles were involved, the matter might be quite simple, but the luxury-ornamentation motive is no less characteristic there than in dress, eyeglasses, bathtubs, telephones, and almost every other item of daily use.

The American standard of living has risen so precipitously that young couples in many instances are able to begin married life on or near the level of comfort which their parents achieved only after years of struggle and thrift. Aspirations for a high level of living, in fact for an increasingly higher level of living, are a part of the American heritage. The common laborer shares it along with the middle and upper classes. An open-class system sets no limits to human aspirations. There is no standard by which one knows when he has reached a satisfactory level and can rest content in his achievements.

Modern business is sales-minded and uses every possible means of contact and communication to whet desire and raise aspirations—the display window, talking mannequin, demonstration, pseudo and real scientific opinion, high-pressure salesmen, advertising by press, radio, and television. There is no end to what a couple can want, for new models and styles, and even new products, are flashed before them in a continuous flow of advertising.

To make it all easy, and nearly painless, there is the generous time contract by which the couple may mortgage their income for two to three years ahead with readily consumable goods, to say nothing of 20–30 year mortgage contracts or life-long insurance contracts. One can mortgage any share of his future income he chooses years before it is earned.

"Keeping ahead of the Joneses" is a favorite American game and no doubt explains some of our remarkable progress as a nation toward new and better things. This spirit keeps the family on its toes, too, but it can readily become a vice, particularly for young housewives whose aspirations far exceed their husbands' earning power. In many marriages, basic conflicts in values of husband and wife center on consumption standards and values. Such conflicts are almost inevitable in many marriages.

We have spoken at length about the need for a feeling of productivity as a motive for the outside employment of housewives. What about the simple consideration of "making ends meet"?

According to one woman who has successfully combined a career with motherhood, women's rights and individual development are no longer the crucial considerations. Among young married women today it has become simply a matter of bookkeeping, a single pay envelope simply will not meet the needs of an average family.

It should be added, however, that the justification for working to supplement income, while sometimes easier to understand, is no greater than working to satisfy personality needs. The woman who "works out" in order to keep up payments on the new car but who worries over neglecting her children, is probably doing herself and her family greater harm than if the car were allowed to revert to the creditors. At the same time, the wife who, because of unjustifiable guilt feelings or because of uncertainty about her role, forces herself to stay at home full time and pass up opportunities for an interesting job is inviting frustration and bitterness that can easily undo many of the advantages of being a full-time wife and mother.

MUTUAL ROLE ACCEPTANCE

Whether the young bride becomes a full-time housewife, combines her new role with a part-time job, or devotes her daytime interests and energies to a full-fledged career is not the point. The important consideration to marital adjustment is whether husband and wife agree on the course of action taken and are mutually satisfied with the kind of family life it entails.

The wife who does not work outside the home, for example, has no right to expect the same amount of sharing her domestic duties as has the wife who works the same length of day as her husband in gainful employment, yet she may do so. The husband whose wife works may expect the same leisure and attention at home as though his wife were not working and be negative toward any suggestion that he share the housework or care of the children. There are no set rules to follow. The husband in this instance is trying to live by the division of labor that may have existed in his parental home, not realizing that he has not established the same sort of family.

The choice of several possible roles is not the exclusive right of wives. Husbands, too, must decide whether they will divorce themselves completely from housework, household interests, and child-rearing activities. A good marital adjustment is seldom achieved unless husband and wife can genuinely accept whatever role the other decides to assume.

Whether or not she decides to work outside the home full or part time, the average wife soon discovers that, in our culture, the husband's work activities usually take precedence over her own. There are numerous exceptions, but they are exceptions nevertheless. A "good wife" is still expected to look up to her husband in the matter of making a living and to show an interest in his productive activities. If she fails to do so before marriage, she is likely to lose her man in spite of her personal attractiveness. A wife who fails to develop an interest in her husband's work, investments, and other productive efforts and to grow in knowledge and understanding of such activity is bargaining for a lonesome future.

He may or may not leave her, but he will find much of his conversation, companionship, and true friendship in quarters where there are men or women who appreciate the things that are vital to him. The most vital interests of most successful males are centered on productivity. If their work is uninteresting, it may be hobbies or avocations that give life zest for them.

This does not mean that a wife should lose her own interests and hobbies and become a drudge of the home. Far from it. To be the wife most men want she must keep alert, informed, have her own vital and stimulating interests, and also understand his world of activity and meaning.

This takes the young wife through one step after another of adjusting to the husband's world. In spite of romantic considerations, most wives must learn early in marriage to share a great deal of the husband's time with his job. Many professional men and others ambitious to get ahead in their work are inclined to spend longer hours with their profession or business than they should, sometimes to the unnecessary neglect of the wife. Some employers also are inconsiderate of their employees, requiring a great deal of overtime work. With men, work tends to come first, although every man should realize that marriage takes time and that the wife's interests must be given consideration.

The demanding, possessive woman had better marry a man who has no deep male recreational or occupational interests. Otherwise, either he or she or both are likely to be unhappy in marriage. For example, she should never marry a doctor. She will either succeed in ruining him as a doctor and as a man, or she will have to suffer from seeing him devote a great deal of his interests and time to his profession. Similarly, if she wants a great deal of attention, she should not marry an ambitious college professor or, in fact, any individual who expects seriously to pursue a highly competitive vocation. She may actually succeed in shaping him to her will, but if she does, his career will be ruined. Few men can forgive a woman for being so demanding.

The same is true for a man who marries a woman with her heart set on a vocation and insists on confining her to the home after marriage. He will have on his hands a person disillusioned with marriage as soon as she realizes that it has robbed her of satisfactions which mean more to her than housekeeping or even marital romance.

Most wives recognize that a great deal of a man's time and energy will be consumed in work; most of them are willing to have the attention of their husband in the family for only a limited portion of the time, recognizing that the husband's devotion to his occupation is essential to the family's economic well-being. But there are some wives who are too demanding to make such adjustments.

In the case of a few highly intellectual individuals, it seems to be possible to have a marriage that permits each member to continue very much the independent life he has lived before marriage, each continuing with his own work and associations, knowing, well before they marry, that married life will make demands on only a relatively small part of their time and attention. Such couples usually do not plan to have children, and each plans to retain a high degree of individual self-interest within marriage. The average marriage, however, cannot be of this character.

For most couples, give and take to a degree never required of them before is necessary in the early weeks and months of marriage. The blending of two distinct personalities into one way of living is for most people something more of a task than they expected. But it can be done by those who are determined to succeed.

The adjustments of the early years of marriage, even in the companionship family, are generally more demanding of the wife than of the husband. This is why, as we have seen in an earlier chapter, a girl looking forward to marriage must have a great deal in the way of character and courage to succeed. It is the wife's way of life that is usually reshaped to fit the husband's. This will probably be true as long as men earn the living in most families. The current feminist movement is changing the law, opening positions, bringing equal pay for equal work, but as long as women are mothers, they will inevitably have to adjust more to the demands of the home than does the male. At some periods in life the job must for them be secondary to caring for the emotional and socialization needs of their children.

While most couples follow in the traditional pattern, the significant issue is not that they do so but that they do so willingly and with a mutual respect for whatever role the other takes in the home as well as in the world of work.

PROBLEMS

1   Describe specific American traditions or customs, and specific instances from American education and advertisements that seem to produce differences in values held by men and women.

2   Modern society has greatly increased the number of areas in which women may play productive roles. Why then is the modern wife likely to feel less productive than the wife of two generations past?

3   Is it possible to educate women away from the need they feel to be productive? Describe a way of life in which feminine productiveness is frowned upon. Why would such a role be unacceptable to most American women today?

4   *Sociodrama:* A young doctor and his wife have come to live in a new community. The wife realizes how important it is to make the right impression in order to gain standing in the community. To make this impression, she is willing to spend all their savings and mortgage most of their future earnings in possessions. The husband is beginning to be concerned about the fact that they have no children, no real savings, no money for relaxation and adventure. Dramatize a discussion or argument between them in which their values are pictured, in which the dangers of overconsumption are suggested, and in which the arguments for the wife's point of view are presented.

5   If a young couple agree that the wife shall work for a limited time, are there any rules they should agree upon as to how her income shall and shall not be spent?

6   Marilyn was a graduate student in interior decoration with a brilliant career awaiting her, when she fell in love with Mike. Mike is not a tyrant, but he firmly

believes that a home can be happy only when the wife devotes herself full time to her roles as wife and mother. He believes that she should channel her professional talents into her own home and forget about the career that might have been. Still, she feels that life would never be complete without a little success in the competitive world outside marriage. Would you advise her to:

a Forget about marriage; Mike is unreasonable?
b Postpone marriage a few years in order to further her interests?
c Marry and try to forget the career?
d Try some other alternative?

In weighing and discussing each alternative, consider its possible risks as well as its advantages.

7 Describe several common customs or practices that illustrate the consumption-mindedness of modern Americans.

8 Poll the class on the problem: If, upon marrying, you were able to live in a comfortably but simply furnished apartment and save $100 a month, would you prefer to:

a Save the $100 without specific purpose?
b Use the $100 for recreation?
c Buy a car?
d Invest the money?
e Begin having children?
f Buy furniture?
g Buy a home or property?
h Travel and have some adventure?
i Use the $100 for attractive wardrobes, eating out, and entertaining?
j Divide it in half and let each mate spend $50 as he chooses?

9 After tabulating the anonymously submitted data, do you find that:

a Most students tend to agree on economic values?
b Students differ according to sex?

10 If no agreement can be reached on how to spend the family's income, how should the dilemma be solved and why?

a Husband's values prevail?
b Wife's values prevail?
c Some other arrangement?

Discuss.

FINANCE MANAGEMENT

23 Married college students are able to excuse their financial self-denial, looking forward to the short time ahead when they will have more income. Most young marriages face financial struggle, but there is the hope that financial success lies ahead. To expect that the time will come when one can have everything one wants, is an illusion. That day probably will never come, for wants will most likely multiply more rapidly than resources. One of the most certain things about the money aspect of marriage is that there will never be enough money. Wise management will be necessary if even a substantial portion of wants of all family members are to be met. The word *wants* is used advisedly; most families in the United States have their *needs* met quite adequately. Wants are as flexible as human aspirations, and tend to grow Veblenian fashion, as members of the family use money to keep pace with the demands of their social circle; the husband with other men in the male subculture—business, club life, recreation—the wife with other women, primarily in the female subculture—clothes, beauty care, household furniture and equipment, club life—and as children grow, each with his age group in toys, appropriate clothes, and gadgets from the cowboy outfit to the first dress suit of the budding adolescent.

Some years ago *Life* carried an editorial based on a study by William H. Whyte, Jr., for *The Wall Street Journal*. It was titled "Is Thrift Un-American?" and described the spending habits of 83 young couples with incomes of $5000–7500. He found typically that their incomes were "hocked" far in advance, so that they never had cash. For example, he found of a $500 gross monthly income, only about $45 remains after all commitments for the month are met: time contracts, food and lunch money, but no savings. The system is to have oneself committed to regular monthly payments for all major items. In buying, cost is disregarded. The question asked is "What is the monthly payment?" There is more concern in the fact that it is $12.73 a month than in the total price. And there seems to be a complete disregard of the fact that 12–18 percent interest piles up. In big expenditures like automobiles, Whyte finds that buyers take dealer "packs" without even calculating the total amount, and often end up suckers.* Not only has Yankee thrift vanished, but so has Yankee shrewdness, he suggests.

His sampling of the $13,000–17,000 junior-executive group showed a similar pattern of being committed far in advance, carrying a large amount of debt in as many as 15 different loans. Saving, he concudes, is no longer identified with morality. In the average family, the difference between success or failure in money matters is largely a matter of money sense, no matter what the income level. One can always be in debt regardless of salary, and with the possible exception of the very lowest income group, savings are usually possible. Barring major illness or other such misfortune, success is a matter of money management.

There is no significant or consistent relationship between the amount of income and marital happiness. The economic security of the family, as measured by the proportion of the income being saved, has been found to bear an association with poor and good adjustment in marriage, as does regularity of employment and income. This may mean that the desire or ability to save is an index to a certain type of character which adjusts well in marriage. It is more definitely established that occupation and steadiness of income are related to successful adjustment in marriage. Managerial and professional occupations, where income is regular, show greater happiness scores than the less-regular-income occupations. (Refer back to Chapter 19.)

MONEY MANAGEMENT

Advice is always cheap, yet in the field of money management it is always in demand. By and large, the American family's success at money management falls far short of an ideal standard. Loan shark offices by the dozens flourish under fancy names in every city. Other finance agencies with greater respectability but excessive interest rates abound in cities, states, and even on a nationwide scale. Installment financing is often offered at more than twice a normal bank rate of interest.

In the field of life insurance and investments, the average couple are "babes in the woods" with little or no knowledge to help them in judging when they are or are not buying wisely. In the daily purchases of the household, many wives have too little knowledge for wise purchases of furniture, fabrics, and nutritious foods. A great deal of consumer education is needed.

Although one cannot assume that wise money management would ease all

---

*This situation became so bad at one point that the government entered the field, requiring that actual interest rates be shown and that the cost of the car be made known, to protect the gullible buyer (see page 393).

the family tensions that arise over money matters, it undoubtedly would help. Not all prospective housewives can take home economics courses, nor can all men be trained in money management, but some money sense is essential to successful home management.

The average young white man who makes it through college will earn about $15,841 for his family. It will be less at the beginning, more as he climbs. To have more for luxuries, either his wife must earn or he must learn to save and invest wisely to increase income later on as family responsibilities increase. There are only two ways to obtain income: (1) earn it as a reward for services performed or (2) add value to investments.

A PICTURE OF FAMILY INCOME

A realistic conception of probable earning power is important to success in marriage. Income is closely related to the schooling of the family head (Figure 23-1). This is inevitable, since a high level of training is prerequisite to both the better-paying and more stable occupations. Whites with less than grade school

Median family income, United States, 1970—by race and years of school completed. **FIGURE 23-1** Education and race are factors affecting family income. Among both whites and nonwhites, the more schooling, the higher the income. At 1970 income rates a college graduate would provide for his family an approximate income of from $580,000 to $650,000 during his working lifetime, depending on his race; a high school graduate $385,000 to $520,000; a grade school graduate $275,000 to $390,000. Schooling is also the most important gateway to occupational security. U.S. Census.

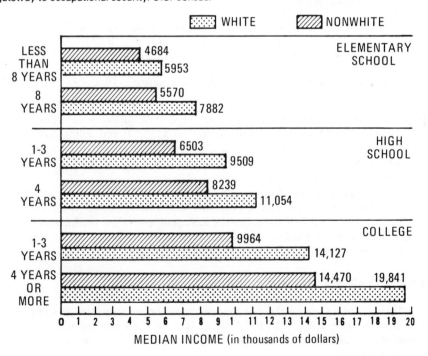

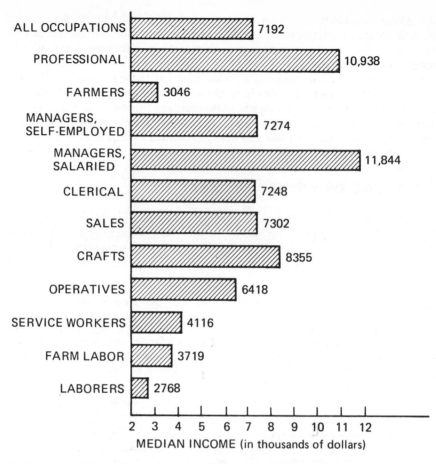

ALL OCCUPATIONS 7192
PROFESSIONAL 10,938
FARMERS 3046
MANAGERS, SELF-EMPLOYED 7274
MANAGERS, SALARIED 11,844
CLERICAL 7248
SALES 7302
CRAFTS 8355
OPERATIVES 6418
SERVICE WORKERS 4116
FARM LABOR 3719
LABORERS 2768

2 3 4 5 6 7 8 9 10 11 12
MEDIAN INCOME (in thousands of dollars)

FIGURE 23–2   Median income, U.S. families and persons, 1970—by occupation. U.S. Census.

education have a median income level of $5953, those with eighth-grade schooling, of $7882; high school graduates, of $11,054; and college graduates, of $15,841. Nonwhite families receive substantially less income than white families at all levels of education, but among them, also, more training brings a higher median level of income.

The occupation decided on will also have a direct bearing on earnings. Most of the college-trained seek positions at the professional and managerial levels. These salaried fields are now the best paid, providing the highest median income, which in each field exceeds $10,000 (see Figure 23–2). More important still to the security of family life, they provide regularity of income.

THE COST OF MONEY

Whether or not a young couple of average or above average income will be economically secure at age 45 or still living beyond their income will depend in considerable part on their learning early in their married life, or before, the cost of money.

Money used for *investment debt* is cheap money. It is used in the purchase of tangible assets which have permanent value and which often increase in value with the passage of time. Investment capital is usually to be had at a simple rate of interest. Land, a house, a business are examples of investment debt.

Money borrowed on *consumer debt* is high-priced money. It is used for consumable items, which perish with the using and the value of which rapidly diminishes with the passage of time. Cars, refrigerators, washing machines, furniture, clothes, and boats are examples of consumer debt.

Investment debt is financed by *simple interest,* that is, interest on the unpaid balance. In other words, the amount of interest declines with each payment on the principal. Consumer debt is financed by *discount interest,* or *hard interest,* that is, interest charged on the whole amount for the whole period of the loan. The interest is charged in advance and does not decline as monthly payments are made, so it is actually almost twice the simple interest rate. Actual interest rates usually range from 12 to 35 percent on consumer debt.

Money is made by the use of borrowed money for investment debt in assets which will increase in value. The borrower pays, say, 8 percent simple interest, expecting with the passage of time that his investment will grow in value far beyond the purchase price and accumulated interest.

AGREEMENT ON WHO IS TO HANDLE FAMILY SPENDING

A seemingly simple but frequently contentious aspect of money management is the handling and spending of the family income. In every marriage an early decision must be made concerning who shall handle the money and how it shall be handled. With some couples, the question does not come out in the open. Circumstances seem to decide the answer before it ever becomes an issue. With others there is a good deal of experimentation, and sometimes quite a contest develops before a mutually satisfactory arrangement can be reached. There are at least five possible methods of handling money: (1) the husband may control all the spending; (2) the wife may control all expenditures; (3) the husband may control the income but give his wife an allowance for meeting household expenses, her own personal needs, and the needs of the children; (4) the husband and wife may have separate incomes and bank accounts, each one controlling his own funds, and each agreeing to meet certain of the family's financial obligations; (5) the husband and wife may maintain a joint bank account, each drawing upon it at will.

This question appears on the surface to be one of simple expediency. It is that, but it is much more, too. The decision reached influences how the family shall live and also has an effect upon attitudes and relationships of family members. Problems of domination, submission, insecurity, inferiority feelings, and many others are frequently created or exaggerated by the circumstances surrounding the spending of the family income.

The following case, reported by a family relations counselor, illustrates a characteristic difficulty as well as the importance of reaching a mutually satisfactory decision:

Jim and Gertrude married during their senior year in college. Jim was receiving veterans' schooling benefits and Gertrude had a part-time typing job. Their combined income allowed for few luxuries and only by careful planning were they able to finish their schooling without outside assistance.

At first, they handled the money together, both planning and worrying about making ends meet. After a few months, however, a budget was worked out and Gertrude took over the routine jobs of bill paying, grocery buying, etc. Since there was no "extra money," no question or argument ever arose as to how any of their income *should* be spent.

After graduation, Jim obtained an excellent position with a local insurance office. His income rose steadily and, by mutual agreement, they invested in a new car and began the accumulation of household furnishings. Gertrude maintained her position as the family money manager and as Jim's pay increased she regularly revamped their budget to allow for larger expenditures on furniture and appliances.

When Jim occasionally complained about his own lack of spending money or about the absence of extra cash for unplanned-for expenditures—magazines, books, records, or a show—Gertrude would reassure him that after next month, "when the TV set is paid off, we'll have plenty for extras."

Months passed but the day when there would be plenty for extras was always a month or two away. Jim finally exploded over a situation in which he, a man earning $9000 a year, should "have to borrow from somebody every time I want a pack of cigarettes or a cup of coffee!"

Gertrude, in turn, felt accused and unappreciated for her hours of budget planning. For several months the atmosphere remained bitter and the problem unsolved. Sometimes Jim handled all of the money himself, but bills went unpaid and insufficient funds were being put aside for groceries and living expenses. Then Gertrude took over and the old problems reappeared.

In their third year, they reached the point of considering divorce because of the constant bickering and frustration over money. A friend induced them to take their problems to a local family relations clinic. They did, and after several weeks of "talking things over" with a counselor they began to understand one another's values and wishes in money matters. After months of effort they finally reached a solution in which both could find satisfaction. Only by giving up a few of the furnishings that Gertrude had set her heart on was Jim able to carry sufficient money in his pocket to regain his sense of confidence and pride in himself as a successful money earner. Gertrude continued to handle most of the routine spending, but whenever the question of a new purchase of any significance arose, they talked over its desirability and the effect it would have upon their regular way of life.

This is but one of an endless number of possible situations which can grow out of money handling. Because of the importance money plays in the satisfaction of needs and wishes, it is desirable that every couple face personality needs, as well as economic considerations, in deciding who shall handle the money and how. There is no one best answer. The policy adopted by one couple

379
is bound to differ from that of others even in the same income group.

It may be said, however, that in general a mutually acceptable routine plan for money spending is more conducive to happiness than the policy of meeting each month's financial demands as if they were a new experience. Money matters can become the foremost issue in every family discussion. To allow this is to invite poor management as well as hard feelings. To prevent it, however, demands mutual concern, give and take, and a real desire to make money a tool of happy family life rather than the family's master.

Since financial patterns are a matter which must vary among families, no one system can be given to suit all needs. There are, however, certain basic considerations in financial planning which should help most couples in working out a program suited to their own needs.

FINANCIAL PLANNING

Every family, regardless of the amount of its income, has to face the problem of dividing up that income according to the use that will be made of it. This may be done according to plan or simply by deciding what one wants and spending the money without any systematic plan, but in either case it will be divided up in some way in an attempt to meet the needs of the family.

To develop a family budget requires, first, an estimate of income; second, an estimate of the various kinds of expenses which the family wishes to accept for a given period of time; and third, a plan for dividing this income among these various expenditures. Usually involved is a cash record of the expenditures, so that it is possible to know whether the plan of the family budget has been carried out.

The amount of income determines not only the amount there is to be spent but also the ratio of income that can be spent for different things. Generally speaking, the smaller the income, the greater the proportion spent for food, clothing, and the necessities of life; the larger the income, the smaller the proportion spent for necessities and the greater the proportion spent for comforts, luxuries, and savings.

By developing a family budget, it is usually possible to make money go further to obtain the things that are most important to the family. It also has the advantage of making all members of the family plan together for the use of money to be spent. Thus, neither partner is so likely to blame the other if the money runs short.

No family should become a slave to the family budget, even though they may plan out in advance each year or each month the amount they are going to spend for a given class of items. Such exact accounting has certain advantages, but it may, like any other exact scheme, become a source of irritation and conflict. Some people can probably do better without any written budget at all, but families should give some thought to the way they will spend their income in order to get the most satisfaction from it.

Frequently, the difficulties over a family budget come not in planning how to spend the money but rather in trying to keep an exact accounting of what each penny was spent for. At least keeping such an account will show where the seepages are. Many couples are amazed to discover how these small expenditures mount into many dollars.

The expenditures for every family are in most respects quite standard, at least for major items, which usually fall into the following categories: food, shelter (which may be broken down into rent or, if the person owns property, taxes, mortgage, and so on), clothing, transportation, operating expenses (under which come the costs of keeping up the home, heat, light, electricity, telephone), charity, and recreation (under which may come expenditures for personal items, vacations, candy), education (under which comes the purchase of books, papers, magazines), and savings (under which come life insurance, a fund for emergencies, other investments).

The amount that can be allotted to these various items depends, first, upon the amount of income the family has to divide, and second, upon the interests of the members of the family.

The American Institute of Family Relations has worked out a practical guide sheet to help couples in setting up a spending plan and in anticipating major items of expense:

STEPS IN SETTING UP A SPENDING PLAN

1   Decide for what you want to plan: the most important thing you want to accomplish; things of lesser importance but desirable.

2   Decide for how long you want to plan. (Six months, a year, etc.)

3   List the income from all sources that can be depended upon each month.

4   Next set down the various fixed expenses, placing the amount of each under the month when it must be paid.

5   Then calculate the amount which must be set aside each month to meet these fixed expenses which occur less often than monthly (insurance, taxes, etc.).

6   Set up some sort of reserve fund to take care of these expenses. This might be done by:

    a   Having a separate envelope for each of these items and placing a specified sum in each, each month.

    b   Adding together the monthly allowances for the various items to make up a reserve fund which must be set aside as a whole each month. This can go into a temporary savings fund or account, or into the checking account provided it is not used for purposes other than those decided upon.

7   Subtract the total of the fixed expenses for each month from the income for each month. This difference is what is available for the less predictable expenses or those that can be adjusted or varied.

8   Out of this, set aside first a small sum to take care of small unexpected demands or miscalculations. If it is not needed, it can be used for some special pleasure or item.

9   Make an estimate of the amount needed for each of the variable expenses. For this, one can go for information to:

   a His own past experience.
   b What he considers essential, or his own standards.
   c The experiences of others.
   d Studies of how others spend.
   e Scientific information.
   f Suggested divisions of the budget.
   g "Standard" budgets.

10 Make adjustments until the total of all these expenses for the month does not exceed the sum available for the variable expenses for that month. Where there are larger expenses which do not occur monthly (larger items of clothing, Christmas gifts, etc.), make some provisions for accumulating the necessary amount through additions to the reserve fund mentioned above, a separate fund, or the like.

11 Select some method for keeping a record of what is spent.

12 Decide who is to be responsible for keeping the record of expenditures, paying the bills, and being responsible for the business management of the household— or which person is to be responsible for which things.

13 Try out the plan for a month, keeping a record of expenditures. Make any adjustments that seem necessary; then try it out again. Continue this until a satisfactory plan is developed.

14 When the budget is running smoothly, simplify the work of account-keeping as much as possible.

15 Measure the success of the plan frequently in terms of what you hoped to accomplish with it.

16 Strive continually to maximize the satisfactions possible from the income available through:
   a Independence and originality in choice making.
   b Careful buying.
   c Intelligent using.

FIXED EXPENSES

Taxes (state, federal, local): personal, income, automobile, real estate, assessments

Insurance: life, accident, health, automobile, fire, theft

Licenses: car, business, pets

Fixed payments for medical or hospital care

Union or professional dues or fees

Rent, after a decision is made

Minimum charges for utilities; telephone

Tuition: fees, special lessons, books, equipment

Newspapers and magazines if on a yearly subscription basis

Installment payments and interest on debts

Obligations for the support of others

Pledges made to church or civic organizations

Savings: government bonds, savings accounts, investments

Reserve fund: fund set aside to take care of larger expenses occurring less often than monthly

VARIABLE EXPENSES

Food

meals at home, lunches, other meals away from home, entertaining

Clothing

outer garments; underwear; footwear; hats, accessories; materials; dressmaker, tailor; clothing repair; cleaning and pressing; laundry (if not under *Household Operation*)

Personal Care

barber and beauty parlor services, shaving supplies and equipment, cosmetics, toilet articles, dental supplies

Housing

rent, if not already determined; improvements, repairs, and depreciation on owned home

Furnishings and Equipment

furniture, rugs, carpets; draperies, curtains, shades; silver, china, glass; linen, bedding; kitchenware; cleaning and laundry equipment; lamps, fixtures, vases; clocks, etc.

Household Operation

utilities, fuel, refrigeration, laundry, household service, household supplies, small equipment, stamps, stationery (if not taken from *Personal Allowance*)

Transportation

car, train, bus fare; running expenses of automobile; car repairs and upkeep

Health

doctor, dentist, hospital, medical supplies, devices or equipment

Education

books, magazines, newspapers, lectures, technical journals, supplies, tuition and special lessons unless a fixed expense, miscellaneous school expenses

Recreation

travel, vacation, sports, hobbies, musical instruments, music, records, toys, club and organization dues, concerts, opera, theater, movies, dances, meals out, entertaining, races

Gifts

to members of the family

to others: wedding, shower, baby, birthday, Christmas, etc.; flowers

to community welfare: Community Chest, church, Red Cross, etc.

Personal Allowance or Spending Money

amount allocated each member of the family for pocket or spending money; in the case of children this might be gradually increased as an educative measure to provide for additional items—school supplies, lunches, clothing, etc.

The Total Cost of a Child, 1969

TABLE 23-1

	DISCOUNTED	UNDISCOUNTED[a]
Cost of giving birth	$ 1,534	$ 1,534
Cost of raising a child	17,576	32,830
Cost of a college education	1,244	5,560
Total direct cost	20,354	39,924
Opportunity costs of the average woman[b]	39,273	58,437
Total costs of a first child	$59,627	$98,361

Source: Ritchie H. Reed and Susan McIntosh, "Costs of Children" (prepared for the Commission, 1972).

[a]Discounted and undiscounted costs—spending $1,000 today costs more than spending $1,000 over a 10-year period because of the nine years of potential interest on the latter. This fact is allowed for in the discounted figures by assuming interest earned annually on money not spent in the first year. True costs are not accurately reflected in the undiscounted estimates, for these are simply accumulations of total outlays without regard to the year in which they must be made.

[b]Depending on the educational background of the mother, the opportunity costs (earnings foregone by not working) could be higher or lower.

ESTIMATING THE COST OF CHILDREN

Family planning has come with urban industrial civilization. Because children are a heavy drain on the family budget, their numbers are limited in most families and the couple tries to save up for the extra cost. In agricultural societies, by contrast, children are workers and are desired in part for the contribution they will make to the family income.

A government commission headed by John D. Rockefeller, 3rd, in its report *Population and the American Future* (1972) calculates the cost of giving birth to and rearing and educating a child (Table 23-1). It is apparent that each child inevitably takes a big share of the family earnings. The share becomes much greater if the potential earnings of the wife while she is out of the labor market are added.

The cost of rearing a child to maturity, regardless of price levels, may be calculated roughly as requiring three years of the father's income. One child will take three years of the father's earnings; three children, nine years, etc.

THREE MAJOR ECONOMIC ISSUES

Three major issues face the newlywed couple, each involving very important financial considerations and each fraught with serious consequences to the success of the marriage. They are (1) life insurance, (2) housing, and (3) installment buying. The way these matters are handled has a great deal to do with the couple's financial security and the long-run success of their joint effort to become a successful economic unit.

The young are relatively propertyless, yet they have major responsibilities once children become dependent upon them. This means that in case of the untimely death of the breadwinner, they will have no estate, unless it is provided for by life insurance. By the mere passing of a physical examination and paying of a premium on a policy, an estate of considerable value can be had immediately; the amount of the estate will depend on the amount of insurance purchased.

This is the only kind of estate that may be had for a small outlay of cash. It is, therefore, the only kind of estate that the young marriage can afford. Even so, unless wisdom is used, even this estate will be too small to provide for the emergency of death of the family earner. Where investment funds are limited, as they are in the average young marriage, the goal should be to buy the maximum protection for the least cash outlay.

Assuming that the couple will soon have three dependent children, the husband is earning $8000 per year, the couple has the average number of debts and the average standard of living for the beginner in the professions, adequate protection would seem to call for an insurance policy that would replace three or four years of his income if he should die. In other words, he should think of providing an insurance estate with a minimum value of $25,000-$35,000. This would help pay off pressing debts, in case of his death, and give the family security while the wife was getting back into the work world. If the husband is covered by Social Security and is paying in the maximum contribution, the insurance load can be cut in half, since income from this source will carry about half the family burdens of the family with a $8000-per-year income.

To be able to afford this much insurance requires that the young man spend his insurance dollar where it will buy the most protection. A glance at Figure 23-3 will show where the greatest protection lies or the least cost—term insurance.

The shorter the term for which he buys insurance, the less it will cost, since the risk of death goes up each year, and therefore the cost of coverage increases slightly with each year of age.

The insurance salesman calls upon a couple when the announcement of the birth of their baby appears in the local paper. At this time, couples uninformed about insurance will do well to make sure that they are dealing with a reliable and well-informed agent. Endowment policies should be bought only by those who are in a position to save money. In an endowment policy, a person is buying not only insurance but a savings plan which returns only 4–6 percent interest on money deposited beyond the cost of insurance—a return that is little if any more than he can get from government bonds.

There is no objection to the endowment or other type of savings policy for the prosperous, but the beginning family usually cannot afford the low interest return. If it is bought, it is usually at the expense of an adequate protective coverage for dependents. Some are talked into these policies, because insurance will cost them a much higher rate later on in life. But they will also be earning more and will have a shorter term to go until they collect by death. The average couple will have very little need for heavy insurance coverage after age 40–45 for their children will have passed the age of dependency. Besides, by

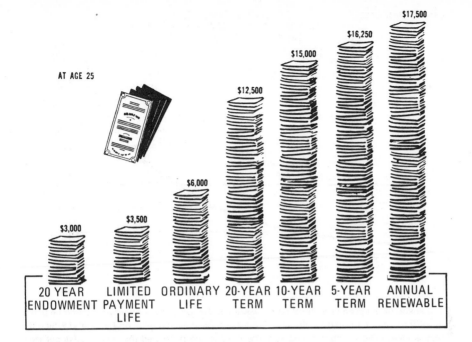

AT AGE 25

$17,500

$16,250

$15,000

$12,500

$6,000

$3,500

$3,000

| 20 YEAR ENDOWMENT | LIMITED PAYMENT LIFE | ORDINARY LIFE | 20-YEAR TERM | 10-YEAR TERM | 5-YEAR TERM | ANNUAL RENEWABLE |

Value of insurance policy bought for $100 yearly premium. Different types of insurance policies provide different kinds of protection. Insurance can have two principal values—protection against risk and savings. Renewable term policies give maximum protection against risk for those with little to spend from present income. The 20-year endowment policy gives least protection but maximum savings. Which is the more appropriate for the young married man with a child and low income? Why?

FIGURE 23-3

then the shrewd couple will have built an inheritance of other business or property assets to protect each other.

Some are enticed into buying high-cost endowment policies by the thought that they will get all their money back in 20 years, or whatever the period of maturity may be. Only the survivor will get the insurance money back, and then only if the insured person dies before his time. At around age 25 it costs about $6 per year. This rate is based on actuarial tables which show the likelihood of death in a given million, or other large number of people in this age group. These premiums go to pay death claims. Some will die in their twenty-fifth year, in a large group some even the day after the policy is written, others the twenty-sixth year, but some will still be living at 100 years of age. The company charged enough to pay off each person's inheritors at his death, regardless of his age, and retain a profit. On endowment policies, one does not get his insurance back. He gets the extra money back which he invested, plus accumulated compounded interest.

Assuming that a young couple can afford, say, $150 per year for life insurance, the choice is clear. For this $150 they can buy around $25,000 renewable term insurance, or at the other extreme, they can buy a 20-year endowment policy worth around $3000. If they choose the latter, the widow may

FINANCE MANAGEMENT

NET LEVEL PREMIUM FOR
STRAIGHT LIFE POLICY ISSUED AT AGE 25
VERSUS NET STEP-RATE PREMIUM

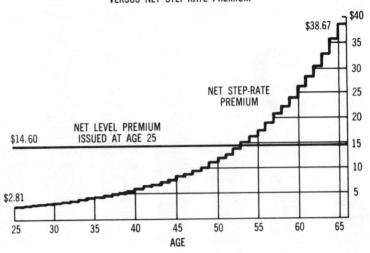

FIGURE 23–4   Comparison of net premiums for $1000 insurance. The cost of a *straight life* insurance policy is level throughout a person's lifetime. The amount he pays depends on the age at which the policy is taken. The younger the person, the less the death risk and the less he pays per year. Of course he pays a larger sum years before death. In this kind of policy he pays far more in the younger years than it costs to cover the risk of his death; he pays in excess of cost until he is into his 50s, as shown above. *Term policies* increase each year in cost, but in the younger ages rates are very low because death risk is low. A five-year term policy, for example, taken at age 25 costs what it costs to cover the death risk between the years 25–30 only. This is why term insurance offers maximum coverage at very low cost for the young family, providing the wife and children an immediate estate in case of the death of the husband. Source: Jerome B. Cohen, *Decade of Decision* (New York: Institute of Life Insurance, 1958), p. 11.

FIGURE 23–5   The 20-year endowment policy. The *endowment policy* insurance offers a maximum amount of protection for the money and the maximum amount of savings. A 20-year endowment policy for $1000 pays $1000 at the end of 20 years because the buyer has paid in a small amount for insurance and a large amount for savings which draw interest at a low rate. If cashed at the end of 20 years, insurance ceases. This kind of policy is not recommended for the young family because premiums are so high that it is impossible to create an adequate estate for those dependent on the father's income. Source: Jerome B. Cohen, *Decade of Decision* (New York: Institute of Life Insurance, 1958), p. 16.

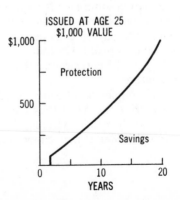

not have enough left to pay medical and funeral expenses, to say nothing of providing for herself and the children during the transition back to a normal life.

For a brief graphic comparison of the more common types of policies, see Figures 23–3 to 23–6. The ideal type of insurance for the young couple who can afford a little more than the average beginner is the type depicted in Figure 23–6. Here one is getting a small amount of permanent insurance. Onto this is attached a reducing-term rider, which greatly increases his protection at very low cost for the term in life when his load of dependents is greatest.

Much insurance is carried through group plans rather than on a personal basis. The military, federal, state, and local governments, public institutions, business corporations, and many other employers have group plans under which employees are covered, usually at advantageous rates. Often the employer assumes part or all the cost. In the teaching field, the Carnegie Foundation has established the Teachers Insurance and Annuity Association, which is nonprofit. A legal-reserve life insurance company, incorporated in New York State and operating without agents, this company, in addition to funding the retirement plans of colleges and universities, also issues specially designed life insurance policies for college staff members. The teachers pay standard rates, but at the close of each year, when the profits are known, refunds are made. Most industries have group plans at very favorable rates.

The need of the young couple for life insurance is depicted statistically in Figure 23–7, which shows the chance of a child's being orphaned now compared with his chance at the beginning of the century. The chances are much less now than then, but still there is sufficient likelihood of the father's dying before the child has reached 18 to justify carrying a reasonable amount of protective coverage.

In case of divorce before the family is reared, there is still need for life insurance protection. In fact, disposition of insurance increasingly enters into divorce suits.

Family income policy protection values. This policy combines *straight life* insurance—giving a small amount of permanent insurance—with a *reducing term* of almost two-and-a-half times the value of the straight life insurance. The reducing term is very cheap since it declines in value with increased age and cuts off entirely before death risk becomes great. This policy costs slightly more than term insurance. For those who have bought costly insurance policies before marriage, adding the declining term rider to the existing policy offers a good solution to the problem of providing a maximum estate while children are most dependent. Source: Jerome B. Cohen, *Decade of Decision* (New York: Institute of Life Insurance, 1958), p. 20.

FIGURE 23–6

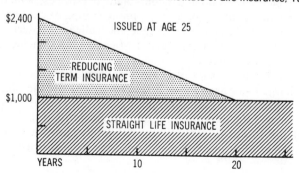

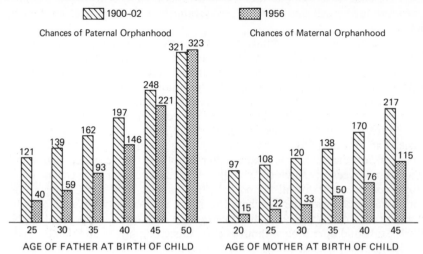

Mortality Experience of White Population, United States, 1900–02 and 1956

▨ 1900–02   ▦ 1956

Chances of Paternal Orphanhood   Chances of Maternal Orphanhood

AGE OF FATHER AT BIRTH OF CHILD   AGE OF MOTHER AT BIRTH OF CHILD

FIGURE 23–7   Chances in 1000 that a newborn child will be orphaned before age 18. Although the chances of death of a parent have greatly decreased, there is still sufficient risk to justify purchase of insurance on a basis which will assure maximum protection for the young couple without property, rather than provide for savings in old age. Study Figure 23–3 and see that $100 a year can buy $17,500 worth of protection or $3000 worth of protection plus the investment feature. Source: Metropolitan Life Insurance Company, "Family Responsibilities Increasing," *Statistical Bulletin,* 40.3–5, April, 1959.

Shopping for Life Insurance

Important as life insurance is in creating an estate for dependents, and although it has been one of the sacred cows of the American economic system, it has recently come under the critical eye. Consumer advocates in February 1973, charged before a Senate subcommittee that many life insurance companies were selling to a gullible public policies that were confusing, overpriced and deceptive (NYT). The star witness was Herbert S. Denenberg, insurance commissioner of Pennsylvania, who has published a booklet comparing the cost of policies of the 50 largest companies operating in the state. He labels the life insurance industry one of the "leading consumer frauds." It confuses the public with policies they do not understand, overprices, and operates with many incompetent agents, and, he says, many companies are unsound. Ralph Nader, consumer advocate par excellence, has called for federal legislation on life insurance. Senator Philip A. Hart of Michigan has concluded that life insurance is of antitrust concern.

Denenberg's comparisons of companies showed that some of the largest companies charge twice as much as others for essentially the same policies. Of the 50 largest operating in Pennsylvania, Banker Life (Iowa), Home Life (New York), National Life (Vermont), Connecticut Mutual Life, and Phoenix Mutual had the lowest-priced policies. None of them were among the ten largest companies. The five companies with the highest-priced policies in the

Home Ownership

In acquiring home-ownership debt, the couple is in the area of simple interest money and investment use of credit. Not only are houses looked upon as investment debt in credit circles, they are considered the safest of all debts. For this reason, home finance is the cheapest in the marketplace of money. In fact, the bulk of insurance company loans, much labor union retirement fund money, and much bank capital is invested in real estate. And throughout the nation are numerous savings and loan associations which use most of their capital in home finance. Those with federal charters guarantee the money deposited by investors on the same basis as deposits are insured in banks with federal charters.

Home ownership should be an aspiration of most young couples, and separate living quarters, even though a rented house or apartment, are almost necessary today, when a rather complete economic break from the parental family is expected at marriage. Whether one can buy a home depends very much on the kind of credit arrangements that can be made, the down payment, and the interest rates. Houses are almost always bought on credit. This kind of debt is creative, in that a house, with a little work by the couple in improving it, usually increases in value.

The general standard is that one can buy a house valued at twice his annual income and not be overreaching himself. In other words, the $7000-a-year man can safely buy a $14,000 house. He may go higher if he gets low interest and a low down payment.

The importance of housing to the success of marriage and family life has never been adequately studied, but certainly living arrangements have much to do with the personal relations of husband and wife, and of parents and children. Living with in-laws results in congested living arrangements and lack of privacy, as well as in a tendency of relatives to interfere with the couple's adjustment to each other. In Great Britain during World War II, when family members were forced to live in one room because of the heating problem, many families found it necessary to impose the rule of silence on the family. Only by this means could they tolerate the close and congested living that was forced upon them.

One only has to investigate the matter casually in Europe to know the terrible strain and frustration of inadequate housing. In France, Holland, and Germany, for example, into the 1950s, people who had more than an average of one and a half rooms per family member were required to take in an addi-

---

*Three states, Connecticut, Massachusetts, and New York, sell savings bank life insurance policies to their own residents. This is the cheapest way to buy up to the limit permitted by these respective states. Teachers Insurance and Annuity Association sells insurance to teachers without profit. The Presbyterian Ministers' Fund offers nonprofit insurance for protestant ministers and their families.

tional family. Many young people could not marry because they were unable to find housing. Some married and had to live apart a good deal of the time. Even in Sweden and Denmark, where such rules of combining households were not in force, many of the same problems of housing shortage existed, hindering marriage and increasing unmarried motherhood and other problems.

Low-cost government-insured bank loans have been a major factor in the development of private family housing in the United States since World War II. It has made possible extensive home ownership even during a period of high building costs. Over half of American nonfarm families now own their own homes. Home ownership is certainly a factor in family stability, both from a psychological and a mobility standpoint.

Undoubtedly some young couples have overextended themselves economically in order to acquire a new home, or too high-priced a home, but there are others who would have been much further ahead had they bought rather than paid high rental rates. When can one afford to buy a house?

It is not necessary to be rich to buy a house, but usually a down payment of about 5–20 percent of the price of the house is required. (More liberal terms have been granted to veterans.) A rough standard by which one may judge what amount he should pay for his home in relation to his earnings is the following:

IF INCOME IS	FAMILY CAN AFFORD A HOME COSTING
$ 5,000	$10,000–12,500
10,000	20,000–25,000
20,000	40,000–50,000

The Chicago Metropolitan Home Builders' Association has set up the following even more specific table to help persons determine how much of the family's monthly income may be invested safely in a home. It does not contradict the preceding—in fact, it agrees quite closely with that standard—but does spell it out in greater detail. Here are monthly payments on a home that families of different monthly incomes can handle ranging from the safe side to the risky side:

MONTHLY INCOME AFTER TAXES	SAFELY	PROBABLY	RISKY
$200	$ 58	$ 66	$ 75
250	64	72	83
300	68	78	91
350	74	84	100
400	78	90	109
450	82	96	118
500	86	102	127
550	89	108	135
600	92	112	142
650	96	118	149
700	99	124	156
750	101	130	161
800	103	136	168

The amount a couple can pay for a home and the monthly payment load they can carry will vary with the number of children, the number of high-interest installment contracts they carry, their habits of thrift, their ability to handle maintenance and make improvements themselves, and many other factors in their living habits and spending practices. But one of the basic factors is the kind of financing they are able to get at the outset in buying a house.

Few pay cash for a house, rather houses are usually bought on contract with a small down payment and monthly payments. The monthly payments include principal and interest. If the buyer pays 10 percent down on a new development house, the balance will be paid in equal monthly payments over a period of 25–30 years. Let us say this house is bought for $15,500. The buyer, then, has paid down $1550 (10 percent). He will owe $14,000 on the mortgage. It will require a monthly payment of $98.95 for 300 months (25 years) to pay off the balance with interest on the declining balance at the rate of 7 percent. On a house of this value, insurance will run around $20 per year and taxes around $220. (Rates will vary from community to community. Small towns usually have lower taxes than this; larger cities have much higher taxes.) Most couples prefer to pay the taxes and insurance monthly. If they are paid in this way rather than in a lump sum annually, the $240 required for taxes and insurance will raise monthly payments by $20. This brings the total monthly payment to $118.95.

Upkeep   Home ownership involves upkeep. How much will be required depends on the condition of the house. Here we are dealing with a new house (an old one would require more upkeep). But even with a new house, plumbing can become clogged, and in time paint and other maintenance will be necessary. At the beginning, landscaping and fencing may be required, or window screens, screen doors, or gutters may be needed. Also, one must allow some money for unexpected upkeep. Let us say the total allowance for upkeep will be $10 per month. The actual cost of ownership then becomes $128.95 per month. Couples who are handy with tools and paint brush can keep maintenance costs low; others can expect them to be much higher.

Interest Costs   In considering home purchase, the interest rate on the contract is very important. Suppose the young couple in shopping for a house are offered the same house with an 8 percent interest rate instead of 7 percent. Then the contract payments for the 300 months would be $108.06 or $9.11 more per month before insurance, taxes, and upkeep. Over the life of the contract this interest rate makes the house cost $2,277.50 more.

House finance is the cheapest money the family can borrow, but even so, a one-half percent difference in interest rate can affect the family budget. Interest rates on home financing rise to 8.5 to 9 percent periodically. At such periods the young buyers with modest income cannot buy, for such interest rates make the monthly payment beyond the scope of the family budget. It is better to wait until interest rates drop.

The Down Payment   If the buyer has an extra $1000 beyond the required down payment, should he add it to the down payment? Old ideas of American thrift would lead one to advise "yes." In the present pattern of American life, the answer is "no." Keep the extra $1000 for other investment or use.

The typical young couple, in three to six years, will be moving to a larger house in a new city or new neighborhood of the same city. They will want to get their equity back for the down payment on a higher priced home. Even with the small down payment and the equity gained from monthly payments, the new buyer must have quite a sizable down payment to repay the seller's investment. This will be particularly true if the sellers have improved the house and landscaping and raised the price $1000 or so to gain a little profit from their investment and effort. The chances are that if the extra $1000 down payment had been made, the buyer would be priced out of the market, if the sellers expected to get it back in cash. To sell, they would likely have to take a second mortgage and take years to get the extra cash back in small monthly payments.

The Buying Situation   There are some localities and some towns and cities where real estate is depressed. If one is certain he is going to live there the rest of his life and in the same house, bargains are plentiful. But for a young couple on the way up, this is not a buying situation. There may be no market when they move on to the new job or the bigger house.

In buying, consultation with someone who knows conditions in the new locality—a banker, builder, or realtor—can reduce risk. It is also important to consider community services and institutions. Distances to a shopping center, schools, and churches are important. On selling, convenience of location with reference to such institutions will be a factor in demand and sale price.

Profit Possibilities   The young couple on the way up should buy only in a community where they can expect to make a profit when the advancement in position requires that they sell. With "do-it-yourself" skills, this is a realistic goal in the average growing community. A great deal will depend, however, on the energy the pair puts into improving the house and landscaping. Improvements usually add more value than they cost, particularly if the couple do the work, and the improvements will add to family comfort. As the family increases in size, the couple will likely want to add a room or two to meet space requirements.

LIQUID INVESTMENTS

In modern urban society, much wealth is in liquid investments, that is, investments for which there is a ready market in case funds are needed. Such investments are more risky and take more sophistication in management. Stocks and bonds are in this class. They vary greatly in safety, liquidity, and chance for steady income, and/or appreciation in value. Young couples should not get speculation fever until they have built a secure foundation. After that, a good rule of thumb is that speculative investments should be limited to 10 percent of one's savings.

Here we enter the world of hard-interest money, or discount interest. Rates usually range upward from 10 percent, with the average in the 15–20 percent range. Credit can run as high as 35 percent. Can one get ahead paying a fifth of his income for the use of money? This is a question to which few young families give serious thought.

The American family is time-contract-minded. The merits of this philosophy of economics is widely debated, and, of course, even from the standpoint of the individual family, there are two sides to the question. There is no doubt that a young couple can get off to a quicker start by buying on contract to the full extent of their credit. But they burden themselves with an interest load which reduces their capacity to buy for one or two years ahead, particularly if they load themselves with contracts with excessive interest rates. Yet in periods of inflation part of the excess interest is offset by price rises in goods over a two-year period.

Interest-charge abuses have been so great that consumer credit is now regulated by the "Truth in Lending Law," passed by Congress to protect the consumer from excessive hidden interest charges. All time contracts must show the true rate of interest in terms of simple interest. In financing cars, for example, the claim of 6 percent interest can no longer be made. Cars are sold at discount or at hard-interest rates. The 6 percent is closer to 12 percent on a simple-interest basis, and this must be shown in the contract. The actual simple-interest charge on credit-card accounts and store-credit balances must also be shown.

On consumer goods interest rates have to be high to cover the cost of collection, bookkeeping, loss on goods not paid for, repossession of goods, and their resale.

Many couples justify purchases with high carrying charges in terms of immediate comfort, convenience, or necessity. There are no doubt instances where such added costs are justified, but to make installment buying a habit in family living is to sell oneself short in making the most of income. In cases where quick credit is needed, those who, after a period of thrift and saving, have established sound credit, can usually borrow on a straight bank loan at 7–10 percent simple interest on the unpaid balance.

FACTORS IN A PERSONAL CREDIT RATING

Banks and other agencies which lend money rate those who apply for credit. Here is a standard form used by many banks that is quite like the I.Q. test used in school placement.

The bank wishes to know the following:
  Income?   _____
  How long on present job?   _____
  Credit experience?   _____
  Equity in real estate?   _____
  Down payment you can make on purchase?   _____
    Total Score   _____

From information below fill out your credit rating.

	Points
Income per week:	
Under $75	0
$76–100	150
Over $100	200
Wife earning	50
Length of time on job:	
Less than a year	0
One to four years	100
Four to ten years	150
Over ten years	250
Credit experience:	
None	0
Favorable for six months (one source)	250
Favorable for six months (from another source)	100
Good record from previous loans from bank	100
Unfavorable credit references	−100
Equity in property:	
Little or unknown but do own	100
Equity twice minimum, or five years' ownership	200
Property owned clear	300
Down payment you can make:	
0–10 percent	0
10 percent to one-third	100
Over a third	200

(A score of 600 will usually be sufficient for small loans.)

Source: "A Guide to Consumer Credit," Public Affairs Pamphlet No. 348, New York.

THERE WILL NEVER BE ENOUGH MONEY

As was stated at the outset, one of the most certain facts that any young couple must face in planning for their economic future is that they will never have enough money to meet all their needs. A nationwide survey of attitudes on this point by the office of Public Opinion Research of Princeton showed that most Americans are not satisfied with the amount of money they make. The less than a third who felt that they were more or less satisfied with their incomes were not necessarily the most prosperous; in fact, they were more likely to be farmers and businessmen who were self-employed and felt that they controlled their own economic future.

The most dissatisfied group of all was the professional group, where income is generally fairly adequate but where aspirations for an improved level of living are apparently extremely high. Another finding of opinion polls is that people who define happiness in terms of making money actually are not as likely to achieve happiness as those who consider love, family, and wisdom the essentials in life.

Probably the greatest worry of the American family is in making ends meet. This struggle between the amount of money the family makes and the number of things they want suggests that perhaps the majority of American families never really learn to live within their incomes.

The family with a $5000 income is sure its members would have everything they wanted with $10,000; but the family with the $10,000 income is just as certain, and perhaps even more so, that it could meet all its needs with $15,000. Yet Spectorsky's (1955) study of "exurbanites"—the high-pressure New York advertisers and promoters who live in the lavish mansions with acreages out beyond the suburbs—shows that not only are they living high on the hog, but they are also so deeply in debt that the $40,000 man must look forward to moving up another $10,000–20,000 a year to ever get out, and the man already up there is as bad or worse off.

Credit counseling clinics are now common in many communities to keep couples from falling into the hands of loan sharks and bankruptcy courts. Help in locating such clinics may be had by writing: National Foundation of Consumer Credit, 1819 H Street, Washington, D.C. 20006.

PROBLEMS

1 Discuss this statement with reference to marriage happiness, "Dollars alone are not enough. You've got to have dollars and sense."

2 Lawrence earns a comfortable income, but he and Jane are only recently married, and there are a hundred ways in which each extra dollar could be spent. When Lawrence handles the money, he and Jane have a lot of fun, but at the end of the month there are always bills he forgot to pay. When Jane handles the money, the bills get paid and they are able to buy some of the extra things they want—furniture, records, etc.—but Lawrence feels that they have no fun and resents the fact that he is given an allowance like a child. What alternative method of money management might you suggest that would satisfy the economic-psychological needs of both Lawrence and Jane?

3 Poll the class on the questions, "What income are you likely to receive in the occupation you plan to enter? Do you believe that it will be more or less than ample for your needs and wishes?" Tabulate and discuss the class expectations with regard to future income. Do the expectations of the group seem to be realistic?

4 A marriage counselor advised a childless couple after their fifth year of marriage, "If you wait until you can afford to have children, you'll never have them." How accurate do you consider his observation? What merit is there in estimating the cost of children?

5 (a) Nat and Alice are 28 and 26 respectively. They have two children, age two months and two years, and plan to have one more after a few years. Nat has a relatively secure position, and Alice has a temporary half-time job. Their combined incomes total $6700 a year before taxes. What type of insurance and what amount would you advise them to buy?

(b) With a saving of only $1000 would you advise Nat and Alice to consider buying a house? If so, what price range should they consider? Under their circumstances, what are the advantages, or disadvantages, of apartment living?

6   What is the appeal of installment buying? Under what circumstances is it justified? Some couples argue that it helps in budgeting if almost everything is bought on the installment plan. In what way is this true? What argument is there against it?

7   One occasionally hears of people with fabulous incomes who are sued for indebtedness. How can this situation be explained in the case of honest, well-meaning people?

8   *Sociodrama:* A young man and wife who have not yet begun their family disagree on how the income should be handled. The play opens as the husband suggests, "Let's pay all the bills at the beginning of each month; put the rest in a big purse, and trust one another to draw from it wisely. We'll save whatever is left over each month."

PART **VI**

PARENTHOOD

FAMILY PLANNING

24   During the long history of man's struggle for survival, having children near the limit of productive capacity was a necessity. Custom and taboo have always regulated productivity to some extent, but a high mortality rate has been the most effective instrument of population control. In parts of the world mortality rates still remain high, but modern medical and nutritional practice have brought precipitous declines in mortality rates. The average length of life has almost doubled and the world population has been increasing at an alarming rate.

Concern over the population explosion, combined with the Women's Liberation movement, the desire of all for a higher level of living, and effective birth control measures, has recently brought the national birth rate down to the approximate level of "zero" population growth. The poor now share the luxury of contraception through Maternal and Child Health federal grant funds to the states for family planning under the Social Security Act.

Having more than two children will become of increasing social concern in Western society, and hopefully throughout the world. Having large numbers may some day be prohibited, or at least heavily penalized by various social sanctions. Nations facing recurrent famine may see moratoriums on births for limited periods, or mass immunization against pregnancy may be introduced through water or food supplies.

College youth even more than others will make childbearing a matter of serious decision rather than biological accident. Fertility can be controlled with a great deal of certainty, and without denial of sexual pleasure. This has never before been so for any group in the population. Planning whether to have children, how many to have, and when to have them are matters of personal decision.

As having children becomes more of a privilege and less an inherent right, children will be a greater source of joy, and many of the burdens of having children will be removed. Resources will be more adequate, children will be more healthy, and parents will have more time to devote to the socialization of each of them.

HOW LIFE BEGINS

Each girl is born with a lifetime supply of many thousands of immature eggs in her ovaries. During her fertile lifetime only some 400–500 eggs will ripen, at the rate of one per 28 days. About the twelfth day after the beginning of menstruation, an egg cell is released from an ovary and floats into the opening of the fallopian tube. Its capacity to survive in the tube is limited, perhaps to a maximum of eight hours. To be fertilized, the thick wall of the cell must be penetrated by a sperm cell. If it is met in the tube by sperm, which have been discharged into the vagina and have swum up through the uterus and into the fallopian tube, the fertilized egg then begins to divide and to move down into the uterus (or womb). Here it attaches itself to the wall, which is fully lined with bloodfilled tissues to cushion the egg and nourish it.

During most of the ovulations that take place in the woman's fertile life cycle, no sperm will be there to meet the egg, or even if they are there, they may not succeed in penetrating its wall. As a consequence, rather than the womb performing its function of nursing the egg, the microscopic-sized unfertilized egg floats on through and is discharged. Since the blood-filled uterine wall is unused, some 14–16 days later it breaks down and passes out in the menstrual flow. After the cessation of the flow, the rebuilding of the womb lining begins again preparatory to another ovulation.

There is a slight rise in temperature near the time of ovulation. The temperature change is due to hormone changes and often does not conform exactly to the period of ovulation. Some women feel the egg burst through the wall of the ovary, with a sharp cutting pain (called *mittelschmerz*), but most are not aware of the time of ovulation.

In sexual intercourse, approximately a tablespoon of semen, containing some 500 million sperm, is deposited in the upper part of the vaginal tract, near the *cervix*, or neck of the *womb* or *uterus*. The cervix is a strong muscle with an opening that is normally very small, but it can stretch to permit the passage of the baby at birth. Vaginal fluids are hostile to sperm, but if pregnancy is to result, some sperm must swim rather quickly through this tiny opening (or be sucked through with the orgasmic contractions of the uterus) and travel the long distance up through the womb to meet the female ovum in the fallopian tube. The five-inch journey of the sperm has been likened to a man's five-mile swim upstream. If the egg meets the sperm, and one finally breaks through its tough wall, the egg is fertilized. The fertilized egg becomes the *zygote*, and as cell division proceeds, the *embryo*, which after birth becomes the child.

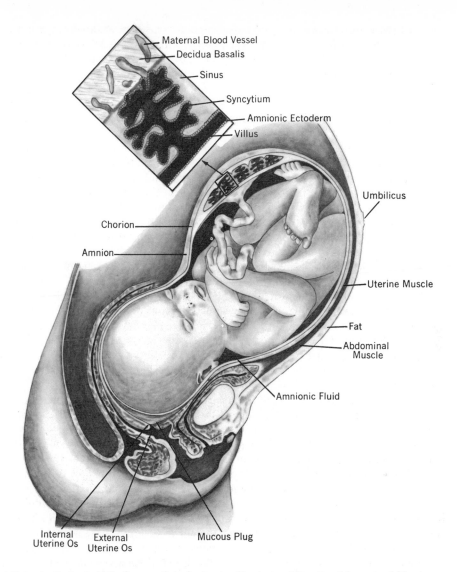

Maternal Blood Vessel
Decidua Basalis
Sinus
Syncytium
Amnionic Ectoderm
Villus
Umbilicus
Chorion
Amnion
Uterine Muscle
Fat
Abdominal Muscle
Amnionic Fluid
Internal Uterine Os
External Uterine Os
Mucous Plug

Fetus just prior to birth. Source: C. L. Anderson, *Physical and Emotional Aspects of Marriage* (St. Louis: C. V. Mosby Co., 1953). Reproduced by permission of the publisher and Dr. Anderson. The magnified section shows the sinuses in which the mother's blood circulates. Only the thick lining of the sinuses separates the maternal bloodstream from that of the fetus.   **FIGURE 24–1**

The point at which the zygote becomes attached to the uterine wall develops into the umbilical cord which provides the nutritional contact between mother and child. Here the bloodstreams of mother and child flow side by side, permitting nutrition to pass through the thin wall by osmosis from the mother's bloodstream to the embryo's, and permitting the embryo's wastes to pass into the mother's bloodstream.

In the womb the embryo grows for nine months (known as the *gestation period*), after which contractions in the uterus warn the mother that the birth of the child is imminent (see Figure 24-1). (For an excellent film showing all these processes, see *Human Reproduction*.)

HEREDITY IN FAMILY PLANNING

At present, genetic capacity for producing normal offspring remains socially untested. Even those of known polluted genetic material may reproduce without the restraint of law or custom. Having children is considered one of those inherent rights of the couple. As more critical attitudes develop toward population numbers, so also will they develop toward the right to produce defective offspring. Plant and animal eugenic control are far advanced. We know much more about human genetics than is practiced, because many are afraid of the consequences of misuse of human eugenics.

To practice human eugenics, a national registration of all families would be necessary, with known transmissible defects, both dominant and recessive. With the rapid strides being made in the study of genetic material, less prohibition would be necessary for some defects, because of ability to determine defects in the uterus and make corrections there. For many transmissible defects, prohibition of reproduction is humane and just. Where the defect is in the male, fertilization by donor semen is a possibility; when in the female, ovary transplant is on the horizon. Then there is always the alternative of adoption.

Many young people enter marriage with groundless fears about their heredity. Others who enter marriage with hereditary defects should be concerned about them, but are not. The field of heredity is a highly technical one and only a competent eugenist can give adequate advice on specific problems. Suffice it here to give some general information.

The marriage of close relatives has been condemned in most primitive and modern societies. Yet the question comes up frequently as to whether cousins can marry. In the Arab culture cousin marriage is still extensive. The difficulty of cousin marriages arises out of the fact that all human strains carry certain undesirable and usually hidden traits in the germ plasma. These pathological genes are recessive. When two recessive genes combine they can produce an individual with the undesirable trait. The likelihood of relatives combining the recessive genes is many times greater than of nonrelatives doing so. Cousins, therefore, have a greater chance of producing offspring with genetic abnormalities than people with completely different bloodlines.

A study of 106 first-cousin marriages showed that while there was little ill effect prior to birth, insofar as spontaneous abortions and stillbirths were concerned, damage began to appear after birth and increased with age. The mortality rate was three times that of marriages outside the bloodline, and abnormalities were twice as numerous—major abnormalities, even more than twice as numerous.

Fortunately for mankind, most defective traits are recessive, and affect offspring only when both husband and wife carry the defective gene. In such cases, the chances are one in four of the offsprings' inheriting it. Cystic fibrosis is a fatal genetic trait, which causes offspring to die after a few weeks, months, or years. It is a chronic disease of the pancreas beginning in infancy and manifesting itself in inability to digest food and difficulty in breathing. About one in every 20 adults carries the defective gene, and about one in 800 white children inherit it. It is rarely found among Negroids and Mongoloids.

The predisposition to diabetes, epilepsy, certain forms of heart disease, high blood pressure, and some forms of mental illness may be inherited. By this is meant that they appear more readily under certain conditions of environmental stress in people with these diseases in their hereditary background than among others, even though the diseases themselves may not be transmissible in the genes.

On diabetes, Amram Scheinfeld (1972) presents these facts: (1) one in four diabetics has a diabetic relative; (2) if one identical twin has diabetes, the other will also, in almost every case; (3) diabetes is inherited in some strains of mice. In addition to the known million diabetics in the United States, the Health Information Foundation says there are a million unknown diabetics.

There are only one in 20 chances that a parent who is an epileptic will have an epileptic child, and in only about one case in 70 will seizures become chronic. The type of epilepsy which develops after age 30 has no hereditary basis at all.

Huntington's chorea (deteriorating brain disease with onset of middle age) is definitely hereditary and dominant. Hemophilia and color blindness are sex-linked hereditary defects (carried by the mother but appearing in the male line). There are numerous other less common diseases which are known to be of genetic origin or predisposition. The unanswered question of all expectant parents is, "Will our child be normal?" One of the heaviest burdens parents have to bear is having a defective child. There is about one chance in 33 that a child will be born with some defect. The time seriously to consider this question is before marriage. Certainly not all defects can be anticipated. Even those of sound heredity may have a defective child—for reasons that will become evident later in this chapter. But most young people do not even think of counsel in this area until they have had one or more defective children. Then they are inclined to react with a sense of guilt: "What have I done to deserve this?"

Unlike Denmark, where all defective families are registered, in the United States it is up to prospective parents themselves individually and together to analyze their backgrounds for similar recessive defective traits. Because of the very common use of drugs for medical reasons and as a means of escape, x-ray effects of radiation, and many other factors, genetic counseling is advisable for many couples. Some have anxieties based on common myths, or about consequences of racial mixture and want to allay their fears in this area.

Genetic counseling for those who have had a defective child helps them decide whether the risk of a repetition of the defect in other children they may wish to have is too great. J. A. Fraser Roberts, of London's Guy Hospital, has worked out the ratio in which hereditary defects will reappear. If the risk is as high as one in ten, it is a high risk. Muscular dystrophy, hemophilia, and some forms of mental retardation are in the high-risk group, as is cystic fibrosis, with a risk of one in four. In the low-risk group, Roberts places diseases with a less than one in 25 chance of reoccurring. Where the risk is statistically too great, the couple may choose sterilization. If they wish to have a family, they can adopt.

Some couples will choose sterilization before marriage. Knowing that they each carry recessive traits that may come out in their offspring, or that one carries a dominant defect, they have to choose between further pollution of the genetic pool, refraining from marriage, or seeking sterilization. Most states have sterilization laws, which were designed to eliminate certain defective strains, but they have not been widely used. Probable reasons are: (1) the uncertainty about what is hereditary and what is not, particularly in the area of mental deficiency and mental disease; (2) uncertainty about hereditary factors involved in many physical diseases and defects which tend to run in families; (3) uncertainty about hereditary factors in such areas as criminality and moral deficiency; (4) resistance of certain religious groups to interfering with man's capability of reproduction; (5) some political resistance to the state's deciding who may and who may not reproduce.*

New techniques now make possible the correction of certain hereditary defects very early in the intrauterine period. As more is being learned about the chemistry of the cell, eugenicists look forward to the time when they can control human heredity by selecting gene combinations. Some predict that this will be the most significant development of the next century.

For those needing genetic counseling, The Society for the Study of Social Biology (230 Park Ave., New York, N.Y. 10017) can provide a list of Human Heredity Clinics in the United States and Canada.

STERILITY

Some 10–15 percent of marriages throughout the world are sterile; at least, this proportion never bears children throughout their married life. This was the conclusion of The First World Congress on Human Infertility, held in New York in May 1953, with 1300 physicians from 53 nations in attendance. United States Census data show that childlessness ranges from 9 percent of rural marriages in the United States to over 17 percent in urban marriages. It is assumed that most of the sterility is involuntary, although a few marriages, of course, are voluntarily childless.

Of the Kinsey Institute for Sex Research sample of women, 20 percent of marriages proved infertile. Women who married youngest proved to be the most fertile, in that they became pregnant most often and in a higher percentage of cases. Of those who married before the age of 21, pregnancy occurred among 90 percent and they averaged 3.5 pregnancies. Pregnancy occurred among 86 percent of those who married between 21 and 25, and they averaged 2.8 pregnancies. Of those who delayed the marriage until after age 30, the institute reports that not more than half became pregnant, although

*The Association for Voluntary Sterilization (14 West 40th St., New York, N.Y. 10018), formerly called Human Betterment Association for Voluntary Sterilization, once published statistics annually on eugenics sterilizations performed in the various states (their report of December 31, 1963, showed that 63,678 such operations had been performed, mostly for the mentally ill and mentally deficient). Now their emphasis is on voluntary sterilization as a means of controlling population.

the sample of this age group was rather small. They cite confirming evidence that after age 30 very few women in any of the samples become pregnant, even those who had previously demonstrated their fertility. From age 46 on there is only one chance in 500 of a woman's becoming pregnant.

Throughout history sterility has been considered a tragedy, and has universally been looked upon as a defect in the wife. This is no longer so. Absolute sterility is thought to characterize only a small percentage of the childless marriages, and where it exists it is now recognized that the husband is as responsible as the wife. In fact, Dr. Edward Tyler estimates that more sterility is caused by lack of male sperm count than any other single factor. He blames this for 40 percent of all cases of infertile marriages.

In general, the treatment of infertile husbands is less successful than the treatment of sterile wives. Hormone and drug treatments have for the most part proved disappointing. A recent development is the use of pituitary hormone to bring about ovulation in women who do not ovulate. The hormone, at first taken from the glands of the dead, is now extracted from the urine of postmenopausal women. The drug (Pergonal, for gonad) often causes ova to break out of both egg sacs at once so that nearly half who become pregnant have twins. A few have quadruplets.

Various medical and surgical techniques have been developed to treat sterility. Knowledge of them may be obtained from doctors, specialists, and clinics. It is, however, important to know that the likelihood of barrenness increases somewhat with delay of pregnancy; each year pregnancy becomes more difficult. This leads some practicing gynecologists to advise the young woman with an underdeveloped uterus or other symptoms which might indicate difficulty in becoming pregnant to have her first pregnancy early in marriage.

That emotions can affect fertility is becoming well-established. The Margaret Sanger Research Bureau in New York studied 500 cases of sterile couples. Of these, 122 couples were found to be sterile because of psychological tensions. Once the tensions were removed by counseling and reassurance, they became pregnant. Only five of the 122 needed psychotherapy. It may well be that this is nature's way of keeping the nervous mother from conceiving offspring who would be damaged during development by her extreme stress. As is discussed later, extreme nervous tension of the mother can produce a child who is neurotic at birth.

ALTERNATIVES TO NATURAL CONCEPTION

In many cultures, perhaps in most of them historically, a fertility ceremony has been institutionalized. This may consist of a sanctioned period of license, in which copulation with others than the spouse is more or less taken for granted. There is a survival of these practices in many advanced cultures. In the West German Catholic areas, for example, especially in the Rhineland, Swabia, and Bavaria, there is an annual ceremony called the *Karneval*. (In rural areas it is called *die Fastnacht*.) It is a Mardi Gras type of celebration, with riotous parties and a carnival atmosphere that takes over the community. Drinking and carousing are the order of the day. It is said that the spouse who would attempt to sue the mate on grounds of infidelity which occurred during Bavaria's carnival time would be laughed out of court.

Such practices are a boon to the wife of an infertile mate, but they are hardly an acceptable solution to this problem in our society. Artificial insemination now offers scientific help to the apparently sterile couple. In cases where both husband and wife are fertile but conception fails to take place, instrumental insemination using the husband's semen is sometimes successful.

Thousands of artificial inseminations have been successfully carried out. It is, however, according to some authorities, still hazardous to the marriage. Husbands rarely suggest artificial insemination. Even when his consent is willingly given, and in spite of the fact that he is present when the act of insemination is performed, the husband may become jealous and suspicious, feeling that the wife has been disloyal. It should not be undertaken using a donor's semen, without being discussed fully.

The emotional impact of artificial insemination is found by Farris (1956) to be less serious than these warnings suggest. He reports, for example, that there may be the same emotional complications in the case of adoption, when there is resentment against the adoption agent. Artificial insemination with donor semen does meet the desire of the couple to experience pregnancy, and promises 50 percent heredity, which gives promise of a closer tie than does adoption. It also protects the husband's pride, in that no one but he and his wife know the child is not his. He also finds that couples he studied who had a child by artificial insemination would unanimously agree to have another.

Student attitudes generally favor artificial insemination by the husband but not by a donor. Vernon and Broadway (1959), studying attitudes toward artificial insemination, both by donors and by husbands at Central Michigan College, reported a great preference for adoption over artificial insemination by any means. Only 73.5 percent would approve artificial insemination using the husband's semen, compared to 90 percent studied by Greenberg (1951) at Colorado, and only 17 percent at Michigan would approve it by a donor compared to 52 percent at Colorado. Religious reasons were among those given for condemning artificial insemination. The more conservative attitudes, as would be expected, were among Catholics. Whether a difference in the classroom atmosphere in which artificial insemination was discussed is the real variable here, or regional differences, or whether students are actually becoming more conservative in this matter is debatable. It seems unlikely that the statistical differences found represent real differences in attitudes. It may well be that attitudes have changed since the latter study was made.

The legitimacy status and inheritance rights of the child sired by the donor's semen are in question. Some courts have ruled such children illegitimate unless the husband adopts the child. Some courts have ruled that the act of siring a child by such means is adultery.

Family Life (July 1968) called a decision of the California Supreme Court without precedent when it ruled that a husband was criminally negligent for the nonsupport of a child born to his wife by artificial insemination, even though they had already been divorced.

Legal problems will no doubt be solved with the increased use of artificial insemination. Scientists are already advocating sperm banks for eugenics reasons, particularly as a protection of human stock from possible radiation damage. The storage of deep-frozen semen was recommended by Nobel Prize winner, Hermann J. Muller to the American Institute of Biological Sciences. It is now done.

Ovary transplant is in its infancy, but already has been carried out successfully. The ovum of another woman is transplanted into the uterus, where it can be fertilized. The ova will contain the genetic traits of the donor, but the processes of pregnancy and birth will be those of the recipient. This too brings new adjustment problems for husbands and wives involved, and new legal, moral, and religious quandaries.

FETOLOGY

Fetology is a new science that has developed techniques for studying the interior of the womb from the time of conception to delivery. By puncturing the mother's abdomen with a hollow needle, fluid is drawn from the sac in which the fetus floats. Its color, chemical composition, and volume indicate the sex of the fetus, health or illness, and can reveal certain genetic abnormalities. It is even possible to remove the placenta from the mother's body in order to perform surgery on the fetus and return it to her body. When genetic abnormalities are discovered by analysis of chromosomes in the fetal fluid early in the pregnancy, an abortion can be performed.

The National Foundation, March of Dimes, is now concentrating research and therapy on the problems of birth defects, which they report to be the nation's second greatest destroyer of life. The foundation has a network of more than 70 March of Dimes Birth Defects Centers, and also helps subsidize The Salk Institute for Biological Studies in San Diego, California. There is great hope that the tragedy of the defective child which visits so many homes can be alleviated.

Treatment of the unborn through injections, surgery, transplants, and removal of the hereditary defective fetus which cannot be corrected, are all part of a rapidly advancing science, fetology. Modifications in genetic characteristics and matching of desirable hereditary traits is a possibility. Social and moral implications of genetic control are emerging as new issues for man.

Prenatal Influence—Myths Versus Science

The womb is a place of activity. In it the child can hear, feel the rhythm of the mother's heartbeat, and the rumblings of her intestines. A survey by the Ministry of Health and Welfare in Japan found that when the mother spent a large part of her pregnancy very close to an airport noises were so severe as to greatly reduce the weight of unborn infants. The child in the womb also responds to endocrine changes in the mother's system which accompany her emotions. In the fluid sac it sucks its finger and drinks in large amounts of the fluids in which it floats.

The old wives tales about the baby's harelip being caused by the mother's being frightened by a rabbit is not so far from the truth as was once supposed. Experiments with animals show that damage to lip and palate can be caused by drug injection or severe emotional stress, which has the effect of releasing chemicals into the bloodstream. Two variables determine the degree of damage to the embryo: (1) time of influence—it must be when the jaws and lips are being formed, (2) extent of influence—it must reach a degree of intensity for damage to result.

Study of harelip and cleft palates among humans shows that most persons with these defects were born to mothers who experienced the damaging influence between the sixth and eighth weeks of pregnancy, the time when jaw structures form in the human embryo.

Such research has led to a reevaluation of the arbitrary opinions regarding the possibility of the mother's health, nervous stability, and emotional experiences affecting the child. Instead of writing all prenatal influences off as old wives' tales, research is now trying to assess the specific effect of the prenatal environment on the unborn child. Briefly, for this is too complex a subject to present in any detail, evidence to date suggests the following:

Prenatal Marking   The idea that if a mother is scared by a snake the child will have the print of a snake on its back; or by a rabbit, and the harelip will result; and many other such folk tales are strictly myth. Extreme fright at a time when given embryo structures are forming can, however, create developmental damage.

Prenatal Chemical Damage   Certain chemicals injected into the body can affect the development of the embryo, as experiments with animals have clearly demonstrated. X-Rays and radiation can damage an embryo. Women should avoid x-ray and fluoroscopic examination during the first half of the month while the egg is forming. Smoking by the mother, while it will not produce a yellow baby as folk myth holds, may cause premature births. It constricts blood vessels in the abdomen and cuts off oxygen supply. A report by the U.S. Surgeon General (1971) reaches this conclusion regarding fetal development:

> Maternal smoking during pregnancy exerts a retarding influence on fetal growth as manifested by decreased infant birthweight and an increased incidence of prematurity, defined by weight alone. There is strong evidence to support the view that smoking mothers have a significantly greater number of unsuccessful pregnancies due to stillbirth and neonatal death as compared to nonsmoking mothers. There is insufficient evidence to support a comparable statement for abortions. The recently published Second Report of the 1958 British Perinatal Mortality Survey, a carefully designed and controlled prospective study involving large numbers of patients, adds further support to these conclusions.

Some of the drugs used for escape in the contraculture may affect chromosome breakdown, and also fetal development. And some nonprescription drugs should be taken sparingly, and only if badly needed, during pregnancy, especially during the first three months and the last few weeks. Alcohol is also a damaging drug. Mothers who are chronically alcoholic produce defective children.

Prenatal Nutritional Damage   Lack of vitamins may damage the embryo. During the stress of war, when carbohydrates were burned up by mothers in excessive amounts, babies were born light in weight but of normal length, since mineral elements that form bone structure were not consumed in excess.

Many American mothers have been wrongly advised about weight gain and nutrition during pregnancy by their doctors. They have been taught that they should not gain weight or gain very little. Research by the National Institutes of Health recommends a 10 pound gain of the mother during the first half of pregnancy and 15–20 pounds during the second half. Shortage in the diet can reduce the brain weight of the child and thereby limit his full capacity. Protein deficiency can result when the total diet of the mother is inadequate. Hungerford (1972) believes that lack of proper nutrition is so widespread that damage may result to both mother and offspring.

Prenatal Disease Damage   Virus diseases of the mother, particularly German measles, have been responsible for as much as 30 percent of cerebral palsy; but even chickenpox and diabetes may also damage the embryo, causing deformity or mental retardation. This is so well-recognized as a hazard during the first three months of pregnancy that having German measles has been legal grounds for abortion as a eugenics measure in Sweden.

Recent research shows that even children who show no symptoms of having been damaged prenatally by German measles, may pass the disease on to others, thus spreading it among women who may be pregnant, and who may come in contact with pregnant women. Fortunately, a new vaccine promises elimination of German measles (rubella), the worst intrauterine crippler and killer.

An untreated syphilitic mother can transmit syphilis to the child during the embryonic stage. Although the bloodstream of the mother and the fetus are separate, syphilis can pass through the placenta wall by osmosis in the same way as food and waste materials.

One of the serious problems of the drug culture is that certain potent drugs pass through the placenta wall by osmosis and cause addiction in the unborn child. *Family Life* (June 1972) reports that in New York City public hospitals, one in every 30–35 children born in ghetto areas is an addict. Withdrawal pains may be from mild to severe—vomiting, sneezing, convulsions. With heroin it depends on how long the mother has used the drug, in what quantities, with what frequency, and the latest usage before the child was born. A more recent observation of hospitals is that the methadone treatment for heroin addiction also produces addiction in the unborn child.

Prenatal Emotional Damage   Extreme emotion causes release of chemicals into the bloodstream, which can very decidedly affect the embryo, just as can externally injected chemicals. Sontag's (1944) studies show such effects in mothers undergoing extreme emotional stress. Fetal activity is greatly increased, too, and the fetal movements last longer than stress of the mother, causing it to burn up excessive carbohydrates. Infants born to mothers undergoing extreme emotional stress are hyperactive after birth, want to be fed frequently, and have frequent bowel movements. They are born neurotic. Ashley Montagu and Schweitzer's (1954) research confirms the fact of the neurotic child being born to the extremely nervous mother. They also summarize other research confirming this view.

In the animal field, breeders have long recognized the necessity of a calm gestation period, particularly for captive wild animals like foxes and mink. Perhaps with continued research we will have equal insight into the effect of maternal temperament on prenatal environment.

Prenatal Damage from Rh Disease   Intrauterine damage to the fetus due to the clash of the mother's and the child's blood is now rare, but it once resulted in jaundice, anemia, heart defects, and mental retardation to some 20,-000 children per year, 10,000 stillbirths, and accounted for 10 percent of cerebral palsy cases.

Rh incompatibility (named for its discovery in rhesus monkeys) occurs when the mother is Rh negative and the fetus is Rh positive like the father.* The mother is normal and healthy but the pregnancy sets up antibodies, as if the fetus were a virulent disease or transplant. There is little of this reaction until the placenta breaks at the birth of the child, causing some of the child's blood to get into her bloodstream. The first child is not affected, but following children, if they are Rh positive, will be damaged. A new injection procedure now keeps the mother from producing the antibodies which can damage the fetus so severely.

Protein Deficiency   As hunger throughout the world has become a matter of increasing social concern, it has been discovered that malnutrition may retard mental and physical development in the womb and after birth. Particularly critical is protein starvation, a factor in prematurity and in retarding brain growth.

Eating clay, a practice of many of the poor in the South, particularly of black women (replaced in the northern city by eating starch), is disastrous from the standpoint of nutrition. It leads to such obstetrical problems as premature birth, low weight of fetus, placenta complications, low resistance to infection, and mental retardation of the newborn child.

THE RISKS OF YOUTHFUL PREGNANCY

Montagu (1957) has found that full female maturity for purposes of reproduction is reached only very slowly, and not until years after puberty. Preg-

---

*The Rh negative factor is found in 15 percent of whites, 7 percent of blacks, and 1 percent of Chinese and Japanese.

nancy before full biological maturity is risk-laden. The principal risks he finds to young mothers are: (1) a high death rate among children born; (2) a high death rate among mothers during or following childbirth; (3) many spontaneous abortions; (4) high stillbirth rate; (5) more frequent toxemia.

Surveying the evidence, he concludes that we should not only discourage young marriages, but that where young people in their teens do marry, they should delay the first pregnancy.

As women approach the end of childbearing at 45 or 50, risks to both mother and child from pregnancy are very high. Fresh male sperm is constantly being produced, but the female ova are all laid down in preegg form while the infant is still in the womb or shortly after birth. "Stale" eggs are likely near menopause. For example, a woman of 25 has only one chance in 2000 of producing a mongoloid; a woman of 45, one in 50.

HAZARDS OF BIRTH AND BIRTH TIMING

Birth damage to children is extensive. Meyer A. Perlstein's (1957) research in the area of cerebral palsy, which affects one child in every 215 born in the United States, suggests that about 3 percent is caused by forceps delivery, but that 60 percent is due to brain hemorrhage and contusions during a difficult natural delivery and to oxygen starvation. Illness of the mother during pregnancy, notably German measles, anemia, and diabetes may account for 30 percent, and the Rh factor, about 3 percent. Childhood injuries account for the rest.

Premature births are another problem of great significance. About half of infant deaths in the United States are among this group. Extremely careful handling is necessary not only to save life but to protect the premature from brain damage due to bile pigments which the liver cannot handle, and from blindness due to an excess of oxygen in the incubator. The excess of bile pigment usually requires blood transfusion.

About 12 percent of births are delayed about two weeks beyond due date, and 4 percent are delayed three weeks. Research by Mitchell J. Nechtow (1959) has found the mortality rate of the latter group three times that of normal term babies. His explanation is that the placenta may shrink, causing the baby to live off its own tissues, thus losing weight. Difficulty of delivery also increases with more frequent breach births and use of forceps and Caesarean sections, all of which bring risk of injury.

MULTIPLE BIRTHS

In most cultures, twins have been considered omens of either good or bad luck. In much of black Africa they are put to death to protect the group from evil. Certain Canadian Indian tribes which accept them as good omens, have elevated them to enviable places in the group. In our sophisticated culture, superstitions concerning twins have disappeared, but twins do attract attention, require special care in rearing, and have become the subject of studies for testing the relative influence of heredity and environment.

Identical twins begin with a single ovum which has been fertilized by a single sperm and which later divides to form two embryos, each having the same pattern of genes and therefore the same common inherited characteristics. They are, of course, of the same sex. If the egg divides late after fertilization, the twins may be *mirror images* of each other rather than identical images; that is, their hair will part on opposite sides, one will be left-handed and the other right-handed, etc.

The handwriting and fingerprints of identical twins are very similar. Their skin is so identical that skin grafts can be made on each other's bodies interchangeably and without difficulty.

Numerous studies of identical twins show that they have the same general characteristics of temperament, interest, and even hereditary weaknesses. Researchers find few twins in the list of distinguished persons. There seems to be frequent intellectual retardation among them, possibly linked to premature birth. Some think a factor of retardation is speech-caused. The twins are able to communicate with each other during early childhood and do not have to learn normal vocabulary.

The statistical chance of twins is about one in 85 births, of triplets, one in 7000, of quadruplets, one in 50 million, of quintuplets, one in 57 million (only 60 sets have been reported in the world during the last 500 years). Twins do tend to run in families; both male and female can carry the twinning characteristic. Older mothers more often have twins than young mothers. The death rate of multiple births is high—of twins even three times as high as in single births.

Fraternal twins (nonidentical) make up 75 percent of all twins. They are born of two different eggs which have been fertilized by two different sperm. The fertilization may even take place in different acts of intercourse, even by different males, as has been proved in tests of paternity. Such twins may be of either sex and are no more alike in heredity than siblings born separately.

A rural myth of long standing holds that mixed-sex twins are sterile. It apparently originates from the "free martin" situation in cattle, where, in the case of mixed-sex twins, the female is almost always sterile. The reason seems to be that the placenta surrounding the calves is very thin, permitting the male sex hormone to dominate the female's sexual development, making it sterile. The situation does not exist in humans.

THE CONTROL OF PREGNANCY

The ability to control conception is at the very heart of the companionship marriage. For the welfare of the children, too, child spacing is considered an essential in providing the maximum social and economic advantages. Effective timing and spacing of children requires medical technology and constant vigilance. Most couples will have consulted a physician or visited a clinic prior to marriage, ideally three months before. Methods of conception control will have been provided so that the marriage insofar as possible is protected from unwanted pregnancy. There are many approaches to conception control. Various devices are used to keep sperm from entering the cervix. The most effective of the mechanical means are the condom, used by the male (effective also in venereal disease prevention and sometimes used for this purpose), and the diaphragm, used by the female. The chemical means include creams, suppositories, and foams introduced into the vagina prior to sexual intercourse (preliminary research suggests that some of these spermicides cut down the incidence of venereal disease infection). They may be used along with the diaphragm for extra safety. Douches are used after intercourse as means of conception control. They are among the least effective means, for the sperm may already have moved through the cervix into the uterus.

Withdrawal prior to ejaculation (*coitus interruptus*) is an ancient method of conception control among peoples who know the relationship between sexual intercourse and conception. It is unreliable, as some semen may be leaked prior to withdrawal; in addition, withdrawal takes more strength of will than many males are able to command.

Intrauterine devices (IUDs) have come into wide usage. They consist of a T, ring, coil, or loop—the shape does not seem to matter—which uncoils after insertion. It is the foreign object in the uterus which protects from pregnancy. Plastic, stainless steel, or copper, it is noncorrosive and when inserted by the doctor may be left for years without side effects. It is inexpensive, requires no daily planning, or preintercourse ritual. It has been widely used in India as the best approach to date to an economical mass method of population control. However, some women's bodies expel the device and many women, for various reasons, remove it.

Rhythm

The rhythm method is based on the assumption that a couple may determine quite exactly the time of ovulation and by avoiding sexual intercourse then, avoid conception. The rhythm method, although usually identified with spacing or limiting births, is of equal importance in achieving pregnancy. It depends for its effectiveness upon accuracy in determining the time of ovulation.

Edmund J. Farris (1956) has reported research which casts considerable doubt on existing theories about the specific period of ovulation. He finds that in 90 percent of the cases, ovulation takes place between the tenth and sixteenth days from the beginning of the menstrual flow, and that in the majority it takes place between the eleventh and fourteenth days, the twelfth day being the most common. He is very doubtful that the ovum can be fertilized later than eight hours after its rupture from the egg sac or that sperm cells are potent for more than 24 hours after ejaculation.

He recommends that women who wish to establish the time of ovulation either for purposes of birth control or conception determine the midpoint of the cycle and subtract two days from this number. This is the time of most likely ovulation. The earliest possible day of fertility then would be two days before this date and the latest five days afterward. He believes that the temperature method of determining ovulation is not reliable in more than half the cases.

Farris has indicated that to assure conception it is desirable to refrain from sexual intercourse until just five days prior to ovulation to assure maximum development of the husband's sperm. Then, at the period when ovulation is expected, the couple should have sexual intercourse daily for three days before the midcycle day.

Rhythm is the only means of birth control approved by the Catholic Church, and even this method is approved with reservations by some of the Church leaders. For limiting offspring it is ineffective. A careful mathematical analysis of the reliability of the "safe period" has been made by André J. De-Bethune (1963). He finds that even if the fertile period is no longer than 12 hours, a couple who wish to space children two years apart are limited statistically to two acts of coitus per menstrual cycle. Those who expect to space children by four years are limited to one act of coitus per cycle. He concluded his analysis with the observation, "It is not surprising that the rhythm method has become a source of mental torture to many couples."

In addition to being ineffective as a means of birth control, rhythm may, when it fails, produce a totally malformed child. The difficulty is stale sperm, or a stale egg. The supposition is based on the substantially higher rate of serious malformations found among Catholic than Protestant or Jewish offspring. Raymond G. Cross (1968) of Dublin found anencephaly (absence of brain, and failure of spinal column to close) to run 2.8 per thousand among Catholics, 2 among Protestants, and 0.7 among Jews. Carlo Sirtori of Milan agrees with this finding and adds mongolism to the list of defects from stale reproductive cells. Alan Guttmacher, president of the Planned Parenthood Federation in the United States, indicates that the stale-egg theory has been confirmed in animal experiments.

"The Pill"

The most revolutionary and surest approach to pregnancy control has been the oral hormone inhibitor. The most frequently used pill employs estrogen, which inhibits ovulation during a woman's pregnancy. When taken in the right dosage 20 times per month on successive days beginning five days after the onset of menstruation, it inhibits ovulation just as pregnancy does. Ovulation begins when the pill is no longer used.

The Side Effect Risks   The extent to which a given device or chemical controls pregnancy is but one significant measure of the desirability of its use. The basic question, particularly with chemical methods, is that of side effects. Using this as a standard, of the two most effective methods, the intrauterine device rates higher in safety. The pill affects the user's entire hormone balance including the pituitary gland and the ovaries. The effect of the IUD is localized, for it lies harmlessly in the uterus.*

The pill has been used by more than 30 million women and is to date the most effective method. The side effect of most concern from the pill has been that its long-continued use may cause blood clots in certain women, as well as other less serious side effects. In September 1969, the Food and Drug

*Some devices have been developed which cause irritation, and we have already mentioned that some women expel the device.

Administration released its in-depth study on oral contraceptives. Although they report that the death risk is 4.4 times greater for pill users than nonpill users, the drug is well within the limits of safety. H. W. Stinson (1969), of the Association for Voluntary Sterilization, commented on the association's findings: "It is well to keep in mind that childbirth deaths are 1700 percent greater than pill death." Use of the pill over long periods of time does require medical supervision, and doctors do not recommend its use for those with a history of cancer or vascular diseases.

Side effects of the pill have been about as few as with most drugs in general use and no doubt will decrease in the future. The dosage of the long-used 20 pills a month has been cut to one-tenth the original dosage, but the pills do require medical approval and supervision. Other pills are being and will be developed also which will mark further improvement insofar as human tolerance is concerned. And pills for "morning after," once a month, once a quarter, and longer periods are in the experimental stage, as are pills providing male sterility for a period of time.

The present most used "morning after pill" has not been approved by the Food and Drug Administration; their report indicates that it may increase the risk of cancer in women with a family history of breast or cervical cancer. At the present stage of development, its use is considered sufficiently safe following rape or unpremeditated sexual intercourse, but it should not be taken as a regular preventive device.

Population pressure is so critical in many parts of the world, and food shortages so recurrent, that it is probable that temporary immunity to pregnancy may be introduced to large populations through chemicals placed in water or food supply. Social concern is so great that new means for the control of pregnancy are receiving much research attention.

Certainly much can be expected in the way of improvement of chemical immunization in the immediate years ahead, by use of pills, injections, implantation of capsules under the skin to release inhibitors continuously, and temporary sterilization agents for the male. The Poverty Program is experimenting with injections which give three month's immunity.

STERILIZATION FOR FAMILY LIMITATION

Vasectomy involves the tying off and cutting of the *vas deferens,* an operation of approximately seven minutes duration, requiring an incision into the scrotum. Usually the male can return to work within a day or so after the operation. Tubal ligation or salpingotomy has until recently required opening the abdominal cavity of the female to tie and cut the fallopian tubes. Since this involved surgery of considerable seriousness, it was usually not used in this country except when the abdominal cavity was opened for other reasons or when serious medical reasons existed. Tubal ligation can now be performed by making a small incision in the naval, inserting a laparoscope (a long, hollow, stainless steel tube about the diameter of a pencil) for vision, and inserting, through a smaller hole below the navel, electrically operated biopsy forceps to seal off a portion of the fallopian tubes. Although greatly simplified over the old operative procedure, it is still more costly and complicated than sterilizing the male. In Catholic countries like Puerto Rico, it has been used extensively by women who usually give as their reason, "one confession is sufficient," whereas with birth control, repeated confessions are necessary.

Vasectomy is being promoted by the government of India as one of the principal means of population control. Some states give a payment to the male submitting to the operation, and some also a reward payment to the recruiter. In some states a fine is imposed on those having more than three children. Vasectomy for family limitation is on the increase in the United States. The male operation is so economical in terms of discomfort and cost (as low as $50) that it offers the best and a final solution to the problem of unwanted pregnancies for couples choosing to use it. The Association for Voluntary Sterilization is promoting voluntary sterilization throughout the world.

The great concern of males considering the operation is with the physical, psychosocial, and marital implications of the operation. Landis and Poffenberger (1965) studied 2007 vasectomy records of physicians and obtained follow-up questionnaires from 330 couples. Most couples appraised the results as beneficial to their sex life and to their marriage; almost none regretted it. Greater frequency of sexual intercourse was reported by most couples. The principal motive for the couple's joint decision to have the operation was their desire to fix the size of their families, even though most of the couples had small families. It is estimated that nearly a million males a year seek sterilization. It is rapidly increasing in popularity (Presser and Bumpass 1972).

The one serious objection to sterilization has been its finality. Some couples change their mind about the number of children they want, and some remarry after widowhood or divorce. In the past, comparatively few operations have been reversible to the point of restoring fertility. Now, removable plugs in the *vas deferens,* or clips to pinch them shut, and even a gold valve which can be opened and shut are available. The extent to which glands atrophy during long periods of shutoff is still a matter of study. Opening of tubes by surgery has not been too successful in restoring fertility. The most certain methods today to assure offspring, should the family situation change, is the sperm bank, where the husband's sperm can be frozen and kept for use by artificial insemination in case further children are desired by his wife or a succeeding wife.

Effectiveness of Contraceptive Practice

Rainwater (1965) published a study of attitudes of Protestant and Catholic couples and of social class levels toward likely success of their ability to limit families to the desired size. Of middle-class Protestants, 63 percent were "planful and self-assured," 37 percent "hopeful but unsure;" of middle-class Catholics, only 23 percent were "planful and self-assured," 63 percent "hopeful but unsure," 14 percent "passive and fatalistic." Of upper-lower-class whites and blacks, only 18 percent were "planful and self-assured," 58 percent "hopeful but unsure," 24 percent "passive and fatalistic." In the lower-lower social class only 5 percent were "planful and self-assured," 32 percent "hopeful but unsure," 63 percent "passive and fatalistic."

The situation has undoubtedly improved greatly for both religious groups and for all social layers. The addition of family planning to family assistance programs has no doubt increased effectiveness, accessibility, and success of contraception, and therefore, faith in it, among the lower-lower classes who are beneficiaries of family assistance programs.

Westoff (1972), working with data of the National Fertility Studies, has reported that unwanted births declined by 35 percent among whites and 56 percent among blacks between 1965 and 1970. He reports that the differentials between economic groups have narrowed, as all now have access to information and techniques of birth control. The great increase in proportion of blacks limiting families to desired levels is indicative of their increasing access to effective contraception. The extent to which abortion has affected these trends among all groups is not known, but the 1970 data precede the new laws permitting abortion. In Table 24-1 is Westoff's complete picture of methods of family limitation used, by age of wife for the nationwide population studied. Those who were practicing no means of family limitation are not included in this summary. In 1965 this group was 36 percent married women, in 1970, 35 percent. (The group was composed of women who were pregnant, postpartum, or trying to get pregnant, and women who were sterile, of low fecundity, and other nonusers.) Observe from the table the increase in use of various methods between 1965 and 1970, and differences in racial and age groups. It is interesting to note that among blacks it is the wife who must seek sterilization in most marriages, even though the female operation is more difficult and costly. The pill is most used of all methods, but use of the IUD is on the increase. Use of condoms and rhythm declined rapidly, as also did withdrawal.

Extreme Women's Liberations have labeled the increased dependence on female methods of conception control as part of the male "chauvinist plot." They see the slower development of the male pill, and other such controls, as part of this plot. The fact remains that until now the male has been responsible for using contraceptive means: the method of withdrawal is old in human history and requires considerable strength of will on the part of the male; and the condom, long in use, has reduced male sensation in the sex act to a considerable degree.

A few years ago, when the black revolution was more militant, extremists saw any attempt to propagate family limitation among the blacks as part of the plot of whites to commit genocide on the blacks, rather than as a way to elevate the race to a position of economic and social equality.

Voluntary Abortion

Induced abortion has a long history as a means of limiting family size. Throughout the world abortion accounts for most control of births, now as always, according to a report of Dr. J. Corbett McDonald, before the 1973 convention of the International Planned Parenthood Association. In his survey of 209 countries, he concluded that less than a third of fertile couples in the world practice any birth control by contraception; they lack the knowledge and facilities to do so. The consequence is that about one in three pregnancies is terminated by voluntary abortion. Folk remedies for inducing abortion are almost as numerous as the cultures of man, but they are highly hazardous to

TABLE 24-1 Methods of Contraception Used Currently by Married Couples, Percentages, by Age and Color: 1965 and 1970

CURRENT METHOD	ALL COUPLES (WIFE < 45)				YOUNGER COUPLES (WIFE < 30)				OLDER COUPLES (WIFE 30-44)			
	WHITE		BLACK		WHITE		BLACK		WHITE		BLACK	
	1965 (N = 2441)	1970 (N = 3273)	1965 (N = 554)	1970 (N = 462)	1965 (N = 922)	1970 (N = 1540)	1965 (N = 276)	1970 (N = 222)	1965 (N = 1519)	1970 (N = 1733)	1965 (N = 278)	1970 (N = 240)
Wife Sterilized[c]	6.3	7.5	14.4	19.3	2.8	2.9	6.9	5.0	8.4	11.6	21.9	32.5
Husband Sterilized[c]	5.4	8.3	0.5	1.1	3.1	3.2	0.4	0.5	6.8	12.9	0.7	1.7
Pill[d]	24.0	34.0	21.7	37.4	42.5	49.4	30.8	54.1	12.8	20.4	12.6	22.1
IUD[e]	1.0	7.3	2.9	7.6	1.4	8.8	4.7	9.9	0.8	5.9	1.1	5.4
Diaphragm[f]	10.4	5.7	5.1	5.2	6.5	3.5	3.3	3.6	12.8	7.7	6.8	6.7
Condom[g]	22.4	14.8	17.0	6.7	19.2	11.9	18.1	6.3	24.4	17.3	15.8	7.1
Withdrawal	4.1	2.2	2.2	0.6	2.3	1.8	1.8	0.5	5.3	2.7	2.5	0.8
Foam	3.1	6.1	6.1	6.1	4.4	8.2	8.0	6.8	2.2	4.3	4.3	5.4
Rhythm	11.6	6.7	2.5	1.7	7.9	4.4	2.9	0.9	13.8	8.8	2.2	2.5
Douche	4.2	2.9	17.5	8.0	3.8	1.9	15.2	5.9	4.4	3.7	19.8	10.0
Others[h]	7.3	4.4	10.2	6.2	6.0	4.0	8.0	6.8	8.1	4.6	12.2	5.8
Percent Total	100	100	100	100	100	100	100	100	100	100	100	100

Source: Charles F. Westoff. "The Modernization of U.S. Contraceptive Practice." *Family Planning Perspectives*, 4:9–13. July. (1972).

[a]Who were living together currently.

[b]Includes nonwhites other than blacks.

[c]Surgical procedures undertaken at least partly for contraceptive reasons.

[d]Includes combination with any other method.

[e]Includes combination with any other method except pill.

[f]Includes combination with any method except pill or IUD.

[g]Includes combination with any method except pill, IUD or diaphragm.

[h]Includes other multiple as well as single methods and a small percentage of unreported methods.

the life of the mother. *Family Life* (Dec. 1972) reports the current condition in Turkey, where it is estimated that 60,500 women abort by folk remedies annually using chicken feathers, crochet needles, matches, tweezers, nails, forks, and other instruments. Most die from the ensuing bleeding.

Such risk-taking is indicative of the dread with which women almost universally face unwanted pregnancy. In underdeveloped cultures the dread is caused by already having too many mouths to feed. In the light of such a history, it is little wonder that the recent Supreme Court Decision in this country is hailed as an historic step in individual rights and in the liberation of women. On January 22, 1973, by a seven to two decision, the Supreme Court held that "the right to privacy . . . founded in the Fourteenth Amendment's concept of personal liberty . . . is broad enough to encompass a woman's decision whether or not to terminate her pregnancy."

For the first time, women throughout the nation may seek abortion without breaking the law. The moral issue remains for many, but the legal issue has been clarified. The religious issue also remains for certain groups, but without legal support. Of course, the liberation of abortion law need not make the practice of contraception of less concern. Contraception is far less costly in terms of moral compromise, financial outlay, and producing risks to carrying another pregnancy when a child may be wanted.

CHILD SPACING

The problem of spacing children is one which must depend largely upon the couple's own desires. A study of maternal and child development by R. W. Woodbury, in 1915, recommended that children be spaced at least two years apart for the sake of the health of the mother. More recent research and medical opinion suggests that the nearer the children can be spaced, the better for the health of the mother.

Close spacing of births does increase the percentage of premature births, according to records of the University of Pennsylvania School of Medicine. Israel and Nemser (1968) find the following:

MONTHS SINCE PREVIOUS PREGNANCY	PERCENTAGE OF PREMATURE BIRTHS
More than 23	7.8
12–23	10.3
Less than 12	18.0

From the standpoint of social development of children there is something to be said in favor of having children as close together as possible. It provides a play group of similar ages in the home, even if a highly competitive one. Of course, it takes a sturdy mother to care effectively for two or three very small children at the same time, particularly if the family does not have the financial resources to hire help with housework and child care.

COITUS DURING PREGNANCY

There is much folklore about sexual intercourse during pregnancy. Actually, pregnancy usually does not reduce interest in sexual intercourse until the later stages. In fact, the wife's desire may actually increase during the early stages of pregnancy. During the final stages, particularly the last two weeks to a month, when the neck of the uterus is likely to be somewhat open and the nearly full-grown embryo may be expanding the uterus down into the vaginal canal, intercourse is not wise, at least intercourse by deep penetration of the vagina. The belief that having sexual intercourse during pregnancy will make the child oversexed is strictly myth, as is also the notion that intercourse will make the delivery easier.

Landis, Poffenberger, and Poffenberger (1950) asked a group of 212 wives who had completed their first pregnancy the question, "What effect, if any, did pregnancy have upon your sexual adjustment?" Husbands and wives generally agreed as to the answer:

EFFECT	HUSBANDS (PERCENT)	WIVES (PERCENT)
No effect	58	58
Unfavorable	23	25
Favorable	19	17

Of those who indicated that the effect had been favorable, most had had poor sexual adjustment previous to conception. Of those who reported an unfavorable effect, a considerable proportion had had a good adjustment before pregnancy. In general, husbands and wives reported a decrease in sexual desire with the duration of the pregnancy. Toward the end of the pregnancy, many women were found to lose interest in sexual contact, or found it painful. Others quit because of doctors' advice for fear of hurting the baby.

A significant effect of pregnancy is the decreasing of the husband's desire. About 10 percent felt "it didn't seem right" or that they did not enjoy intercourse. Almost all the wives felt that their husbands were more considerate of them and exhibited more sensitivity concerning their feelings during the pregnancy than before.

After childbirth, intercourse may begin as soon as the wife feels ready for it. Unless there has been surgical damage, she is usually ready in three to six weeks. The need for contraception by those who wish to space children will be greater after delivery than before. Because of the dilation of the cervix a new pregnancy is often very easy following childbirth. The notion that a nursing mother cannot become pregnant has no basis in fact.

PSYCHOLOGICAL ADJUSTMENTS TO PREGNANCY

Folklore and old wives' tales have given the young wife a picture of what pregnancy may be expected to be. The symptoms are so familiar that the woman who does not have her morning nausea, often accompanied by vomiting and symptoms of dizziness, considers herself almost abnormal. Motion pictures have contributed to this image by having the young husband act solicitous when the young wife announces that they are going to have a baby.

The particular symptoms of pregnancy are, in part, a matter of custom and culture. This is well-demonstrated in Margaret Mead's (1954) analysis of the extent of nausea that exists among women in various cultures. In cultures where the nausea feeling is considered the universal experience of pregnant women, practically all women have it; in societies which ignore the phenomenon, nausea is rare, although it may be felt by some women. She explains this by the fact that nausea and even vomiting are biological capacities of the organism, but that a culture may elaborate these to the point where they become important and customary. Or the culture may neglect, ignore, or even frown on such reactions so that they are not so frequently in the consciousness of the pregnant woman.

She also finds that cultural expectations very much affect the reaction of the woman to the menstrual period. In some cultures where pain is glorified, women may almost all feel severe symptoms during the menstrual period. In cultures where menstrual pain is ignored, the woman may simply rub her body with stinging nettles to obscure a real feeling of menstrual pain and go about her day, attempting to ignore it completely.

Some women do have nausea and vomiting and a great deal of discomfort during pregnancy. A few are even confined to bed for considerable periods of time in order to avoid miscarriage. For many healthy young women, however, none of these symptoms appear at all. In fact, a woman is more likely than not to feel better during pregnancy than at any other time. This may be due to the release of certain hormones which prepare the uterus, particularly, and the entire physiological system to some extent, for handling the fetus.

A current theory is that nausea is possibly due to the mother's system trying to reject the fetus as a foreign object, just as it would a transplant. This view came from the observation that pregnant women reject transplants less violently than nonpregnant women, leading to the presumption that certain restraints against rejection are present in her system during pregnancy. Even so, some women miscarry, thus expelling the foreign object.

CHILDBIRTH

Our culture has lost much of the folklore centering about the dread and pain of childbirth. Natural childbirth, sometimes wrongly called painless childbirth, has been widely accepted. The use of anesthetic drugs, which affected the unborn child, is gone from medical practice. Except in cases of severe complication, there is a growing tendency to accept childbirth as a natural and not too difficult event.

The "Birthsuit" of "Baby Bubble"   O. S. Heyns at the University of Witwatersrand, South Africa, has been using the birthsuit for some years to reduce the pain of labor and to minimize risks of complication for mother and child (Mendels 1963). Various American doctors are experimenting with pressure "bubbles."

The mother sits in the suit with her arms free. She can regulate the pressure in the suit. Regulation of pressure keeps the uterus in a normal position, avoiding the painful muscle spasm in the uterus. Painful labor, shock, and mental distress are eliminated. South African reports say that 90 percent of women who used it got relief from labor pains or eliminated them completely. Labor time has been cut by half in most instances. Chances of brain damage, cerebral palsy, mental deficiency, and stillbirth of the child are greatly reduced. It is estimated that fetal distress is cut 80 percent.

The most amazing aspect of the method is that babies are superior in tone and behavior from the beginning. Researchers feel that the level of mental ability is substantially increased in that there is no longer damaging oxygen deprivation during birth. Use of the pressure suit keeps up the free flow of blood to the fetus, thus keeping up the oxygen supply. It is even recommended that the suit be used for half-hour daily periods during the latter stages of pregnancy to increase the oxygen saturation of fetal blood.

This technique, with various modifications, is in increasing experimental use (Kennedy 1971).

The Hospital Situation   Along with "natural childbirth," another movement of significance has developed—that of rooming-in, also called the *Cornelian Corner*. With the development of the modern hospital, the practice of partially isolating the infant from the mother during the period of her stay in the hospital had become more or less customary. Now, rooming-in provides that the child be placed with the mother a great deal during her period in the hospital; that she nestle and cuddle it, give it affection, and nurse it. It is believed that the basis is laid here for a more secure personality, in addition to the satisfaction and comfort given to both mother and child.

A new group of nurse–midwives has been trained, assuring the mother more prompt and continuous attendance during the uncomplicated childbirth than the busy doctor can give. Women's Liberation has given impetus to midwifery, as a preferred method, and there is also some drift toward home deliveries.

PROBLEMS

1   Few couples consider it necessary to have more than the conventional physical examination prior to marriage. Under what circumstances would an analysis of one's physical heredity seem warranted?

2   A happily married couple who want children have failed to have any by the end of their third year of marriage. Which of the following courses of action would you advise, and why?

   a   Consult a marriage counselor.

   b   Consult a psychiatrist.

   c   Consult a doctor.

    d Consider adoption.

    e Concentrate on keeping their marriage a happy one in spite of their failure.

3 *Sociodrama:* A young woman whose husband is sterile seeks the counsel of her doctor (this doctor may be either male or female) on whether and how she and her husband may have a family. Through a question-and-answer type of discussion the two of them consider the advantages and disadvantages (physical, psychological, etc.) of such alternatives as: *(a)* adoption, *(b)* artificial insemination, *(c)* remaining childless.

4 What do we know about the effect of prenatal conditions on a child? For example:

    a Can a child be physically "marked" as a result of traumatic experiences happening to its mother during pregnancy?

    b Can a child be physically affected by certain physical conditions of its mother during pregnancy?

    c Can a child be psychologically affected as a result of traumatic experiences happening to its mother during pregnancy?

5 Is there any way in which an individual can increase the chances of bearing twins?

6 What are the various common techniques for controlling pregnancy? Which method seems to be the most effective? Are any of them 100 percent effective? What are the psychological advantages and disadvantages of birth control devices?

7 *Sociodrama:* A young mother whose children are one and three years old, respectively, is sorry that she followed the advice of her pediatrician in spacing her children. Her older sister whose two children are now six and eight defends the pediatrician's advice. Show how both have good arguments for their positions.

PARENTS AND CHILDREN

25 Paul Popenoe (1972) reports that more family disputes arise over the way children should be handled than over handling family finances. This reflects not only the lack of preparation for parenthood, but no doubt also an increasing awareness of young parents today of the critical importance of their role as parents. Kirkpatrick (1963) described the entrance of the child on the family scene as follows:

> The young human is interwoven with an entire family situation. With the birth of a baby a total family structure is modified. Figuratively speaking, a grandparent is produced, or a brother. Status relationships are drastically altered. An empire may be snatched away, a war started, or a multimillion dollar fortune redirected. Metaphorically, scripts are issued for new roles to be played by family members in adjustment to the new role of the infant actor (p. 206).

No single relationship in life has greater and more lasting significance than that between parent and child. The connection is more than one of blood; there are deep ties of emotion and lasting marks of influence that affect both throughout their lives. No experience can cause so much growth in the personality as that of parenthood, and certainly no single circumstance in the life of the child is so fateful as his relationship with his parents. Montagu (1958) sees the development of every human being as a loving person who is capable of realizing his full potential in cooperative relationships with others as the great challenge to our society and especially to mothers who are so intimately connected with the development of the individual.

The following chapters do not pretend to substitute for a course in child development, nor can they summarize all of the significant information young couples should consider. They are designed, rather, to point up a few of the basic issues and to give some insight into problems of parenthood.

TIMING PARENTHOOD

We have reached an era when it is theoretically possible for children to be born only when a couple wishes. The child need not be the victim of accident and fate. Many are, of course, particularly those conceived premaritally. Barring this circumstance, the newlyweds may, if they choose, decide the time in their marriage when they will have their children.

The question of the best time to start a family is an important one. It is safer from the standpoint of the wife's health and life to have the first child while she is still in her 20s. With the low maternal death rates of today, however, having a child somewhat later is not a serious risk. Life-conserving techniques improve from year to year. Financial considerations and the status of the couple's marital adjustment are more often the issues which must be faced. Sterility, however, does increase with age. This is a concern only to those who marry when the wife is well past the average age of marriage.

Children should be planned for only after the couple are confident that their own relationship is established on a secure basis. Well-meaning people sometimes advise couples who are in difficulty in their marriage to have a baby, assuring them that this will likely make their marriage a success. There is no scientific opinion to support this view, and the risks of bringing a child into a situation of tension are great indeed. Research and clinical observations indicate that a home in which there is severe tension between parents is the worst possible situation in which a child can be placed. Prenatal damage may result (see pp. 409–10). The additional work and worry accompanying the birth of a child is more likely to add problems to the already difficult situation.

Much research, too, has shown that there is a close relationship between the happiness of the parental home and the happiness of the child. Unhappily wed people usually have a negative attitude toward children, which may account in part for the failure of children in such homes to obtain happiness. Unhappiness as a parental attitude frequently leads to a lack of harmony in the parent–child relationship also.

Differences in the divorce rate of couples with and without children are not so great as has been supposed. Although divorce is more frequent among the childless in the early years of marriage, there is no difference in the rate after 13 years of marriage. Even the differences in rates which exist in the early years of marriage are probably not explained by the presence or absence of children. Young couples who are not happy will seldom become so by having children. If they cannot work out techniques of adjustment during the childless period of family life, there is little likelihood that they will be able to face the complicated adjustments that are involved as the family grows.

The circumstance under which the birth of a child might be expected to save a failing marriage is that in which childlessness itself is at the root of the marital discord. When an otherwise compatible couple begin to find life meaningless and empty but feel, for example, that they cannot yet afford the children they both want, they must reexamine their values and ambitions in order to save their marriage. As one counselor advised a group of newlyweds, "Young couples who are determined to get somewhere in this world will probably never feel that they have reached the place where they can afford children. At some point they must merely decide to compromise ambition for the sake of their own happiness."

All the evidence points up the conclusion that only couples who genuinely want children should have them and that only couples who are well-adjusted in marriage should plan to have children. This generalization becomes more significant in a crowded world where man's survival requires fewer births than at any time in human history.

MARRIAGE HAPPINESS AND CHILDREN

There is some evidence that having a child during the first year of marriage interferes somewhat with the happiness of the couple. This would seem to agree with the popular opinion that the couple should be alone during the first year or so of their marriage and not have the interference of a third member. It is assumed that a period of adjustment to marriage and to the community is desirable before confinement. Marriage books and clinicians usually advise a delay of a year or two to permit time for adjustments in the marriage and in social and community relationship.

Some couples fear that the pregnancy and the child will in some measure interfere with their love life. Studies of marriage happiness show that the happiest years are those early in marriage before children come. (Refer to studies in Chapter 19.) Old people looking back on their lives, however, indicate the years when the children were growing up in the family as their happiest in terms of total life satisfactions.

Some of the early births are a result of marriage forced by pregnancy, which no doubt is a factor in reducing happiness. Evidence shows that the highest rate of failure in marriage is among those who become pregnant premaritally. Happiness ratings for those who become pregnant early in the marriage are lower than for those who become pregnant after a year or more of marriage.

There are, however, arguments in favor of having a baby fairly early in the marriage, provided the wife is physiologically mature. The longer the couple is together in a pair relationship, the greater the difficulty in breaking the established routine and habits in order to make room for a third party. The companionship marriage, which emphasizes the partnership role of husband and wife, is in fact the one most likely to suffer severe problems of readjustment of husband–wife relations. The more traditional family system had no place for marriages in which the role of wife was distinct from the roles of housekeeper and mother. Where a high level of companionship has been established by the couple in their marriage, the effect of a small child, with his rigorous demands on the mother and the requirement that the entire routine of the couple be changed, is often serious.

An English statesman, in commenting on the problems of the contemporary family, observed that the main trouble with the companionship marriage is that couples get to be so companionable that they have no place for children in their lives. This foreboding has certainly not been justified in the United States. Margaret Mead (1960) criticized the young wife for wanting to be a mother to the neglect of her obligations as a wife. She fears the trend toward overdomesticity which draws the young male into the safe shelter of the home, thus curbing his creative, adventurous outlook.

The question of whether there can be a happy marriage without children will be of increasing concern in the days ahead, as the pressure of world population reaches an ever more critical point. The question has not been given the attention it deserves. Burgess and Cottrell's (1939) classic study of 526 married couples is suggestive that a desire for children is the key, not actually having children.

Good adjustments were high among this group. The group which had one or more children and desired them also showed a high percentage of good adjustments. But those who had children that were not desired showed the greatest proportion of poor adjustments, and very few of these couples showed good adjustment.

The precipitous decline of the birth rate in recent years, a slight trend toward marrying later, and the tendency to delay having children so soon after marriage, all point new directions in restricting parenthood. The countertrend is the increase in out-of-wedlock births (many by young teen-agers), and the increase in marriages hastened by pregnancy. One of the great disadvantages in our society in having children when too young is the lowered level of living that may persist throughout a lifetime where schooling is abbreviated. In general, in urban–industrial society, the more children a couple has, the lower their standard of living.

THE BABY AND FAMILY ROUTINE

The coming of the first child into the family calls for numerous readjustments in the habits of the parents. Much of the routine of family life must be centered around the child. Times of rising and retiring, sleep habits, recreational habits, the time spent outside the home—all these things have to be viewed from a new perspective when young people face the responsibilities of parenthood.

The first baby is one of the most significant educational experiences in the life of any person. This is especially true now because an increasing number of young people have had no experience with babies, even in their parental home. Their first experience comes with their own first baby.

The young parent learns that a baby is quite a different physiological mechanism. The heart beats around 135 times a minute, rather than 72 times, as in the adult. The infant breathes 35 times a minute instead of 16. Although much more susceptible to dietary upsets than an adult, he recovers from fevers and many diseases, and from injuries, much more quickly than will the adult. His temperature-adjusting mechanism is much more flexible, permitting quick adjustments to hot and cold. This is true to a considerable extent throughout childhood. And the abounding energy of the young child and older child is unmatched in the adult. Growth and development are very rapid; so also is the repair of damage to tissue.

Parental Adjustments to a Third Member

The coming of the first baby quite frequently creates emotional problems centering around the relationships between husband and wife. This may occur immediately after the child's birth or come when he is a few weeks old, and the couple begins to sense the change parenthood has brought into their lives. The wife goes through a "honeymoon" period with the baby, a time in which the insecure husband is likely to feel sadly neglected. In some cases the mother from that point on makes the child, rather than the husband, the emotional center of her life. The wife who relegates the husband to the position of merely earning the money, giving all her attention and emotional life to the child, cannot expect to continue to have a satisfactory home life.

There are other cases where the wife resents the coming of the child because his birth means sudden and unwanted termination of her career, her independence, or some other special status she enjoys. The wife may also fear that the coming of the child will interfere with the relationship between husband and wife. No matter how much the baby is wanted or how happy the couple may be on its arrival, the home life or the husband–wife relationship will never be the same. Babies are in their own innocent way, tyrants in the home. As Levy and Munroe (1938) have so well expressed it,

No matter how going a concern a marriage may be, the advent of children causes severe strain between parents. Newborn babies cannot be taken in their stride; they have none. Their very physical disorganization sets the pace for their influence on marriage ties. Children are as disturbing to marriage as their own physical eccentricities. Any orderly, smooth, satisfactory relationship carefully worked out between husband and wife is broken up the very first night the child is home from the hospital. The inability of a child to do anything for itself means that demands are made on parents which create a new relationship between husband and wife. Their time and energy are no longer their own for companionship or intimacy. The little tyrant need only raise its voice a tiny bit to break up the parents' closest embrace. The warmth of the adult relationship is forever being disturbed by the child's demands for physical attention. At any hour of the night the newborn youngster can separate husband and wife without repaying them for their loss with even a friendly smile. The child's physical requirements have the right-of-way over their feelings toward each other and toward the child. No matter how much one or both of them may resent this intrusion, their only choice is to obey the child's call and sacrifice their own need for each other. Babies are tyrants (p. 243).

On the other hand, children always bring to the home a new focus of interest which is usually of decided advantage. They also bring new responsibilities which may intensify the loyalty of parents to each other and their loyalty to the family itself. LeMasters (1957b) has made a case-history study of the adjustments of 46 couples to the coming of the first child (also Dyer 1963). Of this group, 38 couples, or 83 percent, reported "extensive" or "severe" crisis in adjusting to the first child. This was a joint rating of the parents. LeMasters concludes that adding a child to the urban middle-class married couple constitutes a crisis.

Most of these couples actually wanted and planned for the child, so this was not a case of unwanted children; and most of them considered their marriages good marriages, so it was not a matter of husband–wife conflicts. Much of the difficulty was due to a romanticized rather than a realistic conception of what parenthood and babies are like. Mothers had not anticipated the loss of sleep, the chronic tiredness and exhaustion, the confinement to the home, the curtailment of social contacts, the drain on income, the isolation, the washing and ironing, the seven-day-and-night week, the worry over the child and their ability to meet its demands adequately, that are a part of parenthood. Women with professional work experience suffered a crisis in every case.

Fathers added to these adjustments the decline in sex interest of the wife, the loss of her earnings, putting a greater burden upon him, and worry about future pregnancies and income. LeMasters reports that the husbands quickly became disenchanted with the parental role.

He concludes that there is a great deficiency in preparing young people for the parent role in our culture. They anticipate with great hope the mate role but not the parent role. The first child destroys the pair role relationship and creates the triangle relationship. The husband no longer has priority in the wife's interests and attentions. The first child painfully forces the couple to take the last step into the adult world.

Most of the group LeMasters studied eventually made the transition into successful parenthood. Even though the transition was painful, most felt it was worth what it cost.

Robert O. Blood, Jr., and Donald R. Wolfe (1960) found, in a study in the Detroit area over a five-year period, that "the arrival of children constitutes the gravest crisis that the average marriage encounters." This they found to be true even though children are more popular than ever and practically all couples want them. The mothers stressed such factors as loss of companionship between husband and wife, economic hardship, loss of sleep and other disruption of their lives, and being tied down to the home.

Alice Rossi (1968) agrees that motherhood exacts a big price on mothers in a society without the kinship group. It is a question of deprivations versus rewards. She feels that women do not have a realistic appreciation of the cost of motherhood. "What has not been seen is the more general point that for the first time in the history of known society, motherhood has become a full-time occupation for adult women." But she thinks it wrong to call it a crisis. Most women do adjust. It is, therefore, to be viewed as a role transition, a developmental stage.

Women used to expect pregnancy soon after marriage. Marriage was, for them, the transition. Now that pregnancy can be delayed, the transition is that to parenthood. The real shock of parenthood is that the role is abruptly assumed, and with it a 24-hour task from which there is no reprieve.

In many cities, infant-care classes are offered for prospective mothers and fathers. These are valuable not only in that they help young people gain confidence in handling and caring for a baby but also they place the couple with others who are enthusiastic about parenthood.

Parent Maturation

One of the rather surprising things the young couple has to learn when the first baby comes is that the role of the mother in the family is quite different from that of the wife and that the role of the father is quite different from that of the husband. The coming of the child, in fact, calls for a recasting of attitudes of the parents toward each other.

Dorothy Canfield Fisher once discussed the topic "How Children Educate Their Parents" in *Progressive Education*. She said:

> Most mothers and fathers at the beginning of their career as mothers and fathers are immature, egotistical, raw, spoiled children, whom society has not been able to "educate" in any real sense of the word; at whom life has not been able to get, through the thick barrier of protection set up around the young; in whom the most careful training has been able only to plant the barest germs of what we know as "character." Their ideal of life, expressed or subconscious, is the childish, shallow unrewarding one of doing as they like, and leaving somebody else to take the consequences. They have been (I speak of course only of the majority of cases) cherished more or less wisely, protected more or less wisely, protected more or less completely, looked out for by their families. In the back of their minds has always been the feeling that if things got too bad, or difficulties too steep, or the water too deep, one could always fall back on the older generation.

She then showed how being a mother or father puts many young people on their own resources for the first time and concluded, "The great majority of ordinary human beings would be unbearable if they had no children to bring them up."

The proper emotional attitude of the parent is all-essential in providing the child with a proper atmosphere for development. The infant at birth has a capacity to learn but no knowledge, emotions but no orientation of them around persons or things. Experience, the social traditions, moral beliefs of parents and other social groups must be acquired. The mind is plastic, highly impressionable, capable from the outset of receiving an almost unlimited number of impressions. This plasticity of mind and receptivity of the nervous system makes possible the cultivation of his emotional life and the passing on to the child of the experiences of the race.

The family atmosphere surrounding the child in early infancy and childhood is the most important single factor in personality development, for he absorbs the atmosphere of the life about him. Impressions and attitudes resulting from these early experiences carry over through the individual's lifetime, affecting many other relationships. The relationships between the parent and the child are important factors in the happiness of the child as he grows to adulthood and to his later success in marriage.

Breast feeding mothers are predominantly college-educated, affluent, and "warmly relaxed about sex." The bottle feeding mothers are reported to have more psychosexual disturbances and to dislike nudity and sexuality. Contemporary research on breast feeding, suggests that the isolation of the infant from the mother, as in many modern hospitals, may be wrong. Research by Montagu (1957) confirms the fact that the child should be allowed to nurse from the beginning. Research by Paul G. Gyorgy shows that the colostrum which is in the mother's breast prior to the flow of milk is necessary to the growth of microorganisms important to the infant, giving it resistance to disease. Cow's milk has only 1/13–1/15 the amount of fortification against disease as has human milk. He has gone so far as to call formula feeding criminal.

Montagu's research shows that, for the mother, the sucking of the infant immediately after birth sets up contractions in the uterus which help to constrict blood vessels, guard against postpartum hemorrhages, and cause the immediate detachment of the afterbirth and its ejection. This immediate nursing of the infant is nature's way of getting the uterus to return to normal size. The contractions in the uterus produced by nursing last as much as 20 minutes after the infant ceases sucking. Where nursing is delayed 20 hours or more, blood oozes into the uterine cavity, causing irregular spasmodic contractions. The mother whose baby has nursed immediately will not suffer afterbirth pains and will return more quickly to her prepregnant condition.

What is known as the "let-down reflex" in the mother may start the milk flowing even before the infant begins sucking. There is a definite erotic feeling in connection with this reflex that is a factor in the emotional bond between mother and child.

The contractions of the uterus which accompany nursing and continue even beyond the completion of the breast feeding seem to be of the same character as those experienced during orgasm in the sexual act. The nursing reaction, therefore, not only brings close contact with the child but also brings emotional and physical satisfaction to the mother. In many primitive cultures, nursing extends beyond a two-year period, in some as long as four or five years, perhaps accounting in part for the built-in security of the child.

On the other hand, the long-nursed primitive child may suffer great trauma when weaning time comes. When a new babe goes to the breast, he may feel greatly rejected. Today, the nursing period is confined to a few months, and the baby gradually shifts to soft foods. There is little trauma at weaning because it is so gradual and takes place well before a rival sibling enters the scene.

THE SECOND BABY

The following is the experience of a young couple, the father with a doctoral degree in sociology, the mother with a masters degree in psychology:

> Well, we seem to have weathered the worst of it; not without scars, however. Five weeks have passed and things are beginning to seem almost normal

again. Our problem came from the least expected source—not the baby, but our two-year-old, Sue. After two days of angelic behavior she hit the baby with a toy truck, grabbed her bottle and finished it off and the battle was on. Since then she has kept us under a more or less constant trial by fire—up late at night, at any and all hours of the night and at 5:30 or 6:00 every morning; temper tantrums, whining ill-humor, and all of the other horrible things that a child of mine "just wouldn't do." At the first signs of what was happening we hastily read all the books we should have read six months ago on the peculiarities of the two-year-old and sibling jealousy. Bill ended up playing mama to the baby, while I became a 24-hour-a-day mama to a very babylike Sue.

Within the last couple of days she has begun to get sick of me, which is the sign I've been waiting for, and to return to much of her former independent activity. If this is really about the end of it, I guess we've gotten off fairly easy, although the weeks since it began seem much more nearly like four months.

At the time the second pregnancy is known, preparation of the first child for the sibling's coming is highly important. This will be a momentous event in the life of the firstborn. He has had a world in which the affection of parents has been his exclusively. He cannot share his rights, privileges, and attention without a great deal of adjustment.

Parents must begin early by telling the child he is to have a brother or sister playmate and helping him to look forward to the coming of the baby with happy anticipation. This also will be a time for a new step in the sex education of the child. If he is old enough, he is certain to ask where babies come from, how they grow, who brings them, or some similar question which opens the way to explain that the baby grows inside the mother. When he asks how it gets out, the question must be answered by a simple statement such as, "through the birth canal," or "it comes out through a very special place that opens at that time." It is important that questions be answered honestly, up to the level of the child's understanding.*

When the mother returns from the hospital, full attention should be given to the child who has been left at home and not to showing off the new baby. As much attention must be given to him in the days following as is possible, to avoid jealousy and the development of aggression of the child toward the new baby. Even then a perfect relationship should not be taken for granted.

Factors Influencing Number of Children

This aspect of family life was very much in the lap of the gods historically. There was little control over reproduction, so the number of children was in ratio to the couple's fecundity and years married. Today, size of family reflects, in part, differences in values and goals and, to some extent, differences in self-control and ability to consistently pursue whatever ideal has been set for the size of the family.

---

*An interesting new development is the location of the maternity ward on the ground floor, with low windows, so the older child may visit his mother while she is in the hospital, and building the nursery on the outside wall, too, and with low windows, so the child can see his new brother or sister while the baby is in the hospital.

There is some evidence that family size is partly a matter of family tradition, for there seems to be a definite family-size relationship running through the generations. Children who come from large families tend to have large families. This is more true if the mother comes from a large family than if the father does, although it holds true somewhat for both. It seems also to hold for all social classes.

Census data on size of family by education show that those with the least education have the largest families; those with the most education, the smallest families. High school and college graduates tend to have small families. One must recognize, of course, that this association between education and size of family is a two-way relationship. Parents with a large number of children are able to give them less education, and therefore the large-family pattern persists. Families with a small number of children can educate their children, so the small-family pattern persists.

Another important variable in determining the number of children has been, and still is, to some extent, religion. The Catholic birth rate has been considerably higher than the Protestant, owing to restrictions placed on birth control by the Church.

Economic factors too have been operative. In Western society it is generally those least able to support children who have the largest families.* This is in part both cause and effect. The large family makes heavy economic demands, but on lower socioeconomic levels birth control techniques are less effective and motives less strong or less implemented.

With any couple, motives governing size of family are certain to be complex, being affected by family tradition, their scheme of values, the way children are viewed in fulfilling or hindering their life purpose. And even with the best resolves and technology, couples do have children they did not plan for.†

NUMBER OF CHILDREN AND QUALITY OF FAMILY LIFE

The number of children in a home has the effect of remaking it as an environment. It is a much different place with one child than, say, with six. It becomes a different environment for the parents and for the children. Both aspects of the problem have been studied.

Happiness of Parents   Happiness tends to decrease with the size of the family. Apparently the pressures of a large family detract from the ability of the couple to enjoy marriage. (Refer back to Chapter 19.) The ability of a couple to control the size of their family seems to be associated with happiness. In the case of many large families, they have failed in this objective and

---

*This issue is of current political concern. The issue now is whether the poor and the nonwhites among them, should be helped with birth control and sterilization by the use of public funds in order to help solve the recurrent problem of poverty through the generations.

†Lynn Landman (1968) claims the nation has 5,300,000 women age 18–44 in need of subsidized family planning. A program for this will cost $100 million a year.

are burdened with children they are not adequately equipped to care for, either emotionally or financially. In this group are undoubtedly many Catholics who have children they felt they could not in good conscience prevent.

Although couples in small families seem to be happier, they resort to divorce more readily if things go wrong. The writer compared divorce rates in large families (six or more children) and small families, using as a sample the parents of 4300 high school seniors and 1424 college students. In this sample only 6 percent of homes in families of six or more children were broken by divorce and 16 percent by death. In the broken only-child families, 11.5 percent had been broken by divorce, 10 percent by death. There was a 50–50 chance of divorce and death in the broken two- and three-child families.

Parent–child Relationships   An intensive study of 100 large families (Bossard and Boll 1956; Bossard and Sanger 1952) led researchers to a comparison of large families with the general small-family systems and to the development of some hypotheses concerning the characteristics of each. In the small family, planning is one of the basic characteristics, along with the spacing of children and a strong emphasis on child-rearing. Educational aspirations are high; the quest for status is conscious and deliberate, pointing toward a career for the child. Parenthood is intensive, with a great deal of professional care being given the child. In many cases, both parents are working; often the mother has a career-oriented personality. Family life is generally democratic, with the child having a voice in the family discussions. The full development of the child is the objective of the family atmosphere, so that the pattern is essentially one of cooperation, with the parent being conscious of numerous emotional problems of the child. The parent is always comparing his child with other children in the social group. There is great pressure on the child to measure up and great anxiety on the part of parents if the child fails to measure up. There is little discipline from siblings and little direct interaction between the child and other children. The child's resentments, because of his limited contacts, are directed against a few persons—often the parents. The same is true of his affections. In most conflict situations, it is two against one, rather than there being a large group in the conflict unit. In the small-family pattern, it may be one parent and child against the other parent—a struggle, in effect, between the parents for the favor of the child.

Summarizing the characteristics of the small family, Bossard and Sanger (1952) say:

> The small family rests upon the ideas of planning, individualization, democratic cooperation, social isolation and intensive pressures. The small family system is the quality system, chiefly at the middle-class level. Its driving force is one of ambition, in an open class system; its social justification, if one may thus speak of it, is that it represents an adjustment to a rapidly changing society, with its train of attendant insecurities.

These writers find that the large family is different in almost every respect and that it produces quite different personality types. Involved in the birth rate itself is a different philosophy of life. When the large family is intentional, it is usually a desire of either husband or wife, rather than of both. In nonplanned large families, children are accepted as a product of fate.

The large family provides an environment in which there are constant readjustments to the vicissitudes of life. Things are always happening in the large family, and there must be a constant shifting of roles, statuses, and responsibilities of various members to meet events. The family group is the unit of first concern in the large family, whereas in the small family the individual is the unit of concern. In the large family, each person's wishes are always subservient to those of the group. Sleeping arrangements, dress, dates, every aspect of living are limited by the economic resources, crowded conditions, and constant pressure of family members upon each other. The large family is more rigidly organized within and therefore tends to be more authoritarian, with one or more persons being dominant. A greater degree of executive direction and arbitrary control is necessary. This control is usually by the father or mother, but sometimes by an older sibling. Authoritarianism is almost an inevitable part of the large-family system. This, the writers suggest, is probably why the early American family was authoritarian in character.

This research also finds that in the large family there is a great deal more specialization of roles among family members. One girl may be a household drudge, a son may be a father substitute. One child may be a gadabout, one a whiner, another a tattletale, and so forth. Obviously such specialized roles cannot be played in the small family. The young child in the large family has fewer choices of roles, as many roles are already taken by the time he appears on the scene.

In the large family, parents and children are likely to be less demanding in attitude and less tolerant of neurotic tendencies of members than in the small family. It is impossible for the child in the large family to receive the much-emphasized individual attention so characteristic of family philosophy in small families. The crowded space of the home, it is believed, tends to lead young people to want to leave home early and to marry early.

The writer has been able to test some of these hypotheses further with a group of more than 4300 high school seniors and 1424 college students. This study gives statistical confirmation to many of the differences suggested by the Bossard and Sanger case studies. It was found that the large family (with six or more children) does tend to be authoritarian, the small family, democratic. The small family was found to be much more education-oriented than the large family. Even representatives of large families who finished high school and went to college were less academically oriented, had lower educational aspirations, and were less successful in their school performance. Those from large families were more certain they knew the vocation they wanted to go into, which probably indicated a limited range of choice rather than actual preparation for a wide range of choice (Paul Landis 1954).

Much evidence of economic pressure and home crowding was found in the large family. This is inevitable in a society where wages and salaries are based on individual performance alone, with no subsidy being made by industry or government for children. The boy from a large family adjusts well; girls from large families do not. In fact, girls from large families have more problems of adjustment in senior high school and college years than others. They are more often friendless or have few friends and seldom exercise leadership. Girls from the small family, particularly from the only-child family, are far superior in their adjustments as measured by number of friendships, number of activities, and leadership roles at this period in life to those from large families and, in fact, have a more prominent place in leadership than any other group.

Historically, this may not have been true. Formerly, the girl's life was submerged in the family. The modern girl who finishes high school, and particularly the girl who goes to college, is venturing far out into the individualistic world of contemporary life. She is sampling competitive values that were once the privilege of the male only. Her training in the individualistic family, under the small-family pattern, has led to the maximum of independence and self-sufficiency, and she has, therefore, formed her personality more appropriately for living in an individualistic society. The girl in the large family, by contrast, has had her personality so submerged in the family that she is not particularly well-fitted for the adjustments of our highly individualistic teen-age world.

It may well be that the personality deficiencies of the teen-age girl in the large family are due largely to the fact that she has been tied down with being an assistant mother or housekeeper to younger children. This is often the case with the older girl in the large family. She is thus hindered from making the plunge into her peer group at the puberty period. This may be for the girl what psychologists call a "critical period"; it must either be done then or she can never feel at home with her peers. In any case, we know that she tends to develop a feeling of friendlessness.

There is much evidence from our study of teen-agers that boys are never so submerged in the family as are girls and are seldom so completely subject to authoritarian patterns, regardless of family size. This is probably a factor in the adjustability of the boy by type of family background. The boy in the only-child family probably suffers from overmothering, making his adjustment outside the family difficult. He is also an only rival of his father for his mother's affection.

The problems faced by teen-agers in large families tend to be largely external in nature—schooling, living space, money, and vocational problems. The only child suffers more from problems that are introspective in character. He more often has problems in his relationships with family members, with his age mates, and in boy–girl relations. He also tends to have more problems in the area of morals and religion.

Elder and Bowerman (1963) studied the effect of family size and composition on child-rearing patterns with a sample of 1261 Protestant seventh-grade pupils. They found that with the increase in family size, the lower-class girl was more likely to perceive her father as being authoritarian and both parents as being less communicative, more controlling, and given more to physical punishment and less to praise than was the case in the smaller family. Among the boys, it was in the middle-class family that authoritarian traits more clearly emerged as the family pattern with increase in size: more physical punishment, more parental dominance, less communication.

Hawkes, Burchinal, and Gardener (1958) found that the small-family environment did not have a detrimental effect on the personalities of children they studied—a fifth-grade group. They found no evidence favoring the beneficial effects of the large family. Generally speaking, they concluded, children from the small family probably fare better psychologically than those from larger families. E. James Lieberman, formerly of the National Institutes of Health, has reviewed studies on size of family that have appeared over a period of many years. He concludes, "children from small families are, on the whole, more intelligent, more creative, more independent, taller, more energetic and healthier mentally and physically—all because parents have the leisure and resources to take good care of themselves as well as of their children" (Rosenfeld 1971). Nye and colleagues (1970) stated that in the largest proportion of cases the small family contains "the most satisfactory spouses, parents, and children."

SIBLING RELATIONSHIPS

There probably never was a family with more than one child in which a certain amount of jealousy, rivalry, and bickering, or hidden suffering, did not take place in the relationship between siblings. An early account of family relationships is the bitter jealousy between Cain and Abel, which led to murder. Joseph's relationship with his half-brothers is an account of the interplay of family relationships in a large patriarchal family—their envy of his coat of many colors given him by a doting father, their sale of him into bondage, his later forgiveness, when as a member of Pharaoh's household he was able to save them from famine. The Cinderella story and numerous other tales, as well as historical biography, tell of struggles, rivalries, jealousies, and resentments, as well as magnanimity of sibling relationships.

These relationships require insight on the part of parents. The nature of the sibling relationship is of lifelong importance. Jessie Bernard (1949), who has studied the literature on sibling relationships thoroughly, concludes her review with this statement:

> If, standing on a crowded street corner, we could see all the adults about us in terms of their sib relationships, we would see not the seemingly independent, self-resourceful individuals who pass before us, but rebellious little sisters fighting against parental discrimination, resentful little brothers hating older sisters whose superiority in age and maturity frustrated their male egos, jealous older sisters resenting the attention bestowed on little sisters, sisters of all ages envying the privileges of brothers of all ages. Most of us, on becoming closely acquainted with men and women of apparent maturity, have found that in certain aspects of their personalities they are still much under the influence of brother or sister, still smarting under childhood patterns. It does not matter that they are now successful in their own right; they must still convince brother or sister of their success. One man's whole life is spent in achieving goals which his sister unconsciously set for him years ago; he must prove to her that he can do it. One woman's life is shattered because of her ambivalent attitude of hatred and love for a brother who dominated her childhood (p. 312).

Parents cannot hope that children will be alike in temperament, disposition, or lovability or that each will be able to accept the other fully. Some children will live under the shadow of a brother or sister for a lifetime, even though they are far separated by marriage. Others carry in their personalities the experience of dominance or submission which was established early in life by a relationship with a brother or a sister. This may affect their choice of a mate. Still others will carry a long resentment against a sibling, always fighting against anyone who interferes with their development because they are still subconsciously fighting a dominating brother or sister.

The autobiographies of college students describe sibling influences as a determining force in the development of their personalities. Take, for example, the young person who has suffered from an overshadowing relationship with a domineering or brilliant brother or sister and who has literally shaped his life in the sibling's image. Some describe how painful and discouraging such a relationship is as they continue to live under this shadow, even when they go to school, being faced by their teachers all the way from grade school to college with the record of an older brother or sister who happened to achieve high standards. Such a person may never get over the feeling of inferiority and hostility this constant unfavorable comparison has brought.

Parents can do much to keep down the bitterness and rivalries between children in the family, but wisdom and understanding and a great deal of patience are required. The best book which has come to the writer's attention for giving insight and removing anxiety of parents in the little rivalries and difficulties that normally develop in the family is that by Edith G. Neisser, *Brothers and Sisters* (Harper & Bros, 1951).

Adoption

For couples who cannot have children because of incapacity or because they do not choose to because of undesirable genetic characteristics, adoption offers a way to parenthood. There has been a relaxing of too stern adoption laws, so that now single women can adopt and in certain instances, single men. Matching parent and child by religion, race, and physical type are being discarded as requirements.

Although adoption of the age and type of child wanted may not be easy because of shortages of children available, there is always a long list waiting among the nonwhite and mixed groups, those with some defect, and the older group. In the case of any adoption, prospective parents must be aware of their own feelings, fears, and resentments, and it is especially necessary that they be when adopting from the leftover group. Often much loving and patience is necessary with any child who is old enough to have formed previous attachments to a mother or mother figure.

It is generally believed that the sound procedure in handling an adopted child is to make his adoption clear to him from the time he is able to first understand it. By frank handling of the situation, without overdoing it, the child will develop normally and naturally without any anxiety about the situation—probably, in fact, with less anxiety than many children who feel insecure with their natural parents. Many of the latter at times day-dream that they are adopted.

1   Childlessness in marriage may result from physical or emotional factors, sterility, voluntary control of pregnancy, continued delaying of parenthood, or the conviction of one mate that children are undesirable. Under which of these circumstances do you think a childless marriage will most likely remain happy? Under which circumstances is the marriage most likely to be doomed?

2   Cases X and Y below are taken from a marriage counselor's file. In the first of the two cases the counselor advised the couple to consider seriously having a child; in the second, he discouraged parenthood. After studying the cases discuss:

   a   Why the counselor advised as he did.

   b   Whether his advice seems justified.

   c   What the future of the two marriages will probably be if the couples follow the counselor's advice.

   d   What the future of the two marriages will be if the couples do not follow the counselor's advice relative to having a child.

      Case X: Wife and husband, aged 26 and 30, respectively. Married six years. Report that, while still compatible and in love, marriage seems to be losing its joy. Both feel despondent and sad. Wife reported, "We just don't have anything to stay married for or even to stay alive for, for that matter." Couple childless because their financial circumstances would not, as husband puts it, "allow us to raise the children with the advantages we would want them to have."

      Case Y: Wife and husband aged 25 and 27, respectively. Married three years, during which they have separated briefly twice but have not considered divorce because of religious convictions of wife. Report that, while they occasionally enjoy things together, marriage has lost much of its meaning. Wife wants to continue working but husband disapproves of a wife's earning money. Husband thinks wife would "settle down" if she had a child. Wife is unsure but tends to think that the way to save their marriage is for both of them to work and make money "so we can start having some fun again."

3   *Sociodrama:* A wealthy but conservative young wheat grower sells his farm, moves to New York, and later becomes engaged to a young office worker. Dramatize a scene in which they disagree about how long they should wait before having their first child. Let their backgrounds, role conceptions, and values determine the arguments they present.

4   A man and his wife in looking back at their early months with their two children admit: "Actually they were both very much alike—neither cried excessively, neither was sick or unusually demanding, both followed much the same sleeping and eating schedules. Why then," they wonder, "did the first seem like such a terrible problem? How could it have so disrupted our lives and spoiled our relationship when the second seemed so angelic and undemanding?" How would you explain the difference in the way they felt about the two infants who acted so much alike?

5   Do you consider the role of the mother or that of the father more important in child-rearing? Do you believe it is unnecessary, rather silly, or very important for men to be formally prepared for their roles as fathers? Why?

6   In terms of social and psychological (rather than economic) advantages, what size family do you consider ideal? What, if any, are the advantages of growing up in a very large family? What, if any, are the advantages of being an only child or one of two children?

7   When couples are unable to have children, adoption is considered by many to be a desirable alternative. Why should couples be urged to think long and hard about the disadvantages of adoption when childlessness is their only alternative?

BRINGING UP
CHILDREN

26

In the nuclear family, the socialization of the child is dependent too much on the central figure of the home, the mother. If she is too young, too soon shifts to the role of worker and fails to provide an adequate caretaker, is too neurotic or frustrated by her confinement to the home, is cruel or demanding, irrational or cold, there is no other person to turn to as in joint family systems. Some groups justify communal living in terms of its advantage to the child. There is a broader base for socialization and for achieving emotional security. It is unlikely that communal living will take hold enough for this to be a solution. Peter Neuberger (Cadden, 1971) has suggested another possible solution which may in time come to be— an inventory of the child's developmental needs would be taken early in life and social support would be given to the mother if she fell short of meeting these needs.

NO ONE BEST WAY

The way children are trained is a part of folk wisdom in all cultures, and, therefore, methods are transmitted through the generations without much reasoning about consequences of methods used to arrive at the end product. For some time our society has struggled to replace folk wisdom in child training with scientific wisdom. This is not an easy thing to do, and it has not been done effectively.*

Learned theories have not been constant. New research has brought changes with great rapidity. Different social classes accept the new with differing degrees of readiness, and there are always critics who challenge the validity of the new as a means of justifying their clinging to the old. The teacher in the college classroom still finds two attitudes prevailing: (1) I want to treat my children as my parents treated me; or (2) I am not going to bring up my children like my parents brought me up. In making these statements, students are commenting on methods of discipline, their parents' ways of informing them about sex, and other such specific matters.

The fact that students still tend to think in terms of folk wisdom does not necessarily mean that they are uninterested in what has been learned in child psychology and child development. They are interested but try to fit the new knowledge in with what folklore has given them. Which will predominate in the training of their children is problematic. Perhaps most will make a combination of both, as they must do when man and wife bring two family cultures to bear on the rearing of their children.

It is doubtful that many young people are fully aware how much the way they handle, teach, and discipline their children will have to do with the kind of people they become in capacity to love, learn, and function well in the society of which they become a part. The parent literally forms the child's self-image. Few societies have placed so much responsibility on the pair, and particularly the mother, for doing the job alone during the most critical early years as ours has. The joint family provides many teachers and disciplinarians. Western cultures once had more kinfolk in the home, and servants and "nannies" to share child training.

Few cultures have provided such a rich environment outside the home, so that by the teen years most of the training is by agencies which supplement the family. Even though the young mother has many professional guides, they do not always quiet her anxiety as to whether she is doing the right thing. Sometimes they give her a guilty conscience because she does not live up to the best she reads or hears about, but she is not likely to run to her mother for assurance and comfort in solving her problems. The college woman, particularly, is likely to trust the guides who speak with the voice of scientific authority.

The leading cultures of the world have a great variety of child-training methods. The end product in adulthood is quite different, of course. Englishmen, Germans, Japanese, Frenchmen, and Tahitians are made by the way infants and children are handled. The product may be a stern, unaffectionate administrator, an overly disciplined military type, or an affectionate, home-loving, domestically oriented type who loves and is loved by the opposite sex.

The differences in training begin at birth. Tight wrapping in swaddling clothes may be customary; there the child lies bound hand and foot for two to three days. Being tucked in beside the mother's warm body and given the

---

*Comment based on the writer's experience in reading thousands of anonymous student autobiographies and class discussions.

breast immediately may be the custom, or the child may be separated by a glass cage in the hospital, comforted by the sounds of a tape-recorded heart beating out the pulselike rhythm to which he was accustomed in the womb.

No people has a panel of experts in child psychology and child development sit down and try to picture the kind of man and woman they want or need in the next generation and then outline steps to achieve the product desired. In sort of a vague way cultures do this, and so does every pair of parents.

Parents want bright children, able to meet intellectual challenges. They want their children well enough mannered to function in social relations and in work situations. They want children who know the moral rules, and practice sexual restraints and social etiquette sufficiently to become dependable community members and eventually marriage partners and parents.

The American philosophy of child training, for instance, is in direct contrast at many points to that of certain European societies. In France and England the visitor gets the impression that children are reared by tea-time etiquette and are made young adults from the very beginning. The French child meets his schoolmate on the street and shakes hands with him as an adult would do. An English boy will ask his boyfriend in for tea in midafternoon. Adult standards of etiquette and behavior seem to prevail. British training methods are stern, perhaps a carryover from the day when the British upper-class male was trained to rule the empire.

In the United States, children are seldom thought of or treated as miniature adults. They are credited with different standards, values, and interests. They are treated as children, and adults are very much surprised if they do not act as such. Scandinavian cultures conceive of childhood in much the same way. The world of a child is believed to be a world of play and independent activity. He is not expected to live entirely, or even primarily, by the manners, codes, and restraints of adults, or to share in their responsibilities and problems. He is to have a warm and affectionate relationship with parents, but otherwise live in a child's world. His attachment to parents is emotional and affectional, whereas the child in other European societies tends to be reared in an attitude of respect, honor, and obedience to parents, much as in the patriarchal family of America some generations ago.

The British want their children quiet, clean, polite, and respectful of adults. They are left outdoors for long periods unattended in perambulators as infants. Their crying is ignored. The child is often left to the care of a "nanny." Even guests of the family do not see the children. They are kept out of the way. By our standards they are "repressed, unresponsive, and unchildlike" (Wintour 1964). It is still the practice of many families to send the child "off to school," which means off to live in a boarding school at an early age. By the age of eight, the boy's training is usually taken over by male schoolmasters.

A study of the home life of 158 children in Milwaukee suggests that there are a great variety of practices and ways of doing things in families within the United States and that good adjustment is associated with no particular technique. Some of the factors that are generally associated with good adjustment, however, are love and affection, wanted, appreciated, trusted, accepted as a person, and looked upon with respect as individuals.

It must always be kept in mind that personality formation is a continuous and never-ending process; that it goes on throughout childhood and the teen years into adulthood; and that forces outside the family have their part in it.

THE LOVE ANCHOR

Love is the basis for feeling secure, as was discussed in Chapter 9. Without it the world is an unfriendly place. Psychologists believe that a sense of belonging is established by relationships with those closest to the child, the mother or mother substitute during the first two or three years of life. If a mother by affection makes her child feel that he is wanted and important to her, he acquires a sense of security which carries over to other relationships. If, on the other hand, she is irritable or hostile and makes him feel that he is unwanted, he develops a sense of insecurity which is difficult to eradicate in later years.

Socialization begins early with the body warmth and loving care of the mother or mother figure. By five or six months of age, a child differentiates between the mother and others to the extent that her absence brings separation anxiety. Up to about three years of age, he has such an undeveloped sense of time that her short absences give him great anxiety. After the child is three, she can begin to increase the length of her absences.

Spock (1963) observes that it is at about five months that the baby begins to discriminate between familiar and strange people. From this time on, through three years of age, he needs a familiar figure for love, comfort, approval, play, gentle kidding, and curbing. Spock feels that this is the critical time of socialization, when the child gets his self-image, which builds in him a sense of being a good or bad person, of a world that is hostile or loving. After three, he believes, the child can be left by the mother in the care of a reliable substitute without anxiety being provoked.

Spitz (1949) finds that if emotional deprivation starts late in the third quarter of the first year, a condition develops which resembles depression in the adult. If the deprivation lasts no longer than three months, reestablishment of sociality is possible. If it lasts longer than five months, no improvement is shown after restoration of social contacts.

THE DEVELOPMENTAL GOAL

The current emphasis in child training is developmental, not regimental. It is assumed that natural growth should be encouraged and directed, but not suppressed. Initiative is to be encouraged rather than curbed. Human nature is good, not evil.

In our culture it has been easy for parents to accept a negative view of human nature and to curb their natural impulse to love the child. Our culture is rooted in a theological conception which held that human nature is evil, that the child is born in sin, and that before he can be good his nature must be changed. A maxim of parental training of an earlier day held that the child is by nature willful, sinful, and carnal, that before goodness could even begin, his will had to be broken. "Spare the rod and spoil the child" was one expression of this philosophy.

Scientific study of human nature leaves no basis for such a view of child-hood. Gesell and Ilg (1946) declare, "The intrinsic charm and goodness of childhood still constitute the best guarantee of the perfectability of mankind" (p. 453). They further observe, "The most ameliorative force ... is an intensified conservation of the development of infants and children" (p. 454). Here we see an expression of the scientific view: That human nature is to be accepted, cultivated, developed, and brought to its full potentialities. Good and bad are in the training system, not in the nature of the child.

Maslow has criticized child training which employs fear, punishment, withholding love, and threat of abandonment. He finds that children and adults who feel safe, loved, and respected were trained by positive rather than negative methods. They were taught to please, to make others happy; they were taught truth, logic, justice, consistency, right, and duty. Their personalities were not built in an atmosphere of anxiety, fear, insecurity, guilt, or shame but in one where reality, fair play, fitness, beauty, and rightness were stressed.

Maslow (1954) sees need for nourishing goodness in human nature, not negative and suppressive tactics, as the route to desirable character. Rather than seeing child–parent relationships as a chance primarily to make mistakes, as a set of problems, he sees them as "a pleasure and a delight, a great opportunity to enjoy."

The Self-Image

Self-image is formed very early, mainly during the first three years of life, as was shown in Chapter 8. It is largely the product of relationships with the mother during the period from five months to three years of age. It is she who makes the child feel he is good or bad, accepted or rejected, that the world is hostile or friendly. Self-image is added to and modified later by others in the primary group, and as the child ventures outside the family, by secondary groups, but the foundation is laid very early.

Freud and his followers no doubt made too much of toilet training as a factor in determining the trend of personality development. The significant fact may well be that the control of elimination is taught during the critical period of socialization. It is then that the attitudes of the mother toward the child have so much to do with the building of his self-image. Whether the child will be a confident and assured person or a fearful and guilt-ridden one depends very much on the mother's early treatment of him.

It is important that the child have self-esteem if he is to meet life with courage and vigor. Lacking this he is cringing in his attitude, fearful of new experiences and new challenges. If the self-image given by parents is that the child is bad, there is a tendency to live up to expectations. Studies in the field of delinquency show that self-image is an important factor in the route a child takes. Those with a good self-image from the family can be insulated against delinquency even in areas where a delinquent subculture makes violating the law seem natural for most.

A Climate for Growth

Few young people realize how much the intellectual growth of their child, the manners and morals, the character formation, the response to responsibility will depend on their attitude toward the child from the date of his birth, in fact, from the time of his conception. Every prospective parent needs a course in child development. But a brief review of some of the developments in the area of child training here will at least give a start toward incorporating current concepts. Every young mother must have some of the vision of the one who said, "I've lived all my life to be ready for this time: *to teach my children the things I have learned that will help them be what they can be.*"

Aspiration Level

Parents do most to set the aspiration level for their children, as they do the patterns of creativity and adventure. Whether a child expects great things of himself or the mediocre is determined in large part by parental expectations and their ways of expressing them. The way the child's imagination and curiosity are treated in the home will have much to do with his mental and emotional growth. Far too often parents dismiss the child's imaginative activities, stories, and dreams in such a way that he becomes discouraged and falls back into the routine which most human beings follow. His "silly ideas" may well have been the ones that indicated a spirit of creativity and originality.

The National Merit Scholarship tests for high school students seek evidence of creativeness in the persons considered. No longer are grades the sole measure for college entrance in even the most exclusive universities.

If one wants to develop a genius, he will do it by encouraging the maximum learning and by encouraging the child's ventures rather than scorning them. Genius is, in part, the product of a home which frustrates least and which provides maximum stimuli toward growth. Children tend to become what parents expect them to become and what parents trust them to become.

Intellectual Growth

One of the most important lessons learned in the study of poverty during the last half of the 1960s was that poverty brings intellectual blight. "Head Start" was a courageous effort to introduce corrective measures. The 1960s brought to focus study on the learning of the very young child. Discoveries have been revolutionary.

Response to stimuli begins in the womb. It is now believed that 20 percent of the child's basic abilities are developed before his first birthday. The most rapid period of learning of his lifetime is the preschool years. By the age of four, he will have gained half of his basic abilities and intellectual growth (White 1971).

From the very beginning, the infant needs an environment rich in sights, sounds, colors, textures, heat and cold, light and darkness; and, as soon as there are toys, articles which offer a great variety of manipulative possibilities.

He needs to lie on his stomach and squirm and reach, twist neck and body. He needs as much freedom from clothing and playpens as can be permitted in order to explore his world and try out his senses. Much is learned by touch, and he should therefore be given a wide variety of textures, coarse and smooth, wet and dry, hot and cold, so that his senses may experience the full range. Objects are tested by his lips, where sensation is most acute (Hunt 1961).

During long periods in bed when he is awake, he should be in a lighted room so that he can learn to focus his eyes and study objects about him, their color and form. There can be no visual learning in darkness. Colors in wide range should be presented to him. Exposure to a wide variety of sounds is important to the cultivation of the auditory sense. He should be read to and talked to, long before he can speak. Learning is going on, even though he can give no vocal response. He learns words long before he can speak. His mind is like a computer, processing information. A wide range of foods and odors are important to cultivating the sense of taste and smell. Different food textures and temperatures are important in the learning process. The infant exhausts the learning potential of most toys in a minute or so, according to critics of toys. As soon as he has seen their color, felt them, tried them in his mouth, their learning value is gone. They offer little chance for manipulation.

Opportunities for wide use of the senses give the child a head start in learning and are important to his development.

The parents need not push the child into learning. It is enough to provide rich opportunity. He already has the motive if it is encouraged, and capacity for learning is unlimited. It was once thought that early learning might damage the child and that those who started later would surpass him. Not so. A head start means a permanent advantage. The whole idea of the national project "Head Start" is based on the knowledge that those who have limited exposure to experience and vocabulary during the preschool years are already seriously handicapped in school competition.

By 1973 protest voices were being raised about the irreversibility of early learning deprivation. Jerome Kagan, of Harvard University, addressing the American Association for the Advancement of Science, declared that "intellectual development is much more plastic and reversible than anyone has surmised." He based his conclusion partly on studies in Guatemala where children without much development in the early years are considered normal, but who none-the-less develop very rapidly when exposed to learning. He feels that part of the problem with American children is the negative attitude of teachers toward children entering school without previous learning. They are not expected to be capable of learning and, therefore, do not learn.

Exceptional Ability

Terman's *Genetic Studies of Genius,* which took a large group of high-ability children and followed them through into productive life, making periodic studies of their life adjustments and achievements, banished the old myths that genius is a form of insanity, "Early ripe, early rot," "Usually one-sided in talent."

The group was high in scholarly achievement, and also in life activities generally. Their high creativity shows up early, and the myth that geniuses are often dull later in school and early in life is found to be just that—a myth. Terman concluded that although children of high ability should not be pushed through school, they should be allowed to progress more rapidly than others so they can move into productive after-school life while at the peak of youthful creativity.*

The most recent follow-up of Terman's gifted group of children, first studied in 1921–1922, found that family environment, and not genius mentality, was a major factor in differential lifetime achievement of the 100 most successful and 100 least successful (Oden 1968). The parental home, in providing emotional stability, in giving motivation and encouragement, seems to be most important in the actual achievement of children of genius capacity.

A composite picture of the home in which genius grows to its maximum potential, as judged by these findings, is one where parents:

1   Place a high value on education.

2   Encourage independence and initiative.

3   Expect a high level of accomplishment.

4   Provide an atmosphere of security and emotional stability.

5   Encourage perseverance, self-confidence, motivate toward leadership, friendships, academic success, excellence in work, and recognition for accomplishment.

Here are a few hints that may help the child in the direction of creative development:

1   Treat the child's questions with respect.

2   Encourage his imagination.

3   Show him that his ideas have value.

4   Let him do things experimentally within the limits of safety.

5   Let him create things for himself.

6   Remember that undirected play is highly creative. As Suttie (1952) has said, "Necessity is not the mother of invention, play is."

GOOD SENSE IN CHILD TRAINING

Being informed about the latest theories is important, as is knowing general stages in child growth and development. Yet every child is very much an individual and has his own distinct problems of growing up and of making adjustments to the family, brothers and sisters, his own age group, and adults outside the family. These adjustments may not follow in the order the parents think they should, and they may not all be made without pain on the part of the

*See Terman (1966) for a summary of his lifelong studies of superior children; see also Lewis (1966).

child and considerable anxiety on the part of the parent. Life is not abnormal when this is so. A lot of trial and error goes into the formation of a personality—difficulties are the norm.

Parents must have confidence that growth itself will work wonders in the experience of the child. The adjustment that he finds so difficult to make at a particular time in his development may be made almost automatically and as a matter of course as he acquires a little more age and experience. Time itself will cure many of his problems.

Neither do parents need to have great anxiety that some serious period of maladjustment in the child's early life is going to maim him permanently as a human being. Personality is a constantly growing and developing affair. Many of the mistakes of the past can be corrected and many of the wounds that have been suffered through rather severe periods of maladjustment can be healed by time. The child's confidence and assurance can be rebuilt as his path into the future is plotted with greater certainty.

Growth and development are most amazing phenomena and very interesting to watch. The parent, if he is not overly anxious, will see in his child's growth and maturation the fascinating and miracle-working power of nature as it transforms the personality with age and experience. A few parental blunders are not going to ruin a child. These are merely some of the bumps he experiences in growing up. It is the long-persistent, seemingly incurable situations in the environment that work the damage, not the little day-to-day ups and downs that are characteristic of the normal experience of childhood.

PROBLEMS

1 Most child-training authorities agree with Father Flanagan's observation, "There is no such thing as a bad boy." Why then is discipline considered essential in training children?

2 In using the word "discipline," people often mean very different things. Give a definition and example of at least two different usages.

3 Hill Street is a busy thoroughfare lined with middle-class homes. In the 900 block there are three houses on the north side of the street and in each there is a child under two years of age. These youngsters frequently play together on one of their lawns while their mothers sit together talking and watching them play. The children, of course, are too young to know about the dangers of the traffic on Hill Street so they frequently venture out toward the exciting highway. When this happens the mothers react in very different ways.

Analyze the typical behavior of each mother described below, and discuss it in terms of:

a Effectiveness in controlling child's behavior.

b Effectiveness in controlling child's future behavior.

c Effect of behavior on child–mother relationship.

d Theory of behavior on child–mother relationship.

Mother A: Runs after child, screaming "Don't!" Grabs the child and spanks it. Repeats this if child goes out again.

Mother B: Calls out in frightening voice, "Don't you go out there. If you do a big car will hit you and kill you." If child continues, mother pulls her back to middle of lawn. Repeats this ritual if child starts out again.

Mother C: Says nothing. When child reaches a certain point, mother calls pleasantly, "Mary," to get her attention. If child does not return, mother goes out and takes her hand and watches the cars. If child wants to go nearer street, mother picks her up and carries her back to center of lawn without saying anything. Repeats this action whenever necessary.

4 Read pages 253–60, entitled "Discipline," in Benjamin Spock's *Baby and Child Care.* What are Spock's views on punishment? Do you think he is correct in his evaluation of its effectiveness?

5 Two very healthy, high-spirited, inquisitive young boys are handled in two very different ways. Both are described by their parents as "difficult to manage."

One is encouraged in his inquisitiveness, urged ahead in all physical activity, and given maximum freedom within the limits of health and safety. The other boy's parents try to curtail his excesses by discouraging his constant questions, and trying to channel his interests into reading. They do not punish him physically, but rebuke him frequently for his tactlessness and forwardness, and remind him that, "where choices are concerned, we know what is best." Which boy is most likely to:

a Be an unmanageable adult?

b Respect his parents most?

c Develop antisocial energy outlets?

d Develop a distaste for reading?

e Be most successful as an adult in terms of leadership and achievement?

6 A well-meaning young mother has read that "permissiveness" is the best method in child-rearing. She feels that she should do what the authorities say is best for the child, but secretly she feels that a good spanking is what her child needs most. What are the dangers of attempting to administer a system of discipline in which one does not sincerely believe? What course would you advise this parent to follow?

7 *Sociodrama:* The scene opens a moment after Mary's 12-year-old. daughter, Jean, has rushed out of the room screaming at her mother, "I hate you! I hate you! I hate you! You're the meanest person I know!"

Mary's mother-in-law, who has witnessed the scene, says, "Call that child back and punish her on the spot. She can't be allowed to talk to you that way. Why, when I was a child. . . ."

Mary interrupts, "I'll do nothing of the sort, Mother. You probably felt just as Jean does many times when you were young, and it would have been better if you hadn't been punished for expressing what you felt."

Let the drama picture the two philosophies of discipline held by the two women. Try to show both philosophies in a sympathetic light.

CHILD DISCIPLINE

27 In the college classroom and in student autobiographies, it becomes clear that male and female subcultures lack a unified perspective on child discipline. Girls are brought up on women's magazines, many have had courses in some aspects of child development, and some have had both training and experience in baby-sitting or in nursery-school management. They are more likely to have a developmental, democratic approach to child training than is the college male, who is confident about his opinions, which are more often derived from folklore or from his own parental home. Often as not, he seems quite as sure of his opinions as a child-rearing expert as the more informed college woman he is going to marry.

This too often means conflict ahead, or else the wife and mother is going to have to take charge and educate the husband along with the baby. As the child gets older, inconsistency and uncertainty make for insecurity in the child. He has difficulty knowing what is expected of him.

The transition from authoritarian methods to the developmental, democratic methods is the basis for much of the conflict. The one parent operates on the philosophy that responding to the child's need and making him an equal partner in the family relationship is important to the development of the young personality. The other assumes that such efforts amount to nothing more than pampering and spoiling the child. The one assumes, for example, that crying indicates discomfort and need and that the baby should be picked up and patted until he burps; the other believes he should be allowed to cry it out and not be pampered and petted lest he become a demanding tyrant, not realizing that the demanding, "spoiled" older child is one suffering from lack of loving care, not overattention. As the infant becomes a child, the father operates under the ordering-and-forbidding technique, which has come down from time immemorial; the mother believes in consideration for the child's wishes and approves of reasoning with him and attempting to understand him. The one believes in punishment; the other believes in correction by nonpunitive methods. The father is more likely to tend toward a harsh extreme in the handling of the child, which the mother considers to be frightening and shocking. In extreme cases, neither parent has any sympathy toward the approach of the other in child care.

In such families, the husband should visit nurseries and nursery schools to learn how children are properly handled, or he should read some of the better books on child development to know the outcome of different systems of discipline, or he should retire from the administrative situation, leaving it to the better-trained wife. Certainly, unless one or the other can change, the marriage is in for turmoil, as well as the children being in for a rough time during their critical years. A day's visit to the college nursery school can be an eye-opener for the average college man. There he can see democratic methods of child discipline in practice.

Young wives with just a smattering of information on permissive child-rearing are often attracted to the method without understanding its full implications or recognizing the degree of thought and effort it requires. Above all it should be understood that this is not a "do-nothing" approach. It does not mean that the mother can stand aside and let the child rear itself, so to speak. Slapping a youngster's hands or shouting "No!" every time he does something wrong is much easier than calmly and repeatedly restraining him until he understands and accepts certain limits. Patience, tact, and ability to see the world as your child must see it are important prerequisites to success in developmental training. All parents ought to get down on their hands and knees occasionally and see how different the world looks to a child who cannot even see what is on the table.

There is much more to the theory behind modern practices than can be set forth in this chapter. All young couples owe it to themselves and to their unborn children to look into the literature before attempting parenthood. "Gentle discipline" can easily deteriorate into "no discipline at all," and a great deal of behavior which may be lastingly detrimental to the young person is often countenanced in the name of "progressive child training."

PARENTAL AUTHORITY

All social control begins in the family. The pattern of family authority is shaped to fit the parents' conception of what the child must become to function in the adult society of his time. The parent is provided with a general framework of patterned behavior by which to be guided. In simple cultures, where each institution and where each group hold like conceptions, the task is an easy one. In complex cultures where institutional patterns are different in their emphasis and where many groups have different expectations of their members, the parents' task is a difficult one indeed.

No society has a place for the individual who ignores all authority. Those who fail to recognize the authority of the law find themselves outcasts or in institutions for the delinquent and criminal. Those who fail to accept the ethical or religious standards and customs of their group may find themselves in moral confusion. Those who fail to recognize that every game has to be played according to its rules find themselves maladjusted in many situations, at odds with their fellows, and in discord with the general tenor of social life.

The child who has never known authority is of all children most unhappy. Adulthood assumes a willingness to recognize the rights and wishes of others and to assume one's share of the load of human responsibilities. The child who grows up without ever having recognized that every human being has obligations to others is not ready to face the compulsory restrictions of an adult society happily.

Margaret Mead (1930; 1939) has described the experience of children of the Manus tribe, primitives on the island of New Guinea. There, children are allowed to grow up with almost no restriction by parents or elders, carefree, and with their every wish indulged by the adults of the group. In adolescence they are initiated into adulthood, a state in which men and women everywhere have to recognize social control and assume their share of the world's duties. These young people enter adulthood sorrowfully and always look back upon their childhood as the happy period of their lives.

Disciplinary failure brings much anguish to the parent and disaster to the child, for discipline is a necessary part of effective socialization. There is no place in society for the undisciplined. They must be banished, caged in prison, or otherwise removed for the safety of the group.

THERE IS NO PERFECT DISCIPLINARY RECIPE

No society has developed the perfect disciplinary system. All produce their misfits. And all pay the price of dealing with the unsocialized portion of each generation. Ours has no perfect disciplinary system and no universal disciplinary techniques by which success in this step in socialization may be assured. Theories are not lacking, and new ones are always in the making. A part of the problem is that society now changes so rapidly that parents are often unsure of the kind of end product they want.

Most any kind of discipline is better than none at all. In the United States it differs markedly between the social classes. Kohn and Carroll (1960) found that "to the middle-class parents, it is of primary importance that a child be able to decide for himself how to act, and that he have personal resources to act on these decisions—to working-class parents ... it is of primary importance that the child act reputably, that he not transgress the proper rules."

A survey of over 400 mothers in Chicago gave a revealing picture of differences between the traditional and modern groups' conceptions of their role as mothers and the goals to be achieved in child training (Duvall 1946).

Those who held the traditional concept, considered their functions to be those of (1) keeping house, (2) taking care of the child's physical needs, (3) training him to regularity, and (4) disciplining him and teaching him obedience and goodness.

Mothers with a modern concept of parenthood considered their function to be a developmental one; they felt that they should (1) train the child for self-reliance and citizenship, (2) see to his emotional well-being, (3) help him develop socially, (4) provide for his mental growth, (5) guide him with understanding, (6) give him love and affection, (7) be calm, cheerful, growing persons themselves.

The first group of mothers thought the child should be judged by whether or not he (1) was neat and clean, (2) was obedient and respectful of adults, (3) pleased adults, (4) respected property, (5) was religious, (6) worked well, (7) fitted into the family program.

The second group of mothers felt they were succeeding as mothers if the child (1) was healthy and well, (2) shared and cooperated with others, (3) was happy and contented, (4) loved and confided in his parents, (5) was eager to learn, (6) was growing as a person.

Obviously these concepts of motherhood are far apart in practice and basic philosophy, yet they are both part of the American scene. The first is more common among the lower classes; the second, among the middle and upper classes; the first, among the uneducated; the second, among the educated; the first, among large families; the second, among small families.

The father's role is also changing. As shorter working hours provide for greater interaction between father and child, the role of fatherhood becomes an increasingly important one. He is no longer primarily the stern disciplinarian. Yet, many fathers today still conceive of their function in terms of the traditional pattern. Like their fathers before them, they willingly leave child-rearing to their wives but consider themselves the final authority in any uncertain situation or in circumstances where the mother's methods prove inadequate. Traditionally the father's chief function was that of providing for the physical support of the family. He entered into the world of the children also as a disciplinarian when the mother asked for help. His attitude toward the children was likely to be one of impatient tolerance rather than understanding companionship. He did not pretend to understand the child or his special needs and did not feel that such understanding was his responsibility. He, like the old-fashioned mother, was inclined to judge children in terms of the children's effect upon his own life, reputation, and comfort. He believed that children have been properly handled if they are obedient, respectful, and useful.

The father with the modern concept of parenthood willingly accepts a much more complex and involved role for himself. He is likely to differentiate very little between the mother's duties in child training and those he himself accepts. He is concerned about each step in his child's development and assumes that he can and must play an important part in it. He considers himself less the disciplinarian and more the companion of his children. He is likely to plan his hours with them not around ritualized activities but around play, hobbies, and other enjoyable pursuits.

While the mother in most modern families must of necessity still take chief responsibility for the actual rearing of the children, present-day fathers generally desire to play as active a part as their time and energy permit. When working hours are long, this may mean that their chief influence over their children is an indirect one—the result of plans and policies agreed upon by husband and wife in late evening talks and put into practice by the wife. Whenever possible, however, most modern couples agree that every effort should be made to provide situations in which father and child can develop an intimate and companionable relationship. Some young men even consider the amount of leisure time for family life a major factor in the selection of a vocation or a particular job.

Although the more favored socioeconomic classes have likely acquired an improved philosophy of child-rearing and may more often practice a democratic type of family administration, some believe that during infancy and early childhood parents of the lower classes are more permissive than are parents of the middle classes. Dale's (1946) study shows that in the middle class (which social-class experts often refer to as the frustrated class), fewer children are breast fed than in the other social classes. In this class, too, three times as many children were thumb-suckers as in the other social classes. It was found that the middle class trains children in bowel and bladder control earlier than do the other classes. In general, the disciplinary pattern throughout childhood was found to be more rigid in the middle than in the lower classes. This study was conducted some time ago with small samples and by personal interviews in which 48 middle-class mothers and 52 lower-class mothers were studied. The middle-class group was selected from nursery schools and child-study groups. The families of both social classes had only normal children. The author expresses the belief that the disciplinary regime employed by the middle class tends to condition the child toward frustration and anxiety. The lower-class infant, by contrast, is permitted a more natural and spontaneous development.

While these results may be taken as suggestive, they should not be accepted as conclusive. The culture has shifted from the view that the infant and the child should be handled by the cold Watsonian techniques of an earlier generation to the view that warm "rooming-in," "self-demand" feeding, and a permissive pattern are the only safe ones. The new approach assumes that discomfort and denial lead to frustration and frustration to a neurotic condition. The new method, like the old, must be taken on faith and the outcome observed in the development of the child.

Parents who still cling tenaciously to yesterday's methods generally do so out of a certain distress at the new or because they have linked their child-training philosophy with religious convictions and justified their practices on moral grounds rather than by their practical results. Those who feel a strong attachment to the methods their own parents or grandparents used need to understand that, while suited to the world and values of yesterday, the authoritarian pattern does not adequately prepare young people for life in modern times.

The goal of yesterday's training system was to make of the child a working member of the household at as early an age as possible. This meant that he was taught to work. He began with simple chores and each year was given an increasing share of the household work load. With work playing so important a part in the child's life, discipline was necessarily strong. A heavy hand was needed to channel energies away from play into routine duties.

Except on farms, and even there to a lesser extent than in the past, children are no longer valued in terms of their ability to make an immediate contribution to the family's economic well-being. Child-labor legislation has eliminated children from industry and greatly limited the number of jobs in which young teen-agers can be gainfully employed. Custom and school pressure further limit the work demands parents can make on their children. The type of discipline which was necessary when children were workers is pointless now that their chief activities are centered around school and play.

Other adults are skeptical of the newer disciplinary pattern because it seems to produce a more casual parent–child relationship. They remember the strong emphasis of the past upon the obligations of children to their parents and they fear that when these obligations are no longer stressed family loyalty and unity will vanish. It is true that the commandment, "Honor thy father and thy mother" was a basic one in generations past, often repeated to the child by parents, grandparents, aunt, and uncle, in fact by all of the elders. Honor and obedience were the criteria of good child training. Disobedience was looked upon as a cardinal sin.

Religious leaders as well as educators of the past lent their full support to the commandment. In orthodox theological terms, this philosophy took the form of an admonition to parents to "break the child's will," it being that the child was almost worthless until his carnal nature was destroyed by discipline and punishment, his will broken, and submission to authority achieved. Only then could he attain to grace and become a submissive member of the church, community, and family.

Although the relationship between parent and child in the democratic family does tend to be more casual (less ritualistic and formalized), it is actually a closer and more mutually satisfying one than existed in the past. The loyalty which young people give their families is much more likely to be given freely; their sense of obligation is much more likely to grow out of real respect than parent-instilled fear. When the break with parents comes, as it inevitably must if the young person is to become a self-directing adult with a family of his own, it is less likely to be the cruel and complete break that it once was. In the old-fashioned American family, far too often father and son came to either physical or verbal blows, leading to an abrupt and unqualified break. This assertion of independence by the son was looked upon as a direct challenge to the father's position of supreme authority. The son was sometimes ordered out of the home and told never to return.

In the modern family, parents accept each new step the child takes toward independence as not only inevitable but also desirable. They visualize for their son or daughter not a life of submission but one of independence, self-respect, creativity, and ambition. To cultivate these qualities, greater rather than lesser freedom of thought, choice, and behavior are permitted.

The democratic system of child discipline has emerged with urban industrial development. It is in direct contrast to the older system of child training at almost every point, and the clash of the two explains the frequent conflict of values of young husbands and wives as they face the task of child training.

Democratic discipline can best be differentiated from the authoritarian by recognizing its focal point. In almost every aspect of its pattern of living, the home is child-centered rather than adult-centered. It assumes that the needs of the child are paramount to those of the father and mother. Parents do not consider that their children "owe" them anything—either love, respect, gratitude, or repayment for their own work and worry in the child's behalf. They hope, however, that by their own attitude of unselfish devotion they can arouse and develop similar attitudes in their offspring.

Even legal statutes recognize the paramount obligation of parent to child, for the state is willing to investigate where there is evidence of neglect or mistreatment of the child, and even to remove the child from the parent. This is a striking contrast to early agrarian cultures, in some of which the child could be stoned to death for disobedience to parents. No question was ever raised then about the parents' right to demand obedience. Now it is assumed that the child has to become an independent and self-sufficient adult. It is taken for granted that some time during his youth he will become almost entirely weaned from the family and lose practically all sense of obligation to it.

This is true in the emotional sense to a degree; it is even more true in the economic sense. The Social Security Act provides through the state means of support for the aged when they are no longer able to care for themselves. Young people have an obligation to carry the support of their own children, but they do not have to care for their own parents.

Because democratic discipline is directed toward the development of independence and individualism, rather than conformity and submission, it tends to be guidance-centered rather than discipline-centered. This does not mean that discipline is absent in the family; it is rather a discipline achieved by cooperation and mutual understanding. It operates by discussion and explanation, by pointing out a better way when error is committed, by giving the child sufficient freedom to make mistakes and gain experience from them to choose and, eventually, through trial and error, choose wisely. Punishment as such is disappearing as a disciplinary concept. Sharing and working together, rather than honor and obedience, have become the bonds.

With individualism rather than familism as the goal, it is the dream of most parents that their children will become creative, independent, self-sufficient persons, able to play a highly individuated, self-directed role in a specialized social order. For this reason a parent cannot stamp his own pattern and philosophy upon the child. He shares the training function with many other institutions. He encourages initiative in the child, smiles upon evidence of independence, even welcomes a certain amount of revolt, for he knows that only through such independence and originality can greatness be achieved.

The democratic parent does not expect a period of sowing wild oats and complete teen-age rebellion. He expects the child gradually to achieve independence and to be ready for the freedom that inevitably comes in the teens. With the recognition of increasing maturity, the parental hand is gradually withdrawn and the child is given greater opportunities to exercise his own judgment within the areas and limits which the parents consider safe. The way he behaves when not in the custody of parents is the final test of the disciplinary system employed.

In a democracy, as Margaret Mead has stated, "A child is a person from the moment of his birth." As a person, his growth is encouraged from the beginning. In a sense he becomes the most important person in the family environment—the most needy, the most demanding, certainly, but also the one with the greatest potentialities for rapid development.

The home now becomes his environment and must be shaped to fit his needs. The routine of the family must be in response to his demands. Here is a little creature demanding an audience and needing a receptive and appreciative rather than a critical and hostile one. As his growth unfolds, he will gain a voice for words and need a sounding board against which to repeat over and over the same words, and new words, and a wide range of sounds. And as he becomes mobile and takes over his environment, he inspects it all by touch and taste and attempts to dismantle it to learn its parts and how they are put together. And to each thing he must attach a name, and later to each, feeling. He is a dwarf in a world of giants but, if given an appreciative adult audience, feels no inferiority, only a consuming desire to learn and conquer the environment about him.

The democratic family wants the child to be free, within established limits, to give him room for maximum development. The authoritarian family quickly tries to curb and restrain, to protect property and adult comforts and routines. This is the easier course. It makes life smoother for parents but curbs growth in the child. The democratic way from the very beginning requires more adaptability by the parents.

To many, the idea of handling young children democratically is overwhelming because of the tremendous drain on patience that such a system implies. To command obedience and to force it by virtue of greater physical strength seems to be much the easier course. Blood's (1953) study of 40 couples shows that the permissive pattern does disrupt parents' lives more. The children are inclined to be more noisy, to encroach on the parents' privacy from morning to night. The parents also must be more alert in controlling the children's activities in order to protect them from harm and to protect the family possessions from damage.

In general, the living quarters of permissive parents were more cluttered by the activities of the children, and the parents had to supervise the picking up of toys or, more frequently, do it themselves. In homes where the pattern of discipline was strict, the children expected little freedom and conformed more or less to the rigid controls of their parents.

In the permissive homes, the ideal was to give the children a chance to grow and learn. In the authoritarian homes, the virtues of obedience, honesty, manners, and neatness were emphasized. The democratic parents were inclined to use the living room as a place to which the children had full access, making its use for guests secondary.

The developmental parent, as Blood states, works on the assumption that in the long run the independence he gives and the sacrifices he makes for his children in early childhood will make them more self-sufficient later on and perhaps more self-directive, requiring a total of less time and worry on his part.

We live in a time when reactionaries blame Spock and more democratic methods of child-rearing for the violence and rebellion of youth. Time will show they are quite wrong.

Olim (1968) has studied "self-actualizing" young people. These are young people reared in democratic homes. They are people with a strong humanitarian outlook. They do challenge tradition in many areas, are particularly critical of judging life by primarily economic motives. They are strongly motivated toward the Peace Corps, the Teachers' Corps, VISTA, civil rights struggles, and student revolts. They may be questioning and nonconformist, but are not violent or destructive.

The violent and destructive are most likely to come from environments of frustration, authoritarianism, and despair. It is much too soon to write off the democratic ideal as a failure. Great masses of American youth have never had any experience with it in their homes.

Below are some principles for a positive approach to discipline developed by Washington State University Nursery School as a guide for baby-sitters. It is a list worth the attention of any young parent:

1   Give a child a choice only when you intend to accept his decision.
2   Redirect the child's interest or activity.
3   State suggestions or directions in a positive way. For example, instead of saying, "Don't throw the ball," say, "You can roll the ball on the floor."
4   Disregard some of his no's and assume he will conform.
5   Give only one direction at a time.
6   Remember that children tend to be slow and tend to dawdle.
7   Maintain necessary limits.
8   If one method does not work, wait a while and try another.
9   Always ask yourself why the child is behaving in this particular way.
10   Try to look at the situation through the child's eyes.

DISCIPLINE WITHOUT PUNISHMENT

Many parents cannot reconcile the idea of a need for discipline of children with the view that the child should be free of punishment. Ellsworth Faris (1952) differentiates the two and makes a strong case for discipline without punishment. He defines punishment as "the intentional inflicting of suffering administered by authority on one who has been guilty of offense." He ably defends the thesis that discipline without punishment is feasible and more effective than discipline achieved by punishment.

He begins his defense by citing his early observations among natives of the Belgian Congo rain forest, who never punish children. He indicates that critics were inclined to look upon his observations as being inaccurate, but reports that all anthropologists have come to recognize that punishment of children is unknown among preliterate people everywhere. The children are taught the taboos, inhibitions, rituals, and customs of tribal life. They are well-disciplined, but they are not subjected to punishment.

Our logic for punishment, he believes, is to deter the offender from future transgression and to deter others by publicizing his punishment. This is particularly true in the field of penal practice with adults.

In applying his theory of discipline to the child, Faris indicated that the child must have its full measure of love. When language begins, discipline takes on new meaning for the child. If, for example, he picks up objects which he should not have, they should be taken away from him with "affectionate inflexibility accompanied by gentle tones." In this way he learns that some things are for grownups and not for him. Close bonds are maintained between child and parent which should never be broken.

Punishment in any form tends to weaken this bond. He should not be given his own way, but by "loving, gentle compulsion be required to do what he is expected to do and do it on time." There should be no violation of the intimacy and trust which exist between child and parent. In the childhood stage, when he is no longer a toddler, praise should be added to the love-and-fun relationship between child and parent. Expressions of approval soon become important factors in discipline. The parent, by rewarding certain conduct with approval, makes the child eager to repeat the conduct and thus win approval again. The never-ending thirst of children for affection and admiration is a parents' most valuable ally in drawing out the best in his child.

The later stage of boyhood or girlhood brings the need not only for love, fun, and praise but also for membership. There is a desire to belong to the group, to be accepted and appreciated by his age mates. Organized games become very important, and the child is eager for the first time to play by rules. Now is the time when abstract moral precepts can be taught "in cozy, intimate moments, when only two are present, the child and one parent." Faris believed that moral teaching should be divorced from particular offenses and that an offense should not be reproved until a day or two afterward, when there is no tendency on the part of the child to want to justify what he did.

The next stage is adolescence. All the teaching that the parent can effectively do has been done before this stage is reached. Those who have done the job well need have little anxiety about the future. Those who have failed can do very little at this time to undo the effects of their serious mistakes.

In concluding his statement of child-training theory, Faris indicated that discipline is essential and that any method of producing it is better than no discipline at all but reaffirms his thesis that discipline without punishment is possible and effective. In summarizing his views, Faris (1952) states:

> The rearing of children is not a science and can never be; it is rather an art, for no two situations are identical. But scientific principles must guide the method, whether these principles are learned systematically or transmitted by tradition.
>
> The young parent can lovingly overpower the runabout, define the objects for the child, give a due measure of love, fun, and praise, avoid producing a sense of guilt, never reprove what has been done accidentally, and, if it is thought important make disobedience impossible by substituting polite requests for arbitrary or semi-military commands. There is a strong close intimate bond between parent and child, given—not acquired—and this precious bond can be kept unbroken. The child's very conception of himself is wholly within the power of the parents in the early years.
>
> The subject here discussed is controversial, highly controversial. Many have

argued the point with me and have contended that discipline without punishment is inferior to the method which visits every offense with its appropriate penalty. This can be argued and I have tried to argue it here. But when I am told that discipline without punishment is not possible, then I insist that there is no argument. It has been done and is being done, and successfully.

Not only is the example of the millions of preliterate children in Africa and the islands of the sea before us but many of my own students have tried this better way and have been successful.

And if I may be pardoned for a more personal reference I will say that I have fourteen (14) grandchildren, ages from two to thirteen, all of whom are, so far, well disciplined but none of whom have been punished in any manner.

RECOGNIZE GROWING INDEPENDENCE

Even though authority and discipline must enter into the child's world, it is equally important that discipline leave room for growing individuality. As the youngster passes from infancy into childhood, the parent must accept his growing need for independence. Each year the normal child develops new interests and an ever-increasing belief in himself and his own power and wisdom. He challenges his parents' opinions and authority, not because he is bad, but because he is developing a normal confidence in his own opinions—a confidence which is necessary in adults but often resented in children. Parents who do not understand the genesis of this growing assertiveness are inclined to "clamp down" before the child gets completely out of hand. Clamping down is an open challenge and may mark the beginning of real disciplinary problems.

THE POWER OF EXAMPLE

In the disciplinary area, example is quite as important as teaching, in fact, much more so. What parents condone in themselves and in their children will become the behavior of the child. The parents' maturity, and lack of it, will form the patterns of the child's reactions to situations.

No such striking statement in concrete terms of this principle in child training has come to the writer's attention as that of Nolte (1954):

If a child lives with criticism, he learns to condemn.
If a child lives with hostility, he learns to fight.
If a child lives with fear, he learns to be apprehensive.
If a child lives with pity, he learns to feel sorry for himself.
If a child lives with ridicule, he learns to be shy.
If a child lives with jealousy, he learns what envy is.
If a child lives with shame, he learns to feel guilty.
If a child lives with encouragement, he learns to be confident.
If a child lives with tolerance, he learns to be patient.
If a child lives with praise, he learns to be appreciative.
If a child lives with acceptance, he learns to love.

If a child lives with approval, he learns to like himself.

If a child lives with recognition, he learns that it is good to have a goal.

If a child lives with sharing, he learns about generosity.

If a child lives with honesty and fairness, he learns what truth and justice are.

If a child lives with security, he learns to have faith in himself and in those about him.

If a child lives with friendliness, he learns that the world is a nice place in which to live.

If you live with serenity, your child will live with peace of mind.

With what is your child living?

THE ULTIMATE TEST OF EFFECTIVE DISCIPLINE

The way the child acts when the parent is absent is the true test of whether the parents' disciplinary patterns have been internalized. Until the child is self-disciplined, the goal of discipline remains unattained. It seems likely that in the authoritarian disciplinary system this goal is often unattainable.

In the early farm home, children were taught never to play with matches and were severely punished if ever caught with them. A not unusual consequence was that when parents were out doing the chores or visiting neighbors, the child set the lace curtains on fire, built a fire under the bed with wastepaper, or set fire to shavings in the woodshed or elsewhere.

In the democratic family, children are as fascinated by matches as children ever were. Parents let them start the fire when a picnic fire is being lighted or when kindling in the fireplace is ready to be ignited. They light the candles on the birthday cake. Since the children have not been taught never to play with matches and have had experience in the correct use of matches, child-started family fires no longer occur with regularity. The child internalizes mature standards with regard to matches.

Blind obedience is the lowest possible standard of discipline. It can be enforced because parents are physically stronger, but what does enforcement accomplish? If it succeeds, it destroys the child. Initiative, inventiveness, and experimentation are the way to learning. Curb these, and growth is curbed. Permit them to develop under an atmosphere of guidance, and unlimited growth is possible.

John Anderson, when director of the University of Minnesota Child Welfare Research Station, in an address many years ago in Los Angeles made the point strikingly clear: "The world is always waiting for the executive in the $100,000 class. Positions are never filled. There are always plenty of people to fill the routine factory jobs where others make all the decisions. These masses are trained to obedience."

DEMOCRATIC PATTERNS AT THE LAUNCHING STAGE

As the child moves toward the teen years, his life becomes oriented outside the home to an increasing degree. This is when the last test of discipline comes, and results become apparent much too late for the parent to remodel his training patterns.

Margaret Mead has likened the American family to a launching platform from which young people are cast to live independent and selfsufficient lives. It is this fact of modern life which makes the democratic family-training pattern have significance in our mobile, urbanized social system.

The evidence is strongly in favor of the democratic family insofar as parent–teen-ager relationships and the adjustment of teen-agers to the peer group, church, community, and school, and in social relations is concerned. Studies of more than 4300 seniors in high school show that the teen-ager in the democratic family has fewer problems than the one reared in an authoritarian family. He feels more ready to enter the world as an independent person, and yet he is more closely attached to his parents. He has less of a sense of rebellion against parents. The bond is one welded out of mutual respect and close emotional ties, rather than being one of honor and obedience.

One way to test the extent to which the child has internalized the values and standards of his parents is the extent to which he wishes to emulate the parents in their life patterns. Figure 27–1 shows in striking contrast, by type of authority, the comparative desires of 4310 high school seniors to emulate their parents. Those under authoritarian discipline* in few cases considered their parents' lives as ones they wished to follow. Those under democratic discipline often wished to pattern after parents, and less than a fifth of the boys and little

Responses of teen-agers, by family disciplinary pattern. The democratic family does not stress honor and obedience, but young people on the threshold of adulthood reared under the democratic pattern are more desirous of emulating parents than those reared in authoritarian homes. Source: Landis and Stone (1952).

FIGURE 27–1

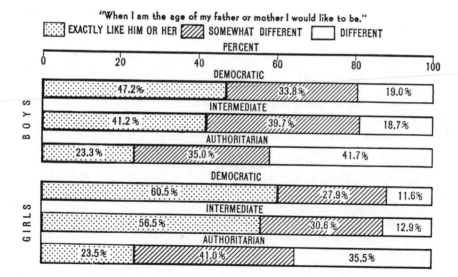

"When I am the age of my father or mother I would like to be."
EXACTLY LIKE HIM OR HER — SOMEWHAT DIFFERENT — DIFFERENT

*Families were classified into the three administrative types on the basis of young people's responses to a lengthy questionnaire which dealt with all aspects of their adjustment. Relationships within the home as checked by teen-agers were used in classifying families, a scale following the Guttman technique being employed in the classification. In other words, young people themselves were not asked to classify their homes into authority types by direct questions.

TABLE 27-1   Average Number of Problems Checked by 4310 High School Seniors Living in Democratic, Intermediate, and Authoritarian Families

			FAMILY ADMINISTRATIVE PATTERNS		
PROBLEM AREAS	NUMBER OF PROBLEMS CHECKED	SEX	DEMOCRATIC (AVERAGE PROBLEMS CHECKED)	INTERMEDIATE (AVERAGE PROBLEMS CHECKED)	AUTHORITARIAN (AVERAGE PROBLEMS CHECKED)
Personal	33	boys	3.5	3.6	4.4
		girls	4.2	4.5	5.1
Family	63	boys	2.9	3.3	5.1
		girls	3.2	3.9	6.5
Social	30	boys	1.8	1.9	2.5
		girls	1.9	2.4	2.7
Boy–girl relations	34	boys	2.0	2.2	2.7
		girls	2.2	2.6	3.0
School	30	boys	2.2	2.4	3.0
		girls	2.2	.2.5	3.0
Vocational	30	boys	2.9	2.9	3.4
		girls	2.6	3.1	3.2
Morals, religion	30	boys	2.2	2.4	2.5
		girls	2.4	2.9	3.0
All problems	250	boys	17.5	18.7	23.6
		girls	18.7	21.9	26.5

Source: Landis and Stone (1952).

more than a tenth of the girls wished to be entirely different. This is striking testimony to the stronger influence of parent over child in the democratic family. Elder (1963) also found that adolescents more often model their roles after parents who are democratic than after those who are either authoritarian or permissive.

A second index of comparative adjustment of the democratically disciplined and authoritarian by discipline child is shown in Table 27–1, which summarizes responses of 4310 high school seniors to a checklist of 250 adjustment problems. These problems are classified by area and sex. It will be seen that in all areas, and in total problems, the more democratic the family, the fewer the problems checked.

These are but a few aspects of the problem studied, but they illustrate the kind of conclusions which were found in almost every aspect of teen-age adjustments and relationships.

Rose (1959) finds, from an analysis of 183 male and 206 female University of Minnesota students, that the transition of the adolescent to maturity seems to be made much more easily by those who have secure family relationships. He advances the hypothesis that difficult family relationships, particularly when their origin is in relationship to the mother, cause the adolescent to withdraw from the family before he is fully socialized and/or emotionally

The home atmosphere—relationship of parents to each other, of father to child, and, above all, of mother to child—is the key factor in juvenile delinquency. A long-time study of delinquent children, begun in the 1930s and following them into adult life (to 1955), indicates that where the home is a destructive environment, community efforts, social-work programs, and counseling show little results in improvement. The absent father, or the cruel neglectful one, tends to produce criminality in the child. Mothers who are absent, passive, cruel, rejecting, or neglectful tend to produce criminal sons. A home marked by a great deal of quarreling, with or without affection, produces delinquents, as do also lack of discipline and erratic punitive discipline. A firm but kindly discipline is preventive. The study concluded that the treatment of the young delinquent is primarily a problem of working with the family.

The Glueck (1956) study of delinquency rated overstrict and erratic discipline high as the factor predictive of delinquency.

PROBLEMS

1   A young man leaves his home in a small town and moves into a dormitory of a large state university located in a metropolis. Describe the adjustments that face this young man and discuss the way he will react to them if he is:

   a   The product of a highly authoritarian training pattern.

   b   The product of a democratic training pattern.

2   What type of personality is best suited to parenthood in a democratic family? Describe common traits that would be assets to parents adhering to the democratic pattern. Describe traits that would handicap the practice of modern child-rearing techniques.

3   Describe several aspects of the childhood training patterns in typical middle- and lower-class homes. Consider the differing degrees of emphasis put on toilet training and, a little later, on training in manners and early formal learning. Which training pattern do you consider superior? Why?

4   In what respects do the training patterns of rural America still differ from those common in urban centers?

5   When conscientious parents find themselves disagreeing on disciplinary philosophy and techniques, which course of action is best? Discuss advantages and disadvantages of:

   a   Leaving the discipline entirely in the hands of one parent.

   b   Getting an authoritative handbook on child-rearing and doing exactly as it advises.

   c   Reading books on child discipline and consulting a specialist in the field.

   d   Leaving the discipline in the hands of one parent until an agreement on techniques and philosophy can be reached.

6   *Sociodrama:* Two young wives, both of whom consider themselves "modern" in their child-rearing practices, find that they disagree on some basic principles. One

argues that modern theory "teaches you to keep your hands off and let nature take its course." The other feels that modern practices call for "greater thought, patience, and hard work for the parent than ever before."

7 Does the democratic pattern of family living require that young people have a voice equal to that of their parents in family matters?

8 List on the chalkboard several of the traits and characteristics which are admired and encouraged in young people in authoritarian homes. Make another list of youthful traits that are most admired by democratic parents. With these traits in mind, discuss the probable adult personality which would emerge from each training pattern.

PART VII

MARRIAGE PROBLEMS

DIVORCE AND
REMARRIAGE

28 Marriage always has an escape clause, as far as social systems are concerned. Few religious systems hold that it must be lasting for all until the final parting of death. The requirements for terminating marriages by choice differ greatly from society to society, and, in our nation, from state to state. A book designed to help youth toward successful marriage cannot deny the reality of divorce as a significant part of our culture.

The divorce-as-sin concept is all but gone from the value systems of the majority. Even the idea that someone is to blame is slowly vanishing. Not that all persons can terminate a marriage without feelings of guilt and self-condemnation, for many cannot. Conscience and fear of social condemnation are still much a part of the process. But logically, divorce is coming to be looked upon as remedial; a way of solving the problem of mates, and often of their children too—the problem of tension and conflict to which there is no better solution.

THE SOCIAL VERSUS THE LEGAL APPROACH
TO DIVORCE

Divorce in advanced societies requires some formal action by which the community is made aware that the couple have permanently ended their relationship. In primitive societies, the woman may set the man's gear outside the hut, and he and others will know the marriage is ended. In a complex society there is too much gear to be divided, too many contractual obligations that must be carried on, like the automobile contract, furniture installments, house payments, etc., and there are the inheritance rights and continuing support of the child, which must be settled by law.

In theocratic societies, this may all be settled by the religious leaders, but in Western industrial cultures the state issues the license to marry and the state must pronounce the end as well. Historically this has involved adversary procedure—the pitting of one party against the other to determine guilt and innocence. A legal case was required for divorce. This meant presenting causes, and causes had to be those recognized by the state's law as justifiable ones. If the state recognized adultery as the only proper cause for legal action, adultery must be proved, even if it meant a hotel scene set up for an appropriate photograph to be introduced into court. Where state laws acknowledged a wider range of causes, couples had a greater choice of reasons.

Sociologically speaking, establishing guilt is nonsense in most cases of marital incompatibility. And it has long been known that adversary proceedings were often completely dishonest as to cause for seeking the divorce. Figure 28–1 shows reasons given in courts for a typical year. They reflect what states accepted much more than couples' real reasons. In fact, students of divorce, counselors, social workers, ministers, as well as researchers have long known that couples seek divorce for many reasons, and that some are so

FIGURE 28–1   Reasons given in court for wanting divorce: divorce registration area, 1965. Divorce is considered a legal farce. Reasons given in court and the real motives for divorce may have little similarity. Source: "Excerpts from Vital Statistics of the United States, 1965, Vol. III—Marriage and Divorce," U.S. Department of Health, Education, and Welfare, Table 2–21, p. 2–18.

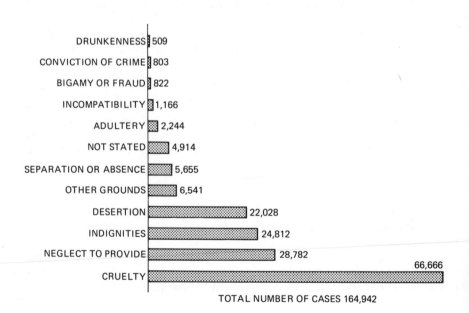

TOTAL NUMBER OF CASES 164,942

disturbed in their relationships that they could not pick a reason or set of reasons. For them it may be a choice between shedding the mate or heading for a mental institution; in others there is violence or threat of violence. Judges recognize the farce of legal proceedings and the fraud of many divorce complaints.

It is out of this background that divorce for "irreconcilable differences," the so-called "no-fault" divorce laws, have emerged in an increasing number of states. It may well be a long time before adversary proceedings vanish in all of them. California set the pace in 1969 with the Family Law Act which went into full effect in 1970.

Nationwide, the right to divorce proceedings for those without income is now law. Free counsel must be provided. In California anyone can, and many do, appear (10–15 percent) in divorce court without counsel by choice. In Los Angeles, where the lawyer may charge $350 or more, the do-it-yourself filing fee is only $44. *How to Do Your Own Divorce in California,* by Charles Sherman, a Berkeley lawyer, is said to be the most thumbed book in some law libraries. Where there is no need to prove fault to obtain a dissolution of marriage, the adversary procedure is eliminated as far as getting the marriage terminated is concerned. For those with property to divide, the custody of children to be settled, and other such worldly matters, there may be great need for legal counsel.

THE MARRIAGE, DIVORCE, REMARRIAGE TREND

The United States now has the highest divorce rate of any nation for which adequate statistics are kept, and is going through a period of slowing first marriage rates, rapidly rising divorce rates, and rapidly rising remarriage rates. Glick and Norton (1972) show that the number of marriages has risen about a third since 1960, the annual number of divorces has risen 80 percent, and the annual number of remarriages has risen 40 percent.

Figure 28–2 shows the 50-year trend of first marriages, divorces, and remarriages for women 14–44 years of age. The divorce and remarriage rates have passed the prior peak of 1946, reached following the return of the World War II military men. The rise in remarriage rates is logically related to the rise in divorce rate, since, as will be shown later, most divorces are followed by remarriage after a brief time interval. The decline in the first marriage rate, the researchers say, "suggests an unprecedented modification of life styles and values relating to marriage."

DIVORCE BY SOCIAL CHARACTERISTICS: AGE AT MARRIAGE, EDUCATION, INCOME, OCCUPATION, AND RACE

The half century of notoriety given to Hollywood divorces may well have given many the thought that divorce is highest among the educated and prosperous. This is not true. Divorce, like unhappy marriage, is an escape primarily of those of little education and of low income. It is among these that divorce rates

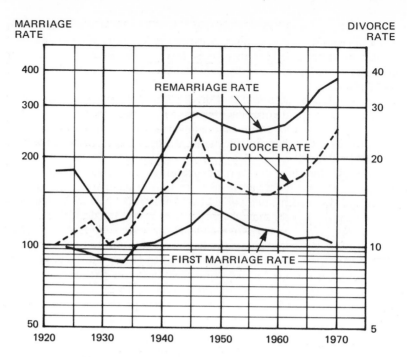

MARRIAGE
RATE

DIVORCE
RATE

FIGURE 29-2   First marriage, remarriage, and divorce rates per 1000 single, widowed, or divorced, and married women: three year averages 1920–1970.

are highest and that divorce comes earliest in the marriage. And as is so well-known, the rate is highest and comes earliest after marriage among those who marry young. These socioeconomic variables and their impact on divorce have been most comprehensively studied by Glick and Norton (1971), who analyzed a sample of 28,000 households selected nationwide. In Figure 28–3 only white males from the sample are used.

Age   It will be seen that the probability of divorce during the first five years of their first marriage is 16 per 1000 for those marrying at ages 14–19; only 5 per 1000 for those marrying during ages 25–29. (It is interesting to observe that as early as the late 1930s, sociologists found that the under 20 group had low chances of successful marriage; the 25–29 group the best chances (Burgess and Cottrell 1939).

Schooling   Note that education is favorably related to survival of the marriage during the first five years, with those of the college group having twice the chances of survival as the high school educated, and almost three times as great as those of the eighth grader.

MARRIAGE PROBLEMS

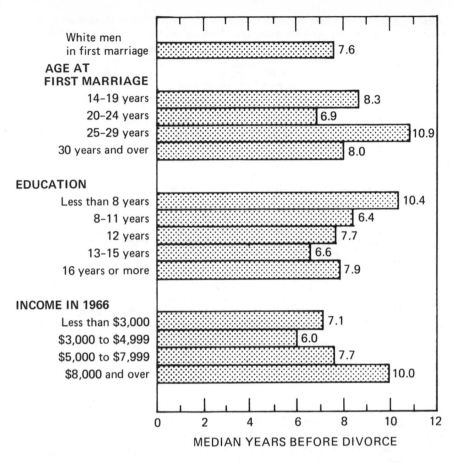

White men in first marriage 7.6

AGE AT FIRST MARRIAGE
14–19 years 8.3
20–24 years 6.9
25–29 years 10.9
30 years and over 8.0

EDUCATION
Less than 8 years 10.4
8–11 years 6.4
12 years 7.7
13–15 years 6.6
16 years or more 7.9

INCOME IN 1966
Less than $3,000 7.1
$3,000 to $4,999 6.0
$5,000 to $7,999 7.7
$8,000 and over 10.0

MEDIAN YEARS BEFORE DIVORCE

Socioeconomic factors related to divorce. Source: Paul C. Glick and Arthur J. Norton, "Frequency, Duration, and Probability of Marriage and Divorce," *Journal of Marriage and the Family,* 33:314, May, 1971. **FIGURE 28–3**

Income   Statistically speaking, the $8000 a year man had more than three times the chances of surviving his first five years in his first marriage as the $3000 a year man. The more earning power a man has the greater the likelihood of his first marriage lasting five years. Of course, we know from many studies that the first five years are the critical ones; those who make the adjustments of these first years, usually make it together for a lifetime.

Race   Blacks have a much higher divorce rate than whites regardless of their age of marriage, but black marriages last longer before breaking up than do white marriages. Analysis of a nationwide sample by Glick and Norton (1971) provides convincing evidence. Table 28–1 shows the percentage of each race married and divorced by age at first marriage and by years since first

TABLE 28-1   Percentage of Persons Ever Married Under 70 Years Old Who Were Known to Have Been Divorced, by Age at First Marriage, Number of Years Since First Marriage, Race, and Sex: United States, 1967 (Numbers in Thousands).

AGE AT FIRST MARRIAGE	WHITE PERSONS UNDER 70, BY YEARS SINCE FIRST MARRIAGE			BLACKS UNDER 70, BY YEARS SINCE FIRST MARRIAGE		
	UNDER 10	10–19	20 AND OVER	UNDER 10	10–19	20 AND OVER
Men ever married	9,514	10,456	19,537	1,007	971	1,748
Percentage known to have been divorced:total[a]	7.5	13.6	16.7	10.4	28.0	37.1
14–21	9.1	17.5	25.4	12.2	31.7	45.6
22–27	5.3	11.1	12.6	8.5	27.9	30.9
28 and over	8.5	10.9	10.1	10.2	21.1	24.6
Women ever married	9,959	10,877	24,697	1,309	1,228	2,522
Percentage known to have been divorced: total[a]	8.1	14.6	18.2	14.4	32.3	40.2
14–19	10.7	21.3	24.8	16.9	41.1	46.5
20–24	5.1	8.5	13.2	13.3	22.4	31.0
25 and over	5.7	8.0	11.5	9.1	21.3	31.0

Source: Paul C. Glick and Arthur J. Norton, "Frequency, Duration, and Probability of Marriage and Divorce," *Journal of Marriage and the Family*, 33:309, May, 1971.

[a]Persons whose first and/or most recent marriage ended in divorce.

marriage to the divorce. Data are shown for both males and females. The high divorce rates for both sexes are for men marrying under 22 and for women marrying under 20. Of black males married under 22 who were first married 20 years before the date of the survey, 45.6 percent had been divorced; of white males, 25.4 percent. Of females in this classification, 46.5 percent of blacks had been divorced; 24.8 percent of whites.

The authors report that 15 percent of men and 17 percent of women under 70 of all races who have ever been married have been divorced. For males, the white rate was 14 percent, the black rate, 28 percent; for females, 15 percent for whites, 32 percent for blacks.

Cutright (1971) has suggested that the frequency of illegitimate children born to each group may be a factor in relative stability of white and nonwhite marriages. Such births historically have been seven times as high for non-whites. He compares the rate for the years 1950–1964 and finds that nonwhite brides in 28 percent of cases have borne one or more illegitimate children prior to their first marriage; white brides have done so in only 4 percent of cases. These great differentials are declining, so this may be less a factor in future divorce rates of the races than historically.

Glick and Norton compare white and black groups as to age at first marriage, median years marriage lasted before divorce for those who divorce, median years before the divorced remarry, and median years before the second marriage ends in divorce for those who end their second marriage by divorce

(Table 28–1). Blacks marry somewhat later; those who divorce stay with their first mate longer than do whites. The blacks also delay their remarriage much longer after their first divorce.

Trend of the Marriage–Divorce Ratio

Glick and Norton have plotted the trend in marriage and divorce ratios, relating divorce to the marriages of seven years earlier (the reason for this is that the median duration of first marriages over a period of 50 years has been seven years). These ratios are plotted by three-year averages since 1914. It will be seen that by this measure, there was one divorce for every 6.5 marriages contracted seven years earlier for the earliest period (1921–1923); for the latest, there was one divorce for 2.4 marriages contracted seven years earlier (Figure 28–4). There is already a higher ratio of marriages terminating in divorce than that reached following World War II. Whether this is a permanent situation, or whether it is temporary is too early to know. If it should prove to be permanent, sequential polygamy is becoming an established fact, particularly among the young.

Three-year averages, marriages (1914–1964) per each divorce (1921–1971). Source: Glick and Norton (1972). **FIGURE 28–4**

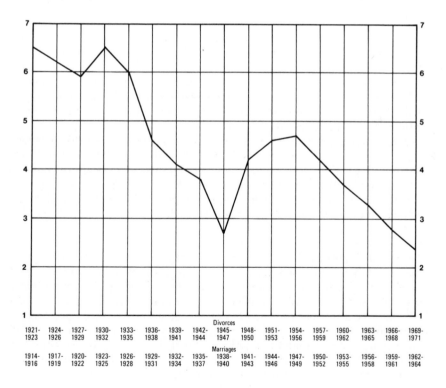

Glick and Norton conclude that the percentage of divorced women in the younger ages has increased greatly as follows:

AGE GROUP	PERCENTAGE DIVORCED	
	1940	1970
20–24	2.1	6.3
30–34	6.3	15.8

Note that as high a proportion of the younger group was already divorced in their early 20s as in the early 30s in the 1940 generation, and that in 1970 almost three times as many in the early 30s had already been divorced as women of these ages in 1940.

Divorce data greatly underrate the actual number of marriages which dissolve among the poor. Social workers have long considered desertion the divorce of the poor. Unable to bear the cost of divorce, and having no property of consequence to divide, the male takes to the road. "Missing males" are usually poor males. In March 1971, the U.S. Supreme Court ruled that the poor can participate in divorce proceedings without cost to them. This will no doubt release a great number of the poor from broken marriages they now endure, temporarily greatly raising their divorce rate.

Occupation   Occupation is related to income, yet in itself is a variable in the divorce rate. Some occupations are protected by more social pressure than others. There is greater need to retain a favorable public image.

Using occupational categories, Monahan (1955) studied couples involved in divorce in the state of Iowa. Employing vital statistics data for the state, he found that marriage problems are very closely related to socioeconomic status. The divorce measure shows that generally the higher the occupational level the lower the divorce rate. His divorce data for the year 1953 show ratios to employed males in the various occupational categories. Although labor constituted less than 10 percent of the population, they had almost one-third of the divorces. Professional people had less than half the divorces that would be expected on the basis of their ratio of the population. Owners and officials had a few more than one-third of the expected divorces.

The Social Transmission of Divorce   General statistics are a very poor index of whether any given individual or couple are likely to end up in the divorce court. Studies by Judson T. Landis (1956) indicate, however, that divorce, like stability, runs in families. There are many families that have never had a divorce as far back as memory or geneologies carry them, and there are other family lines that are divorce-prone. He studied the ancestors of 1977 college students and found this to be strikingly so. Taking the students' own parents, and aunts and uncles, he related the divorces of this generation to whether the students' grandparents had been divorced. In the group of parents, and aunts and uncles, there were 13,255 persons. Where there had been no divorces in the grandparent generation, only 14.6 percent of parents, and aunts and uncles had been divorced; where one set of grandparents had been divorced, 23.7 percent had been divorced; where both sets of grandparents had been divorced, 38 percent had been divorced.

Since this study dealt with a college population, it may not be representative of the total population. It does, however, seem logical to assume that a divorce tradition in the family is as likely to be transmitted, as are other family traditions, among the lower classes as among the more favored classes.

DIVORCE—A SOCIAL PROCESS

People abroad get the impression that divorce in the United States is a very casual experience. It is not so. There is a revival of hope and return to despair; a period of good adjustment and a glimpse of happiness, then a slipping back. Often this goes on until misery is so great that temporary separations are necessary. Love may revive only to be followed with disillusionment and near despair. For most couples there is a long time lapse (an average of about two years) between the first consideration of divorce and the decree.

Under the companionship-family social system, divorce is a social process which in outline is not unlike the process of dating, courtship, engagement, and marriage. It is, in fact, those processes in reverse. Instead of a series of experiences creating greater intimacy and involvement and culminating in marriage, divorce is a series of experiences beginning with the initial frictions and climaxing in emotional indifference or even violent hatred.

The late Willard Waller traced the various steps which lead to the divorce court (Waller and Hill 1951). The first stage is a disturbance in the love life of the pair. This eventually leads to the point where friction is so intense that the possibility of divorce is mentioned. The next stage is that in which husband or wife tells some outside person or persons of their difficulty. This puts the marriage on a different basis, since the couple loses face with other people. Usually this does not end the marriage; discussions ensue concerning a course of action. Finally, there comes the stage when the husband and wife definitely decide to make a break. This is followed by a separation, which is followed later by the divorce action itself. The divorce does not end the relationship. There is still the important period of mental conflict, during which both individuals are confronted with the problem of reconstructing their lives to fit the new situation.

There is also the problem of emotional readjustment. Waller has stated that, in his studies of divorce cases, he had yet to find a divorce which was not followed by a serious form of bereavement, along with problems of loneliness, sex tensions, and problems of lowered income and social standing among friends. In many cases the bereavement following divorce for one or sometimes for both parties is much more serious than bereavement (grief and shock) following the death of a mate. Death is always classed among the inevitable occurrences of life. The shock of death may be more sudden, but it can be charged to Providence, accident, or natural causes, and one can absolve oneself of blame. But in the case of divorce, there is always the knowledge that it might have been avoided and awareness of disappointed happiness against which to project the divorce.

This early analysis of Waller's, based on the case history analysis of 33 couples involved in divorce, shows great insight. Much of it is still irrefutable. It does, however, need some modification and elaboration to suit current conditions.

First, it should be stressed that the divorce process may be arrested at any step, and adjustment turned toward better rather than worse relationships. This is particularly true today when more specialists are available for counsel and where many ministers, teachers, and others are sufficiently informed to help a couple in conflict gain insight into their problems, thus helping to solve them. Waller's basic thesis that marriage relationships are dynamic, always tending either to get better or worse at any stage of the relationship, is probably more true now than when he made the observation.

Second, bereavement and shock do not inevitably follow divorce. Some find in it genuine relief from tension. Greater public tolerance may be a factor here, although it is doubtful that the shock reaction was ever universal. Locke's case histories show that in many instances there is no shock at all (Burgess et al. 1971). He also suggests the probability that where there is emotional trauma, it may be eased by early remarriage. Goode (1949) studied 100 urban mothers who had been divorced. He found that there is no consistent traumatic pattern following divorce. Half of the subjects studied indicated an attitude of indifference toward the former spouse.

DIVORCE IN THE MARRIAGE CYCLE

Generally speaking, the longer the marriage survives, the less likelihood that it will end in divorce. The divorce rate is highest during the first few years of marriage, when major adjustments must be made or the marriage declared a failure. The peak in number of divorces comes in the third year of marriage and drops sharply after the seventh (see Figure 28–5).

In about three-fourths of all cases, the wife initiates the divorce action. In most cases, collusion is involved; the couple agrees that the wife is most likely to succeed in obtaining a decree. Most divorce cases are uncontested, indicating that there has been prior agreement as to obtaining a divorce. It must, however, be granted that women use divorce as a solution to marriage problems more often than do men. The wife's happiness, success, mental health, and general well-being are much more identified with success of the marriage than are those of the husband. He may use outside recreation, work, an extramarital affair, or even desertion as an escape much more readily than she. He becomes the overt offender against the marriage. She requests the divorce on the grounds of his offense.

REMARRIAGE AS A POSTDIVORCE ADJUSTMENT

Some churches try to discourage divorce by hindering remarriage or forbidding it altogether. Some states require a waiting period of months or even

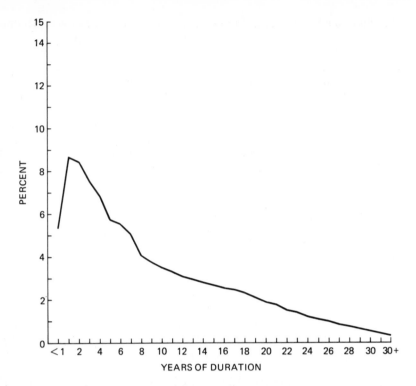

Percentage of divorces and annulments—by duration of marriage: divorce registration area, **FIGURE 28-5**
1965. Note the high rates during the early years of marriage. Source: "Excerpts from Vital
Statistics of the United States, 1963, Vol. III—Marriage and Divorce," U.S. Department of
Health, Education, and Welfare, Table 2–5, p. 2–8.

years before a new marriage license will be granted. Yet most persons separated from a spouse by divorce or death do remarry.

Marriage rates drop with increased age for all groups and for both sexes,
dropping faster for females than males, but throughout life the divorced
person continues to have much better chances of marriage than the other
groups. For example, at age 40, the divorced woman has a 65 percent chance
of remarriage; the widowed woman, only 29 percent; and the single woman,
only 16 percent. Or to approach it differently, a spinster of 30 has approximately a fifty–fifty chance of marriage; the widow of 33 has a similar
chance; but the divorcee of 45 has a fifty–fifty chance of remarriage.

How soon does remarriage take place? There are as yet no specific and
comprehensive data on this subject, but data for a five-year interval indicate
that remarriage after divorce usually comes within the first five years. Glick
(1949) made estimates from large samples and concluded that of those divorced in the five years preceding the 1948 U.S. Bureau of the Census survey,
all but one-fourth had remarried. Of those who had been divorced 5–14 years,
only about one-seventh had not remarried. While Glick advises caution in the
acceptance of his data, he suspects that the estimates may be low in that unat-

tached adults tend to be missed in sample census surveys, and a certain proportion of divorced persons fail to report themselves as divorced.

Using the same series of data, Glick found that approximately half of the men and three-fourths of the women who had lost their spouses by death during the preceding five years had not remarried. Of those losing their spouses by death during the 5–14-year period preceding the survey, about one-third of the men and two-thirds of the women had not remarried.

Glick and Norton's (1971) analysis of more recent trends in marriage, divorce, and remarriage find that the median number of years after termination of the first marriage by divorce before entering a second marriage between the years 1960 and 1966 was 7.6 years for white males, and 8.2 years for black males; for white women, 7.7 years, for black women, 8.6 years.

SUCCESS OF REMARRIAGE AFTER DIVORCE AND WIDOWHOOD

There have undoubtedly been great changes in this area with the greater acceptance of divorce, but various studies over the years indicate that marriages after widowhood are generally more successful than those following divorce. This is to be expected, since the widowed person has a more likely record of success in marriage. Divorced persons are a much greater risk in remarriage than persons who are in their first marriage, and divorced women are a greater risk than divorced men.

Those divorced and remarried persons, if they divorce again, do so after a shorter period of marriage on the average, than they did in their first marriage: for white men, the first marriage lasted 7.7 years, the second only 6.0 years; for white women 7.9 and 7.4 years, respectively (Glick and Norton, 1971).

Statistics aside, there are divorced persons who make a great success of remarriage, and some divorcees even remarry each other and succeed in the remarriage. For some, divorce has a maturing effect. For many, it makes the road of escape from a subsequent marriage easier.

DIVORCE AND THE CHILD

A special study dealing with 1960 data showed that 57 percent of homes broken by divorce had children under 18, the average being 1.18 per family. A 1966 study of census data showed that divorced women head most such families, and there was an average of 1.65 dependent children per family (*Statistical Bulletin* 1970). Even large families are not immune to divorce and annulment. A special analysis of data gathered by the census of 1965 shows the number of families of different sizes involved in divorce (see Figure 28–9). Only-child families are more exposed to divorce, but a substantial number of families of all sizes are affected.

The total picture of broken homes for the nation where children are involved is shown in Figure 28–10 (see also Glick 1963). These data include homes broken by death and desertion, as well as by divorce. The major cause

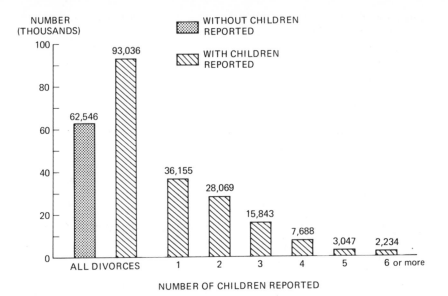

NUMBER (THOUSANDS)

WITHOUT CHILDREN REPORTED

WITH CHILDREN REPORTED

93,036

62,546

36,155

28,069

15,843

7,688

3,047

2,234

ALL DIVORCES — 1 — 2 — 3 — 4 — 5 — 6 or more

NUMBER OF CHILDREN REPORTED

Divorces and annulments by number children under 18 reported: divorce-registration area, 1965. Almost half a million children in the nation under 18 years of age have lived through the divorce or separation of their parents. According to this sample, well over half of all divorces are in families with dependent children. Source: "Excerpts from Vital Statistics of the United States, 1965, Vol. III—Marriage and Divorce," U.S. Department of Health, Education, and Welfare, Table 2–18, p. 2–15.

FIGURE 28–9

is, of course, divorce, since most parents live to the age when their children have already passed 18 years of age. Data on this are presented on p. 388.

Divorce May Be the Better Alternative   Social concern for the welfare of children affected by divorce is of great importance. Yet sociologists, counselors, domestic relations court judges, and child-guidance clinic professionals have long known that divorce may be a better alternative for the child than living under the tensions of a home in which there is no solution to the marriage relations problem.

One of the most convincing analyses on this point is that by Plant (1944). Writing for judges involved in the legal processes of the divorce courts, he stated that in many cases divorce is the best possible solution for the child. He found that ten times as many children were sent to the Essex County, N.Y., Juvenile Clinic from separated parents as from divorced parents. Less disturbance was shown in the lives of children of divorced parents than in those of separated parents. He believed the divorce court, in granting the decree and in assigning the child to one parent, making whatever financial arrangements are necessary, is often doing the most that can be done to remedy the situation from the standpoint of the welfare of the child. Divorce is not an ideal solution, but is the only one possible in certain instances. In such cases, it comes as a great relief to the child.

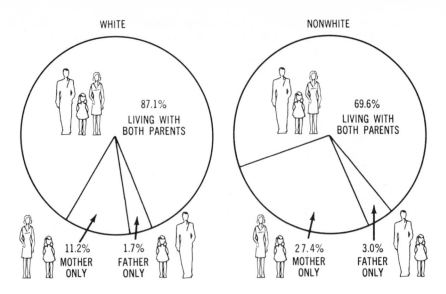

WHITE

87.1%
LIVING WITH
BOTH PARENTS

11.2%
MOTHER
ONLY

1.7%
FATHER
ONLY

NONWHITE

69.6%
LIVING WITH
BOTH PARENTS

27.4%
MOTHER
ONLY

3.0%
FATHER
ONLY

FIGURE 28–10 Children in broken families. Distribution by race of children under 18 living with one parent. See also Paul C. Glick, "Marriage Instability: Variations by Size of Place and Religion," *The Milbank Memorial Fund Quarterly*, 41:43–55, January, 1963. U.S. Department of Commerce, Bureau of the Census, *Current Population Reports: Population Characteristics*, Series P–20, No. 112 (December 29, 1961, p. 13).

There has been much publicity of the fact that children of divorced homes make up an undue proportion of delinquents. As a consequence of such reports, the public generally blames divorce for these problems. Actually, this kind of thinking is erroneous. Divorce itself is simply the legal incident in the conflict of marriage partners.

Far from being the cause for children's problems, divorce is often the solution. The damage to the child was done long before the divorce decree was sought and might have been avoided had the divorce come sooner. The damage to the child comes from perpetual conflict between parents; from his being used as a pawn in their conflict. Those who work with children's problems and with courts of domestic relations observe that parents in conflict are rarely fair to the child. Each parent will try to influence the child against the other parent. In some cases, one parent will use the child as an excuse for holding the marriage together. Without any regard for his feelings or interests, a parent may pour out his miseries and condemnations of the other parent into the innocent child's ears.

Paul W. Alexander (1952), who presided over 30,000 divorces and who on alternate days presided over the juvenile court, observed that during some years as many as 40 percent of couples with children who come for divorces have been to the juvenile court previously with their children's problems. Certainly this is striking evidence that problems of delinquency appear before the divorce.

There is an increasing body of evidence that divorce in and of itself is not seriously harmful to children. The aftereffects depend a great deal on the kind of relationship that preceded the breakup. There is the strong likelihood in many instances that the effects on the child might have been more disastrous had the divorce not taken place. Burchinal (1964), in one of the most refined pieces of research to date, compared five types of family groups in their effects on some 1500 young people in seventh through eleventh grades: unbroken families, mothers only, mother and stepfather, both parents remarried, and fathers and stepmothers. For the most part, he finds no differences in personality and social relationship scores. He concludes that the broken family, and even the reconstituted family, where remarriage of a parent or parents takes place, "was not the overwhelming influential factor in the children's lives that many thought it to be."

Perhaps the social adjustment process is far different today, even for children, than it was in an earlier day when divorce was a more definite challenge to the mores. Greater tolerance has no doubt permeated both community and school.

Judson T. Landis (1960a) has found that the effect of divorce on the child varies greatly with the age of the child at the time of divorce—it is less traumatic for younger children—and how the child viewed the parent relationship prior to the divorce—those who considered the home happy suffered more trauma.

Bernard (1971) studied attitudes of men and women toward children acquired through remarriage. Almost two-thirds of divorced men and 56 percent of divorced women were affectionate toward children acquired. Only about 5 percent of divorced men and 7 percent of divorced women rejected them. About a third neither rejected nor were affectionate.

Schlesinger's (1969) study in-depth of 84 Canadian couples who had made a success of remarriage, finds that couples are keenly aware of the dual adjustment the marriage requires—that to each other and to any children brought into the marriage.

The problem for the one who has no children, usually the male, is to learn to be a father, which involves loving children he did not sire, and learning to establish effective discipline. This study of successful marriages shows that there was a strong tendency on the part of both parents and stepchildren to want to adjust. About half of stepparents admitted some difficulty in adjusting.

Another unique problem of the remarried with stepchildren is equality of treatment with any children born into the new marriage. Here couples have to rationalize and resolve in a way that is not done when siblings are being added to a first marriage. Schlesinger finds that parents do have the new children with a resolution to treat all children equal. In the successful marriage, they are apparently usually able to carry out the resolutions. It is probable that in marriages which fail, reasonableness cannot be carried over into emotional acceptance.

Margaret Mead (1968) expresses the view that the shock of divorce could be eased by bringing up children to realize that people today live a very long time and may not wish to spend their full lifetime together. She feels women should also be taught not to feel abandoned and hurt when a marriage ends after 20 years. She believes that we have not even accepted the fact of divorce yet.

It will be quite a different world when children are brought up to believe that a parent may leave at his discretion for another mate, and when wives do not feel abandoned if their husband chooses to leave them for another. It seems not to be in the making now.

Psychiatrist Lawrence S. Kubie recommends that custody of children be assigned to a committee. Parents would agree on custody arrangements, as is now usually the case, but would select a committee composed of a pediatrician, a child psychologist, an educator, and a lawyer or clergyman, who would arbitrate disagreements between parents rather than have custody disputes thrown into court. Another child specialist would serve as an "adult ally" for the child, winning his confidence and keeping informed as to the child's feelings about the custody relationships. This ally would report to the committee.

Although this sounds like a cumbersome arrangement, a growing number of parents are using it and finding it better than a court for settling custody disputes and for holding down quarrels about custody. It also relieves the courts of a heavy burden.

POSTDIVORCE ADJUSTMENT

Under the 1969 California Family Law Act, the judge alone hears the case, and without witnesses or adversary proceedings of any kind, may grant the divorce if it appears to him that there are irreconcilable differences. If he feels that there is a possibility of reconciliation, the couple is referred to the Domestic Relations Court. The act even does away with the term *divorce,* using instead the term, *dissolution of marriage.* Child support and alimony may still be given, and community property division is equal between spouses.

It is believed that by eliminating the adversary situation, there will be less opening of old wounds. Private matters will not be aired in court, false testimony given by witnesses to bolster the claims of one or the other mate will no longer be necessary, and other damaging exposures will cease. There is more likelihood that both the couple and the children will suffer less damage and carry over less hostility as they take up their new life. There will be greater possibility of later reconciliation, too, or at least of genuine cooperation in sharing the child where children are involved.

There is likely to be a great deal of insecurity after divorce, particularly for the woman. She has had to acknowledge defeat in the relationship that means most to women. She is likely to feel abandoned, and she may feel bereaved. She faces a world in which she must accept both masculine and feminine roles, as far as business and managerial affairs are concerned and in supporting and disciplining the children.

When she begins to circulate among friends again, she is more suspect than is the widow in that insecure wives consider her a threat to their marriage and a competitor for the attentions of their husbands. Males are likely to consider her fair game, although for a time she may feel as though she never wants anything to do with men again.

In our day of Women's Liberation, it may seem inappropriate to call attention to the fact that the male may actually suffer severe postdivorce adjustments, perhaps more than the divorced wife. She usually retains the home which he has helped provide, with whatever comforts they have earned together. She usually retains a family environment, since she customarily has custody of the children. She perhaps has more social support of the community and friends. She is less often blamed legally and by social censure. He leaves his home and children, perhaps community. He may feel that the wife, courts, and lawyers have "taken" him, no matter how gallant he may have been in refusing to challenge charges of adultery, cruelty, etc. He is more likely to be overcome by loneliness and a feeling of social rejection. He is more likely to suffer from emotional disorders, mortality risks, and suicide or attempted suicide. Although the exwife's economic problems are severe, his may be also if child support is heavy. And this may hinder his willingness or ability to seek remarriage.

Divorce Anonymous P.O. Box 5313, Chicago, Ill. 60680 now exists nationwide for mutual help and understanding, and many churches have "divorcee clubs" to try to give support to the many who feel shame and stigma and yet who are religiously inclined. Many divorced persons need the church to help them find new purpose in life. Parents Without Partners 7910 Woodmont Ave. Suite 1000, Washington, D.C. 20014 is a nationwide organization designed to help the divorced and the widowed with their special problems.

PROBLEMS

1   Which of these philosophies do you consider most desirable in a young bride or groom?

   a   "I said it and I meant it, 'until death do us part.' I shall never never consider divorce."

   b   "If things don't work out well, there is always the divorce court."

   c   "I believe in this marriage and I'll do my best to make it a happy one. If my best isn't good enough, however, I won't let pride or pressure frighten me of divorce."

2   Dividing the class into two opposing groups, discuss divorce as: *(a)* an indication that marriage is taken less seriously than in the past, *(b)* an indication that marriage is taken more seriously than in the past.

3   Upon what legal grounds are most divorces obtained? Compare these reasons with the actual grounds.

4   Divorce, unlike death, is a separation usually preceded by tension and antagonism. Why, then, are so many divorces accompanied by tears and a period similar to bereavement?

5   Charles and Hannah have read about the undesirable effect divorce has on children. They no longer love one another, seldom ever speak, and Charles, who is deeply in love with another woman, spends most of his time in town to escape Hannah's bitter tears. They have agreed, however, that until their children, five and seven, are fully grown, they will not consider separation.

   a   How wise do you consider their decision?

   b   What might the effect of their relationship be on the two children?

c Do you think their two children might profit if Charles and Hannah obtained a divorce?

6 Considering the statistical evidence, would you say that a marriage ending in divorce tends to embitter most individuals against the institution of marriage?

7 Marriage is, after all, a relationship between two people that is capable of producing intense and lifelong misery as well as happiness. Do you think that it is justifiable for any individual judge to have the power to deny a divorce to an unhappy couple? Discuss.

8 Upon what grounds may divorces be obtained in your state? In what ways could divorce laws be improved?

9 *Sociodrama:* A young divorcée returns to her parents' home but receives a rather cool reception. The drama might open with the observation of one of her parents: 'Now, you've been bitten once, I hope you don't expect to try marriage again. You just aren't the type!"

"Nonsense!" The girl might reply. "This has been sad, but it has also been the best thing that ever happened to me."

Go on to picture the therapeutic results of the divorce.

BETTER MARRIAGES

29 There are undoubtedly many who think trial marriage, premarital sex, and experimental marriage of various kinds before the real thing will prove to be the way ahead for marriage. There is little in sociological research to make one hope that this is the way to greater stability of marriage or greater happiness for mates. There is even less to make one believe that such a background is the preferable one for parenthood. It is proven fact that those who experiment before marriage are most likely to do so after marriage. Satisfactory marriage needs an attitude of commitment rather than one of experimentation.

Today an increasing part of the case load of marriage counselors is made up of young people in various stages of experimental living together. They become involved and do not know how to break it up, or one wants to marry and the other does not. The couple thought they were free, but emotional involvement does not work equally for both. One may want to do as he pleases, and the the other feels used and abused. They try therapy, but usually do not stay with the counseling program to see it through. It is easier to shift to another partner than to solve emerging problems in the relationship with the present one. This kind of running away may well carry over into marriage.

THREE APPROACHES TO MARRIAGE IMPROVEMENT

Improvements may be expected from the (1) legal and governmental policy-making, (2) educational, and (3) remedial directions. These are not mutually exclusive approaches; in fact, they overlap at points.

The legal and governmental has the advantage of quick and decisive action in that it can exercise the prohibitive function, "Thou shalt not." In areas of promotion, the legislative process is much slower, but even that is fast compared with education, where one must often work a generation ahead for results. Urban–industrial society has come to depend so much on governmental action for social improvement that it is often referred to as "the welfare state."

The educational has no power to compel change, rather it controls by internalizing values and goals, it guides and presents evidence and incentives. It shows that if better methods of living and doing are adopted, outcomes will be more satisfying. It selects from the culture, transmits the better parts of it to the young, and uses the lessons both of failure and success.

The remedial approach is the proverbial method of "locking the stable after the horse is stolen," but society is never without its need for cures, for there is no way of keeping all men from error, no way of educating for marriage or of restricting youth adequately by law, so as to prevent many from making unwise marriage choices. And married people do encounter difficulties and must seek remedial measures. In the area of marriage and of children's problems, the remedial is so much in demand that neither sound techniques nor trained personnel are accessible in sufficient numbers to deal with them.

LEGAL RESTRICTION OF MARRIAGE

States have jurisdiction over marriage and divorce. Until this changes, and there are uniform marriage and divorce laws throughout the country—a highly desirable objective from a sociological point of view—the most to be hoped for is that the various states will adopt measures that have proved effective in states having them and that all states will improve on their best measures.

Age Requirements   Age regulations have to do with (1) age below which one cannot marry at all, (2) age below which parents' or guardians' consent is required, (3) age at which one is free to marry of his own choice. Most states require that girls be 16 before they can marry with parental consent and that boys be 18. The usual age for marriage without parental consent is 18 for girls and 21 for boys. Age restrictions may be waived when the girl is pregnant. A few states have no age restrictions at all. A few states recognize common-law marriages at age 12. A few states permit marriage of girls age 13 or 14 with parental consent. In requiring the male to be older, the state recognizes the difficulty the young male is likely to have in supporting a wife and family.

A nationwide goal of a minimum age of 18 for girls and 21 for boys would seem to be a reasonable objective for every state. The problems of teen-agers are so many in urban society that this rule would be a quick way to cut the divorce rate and ease the social burden of dependent children. Exceptions would have to be made in cases of pregnancy, but even in such cases, the right to marry might well be prefaced by a requirement of counseling and other guidance and help.

Waiting Period   States with stricter laws purposely delay marriage, thus hindering hasty and ill-advised marriages. All states require a marriage license, common-law marriages being the exception. Except in some cities, a license usually can be bought only during working hours and on weekdays, when county officials have office hours. This fact alone hinders many marriages of couples who otherwise would marry without much forethought.

Some states require that the license be applied for a few days before it can be issued. Some require a lapse of time between acquiring the license and marriage. A medical certificate clearing the pair of venereal disease must have been obtained in advance in most states, and be presented to the clerk as part of the license application.

Research indicates that where people are compelled to wait, many do change their minds and fail to follow through to marriage (Plateris 1966; Shipman and Tien 1965). Others, of course, cross the line into states which have no waiting period. Uniformity of law in the various states would hopefully require that all go through a period during which they could reconsider. Lengthening the waiting period beyond that now in effect in any state would undoubtedly cut down on ill-advised marriages further still. Few states have a waiting period of more than three days. Oregon has the longest waiting period, seven days. It is likely that the goal of a 30-day waiting period nationwide would be a realistic one.

CONTROL OF DIVORCE

In the area of restrictive legislation, a period of separation prior to divorce seems to offer some promise as a way of lowering divorce rates and thus avoiding the tangled web of relationships, emotional and financial, that the ill-considered divorce brings. The period of separation prior to divorce, required in several states, gives the couple a chance to compare their marriage with return to single life, to sense to an extent what it will mean to them, and if there are children, to the children also. We know that some couples divorce and later remarry each other. A waiting period could forestall some of this legal burden and family disruption.

A waiting period before remarriage, now in effect in some states, may be of value also. It may not deter divorce, but it can be a factor in a new marriage's being considered more carefully than in the case of two couples who divorce, then go to the other floor of the courthouse and remarry, as they now can, and sometimes do, in Reno.

Divorce Reform   Courts of reconciliation have their place, but the remedy usually comes too late. By the time a couple goes to court, most bridges have already been burned behind them. Uniform divorce laws between the states would stop some divorces entered into too hastily. More readily available counseling services would be a better deterrent. In the court procedure of divorce itself, reform must be in the direction of eliminating the adversary approach in all states and settling the case in the interest of the children and the couples with the fewest possible battles. The case-history approach has as the first objective the welfare and rehabilitation of the persons involved.

GOVERNMENT SOCIAL POLICIES

In the supportive area, numerous welfare programs and policies have built minimum security about the family. We look to the government still as the action agency from which further help must come in urban–industrial society. The broad areas of Social Security have given mothers with dependent children and the widowed a minimum of protection. Medicare has lifted another load from the young couple for the care of elderly parents. All these programs can be improved.

There are two important areas where our nation lags behind most industrial nations: (1) adequate medical care for the entire family, and (2) family allowances to equalize in part the economic load of the couple with and the one without children.

Medical Care　　We are backward among Western industrial nations in medical care. Most of them have a lower infant and maternal mortality rate, and we lag in many other indices of health. We have some of the best medical facilities in the world, but a poor system of medical administration. Millions have inadequate medical care.

Our medical system is very much profit-oriented. We are one of the few industrial nations without a salaried medical profession and a system of tax-supported medical and dental care. It is in the nations with such care that health records exceed ours.

Annual Wage　　The annual wage for industrial workers is full of promise for greater happiness in marriage. Research has shown that regularity of income is associated with successful marriage. The industrial classes, which now show the greatest amount of unhappiness in marriage, might well enjoy a higher level of marital happiness with a regularity of income that would provide for greater stability and permit more meaningful planning.

Family Allowances　　In the economic field, too, the family allowance systems now in effect in practically every other major industrial nation represent a means of bringing about greater equality between the sexes. This system is also conducive to a greater feeling of economic security and to greater marital stability. Family allowances, paid by taxation, usually are paid to the mother, giving her a new sense of independence and equality. The family allowance also gives her vocation a new dignity. By providing a regular guarantee for the minimum support of all children, it places marriage on a safer foundation. Family allowance systems exist in almost all industrial nations, including our neighbor, Canada.

In an agrarian society, security is in the land, and all members of the family, as workers, increase that security. In an industrial society, a man and wife's security is in their own earning power. The economic disadvantage of having children in an industrial society is clearly shown by data presented in Figure 29-1. Democratic industrial society must, through such social policies as those suggested above, make life safer for marriage and the family.

Population Control   The time has come when complete control of fertility is possible, yet we have many working-class families, particularly among the nonwhites, who are propagating themselves into the third generation on relief. There is little hope of successfully attacking poverty or raising the standard of

Relationship of children and income. Couples without children have an average per capita income of $3614. Add a child and that average drops to $2391 per capita. Add six children and it drops to $736 per capita. Source: "Consumer Income," *Current Population Reports,* Series P-60, No. 53, December 28, 1967, Table 5, p. 26.

FIGURE 29-1

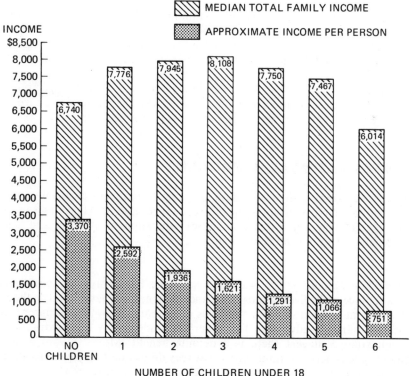

living of this great dispossessed group in the city slums and rural poverty pockets except by bringing fertility under control. Family-assistance programs have been expanding in the family-planning area.

Children in all families, the privileged and underprivileged alike, should be the voluntary issue of the family. This can be only as we develop a national policy of birth control which seeks aggressively to make parenthood voluntary. It will require a system of birth-control clinics throughout underprivileged rural areas and slum sections where such programs can be promoted as an end toward raising the standard of living and economic and educational aspirations.

Planned Parenthood now has offices in many cities where advice and help is given. The American Association for Voluntary Sterilization has carried out experimental projects in selected areas. It is now possible to use "poverty" funds for birth control. Abortion has become a woman's legal right. The projected family-planning budget for 1974 is $122 million (Rosoff 1973). An Internal Revenue ruling of April 1973, held that the cost of birth control was a deductible expense.

Quality Control   Quality control is the goal of industry. Its practice in American agriculture through selective plant and animal breedings has doubled production and made our agriculture second to none. Quality control in human population is no less necessary and deserves attention in a world where numbers must be limited.

The first step is registration of all families with known defective traits. A computerized national register is now possible to the point where each engaged pair could be compared for like recessive traits. Social policy could determine the degree of risk tolerated. The too risky could be permitted to marry only if first sterilized.

There could be endless debate as to the rightness of such measures, but few could face the evidence and make a case against the resulting improvement in the welfare of children, and in the happiness of married pairs.

THE EDUCATIONAL APPROACH

America has great faith in education as a long-term means of social improvement. In the marriage field the most direct approaches are (1) courses in marriage preparation, (2) instruction in sex education of children and young people, and (3) premarital counseling.

Family-Life Education   Although marriage has always occupied an important place in the lives of most men and women, there has been little thought of any formal preparation for the roles of husband and wife and parent. The case for marriage education has never been adequately demonstrated, but certain studies suggest there is a definite benefit. Moses' (1956) study of students and married alumni shows that they do feel that they gain insight and learn to solve problems as a consequence of their training for marriage.

One of the aims of family-life education is to help young people approach marriage and family living realistically. This requires providing information concerning what can make marriage a success. Family-life education helps to develop an understanding of interaction patterns which make for greater marriage competence. The fact that it helps young people to discard certain folklore conceptions can be of great value. Most colleges now teach a general marriage course and a course in the history of the family, as well as various courses in child psychology and development. Unfortunately, these courses are still taken primarily by women, even though men need them.

One of the interesting developments in this field has been the tendency for the content to become increasingly functional, that is, directed at the specific problems young people face in their adjustments to the opposite sex during the premarital period and the early years of marriage. The greatest handicap in the development of this approach to date is the lack of sufficient research material to provide an adequate guide, but an increasing amount of sociological and psychological research is in the making.

Family-life education must be extended into the high school to provide both boys and girls with opportunity to observe nursery schools in operation, observe the care of small babies, and learn more about parenthood and child training. One of the barriers to popular acceptance of broad courses in preparation for marriage, particularly on the elementary and high school level, is that they are frequently equated with sex education courses. Many parents are still frightened or suspicious of group teaching in this area. Sex education has an important place in these courses because of its importance in marriage, but it is not the only, not even the primary, purpose of the course. Combating folklore notions of mate finding and marriage adjustment and instilling some appreciation of the full possibilities of marriage and family life—these are more often the basic goals.

Sex Education　　High on the list of personal needs which marriage now seeks to satisfy are those of intimacy, companionship, and love. These needs, as has been observed, derive their fulfillment in large part from the sex relations of man and wife. This elevates sex to a position of new importance in marriage. Most couples now consider satisfactory sex relations a necessary part of marriage and unsatisfactory relations as ample justification for divorce.

Sex education is gaining increased acceptance on the elementary and secondary level of the public school system. Were it practical to delay this formal education until later adolescence, the program would probably arouse much less opposition. Many parents feel that instruction in the lower grades is either unnecessary or dangerous. They argue that it may only raise questions and arouse curiosity. But sex education does begin in a child's early years. During the first six years of a child's life, he inevitably begins to wonder about such obvious and fascinating matters as "where babies come from." How this and similar questions are handled—the atmosphere in which they are discussed, the individual answering them, the facts or fictions that are passed along—can have a serious and lasting effect upon a young person's attitudes toward sex, marriage, and parenthood.

Sex education must begin at home, for that is where the child's questions begin. Parents must be sufficiently prepared for these early questions to answer them honestly and without evasion or shame. This education is readily carried forward in the nursery school, where both sexes use the same toilets and have a chance to observe each other and to have questions answered by trained personnel, who answer without undesirable emotional overtones.

The older the child is, the less likely is the parent to give adequate information, or even to guide at all. Many parents do not have the vocabulary, and some allow the communication gap to close before they get around to the subject of sex in its various aspects. Perhaps even the well-informed parent will not be able to handle the subject naturally and fully. Mace (1962) suggests that incest taboos may make parents reticent to discuss sex subjects with their own children. This would be particularly true with older sons and daughters.

We know that appalling ignorance abounds. Poffenberger (1959) reports that anonymous questions put in a question box by eighth-grade girls in a marriage and family life course indicate a shocking lack of information. About half of the girls asked questions about sexual intercourse using vulgar terms.

Hillman's (1954) study of letters to an advice column showed that more informational inquiries centered around sex than around any other single topic. Second were queries about birth control. This would seem to indicate a great deficiency in the sex education in the typical person writing to such a source for information.

Landis and Landis (1973) find no improvement in the number of parents giving sex education to their children among the thousands of college students studied, comparing 1967 students with 1952 students. This may in part reflect the fact that college enrollments now reach into lower status groups with the mass movement into college. But even allowing for this factor as a possible influence, there is much room for improvement.

Sex education is best presented as part of a broader course in family-life education. This fits it into proper context and helps ward off community attack. Any sex education program, presented in isolation from such a context, tends to bring strong protest from a vocal minority in the community and risks causing principals and superintendents of schools to clamp down on the program.

Premarital Counseling   One of the aims of professional counseling is to discover the unmarriageable person or incompatible pair before marriage. Research gives some clues here. In fact, tests of considerable reliability are now available for predicting the success or failure of a marriage. Greater development can be expected in this field, but aside from this, counseling can be of great value in helping people understand themselves and each other prior to marriage. Objectivity at this stage, when change is easy, involves little personal and social damage.

Measurements of temperament and personality are becoming more dependable. Tests for predicting marriage outcome are based on more dependable norms. It is increasingly possible that the premarital counseling clinic can be helpful in the area of psychological and emotional relationships, in addition to the psychosexual. All clinics employ various tests as counseling aids.

Perhaps it is premature to expect that all contemplating marriage be required to submit to certain tests and examinations. Facilities are not adequate, nor is sufficient personnel available. But the goal is worth seeking. Perhaps even now all teen-age marriages for which pregnancy is the cause should have to undergo counseling and be assigned social service counsel for their beginning years. This would seem to be in the interest of protecting the child from immature parents.

THE REMEDIAL APPROACH

Popenoe (1970) says there are 40 million husbands and wives who need counseling, but there are only a few thousand counseling specialists in the marriage field. Psychologist Carl Rogers estimates that there are at least 80 million people in the nation who would immediately seek help in the general counseling area if it were available at a price they could afford. And there are many young people looking toward marriage who would like counsel with someone broadly trained and nonjudgmental in their approach.

The remedial approach includes not only preparatory and marital counseling in clinics but also help from the minister or the family doctor, who actually do most of the counseling according to the study of Gurin, Veroff, and Feld (1960; see Table 29-1), going to relatives, and in serious cases seeking out the psychiatrist, psychologist, or lawyer for advice.

Now, when many have no close relative or friend in whom to confide, there is great need to confide and to shed burdens in the counseling situation. How many of these counseling sources are qualified to render assistance, no one knows, and what their motive is in rendering the assistance varies with individual and by profession. But it is likely that just being able to talk with someone and to get problems out into the open brings relief.

Presumably the professional counselor is the ideal source in that he is not oriented toward a moral solution or a religious goal in his work, but toward a solution to the person's problem, but the fact remains that in most states the counseling profession is unlicensed and passes no qualifying tests. Counselors who belong to the American Association of Marriage Counselors meet the

Relationship of Source of Help Used to the Problem Area (First-Mentioned Responses Only)   **TABLE 29-1**

PROBLEM AREA IS SPOUSE OR MARRIAGE	CLERGY	DOCTOR	PSYCHIA-TRIST	COUN-SELOR	OTHER PSYCHO-LOGICAL AGENCIES	NONPSYCHO-LOGICAL AGENCIES	LAWYER
				SOURCE OF HELP			
Frequency	60	32	16	11	9	1	8
Percentage	43.8	23	12	8	6.5	.7	5

Source: Gerald Gurin, Joseph Veroff, and Sheila Feld, *Americans View Their Mental Health* (New York: Basic Books, 1960, p. 309).

standards of this professional group. Most practicing marriage counselors are not members.

Psychiatrists, psychoanalysts, and clinical psychologists are trained but also highly individuated in theoretical perspective, conceptual premises, and methods of treatment. Their results are not submitted to scientific verification and are often suspect, even among more critical members of their own professions. Their services are costly and there is great scarcity of personnel. For the most part they serve the affluent.

Various group methods of treatment are now in use, which helps spread the limited time available. Some methods of treating groups are also highly individualistic, being perhaps more a reflection of a particular man and his theoretical premises rather than of a proved sound method of rendering permanent help to the couple in trouble. Whether they provide more than a place where one can relieve his frustrations by talking or acting is to be proven. In many instances, time may be the real healer, rather than the particular ritual through which one specialist or another leads the person or the pair in trouble. All approaches must be considered experimental.

The ministerial profession begins with a bias in the counseling approach. Ministers are apostles of the good life. This predisposes them to seek certain values in their guiding people in marital difficulties. Whether they are more inclined to save a marriage which cannot and should not be saved for the sake of parents, and particularly for the sake of children, than other counselors is not known from research. Probably they lean in this direction more than, say, doctors or psychiatrists, or even bartenders, who no doubt listen to many marriage confessions and may also be generous with advice.

Doctors are more involved with physical and sexual problems of marriages, but these carry over into the psychosomatic; any doctor with experience and insight knows that he is very often dealing with problems that exceed those of the flesh. Perhaps the majority avoid giving advice beyond the physical, and provide for relief with placebos and tranquilizers, but they do listen, even if briefly, and no doubt at times drop hints as to a wise alternative.

William M. Sheppe, Jr. (1969) finds doctors very inadequate in the field of sex counseling, owing to "the physician's own personality structure, his life experience, and inadequate medical curricula." He reports that in working with both doctors and clergy, the better-educated clergy are "far more knowledgeable and emotionally free in discussing human sexuality and marital problems than their medical peers."

More and better-trained marriage counselors and more strict licensing requirements are goals to be reached, but it is likely that most people will still go to their minister as the first source of help. He is a trusted source of sympathy; he is accessible; his services are free to the parishoner, and in many instances to any who come; and there are more ministers than there can ever be professional counselors. Ministers in the better seminaries are being given much more extensive training in counseling and related disciplines. There will continue to be the great mass without seminary training, whose qualifications for duty are "the call" and whose counseling will be authoritarian admonitions, "Thus saith the Lord."

The Ministerial Association of Prescott, Arizona, illustrates what united action in a community can do in putting bars in the way of unwise marriage and in making the pair consider the step they are taking. Here are their resolutions ("Clergymen Act" 1968):

497

1   Outright refusal to perform "doorbell" marriages (couples seeking immediate ceremony).
2   A minimum of three premarital counseling sessions with the engaged couple, reserving the right to refuse to perform the service if the first session indicates the wisdom of such a decision.
3   The minister shall secure from the engaged couple written permission to intervene voluntarily and at his own discretion if the marriage appears at some later date to be threatened with dissolution.
4   The minister shall exert the strongest possible persuasion to discourage marriage of girls under 18 and men under 21 years of age.
5   The minister shall consider with the couple and other interested parties the possibility that marriage is not necessarily the best solution to out-of-wedlock pregnancies.

The association also agreed to arrange at least one annual school for engaged couples and to promote in every way the sanctity of marriage.

Medical training has been seriously deficient in sex education and in providing background for understanding psychosomatic complaints. It has not given a broad basic background such as is needed for either premarital counseling or remedial counseling. Conditions are improving, but the pressure for more and more technical training, and the growing body of medical knowledge, is likely to threaten this broader training. The doctor, by law, is the only professional person with whom persons must consult prior to marriage, and he is the one to whom they are certain to go after marriage.

PROBLEMS

1   List and discuss various attitudes and skills which might be taught to young people in courses in family-life education.
2   Which goals do you believe should be uppermost in such courses—teaching specific homemaking skills or developing specific homemaking and family-oriented attitudes?
3   At what grade level do you believe sex education should begin in school?
4   What are the chief arguments presented by some parents in opposition to sex education at any level in public schools? How might these arguments best be met?
5   Ideally, should sex education be handled chiefly by the home or the school? Why?
6   Discuss the views presented in the following conversation:
    One mother, "I'm opposed to sex education in or out of school. I believe that young men and women should be given the necessary facts when they're old enough to need them, not before." She adds, "All of this fuss about children

being 'naturally curious' is just poppycock. Why my 11-year-old daughter has never once asked a question having to do with sex, reproduction, or the like."

Her companion answers, "If I had an 11-year-old daughter who hadn't asked about anything associated with sex, I would not brag, I'd be alarmed."

7 A respected marriage counselor in a New York community was recently sued for a divorce. As a result he lost many of his clients who seemed to feel, as one woman put it, "If he can't make a success of his own marriage, how can others have faith in him?" Among those who remained with him was a young husband who answered this charge with, "My physician is often sick, but this does not reflect upon his professional skill."

What would your reaction have been to this divorce had you been a client? Justify your position.

8 In the West Haven Marriage and Family Relations Clinic there are two marriage counselors using very different techniques in their counseling. Of the two, Dr. Robell is the more popular. He is generous with his advice and not at all reluctant to suggest specific action as a cure for a couple's problems.

Dr. Murry seldom gives advice. His chief goal seems to be getting man and wife, or an engaged couple, into the clinic together. Once there, Dr. Murry speaks only enough to keep the two of them going in their conversation together about their differences.

a Upon what principle is Dr. Murry operating?
b Why is Dr. Robel more popular?
c Which counselor do you believe is the more successful in helping couples work out solutions to their problems?

9 Which of the areas of legal action do you think is the most promising as a way to improve marriage?

10 Debate: *Resolved:* That the United States should adopt the family allowance.

APPENDIX:
AUTOBIOGRAPHICAL
TERM PAPER

On each topic trace your background, and show how each trait or characteristic is likely to affect you as a marriage partner and parent.

I. Love

A. Affection: Can you give and receive affection? Is love or hostility the dominant trait of your personality? Relate to family background. Relate to marriageability and parenthood.
B. Romantic love: (1) On separate sheets of paper, chart your completed love affairs; love, attraction, indifference, dislike. . . . (2) Chart course of your emotions after breakup—love, attraction, indifference, dislike . . . (see p. 142 of text for pattern).

II. Work Duty Patterns

What is your balance between work and pleasure? Can you pursue goals to their conclusion? Are you willing to assume the obligations of caring for others, particularly children? Is your orientation primarily toward consumption or production; acquiring goods or display? Relate to the past and the future.

III. Psychological Patterns

A. Ego needs: Are you essentially ego-centered or love-centered? Why?
B. Basic emotions: What is your dominant emotion—love, hate, fear, anxiety, etc.?

Completing statements like the following will be helpful, "I hate most deeply"; "I fear most deeply"; "I am most anxious about"; etc.

C. *Approach:* Is your approach to people and to life essentially negative or positive?

D. *Psychosexual orientation:* Here consider the physical, psychological, and moral orientation of your personality. Is your personality in this area primarily guilt-centered, pleasure-centered, love-centered? Are your attitudes those of disgust or wholesome anticipation?

IV. Life Goals

Dominant aspirations: What do you want most in life? Wealth? Happiness? Learning? What influences built this goal? How will if affect your mate choice and the development of your family life?

V. Role Orientation

Male and female grow up under different subcultures. Do you accept the role of your sex or protest it? What do you expect in the way of behavior of the person you marry? Do you anticipate a role of equality or the traditional male–female pattern of roles? Can you readily compromise your role expectations for a member of the opposite sex whom you expect to marry? If you are already engaged, what role changes do you expect of your future spouse?

VI. Sibling Position

What is your place among brothers and sisters? How has this affected your personality as it relates to your marriageability? If an only child, how has this affected your adjustments to the opposite sex?

VII. Conventionality

Are you a rebel or an easily institutionalized person? Do you regard conventions of marriage important? Does marriage make sense in the obligations and vows it imposes? Do you want children in marriage? Do you consider a similar religion important to your marriage? Were the ceremonial occasions in your parental family that you plan to reproduce in your family?

Specifications:

1   Paper should range between 2000 and 5000 words.
2   Place your name on a face sheet, which will be keyed and removed before papers are read to assure anonymity.
3   Papers will be held in complete confidence for two years, after which the file will be available to marriage classes.

BIBLIOGRAPHY

ADAMS, CLIFFORD R., and PACKARD, VANCE O. *How to Pick a Mate: The Guide to a Happy Marriage.* New York: Dutton, 1946.

ADAMS, ROMANZO. *Interracial Marriage in Hawaii: A Study of Mutually Conditioned Processes of Acculturation and Amalgamation.* New York: Macmillan, 1937.

ALBERT, ETHEL M. "The Roles of Women: Questions of Values." In Farber and Wilson, 1963, pp. 105–15.

ALEXANDER, PAUL W. "A Therapeutic Approach to Divorce." In *Conference on Divorce.* Chicago: University of Chicago Law School, 29 Feb. 1952.

ANDERSON, C. L. *Physical and Emotional Aspects of Marriage.* St. Louis: C. V. Mosby, 1953.

ANSBACHER, HEINZ L., and ANSBACHER, ROWENA R., eds. *Individual Psychology of Alfred Adler: A Systematic Presentation in Selections from His Writings.* New York: Basic Books, 1956.

BABER, RAY E. "A Study of 325 Mixed Marriages." *American Sociological Review* 2 (1 Oct. 1937):705–16.

BACH, GEORGE, and WYDEN, PETER. *The Intimate Enemy: How to Fight Fair in Love and Marriage.* New York: Morrow, 1969.

BARIZ, KAREN WINCH, and NYE, F. IVAN. "Early Marriage: A Propositional Formulation." *Journal of Marriage and the Family* 32 (1970):258–68.

BARNETT, LARRY D. "Research on International and Interracial Marriages." *Marriage and Family Living* 25 (Feb. 1963):105–7.

BELL, HOWARD M. *Youth Tell Their Story*. Washington, D.C.: American Council on Education, 1938.

BENEDEK, THERESE. "Some Problems of Motherhood." In Krich, 1953.

———. "The Psychodynamics of Love." In Krich, 1960.

BERGLER, EDMUND. *Unhappy Marriage and Divorce: A Study of Neurotic Choice of Marriage Partners*. New York: International Universities Press, 1946.

BERMAN, LOUIS A. *Jews and Intermarriage: A Study in Personality and Culture*. New York: Thomas Yoseloff, 1968.

BERNARD, JESSIE. *American Community Behavior: An Analysis of Problems Confronting American Communities Today*. New York: Dryden Press, 1949.

———. "Marital Stability and Patterns of Status Variables." *Journal of Marriage and the Family* 28 (Nov. 1966a):421–39.

———. "Notes on Educational Homogamy in Negro-White and White-Negro Marriages, 1960." *Journal of Marriage and the Family* 28 (Aug. 1966b):274–76.

———. *Remarriage: A Study of Marriage*. New York: Russell & Russell, 1971.

———. *The Sex Game: Communication Between the Sexes*. New York: Atheneum, 1972.

BETTELHEIM, BRUNO. "Growing Up Female." *Harpers* 225 (Oct. 1962):120–28.

BILLER, HENRY B. *Father, Child and Sex Role: Paternal Determinants in Personality Development*. Lexington, Mass.: D.C. Heath, 1971.

BINGOL, NESRIN. Quoted in *Family Life* 32 (Nov. 1972).

BLOOD, ROBERT O., JR. "Consequences of Permissiveness for Parents of Young Children." *Marriage and Family Living* 15 (Aug. 1953):209–12.

———. "A Retest of Waller's Rating Complex." *Marriage and Family Living* 17 (Feb. 1955):41–47.

———. "Uniformities and Diversities in Campus Dating Preferences." *Marriage and Family Living* 18 (Feb. 1956):37–45.

———. "Experiences of Foreign Students in Dating American Women." *Marriage and Family Living* 24 (Aug. 1962):241–48.

———. *Love Match and Arranged Marriage*. New York: Free Press, 1967.

———, and WOLFE, DONALD R. *Husbands and Wives: The Dynamics of Married Living*. New York: Free Press, 1960.

BOGARDUS, EMORY S. "Comparing Racial Distance in Ethiopia, South Africa, and the United States." *Sociology and Social Research* 52 (Jan. 1968):149–56.

BOSSARD, JAMES H. S. "Private Worlds of Men and Women." *Family Life* 18 (Oct. 1955):1–3.

———, and BOLL, ELEANOR STOKER. *The Large Family System: An Original Study in the Sociology of Family Behavior*. Philadelphia: University of Pennsylvania Press, 1956.

———, and LETTS, HAROLD C. "Mixed Marriages Involving Lutherans—A Research Report." *Marriage and Family Living* 18 (Nov. 1956):308–10.

———, and SANGER, WINNOGENE PRATT. "The Large Family System—A Research Report." *American Sociological Review* 17 (Feb. 1952):3–9.

BOWLBY, JOHN. "The Nature of the Child's Tie to His Mother." *International Journal of Psychoanalysis* 39 (1958):350–73.

_____. "Child Care and the Growth of Love." Article 25 in Haimowitz and Haimowitz, 1966.

BURCHINAL, LEE G. "Characteristics of Adolescents from Unbroken, Broken, and Re-constituted Families." *Journal of Marriage and the Family* 26 (Feb. 1964):44–51.

_____, and CHANCELLOR, LOREN E. "Survival Rates Among Religiously Homoga-mous and Interreligious Marriages." *Agricultural Experiment Station Research Bulletin* 512 (Dec. 1962). Also in *Social Forces* 41 (May 1963):353–62.

BURGESS, ERNEST W., and COTTRELL, LEONARD S. *Predicting Success or Failure in Marriage.* Englewood Cliffs, N.J.: Prentice-Hall, 1939.

_____; LOCKE, HARVEY J.; and THOMES, MARY MARGARET. *The Family: From Tradi-tional to Companionship,* 4th ed. New York: Van Nostrand Reinhold, 1971.

_____, and WALLIN, PAUL. *Engagement and Marriage.* Philadelphia: Lippincott, 1953.

CADDEN, VIVIAN. "Yes to Love and Joyful Faces." *Life* 71 (17 Dec. 1971):68 ff.

CAMPBELL, ARTHUR A. "The Role of Family Planning in the Reduction of Poverty." *Journal of Marriage and the Family* 30 (May 1968):236–45.

CAMPBELL, BERNARD, ed. *Sexual Selection and the Descent of Man.* Chicago: Aldine, 1972.

CASSEL, JOHN C. "Love Plays a Vital Role in Preventing Disease." *Los Angeles Times* news release, 1972.

CAVAN, RUTH S. *The American Family,* 4th ed. New York: Thomas Y. Crowell, 1969.

CAVAN, SHERRI. *Hippies of the Haight.* New York: Dutton, 1972.

CHESSER, EUSTACE, et al. *The Sexual, Marital and Family Relationships of the English Woman.* New York: Roy Publishers, 1957.

Chicago's Alcoholic Treatment Center News 1 (Sept. 1964):2.

CHRISTENSEN, HAROLD T. "Dating Behavior as Evaluated by High School Students." *American Journal of Sociology* 57 (May 1952):580–86.

_____, and BARBER, KENNETH E. "Interfaith versus Intrafaith Marriage in Indiana." *Journal of Marriage and the Family* 29 (Aug. 1967):461–69.

_____; BOWDEN, O. P.; and MEISSNER, H. H. "Studies in Child-Spacing: III—Pre-marital Pregnancy as a Factor in Divorce." *American Sociological Review* 18 (Dec. 1953):641–44.

_____, and JOHNSEN, KATHRYN P. *Marriage and the Family,* 3rd ed. New York: Ronald Press, 1971.

_____, and PHILBRICK, ROBERT E. "Family Size as a Factor in the Marital Adjust-ments of College Couples." *American Sociological Review* 17 (June 1952):306–12.

_____, and RUBINSTEIN, BETTY B. "Premarital Pregnancy and Divorce: A Follow-Up Study by the Interview Method." *Marriage and Family Living* 18 (May 1956):114–23.

_____, and SWIHART, M. "Postgraduation Role Preferences of Senior Women in College." *Marriage and Family Living* 18 (Feb. 1956):52–57.

CHRISTOPHERSON, VICTOR L. "Women in Modern Society." *Journal of Home Eco-nomics* 57 (1965):99–102.

"Clergymen Act." *Family Life* 28 (July 1968):5.

COHEN, JEROME B. *Decade of Decision.* New York: Institute of Life Insurance, 1958.

"Consumer Income." *Current Population Reports,* Series P-60, no. 53 (28 Dec. 1967).

COOKE, W. R. *American Journal of Obstetrics and Gynecology* 49 (1945):457.

COOMBS, ROBERT H. "A Value Theory of Mate Selection." *Family Coordinator* 10 (July 1961):51–54.

———. "Reinforcement of Values in the Parental Home as a Factor in Mate Selection." *Marriage and Family Living* 24 (May 1962):155–57.

———. "Sex Attitudes of Physicians and Marriage Counselors." *The Family Coordinator* 20 (July 1971):269–77.

COSER, ROSE LAUB, ed. *The Family: Its Structure and Functions.* New York: St. Martin's, 1964.

CROCKETT, HARRY J., JR.; BABCHUK, NICHOLAS; and BALLWEG, JOHN A. "Change in Religious Affiliation and Family Stability: A Second Study." *Journal of Marriage and the Family* 31 (Aug. 1969):464–68.

CROSS, RAYMOND G. "Contraception: Hazardous Rhythm." *Time* (30 Aug. 1968).

CUBER, JOHN F., and HARROFF, PEGGY B. "The More Total View: Relationships of Men and Women of the Upper Middle Class." Article 8 in Rodman, 1965.

CUTRIGHT, PHILLIPS. "Income and Family Events." *Journal of Marriage and the Family* 33 (May 1971):161–73, 291–306.

DALE, MARTHA ERICSON. "Child-Rearing and Social Status." *American Journal of Sociology* 52 (1946):191–92.

DALTON, KATHARINA. *The Premenstrual Syndrome.* Springfield, Ill.: Charles C Thomas, 1964.

———. *The Menstrual Cycle.* New York: Pantheon Books, Paperback Library, 1972.

DAVIS, KATHERINE B. *Factors in the Sex Life of 2200 Women.* New York: Harper & Bros., 1929. Reprinted in 1972 by Arno.

DAVIS, KINGSLEY. "The Early Marriage Trend." *What's New,* summarized in WSC News 7 (Oct. 1958):3.

DEBEAUVOIR, SIMONE. *The Second Sex.* Edited and translated by H. M. Parshley. New York: Knopf, 1953.

DEBETHUNE, ANDRÉ J. "Child Spacing: The Mathematical Probabilities." *Science* 142 (27 Dec. 1963):1629–34.

DEBURGER, JAMES E. "Marital Problems, Help-Seeking, and Emotional Orientation as Revealed in Help-Request Letters." *Journal of Marriage and the Family* 29 (Nov. 1967):712–21.

DECTER, MIDGE. *The New Chastity and Other Arguments Against Women's Liberation.* New York: Coward-McCann, 1972.

DEDMAN, JEAN. "Relationship Between Religious Attitude and Attitude Toward Premarital Sex Relations." *Marriage and Family Living* 21 (May 1959):171–76.

DEUTSCH, HELENE. *The Psychology of Women, A Psychoanalytic Interpretation.* New York: Grune & Stratton, 1944.

DICKS, HENRY V. *Marital Tensions: Clinical Studies Toward a Psychological Theory of Interaction.* New York: Basic Books, 1967.

DOTY, ROBERT C. *The New York Times,* western edition (27 Dec. 1963).

DRUCKER, A. J.; CHRISTENSEN, HAROLD T.; and REMMERS, H. H. "Some Background Factors in Socio-Sexual Modernism." *Marriage and Family Living* 14 (Nov. 1952):334–37.

DUVALL, EVELYN. "Conceptions of Parenthood." *American Journal of Sociology* 52 (1946):193–203.

DYER, EVERETT D. "Parenthood as Crisis: A Re-Study." *Marriage and Family Living* 25 (May 1963):196–201.

EHRMANN, WINSTON W. "Student Cooperation in a Study of Dating Behavior." *Marriage and Family Living* 14 (Nov. 1952):322–26.

––––––. *Premarital Dating Behavior.* New York: Henry Holt & Co., 1959.

ELDER, GLEN H., JR. "Parental Power Legitimation and Its Effects on the Adolescent." *Sociometry* 26 (March 1963):50–65.

––––––, and BOWERMAN, CHARLES E. "Family Structure and Child-Rearing Patterns: The Effect of Family Size and Sex Composition." *American Sociological Review* 28 (Dec. 1963):891–905.

ELLIS, HAVELOCK. *Man and Woman: A Study of Human Secondary Sexual Characters,* 5th ed. New York: Scribner's, 1915.

EPSTEIN, GILDA F., and BRONZAFT, A. L. "Female Freshmen View Their Roles as Women." *Journal of Marriage and the Family* 34 (Nov. 1972):671–72.

ESHLEMAN, J. ROSS, and HUNT, CHESTER L. "Social Class Influences on Family Adjustment Patterns of Married College Students." *Journal of Marriage and the Family* 29 (Aug. 1967):485–91.

FALK, LAWRENCE L. "Comparative Study of Problems of Married and Single Students." *Journal of Marriage and the Family* 26 (May 1964):207–8.

Family Life 29 (May 1969):5.

Family Life 32 (Aug. 1972):4.

Family Planning Digest (Nov. 1972).

FARBER, SEYMOUR M., and WILSON, ROGER H. L., eds. *Potential of Woman.* New York: McGraw-Hill, 1963.

FARIS, ELLSWORTH. *Discipline Without Punishment.* Salt Lake City: University of Utah Press, 1952. Pamphlet.

FARRIS, EDMUND J. *Human Ovulation and Fertility.* Philadelphia: Lippincott, 1956.

FERRER, TERRY. "Rosemary Park: New President of Barnard." *Saturday Review* (20 Apr. 1963):66–68.

FOLEY, PAUL. "Whatever Happened to Women's Rights?" *Atlantic* 213 (March 1964):3–5.

FOOTE, NELSON N. "New Roles for Men and Women." *Marriage and Family Living* 23 (Nov. 1961):325–29.

FORREST, TESS. *Family Life* 28 (Nov. 1968):6.

FREEMAN, LINTON C. "Marriage Without Love: Mate-Selection in Non-Western Societies." In Winch, McGinnis, and Barringer, 1962, pp. 439–55.

FREUD, SIGMUND. "The Most Prevalent Form of Degradation in Erotic Life." No. 10 in Krich, 1960.

FRIEDAN, BETTY. *The Feminine Mystique.* New York: Norton, 1963. Published in paperback in 1970 by Dell.

––––––. "Woman: The Fourth Dimension." *Ladies Home Journal* 81 (June 1964):48–55.

GABRIELSON, IRA W. *Journal of Public Health,* 1970.

GESELL, ARNOLD, and ILG, FRANCES L. *The Child from Five to Ten*. New York: Harper & Row, 1946.

GILLESPIE, DAIR L. "Who Has the Power? The Marital Struggle." *Journal of Marriage and the Family* 33 (Aug. 1971):445–58.

GINZBERG, ELI, et al. *Educated American Women: Life Styles and Self-Portraits*. New York: Columbia University Press, 1966.

GLICK, PAUL C. "First Marriages and Remarriages." *American Sociological Review* 14 (Dec. 1949):726–34.

_____. "The Life Cycle of the Family." *Marriage and Family Living* 17 (Feb. 1955): 3–9.

_____. *American Families*. New York: John Wiley, 1957. Reprinted in 1974 by Russell.

_____. "Marriage Instability: Variations by Size of Place and Religion." *The Milbank Memorial Fund Quarterly* 41 (Jan. 1963):43–55.

_____, and NORTON, ARTHUR J. "Frequency, Duration, and Probability of Marriage and Divorce." *Journal of Marriage and the Family* 33 (May 1971): 307–17.

_____, and NORTON, ARTHUR J. "Perspectives on the Present Upturn in Divorce and Remarriage." Paper presented at the annual meeting of the Population Association of America, Toronto, Canada (15 Apr. 1972).

GLUECK, ELEANOR T. "Spotting Potential Delinquents: It Can Be Done." *Federal Probation* (Sept. 1956), p. 9.

GOODE, WILLIAM J. "Problems in Postdivorce Adjustment." *American Sociological Review* 14 (June 1949):394–401.

_____. *After Divorce*. New York: Free Press, 1956. Published in 1965 as *Women in Divorce*.

_____. "The Theoretical Importance of Love." *American Sociological Review* 24 (Feb. 1959):38–47.

_____. *World Revolution and Family Patterns*. New York: Free Press, 1963.

GORDON, ALBERT. *Intermarriage: Interfaith, Interracial, Interethnic*. Boston: Beacon Press, 1964.

GREEN, RICHARD, and MONEY, JOHN, eds. *Transexualism and Sex Reassignment*. Baltimore: Johns Hopkins, 1969.

GREENBERG, JOSEPH H. "Social Variables in Acceptance or Rejection of Artificial Insemination." *American Sociological Review* 16 (Feb. 1951): 86–91.

GREER, GERMAINE. *The Female Eunuch*. New York: McGraw-Hill, 1971.

GURIN, GERALD; VEROFF, JOSEPH; and FELD, SHEILA. *Americans View Their Mental Health: A Nationwide Interview Survey*. New York: Basic Books, 1960.

HABERMAN, PAUL W. "Childhood Symptoms in Children of Alcoholics and Comparison Group Parents." *Journal of Marriage and the Family* 28 (May 1966):152–54.

HACKER, HELEN MAYER. "New Burdens of Masculinity." *Marriage and Family Living* 19 (Aug. 1957):227–33.

HAIMOWITZ, MORRIS L., and HAIMOWITZ, NATALIE R., eds. *Human Development: Selected Readings*. New York: Thomas Y. Crowell, 1966.

HARBESON, GLADYS E. *Choice and Challenge for the American Woman*, 2nd ed. Cambridge, Mass.: Schenkman Publishing Co., 1972.

HARLOW, HARRY F. "The Nature of Love." *The American Psychologist* 13 (Dec. 1958):673–85.

———, and HARLOW, MARGARET K. "Social Deprivation in Monkeys." *Scientific American* 207 (Nov. 1962):34, 136–46.

HART, HORNELL. *Chart for Happiness*. New York: Macmillan, 1940.

———, and HART, E. B. *Personality and the Family*. Boston: D.C. Heath, 1935.

HAWKES, GLENN R.; BURCHINAL, LEE; and GARDENER, BRUCE. "Size of Family and Adjustment of Children." *Marriage and Family Living* 20 (Feb. 1958):65–68.

HEER, DAVID M. "Negro-White Marriage in the United States." *Journal of Marriage and the Family* 28 (Aug. 1966):262–73.

HILLMAN, CHRISTINE H. "An Advice Column's Challenge for Family-Life Education." *Marriage and Family Living* 16 (Feb. 1954):51–54.

HOBART, CHARLES W. "Disillusionment in Marriage, and Romanticism." *Marriage and Family Living* 20 (May 1958):156–62.

HOCHMAN, SANDRA. "Sandra Hochman: Thoughts on Children." *Look* 32 (24 Dec. 1968):14.

HORNER, MATINA S. "No Fear at Radcliffe." *Time* 99 (29 May 1972):47.

HUNGERFORD, MARY JANE. "Preventing High School Marriages." *Family Life* 28 (Sept. 1968):1–4.

———. *Childbirth Education*. Springfield, Ill.: Charles C Thomas, 1972.

HUNT, JOSEPH M. *Intelligence and Experience*. New York: Ronald Press, 1961.

ISRAEL, S. LEON, and NEMSER, SONDRA, "Family-Counseling Role of the Physician." *Journal of Marriage and the Family* 30 (May 1968):311–16.

JACKSON, JOAN K. "The Adjustment of the Family to Alcoholism." *Marriage and Family Living* 18 (Nov. 1956):361–69.

JACOBSON, PAUL H. *American Marriage and Divorce*. New York: Holt, Rinehart & Winston, 1959.

JAY, PHYLLIS C. "The Female Primate." In Farber and Wilson, 1963, pp. 3–12.

JOHANNIS, THEODORE B. "The Marital Adjustment of a Sample of Married College Students." *The Coordinator* 4 (June 1956):4.

JOHNSON, W. B., and TERMAN, LEWIS M. "Some Highlights in the Literature of Psychological Sex Differences Published Since 1920." *Journal of Psychology* 9 (1940):327–36.

JONES, E., and WESTOFF, C. F. "Attitudes Toward Abortion in the United States in 1970 and the Trend Since 1965." In Westoff and Parke, 1972.

JOSEPHSON, ERIC. "The Matriarchy: Myth or Reality." *Family Coordinator* 18 (July 1969):268–76.

KAGAN, JEROME. *Time* (20 March 1972), pp. 43–46.

KALASHIAN, MARION M. "Working with the Wives of Alcoholics in an Out-Patient Clinic Setting." *Marriage and Family Living* 21 (May 1959):130–33.

KANIN, EUGENE J. "Premarital Sex Adjustments, Social Class, and Associated Behaviors." *Marriage and Family Living* 22 (Aug. 1960):258–62.

———. "An Examination of Sexual Aggression as a Response to Sexual Frustration." *Journal of Marriage and the Family* 29 (Aug. 1967):428–33.

508 _____, and HOWARD, DAVID H. "Postmarital Consequences of Premarital Sex Adjustments." *American Sociological Review* 23 (Oct. 1958):556–62.

KANTNER, JOHN F., and ZELNICK, MELVIN. "Sexual Experience of Young Unmarried Women in the U.S." *Family Planning Perspectives* 4 (Oct. 1972):9–18.

KATZ, ELIA. *Armed Love.* New York: Bantam, 1972.

KATZ, JOSEPH. News item in *Family Life* 24 (May 1968):4.

KAVINOKY, NADINA. "Premarital Examination." *Western Journal of Surgery, Obstetrics, and Gynecology* 51 (Oct. 1943):315.

KEE, CYNTHIA. News release, London, 1971.

KENNEDY, ELIZABETH. "Baby Bubble Sequel." *Ladies Home Journal* 88 (Oct. 1971):56 ff.

KEPHART, WILLIAM M. "Some Correlates of Romantic Love." *Journal of Marriage and the Family* 29 (Aug. 1967):470–74.

KINSEY, ALFRED C., et al. *Sexual Behavior in the Human Male.* Philadelphia: Saunders, 1948.

_____. *Sexual Behavior in the Human Female.* Philadelphia: Saunders, 1953.

KIRKENDALL, LESTER A. "Premarital Sexual Relations: The Problem and Its Implications." *Pastoral Psychology* 7 (Apr. 1956):46–53.

_____. "Why Teen-age Boys Visit Prostitutes." A paper presented before the 1959 meeting of the Pacific Northwest Conference on Family Relations, Seattle, Washington.

_____. *Premarital Intercourse and Interpersonal Relations, A Research Study of Interpersonal Relationships Based on Case Histories of 668 Premarital Intercourse Experiences Reported by 200 College Level Males.* New York: Julian Press, 1961.

_____. "Understanding Premarital Sex Problems." In *Sex in the Adolescent Years.* New York: Association Press, 1965, chs. 24 and 25.

KIRKPATRICK, CLIFFORD. *The Family: As Process and Institution,* 2nd ed. New York: Ronald Press, 1963.

_____, and CAPLOW, THEODORE. "Courtship in a Group of Minnesota Students." *American Journal of Sociology* 51 (Sept. 1945):114–25.

KLEMER, RICHARD H. *Marriage and Family Relationships.* New York: Harper & Row, 1970.

KNEBEL, FLETCHER. "Identity, The Black Woman's Burden." *Look* 33 (23 Sept. 1969):77–79.

KOHN, MELVIN L., and CARROLL, ELEANOR E. "Social Class and the Allocation of Parental Responsibilities." *Sociometry* 23 (Dec. 1960): 372–92.

KOLLER, MARVIN R. "Some Changes in Courtship Behavior in Three Generations of Ohio Women." *American Sociological Review* 16 (June 1951):366–70.

KORSON, J. HENRY. "Dower and Social Class in an Urban Muslim Community." *Journal of Marriage and the Family* 29 (Aug. 1967):527–33.

KRAUSE, JEANNE. "Are There Sex Differences?" *Fortune* (Feb. 1971), pp. 76 ff.

KRICH, A.M. *Women.* New York: Dell Publishing Co., 1953.

_____, ed. *Men: The Variety and Meaning of Their Sexual Experiences.* New York: Dell Publishing Co., 1954.

_____. *The Anatomy of Love.* New York: Dell Publishing Co., 1960.

Ladies Home Journal. "Medicine Today." (Oct. 1968):55.

LANDIS, JUDSON T. "Length of Time Required to Achieve Adjustment in Marriage." *American Sociological Review* 11 (Dec. 1946):666–77.

————. "Marriages of Mixed and Non-Mixed Religious Faith." *American Sociological Review* 14 (June 1949):401–7.

————. "The Women Kinsey Studied." *Social Problems* 11 (April 1954): 139–42.

————. "Pattern of Divorce in Three Generations." *Social Forces* 34 (March 1956):213–16.

————. "Physical and Mental-Emotional Changes Accompanying the Menstrual Cycle." *Research Studies of the State College of Washington* 25 (June 1957):155–62.

————. "The Trauma of Children when Parents Divorce." *Marriage and Family Living* 22 (Feb. 1960a):7–13.

————. "Religiousness, Family Relationships and Family Values in Protestant, Catholic, and Jewish Families." *Marriage and Family Living* 22 (Nov. 1960b):341–47.

————. "A Re-examination of the Role of the Father as an Index of Family Integration." *Marriage and Family Living* 24 (May 1962):122–28.

————. "Social Correlates of Divorce and Nondivorce Among the Unhappy Married." *Marriage and Family Living* 25 (Aug. 1963a):178–80.

————. "Dating Maturation of Children from Happy and Unhappy Marriages." *Marriage and Family Living* 25 (Aug. 1963b):351–53.

————, and LANDIS, MARY G. *Building a Successful Marriage,* 4th ed, 1963; 5th ed., 1968; 6th ed., 1973. Englewood Cliffs, N.J.: Prentice-Hall.

————, and POFFENBERGER, THOMAS. "Marital and Sexual Adjustment of 330 Couples Who Chose Vasectomy as a Form of Birth Control." *Journal of Marriage and the Family* 27 (Feb. 1965):57–58.

————; POFFENBERGER, THOMAS; and POFFENBERGER, SHIRLEY. "The Effects of First Pregnancy Upon the Sexual Adjustment of 212 Couples." *American Sociological Review* 15 (Dec. 1950):766–72.

LANDIS, PAUL H. "Marriage Preparation in Two Generations." *Marriage and Family Living* 8 (Nov. 1951):155–56.

————, and DAY, KATHERINE H. "Education as a Factor in Mate Selection." *American Sociological Review* 10 (Aug. 1954):558–60.

————, and STONE, CAROL. *Two Generations of Rural and Urban Women Appraise Marital Happiness.* Pullman, Wash.: Washington Agricultural Experiment Station, Bulletin No. 506, March 1951.

————, and STONE, CAROL. *The Relationship of Parental Authority Patterns to Teenage Adjustment.* Pullman, Wash.: Washington Agricultural Experiment Station, Bulletin No. 538, Sept. 1952.

LANDMAN, LYNN. "United States, Underdeveloped Land in Family Planning." *Journal of Marriage and the Family* 30 (May 1968):191–201.

LANG, RICHARD. Ph.D thesis at the University of Chicago, summarized in Burgess and Cottrell, 1939.

LeBARRE, WESTON. "Wanted: A Pattern for Modern Man." *Mental Hygiene* 33 (Apr. 1949):2–8.

LEES, HANNAH. "How to Be Happy Though Incompatible." *Saturday Evening Post* (16 Feb. 1957).

LeMASTERS, E. E. *Modern Courtship and Marriage.* New York: Macmillan, 1957a, pp. 192–93.

_____. "Parenthood as a Crisis." *Marriage and Family Living* 19 (1957b): 352–55.

LEVY, JOHN, and MUNROE, RUTH. *The Happy Family.* New York: Knopf, 1938.

LEWIS, W. DRAYTON. "Some Characteristics of Very Superior Children." Article 73 in Haimowitz and Haimowitz, 1966.

Life. "The Drop Out Wife." (17 March 1972) p. 34B.

LINDSEY, BEN. *Redbook* (March 1927).

LINNER, BIRGITTA. *Sex and Society in Sweden.* New York: Harper & Row, 1972.

LOCKE, HARVEY J. *Predicting Adjustment in Marriage: A Comparison of a Divorced and a Happily Married Group.* New York: Henry Holt, 1951. Reprinted in 1968 by Greenwood.

_____, and KLAUSNER, W. J. "Prediction of Marital Adjustment of Divorced Persons in Subsequent Marriages." *Research Studies of the State College of Washington* 16 (March 1948):30–32.

_____; SABAGH, GEORGES; and THOMES, MARY MARGARET. "Interfaith Marriages." *Social Problems* 4 (Apr. 1957):329–33.

LOPATA, HELENA ZNANIECKI. "The Life Cycle of the Social Role of Housewife." *Sociology and Social Research* 51 (Oct. 1966):5–22.

LUCKEY, ELEANORE BRAUN. "Number of Years Married as Related to Personality Perception and Marital Satisfaction." *Journal of Marriage and the Family* 28 (Feb. 1966):44–48.

MACCOBY, ELEANOR E. In Farber and Wilson, 1963.

MACE, DAVID R. "Personality Expression and Subordination in Marriage." *Marriage and Family Living* 15 (Aug. 1953):205–7.

_____. "Some Reflections on the American Family." *Marriage and Family Living* 24 (May 1962):109–12.

_____. *Getting Ready for Marriage.* Nashville: Abingdon, 1972.

MANNES, MARYA. "The Problem of Creative Women." In Farber and Wilson, 1963, pp. 116–30.

MARKER, MARY. "Confidentially Yours." *The Deseret News Telegram,* Salt Lake City (14 June 1956).

MARKLE, GERALD E. "Most Couples Prefer Boy as First Child." *Family Digest* 3 (March 1974):14–15. [This is a digest of his studies. Another such digest appears in *Family Digest* 1 (1972), no. 6, p. 13.]

MARSHALL, WILLIAM H., and KING, MARCIA P. "Undergraduate Student Marriage: A Compilation of Research Findings." *Journal of Marriage and the Family* 28 (Aug. 1966):350–59.

MASLOW, A. H. *Motivation and Personality.* New York: Harper & Row, 1954; 2nd ed, 1970.

MASTERS, WILLIAM H., and JOHNSON, VIRGINIA E. *Human Sexual Response.* New York: Little, Brown, 1966.

————, and JOHNSON, VIRGINIA E. *Human Sexual Inadequacy*. New York: Little, Brown, 1970.

McCANDLESS, BOYD. "The Devil's Advocate Examines Parent Education." *Family Coordinator* 17 (July 1968):149–54.

McHUGH, GELOLO. "What Ministers Are Learning About Sex." Edited by J.R. Moskin. *Look* 22 (25 Nov. 1958):79–86.

MEAD, MARGARET. *Growing Up in New Guinea: A Comparative Study of Primitive Education*. New York: Morrow, 1930.

————. *From the South Seas: Studies of Adolescence and Sex in Primitive Societies*. New York: Morrow, 1939.

————. *Male and Female: A Study of the Sexes in a Changing World*. New York: Morrow, 1949.

————. "Introduction." In Krich, 1954.

————. "Student Marriage: Good or Bad?" *U.S. News and World Report* 48 (6 June 1960):80–86.

————. "Margaret Mead's Sound Insights into the Furor over Shifting American Morals." *Life* 65 (25 Aug. 1968a):30–35.

————. "Margaret Mead Answers Questions." *Redbook* 130 (March 1968b):10 ff.

MEIERHOFFER, MARIE. *Parade* (2 July 1972).

MENDELS, ORA. "A Revolution in Childbirth?" *Ladies Home Journal* 80 (Jan. 1963):40.

METROPOLITAN LIFE INSURANCE COMPANY. *Statistical Bulletin* 34 (June 1953a):6–8; (Sept. 1953b); 45 (July 1964a):8–9; (Nov. 1964b); 47 (Nov. 1966):6–8; 49 (Oct. 1968):7–8; 50 (Apr. 1969):3–5.

MIDDLETON, RUSSELL. "A Deviant Case: Brother-Sister and Father-Daughter Marriage in Ancient Egypt." In Coser, 1964, pp. 92–94.

MONAHAN, THOMAS P. "Divorce by Occupational Level." *Marriage and Family Living* 17 (Nov. 1955):322–24.

————. "The Changing Nature and Instability of Remarriage." *Eugenics Quarterly* 5 (June 1958):73–85.

MONEY, JOHN. "Developmental Differentiation of Femininity and Masculinity Compared." In Farber and Wilson, 1963, pp. 51–65.

MONTAGU, ASHLEY M. F. *Anthropology and Human Nature*. Boston: Porter Sargeant, 1957.

————. *The Reproductive Development of the Female, with Especial Reference to the Period of Adolescent Sterility; A Study in the Comparative Physiology of the Infecundity of the Adolescent Organism*. New York: Julian Press, 1957.

————. *Education and Human Relations*. New York: Grove Press, 1958.

————. *The Natural Superiority of Women*, rev. ed. New York: Macmillan, 1968.

————, and SCHWEITZER, GERTRUDE. "There Is Prenatal Influence." *Ladies Home Journal* 71 (Feb. 1954):43 ff.

MOORE, HANNA. *Strictures on the Modern System of Female Education*. Boston: J. Loring, 1883. Vol I, p. 61.

MORGAN, THOMAS B. "The Vanishing American Jew." *Look* 28 (5 May 1964):42–46.

MORTON, J. H. *American Journal of Obstetrics and Gynecology* 65 (1953):1182.

Moses, Virginia Musick. "Study of Learning Derived from a Functional Course in Marriage and Family Relationships." *Marriage and Family Living* 18 (Aug. 1956):204–8.

Moskin, J. Robert. "Arnold Toynbee Talks of Peace, Power, Race in America." *Look* (19 March 1969a), pp. 25–27.

———. "The New Contraceptive Society." *Look* 33 (4 Feb. 1969b):50 ff.

Murdock, George P. "Sexual Behavior: What Is Acceptable?" *Journal of Social Hygiene* 36 (1950):1–31.

National Center for Health Statistics. *Trends in Illegitimacy: United States 1940–1965*. Series 21, No. 15. Washington D.C., Feb. 1968.

Nechtow, Mitchell J. "Premature and Past Due." *Time* (20 Apr. 1959), p. 77.

New York Mattachine Society. *Family Life* 28 (Aug. 1968):1.

Newsweek (12 Feb. 1967).

Nimkoff, Meyer F., and Wood, Arthur L. "Courtship and Personality." *American Journal of Sociology* 53 (1948):263–69.

Nolte, Dorothy Law. "Creative Family Living." *Torrance* (Ca.) *Herald* (1954).

Nye, F. Ivan; Carlson, John; and Garrett, Gerald. "Family Size, Interaction, Affect and Stress." *Journal of Marriage and the Family* 32 (May 1970): 216–26.

Oden, Melita H. *Genetic Psychology Monographs* 77 (1968):3–93.

Olim, Ellis G. "The Self-Actualizing Person in the Fully Functioning Family: A Humanistic Viewpoint." *Family Coordinator* 17 (July 1968):141–48.

Ottinger, Katherine Brownell. News item in *Family Life* 29 (Feb. 1969):5.

Packard, Vance. *The Sexual Wilderness*. New York: McKay, 1968.

———. *A Nation of Strangers*. New York: McKay, 1972.

Parke, Robert, Jr., and Glick, Paul C. "Prospective Changes in Marriage and the Family." *Journal of Marriage and the Family* 29 (May 1967):249–56.

Pavela, Todd H. "An Exploratory Study of Negro-White Intermarriage in Indiana." Chicago: Urban League, 1958–1959.

Peck, Robert F., et al. *The Psychology of Character Development*. New York: John Wiley, 1960.

Perlstein, Meyer A. "Against Cerebral Palsy." *Time* 70 (16 Dec. 1957):39.

Perr, Irwin N. "Medical, Psychiatric, and Legal Aspects of Premenstrual Tension." *American Journal of Psychiatry* 115 (Sept. 1958):211–19.

Peterson, Esther. "The Impact of Education." In Farber and Wilson, 1963, pp. 188–98.

Phillips, Clinton E. "Some Considerations for the Newlyweds." *Family Life* 28 (Dec. 1968):4–6.

Plant, James S. "The Psychiatrist Views Children of Divorced Parents." *Law and Contemporary Problems* 10 (Summer 1944):807–18.

Plateris, Alexander. "The Impact of the Amendment of Marriage Laws in Mississippi." *Journal of Marriage and the Family* 28 (May 1966):206–12.

Poffenberger, Thomas. "Family Life Education in This Scientific Age." *Marriage and Family Living* 21 (May 1959):150–54.

Poloma, Margaret M., and Garland, T. N. "Married Professional Woman: A

Study in the Tolerance of Domestication." *Journal of Marriage and the Family* 33 (Aug. 1971):531–40.

POMEROY, RICHARD, and LANDMAN, LYNN C. "Public Opinion Trends: Effective Abortion and Birth Control Services to Teenagers." *Family Planning Perspectives* 4 (Oct. 1972):44–55.

POPENOE, PAUL. "Divorce and Remarriage from a Eugenic Point of View." *Social Forces* 12 (Oct. 1933):48–51.

———. "A Study of 738 Elopements." *American Sociological Review* 3 (Feb. 1938):47–53.

———. *Marriage, Before and After.* New York: W. Funk, 1943.

———. "Farm Marriages Are the Happiest." *Family Life* 8 (May 1947):1–2.

———. "Premarital Experience No Help in Sexual Adjustment After Marriage." *Family Life* 21 (Aug. 1961):1–2.

———. *Family Life* (Feb. 1970).

———. *Family Life* (July 1972).

———, and WICKS, DONNA. "Marital Happiness in Two Generations." *Mental Hygiene* 21 (1937):218–33.

Population and the American Future. Washington, D.C.: U.S. Government Printing Office, 1972.

PRESSER, HARRIET B., and BUMPASS, LARRY L. "The Acceptability of Contraceptive Sterilization Among U.S. Couples, 1970." *Family Perspectives* 4 (Oct. 1972):18–26.

PRINCE, ALFRED J. "A Study of 194 Cross-Religion Marriages." *Family Coordinator* 9 (Jan. 1962):3–7.

RAINWATER, LEE. *Family Design: Marital Sexuality, Family Size, and Contraception.* Chicago: Aldine, 1965.

RAMEY, JAMES W. "Emergent Patterns of Innovative Behavior in Marriage." *Family Coordinator* 21 (Oct. 1972a):436–56.

———. "Communes, Group Marriage, and the Upper-Middle Class." *Journal of Marriage and the Family* 34 (Nov. 1972b):647–55.

REEVY, WILLIAM R. "Premarital Petting Behavior and Marriage Happiness Prediction." *Marriage and Family Living* 21 (Nov. 1959):349–55.

———. "Child Sexuality." *Encyclopedia of Sexual Behavior.* New York: Hawthorn, 1961.

REIK, THEODOR. *Sex in Man and Woman: Its Emotional Variations.* New York: Noonday Press, 1960.

REISS, IRA L. *The Social Context of Premarital Sexual Permissiveness.* New York: Holt, Rinehart & Winston, 1967.

———. *The Family System in America.* New York: Holt, Rinehart & Winston, 1971.

RENNE, KAREN S. "Health and Marital Experience in an Urban Population." *Journal of Marriage and the Family* 33 (May 1971):338–50.

RICHARDSON, ELLIOTT L. Associated Press release (22 Dec. 1972).

RIESMAN, DAVID. "Permissiveness and Sex Roles." *Marriage and Family Living* 21 (Aug. 1959):211–17.

514   RODMAN, HYMAN, ed. *Marriage, Family and Society: A Reader*. New York: Random House, 1965.

ROGERS, EVERETT M., and HAVENS, A. EUGENE. "Prestige Rating and Mate Selection on a College Campus." *Marriage and Family Living* 22 (Feb. 1960):55–59.

ROLLINS, BOYD C., and FELDMAN, HAROLD. "Marital Satisfaction over the Family Life Cycle." *Journal of Marriage and the Family* 32 (Feb. 1970):20–28.

ROSE, ARNOLD M. "Acceptance of Adult Roles and Separation from Family." *Marriage and Family Living* 21 (May 1959):120–26.

ROSENFELD, ALBERT. "What Is the Right Number of Children?" *Life* 71 (17 Dec. 1971):99 ff.

ROSENTHAL, ERICH. *Studies in Jewish Intermarriage in the United States*. Vol. 64. American Jewish Year Book, 1963.

ROSOFF, JEANNIE I. "The Future of Federal Support for Family Planning Services and Population Research." *Family Planning Perspectives* 5 (Winter 1973):7–18.

ROSOW, IRVING, and ROSE, K. D. "Divorce Among Doctors." *Journal of Marriage and the Family* 34 (Nov. 1972):587–98.

ROSSI, ALICE S. "Transition to Parenthood." *Journal of Marriage and the Family* 30 (Feb. 1968): 26–39.

DEROUGEMONT, DENIS. "The Crisis of the Modern Couple." In Krich, 1960, no. 6.

SADOCK, VIRGINIA ALCOTT. "Where Are the Women Doctors?" *Parents* 46 (Nov. 1972): 66 ff.

SCANZONI, JOHN. "A Social Systems Analysis of Dissolved and Existing Marriages." *Journal of Marriage and the Family* 30 (Aug. 1968):452–61.

SCHEINFELD, AMRAM. *Heredity in Humans*, rev. ed. Philadelphia: Lippincott, 1972.

SCHLESINGER, BENJAMIN. "Successful Remarriage After Divorce." *Family Life* 29 (Jan. 1969):1–4.

SCHNEPP, GERALD, and YUI, AGNES M. "Cultural and American Adjustment of Japanese War Brides." *American Journal of Sociology* 61 (July 1955):48–50.

SCHWABACHER, ALBERT E., JR. "The Repository of Wealth." In Farber and Wilson, 1963, pp. 241–54.

SCOTT, J.P. "Critical Periods in Behavioral Development." *Science* 138 (30 Nov. 1962):949–58.

SEARLES, HAROLD F. *Time* (Apr. 1959), p. 73.

SHEPPE, WILLIAM M., JR. Address before the Kentucky Medical Association, reported in *Family Life* 29 (March 1969):3.

SHERMAN, JULIA A. *On the Psychology of Women: A Survey of Empirical Studies*. Springfield. Ill.: Charles C. Thomas, 1973.

SHIPMAN, GORDON. "The Psychodynamics of Sex Education." *Family Coordinator* 17 (Jan. 1968):3–12.

———, and TIEN, H. YUAN. "Nonmarriage and the Waiting Period." *Journal of Marriage and the Family* 27 (May 1965):277–80.

SHLIEN, JOHN M. "Mother-in-Law: A Problem in Kinship Terminology." Article 16 in Rodman, 1965.

SHOPE, DAVID F., and BRODERICK, CARLFRED B. "Level of Sexual Experience and

Predicted Adjustment in Marriage." *Journal of Marriage and the Family* 29 (Aug. 1967):424–33.

SHUTTLEWORTH, FRANK K. "Biosocial and Developmental Theory of Male and Female Sexuality." *Marriage and Family Living* 21 (May 1959):163–70.

SIRJAMAKI, JOHN. "Cultural Configurations in the American Family." *American Journal of Sociology* 53 (1948):464–70.

SLOCUM, WALTER L. *Family Culture Patterns and Adolescent Behavior.* Pullman, Wash.: Washington Agricultural Experiment Station, Bulletin 648. (Oct. 1963).

SMITH, ROCKWELL. In Howard Becker and Reuben Hill, *Family, Marriage and Parenthood,* rev. ed. Boston: D.C. Heath, 1954. ch. 20.

SONTAG, LESTER. "War and the Fetal-Maternal Relationship." *Marriage and Family Living* 6 (1944):3–4.

SPECTORSKY, A. C. *The Exurbanites.* Philadelphia: Lippincott, 1955.

SPITZ, RENÉ A. "The Importance of Mother-Child Relationship During the First Year of Life." Seattle: Washington Society for Mental Hygiene and the Graduate School of Social Work, University of Washington, 1947. Based on a series of film lectures presented in Seattle, 15–17 June 1947.

———. "The Role of Ecological Factors in Emotional Development in Infancy." *Child Development* 20 (1949):145–56.

SPOCK, BENJAMIN. "When Mothers Work." *Ladies Home Journal* (March 1963), p. 142.

———. *Baby and Child Care,* rev. ed. New York: Pocket Books, 1968.

Statistical Bulletin (Dec. 1970), p. 8.

STEINEM, GLORIA. *McCalls* (Jan. 1972), p. 67.

STINSON, H. W. Association for Voluntary Sterilization, news release (5 Sept. 1969).

STOKES, WALTER R. "Premarital Sexual Behavior." *Marriage and Family Living* 15 (Aug. 1953):234–42.

STONE, CAROL L. "Church Participation and Social Adjustment of High School and College Youth." Pullman, Wash.: Washington Agricultural Experiment Station, Bulletin 550, May 1954.

STRAUSS, ANSELM L. "The Influence of Parent-Images upon Marital Choice." *American Sociological Review* 11 (Oct. 1946):554–59.

———. "A Study of Three Psychological Factors Affecting Choice of a Mate." Ph.D thesis, University of Chicago, 1945. Cited in Burgess and Wallin, 1953.

———. "Strain and Harmony in American-Japanese War-Bride Marriages." *Marriage and Family Living* 16 (May 1954):99–106.

STRECKER, EDWARD A. "A Doctor Looks at Marital Infidelity." *This Week Magazine* (8 June 1952), p. 22.

SUTTIE, IAN D. *The Origins of Love and Hate.* New York: Julian Press, 1952.

SWANSON, ETHEL. "Menstruation Dreams." *Today's Health* (Sept. 1967), pp. 45–80.

SWEENEY, WILLIAM J., 3rd, and STERN, BARBARA L. *Woman's Doctor: A Year in the Life of an Obstetrician-Gynecologist.* New York: Morrow, 1973.

SWITZER, ELLEN. "How Sex Clinics Help." *McCalls* (July 1974), pp. 33–34.

TERMAN, LEWIS M. *Psychological Factors in Marital Happiness.* New York: McGraw-Hill, 1938.

516 _____. "The Discovery and Encouragement of Exceptional Talent." Article 72 in Haimowitz and Haimowitz, 1966.

This Week (May 1964), pp. 14–16.

THOMAS, JOHN L. "The Factor of Religion in Selection of Marriage Mates." *American Sociological Review* 16 (Aug. 1951):487–91.

_____. *The American Catholic Family.* Englewood Cliffs, N.J.: Prentice-Hall, 1956.

TIGER, LIONEL, and FOX, ROBIN. *Imperial Animal.* New York: Holt, Rinehart & Winston, 1971.

TIME–LOUIS HARRIS. "Changing Morality: The Two Americas." (6 June 1969), pp. 26–27.

Time. (20 March 1972a), p. 20.

_____. (6 Sept. 1971b), p. 49.

_____. "ITT's Big Conglomerate Troubles." (1 May 1972), pp. 72–78.

_____. "Blacks vs. Feminists." (26 March 1973), p. 64.

TROPMAN, JOHN E., quoted by Mary Salpukas in New York Times News Service (5 Aug. 1972).

UDRY, J. RICHARD; BAUMAN, KARL E.; and CHASE, CHARLES. "Skin Color, Status, and Mate Selection." *American Journal of Sociology* 74 (Jan. 1971):722–33.

U.S. DEPARTMENT OF COMMERCE, BUREAU OF THE CENSUS. "Marital Status, Number of Times Married, and Duration of Present Marital Status, April 1948." Series P–20, No. 23 (4 March 1949).

_____. "United States Census of Population, 1960, Marital Status." (1960).

_____. "Population Characteristics." Series P–20, No. 122 (22 March 1963).

_____. "Marital Status and Family Status: March 1967." U.S. Census, Population Characteristics, Series P–20, No. 170 (23 Feb. 1968).

_____. "Marital Status of the Population: 1972." *Supplemental Reports,* 1972.

U.S. DEPARTMENT OF HEALTH, EDUCATION, AND WELFARE. "Excerpts from Vital Statistics of the United States, 1965. Vol. III—Marriage and Divorce."

U.S. DEPARTMENT OF LABOR. Women's Bureau. *American Women.* Report of the President's Commission on the Status of Women, 1963.

_____. *Special Labor Force Report No. 94.*

_____. "Current Population Reports: Population Characteristics." Series P–20, No. 112 (29 Dec. 1961).

U.S. News and World Report. "Does It Really Pay for the Wife to Work." 42 (15 March 1957):154–58.

U.S. PUBLIC HEALTH SERVICE. National Vital Statistics Division. "Trends in Divorce and Family Disruption." (Sept. 1963).

_____. *Vital Statistics Report,* Supplement 17 (12) (25 March 1969):9.

U.S. SURGEON GENERAL. *The Health Consequences of Smoking.* Washington, D.C.: U.S. Government Printing Office, 1971.

VAN DEN HAAG, ERNEST. "Love and Marriage." In Coser, 1964, pp. 192–202.

VEBLEN, THORSTEIN. *The Theory of the Leisure Class.* Boston: Houghton Mifflin, 1973. Originally published in 1899.

VELIE, LESTER. "The Intimate Life of a Commune." *Reader's Digest* (March 1973), pp. 94–99.

VERNON, GLENN M. "Bias in Professional Publications Concerning Interfaith Marriages." *Religious Education* 55 (July–Aug. 1964):261–64.

———, and BOADWAY, JACK A. "Attitudes Toward Artificial Insemination and Some Variables Associated Therewith." *Marriage and Family Living* 21 (Feb. 1959):43–47.

VINCENT, CLARK E. *Unmarried Mothers.* New York: Free Press, 1961.

———. "Interfaith Marriages: Problem or Symptom?" In Marvin B. Sussman, ed., *Sourcebook in Marriage and the Family,* pp. 349–59. Boston: Houghton Mifflin, 1963.

WALLACE, KARL. *Love Is More Than Luck.* New York: Wilfred Funk, 1957.

———. "Factors Hindering Mate Selection." *Sociology and Social Research* 44 (May 1960):317–25.

WALLER, WILLARD. *The Old Love and the New.* New York: Horace Liveright, 1929.

———, and HILL, REUBEN. *The Family.* New York: Holt, Rinehart & Winston, 1951.

WALLIN, PAUL. "Religiosity, Sexual Gratification, and Marital Satisfaction." *American Sociological Review* 22 (June 1957):300–305.

WARD, HILEY H. *The Far-Out Saints of the Jesus Communes: A First-Hand Report and Interpretation of the Jesus People Movement.* New York: Association Press, 1972.

WATTS, ALAN. "The Woman in Man." In Farber and Wilson, 1963.

WEEKS, H. ASHLEY. "Differential Divorce Rates by Occupations." *Social Forces* 21 (March 1943):334–37.

WESTOFF, CHARLES F. "The Modernization of U.S. Contraceptive Practice." *Family Planning Perspectives* 4 (July 1972):9–13.

———, and PARKE, ROBERT, JR., eds. *Demographic and Social Aspects of Population Growth.* Washington, D.C.: U.S. Government Printing Office, 1972.

WHITE, BURTON. *Human Infants: Experience and Psychological Development.* Englewood Cliffs, N.J.: Prentice-Hall, 1971.

WHYTE, WILLIAM H., JR. "Wives of Management." *Fortune* 44 (Oct. 1951):86–88.

WINCH, R.F. "Courtship of College Women." *American Journal of Sociology* 55 (1949):269–78.

———. *The Modern Family.* New York: Holt, Rinehart & Winston, 1952. 3rd ed, 1971.

———. *Mate Selection: A Study of Complementary Needs.* New York: Harper & Row, 1958.

———; McGINNIS, ROBERT; and BARRINGER, HERBERT R. *Selected Studies in Marriage and the Family.* New York: Holt, Rinehart & Winston, 1962.

WINTOUR, ELEANOR. "Bringing Up Children: The American vs. the British Way." *Harper's* 229 (Aug. 1964):58–63.

Work in the Lives of Married Women. New York: Columbia University Press, 1958.

WYDEN, PETER, and WYDEN, BARBARA. *Growing Up Straight: What Every Thoughtful Person Should Know About Homosexuality.* New York: Stein and Day, 1968.

YOUNG, WILLIAM O.; GOY, ROBERT W.; and PHOENIX, CHARLES H. "Hormones and Sexual Behavior." *Science* 143 (17 Jan. 1964):212–18.

ZETTERBERG, HANS L. "The Secret Ranking." *Journal of Marriage and the Family* 28 (May 1966):134–42.

⸻. *On Sexual Life in Sweden.* Report on the Royal Commission on Sex Education, summary in Moskin, 1969b.

ZIMMERMAN, CARLE C., and CERVANTES, LUCIUS F. *Successful American Families.* New York: Pageant Press, 1960.

ZORBAUGH, HARVEY. *Gold Coast and the Slum.* Chicago: University of Chicago Press, 1929.

INDEX

#26